THE WHICH? GUIDE TO

SCOTLAND

Edited by

Andrew Leslie

WHICH?
BOOKS

CONSUMERS' ASSOCIATION

Which? Books are commissioned and researched by
The Association for Consumer Research and published by
Consumers' Association, 2 Marylebone Road, London NW1 4DF.
Distributed by the Penguin Group:
Penguin Books Ltd, 27 Wrights Lane, London W8 5TZ

Written and edited by Andrew Leslie with contributions from
Deborah Buzan
Editor for *Holiday Which?*: Anna Fielder

Additional research and assistance: Morag Aitken, Ben Hall, Helen
Oldfield, Polly Phillimore, Nick Riddiford, Caroline Sanders, Lucy
Smith and Diana Vowles

Typographic design, line illustrations, cover design and illustration by
Paul Saunders
Maps by David Perrott Cartographics

The illustration on page 196 is based on a photograph in the Original
Coll., Hunterian Art Gallery, University of Glasgow, Mackintosh
Collection

First published April 1992
Revised April 1994
Copyright © 1992 Consumers' Association Ltd

British Library Cataloguing in Publication Data
'Which?' Guide to Scotland – 2 Rev. ed
I. Leslie, Andrew
914. 1104859
ISBN 0 85202 517 3

Typeset by The Electronic Book Factory Ltd, Fife

Printed and bound in Great Britain by
Richard Clay Limited, Bungay, Suffolk

CONTENTS

ABOUT THIS GUIDE

T HIS guide to the whole of Scotland is the culmination of a long tradition of reporting on the country's regions in *Holiday Which?* magazine. It aims to combine the best in travel writing with solid advice and recommendations, as well as a knowledgeable insight into the country's past and present.

The 13 chapters that follow the general introduction and history cover all the mainland regions as well as the islands; the general map of Scotland on page 28 gives an overview of how the regions relate to each other. Within each chapter is an easy-to-follow gazetteer round the region aided by a map and two boxed sections that give travel planning information and advice on good bases – the good bases are highlighted by a black strip on each map.

WHERE TO STAY

Our recommended hotels – all inspected by the *Holiday Which?* team – have bedrooms with bathrooms or showers en suite and serve evening meals, unless we say otherwise. The price categories are based on the cost, per night, of a double or twin-bedded room in 1994, including VAT and breakfast. Tariffs quoted by hotels sometimes include dinner – check when you book. You can expect to pay £12 to £20 for a set meal in a simpler hotel, up to £35 in a luxury one.

£ – under £70 per room per night
££ – £70 to £110 per room per night
£££ – over £110 per room per night

WHERE TO EAT

Our recommendations for places to eat at were compiled with the help of *The Good Food Guide* and many are featured in the 1994 edition and/or in *Out to Eat* (1991), both published by Consumers' Association. Hotels featured in this section are recommended primarily for their food. A ★ marks a place that is particularly good value for money.

OPENING TIMES

We give opening times, in brackets, following the name of each sight – but always double-check, particularly if you are visiting early or late in season.

HS, standard times means Historic Scotland's standard opening times: Apr to end Sept, Mon to Sat 9.30 to 6.30, Sun 2 to 6.30 (last ticket at 6); Oct to end Mar, Mon to Sat 9.30 to 4.30, Sun 2 to 4.30 (last ticket at 4).

NTS means that the sight is run by the National Trust for Scotland.

For more details about these organisations, see pages 24 and 25.

INTRODUCTION

THE best reason for choosing to go on holiday to Scotland is this: it is one of the last places inside the crowded and frenetic European Community where it is possible, indeed easy, to be alone in empty countryside. This is not to say that Scotland, like everywhere else, does not have its tourist traps, its crowded roads or its popular beauty spots. It is merely to stress that it is easy to escape from them. Nor is it to imply that Scotland is a deserted wilderness – it has its great cities, its country hotels and its many festivals. But again, if you wish, it is easy to get away from them.

In fine weather, Scotland is one of the most beautiful countries in the world. The quality of the light is not to be matched further south, while the variety of vegetation and landscape makes for constant change. At every season of the year, except in bleakest November or March, the Scottish landscape is an extraordinary blend of subtle colours. Blues predominate – in the sea and the lochs or in the distant hills. Green and white add their shades in spring, lilac and purple in summer, and, perhaps most magnificent, the tans, caramels and russets of autumn, with, by the sea lochs, the intense orange of the seaweed. A frosty winter's day in sharp white, grey, black and intense blue shows a landscape less subtle, more magnificent. The way in which these hues change over a single slope of hill as trees give way to patches of grass, heather, moss or bracken, broken by outcrops of rock, is worth contemplating in detail. It does not much matter whether it is mountainous coastal scenery or a quiet Border valley – something of the same richness will be found in both.

Curiosity alone may lead you to Scotland. For a thinly populated mountainous country on the fringe of Europe, it has had a disproportionately large impact on the world. The Scot abroad, whether as a mercenary soldier in the European wars of the sixteenth and seventeenth centuries, an explorer, a missionary, a Hong Kong merchant, a New World statesman or a football fan, has long been a distinctive figure. Equally, Scottish inventors, philosophers and scientists have been responsible for many of the ideas on which our understanding of the world is based. The tensions which have turned the Scots into a paradoxical mixture of hard-headed realists and sentimental patriots, which have drawn them to be tempted by idealism and self-interest alike, or which have made them into a nation of reluctant emigrants, can best be understood by going there.

It is a mistake to think that Scotland is merely an extension of England. Indeed no attitude is capable of causing greater offence. The Scots successfully resisted English attempts at domination for seven hundred years, and the mere fact that the two countries now have the same monarch, parliament and currency does not mean that visiting Scotland is much the same as visiting the Lake

District. Many differences between the countries remain – in law, culture, education, church and language, not to mention politics. Scotland's history, traced in its castles, battlefields, ancient trading towns and folk museums, in its cultural and architectural links with France, Flanders and Scandinavia, is distinct. This is again a reason for coming to Scotland – to learn what life looks like on the other side of an old frontier.

To enjoy Scotland to the full, you must enjoy being out of doors, and not just in fine weather. For the naturalists, the anglers, the walkers, the golfers or the rock-climbers who are sometimes prepared to suffer for their hobby, the country is a delight. It is a delight too for those who are happy to track down Neolithic sites, old castles, old hill roads or interesting geological outcrops across rough and sometimes boggy country. To those who are, for one reason or another, tied to their transport, a holiday in Scotland is a more chancy affair. As a country to tour through it can be magnificent, but much depends on the weather, and the weather is unpredictable. This is not necessarily a cause for despair. Edinburgh and Glasgow, Stirling, Perth or Aberdeen have enough attractions to provide solace in a rainy spell and are even better in a fine one. Both Edinburgh and Glasgow deserve better than to be tacked on to a general Scottish holiday. Both are ideal short break cities: Glasgow for its energy, its wealth of galleries and its shopping habit, Edinburgh because it is one of the most beautiful cities of Europe and has a host of sights – historic and otherwise.

IRRITANTS

Wet weather

It does not always rain in Scotland, far from it, but to prepare yourself, mentally and physically, for a spell of wet, possibly windy, weather is vital. On a damp, drizzly day, with low cloud shrouding the mountains to their feet, the Scottish countryside is about as interesting as the inside of a cardboard box. It is impossible to predict what sort of weather you will meet, so be prepared for the worst. If a week of blue skies and high temperatures is your reward, so much the better.

• Take waterproof clothing – trousers too if you intend to walk much – and a pair of wellington boots.

• There is often a difference in weather between the western and eastern sides of the country. If the west is wet, head east; if the east is cold, the west may be warmer.

• If you are going self-catering, make sure you will have enough space for you and your family to be able to endure each other's company in wet weather.

Midges

In all the swathes of literature pumped out to encourage visitors to Scotland, there is seldom any mention of the humble midge. This is unfair, for midges rank close to bad weather as the greatest barrier to the full enjoyment of an outdoor Scottish holiday, and they are at their peak in July, August and September.

Midges are a menace everywhere in Scotland, but they are at their worst in the Highlands, where the damp ground provides ideal breeding territory. Midges are tiny (but not invisible) blood-sucking insects, and they descend upon warm-blooded humans in swarms. Their activity seems to be governed by light: the dim conditions of early morning, evening, or overcast days bring them out in thousands, while sun, strong wind or darkness makes them vanish.

Except to the few people who suffer strong allergic reactions to them, midge bites themselves are little more than an itchy irritant. What is intolerable is the attack itself, for the insects get into hair, scalp, eyes, ears and onto every exposed piece of skin, until the itchy prickle of their biting provokes frenzy in the most patient of creatures. Activities such as bird-watching or fishing, which require stillness, are most easily disrupted by midges. Picnics are vulnerable too, as are evening walks. But it is probably the innocent camper who chooses a sheltered site who will suffer most. Few tents are truly midge-proof, and there are few experiences more awful than attempting to eat breakfast while the midges are eating you.

- Take plenty of repellent.
- Wear light-coloured clothing for preference. A hat helps too.
- Seek the company of a smoker.
- Regard the wind as your friend. Do not camp or attempt an evening picnic in sheltered, dimly-lit places.
- If camping, take a can of insecticide or a mosquito coil.

Trees

Sooner or later, someone must decide whether forestry or tourism is more important to Scotland's economy. From the point of view of the visitor, the wholesale planting of spruce in the Scottish uplands has been little short of a catastrophe. The attraction of the Scottish landscape lies in the sweeping panoramas over hillsides rich in colour and light, so there is little pleasure in contemplating a countryside of monotonous green of which you quickly tire. Whole tracts of Scotland have been ruined by forestry. Galloway is smothered, the high Liddesdale hill routes impenetrable, Loch Tummel irreparably damaged, and much of Sutherland besmirched. The Forestry Commission does its best to make its plantations more attractive to visitors – other commercial enterprises do not have to be so public-spirited. Whoever owns the trees, the point remains: commercial forestry plantations are two a penny throughout Europe; the Scottish landscape is unique.

If you want to see what a Scottish forest can be like at its best, head for the fragments of the old Caledonian forest at Rothiemurchus, or the Black Wood of Loch Rannoch, or even some of the man-made plantations of Scots pine round Nairn. These pinewoods are places of light, colour and birdsong, in contrast to the barren darkness of the spruce plantations. Whenever you see the pattern of lines on the slope of a hill, which denotes a new plantation, look carefully at the view. You won't see it again for the better part of a century.

Gift-wrapped Scotland

Walter Scott started it with *The Lady of the Lake*, the poem which brought the first tourists flooding to the Trossachs. Since then, the Scotland which has been assiduously sold to visitors is a soft-focus land of high romance, full of fierce but noble chieftains, tartan-clad clansmen and the drama of lost causes. To this the twentieth century has added bad jokes about haggis, the kilt and the cult of Nessie, the Loch Ness Monster. Much of this kitsch may be enjoyable, and a good way of selling kilts, bottles of whisky or cuddly monsters, but it bears little relation to the truth about Scotland, past or present.

SCOTLAND'S HISTORY

Scottish history is often baffling to the visitor. It is seldom taught beyond the borders of the country, so few outsiders have any idea of what went on before the union of the parliaments in 1707. However, some knowledge of it is useful, not simply for visiting castles, but because it helps to explain modern Scotland and some of the tensions within it. Scottish history, read from one angle, is a litany of dashed hopes: the silence into which the Declaration of Arbroath fell in 1320; the long sequence of military incompetence at Falkirk, Halidon Hill, Flodden, Solway Moss, Pinkie, Dunbar and Culloden; the gradual realisation in the sixteenth century that the 'Auld Alliance' with France was a double-edged sword; the sense of having been abandoned by the later Stuart kings; the terrible failure of the Darien colony and the discontent felt after the Act of Union. Add to these the devastation of the Highland way of life in the eighteenth and nineteenth centuries, the destruction of the Lowland heavy industry in the twentieth, the failure to achieve any degree of administrative independence from England and the increasing sense of being once more isolated on the edge of a continent whose centres are Strasbourg and Brussels, and it would be surprising if there were not some truth behind the old clichés about the insecurity and touchiness of the Scottish character.

Looked at from another angle, the Scottish tendency to divide into factions or to put self-interest first can be held to blame for most of the country's past troubles. The endless squabbling between powerful barons and kings trying to exert their authority went on longer in Scotland than almost anywhere else. The religious sectarianism which plagued seventeenth-century Scotland was an outbreak of the same tendency. It can be argued that almost every failed enterprise undertaken by the Scots has been doomed from the start by argument and failure to work in unity. It is perhaps no surprise that Wallace and Robert the Bruce, who managed to provide Scotland with a brief flicker of united endeavour, are two of the most revered of Scotland's heroes.

Unity

ROMANS
The difficulties of communication over Scotland's mountainous, boggy and sea-loch-riddled terrain long made the establishment of an effective centralising authority difficult. The Romans were the first to try, moving

north from England in at least three separate campaigns between AD 81 and AD 208, defeating the inhabitants of Caledonia at Mons Graupius in AD 84. Only the area south of the Forth and Clyde was subdued for any length of time. Gibbon describes the Romans as giving up in disgust, turning 'with contempt from gloomy hills assailed by the winter tempest, from lakes concealed in a blue mist, and from cold and lonely heaths, over which the deer of the forest were chased by a troop of naked barbarians'.

PICTS, SCOTS, ANGLES, NORSEMEN AND BRITONS

The sixth century saw what is now Scotland parcelled up into four kingdoms, three of them inhabited by Celtic peoples: Picts, Scots and Britons. The Picts, in central and eastern Scotland, held the greatest area of territory, the Scots (from Ireland) had formed the kingdom of Dalriada in what is now Argyll and the Britons held Galloway and Cumbria. The Angles, from their power base in Northumbria, had extended their rule northward into Lothian. In the ninth century, the Norsemen added to the brew by extensive coastal raiding and by establishing themselves in Shetland, Orkney, the Hebrides, Sutherland and Caithness. Warfare between the rival kingdoms was constant, the battle of Nechtansmere in 685 (when the Picts defeated the Angles) being particularly notable because it stopped Anglian expansion northwards. Marriage brought some kind of unity between Picts and Scots under Kenneth MacAlpine, King of Scots, around 843 and by 1034 the old kingdoms of Britons and Angles had also been absorbed.

MALCOLM CANMORE AND WILLIAM THE CONQUEROR

Several bloody conflicts took place before Malcolm Canmore emerged as king in 1057, killing Macbeth in the process (here at least Shakespeare is accurate). Two important events occurred during his reign – his marriage to Margaret, the English princess, who was a refugee from the Norman invasion, and the act of homage which Malcolm paid to William the Conqueror in 1072 at Abernethy (see Independence and Religion below). Malcolm, often seen as a big barbarian married to a cultured and holy wife whom he adored, spent much time trying, and failing, to establish Scotland's southern frontier along the River Tyne.

DAVID I AND THE NORMAN INCOMERS

There was no Norman conquest of Scotland – the Scottish kings did the job themselves. Malcolm's successors, holding lands in England and with increasingly strong ties there, encouraged Norman families to settle in Scotland, granting land and promoting the building of castles. Many of the most famous names in Scottish history have Norman origins. David I (1124–53) hastened Norman-style feudalism by the establishment of abbeys and cathedrals and the system of royal burghs. Under David, Scotland began to develop an administrative system to match that of England, while the authority of the king was much increased.

LAST OF THE NORSEMEN

Under the improbably named Magnus Barelegs, the Norse settlers in the Hebrides had forced the Scottish crown to concede all the western islands to them (and Magnus shiftily added Kintyre to the list by dragging his boat across the Tarbert isthmus). The Norse-Hebridean chiefs were a menace to the Scottish kings, supporting rebels and making forays of their own. Somerled, ancestor of Clan Donald, was a particularly forceful character in this respect. In 1263, King Haakon of Norway assembled a huge fleet for an attack, but was routed at the battle of Largs. After this defeat, Norway gave up all her Scottish possessions apart from Orkney and Shetland under a treaty of 1266. A royal marriage with Norway in 1468 brought Orkney and Shetland to the Scottish crown.

HIGHLANDS, LOWLANDS AND ISLANDS

For centuries, the clans of the islands and glens continued a law unto themselves, sometimes allied to the crown, sometimes hostile to it. It could be argued that they never became fully part of a united Scotland. Despite expeditions mounted by various Scottish kings, it was not until the defeat of the last Jacobite rebellion at Culloden in 1746 that the power of the clans to act independently was broken. There is still a division between Highlander and Lowlander today – sometimes exaggerated, sometimes glossed over.

Independence

If there is one theme that infects Scottish history, right down to the present day, it is the independence of the nation, and in particular, independence from England. Currently, 37 per cent of Scots wish to have more independence – a substantial proportion for a country which has been unified with England for approaching 300 years.

THE WARS OF INDEPENDENCE

The conflict between England and Scotland really started in 1290 with the death of the child-queen Margaret, 'The Maid of Norway'. The blame for it must be carried almost entirely by Edward I of England, popularly known as 'Hammer of the Scots'. Edward had a clear idea that he was feudal overlord of Scotland, and was able to point to the homage done by various Scottish kings to various English kings to make his point (though what, exactly, they were doing homage for is still disputed). Edward's chance came when he was asked to judge between 13 rival claimants for the Scottish throne. He made his judgement in favour of John Balliol, but proceeded thereafter to treat this weak-minded man as such an underling that even 'Toom Tabard' (empty coat) as he was known, was forced into revolt in 1296. Edward's response was to sack Berwick, invade Scotland, plunder the stone of Scone on which Scottish kings were traditionally crowned, depose John Balliol, and set up a government similar to the one that he had already imposed on conquered Wales. Scotland was to be a little-regarded province of England.

Revolt started almost at once, especially among the small land-owners who had no holdings in England to put in jeopardy. William Wallace defeated the English at Stirling Bridge, but was defeated in turn at Falkirk in 1298. He was captured in 1305 and executed as a traitor in London. Scottish resistance collapsed and Edward set up a new, less repressive government.

In 1306, Robert the Bruce, grandson of one of the claimants to the Scottish throne whom Edward had rejected, killed his Comyn rival in a church, thus laying himself open to charges of murder and sacrilege.

His reaction was to have himself crowned King of Scotland at Scone. Edward immediately swore that he would never rest until Scotland was conquered and set about defeating Bruce. Bruce's deliverance came in May 1307 with the death of Edward, whose son, Edward II, turned back from the Scottish campaign.

Bruce proceeded to defeat his Scottish enemies, then turned on the English-garrisoned castles, until, by 1314, only Stirling remained in English hands. The Battle of Bannockburn (page 274) put the seal on Bruce's triumph and made his kingship undisputed, but it was not until 1328 that Scotland's independence was recognised by the English king.

FURTHER WARS WITH THE ENGLISH
The conflict did not end there. By 1333 everything that Bruce had achieved had gone. John Balliol's son, with the support of Edward III of England, invaded, defeated the Scots at Halidon Hill, and promptly paid homage to the English king. His reign did not last long, but it set the pattern for the following centuries. English kings claimed feudal overlordship or supported discontented Scottish nobles, and occasionally invaded. Scottish resistance, usually marked by internal strife and military weakness, was sporadically successful, but owed its survival to the fact that English kings had more pressing tasks than subduing Scotland, notably that of maintaining their claim to France. Scotland's worst defeat by the English was entirely self-inflicted when James IV invaded England on behalf of his French ally. The result was the terrible battle of Flodden in 1513.

HENRY VIII AND THE ROUGH WOOING
James V of Scotland, the nephew of Henry VIII of England, was not inclined to follow his uncle in throwing off the Pope's authority. Rather, he chose a French bride and kept faith with the Vatican. In 1541, Henry summoned him to confer at York but James chose not to go. Henry dispatched an army northwards and James replied by sending one south, only to have it defeated at Solway Moss in 1542. James died soon afterwards, leaving the infant Mary Queen of Scots as his heir.

Henry saw his chance of bringing Scotland into his orbit by arranging for his son, Edward, to marry Mary. There were enough Protestant (and hence anglophile) lords in Scotland to make this attractive to the Scots, and a treaty was even signed at Greenwich to confirm it. But a putsch by those in favour of the old alliance with France led to Scottish rejection of the match. Henry, typically, overplayed his hand by replacing diplomacy with force. The burning of the south of Scotland in 1544 and 1545, ironically called the Rough Wooing, merely strengthened Scottish determination. Defeated at Pinkie in 1547, the Scots spirited the young queen to France and agreed to her marriage with the French dauphin, the future François II.

A FRENCH PROVINCE?
The mother of Mary Queen of Scots, the redoubtable Mary of Guise, was now regent of Scotland and her response to the English invasion of the country was to bring in French troops to defend it. A military stalemate resulted, but Scotland found itself increasingly governed by French administrators. When, in 1559, a group of Protestant lords

rebelled, they did so as much to rid Scotland of the French as to promote their religion. After the death of Mary of Guise in 1560, the matter was sealed: the French left.

THE NEGLECTED OUTPOST (1603–1707)
When James VI, son of Mary Queen of Scots, inherited the throne of England in 1603 and travelled triumphantly south, he promised his Scottish subjects he would return every three years. He did not keep this promise. For a brief period during the conflict with Charles I (see Religion below), the Scottish parliament asserted its independence, but the invasion of Scotland by Oliver Cromwell in 1650, the enforced, if temporary, union with England, and the absolutist policies of Charles II after the Restoration left Scotland with little independent voice. The hesitation in Scotland after the Glorious Revolution of 1688 had deposed James VII from the British throne was brief – the Scottish crown was offered to William and Mary only two months after the English.

THE UNION OF PARLIAMENTS (1707)
In the years before the final union of Scotland and England, the relationship between the two countries was extremely frayed (see page 128). To many Scots, union with England seemed to be the only way of avoiding bankruptcy and war. When the Scottish parliament voted itself out of existence it seemed the end at last of an independent Scotland.

THE JACOBITES (1715–1745)
The uprisings of 1715, 1719 and 1745, which sought to restore the Stuarts to the British throne, were not in any sense a popular struggle for Scottish independence. While the unpopularity of the Union was a factor that led some people to join the Jacobites, Lowland support for the Jacobite risings was patchy at best, and Highland support was far from solid. Nor were the ambitions of the 'Old Pretender' (James VIII) or his son, Prince Charles Edward Stuart, confined to ruling Scotland – the invasion of England in 1745 was undertaken with the purpose of gaining the British crown. Nevertheless, the uprisings showed that the old link between Scotland and France and the loyalty of many Scots to the person they saw as their legitimate king had not been entirely destroyed by union with England.

HOME RULE MOVEMENTS (1920–1979)
The first serious attempts in modern times to regain home rule for Scotland were made between the two World Wars, at a time of economic depression and, on Clydeside, left-wing radicalism. The nationalist movement was given added fuel by the 'Scottish Renaissance' literary revival, led by Hugh MacDiarmid. All attempts to attain a measure of self-government for Scotland came to nothing, except that they eventually resulted in the formation of the Scottish Nationalist Party (SNP) in 1934. Hampered by factionalist infighting for years, the SNP made something of a breakthrough in 1974, winning seven seats and polling 21 per cent of the vote, largely because the discovery of 'Scotland's Oil' held out the prospect of independence in wealth rather than penury. An extremely confused period, in which the word devolution came to mean many different things to different people, ended in a controversial and inconclusive referendum of 1979 when a

proposal for a form of devolution was rejected by a majority of the Scottish electorate, an abstention being held to count against.

Religion

THE CELTIC CHURCH
The first Christian missionary to Scotland was St Ninian, who, from a base in Galloway, set out to convert the southern Picts around AD 400. He was followed, in 563, by St Columba, whose foundation at Iona became a centre of learning and spirituality which was to have enormous influence throughout Scotland. The Celtic church, its gospel spread by missionaries whose names still crop up in remote place-names, eventually made contact with the Roman church, whose doctrine, brought to England by St Augustine, had spread up to Northumbria. In various conflicts over practice (the date of Easter was one point at issue), the Celtic church gave way. Its influence was weakened by Norse raids on Iona and the Roman doctrine gained increasing hold.

THE NORMAN PERIOD
Just as the Anglo-Norman settlement of Scotland established feudalism, so it placed the Roman doctrine on a firm basis. The remnants of the Celtic church, many of whose priests were not celibate, could not exist within the new system. Malcolm Canmore's wife Margaret, who founded the monastery at Dunfermline, rebuilt Iona but was firm in suppressing the erroneous ways of the older church. By the time dioceses and parishes had been established, continental monastic orders invited in and great abbeys founded, the church in Scotland was almost identical in practice to that in England. The Celtic church, except perhaps in the Highland fastnesses, had vanished.

CHURCH AND CROWN (1153–1560)
Just as the English kings claimed jurisdiction over Scotland, so did the English church – but in this case the Scots had an easier victory, for the Pope recognised the Scottish church as directly responsible to Rome in 1192. In 1472, St Andrews became an archbishopric. During the Middle Ages, the church, wealthier than the king and wielding immense influence, was a strong force for stability in the face of recurring crises. However, in common with the church in so many European countries before the Reformation, it grew fat and lax. When the Lutheran doctrines began to be heard in Scotland, they found fertile ground, although reformers were burnt – notably George Wishart in 1546. The energetic Cardinal Beaton, doing his best to counter the anglophile, Protestant party, was murdered in his turn at St Andrews in the same year. The regency of Mary of Guise, during the time when the young Mary Queen of Scots was in France, saw open warfare, when Protestant lords, aided by the English, confronted the government.

REFORMATION (1560)
In the brief period between the death of Mary of Guise in 1560 and the return to Scotland of Mary Queen of Scots in 1561, the Scottish Reformation took place. The preacher John Knox laid before the Scottish parliament a Confession of Faith, which was accepted; the authority of

the Pope was denied, and the mass declared illegal. Scotland achieved, in one step, a radical transformation of her church. At the same time, the principle that the church was independent of state control was laid down and the basis for Presbyterianism established. This essential difference between the reformed Scottish church and the Church of England was to cause much anguish. The Confession of Faith was followed by the Book of Discipline, which laid out not only how the new church might be organised but envisaged a complete scheme of education from primary schools to university, astoundingly in advance of its time.

MARY QUEEN OF SCOTS

In 1561, Mary, a Catholic queen, returned to a country in the first uneasy aftermath of a Protestant revolution. Fear of a reimposition of the old faith was strong, and the Catholic powers of Europe encouraged Mary to undertake a counter-revolution. The religious tolerance with which Mary attempted to rule was no solution to the polarisation of attitudes within Scotland. Although she suppressed the Catholic Huntly family, she did herself no good by marrying the Catholic Darnley. Part of Mary's tragedy is that she attempted to steer a middle course between two extremes. The nobles who rebelled against her did so largely out of self-interest, but religious concerns were not far beneath the surface.

ABSOLUTISM AND CIVIL WAR (1567–1689)

The turmoil which gripped Scotland throughout much of the seventeenth century was the result of monarchs attempting to impose their will on a church unprepared to accept interference in its affairs. James VI succeeded in reimposing bishops upon the reformed Scottish church, thereby gaining a means of exerting authority, but he achieved this only after long struggle. Charles I, in attempting to dictate particular forms of worship, went too far. The signing of the National Covenant in 1638 led indirectly to civil war in Scotland, England and Ireland, to the throwing off of the king's authority in Scotland and to the appearance of a temporary theocracy, which crumbled in the face of Oliver Cromwell's invasion. After the restoration, Charles II reimposed bishops and let loose troops to persecute the Presbyterian extremists who refused to be reconciled to his policies. The 'Killing Times' round the year 1685 saw the worst of the unequal contest. The accession of James VII, himself a Catholic, led to another swing of the pendulum. Extreme Presbyterianism would not be tolerated in Scotland, but a Catholic monarch was not acceptable in either country. The Glorious Revolution of 1688 deposed James and made way for the Protestant William of Orange and his wife, Mary.

DISRUPTION

The Reformed Church of Scotland, now once more in the ascendant, was an austere body, with the authority to enforce its discipline at the 'repentance stool' in church if need be. One major point of dissent remained – the issue of lay patronage, or whether or not congregations had the right to choose their own ministers. Conflict over this matter led to the withdrawal of more than 470 ministers from the established church in 1843, an event known as the Disruption. During the nineteenth century, other branches of the Kirk split and rejoined. The Church of Scotland remains strong throughout the country; more extreme Presbyterian churches are found in some parts, notably Skye and Lewis.

HOLIDAY CHOICES

- **Self-catering** Self-catering properties range from traditional croft cottages to chalet complexes and caravans and are found everywhere. Having a place of your own to return to for drying your clothes and spreading yourself in can make a lot of sense but remember that the local shops in remote areas will probably only stock essentials. If you fancy doing some complicated cooking, take the ingredients with you. The Scottish Tourist Board publishes a listing, *Scotland Self-Catering*, and regional tourist boards have their own lists too. Other sources worth trying are: Association of Scotland's Self-Caterers (08357 481); Blakes Holidays (0603 782141); Hampster Cottages (08993) 775; Hoseasons Holidays (0502 500500); Mackay's Agency (031-225 3539); National Trust for Scotland (031-226 5922); Summer Cottages (0305 267545). The 'small ads' pages of Sunday newspapers also often carry a selection.

- **Caravanning** There are caravan sites in abundance in Scotland, many of them well positioned on the coast. Do not expect every site to have masses of facilities, however; some may simply be a field which is put to other uses out of season. The Scottish Tourist Board publishes *Scotland Camping and Caravanning*, or, if a member, you can contact the Camping and Caravanning Club (0203 694995), the AA (0256 20123), the RAC (081-681 8512) or the Forestry Commission (031-334 2576).

- **Bed-and-Breakfast** Large numbers of Scots offer bed-and-breakfast, and moving round the country staying in one home after another is an extremely popular way of touring. Staying in bed-and-breakfast accommodation is cheap, and a good way of meeting local people, but it does leave you disadvantaged in bad weather. The Scottish Tourist Board operates an advance booking service and publishes *Scotland Bed & Breakfast*; all regional tourist boards have lists of those bed-and-breakfast establishments who are members. But a number of households are not members, and they may be just as good.

- **Island-hopping** Only masochists will try to reach as many Scottish islands as possible in the course of a holiday. But choosing to move in a leisurely fashion between one island and another is a different matter. You will have to plan and book in advance if you intend taking a car on ferries during high season; you will have more flexibility if you can do without. Island-hopping by aeroplane, using hired cars on the ground, is a good alternative if you can afford it. *Getting Around the Highlands and Islands* (FGH Publications), which gives timetables for all ferry, bus, rail and air services, is essential and comes out twice yearly. Caledonian MacBrayne (CalMac), the main ferry operator, offers unlimited travel island rover tickets (with or without a car) which are valid for eight or fifteen days. Ring (0475) 650100 for details.

- **Hotel-based touring** The days when you had to exist on white bread and tinned vegetables in remote areas are long gone. Several hotels miles from anywhere, ranging from the luxurious to the relatively simple, are purpose-made for a comfortable holiday in the wilderness. In the cities there is less of a range: your best chance here is to look for off-season or weekend rates at one of the more modern business hotels or to spend time in seeking out a guesthouse that pleases you. Small-town hotels away from the most popular tourist areas are apt to be unmemorable, though not necessarily bad value. Fishing hotels are a Scottish speciality. Usually with water of their own, and with ample understanding of anglers' needs, they make an ideal base from which to foray out in pursuit of trout or salmon. Seek out a copy of *Scotland for Game, Sea and Coarse Fishing* (Pastime Publications/STB, 031-556 1105).

● **Packages** There are package holidays to suit most tastes and most activities. The Scottish Tourist Board (see 'The support system' below) has details. Write, explaining what kind of holiday you are looking for, or ask for the free *Activity and Special Interest Holidays* booklet.

Birdwatching

The many different habitats – mountains, sea-cliffs, islands, remains of ancient forest, moorland and lochs – make Scotland a superb place for birdwatching. Areas most favoured by birds include the Highlands and the myriad islands. You can also spot birds in the central lowlands and southern uplands, by the large firths and other coastal waters. The specialist birdwatcher visits Scotland and its islands in spring and autumn for migrants and in winter for coastal waterfowl and abundant geese; May, June or July are good for watching seabirds thronging the cliffs and for moorland and mountain birds – but remember to avoid disturbing individual breeding birds.

Birds of prey are particularly abundant in the Highlands, from the frequently encountered buzzard to the merlin, a small dashing moorland falcon. Cruising along mountain ridges may be the king of the Scottish skies, the golden eagle. Lochs in the vicinity of pine forests may attract an osprey. Scotland's most celebrated conservation success, ospreys are now widespread, though Loch Garten remains the main sighting spot. The area around Loch Garten is excellent for other birds too. The ancient Caledonian forest, with its native Scots pine, hosts some spectacular birds including the capercaillie, a turkey-sized forest grouse.

In more open woodland, you may spot the smaller black grouse, while the trees support crested tits and the Scottish crossbill, its strangely shaped beak a perfect tweezer for extracting seeds from pine cones. Various rare birds live on mountain tops, including the ptarmigan, a grouse which dons white plumage in winter. On bleak moorlands you can hear the melancholic call of the golden plover. A walk through the heather may provoke an explosion and a whirring of wings as a covey of red grouse breaks cover. Upland lochs and lochans are home for a number of birds, including elegant divers, with their eerie, wailing calls in the half-light of summer nights.

It is well worth taking binoculars on a visit to the islands as their cliffs host some of the most impressive seabird colonies in Britain, especially the rows of enchanting, comical puffins along the clifftops in June and July. Many of the islands have their own special birds such as corncrakes in the Hebrides, white-tailed eagles recently introduced to Rum, Fetlar's snowy owls and red-necked phalaropes and, on a number of islands, skuas prepared to attack unsuspecting visitors in defence of their moorland nests.

You can spot birds anywhere, but, especially for trainee birdwatchers, the protected areas offer the best opportunities. The Royal Society for the Protection of Birds (17 Regent Terrace, Edinburgh EH7 5BN; 031-557 3136) has 50 reserves in Scotland. You can write (enclose an s.a.e.) for the comprehensive booklet on reserves. Facilities vary; RSPB members get in free where a charge is made. Other organisations with responsibility for natural areas include Scottish Natural Heritage (031-447 4784), the National Trust for Scotland and the Scottish Wildlife Trust (for addresses, see 'The support system' below). Fair Isle has a bird observatory, open May to Oct, (03512 258), which provides hotel-standard accommodation and the opportunity to learn more about breeding and migrant birds. There is also an observatory, with more basic accommodation, on North Ronaldsay in Orkney (08573 267). The tourist boards are also useful sources of information about birdwatching.

● **Useful books** For identifying birds: *The Shell Guide to the Birds of Britain and Ireland* by James Ferguson-Lees, Ian Willis and J T R Sharrock (Michael Joseph). For the best places to visit: *Where to Watch Birds in Scotland* by Mike Madders and Julia Westwood (Christopher Helm). For background information: *Birds in Scotland* by Valerie M Thom (Poyser).

Golf

Scotland has the oldest golf courses and golf clubs in the world. Although the first rules were not formalised until 1744, there are records of bets on a game of golf in 1504. The home of the Royal and Ancient Golf Club which administers the game is in St Andrews overlooking the first tee and eighteenth green.

For the holiday golfer there are over 400 courses to choose from; the most famous five play host to the British Open. Not surprisingly it is hardest to get a game on these courses. If you are less concerned with emulating golf's great players, there are an exceptional number of other superb courses where the casual visitor has a better chance of getting a game. Fees for the open championship courses start at around £40 a round, although you can get a cheaper round on some of the others which are equally picturesque and challenging. For the real holiday hacker there are municipal courses where you pay £5 for a round.

If you are setting out to play the championship links, arm yourself with a valid handicap certificate (preferably showing a reasonable level of competence) and settle down with the phone early in the year to book your start times. If you are planning a golfing holiday you should avoid the peak months of July and August.

THE OPEN COURSES
● **St Andrews Old Course** You need to book months in advance to be assured of a tee-time, or you can put your name down for the daily right-to-play lottery. Two-thirds of all start times are allocated by ballot. To be included, contact the starter before 2 on the day before you wish to play. Handicap certificate or letter of introduction required; handicap limits are 28 for men, 36 for ladies. (0334) 75757, closed Sunday.
● **Carnoustie** Like St Andrews, Carnoustie is a public course. Demand for tee-times is not as heavy as at St Andrews but you are still advised to book at least a month in advance. Handicap certificate preferred. Visitors not allowed before 1.30pm Saturday and 11.30am on Sunday; handicap limits are 20 for men, 28 for ladies. (0241) 53249
● **Muirfield** Home to the Honourable Company of Edinburgh Golfers, this course has some of the highest green fees in the country. Handicap

19

certificate required; handicap limits are 18 for men, 24 for ladies; ladies can play only if accompanied by a man and are banned from the clubhouse. (0620) 842123

● **Royal Troon** This course has limited start times for visitors – the main days are Monday, Tuesday and Thursday. Fees are quoted per day and include two rounds and lunch or high tea. No ladies are allowed on the Championship course; a handicap certificate is required; handicap limits are 22 for men, 26 for ladies (on the Portland course). (0292) 311555

● **Turnberry Hotel** This course is now Japanese-owned and visitors take second place to hotel guests in the allocation of start times. The course is open to visitors on most days at midday; booking is recommended at least one month in advance. (0655) 31000

THE BEST OF THE REST

● **Royal Aberdeen** Handicap certificate required; handicap limits for play on the championship course are around 20 for men and 24 for ladies – there is a little leeway. No advance bookings, but phone the day before to check. No visitors before 3.30 on Saturday. (0224) 702571

● **Blairgowrie** Handicap certificates are desirable; limits are 28 for men and 36 for ladies. Advance booking required on Monday, Tuesday, Thursday and Friday, but not at weekends. (0250) 872 622

● **Cruden Bay** Handicap certificates required at weekends; no visitors between 4.30 and 6.30 on Wednesday. (0779) 812285

● **Royal Dornoch** Handicap certificate required; handicap limits are 24 for men, 35 for ladies. Advance booking advisable. (0862) 810219

● **Nairn** Advance booking advisable. (0667) 53208

● **Prestwick** No visitors at weekends. Handicap certificate required; handicap limits are 24 for men, 28 for ladies. Advance booking necessary. (0292) 77404

Hill-walking in Scotland

Scotland's mountains are not to be treated lightly. They are not especially lofty – there are few over four thousand feet – but they are both northerly and close to the sea, which means that the weather can turn foul very rapidly and kill the under-equipped or inexperienced walker who has got into difficulty in a matter of hours. A mountain which looks easy to tackle in bright sun can become a death-trap if the clouds come down suddenly and you are left without a map, compass, or other essential equipment.

As a minimum, wear proper boots, pack extra layers of clothing, take a map and compass and know how to use them, and make sure someone else knows where you are going and your estimated time of return. If you are sensible, you will add some high-energy food, a first-aid kit, a lightweight survival blanket, a torch (with spare batteries) and a whistle to your equipment.

There are hills and mountains in Scotland to suit every taste and every degree of experience. With the exception of the Black Cuillin on Skye, which demand rock-climbing ability, most are within the reach of the experienced rock-scrambler or hill-walker. If you do not enjoy heights or rocks, excellent walking is still to be found on the Cheviots, the Pentland or Ochil Hills, or on the gentler slopes of the Perthshire or Angus mountains.

On the hills, you will come across the 'Munro-bagger', the walker who is aiming to climb every one of the tops over 3,000 feet listed in the tables compiled by Sir Hugh Munro. There are 279 of them, and working through them can become something of an obsession for many. You may well find fewer people and gain just as much satisfaction if you make for the mountains which do not reach the magic three thousand foot level. There are two long-distance walks, the West Highland Way, which runs from Milngavie to Fort William, and the Southern Uplands Way, which runs from Portpatrick to Cockburnspath. A section of the Speyside Way, from Tomintoul to Spey Bay, is also open.

• **Access to the countryside** Most landowners are tolerant of walkers on their land, particularly in moorland and mountain areas, although there is a law of trespass in Scotland. If a path is defined on the ground you can usually assume that you may follow it. In fields, keep to the edges. Many walks take advantage of rights of way, defined in Scotland as routes between public places that have been in use for more than 20 years. Rights of way are not officially registered as they are in England and Wales, although the planning departments of local authorities may keep records and maps. Rights of way are not distinguished from other paths on Ordnance Survey maps, although they are often signposted. For more information, contact the Scottish Rights of Way Society (031-652 2937), who can advise on specific routes.

During the stalking and shooting seasons in the Highlands (usually August to October) access to private land may be restricted – check your intended route with the local tourist office.

WHEN TO GO

The Scottish tourist season is short. Outside Edinburgh and Glasgow, many sights do not open before May, and they often close at the end of September. Yet Scotland is arguably at its most attractive in October, when autumn colour is beginning to suffuse the hill-sides and the woods and when the first frosts sharpen the air. June is also an attractive month. The midges have not got into their stride and the wild flowers of the Hebridean machair beaches are stunning. There is generally less to be said for July. August is redeemed by the coming into flower of the heather, which transforms the Scottish moorland into a wide brush-stroke of purple. November can be a good month to take a short break to Edinburgh or Glasgow: hotels may have off-season rates, those sights that remain open will be peaceful, and there will be warm spots to shelter in if the weather turns nasty. In winter, when there is a spell of clear weather with snow on the ground, Scotland can be fabulously beautiful. Otherwise, it is best avoided between December and early April.

Every region of Scotland has its own local festivals, games or sporting events. Tourist offices compile local lists and the Scottish Tourist Board publishes the yearly free *Events in Scotland* booklet.

TRAVELLING TO SCOTLAND

• **By air** From south of the border you can fly direct to Aberdeen, Edinburgh, Glasgow and Inverness from London (Heathrow or Gatwick) and many regional airports. Airlines flying these routes include British Airways, British Midland, Air UK, Loganair, Manx, Gill Aviation and Business Air.

• **By train** There are InterCity services to Scotland from 93 stations in England. Motorail services run between London Euston and Edinburgh, Glasgow, Aberdeen, Inverness and Fort William, and between Bristol and Edinburgh. Sleeper services operate between London Euston and Edinburgh, Aberdeen, Inverness, Fort William, Perth and Glasgow, as well as between Plymouth/Poole and Edinburgh/Glasgow. APEX fares are available on many routes – these must be booked at least seven days in advance and offer considerable savings. Scotrail also has a range of rail passes for travel in Scotland, though there is uncertainty whether these will still exist after privatisation in April 1994. For information, call 031-556 2451 or 071-387 7070 (British Rail) and (0345) 090700 (Motorail).

• **By coach** National Express (071-730 0202) is the main coach operator for journeys from south of the Border. It runs day and night services between the main English and Scottish towns. Fares are cheaper if you book a week in advance. Scottish Citylink (041-332 9191) operates services within Scotland.

SHOPPING

• **Tartan** The whole elaborate mythology surrounding tartan dates from only 1822, the time of George IV's visit to Edinburgh, when Highland dress suddenly became fashionable. Tartans were probably originally associated with districts rather than individual clans, so the whole process of finding the tartan that goes with your name (and most shops have lists) need not be taken more seriously than you want. Tartan travelling rugs, scarfs or headsquares are all good buys.

• **Tweed and knitwear** Shops all over Scotland specialise in these, but you are likely to find the best bargains if you look for mill shops or individual weavers and knitters. The textile towns of the Borders, especially Hawick, Selkirk and Galashiels, are fertile hunting grounds and there are mill shops too on the southern fringe of the Ochil Hills. The bargains you find on Harris, source of the renowned Harris tweed, may not actually cover the cost of getting there, but you can have the satisfaction of watching the cloth being woven by hand. Garments made from high-quality Shetland wool are sold all over the country, but the best bargains are to be found on Shetland itself. The Fair Isle jumper, with its distinctive patterns, is often imitated. The genuine article, knitted on Fair Isle, is rare. You can order one, or visit the island and see if you can persuade a local producer to put you top of the list.

• **Smoked produce and other foods** Smoked salmon, smoked trout and smoked venison can be found in shops or in the many smokeries which dot the Highlands. Many will send your order by post. If you can get them home fast, or can cook them on the spot, Scottish kippers, especially the lightly smoked Loch Fyne ones, are delicious. Look out too for Arbroath 'smokies'.

Oatcakes – dry, sustaining oatmeal biscuits – are easily found and easily transported. So is Scottish shortbread, sweet and crumbly. Cheese-making in Scotland is undergoing a revival and there are a number of varieties, including Lanark Blue and Bonchester, worth looking out for. Buy a black bun for New Year – highly spiced dried fruit and peel are packed into a thin pastry casing which will keep almost indefinitely until opened. Dundee cakes, light fruit cakes with a handsome topping of golden almonds, are extremely filling, good for a long day on the hill. Buy one in a tin to take home.

• **Silver and semi-precious stones** There is a big market in small silver items, especially brooches. Scottish silver-work has a long tradition behind it, and you can buy contemporary silversmiths' work in craft shops up and down the country. If you are feeling rich, a silver 'quaich' (a traditional flat drinking cup more usually made in wood or horn) makes a good present for someone. The best-known Scottish gemstone is the whisky-coloured 'Cairngorm'.

FOOD AND DRINK

Scotland produces some of the best fish, meat and game in Europe, has a long tradition of baking and confectionery, and grows some of the best soft fruit in the world. Increasingly, Scottish restaurants and hotels are waking up to the fact that people may wish to enjoy these fine things within Scotland, rather than having them shipped to London or Paris. The seafood is especially fine: lobsters, prawns, mussels and oysters are common, especially round the lochs and islands of the west. Aberdeen Angus beef and Border hill lamb are both renowned. So of course is Scottish salmon (though eat wild fish rather than farmed if you have the choice). If you are in Scotland during the raspberry season, make sure you find a plateful somewhere. The reputation of both porridge and haggis has suffered at the hands of comedians. Porridge should be made from oatmeal which has been steeped overnight. Purists insist it should be eaten with a horn spoon, standing up, and never adulterated with sugar (salt is all right), but try this in your guesthouse and you may get funny looks. Haggis is made from minced sheep's 'pluck' (usually heart, liver and lungs), mixed with oatmeal, suet and spices and stuffed in the sheep's stomach. It is very much more tasty than this description may suggest. Most butchers have their own recipes. Haggis is traditionally eaten with mashed potatoes and pureed turnip (called bashed neeps, and known further south as swede).

If you want to buy whisky, you can choose between a blended whisky, a de luxe whisky (a blend of particularly old or fine whiskies), a single malt whisky (see box on page 364) or a whisky-based liqueur, such as Drambuie or Glayva. There is considerable variation in flavour and 'smoothness' between the various brands of both blended and single malt whisky. Island malts (from Islay and Jura) are fiery and smoky; Speyside malts are lighter and smoother. If you have not developed your own preferences in malt whiskies, a bottle of Glenfiddich or Glenmorangie will appeal to most tastes.

THE SUPPORT SYSTEM

On your travels in Scotland you will run across a number of organisations which manage sights, can provide you with information, or specialise in some activity.

• **The Scottish Tourist Board (STB)**, 23 Ravelston Terrace, Edinburgh EH4 3EU (031-332 2433). The STB, like its English equivalent, is divided into regional boards. At local level, there is a network of Tourist Information Centres (TIC), many of which are only open seasonally. The STB has publications of general or specialist interest to visitors. The regional boards can provide lists of accommodation and usually a gazetteer of things to see or do, as well as their own publications. In local offices you will also often find town trail leaflets, or descriptions of walks in the area as well as a range of other publications. Staff in Tourist Information Centres are often extremely knowledgeable, and will pursue obscure enquiries for you if they have time. The size and efficiency of the local TICs varies, as does the quality of the leaflets they provide, but in general they are excellent. A major re-organisation of the Scottish Tourist Board is about to take place.

Although many hotel owners, tourist attractions or owners of local businesses are members of the tourist board, some choose not to be, so the accommodation lists, for example, may not be comprehensive. Excellent hotels and guesthouses exist which have chosen to go it alone.

The STB pioneered the 'dual rating' system, by which hotels, guest houses, bed-and-breakfasts and self-catering accommodation are classified according to the facilities they have and separately graded for their quality. The scheme is now widespread throughout Scotland, though not every establishment on the STB's list has been inspected, and not all choose to join the grading system.

Facilities are shown by crowns, and there are six steps, ranging from 'Listed' for simple accommodation to five crowns for a place with all the trimmings. The quality of the accommodation (which has nothing to do with the facilities) is shown in four steps by the words 'Approved', 'Commended', 'Highly Commended' and 'Deluxe'.

The scheme has had its teething troubles, and can cause confusion if you forget how it works and take the number of crowns to be an indication of quality. In general, we have found the quality gradings useful, but rather limited. Establishments carrying the 'Highly Commended' award usually deserve it, and are worth keeping an eye open for. 'Commended' covers a wide range, rather too wide a range for one award. The 'Approved' award is defined by the STB as 'acceptable'. In our experience, this can mean anything from perfectly adequate to fairly dingy. It is hoped that the fourth step recently introduced by the STB in its grading system ('Deluxe') will allow finer discrimination.

Apart from the publications mentioned in the relevant sections above, useful publications produced by the STB include *Scotland Short Breaks*, *Practical Information for the Traveller to Scotland*, and *Scotland Home of Golf*.

● **Historic Scotland (HS)**, 20 Brandon Street, Edinburgh EH3 5RA (031-244 3101). This is a government agency responsible for the care of Scotland's historic buildings and monuments. Most of Scotland's prehistoric sites, ruined castles, abbeys and cathedrals are looked after by Historic Scotland. Its custodians are often experts on the building in their care, and while they manage not to be obtrusive, they are well worth chatting to, especially if you want to know something obscure that is not in the guidebook. They keep the lawns round their monuments in first-class condition, too. If you are going to visit a number of ancient buildings, the seven- or 14-day 'explorer' pass by the 'Friends of Historic Scotland', allowing you free entry to all their sights, will probably save you money. For details, ring 031-244 3099. Historic Scotland also produces an excellent range of books on aspects of the country's past (ring 031-244 3102 for details).

● **The National Trust for Scotland (NTS)**, 5 Charlotte Square, Edinburgh EH2 4DU (031-226 5922). Like its sister organisation in England, the NTS is a charity, independent of government support, charged with the preservation of the properties in its care. It looks after over one hundred of these, including castles, historic sites, gardens and tracts of Scottish land. Of its many responsibilities, the NTS is particularly good at maintaining and running its gardens. Its duty to preserve the buildings in its care sometimes leads to short opening hours, especially out of season. NTS houses gleam with polished furniture, and guides are enthusiasts, if not experts. But despite attempts to give them a lived-in feeling, houses are inclined to lack the personal touches or downright eccentricity of those which are still privately owned. NTS membership allows you free entry to its properties in Scotland, and to those of its sister organisations in England and Ireland. NTS also organises conservational holidays, working in such places as Fair Isles.

• **The Forestry Commission**, 231 Corstorphine Road, Edinburgh EH12 7AT (031-334 0303). The Forestry Commission manages over 500,000 hectares of woodland in Scotland. Visitors are allowed to walk on forest roads, and there are trails for cyclists and horses too. The Forestry Commission picnic site, with its wooden benches, is a common occurrence throughout the country. Individual Forest Districts publish leaflets with details of walks and facilities, which can be obtained from the local district office.

• **Scottish Youth Hostels Association**, 7 Glebe Crescent, Stirling FK8 2JA (0786) 451181. The SYHA runs 72 hostels ranging from cottages to Highland castles, and organises various activity holidays, including skiing, sailing, walking and pony-trekking (ask for the *Breakaway Holidays* leaflet).

• **Scottish Wildlife Trust**, Cramond House, Kirk Cramond, Cramond Glebe Road, Edinburgh EH4 6NS (031-312 7765). Most of the SWT's 89 wildlife reserves are open to the public and the Trust will advise on ranger services, guided walks, best times to visit and any restrictions on wildlife photography. Publications include *Scottish Wildlife* magazine and leaflets on individual reserves.

HINTS AND TIPS

• In the reorganisation of local government of 1975, the old Scottish counties were replaced by nine regions and three island areas, subdivided into districts. Dislike of belonging to administrative areas with uninspired names, such as Central, has led many Scots to continue referring to the old counties, such as Stirlingshire, even in postal addresses. A number of even older names such as Lochaber or the Mearns are also used – some of them, to add to the confusion, have been adopted as names for the new districts. The boundaries of the various tourist boards often match those of neither the new districts nor the old counties, with unique creations, such as the Forth Valley Tourist Board, making their appearance.
• In the Highlands and islands, many of the smaller roads are single-track with passing places. Driving on them demands a slow speed and awareness of cars coming the other way. There is no rule of precedence at passing places, though the satisfaction of getting polite waves from other drivers is motivation for being the first to give way. It is very useful to have a tow rope in your car, in case you come across a driver who has been gazing at the scenery and has put a wheel in the ditch, blocking the road to all traffic.

• Scottish beer comes in many varieties, but is generally stronger, darker and sweeter than its English equivalent. Draught beer is traditionally either 'heavy' or 'export'. Asking for 'bitter' may cause puzzlement.

• Scottish banks issue their own notes, and the one-pound note is still widely used. There is seldom any problem in getting them accepted south of the Border.

• Scotland does not share the same public holidays as England and Wales, and on Scottish public holidays usually only the banks and perhaps some chain stores close. Instead, towns will have their own local or 'trades' holidays. It may be worth finding out when these are, especially in the case of Glasgow and Edinburgh.

• In the far north, London newspapers may not arrive until late in the day. The three main daily Scottish papers are *The Scotsman*, *The Herald* and *The Aberdeen Press and Journal*. All are worth reading for their insights into Scottish thinking. Local papers flourish and are a valuable source of information on local events and attractions.

• October is a favourite holiday time for Historic Scotland's custodians, so check that the smaller sights will be open before you visit them.

BACKGROUND READING

GENERAL HISTORY
J D Mackie *A History of Scotland* (Penguin)
John Prebble *The Lion in the North* (Penguin)
T C Smout *A History of the Scottish People 1560–1830* (Fontana)

SPECIFIC HISTORIES OR HISTORICAL NOVELS
Antonia Fraser *Mary Queen of Scots* (Mandarin)
John Prebble *The Highland Clearances*, *Culloden*, *The Darien Disaster* and *Glencoe* (all Penguin)
John Buchan *Montrose* (Greenwood Press, out of print)
Eric Linklater *The Prince in the Heather*, Prince Charles' wanderings after Culloden (Panther, out of print)
George Macdonald Fraser *The Steel Bonnets*, a companion to border warfare by the author of the *Flashman* books (Collins)
The Wallace and *The Bruce Trilogy* (Hodder & Stoughton) by Nigel Tranter add colour to Scotland's medieval history.
Sir Walter Scott's *Waverley*, about the 1745 rising (Oxford University Press), and *Old Mortality*, on the Covenanters (Penguin), are worth trying.

MEMOIRS
Lord Cockburn *Memorials of his Time* (post-Enlightenment Edinburgh) (Mercat Press)
Elizabeth Grant *Memoirs of a Highland Lady* (Canongate)
Johnson and Boswell *A Tour to the Hebrides and a Journey to the Western Isles* (Oxford University Press)

NOVELISTS OR POETS FOR PARTICULAR AREAS
Neil Gunn (Caithness and the far north)
George Mackay Brown (Orkney)

Lewis Grassic Gibbon (Aberdeenshire)
Sir Walter Scott *Heart of Midlothian* (Edinburgh) and *Rob Roy* (the Trossachs) (Everyman Classics)
Alasdair Gray, William MacIlvanney and Neill Munro (Glasgow)
Robert Louis Stevenson's *Kidnapped* (World International Publishing), Compton Mackenzie's *Whisky Galore* (Penguin) and Derek Cooper's *Hebridean Connection* (Fontana) (West Highlands and Islands)
David Thomson *Nairn in Darkness and Light* (Arrow Books)
Poems by Robert Burns (South-West)
Robert Garioch (Edinburgh)

Maps

The Michelin map of Scotland (1:400,000) covers the whole country; the Ordnance Survey Routemaster series (1:250,000) would be a good choice for those on touring holidays; walkers will need the Landranger (1:50,000) or Pathfinder (1:25,000) maps.

KEY MAP OF SCOTLAND

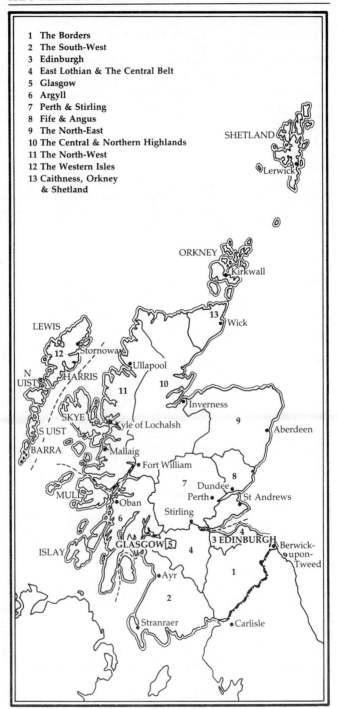

1 The Borders
2 The South-West
3 Edinburgh
4 East Lothian & The Central Belt
5 Glasgow
6 Argyll
7 Perth & Stirling
8 Fife & Angus
9 The North-East
10 The Central & Northern Highlands
11 The North-West
12 The Western Isles
13 Caithness, Orkney
   & Shetland

SHETLAND

Lerwick

ORKNEY

Kirkwall

LEWIS

13 Wick

12 Stornoway

Ullapool

N UIST

HARRIS

11

10

SKYE

Inverness

S UIST

Kyle of Lochalsh

9

BARRA

Mallaig

Aberdeen

Fort William

MULL

8

7 Dundee

Oban

Perth

St Andrews

6

Stirling

GLASGOW 5

4

3 EDINBURGH

Berwick-upon-Tweed

ISLAY

4

Ayr

1

2

Stranraer

Carlisle

THE SCOTTISH BORDERS

- An exceptionally varied landscape, ranging from windswept sheep pasture to fertile woodland or rocky coast
- A fascinating, violent past, which has left castles, abbeys and a rich folk tradition in its wake
- Compact, ancient burghs, all different, surrounded by unfrequented countryside

Jedburgh Abbey

FOR the better part of three centuries, between the first invasion by Edward I of England in 1296 and the union of the crowns of England and Scotland in 1603, the Borders were the battleground for two warring nations. Those three hundred years of constant invasion, counter-invasion, siege, burning and plunder have shaped the land and its people more significantly than anything that has happened since. They left the countryside scattered with ancient fortresses, with the ruins of once-great abbeys, and with small towns which may have seemed in the twelfth century to have a prosperous future ahead of them, but which were to be burned and burned again, while trade and influence moved elsewhere. They also left an obsession with riding, a fierce local pride and a vivid folk-culture – the ballads.

For the inhabitant of those times, on both sides of the frontier between England and Scotland, nothing was worth possessing which was not portable. Horses, weapons and cattle were the currency of the Borders, and 'gear' was accumulated by raiding, not by trade. This was the age of the reiver – the horseman with his lance and his steel bonnet riding secret hill routes by night, descending in a flurry of violence on village or farmstead, driving his slow, mooing plunder homewards.

The predation was by no means a simple question of Scots against English. Constant feuding between families, cross-Border connivance, protection rackets and bribery by the agents of one or other government meant that the Borderer was accustomed to putting his own interest before that of his neighbour, and was as ready to steal the cattle next door as to rustle those across the frontier. The frontier provided an easy refuge for those on the run and, for both the Scottish and English authorities, attempts to impose order were a nightmare. Over the years a whole canon of frontier law involving a degree of cross-Border co-operation came into being. It was enforced by the six Wardens of the Marches, three on each side of the frontier, with varying degrees of success. Yet it never succeeded in stopping the raiding; it took the Union of the Crowns in 1603 to do that. Sixty hours' hard riding brought Robert Carey from London to Edinburgh with Queen Elizabeth's coronation ring to hand to her successor, James VI, King of Scotland, and the frontier disappeared for ever.

Today, crossing from England into Scotland, it is hard to believe that the frontier ever existed. Only on the high pass of Carter Bar across the Cheviots, with its sudden panorama of the Tweed Valley beneath, is there any sense of climax. Indeed, the history and culture on either side of that old frontier are so intimately bound together that the Borderers of Scotland and England can be said to have more in common with each other than with the rest of their respective nations: to confine your exploration to one side is to see only half the picture. We cannot cover the whole English Border country in this guide, but we have included Berwick-upon-Tweed. The town was part of Scotland for four centuries; it is the logical place to base yourself if you want to explore the east coast, and its football team still plays in the Scottish league. So, for the purposes of this book, we are bringing Berwick home.

Border country

It is surprising to anyone who knows the area that the Borders are the least visited region of Scotland; less than 5 per cent of Scotland's tourists stay here for any length of time. Most people pass through on their way to better-known areas further north. If you choose to go against the trend, you will find your enterprise well rewarded.

The region's pleasures are subtle, for the hills are lonely rather than dramatic, the towns quirky but unassuming, the coastline rugged but not wild, the people hospitable but reticent. Yet in all of Scotland there are few other regions with such a mixture of landscapes; bleak moorland lies only a few minutes' road journey from thick beech woods and lush pasture. The character of the countryside changes with a peculiar rapidity, often between one river valley and the next.

In the Borders, the past intrudes on the present with an equal suddenness as you come across a ruined tower half concealed by trees, spot a place name from a sixteenth-century ballad, or see the outline of Iron Age ramparts on the crest of a hill. It pays to become a little obsessive about the past here. Tracking down old castles will lead you from end to end of the region, but you can equally well pursue Roman remains, old churches, drove roads, Iron Age settlements, eighteenth-century bridges or the relics of the once-magnificent railway network, whose stark embankments and broken bridges bear witness to the most recent vandalism inflicted on the region.

There is a final consideration: in foul weather the Scottish Borders are much less depressing than the wilderness areas north of the Highland Line. There is more to be seen under

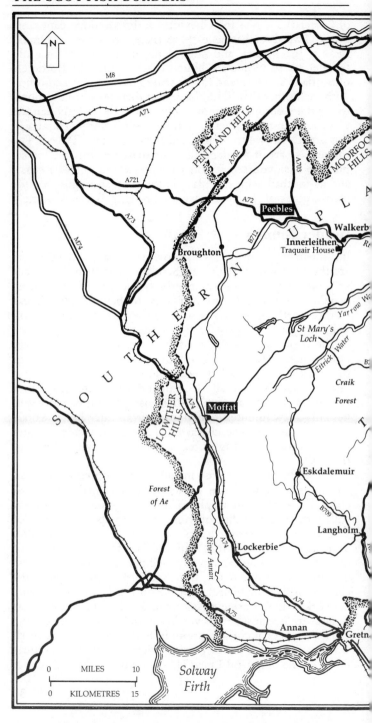

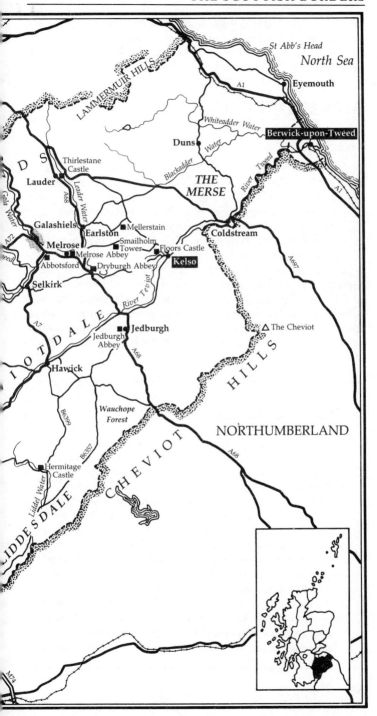

cover; you do not suffer the frustration of being unable to see magnificent landscape because it is shrouded by low cloud and driving rain and, if the worst comes to the worst, Edinburgh and Glasgow are within easy reach.

ANNANDALE

Gretna Green

For many visitors travelling up the western route from England on the A74, Gretna Green is their first taste of Scotland. Even if you did not guess from the coach parks and the piper touting for tips, the signs would remind you that the place is world-famous. The romance of runaway lovers is the draw: Gretna Green owes its celebrity to a long-gone difference of law between England and Scotland, whereby a declaration in front of witnesses was enough to formalise marriage in Scotland after such marriages had become illegal in England. For the self-styled Gretna 'priests' elopement was a lucrative trade. Traditionally these priests are supposed to have been blacksmiths – which is why anvils play such a central part in Gretna mythology, and why you can undergo a mock ceremony over one if you so desire. In its modern

Practical suggestions

The Scottish Borders are sufficiently compact to make it unimportant where you choose to stay, but a car is virtually essential for proper exploration. For family holidays by the sea, consider **Eyemouth** or the tiny coastal outpost of **St Abbs**.

Border hills are rounded, grass-covered and lonely. In the south-west, round **Liddesdale** and **Eskdale**, conifers cover many of them. The best walking areas are either the **Cheviots** to the south or the high, bleak ground at the head of the River Yarrow. Sections of the **Southern Upland Way**, a coast-to-coast footpath across southern Scotland (a guide is obtainable from tourist offices), cut across the high ground here and make for good walking. If you prefer driving to walking, the **Lammermuir Hills** are probably the best area to explore, with small roads winding across open moorland and deep, hidden valleys.

Serious anglers should get hold of the *Scottish Borders Angling* incarnation Gretna Green is a sorry tourist trap. The Old Smithy, apart from its anvil and a collection of coaches, is otherwise a large gift shop glittering with brass, and its more genteel rival down the road, Gretna Hall Hotel (with another anvil and a bridal chamber), has plenty of selling space too. The most incongruous object in the whole place is a modern statue called, pretentiously, Smith God – a human figure struggling to escape from the spears, swords and bits of old iron into which he seems to have fallen. Gretna Green thrives on cash, though endearing graffiti with hearts and arrows show that some people are still somehow determined to get their money's worth.

The Debatable Land

Head east from Gretna on the back roads towards Canonbie and you enter one of the bloodiest parts of the Borders. The landscape is now innocent, rolling farmland, but for more than three hundred years it was a no man's land between the Scots and English, claimed by both but subject to the rule of neither, a haven for those who lived by thievery. In 1552 it was divided, with the French ambassador acting as referee. A dike was dug, cutting the land in half. Its line is still clearly marked by a plantation of trees. **Canonbie**, on the Scots side

Guide, available from the Scottish Borders Tourist Board (for address, see page 66).

Bargain-hunting round the mill shops of the region's textile factories is a favourite occupation. **Hawick** is the place to go for woollens, **Selkirk** and **Galashiels** for tweeds or tartans. **Walkerburn**, in the Tweed Valley, is another possibility.

Borders life is at its most vivid at the rugby grounds and at the Common Riding festivals. Rugby (especially the 'sevens' variety) is a Borders obsession. April is the month to catch these tournaments, the Melrose Sevens probably being the best known. The Common Ridings mostly take place between May and July. Almost every sizeable town has its local celebration, some with a tradition extending back hundreds of years, others more recent creations or revivals. Those in the central Borders are firmly horse-centred and may combine a riding of the town's old boundaries with pageantry associated with heroic events of the past. They are serious and deeply felt occasions, not just put on for the tourist.

of the line, is the site of an old priory, and now boasts a good place for lunch at the Riverside Inn, beside the Esk.

In the squelchy morass of Solway Moss near Gretna a few hundred English Border riders shattered the Scottish army of James V in 1542 as it ploughed southward into England. The defeat ushered in the destructive campaigns of the 'Rough Wooing', when Henry VIII of England tried to persuade the Scots to marry the infant Mary Queen of Scots to his son by indiscriminately burning and looting southern Scotland.

Good bases

- **Moffat** This small town was once a spa, and retains the atmosphere of an early Victorian hill resort. Poised between hill country and the lowlands leading down to the Solway Firth, it is in an ideal position for exploring the western edge of the Borders, for touring into Dumfries and Galloway, or for travelling up to the Clyde Valley and Glasgow. There is plenty of accommodation here, mostly bed-and-breakfast.
- **Peebles** An ancient royal burgh, fortuitously placed among some of the best of Tweed Valley scenery, Peebles is a thriving one-time county town and a bustling centre for day excursions from Edinburgh and Glasgow. There are notable things to see in the town itself, some interesting shops and a large range of hotels and guesthouses. The best sights in the Tweed Valley are only a few minutes away by car, and good walks abound.
- **Kelso** The most appealing of all the Border towns, thanks to its graceful square, the ruined abbey and the River Tweed which flows round it, Kelso is well placed for exploring the central Borders, especially the abbeys and stately homes. The Cheviot Hills, with their intricate valleys and fine walks, are about 20 minutes' drive away. Accommodation in Kelso is sparser than in Peebles or Moffat, for the town is less obviously on the holiday trail, but there is a reasonable range.
- **Berwick-upon-Tweed** The town has been English since 1482, but Scotland laps up to its doorstep. Once an important port, now a quiet river-mouth town, old Berwick is enclosed by sixteenth-century ramparts and has streets lined by elegant eighteenth-century buildings. You will find old coaching-inns within the walls and plenty of guesthouses outside. Berwick is a logical base for exploring the east coast up as far as Edinburgh, or down into Northumbria.

The Romans were here too, leaving, at **Burnswark**, a kind of assault course for attacking hilltop forts. The climb up the hill above the earthworks of the old camp is short, but gives you good views of the Solway estuary to the south and the hills above Moffat to the north.

Thomas Carlyle, one of the graver of Scotland's Victorian sages, was born in the skittish-sounding **Ecclefechan**. 'One life, – a little gleam of time between two Eternities,' he wrote. The village, a quiet place of trees and harled cottages, seems unsuited to such a weighty sentiment. The **Arched House** (NTS, open Apr to Oct, daily 12 to 4.30), where he was born, was built by his father. Inside it is more like a shrine than a museum – and the custodian is primed to make a convert of you if you show signs of interest.

Lockerbie is now irrevocably linked to the tragedy of

THE BORDER BALLADS

We can only guess at the reasons why the bloodstained Borderland produced the stirring poetry it did. Sir Walter Scott, who first started collecting the old ballads which had been handed down for generations, put it down to a link between a wild society and the wild violence of poetry. Whatever the case, reading the ballads while touring the Borders gives immediacy to the history. Among them you will find the tale of Thomas Rhymer's journey into fairyland, the rescue of Tam Lin from enchantment, the battle of Otterburn where Douglas and Percy met in a fierce night–time encounter, the slaying of Lord Douglas and his seven sons, and the lament of the Border Widow. Four of the best ballads come from Liddesdale, among them the tale of Kinmont Willie's rescue from Carlisle Castle, and the raid suffered by Jamie Telfer in the Fair Dodhead and how it was avenged.

Irritatingly, since the *Penguin Book of Border Ballads* (edited by William Beattie) went out of print, there is no comprehensive and compact collection. The *Penguin Book of Folk Ballads*, which contains the most famous examples of the genre, is now also out of print. When in the Borders keep an eye open for the locally published *The Ballads of Liddesdale*, by Michael Robson.

December 1988, when a fully laden aircraft, blown apart by a terrorist bomb, descended on the town. At the far end of the town's graveyard (out on the Dumfries road) lies a still-raw garden of remembrance, and a simple memorial to those who died, the majority being from the United States. It is a corner of a sad America in a sad Scotland.

Moffat

Where the Southern Uplands close in on Annandale lies Moffat, reached in a couple of minutes from the A74 yet happily out of earshot of it. It seems a town of unlikely size and dignity until you realise it was once a spa and even had the distinction of its own branch railway line from Beattock. Its huge hydro hotel burned down early in the century, but it is still possible to visit the two mineral springs where Moffat's health-seeking visitors used to gather before breakfast. The stench of rotten eggs and the skeins of white gunge in the water are hardly tempting. Today, Moffat is bed-and-breakfast land – its sedate Victorian villas are thick with signs. It has everything you need for a couple of days – good walks close by, a broad, sedate High Street with shops selling woollens, antiques and sweeties (especially the renowned Moffat toffee), a little local museum, and the best of the sun if there is any. It also claims the narrowest detached hotel in Britain. Where most towns have statues of local worthies, Moffat's High Street boasts a huge sculptured ram. This is prosaically supposed to symbolise the links between the town and the woollen trade, but it is more fun to think it might be a fertility symbol.

Round Moffat

Moffat is backed by the high, bleak hills which separate the valleys of Annan, Clyde and Tweed (the sources of all three rivers are within walking distance of one another). From the town you can drive and then walk into the **Devil's Beef Tub**, a huge and gloomy declivity in the hills, at its best in mist. This is the best-known of the many 'beef tubs' in the Border hills, where stolen cattle could be hidden and easily guarded. Eight miles up the narrow valley of the Moffat Water, on the A708, you reach the **Grey Mare's Tail**, a waterfall which drops from a hanging valley. This is a popular spot for outings, though the crowds seldom reach oppressive numbers. Beware of coaches on the narrow road.

To see the waterfall, you must walk a short distance from the car park on a slightly vertiginous track (the most dangerous section is now barricaded off).

Alternatively, a longer, steeper walk on the northern side of the Tail Burn leads you to the top of the fall, and eventually to Loch Skeen above it, set in some of the wildest country in the Borders. There are usually feral goats in the area, although they keep themselves to themselves – unlike the local sheep, which have learned that tourists are a soft touch.

Another good, and unfrequented, walk near Moffat is along **Glen Wamphray** (take the minor road south towards Boreland to reach it), where a burn of limpid clarity boils in rock cauldrons among the trees. Well-engineered duckboards and steps save you from the bogs.

The Kagyu Samye Ling Tibetan centre is also within easy reach.

LIDDESDALE

Liddesdale, valley of the Armstrongs, was for centuries the most piratical, the least law-abiding, the worst (in the eyes of the authorities) of all the Border valleys – and from Liddesdale have come the most stirring ballads: *Jock o' the Side*, *Jamie Telfer*, and *Dick o' the Cow*. All are scattered with Liddesdale place names such as Mangerton and Pudding-Burn.

Detour down to the iron bridge over the river at **Kershope-foot**. The English border runs away from you up the burn opposite, into the outlying conifers of the Kielder forest. The junction of burn and river was one of the meeting places for the English and Scottish Wardens of the Border Marches. On designated days of truce, both sides would meet at places like this to settle cross-border disputes under the complicated procedures of the law of the Marches. They were tense occasions, more than once degenerating into fights. It is curious to think, sitting on the peaceful banks of the Liddel, that this place was once a hair-trigger frontier.

Somewhere round here the refugee Earl of Westmorland, after a failed rebellion in support of Mary Queen of Scots, changed clothes and swords with Jock o' the Side, and it was near this ford, if we are to believe the ballads, that the Captain of Bewcastle was shot through 'the left ba' stane'. Now it is all farmland and forestry. There is no heritage centre at Kershopefoot yet, so you will need to have a good imagination, and preferably a copy of George Macdonald Fraser's *The Steel Bonnets*.

There is a heritage centre at **Newcastleton** (open end May to end Sept, daily 1.30 to 4.30), a little way up the valley, where the Armstrongs will tell you all you could ever want to know about their clan. On show are many documents and some photographs. From Newcastleton a back road leads to Langholm, crossing the Tarras Moss. This bleak stretch was an invaluable refuge for the inhabitants of Liddesdale whenever the law tried to catch up with them, and if you cross it you can see why.

If you need a picnic spot, wait until you get to the valley of the Tarras Water, where the landscape suddenly softens.

Hermitage Castle

(HS, standard times, weekends only in winter)

This is the most menacing castle in Scotland, once the stronghold of the Keeper of Liddesdale. It is a great square lump of virtually windowless masonry, pierced on two sides by flying arches like sharks' mouths – a cross between prison and frontier fortress. The massively thick walls are stained algae-green where the light does not reach them and nothing in the remains of the interior suggests comfort, least of all the horrible pit prison.

Throughout most of its early history the castle changed hands between Scots and English and was held successively by Douglases, Dacres and Hepburns, with plenty of plotting and cross-border treachery revolving round it. One of its earliest lords, William de Soulis, supposedly dabbled in demonology within the walls until he met his fate (according to Leyden's ballad) by being wrapped in sheets of lead and boiled alive in a cauldron at the nearby stone circle of Nine Stane Rig.

In 1342, Sir Alexander Ramsay, rescuer of Black Agnes at the siege of Dunbar Castle (page 165), was starved to death in the pit prison by Sir William Douglas, his torment horribly prolonged by a trickle of grain from a storeroom above. In 1566 Mary Queen of Scots rode the 40 or so miles from Jedburgh and back again in a single day when her future husband James Hepburn, fourth Earl of Bothwell, was lying wounded at Hermitage after a tangle with one of the local villains, 'little' Jock (wha daur meddle wi' me?) Elliot. It was an unfortunate journey for the Queen, who lost her watch in a mire (see Jedburgh, page 43) and caught a fever from which she nearly died.

Hermitage Castle was restored in the early nineteenth century, extremely effectively in view of its current air of nastiness. Although it has played no part in history since the union of the crowns, it is one of those places you sense to be dormant, not extinct.

ESKDALE

Langholm is the southernmost – and perhaps the most fanatical – of the Border rugby-playing towns. Situated at the meeting of three valleys, it is full of bridges and people on their way to somewhere else.

The best approach is from the east down from the Tarras moors (see Liddesdale, page 39). From this road, you will see a piece of sculpture, shaped like an open book pierced by cut-outs, which is a memorial to Hugh McDiarmid, Scotland's greatest modern poet, whose childhood was spent in Langholm. The memorial's appearance, its siting and its very existence aroused huge local controversy (McDiarmid not having been at all popular with some elements in his home town), and the fact that it ended up in this little-travelled spot in the moors can still arouse the ire of Scottish literati.

The village of **Eskdalemuir** is surrounded by miles of trees, but is worth visiting to see the **Kagyu Samye Ling Tibetan Centre** (service 1.30 to 3 daily – visitors welcome; office closes at 5.30). Prayer flags flutter outside an old shooting-lodge, whose brightly coloured window frames provide another clue that the building has departed from its original purpose.

At the back, hidden from the road, lies the largest Tibetan temple in Europe. In this high, bleak landscape it is an astonishing burst of colour; inside, the red and the gilt dazzle, while rows of Buddhas gaze contemplatively down at you. The centre runs residential courses on aspects of Buddhism (write for a brochure to Eskdalemuir, Dumfriesshire DG13 0QL).

TEVIOTDALE

The A7 between Langholm and Hawick is not the most attractive of roads, running for most of its distance in a trench between undistinguished hills. However, it is certainly the most convenient route from the west coast to the centre of the Scottish Borders.

It is easy to miss Teviothead, which is just a few scattered cottages beyond the watershed where the burns start to run north-east to the Tweed. A craft shop with a totem pole outside houses the **Museum of Border Arms and Armour** (open all year), worth a stop to pick the brains of its knowledgeable curator about the weaponry on display and how the Borderers used it to slaughter each other. Teviothead is also where the notorious raider Johnnie Armstrong was 'convicted of common theft' and strung up by his King, James V. 'What wants yon knave that a king should have?' said James, seeing Armstrong's finery. Legend rapidly turned Johnnie into the betrayed patriot; 'I am but a fool to seek grace at a graceless face,' he is supposed to have said, before meeting his fate. Whatever the truth, the memorial in the old churchyard here is firmly on Johnnie's side.

Hawick

This is a busy textile town, with none of the gentility of Melrose or the county-town atmosphere of Kelso. It is grey, grainy, and has enough bleak-fronted mills left to remind you that woollens, especially stockings, have long been its *raison d'être*. Mill shops with bargain bins offer splendid opportunities for a rummage.

Shopping apart, there is an excellent reason to visit Hawick on a grey day: the Teviotdale Leisure Centre, with its steamy tropical pool. In Wilton Park, the local museum's displays are in need of an upgrade, but there is plenty of fascinating material about the hosiery industry and the working conditions of a previous century. Perhaps the most notable exhibit is the jumper which established the world record for the time taken to produce a garment from the back of a sheep – a feat accomplished in as short a time as four hours and thirty-five minutes.

Jedburgh

Jedburgh is a long, thin town, running along the Jed Water in a steepish valley, and is the first you will reach in Scotland if you come up the A68 over Carter Bar. Only 10 miles from the frontier and in the heart of Teviotdale, it has seen plenty of violence in its time; its inhabitants gained a reputation for obstinate independence, and for playing football with Englishmen's heads – the streamers attached to the ball in today's festive version represent the hair. Jedburgh has lent its name to the Jeddart axe (one of the most common Border weapons) and to Jeddart justice (hang first and try later). The Jeddart snail (a curly peppermint) ranks alongside Hawick Balls, Berwick Cockles and the Galashiels Soor Plooms in the list of Border confectionery, and was apparently invented in the eighteenth century by a bored French prisoner. Jedburgh was once a textile town, with a polluted river and a huge rayon factory, but all industrial dereliction has been swept away and the main road now runs past open spaces fringed by modern housing.

Jedburgh Abbey

(HS, standard times)
The excavations of 1984 and the opening of a small visitor centre have allowed Historic Scotland to make a first-class job of interpretation here. The plainsong in the visitor centre, the scale model, the helpful explanations at viewpoints within the site and the clear, concise guidebook make Jedburgh the best starting point for exploration of the Border abbeys.

It is an austere ruin, much of its architecture being Romanesque and some of it dating from the fifteenth century, when repairs were made after English raids. There are plenty of architectural curiosities for enthusiasts. Jedburgh, like other Border abbeys, was founded on the initiative of King David I in 1138 for a community of Augustinian canons, and, like the others, suffered not only from the depredations of the English but also from the eventual diversion of resources into the pockets of commendators – officers appointed by the crown, usually with only the most spurious religious qualifications – shortly before the Reformation of 1560. The abbey church at Jedburgh remains remarkably intact despite this, but most of the surrounding buildings have not survived above their foundations.

43

Jedburgh Castle Jail

(Open Easter to Sept, Mon to Sat 10 to 5, Sun 1 to 5)

The jail is well worth the steep walk from the town centre. There is nothing left of the old castle: it was long ago demolished by the Scots to stop the English using it. A jail was built on its site in the eighteenth century on the lines of the best contemporary model, and remains complete. The old cell blocks, the governor's office and the kitchen are sufficiently unchanged to give you a good idea of what life was like for the prisoners.

The first floor contains a local museum with plenty of insights into Jedburgh life.

Mary Queen of Scots House and Visitor Centre

(Open Easter to mid-Nov, daily 10 to 5)

There is something a little unsettling about this museum. The late sixteenth-century fortified house is lovely but it is not entirely certain that Mary stayed here when she was in Jedburgh, though the guidebook does not admit to any such doubts. This would matter less if it were not that the museum chooses to plunge you into a kind of Shakespearean tragedy rather than tell a straight story. Mary's life is split into Prologue, Drama and Epilogue, all linked (we are told) to Mary's motto 'in my end is my beginning'. Early music echoes through the rooms and snippets of text are displayed on engraved glass panels: they are so hard to read that they have to be repeated on printed cards.

The highest point of this high-minded kitsch is the empty white chamber which 'symbolises the full circle of Mary's drama', but is a more telling symbol of the size of the house in comparison to the small number of genuine exhibits. By far the most intriguing object in the place is the French watch unearthed by a mole in 1817 on the route of Mary's ride to Hermitage. You may come away with a lot of odd ideas about Mary, but the house and the watch are certainly worth going to see.

Near Jedburgh

Down by the Teviot, off the B6400, the **Harestanes Visitor Centre** (open Easter to end Oct, daily 10.30 to 5.30) has a

BORDER CASTLES

One hundred and forty-seven castles are listed in Mike Salter's gazetteer *Discovering Scottish Castles* (Shire) in the area covered by this chapter. Half-crumbled into the fields, hidden by trees or restored and converted into homes, they are everywhere. The biggest, such as Roxburgh or Jedburgh, were too vulnerable to being taken and held by the English and were often demolished by the Scots themselves, so the ruins that remain are usually simple rectangular towers or 'peles', mostly dating from the sixteenth century. They are simple structures, usually with a vaulted ground-floor room, the main hall directly above, and a further one, or perhaps two, storeys. Entrance was on the first floor. Much of the life went on outside the tower in the surrounding enclosure called the 'barmkin', where cattle could be sheltered in times of trouble. Pele towers were designed to hold off small raids. They did not catch fire easily and could act as a rallying point and defensive centre whenever a raid was threatened. Even so, they were not entirely invulnerable – there are records of raiding parties climbing the walls and breaking in through the roof – but they did give some protection to humans, even if the cattle were rustled from under the walls.

Most of the ruined towers are still on private land, and you should obtain permission before exploring. The ruins are often precarious, so you venture into them at your own risk. As well as the castles mentioned in the text, look out for:

• **Cessford** (near Jedburgh), stronghold of the Cessford Kerrs, now a riven hulk of red stone, easily visible from a nearby road.

• **Ferniehurst** (near Jedburgh), belonging to the Ferniehurst Kerrs and open to the public on Wednesdays, May to Oct, 1.30 to 4.30.

• **Fatlips** (near Minto), an inaccessible jagged ruin perched on top of Minto crags near Jedburgh.

• **Whitton** (near Morebattle), a ruin in a farmyard, surrounded by hens.

• **Gilknockie** (near Langholm), now restored, may have been the hold of Johnnie Armstrong, the notorious raider. You can see round by making an appointment – enquire at the tourist board, address and telephone number on page 66.

series of pleasing walks centred on the steading of an old estate. Much imagination has gone into providing original puzzles, games and exhibitions – all about, or using, wood.

Off the A68 to the south of Jedburgh, at Mervinslaw, you will find the **Jedforest Deer and Farm Park** (open May to end Oct, daily 10 to 5.30), which is refreshingly unpatronising and is good for families. For picturesque villages, try Ancrum or Denholm; for views, climb Rubers Law. For excellent smoked produce, visit the Teviot Smokery, just beyond Eckford, and for drives through splendid Border scenery, the patchwork of roads round Oxnam and Hownam (a short stretch on the line of the Roman Dere Street) is recommended.

SELKIRK

Selkirk would have had its own abbey if the Tyronensian monks had not been moved to Kelso in 1128. They may have been grateful, for Selkirk's position on a steep hillside is rather exposed. The long High Street has a statue of Walter Scott at one end and one of Mungo Park, the explorer of the Niger, at the other. Here, too, is the fierce Flodden Memorial by Thomas Clapperton, who was also responsible for the magnificent war memorial in Galashiels. Of all Border towns, Selkirk seems to have taken the terrible battle of Flodden in 1513 most to heart. **Halliwell House** (open Apr to Oct, Mon to Sat 10 to 5, Sun 2 to 4; July, Aug daily 10 to 6) is one of the best local museums in the Borders, with a complete ironmonger's shop and much well-presented information on the growth of the town; here you can see the Flodden flag, brought home by the town's sole survivor of the disaster, while the centrepiece of the town's Common Riding ceremony is a re-enactment of the wordless casting down of that tattered standard five centuries ago. This battle, in which Scotland lost one of her best kings (James IV) and 10,000 men, turned one of the most promising periods in Scottish history back into the more usual course of internal strife and misery.

Directly beneath the High Street, Selkirk's textile mills are gathered in a solemn row by the river. A number are deserted (and make good subjects for atmospheric photography), but there are still enough working for this to be profitable hunting ground if you are looking for tweeds and tartans. Seek out a Selkirk bannock before leaving the town – this sweet, sultana-packed variety of bread tastes addictive.

Ettrick

A drive up the Ettrick takes you through the whole range of Borders scenery. At first, you travel through rich farmland, with cows chewing the cud in the fields and a large mansion (Bowhill) distantly glimpsed through the trees. The river is wide and alluring, with hardly a bridge. Ettrickbridge, a tiny village, marks the start of the sheep country, the river narrowing and flowing faster through defiles, or flattening into shingly stretches, the haunt of oyster-catchers. Higher still, the village of Ettrick is just a few houses and a red sandstone memorial to James Hogg, the 'Ettrick Shepherd', who is better known today for his psychological novel *Confessions of a Justified Sinner* than for the poetry that originally made him famous. Now the road becomes single track and the hills close in, forming barriers so that it is hard to see where the valley is going to turn next. However, at the very head of Ettrick, once one of the most unspoilt and beautiful places in the Borders, the landscape has been ruined by spruce plantations. It is a depressing climax to a lovely drive.

Yarrow

It was in the flat ground between Ettrick and Yarrow, just upstream of Selkirk, that Montrose fought the disastrous engagement of Philiphaugh – his first major defeat by the Covenanters (see page 134). The victory was stained by massacre: in accordance with their battle-cry of 'Jesus and no quarter', the zealots slaughtered Montrose's camp-followers in the courtyard of Newark Castle nearby. You can reach the atmospheric remains of this stark tower above the Yarrow through the Bowhill estate.

Bowhill and beyond

(House open July, Mon to Sat 1 to 4.30, Sun 2 to 6; country park open end Apr to end Aug, Mon to Thurs and Sat 12 to 5, Sun 2 to 6, July as for house)
The family of Scott of Buccleuch was once among the most prominent of the Border 'riding families', and since the days of 'Bold Buccleuch', who replied to Elizabeth of England's accusation of presumptuous daring with 'What is there that a

man dare not do?', the family has tied itself to the Douglases, the Montagues, and the Royal Family too. Many of the treasures they have accumulated over the centuries now rest at this mansion hidden in the trees a few miles west of Selkirk. It is not the most elegant of houses, for its simple lines were considerably altered during the nineteenth century, but the quality of what lies inside makes it essential visiting for those who like stately homes; nearly all the best Scottish portrait painters, French furniture masters, miniaturists and makers of fine porcelain are represented. The Raeburn portrait of Sir Walter Scott with Hermitage Castle in the background and the extraordinary painting of George IV in Highland dress are, in their separate ways, wonderful. So too are the Venetian scenes by Guardi, the early Lorrains and the portrait of Lady Caroline Scott by Reynolds. There are monstrosities too – particularly the silver candelabrum weighing 13 stone – and the unconsecrated chapel given over to relics of the Duke of Monmouth (who married a Scott) is a little too like a shrine. Perhaps the most intriguing object in the house is the Pittenweem-made clock of 1775, which, in good Presbyterian taste, plays tuneful airs six days a week, but ceases on Saturday and does not start again until the Sabbath is over.

Above Bowhill, the valley of the Yarrow is less beautiful than that of the Ettrick, though more celebrated by the ballads. The two roads which run over the hills to Ettrick have much to commend them as short diversions to obtain good views of both river valleys. The river starts at **St Mary's Loch**, a well-known beauty spot, apt on fine weekends to become a little too filled with the sails of yachts and sailboards to be called tranquil. The centre for most of the activity is the equally well-known **Tibbie Shiel's Inn**, once a convivial meeting place for Scott, Hogg and fellow writers, and equally convivial, if not quite so literary, today. Over the watershed beyond St Mary's, you come eventually to the Grey Mare's Tail, and so down to Moffat (page 38).

THE TWEED VALLEY

The run down the Tweed from the watershed north of Moffat is the classic Border tour. The landscape is gentle, with heather replacing grass on many of the hills; the castles and houses are grand or imposing, the towns prosperous and sunny. The river itself, moving from upland shingle runs to deep salmon pools, is consistently lovely.

The Upper Tweed Valley

Tweedhope Sheep Dogs (signposted from the A701) is an enterprise run by two veterans of *One Man and His Dog*, and if you can not attend a formal sheepdog trial you will find it offers a good substitute (displays at 11am, 2pm and 3pm). It is all small-scale and very friendly; a large Cheviot sheep gives rides to small children, and there are often collie puppies around. The smallest school ever to exist in Scotland, closed in the 1930s, stands in the grounds.

At **Tweedsmuir**, a detour on the minor road through the hills past the Talla Reservoir to St Mary's Loch takes you straight into the high, bleak and isolated country which fringes the Tweed to the east. If you stay on the A701, the valley begins to open out near Drumelzier. Here you are in Arthurian country, for at **Drumelzier** lies Merlin's grave. King Arthur fought his seventh battle (in the wood of Caledon) at Cademuir Hill above Peebles, and Merlin met St Kentigern at the 'altar stone' at Stobo. Such, at least, is the tradition.

At **Broughton**, you come to the boyhood haunts of John Buchan, author of *The Thirty-Nine Steps* and other tales of derring-do. A converted church, the **John Buchan Centre** (open May to end Sept, Mon to Sat 2 to 5), holds an excellent museum of his extraordinary career. Buchan was not only a novelist but Governor-General of Canada too, and the museum has photographs, mementoes and books in plenty, as well as knowledgeable curators happy to answer all questions. If you are in a mood to visit more museums, drive over the regional boundary to visit Biggar (see page 184), where there are another four.

Dawyck Botanic Garden

(Open mid-Mar to mid-Oct, daily 10 to 6)
The arboretum in this estate on the banks of the Tweed, just off the B712, is now an outstation of the Royal Botanic Garden in Edinburgh. Among the redwoods, Nootka cypresses and Douglas firs are many specimens over a century old. Most of the older planting runs along a small burn, where rhododendrons, azaleas, meconopsis and rodgersias lend colour in spring and autumn. A chapel sits in the middle of the wood; it was designed by William Burn, doyen of the Victorian version of the Scottish Baronial style, as was the house nearby. The gardens seem to be populated largely by enthusiasts –

tracks are worn through the long grass where visitors have detoured to read the labels. Nevertheless, this is a good spot for non-gardeners too.

Peebles

Not many towns are the subject of poems by kings, but James V wrote one about Peebles, describing the bustle and raucous excitement of the town's Beltane festival, which still takes place in mid-June. Peebles was a hunting base for Scottish kings, a former county town, and is a popular place for a day trip from Edinburgh. It has also been blessed by the perfect marketing slogan, uttered by a resident returning from abroad, 'Give me Peebles for Pleasure'. The town's pleasures are gentle ones – golf, fishing, walking, and above all excursions into the scenery, for it is well situated in the best of Tweed Valley countryside. It is an excellent place from which to tour: historic houses, castles and gardens lie nearby, and it is easy enough to lose the crowds by striking out a short distance into the hills.

The High Street fills up fast at weekends: buyers of gifts, antiques and woollens contend with people in town to do the Saturday shopping. There are craft shops and 'The Legendary Cake Company' down a wynd, a bookshop for browsing by the ancient Cuddy's brig, and old weavers' cottages beyond. There is no shortage of hotels, of which there is a good range, though they have to live in the shadow of the enormous Peebles Hotel Hydro, a vast, much-altered nineteenth-century spa hotel which sits in cheery splendour on the edge of town, host to family holidays and conferences alike.

In and near Peebles

Prominent on the High Street lies the **Chambers Institute** (open all year, Mon to Fri 10 to 1 and 2 to 5; Apr to Oct, Sat and Sun 2 to 5). This philanthropic foundation by the eponymous publisher comes in three parts – the Tweeddale museum, an art gallery and the Secret Room (in fact merely a gallery off the main stair), which is an unusual survival of the high-minded Victorian idea that a museum should uplift and enlighten its visitors. Quiet greys and clarets are the background to two large classical friezes – one a copy of a section from the Parthenon, the other the Alexander Frieze, done in similar heroic style by nineteenth-century Danish sculptor Bertil Thorvaldsen. It is worth a peep for the incongruity and the atmosphere of quiet erudition.

In a small wynd off the High Street, you will find the **Cornice** (open daily in summer, weekends spring and autumn), subtitled the Scottish Museum of Ornamental Plasterwork. This is a recreation of a plasterer's workshop from around the turn of the century, closely associated with an old local firm, L Grandison, whose work you will see in the restoration of Thirlestane Castle (page 59). This is a very small museum, and there is a real possibility of bumping into moulds or knocking busts of goddesses off shelves. The roof sprouts a jumble of patterns for flowers, fruits, geometrical abstracts and faces of nymphs or cupids. Explanations are rather vague, but it is possible to puzzle out the techniques of moulding work and of building running cornices with laths and templates. You are sometimes allowed to play at plastering on a wall; wellies and apron are provided.

Just outside the town, a little way upstream off the A72, **Neidpath Castle** (open Easter to end Sept, Mon to Sat 11 to 5, Sun 1 to 5) stands above a dark and swirly bit of the Tweed. This is a good, atmospheric ruin, with massively thick walls, tiny windows and a gloomy pit prison, in which you are invited to deposit your children. More seriously, Neidpath is an excellent place for learning about castle-building techniques, for the fourteenth-century triple-vaulted structure is clearly visible beneath the seventeenth-century alterations and the interior is bare. You can prowl right through the castle up to the roof, for most of it remains remarkably well preserved. Above Neidpath a waymarked path runs up either bank of the river, giving a round walk of six miles (a leaflet is obtainable from the tourist office).

For picnics or a view of gentle scenery, try the Meldon Hills or the valley of the Manor Water, both within easy reach of the town.

Traquair House

(Open Easter week, May, Sun and Mon; end May to end Sept daily 1.30 to 5.30; July, Aug daily 10.30 to 5.30)
Traquair is one of the most rewarding houses to visit in Scotland. There are plenty of sound historical reasons for coming here, as Traquair is the oldest continuously inhabited house in Scotland, possibly dating in part back to the tenth century. Twenty-seven monarchs are said to have visited over the centuries, and there are connections between Traquair and

many of the best-known figures of Scottish history. Mary Queen of Scots was here with her young son; Montrose may have been betrayed by the second Earl before the battle of Philiphaugh, while Prince Charles Edward was made welcome by the staunchly Jacobite household. The 'Bear Gates' on the main avenue were closed behind him as he left, and they will not be reopened until a Stewart sits on the throne again. Traquair also has the romance of having been a Catholic house in hostile country, with a priest's room where the incumbent could escape by a secret staircase.

The history, though, is somehow incidental to the charm that Traquair powerfully exerts on its visitors. What you remember is the odd yet harmonious shape of the house, which is mainly seventeenth-century and looks as if a large château had been grafted on to the back of a smaller one in similar style, the whole turned into a stage setting by the addition of side wings and iron gates. Part of the strangeness comes from seeing it at an angle as you arrive – for a Windsor is on the throne, and you come in by a side road.

This is an ancient house, not a stately home. The steep stone stairs, thick walls and small rooms are tortuous rather than elegant, and certainly do not distance you by their grandeur. Everywhere lies an array of objects, some ancient, some mysterious, others merely endearing.

The cleverness of the Traquair style, established by Peter Maxwell-Stewart and now continued by his daughter, is to recognise that museum-pieces are not all that visitors want to see. Consequently, a chest of musty documents, perhaps labelled merely Bundle XXVIII and tantalisingly unreadable, is displayed with the same degree of prominence as the fragile collection of Jacobite glassware or the rosary which belonged to Mary Queen of Scots. The tale of the house is brought right up to date with a modern letter from a firm of solicitors justifying a bill. Each has its place in the tale of the house and its family, and visitors are encouraged to speculate as well as to admire (and occasionally have their leg gently pulled too). Do not leave without sampling some Traquair ale, brewed on the premises, and taking a stroll round the craft workshops in nearby buildings.

Innerleithen

Peebles was given a poem by a king, Innerleithen a novel by Sir Walter Scott – *St Ronan's Well*. By turns a spa resort and a textile town, Innerleithen is still on the Woollen Trail, with intarsia work a speciality. It is not a big place, and the through traffic can be daunting, but do not miss **Robert Smail's Printing Works** (NTS, open Easter to end Oct, Mon to Sat 10 to 1 and 2 to 5, Sun 2 to 5) at the eastern end of the High Street. This little family business, whose technology, in the words of the guidebook, was 'as obsolete as the steam engine', was saved with all its equipment and business records intact in 1986. Excellent, imaginative work by the National Trust for Scotland (all the information is printed on the firm's machines, for example) allows a close-up of the life of a jobbing printer from the early nineteenth century onwards. The machines still run and you can practise setting type by hand or simply leaf through the guardbooks that are packed with the work done over a century or more – advertisements for sales, announcements of concerts, business cards, hymn sheets, menus and postcards.

Galashiels

Gala, as it is called, is home of the Scottish College of Textiles, centre of the tweed industry and the largest town in the area, with a rash of housing estates and light industry extending towards Melrose. Its tourist office is a sort of Portakabin, reflecting the town's low score in the sightseeing stakes, but Galashiels is one of the few towns in Britain that is worth visiting just to see the war memorial: under the clock tower, a Border reiver astride his horse seems to shout brave defiance across the centuries. Information about the sculptor, Thomas Clapperton, is on view at Old Gala House, on the hill behind the High Street. There is an excellent little historical display about the woollen industry in Peter Anderson's mill, where you can also see the modern machines at work (formal tours twice a day, but ask anyway).

Abbotsford

(Open mid-Mar to end Oct, Mon to Sat 10 to 5, Sun 2 to 5) This is the house that Sir Walter Scott built (most of it around 1822), and an odd one it turned out to be. It stands beside the B6360, and is well signposted. Few people would call its turreted, corbelled and battlemented architectural mish-mash pretty, but it is certainly intriguing. Inside, Abbotsford is less a literary shrine than a high-class junk shop. Most people would not have salvaged a door used by condemned criminals on their way to execution and set it into their own house, or hung the skull of an elk dug out of a Roxburgh bog in their entrance hall, but Scott loved curiosities such as these. The whole house is stuffed with a jumble of objects, many of them reputedly once belonging to the most famous figures in Scottish history. On show is a model of Robert the Bruce's skull, Montrose's sword, Rob Roy's sporran purse, a pocket book belonging to Flora Macdonald, plunder from the battlefields of Waterloo and Culloden, and more. Much was given to Scott by admirers, but most of it, including the collection of about 9,000 books, he assembled himself. It is in bad taste to ask how many of the relics are genuine: a wry grin is about all you will get by way of a response from the guides. Scott drew sightseers during his lifetime, but in nothing like the numbers that flock to his house today. Abbotsford was not constructed with coach parties in mind, and you can feel like a herring in a barrel if you go round when visitors are at their thickest. But Sir Walter's descendants and their staff cope cheerfully, and there is ample space in the ground and gardens (which contain their own curiosities).

MELROSE

The rugby ground and abbey car park are about the biggest things in this quiet red sandstone town, but its attractions are remarkably diverse. As well as the abbey, there is the wonderful **Melrose Motor Museum** (open mid-May to mid-Oct, daily 10.30 to 5.30, part-time from Easter), housed in an old garage down beyond the abbey. Almost all the cars and motorcycles on display were locally owned, and each has its snippet of history attached. The star is the 1909 Glasgow-built Albion, with massive coachwork and a speaking-tube through which to give the chauffeur orders. There are shelves and cupboards stuffed with ancient accessories, from 1930s motoring coats to a stove to heat your 'motor-house'. Children are kept off the most precious exhibits, but are allowed to romp on the 1943 Jeep.

Railway enthusiasts (and others) should not miss seeing the graceful spans of the **Leaderfoot Viaduct** which carried the old railway across the Tweed east of Melrose. It is one of the most delicate bridges to be found in the Borders.

Priorwood Gardens (NTS, open Easter to end Apr and Nov to Xmas, Mon to Sat 10 to 5.30; May to end Oct, Mon to Sat 10 to 5.30, Sun 2 to 5.30), near the abbey, specialise in flowers suitable for drying, and are much nicer than this bald description suggests. The flower-beds are small (but well-labelled) and the displays of preserved flowers and of preserving techniques persuade you to think what a pleasant hobby this might be. Beyond the garden, a quiet orchard, ideal for a picnic, is laid out to show the history of apple-growing from Roman times.

Melrose lies in the shadow of the **Eildon Hills**, a triple-peaked volcanic plug visible from all over the central Borders, and the focus of many legends. Michael Scott, the wizard who lies buried at Melrose, instructed the Devil to split the hill into three, and King Arthur's knights are said to sleep in its fastnesses. The Roman fortress of Trimontium was built beneath the Eildons too (a pillar marks the site). Views from the top of the Eildons are all you might expect: the climb up starts just south of the by-pass off the B6359.

Melrose Abbey

(HS standard times)
Melrose Abbey was thrust into prominence by Sir Walter Scott, who used the combination of moonlight, a wizard's grave and the old ruins to good effect in his poem *The Lay of the Last Minstrel*, and sent many people, as he later confessed, 'needlessly bat-hunting' to savour the gothic shivers for themselves. More prosaically, Melrose is widely agreed to be Scotland's finest Gothic building, with stone carving to rival the best in the United Kingdom. The first impression the ruins give is of delicate precariousness. Flying buttresses, reduced to a single course of stone, hang perilously between ruined masonry, while the east window, its internal tracery missing, is divided by pencil-thin columns of stone, ready to be blown down by the slightest wind. Scott chivvied the Duke of Buccleuch into preserving the crumbling remnants.

The interior would be quite lovely, even in its ruined state, if it were not for the hideous remains of the seventeenth-century parish kirk which was built inside the nave after the Reformation. Where there was once soaring fifteenth-century vaulting (the original twelfth-century building was almost entirely destroyed by the English), there is now a tunnel like a stone Nissen hut. To see what Melrose must once have been like you need to make for the presby-tery and the north transept, where some of the vaulting has survived the fall of the tower. The elaborations of stonework here, fragmentary though they are, are wonderful. Under the east window an embalmed heart in a casket was discovered in 1920 – perhaps that of Robert the Bruce.

The best views are from the outside, for here the seventeenth-century intrusions are not visible and the harmony of the architecture is undisturbed. The remains of the old cloisters (copied by Scott for the Abbotsford garden) are especially worth spending time on. Lawns fill the spaces between the foundations of the old abbey buildings, and although the on-the-spot explanations are not up to the standard of nearby Jedburgh, it is altogether a more rewarding place in which to linger. The Commendator's house (mostly built in 1590 with stones from the abbey church) now contains fragments of stone, allowing you to see details of carving and construction in close-up. Melrose Abbey finally fell victim to the English during the Rough Wooing in 1545, though some

SIR WALTER SCOTT (1771–1832)

If one man can be said to be responsible for starting tourism to Scotland, it is Sir Walter Scott. At the height of the early nineteenth-century passion for the Romantic, his poems (especially *Lady of the Lake* and *Marmion*) thrilled readers with their tales of passion and legend among stirringly described scenery. When he gave up poetry (recognising the superior talent of Byron) and turned to writing novels drawn from Scottish history – *Waverley*, the first, was published in 1814 – the impact was just as great. The novels were at first published anonymously, though many guessed Walter Scott to be the author.

In his childhood, staying with his grandparents in the Borders, Scott became infected with the passion for history and legend which informs his writing. Called to the Bar in 1792, he travelled extensively through Scotland, and there is scarcely a sight on today's tourist trail that he does not seem to have visited. From the valleys of the Borders, where his work as Sheriff of Selkirkshire took him, he collected the songs and ballads which had been handed down over the centuries and published them as *Border Minstrelsy*. With the money from his poems and novels he bought land by the Tweed and built Abbotsford, for Scott, a Tory by inclination, loved playing the country gentleman. Prosperous, admired, granted a baronetcy and at the centre of a of the Cistercian brethren lingered on, denied money to repair the building, well into the Reformation.

Dryburgh Abbey

(HS standard times)
This is the best positioned of the four Border abbeys, virtually surrounded by a bend of the Tweed near St Boswells and set round with fine old trees. You reach it via a spur from the B6356. Dryburgh, the home of White Canons (Premonstratensian monks) from 1150, never quite achieved the magnificence of Kelso or Melrose. Today, there is little left of the abbey church, apart from the transepts, but the surrounding buildings are well preserved – there are even the remnants of painted walls in the chapter house. Most of what is visible dates from the thirteenth century. On a sunny day, the cloister is an extremely peaceful haven. Like Melrose,

---

legal and literary circle, Scott's happiness seemed assured until the sudden bankruptcy of his publisher in 1826 left him with debts of £116,000. Determined to pay these off, he flung himself into his writing and eventually succeeded in doing so, but at a cost in mental and physical health which are only too well charted in his *Journal*. He was 61 when he died.

How his contemporaries felt about him is best symbolised by the magnificence of the Scott monument in Edinburgh. He had single-handedly restored the nation's pride by pointing out and popularising the richness of its past. He was responsible for the rediscovery of the long-forgotten crown jewels of Scotland, had stage-managed the first royal visit to Scotland (George IV in 1822) since Charles II, and had created, in the historical novel, a new literary form.

It is difficult, even today, to escape the influence of Sir Walter Scott. His poetry may remain largely unread and his novels be too tortuous and prosy for today's taste, but the Romantic Scotland he created, with its fierce passions, its unyielding scenery and its gallery of noble or villainous characters, is still happily sold to the modern visitor. He left a more solid legacy, too, for he was assiduous in encouraging the preservation of the past. It is largely thanks to him that Melrose Abbey is not more ruinous, that the Border Ballads are not lost and that Mons Meg (see page 123) draws visitors to Edinburgh Castle.

Dryburgh was more or less finished off by the Rough Wooing in 1545, though religious activity lingered on until the end of the century. Since then its buildings have been used as a house, a cow byre and as a romantic folly. Sir Walter Scott is buried here, squeezed into the north transept among other Scotts. Earl Haig, the British Commander-in-chief on the Western Front from 1915–18, lies here too.

LAUDERDALE

The valley of the River Leader runs north from the Tweed near Melrose and is followed by the A68, the fastest route from the Borders to Edinburgh. Many drivers hurry through, but the valley has its attractions.

Just behind the filling station on the southern outskirts of **Earlston**, a crumbling, ivy-clad heap of stone is all that remains of **Rhymer's Tower**, said to have been the home of Thomas of Ercildoune, or True Thomas, the Border country's best-known prophet-poet. Taken into fairyland after boldly kissing the queen of the fairies, Thomas returned gifted with second sight, prophesying, among other disturbing intuitions, that 'Kelso Kirk would fall at its fullest'. No one knows whether a relatively harmless collapse of the roof in 1771 was what he meant, or whether there is worse to come. Earlston straggles away from the main road, and is one of those large villages that seems about to become picturesque, but never quite does.

One of the best-hidden sights of the Borders is **Legerwood Church**. To find it, take the minor road east off the A68 at Birkenside. Legerwood itself is merely a few cottages around a crossroads; its church lies behind a farm-steading about half a mile further on the road towards Corsbie, and is hardly signposted at all. Once you have discovered it, read the framed history in the porch, then go in to be amazed by the beauty of the pinkish sandstone Norman archway which stands between you and the chancel – a thing of sensuous magnificence in an otherwise bare kirk. Its colour, its carving and its warmth have the intriguing quality of a revealed secret and indeed the arch was hidden behind a wall for centuries. Before you leave, thumb through the visitors' book to see how widely the parish has scattered its sons and daughters.

Lauder has not expanded much beyond its medieval boundaries, so is a good place to discover the typical layout of an old Scottish burgh. A single High Street was bordered by strips of land called tofts, tenements or burgages extending at right angles to the town walls, with closes or wynds running between them and perhaps further linking streets at the back. Lauder is where several unfortunate favourites of James III were hung from a bridge by Archibald 'Bell-the-Cat' Douglas, the leader of a baronial faction discontented by the King's policies.

Thirlestane Castle

(Open Easter week, May, June and Sept, Wed, Thurs and Sun; July and Aug, Sun to Fri; castle 2 to 5, grounds 12 to 6)
Just south of Lauder, the pinnacles, turrets and ogee-roofed tower of Thirlestane stand strategically over the River Leader, looking like something from a peaceful French landscape. Many of the more ornate details are Victorian, but done in keeping with the work of Sir William Bruce, who transformed the original keep in the 1670s. Thirlestane was once the seat of the first (and only) Duke of Lauderdale, Charles II's Scottish Secretary – an unscrupulous man who made the most of his powerful position. His second wife stripped the castle of 14 cartloads of furniture for her London house. The last cart was turned back by outraged locals.

This is a very friendly stately home to visit. Part of it is still lived in by the Maitland family, who have held Thirlestane since the thirteenth century. Each of the long sequence of rooms has its own attendant, many of whom are locals and will fill you in on the history of both family and house, from the photographs taken by the fourteenth Earl of Lauderdale early this century to the magnificently ornate plasterwork on the ceilings of the state rooms. The restored nursery wing has splendid dolls' houses and Victorian and Edwardian toys, as well as a rocking horse, masks and a dressing-up box for children to use. Some of the outbuildings contain exhibitions of Border country life, with various rural implements rather stolidly displayed.

KELSO

Although, according to a local historian, Kelso was more important before 1500 than it has ever been since, it is nevertheless the most attractive of the Border towns thanks to its eighteenth-century square, which gives it the air of a French market town. The ruins of the abbey close to the town centre, the sweep of the Tweed past the backs of houses and on through green parkland and Rennie's elegant bridge across the river contribute to the easy atmosphere. Add some good shops, some interesting domestic architecture and the relaxed bustle of an agricultural centre, and it is plain why Kelso is a good base. It does not have as many places to stay as either Moffat or Peebles, but there are enough.

It is worth exploring the strange octagonal parish church, the old Cross Keys coaching-inn, and the fine Georgian Ednam House as well as the small streets running down to the Tweed. The tiny local museum (open Easter to end Oct, Mon to Sat 10 to 5, Sun 1 to 5) provides the background, or, for more details of local history, you can arm yourself with a copy of Alistair Moffat's *Kelsae* (Mainstream Publishing) which you can get at the local Tourist Information Centre.

Kelso Abbey

(HS standard times)
There is less left of Kelso Abbey than of the other three abbeys nearby – in fact, not much more than a stump is visible – but what does remain shows the monumental scale of what is now thought to have been the biggest and grandest of the Border abbeys. A document discovered in the Vatican suggests that it had towers and transepts at both eastern and western ends, making it one of the most impressive Romanesque buildings in Britain. The Rough Wooing put an end to that in 1545 despite the resistance put up by monks and townsfolk, and all that remains is part of the west galilee and the north-west transept with its turreted façade and its 'surprising disregard for the structural prudence of placing arch above arch, solid above solid'. The memorial cloister of the Dukes of Roxburghe is modern and not particularly attractive.

Floors Castle

(Open Easter, end Apr to end Sept, Sun to Thurs; July and Aug daily 10.30 to 5.30; Oct, Sun and Wed 10.30 to 4)
The seat of the Dukes of Roxburghe, this is a huge folly of a palace. For some years Vanburgh was thought to have had a hand in it, but now it seems that William Adam and William Playfair were dually responsible. If you come upon it from the side, your eye is immediately caught by the roofscape – dozens of little turret caps like columbines and forests of

chimneys and finials, which look more like an aerial pinball table than anything else. Once past the gift shop and café, you enter the castle proper, feeling suitably humbled by the grandeur. The interior, however, is on a much more human scale, with ducal views across the policies down to the Tweed and to a yew tree which marks the spot where James II was killed by a bursting cannon while besieging Roxburgh.

The quality of the items on view is not, in general, as good as at Bowhill (see page 47), though there are fine tapestries, a small collection of post-Impressionist paintings and some Chinese porcelain. There are also some strange collections – very solid stuffed birds, whole cases of snuffboxes, minerals, coins, robes, potties and carriages, which leave you feeling you have visited a gigantic magpie's nest. In the old walled garden the good play area will keep energetic children happy, and there is a garden centre too.

Smailholm Tower

(HS standard times)
Of the many simple sixteenth-century fortalices known as pele towers which litter the Border landscape, Smailholm is the best preserved. It has the advantage of a superb setting on a craggy outcrop above a small loch, making it frequently photographed for calendars and postcards. As a child, Sir Walter Scott stayed with his grandfather at the adjacent farm of Sandyknowe, and later set his ballad *The Eve of St John* at the tower. The approach, signposted from the B6404 or the B6397 to the north-east of Kelso, leads you through a farm with the stone tower looming above. Once inside, you are confronted with Historic Scotland's restoration. The new flooring, the atmospheric music and the displays of dolls and tapestries illustrating various Border ballads may grate on the purist, but they do not spoil the strong sense of the past with which the fort is imbued. From the guard post on the roof there are views down the Eildons and the Cheviots, and you can readily imagine the raiders from Tynedale storming the crags and making away with the cattle.

For a contrast to Smailholm, seek out **Greenknowe Tower** (HS, standard times, apply to the keykeeper – a notice locates him in Gordon) on the A6105 just west of the dull village of Gordon. Built in 1581, the red sandstone ruin marks how the Scottish tower house grew out of the defensive keep, for Greenknowe was built more to impress the neighbours than for defence. A nasty gun-loop, placed to emasculate unwanted visitors, is, however, a reminder that the times were still uncertain.

Mellerstain

(Open Easter, May to Sept, Sun to Fri, 12.30 to 5) Signposted from the A6089 north-west of Kelso, Mellerstain is, for many, the most beautiful Adam house in Scotland. It was started by William Adam, who was responsible for the wings, and finished by his son Robert in a style which approaches the perfection of neo-Classicism. The exterior of Mellerstain is severe and uncompromising, but the interior, with its sequence of breathtaking ceilings, its fireplaces, its Adam-designed side tables, mirrors and cupboards, is a place of light and harmony, created for gracious family living rather than for stately processions. The library is the most perfect of the public rooms, where the eighteenth-century bindings on the shelves are complemented by the figures of Teaching and Learning.

After the splendour of the ground floor the bedrooms seem distinctly ordinary, though the main staircase is again wonderful. At the very top of the house Adam designed a ceiling for the magnificent long gallery, but unfortunately it was never put into execution.

Visitors to Mellerstain tour in the usual stately home fashion. Roped-off routes lead from room to room, while you long to relax in one of the armchairs and put your feet up in front of a roaring fire. Do not become so engrossed in the architecture that you overlook the family portraits. The strength of the Baillie-Hamiltons (Earls of Haddington) lies in the women they married – you can see it in their dignity and power. One in particular – Grisell Baillie – spent a legendary childhood dodging government forces to help her covenanting father. She later became mistress of Mellerstain and left meticulous household records from the early eighteenth century, some of which are displayed in the long gallery. Mellerstain's landscaped gardens are also held to be among the best of their kind, though there are too few flowers for modern eyes, and the lake looks better from a distance than from its boggy margins.

THE MERSE

The flat, richly agricultural basin of the lower Tweed north-east of Kelso does not make for interesting touring, although there are several curiosities hidden away in among the narrow lanes peopled by tractors and horseboxes. Wherever you travel you will see the planned agricultural cottages and hollow square farm-steadings of the eighteenth-century improvers, who helped usher in the agrarian revolution.

The knobbly outline of **Hume Castle**, off the B6364 north of Kelso, is a distinctive landmark. The old stronghold is long gone, and the walls on a craggy outcrop are a romantic folly. Even they are crumbling, but the views you get from beneath them are first class.

Duns, tucked under the Lammermuir hills on the A6105, lacks character, though it was once the county town of Berwickshire after Berwick was lost to the English. Its nature reserve, in the grounds of Duns Castle, has the unhappy name of Hen Poo. Stop at the **Jim Clark Memorial Room** (open Easter to end Sept, Mon to Sat 10 to 1 and 2 to 5, Sun 2 to 5) even if you are not a motor-racing fan, for the memorabilia of the former farmer turned world champion are extensive and moving. There are 122 trophies on the shelves, and photographs and letters from all over the world.

Just to the east of Duns, **Manderston House** (open early May to end Sept, Thurs, Sun and public holidays 2 to 5.30) bills itself as the swan-song of the Edwardian country house. Most of the ideas for this early twentieth-century statement of wealth came from an earlier age – imitations of Adam work in particular. However, the silver staircase – which must be dismantled and polished now and again, is unique to Manderston. Keep an eye open for the collection of biscuit tins – the present owner is a member of the Huntley and Palmer dynasty.

If you follow the banks of the Tweed downstream from Kelso you arrive at **Coldstream**, from where the regiment of guards which now bears the town's name marched south to aid the restoration of Charles II. There is a small museum for the regiment in the town. Coldstream is a quiet place away from the main road, and it is easy to find your way down to the river bank and gaze at the dark swirls of the Tweed. Just outside the western edge of the town, the grounds of the **Hirsel**, seat of Lord Home, are open daily and make a good spot for Sunday walks or dalliance beside the lake. An old steading has been turned into a craft centre and estate museum. Dundock Wood – reached from the A697 – is generously endowed with rhododendrons and azaleas and is extremely colourful on a bright spring day.

The Lammermuir Hills

Forming a natural boundary to the northern edge of the Merse, the Lammermuirs are a low, heather-covered range. Several small roads run across them into East Lothian from Duns, all of which make good drives. It is worth looking out for **Edinshall Broch**, one of the most southerly of the curious Iron Age towers which are found nowhere else but Scotland. The walk to the broch is pleasant, and there are enough stones still on top of one another for you not to feel your time has been wasted. **Abbey St Bathans** is a tiny village tucked into the depths of the Whiteadder valley. The road leading up towards the Whiteadder Reservoir is wooded and grassy by turns, finally rising up on to the treeless moor, with long views across the hills.

BERWICK-UPON-TWEED

If you have been touring the Scottish Border towns, Berwick may not seem particularly different at first, until you notice that the banks are English, the railway station lacks the Scotrail logo and the tourist literature carries a rose on the front cover. For 400 years of its history the town belonged to Scotland, and was a Scottish royal burgh while Glasgow was still a village. During the twelfth and thirteenth centuries (a time of comparative peace), Berwick was Scotland's chief port, trading with the Low Countries and the Baltic. It is a measure of Berwick's importance that, when Edward I of England decided to make an example of it, he seems to have found 12,000 inhabitants to massacre.

It was Berwick's misfortune to be in the worst possible position during the ceaseless wars between Scotland and England. It changed hands 12 times and was finally seized for England in 1482. Even so the town did not legally become part of England until 1836, and used to be separately referred to in charters. While the loss of Berwick was a disaster for Scotland, it had even worse consequences for the town itself. From a flourishing port it turned into an isolated frontier fortress; the massive Elizabethan fortifications show how much England felt it to be under threat. These fortifications are the only complete sixteenth-century example in Britain. For the military historian they are a delight, for here are the bastions and flankers which replaced stone walls as a defence against artillery, intact and built with no expense spared. For the layman the ramparts make a magnificent walk round the perimeter of Berwick, with glimpses of the Tweed, the sea, the Scottish hills and of lovingly tended back gardens.

Berwick makes an excellent base for exploring the eastern half of both the Scottish Border country and the English, and it is an attractive town into the bargain. Behind the ramparts the buildings are eighteenth- and nineteenth-century, with some fine Georgian houses. The modern developments at Berwick are all outside the ramparts, so you feel that you are living in a small, rather old-fashioned county town. There are plenty of places to stay, ranging from town-centre coaching-inns to bed-and-breakfasts on the outskirts.

The Barracks (open Easter to end Sept, Tues to Sun 10 to 6, rest of year 10 to 4, closed Xmas and 1 Jan) are the earliest purpose-built barracks in the United Kingdom, dating from 1721, and are now in the hands of English Heritage. The Berwick local museum is here, too, as is a display about the life and times of the British infantryman. The most surprising thing in the museum is Berwick's very own Sir William Burrell collection (open Easter to end Sept, Mon to Sat 10 to 12.30 and 2 to 6, Sun 11 to 1 and 2 to 6; rest of year Tues to Sat 10 to 12.30 and 1.30 to 4), hardly a rival to the one in Glasgow (page 218) but well worth a visit. The wealthy steamship magnate and art collector Sir William Burrell lived in Berwickshire for much of his life and made a number of gifts from his collection to the town, including some works by Degas. The museum is laid out in a quirky fashion (a promenade through the bowels of a dragon, for example) which will not appeal to everyone, but which certainly enlivens the atmosphere.

THE BORDERS COAST

The Tweed at Berwick is not in fact the frontier between Scotland and England, despite the Royal Border Bridge which crosses it. You must follow the A1 northwards for about two miles before you reach the edge of the old liberty (lands belonging to the burgh) of Berwick, where the Border signposts appear.

Eyemouth

Where the main road veers inland, the coastal A1107 brings you to this mixture of fishing port and seaside resort.

USEFUL DIRECTORY

Main tourist offices
Scottish Borders Tourist Board
Tourist Information Centre
Murrays Green
Jedburgh
Roxburghshire TD8 6BE
(0835) 863435

Dumfries and Galloway Tourist Board
Campbell House, Bankend Road
Dumfries DG1 4TH
(0387) 50434

Northumbria Tourist Board
Aykley Heads
Durham DH1 5UX
091-384 6905

Tourist Board publications Very useful: annual *Visitor's Guide*, Scottish Borders and Northumberland – everything listed, from site opening times to golf courses and cycle hire. Dumfries and Galloway publishes a similar *Explore* guide. Special interest: *Scottish Borders Angling Guide*, *Activity/Special Interest Holiday Pack*; guides on walking, including the *Southern Upland Way Guide*. Postal or credit card phone orders from the above addresses.

Eyemouth is a larger place than you might expect, with fish-processing industries on the outskirts – not such a romantic trade as the smuggling for which Eyemouth was once notorious. Kegs of contraband liquor came straight into the harbour and were stored in the warren of caverns lying beneath Gunstone house, an innocent-looking Georgian building standing on its own above the fishing boats. Ploughs have been known to vanish from the fields as the roofs of old underground passages caved in. The higgledy-piggledy layout of the old town was ideal for smugglers on the run; much of it has been rebuilt in modern fishing village vernacular style. A respectable semi-circle of sand fringes the bay beneath the sea front and there are seaside resort touches, such as the buckets and spades sold in newsagents.

Start your exploration of Eyemouth at the museum (open

Local tourist information centres
Berwick-upon-Tweed (0289) 330733
Eyemouth (08907) 50678 (Apr to Oct)
Coldstream (0890) 882607 (Apr to Oct)
Galashiels (0896) 55551 (Apr to Oct)
Gretna Green (0461) 337834 (Easter to Oct)
Hawick (0450) 72547 (Apr to Oct)
Jedburgh (0835) 863435
Kelso (0573) 223464 (Apr to Oct)
Melrose (089 682) 2555 (Apr to Oct)
Moffat (0683) 20620 (Easter to Oct)
Peebles (0721) 720138 (Apr to Oct)
Selkirk (0750) 20054 (Apr to Oct)

Local transport
Carlisle Railway Station (0228) 44711
Berwick Railway Station (0289) 306771
Lowland Scottish Omnibus (covers the Borders)
(0896) 58484
Western Scottish Omnibus (covers South-West Scotland)
(0387) 53496
Northumbria Buses (0289) 307283

Timetables and bus guides available from the Public
Transport Department, Borders Regional Council –
(0835) 23301 – or from any Tourist Information
Centre.

Easter to end Oct, Mon to Sat 10 to 12 and 1.30 to 4.30;
July, Aug 10 to 6.30, Sun 2 to 6.30) in the Old Kirk near
the harbour, which also houses the Tourist Information
Centre. Central to the museum is the tapestry stitched
locally to commemorate the tragedy of 1881, when 129
local fishermen were drowned within sight of land. There
is also much well-displayed information about Eyemouth's
fishing connections. The town trail leaflet takes you through
some of Eyemouth's streets, down to the harbour, and up to
the bluffs north of the town where Scots and English both
had forts at different times.

You need only bother with **Coldingham Priory**, north of
Eyemouth on the A1107, if you are an expert on church archi-
tecture, for although it was once rich and important the Rough
Wooing almost destroyed it and Oliver Cromwell finished it

off. Only part of the old Norman choir remains, roofed over, extensively rebuilt and turned into a barn-like church. If it is a fine day you will have more fun at Coldingham Bay, where there is sand.

Sheer cliffs, stained white by seabird guano and echoing to the raucous shouts of nesting gulls, mark **St Abb's Head**, now a National Nature Reserve (NTS and Scottish Wildlife Trust), which is reached by turning off at Coldingham. The cliffs are less inaccessible than those of many seabird colonies and are consequently popular with bird-watchers. A half-mile walk from the car park takes you to the clifftops, and there is a network of paths along them. There are fine views from the cliffside paths, interesting flowers and an offshore Marine Reserve (called the St Abbs and Eyemouth Voluntary Marine Reserve; there is a special car park for divers). Wardens organise guided walks in the reserve throughout the summer – information from the Eyemouth tourist office or Borders Regional Council (page 67).

Fast Castle

This presents a good, if rather dangerous, goal for a short walk. One and a half miles of narrow road lead from the A1107 to a row of farm cottages. After that you take to your feet for a further 20 minutes across the clifftops until the path plunges down and you see fragments of stone decking a headland which is little more than a large rock. A path across a narrow isthmus, barely protected by some very ancient chains, takes you to this rock, into what was one of the most remarkable fortresses in the area.

There is nothing much left now except for grass-covered heaps and the odd wall, but there is enough to show how hard it must have been to build here, how intolerable it must have been to live here, and how difficult the castle must have been to besiege. Despite this, it seems to have been captured and destroyed with the usual frequency. Walter Scott may have used it for Wolf's Crag in *The Bride of Lammermoor*, but he certainly described it with a lot of artistic licence. It is a splendid, rather scary spot, with seabirds wheeling and mewing all round the cliffs in the breeding season, and there is a legend of buried treasure to go with it (one of those who searched was John Napier, inventor of the logarithm). It is not a place for children or those who cannot stand heights.

WHERE TO STAY

CANONBIE

Riverside Inn £

Canonbie
Dumfriesshire DG14 0UX   *Tel (038 73) 71512/71295*

A useful stop-over on the journey northwards, the inn revolves around the consumption of food, whether in the restaurant or in the bar. The small residents' lounge is comfortably simple, as are the bedrooms, though they have everything you need and space to sit in, with up-to-date, functional bathrooms.

Open: all year, exc Xmas and New Year, also first 2 weeks Nov, last 2 weeks Feb   **Rooms**: 6   **Credit/charge cards**: Access, Visa

ETTRICKBRIDGE

Ettrickshaws £–££

Ettrickbridge
Nr Selkirk, Selkirkshire TD7 5HW   *Tel (0750) 52229*

A slightly eccentric hotel set in one of the most scenic spots in the Borders. The hallway and beautiful light drawing-room with views down towards the River Ettrick belong firmly to the Scottish Edwardian tradition. Bedrooms and bathrooms are curious, but comfortable. The food is plain and reasonably priced.

Open: all year, exc Dec and Jan   **Rooms**: 6
Facilities: fishing   **Credit/charge cards**: Access, Diners, Visa

GALASHIELS

Woodlands Country House £

Windyknowe Road
Galashiels, Selkirkshire TD1 1RQ   *Tel (0896) 4722*

A stone archway and bare stone steps in the hallway of this imposing Victorian mansion bring to mind a Gothic chapel, but the bar is bright and cheery, and the bedrooms, apart from the singles, are large and well equipped. The old panelled billiard room is especially attractive. Bar meals provide a substantial alternative to the fairly traditional food in the restaurant.

Open: all year, exc Boxing Day **Rooms**: 9
Credit/charge cards: Access, Visa

INNERLEITHEN

The Ley £££
Innerleithen, Peeblesshire EH44 6NL Tel (0896) 830240

Set on the hillside above the Leithen Water and hidden away in the trees, this excellent, good-value Victorian guesthouse is run as a Wolsey Lodge (you are treated as a paying guest in somebody's home). The bedrooms are beautifully furnished, the drawing-room is large and comforting, and the dining-room, where the owner serves up good home cooking, is formal and gleaming.

Open: all year, exc mid-Oct to mid-Feb **Rooms**: 4
Facilities: croquet **Credit/charge cards**: none accepted

JEDBURGH

Hundalee House £
Jedburgh, Roxburghshire TD8 6PA Tel (0835) 863011

A friendly welcome greets you at this large, old, grey-stone house set on a tranquil plateau of farmland high above the Jed Water. Bedrooms, some with bathroom, are well decorated (the 'blue room' is the one to go for), and breakfast is served in a magnificently Georgian dining-room with views over the lawn. Good value. No evening meals.

Open: all year, exc Nov to Mar **Rooms**: 5
Credit/charge cards: none accepted

The Spinney £
Langlee, Jedburgh, Roxburghshire TD8 6PB Tel (0835) 863525

This three-room bed and breakfast has everything you need: a warm welcome, spacious bedrooms and plenty of comfort upstairs and down. The spacious sitting-room has leather chesterfields and the dining-room displays fresh flowers. The modern house is well shielded from the road and the garden is immaculate.

Open: all year, exc Nov to Feb **Rooms**: 3
Credit/charge cards: none accepted

KELSO

Ednam House £-££
Bridge Street
Kelso, Roxburghshire TD5 7HT Tel (0573) 224168

A beautiful Georgian house in the centre of Kelso, with lawns stretching down to the Tweed – this is chiefly a fishing hotel. The atmosphere is one of peaceful, if old-fashioned, gentility. Most of the bedrooms are small, though not the pricier rooms in the oldest part of the house.

Open: all year, exc 24 Dec to 9 Jan **Rooms**: 32
Credit/charge cards: Access, Visa

MOFFAT

Beechwood   ££
Harthope Place
Moffat, Dumfriesshire DG10 9RS   *Tel (0683) 20210*

Backed by acres of its own woods, this is a peaceful, very friendly hotel on a hill overlooking Moffat. The small bedrooms are not lavish and bathrooms are rather tucked away, though they offer all sorts of thoughtful extras. Decoration is conventional but there is ample space and you can lunch in the sunny conservatory. The food is unlikely to disappoint: breakfasts include fresh orange juice and scrambled eggs with fresh chanterelle mushrooms.

Open: all year, exc Jan and Feb **Rooms**: 7
Credit/charge cards: Access, Amex, Visa

PEEBLES

Cringletie House   ££
Peebles
Peeblesshire EH45 8PL   *Tel (0721) 730233*

Bedrooms are scattered all over this old, turreted baronial mansion, but are universally comfortable with luxurious bathrooms: all are priced the same, despite great variety in size. The food here is a treat: there is Cringletie honey for breakfast, and produce from the walled vegetable garden. Public rooms are club-like with views of the lovely grounds – banks of daffodils and extensive lawns. Good value.

Open: all year, exc 2 Jan to 5 Mar   **Rooms**: 13
Facilities: tennis, croquet, putting green
Credit/charge cards: Access, Visa

SELKIRK

Philipburn House   ££
Selkirk TD7 5LS   *Tel (0750) 20747*

A good, friendly base in the Borders, especially for families. The
bedrooms, furnished with pine and stripy fabrics, are cheery and
warm, with the spacious poolside suites the best choice. There is
a smallish lounge, a gleaming bar and a kind of conservatory, and
the imaginative food concentrates on local produce. Walking is the
most keenly promoted activity, with offers of a local guide and a
corner of the house devoted to maps and plenty of local literature.

Open: all year   **Rooms**: 17   **Facilities**: table-tennis, heated
outdoor swimming-pool, badminton, adventure playground
Credit/charge cards: Access, Visa

WALKERBURN

Tweed Valley Hotel   ££
Walkerburn
Peeblesshire EH43 6AA   *Tel (089 687) 636*

Ask for a room in the main house – those in the annexe are small and
don't have the views of the Tweed Valley. The lounge and bar shine
with polished knick-knacks, and though there is not a great deal of
space, there is enough. The best room is the restaurant, where the
food is substantial and where anglers mix happily with tourists. The
newest addition is a smokehouse where the hotel smokes its own
salmon, ham and so on – the hotel also runs courses for guests to
teach them the art of smoking foods.

Open: all year, exc 25, 26 Dec   **Rooms**: 16   **Facilities**: sauna,
solarium, gym   **Credit/charge cards**: Access, Visa

WHERE TO EAT

HAWICK

Old Forge
Newmill-on-Teviot
Nr Hawick TD9 0JU   *Tel (0450) 85298*

The Old Forge can get busy but is worth visiting for its delicious bread and wonderful selection of wines (which was singled out with an award in the 1992 *Good Food Guide*), as well as the imaginative main courses. The restaurant has been under new ownership since May 1993 so things may have changed – reports please.

Open: Tues to Sat 7 to 9.30; closed 2 weeks May and Nov
Credit/charge cards: Access, Visa

INNERLEITHEN

Traquair Arms Hotel
Traquair Road
Innerleithen EH44 6PD   *Tel (0896) 8302299*

The bar meals offer good value, and there is also a restaurant which serves Scottish dishes and reputedly excellent breakfasts.

Open: Breakfast daily 8 to 9 (available to non–residents), weekends 8.30 to 9.30; bar menu 12 to 9; dinner 7 to 9; closed Xmas, 1 and 2 Jan   **Credit/charge cards**: Access, Visa

MOFFAT

Well View Hotel
Ballplay Road
Moffat DG10 9YU   *Tel (0683) 20184*

Named 'County Restaurant of the Year' by the 1992 *Good Food Guide*, this hotel offers well-cooked, imaginative dishes that are changed daily. The price is also a bonus.

Open: daily 12.30 to 2, 6.30 to 8.30; closed 1st week Jan
Credit/charge cards: Access, Visa

NEWCASTLETON

Copshaw Kitchen
4 North Hermitage Street
Newcastleton TD9 ORB   *Tel (038 73) 75250*

A good choice of home-made dishes at this tea–room and restaurant includes delicious scones, shortbread and cream cakes. You might also get barley fadge (Scottish wholemeal bread) with your soup.

Open: tea-room daily 9.30 to 6, restaurant 7 to 9; closed Jan, Feb
Credit/charge cards: Access, Diners, Visa

PEEBLES

Sunflower
4 Bridgegate
Peebles EH45 8RZ   *Tel (0721) 22420*

Snacks are served all day here, or you can go for the three-course menu which offers about half a dozen interesting choices (vegetarian and non-vegetarian) at each course. The wine list is fair.

Open: summer Mon to Sat 9.15 to 5.30, Tues to Sat 7.30 to 9; winter Thurs to Sat 7.30 to 9; closed 11 to 18 Nov and local hols
Credit/charge cards: none accepted

SWINTON

Wheatsheaf Hotel
Main Street
Swinton TT11 3JJ   *Tel (089 086) 257*

Expect the same high quality of food in both the bar and the restaurant. Dishes include staple Borders favourites.

Open: Tues to Sun 12 to 2, 6 to 9.30; closed Xmas
Credit/charge cards: Access, Visa

THE SOUTH-WEST

- A rocky and, in part, marshy coast surrounding an often lonely interior of moor or pastureland, tree-covered hills and isolated lochs
- A past of religious and political turbulence, well illustrated by Christian monuments and fortified castles
- Robert Burns' home country
- A good variety of towns and villages, most of them tranquil and neatly kept

Statue of Robert Burns

DUMFRIES and Galloway region, divided into ridges and valleys by south-flowing rivers, takes up most of the broad bulge of land of south-west Scotland. Nearly a quarter of it is covered by trees, mostly Sitka spruce plantations, and further vast tracts are barely inhabited moorland. Merrick rises high out of the compact central group of mountains that dominate the Galloway Forest Park.

The coastline dithers between ragged and smooth, the shoreline between murky brown mudflats at the eastern end of the Solway Firth, and rocky or sandy beaches at the wilder western end where smugglers once beached contraband. This is not an area plagued by mass tourism, and you are less likely to find ice-creams and postcard stands than to come across solitary birdwatchers lurking beside the mudflats, or waiting for rarities in the coastal nature reserves.

The Ayrshire coast to the north-west extends from near Stranraer in the south to the mouth of the Clyde and Glasgow's outskirts in the north. Here are long stretches of beach (often monopolised by Glaswegian weekenders) and some of the least expensive golf courses in Scotland. Nearby islands decorate the horizon, so the seaward views are frequently splendid. One such island, Arran, is only a short hop by ferry from Ardrossan, and provides a rugged contrast to the gentle farmland of the mainland. Inland, Ayrshire is strewn with small, once prosperous coal or weaving towns from the eighteenth and nineteenth centuries.

Most visitors come to the South-West on the trail of Robert Burns, who was born near Ayr and died in Dumfries, and the figure of Scotland's most famous poet is apt to eclipse the region's other claims to fame. Burns trails, sights, souvenirs and postcards are inescapable, but this corner of Scotland had influence long before the 'Ploughman-Poet' was born.

Galloway was the site of the earliest Christian settlement in Scotland, for St Ninian founded his *candida casa* here in the early fifth century, and the region has some important early Christian monuments, and three fine abbeys from later centuries. During the persecution of Covenanters following the Restoration of Charles II, this part of Scotland became the last refuge of the most extreme Presbyterian sects.

Galloway gets its name from the Gall-Ghaidhil, the stubborn Norse-Gaelic peoples who kept the South-West a thorn in the flesh of the Scottish kings until the thirteenth century. When the region had been assimilated into feudal Scotland, it became the fief of powerful families, among them Bruce,

Douglas, Maxwell and Johnstone. Their rise and fall can be traced in the ruined strongholds of the region. The many planned villages of the eighteenth century tell of a more peaceful life.

DUMFRIES

Unlike other villages and towns along the Solway coast, many of which are built of dour granite, Dumfries is largely reddish sandstone. Its handsome Georgian and Victorian buildings are set along tidy streets, and the broad River Nith has a weir, wide banks and bridges of every dimension and age.

The old town nestles within a bend of the river. The wide esplanade, Whitesands, once teemed with cattle on market days; nowadays, it is cars and buses that are nose to tail. One of Scotland's oldest streets, Friars' Vennel, leads from the river up to the now pedestrianised centre of the town.

Almost certainly an important Roman settlement, this gateway to Galloway was made a royal burgh in the twelfth century. Edward I seized the castle (now gone but commemorated by a street name) in 1301. The weightiest event in the town's history came five years later when King Robert the Bruce murdered his rival, the Red Comyn (see the box on page 82). Dumfries suffered at the hands of the rampaging English several times during the fifteenth and sixteenth centuries, and little of the medieval town remains.

Most sights concern the poet Robert Burns, and all are listed on the *Burns Heritage Trail* leaflet available from the Tourist Information Centre. The town is the best touring base on the Solway coast, with good shopping facilities, and accommodation and restaurants ranging from simple to fairly grand.

In and near Dumfries

The slightly listing **Midsteeple**, in the High Street, was built in 1707 to provide more prison space, a town council meeting house, a court room and, almost as important, the town's first steeple. A table gives distances to far-flung cattle markets, and a relief map shows Dumfries as it was in Burns' time. Burns' favourite howff (tavern), the **Globe Inn**, further along the High Street, is a long, whitewashed pub, worth visiting for

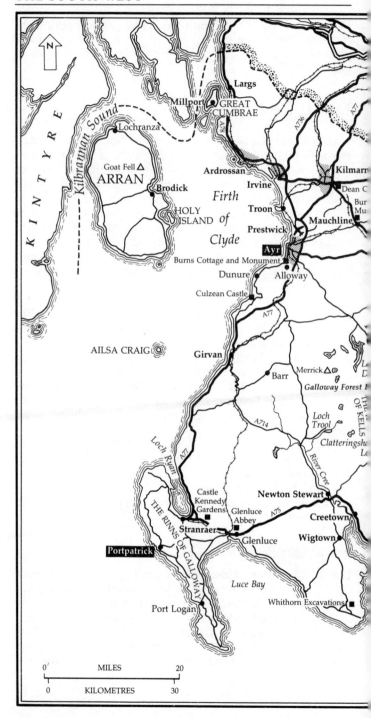

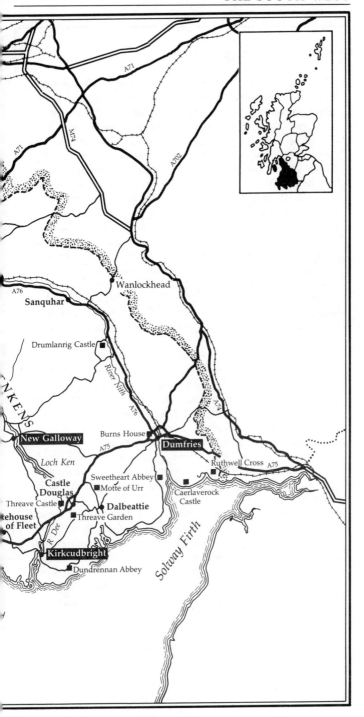

Practical suggestions

Many people have been through Dumfries and Galloway. From England you must cross it to reach Stranraer or Cairnryan for the ferries to Northern Ireland. And you must drive through part of it to reach the Highlands and central Scotland. Comparatively few come for a holiday, which, as tourist offices are eager to point out, gives it that desirable 'undiscovered' status. The South-West is also sparsely populated, so you can expect space and little traffic. It would not be the first choice for new visitors to Scotland, however, since the scenery and sights are not the best that Scotland has to offer.

Bird-watching, golfing, swimming, fishing, boating and camping are major holiday activities here. Good golf courses – links in most cases – are plentiful and notable for being neither stuffy nor pricey. For the best beaches, head for the western end of the Solway Firth or the southern Ayrshire coast. The many lochs and bays offer good fly and coarse fishing as well as sea-angling, and the season, unlike that in England, is open. The few mountains are not spectacular and they are surrounded by forestry plantations, but there is greater scenic variety in the coastal regions. The narrow Rinns of Galloway has miles of remote coastline. Offshore islands, such as Arran and Cumbrae, are compact and satisfying for the island-hungry visitor who does not wish to venture to the more remote islands to the north. On Arran, there is golfing, water-skiing, sea-angling, yachting, bicycling and pony-trekking.

Gardens thrive in the acid soil and the warm and moist air brought by the Gulf Stream, and the region's public gardens, Threave and Kennedy, for instance, are known throughout Britain for their variety of flora, including many tropical species.

Sights associated with Robert Burns, concentrated around Dumfries and Ayr, are plentiful, and illuminate both his life and times. Amongst the best are his house in Dumfries, now a small museum; his farm (Ellisland), just north of Dumfries; the thirteenth-century bridge, Brig o' Doon, near Ayr, which features in his poem, *Tam O'Shanter*; and the Bachelors' Club in Mauchline, a fascinating museum of Burns memorabilia.

The Tourist Board's *Burns Heritage Trail* leaflet describes all the major and minor Burns sights.

The South-West has plenty of good caravan parks, many in out-of-the-way, seaside settings. Hotels, guesthouses and bed-and-breakfast accommodation are concentrated in and around towns or near tourist spots around the coast.

Good bases

• **Dumfries** An obvious stop-over en route to Ireland or the Ayrshire coast and a convenient base for touring eastern Dumfries and Galloway, Dumfries is an upbeat sort of place. It has a busy centre, wide winding river and solid, ruddy Victorian architecture, and is well stocked with hotels, bed-and-breakfasts and restaurants. In and around it, there is no shortage of things to do and see. Fans of Robert Burns can pass several days without leaving town. The new by-pass has improved life for visitors and residents alike.

• **Kirkcudbright** Old but spry, the capital of the district of Stewartry has many virtues: riverside setting, quirky architecture, handsome broad streets, plenty of craft and antique shops and good sightseeing. It manages to feel intimate yet is large enough to cater to fussy tourists, and is not commercialised. Its position along the Solway Firth is handy for water-minded visitors.

• **New Galloway** The smallest royal burgh in Scotland sits on the River Ken with Loch Ken to the south. It would be an obvious base for anglers using these waters, but the Galloway Forest Park is also nearby. There is only one main street so you could soon exhaust its facilities, but it is a cheerful town.

• **Portpatrick** Situated on the stormy western side of the Rinns of Galloway, this fetching little harbour town fills up with tourists in summer. There is lots of self-catering hereabouts, as well as a large hotel and harbour-side pub.

• **Ayr** A good departure point for visiting the Ayrshire coast, with fast roads up and down, and resort facilities right in town. Ayr's race course is one of Scotland's best. The town's fame is based on its close links with Robert Burns, and there are plenty of associated sights. Shops and restaurants are sophisticated, and accommodation ample.

the small dining-room with its period furniture and the poet's favourite chair.

The family rooms and study of **Burns House** in cobbled Burns Street (open Easter to Sept, Mon to Sat 10 to 1, 2 to 5, Sun 2 to 5; Oct to Easter, Tues to Sat 10 to 1, 2 to 5) now constitute a small museum, furnished in the style of the poet's day and displaying a good cross-section of letters and personal ephemera (snuff mills, sword stick and gun, for example). The box bed is original, indeed it is the one in which he died. Look for his name on a window pane in the tiny study where he wrote over 100 poems and songs; though he may have scratched it in frustration over a temperamental muse, he seemed to fancy this form of calling card – look for his autograph in the glass at the Globe Inn, too. Burns spent the last three years of his life in this house and was buried a few hundred yards away, in **St Michael's Churchyard**. First interred in 1796 in one

ROBERT THE BRUCE (1274–1329)

'The Bruce' remains a revered half-legendary figure to many Scots, perhaps because of the fact that his ambition and persistence culminated in success against the odds, but more importantly because his reign marks the emergence of a distinctly Scottish patriotism from among the welter of Anglo-Norman and Celtic loyalties.

Robert the Bruce was grandson of that Robert Bruce whose claim to the Scottish throne Edward I of England had rejected. His behaviour during Edward's invasion of Scotland in 1296 had been ambiguous and indeed his name appears on the 'Ragmans Roll' of Scots who had sworn allegiance to Edward at Berwick. But in 1306 Robert Bruce killed his rival John Comyn in the church of Greyfriars at Dumfries, laying himself open to charges of murder, treachery and sacrilege. His reaction was to make a bid for power, and he had himself crowned King of Scots at Scone.

His revolt against Edward seemed doomed. He was defeated almost at once by the Earl of Pembroke near Methven; within a year three of his brothers were captured and executed, and his wife and daughter imprisoned. Bruce fled, possibly to Arran, spending the winter as an excommunicated outlaw. The spring of 1307 saw him back in Scotland, in Galloway. He won a skirmish with the English who were pinning him in Glen Trool, and beat of the closely packed graves (several of which are those of Covenanters), his body was transferred 21 years later to a more imposing, if inappropriate, Grecian-style domed and pillared mausoleum.

The **Robert Burns Heritage Centre**, in a converted grain mill on the riverbank opposite Whitesands, is a modern, well-organised display with a 20-minute audio-visual show to take you through the poet's life and works (open Apr to Sept, Mon to Sat 10 to 8, Sun 2 to 5; Oct to Mar, Tues to Sat 10 to 1, 2 to 5). There is a café, and from the riverside picnic tables you get a fine view of the weir (or caul) and most of the town. The little **Old Bridge House Museum** (open Apr to Sept, Mon to Sat 10 to 1, 2 to 5, Sun 2 to 5) is packed with furniture and every-day articles (as well as some chilling dental instruments), covering the Edwardian and Victorian as well as Burnsian periods.

them more thoroughly at Ayr. But his real salvation in July of that year was the death of Edward I, who was already in Cumberland on his way north to flatten Bruce for once and for all. Edward II had no stomach for the Scottish campaign, and Bruce was left to himself.

He still had plenty of enemies within Scotland, but his greatest, the Comyns, were beaten at Inverurie and their lands of Buchan mercilessly harried. He then turned on the MacDougalls of the west while his supporters cleared south-west Scotland. The French King secretly recognised him and the clergy, despite his excommunication, gave him support. English-occupied castles fell one by one, and Bruce instigated the sensible policy of dismantling many of them so that they could not again be used against him.

With the Battle of Bannockburn in 1314 (see page 274), Bruce set the seal on his military success. Political success followed only some years later with a thirteen years' truce with England in 1323, the absolution of Bruce by the Pope in 1328 and the recognition by England of Scottish independence in the same year.

Bruce, increasingly ailing, was unable to go on the crusade he had vowed. Sir James Douglas, one of his companions from the start, promised to take his heart to the Holy Land (he was killed fighting Saracens in Spain and the heart was supposedly brought home to Melrose Abbey). Bruce died, possibly of leprosy, in 1329, and was buried at Dunfermline.

SOUTH-EAST FROM DUMFRIES

Caerlaverock Castle

(HS, standard times)
Some seven miles south of Dumfries, this is one of the most striking castles in Scotland, thanks to its unique triangular shape, double-towered gatehouse, water-filled moat and earthen rampart. On flat land by the shore, it may have been built on the site of an old Roman harbour. This stronghold of the powerful Maxwell family was probably built around 1290 and suffered its first siege in 1300 when Edward I of England captured it. His chronicler left an account of the ruthless efficiency with which the siege was conducted. Restored during the fifteenth and sixteenth centuries, the castle fell to the Covenanters in 1640, when it was partially demolished. What remains is very much a mix of styles, from the massive defensive walls of the fourteenth and fifteenth centuries to the Renaissance elegance of Lord Nithsdale's Building (1634), which stands within the walls. In complete contrast to the fortified exterior, this is a stately, three-storeyed dwelling built during the relatively tranquil reign of James VI. Much of it still stands.

Caerlaverock Wildfowl and Wetlands Centre

The flat, grassy moorland and endless mudflats of this coast attract birds in their millions, and at any time of year you can wander around and enjoy the wildlife. Amongst the many birds that live or come to feed and rest after their long migrations at the Caerlaverock Wildfowl and Wetlands Centre (open daily 10 to 5) are Bewick's swan, the white-fronted goose and at least nine species of duck. Towers and hides are well arranged by several ponds for close-up views. If you hit the right day in late September you will see the sky darken as the entire Spitzbergen flock of barnacle geese (around 10,500) arrive to winter here. Caerlaverock also has the northernmost colony in Britain of the rare natterjack toad.

Ruthwell

The small town of Ruthwell is home to the world's first savings bank (now a small museum), founded in 1810. The most important sight here is the early eighth–century **Ruthwell Cross** (HS, access from keyholder at all reasonable times; details at site) in the parish church. Eighteen feet tall, rising majestically from a sunken pit, the grey stone cross is Northumbrian rather than Pictish work. Runes spell out parts of the earliest known Anglo-Saxon poem, *The Dream of the Rood*. The thin sides are carved with more runes and decorative birds and beasts entwined. The cross-piece is modern, but hard to distinguish from the original shaft.

NORTH AND WEST OF DUMFRIES

Nithsdale

Nithsdale runs along the fertile Nith valley from Dumfries north to Sanquhar. The A76, the old stage-coach route from Dumfries to Glasgow, stays fairly close to the river, threading its way through pastures, pine trees and moorland.

Six miles north of Dumfries, the road passes the single-storeyed **Ellisland Farm** (open at all reasonable times), which Burns leased with the proceeds of the Kilmarnock edition of his poems. It is still a working farm and, though a popular tourist attraction, is refreshingly low-key. Burns memorabilia and period furniture are displayed in several rooms warmed by real coal fires. (One is in a kitchen range which Burns himself installed.) Old farming machinery and methods are displayed and explained in the granary. Burns made his last futile stab at experimental farming at Ellisland during 1788. Poetry came easier: he wrote *Tam O'Shanter* during his stay here.

Drumlanrig Castle

(Open early May to Aug, daily 11 to 5; closed Thurs; park open early May to Sept, daily 11 to 6)
This theatrical, turreted quasi-palace surrounded by lawns and peacocks is now owned by the Duke of Buccleuch, although it was built in the seventeenth century for William Douglas, the first Duke of Queensberry. Inside, the collection of paintings rivals that of the other great Buccleuch house at Bowhill and includes the last oil painting by Leonardo da Vinci to remain in private hands – the *Madonna with the Yarnwinder* – and Rembrandt's marvellous *Old Woman Reading*. There is much of Scottish interest, too, including memorabilia of Mary Queen of Scots and of Prince Charles Edward Stuart, who spent a night here on his long retreat from Derby.

Wanlockhead

On the B797, at 1409 feet above sea level in a dip in the Lowther Hills, Wanlockhead is Scotland's highest village and a correspondingly bleak place. From the Middle Ages until 1928 it was the centre of Scottish metal mining: gold and silver have both been found here, but lead was always the mainstay of the industry. At the **Museum of Scottish Lead Mining** (open Easter to mid-Oct, daily 11 to 4.30) you can visit a slightly claustrophobic mine with tool marks on the walls and abandoned machinery, and admire the carefully restored water-powered beam engine.

Glenkiln Reservoir

This clear blue lake off the A75 west of Dumfries has become a tourist attraction because of the three sculptures poised around it. A large bronze standing man by Rodin is at the furthest end and Henry Moore's seated *King* and *Queen* are on the top of a hill above the lake, their curving figures silhouetted against the sky. The Epstein is more elusive, about half a mile away.

SOUTH OF DUMFRIES

There are enough things to see on the 35-mile circular route from Dumfries via the A710 and the A711 to take up a day. The village of New Abbey is not a peaceful place because the main road disects it, and parking, other than in the abbey car park, is almost impossible. However the thirteenth-century **Sweetheart Abbey** or Dulce Cor (HS, standard times, closed Thurs pm and Fri in winter) must be seen (joint ticket also covers New Abbey Corn Mill and New Abbey Village). This was the last of Galloway's three Cistercian monasteries to be founded. It is big, red, remarkably complete, and has a romantic history to go with its lovely setting. The abbey was founded in 1273 by Dervorguilla de Balliol (mother of the luckless 'Toom Tabard', whom Edward I chose to be puppet king of Scotland) in memory of her husband with whom she founded Balliol College at Oxford. Devastated by his death in 1268, she carried his embalmed heart in a casket around with her during the 22 years she outlived him, and was buried with it. Little remains of the monastic buildings apart from the abbey church; though it is roofless, the wheel and lancet windows on the west wall and the arches of the nave are in amazingly good shape.

Arbigland is the birthplace of John Paul Jones (1747–92), father of the American Navy. His cottage can be seen in the grounds of the private stately home, but most people come for the gardens and beach (open May to Sept, daily 2 to 6; closed Mon, exc public holidays). Huge pine trees, fine lawns, a handsome rose garden and a water garden are formally arranged but there are no 'keep off the grass' signs. A broad tree-lined avenue leads to a wide, often empty beach, with the Cumbrian mountains visible across the Solway Firth. You can picnic as well as swim here, and there is a tea-room.

Sandyhills Bay, near the junction with the B793, is wide and curved, with fine sand and craggy rocks. It is never crowded, unlike the popular beaches at Southerness Point to the east, perhaps because it is one of the few places in the whole region where you have to pay to park. **Kippford** and **Rockcliffe**, yachting and fishing villages with a population of just over 100, are reached via a short detour at Colvend.

The sixteenth-century, L-shaped **Drumcoltran Tower** (always open) is north of the A711. Severe, square and built to last, it stands amongst trees next to several eighteenth-century farm buildings. High above the door a Latin inscription exhorts: 'Keep hidden what is secret; speak little; be truthful; avoid wine; remember death; have pity.' There was some concession to creature comforts indoors, with heated bedrooms and vented latrines. The view from the parapet over gentle hills takes some beating.

Dalbeattie to Castle Douglas

Dalbeattie can claim some fame for having supplied granite to build London's Embankment and the Bank of England. Most of the town's buildings are also granite, and there is an old-fashioned feel to the place. A pleasant riverside park has a good play area.

Two miles north of the town, just off the B794, is one of Scotland's largest twelfth-century motte and bailey castles, the **Motte of Urr** (always open). This is one of the best examples of the type of defensive structures built by the earliest Norman settlers in Scotland. The motte, a tall, pudding-shaped mound surrounded by a ditch, sits inside and at one end of an oblong outer ditch, 164 yards long. You will need an Ordnance Survey map to locate it as there are no signposts.

Castle Douglas, the site of an ancient settlement, is now an orderly market town laid out on a grid. The 100-acre Carlingwark Loch, on the southern border, has two crannogs (artificial islands created from logs driven into the bottom) that served as protection for Bronze Age homesteads.

Threave Garden

(NTS, garden open all year, daily 9 to sunset; visitor centre open Apr to Oct, daily 9 to 5.30)

Threave Garden, a training centre for gardeners, is one of the wonders of Scotland's south-west. The range of plants and flowers is impressive, especially of heather, and it is colourful even on wintry days. However, it is the composition and design, by students and staff from the horticultural school, that make Threave exceptional. In all directions are delicate patterns, shapely bushes and, beyond, pastures that seem to have been designed to match.

Threave Castle

An expedition to the fourteenth-century Douglas or Threave Castle (HS, standard times; closed in winter; charge includes ferry trip), which begins with a ten-minute walk and a two-minute ferry ride, is great fun. The tall rectangular tower is in fine shape, despite being taken by the Covenanters in 1640, and its stark outline and remote site on a small, flat, grassy island on the River Dee give it added appeal, the more so in grey weather. A fittingly large stronghold of the Black Douglases, and the last of their castles to surrender to James II during his campaign to bring the over-mighty family to heel, Threave later became a Maxwell seat. The five-storey tower, with a room on each floor, connected by a spiral stair, follows the conventional pattern for fourteenth-century towers, if on a rather larger scale than usual. The scramble to the top is rewarded by timeless views from all levels and in all directions. Archaeological excavations conducted this century have uncovered Scotland's most complete medieval riverside harbour, a small but remarkably well-preserved walled inlet.

Dalbeattie to Kirkcudbright

Four miles south of Dalbeattie, well off the A711 in remote farmland, sits the fifteenth-century **Orchardton Tower** (HS, access from keykeeper at all reasonable times; details at site), as solid and austere as other self-respecting castles, but unique in Scotland for its cylindrical shape, a pattern common in Ireland. It is in good condition, but do not go too near the low parapet if you dislike heights.

Further along, beside the A711, stand the pinkish-grey ruins of the once formidable **Dundrennan Abbey** (HS, standard times; closed in winter), probably founded by King David in 1142 to become one of Galloway's three Cistercian abbeys (the others are Glenluce and Sweetheart). On 15 May 1568, Mary Queen of Scots stopped here on the last day of her flight after the Battle of Langside. The next day she sailed across the Solway Firth to Workington and to her final exile. The abbey passed into secular use at the Reformation and by the seventeenth century had been substantially dismantled to provide building stones for the town. The north and south transepts and chapter house are in reasonable condition; the carving throughout is exceptional. The transition from Romanesque to Gothic can be seen in the pointed and semi-rounded arches, and while the nave is missing, a row of column bases and wall foundations mark the aisle.

KIRKCUDBRIGHT

At the mouth of the Dee halfway along the Solway coast, Kirkcudbright is arguably the most delightful town in the whole of the south-west (especially when the tide is in). It is thus a popular tourist haunt, but neither commercialised nor self-consciously gentrified. The likely origin of the name is the Kirk of St Cuthbert; his bones are said to have spent some time in the ancient church. Colourful houses flank the L-shaped High Street, the west side of which is the most ancient part of town. Several of them have dormer windows on sloping roofs and a few are Georgian. Despite the sprawling car park in Harbour Square it is not hard to appreciate how the seventeenth-century town might have looked, with the houses splayed out behind the castle and harbour. With its quaint houses and bobbing boats in the harbour, Kirkcudbright is an artists' colony. Dorothy L Sayers often visited the town, and set her novel *Five Red Herrings* here.

In and near Kirkcudbright

● **MacLellan's Castle** (HS, standard times; weekends only in winter), the town's most easily spotted attraction, stands overlooking the harbour at the junction of High, Castle and St Cuthbert Streets. A grand tower-house sitting in the middle of a small green, it was built by Thomas MacLellan of Bombie, provost of Kirkcudbright, at the end of the sixteenth century. The fortified exterior of turrets and gunloops is deceptive: the interior was conceived as a well-organised dwelling. More than a dozen rooms were heated, and there were large windows and enclosed water closets. A huge fireplace dominates the great hall, and within it is a spy-hole or 'laird's lug', used for keeping tabs on guests and staff. MacLellan's heirs were ruined following their support of the royalist cause, and it is unlikely that anyone lived in the castle after the end of the seventeenth century. MacLellan's elaborate monument, showing him in a full suit of armour, is in nearby Greyfriar's Church.

● **Tolbooth** Where the High Street turns a corner, the large Tolbooth looks rather like a church. It is half a century younger than the castle, and an endearing jumble of different stones and styles. Both ends, including the spired tower, were added on to the original building. On the forestair is a corroded stone mercat cross and iron 'jougs', used to shackle offenders for public ridicule. At the base is a well.

● The **Stewartry Museum** in St Mary Street is sure to entertain (open May, June, Sept, Mon to Sat 11 to 5; July, Aug, Mon to Sat 11 to 7.30, Sun 2 to 5; Apr, Oct, Mon to Sat 11 to 4; Nov to Easter, Sat only 11 to 4). In the galleried main room is a first-rate collection of archaeological finds and bizarre objects including curling and quoiting gear, a crystal radio set, a witness box on castors, snuff boxes and spinning materials. A small room is devoted to shipping, and in the upstairs gallery stuffed animals and birds occupy glass cases.

● **Broughton House** (open Easter to mid-Oct, Mon to Sat 11 to 1, 2 to 5; closed Sun am and Tues), a speci-men of Georgian architecture at its most dignified was bequeathed to the town by the painter E A Hornel, one of the 'Glasgow Boys' and a leader of the local artists' colony. The library is handsomely panelled. There are paintings, many by Hornel himself (Pre-Raphaelite meets Arthur Rackham), and a Japanese-style garden behind.

● **Tongland Power Station** (open late May to early Sept, daily exc Sun, last tour 3.30) This enormous hydro-electric power station mounts well-organised tours that collect you in Kirkcudbright and carry you off to the bold Art Deco headquarters two miles to the north. The one-and-a-half hour tour begins with a 15-minute video and a visit to the turbine hall. A mile's drive then takes you to the giant curved dam, which you can walk along.

THE COAST TO NEWTON STEWART

Gatehouse of Fleet and around

Sitting amongst green hills at the head of the Fleet estuary, Gatehouse of Fleet is a pretty, colourful town. In the eighteenth century, the Murrays of Broughton built up a thriving cotton-spinning and weaving business here, along with tanning and brewing. Leave the town by the southern road and follow signs for Cally House Hotel to find the **Murray Forest Information Centre** and two-mile **Fleet Oakwoods Interpretive Trail**, which takes in the natural (broad-leaved trees, wetland flora, pheasants, woodpeckers, deer, foxes) and the man-made (twelfth-century Anglo-Norman motte and ditch), with explanation boards and demonstrations of tree maintenance along the way.

The fifteenth-century **Cardoness Castle** (HS, standard times; weekends only in winter), sitting on top of a small neat hill just south of town, is set off by perfect lawns and especially pretty flower beds. Its four-storeyed, well-preserved mass is an object lesson in medieval castle building, with impressive defences (including inverted keyhole gunloops), well-organised accommodation (plenty of vented latrines, window benches, intramural vents) and more than a nod towards aesthetics (moulded fireplace surrounds). Note the 'murder hole' above the gateway, used for pouring boiling liquids on uninvited guests. The view from the top, which takes in the Water of Fleet, is magnificent. There are informative and readable signs everywhere. Look for the copperplate signature of John Bell, a frequently encountered early nineteenth-century graffiti enthusiast, on the outside wall by the entrance.

NEWTON STEWART

Newton Stewart lies on the banks of the Cree in a wooded valley. It is hard by the main A75 Carlisle to Stranraer route and is served by several major north–south roads, too. Like most of the towns of the south-west it is untouristy but not lacking in good tourist facilities. The **Newton Stewart Museum** (open May, June, Sept, Mon to Sat 2 to 5; July, Aug, Mon to Sat 10 to 12.30, 2 to 5; also July to Sept, Sun 2 to 5), formerly St John's Church, on York Road above Victoria Street has a fairly new collection and documentation of local and regional daily life. **Minnigaff**, across the bridge, is older and quainter than Newton Stewart. On working days you can watch mohair being woven at the **Creebridge Mill** (and visit the shop). Of Minnigaff's numerous prehistoric cairns, standing stones and circles, the best known are the **Thieves** standing stones beyond Cumloden, around five miles to the north of Minnigaff.

THE GLENKENS

The A713 from Castle Douglas to Ayr follows Galloway's largest glen through an area known as the Glenkens. The farmland, forest and moorland crisscrossed by rivers and lochs are typical of Galloway, but walks are well signposted and are less frequented than those in Galloway Forest Park just to the west. The mountains known as the Rinns of Kells rise to 2600 feet above the forests lining the west of the A713 and form the boundary with Galloway Forest Park; a path runs along their ridge. The Glenkens are a good spot for fishing. The narrow **Loch Ken**, which meanders past flanks of pine trees, is home to roach, perch and pike. Sailing boats are found here, too (contact Galloway Sailing Centre 06442 626), as are water skiers. The River Ken, to the north of Dalry in an isolated valley, is autumn salmon-fishing territory.

GALLOWAY FOREST PARK

Covering 250 square miles of conifer plantation and open spaces in the middle of Scotland's south-west, Galloway Forest Park has a few sights and dozens of lochs and lochans. Merrick, at 2776 feet, is its highest point. Most of the forest is traversed by well-marked trails, and the 200-mile Southern Upland Way passes through some of the south-west's most dramatic inland scenery.

The A712 between New Galloway and Newton Stewart is known as the Queen's Way. Along it you will find a wild goat enclosure and a red deer range, the large, artificial **Clatteringshaws Loch** (good views from outdoor picnic tables near the Wildlife Centre) and a boulder in a clearing against which Robert the Bruce supposedly leaned after winning the Battle of Rapploch Moss (1307). Named after the novel *The Raiders*, by S R Crocket, the unpaved, single-track Raiders Road off the main road (speed limit 20mph) follows the River Dee. You can see most of its ten-mile length from the Bennan Viewpoint. (The turn-off is signposted near Bennan just north of the eastern entrance of Raiders Road.)

Four miles of lovely road through Glentrool Forest wind, dip and climb, ending at the car park high above Loch Trool. The view over the loch, which takes in miles of lovely wilderness, must be the area's best. A plaque on Bruce's Stone just above the car park commemorates the Battle of Glentrool (1307). Park here if you are mounting an assault on Merrick.

Stroan Bridge, between Glentrool Village and Loch Trool, is good for less ambitious walking. Better still are the four marked trails in **Kirroughtree Forest**, just south of Glentrool, which take in a forest garden, lochs, long-distant views and disused lead mines. To see farm animals at work, go to **Palgowan Open Farm**, four miles north of Glentrool village; tours last two hours (0671 840231). The small town of **New Galloway** is a major lifeline for the Galloway Forest Park, and the region's smallest royal burgh. Along the one main street can be found all that any walker can ask for: sports shops, restaurants, and a reasonable choice of hotels and guesthouses, as well as the licensed Smithy tea-room.

THE MACHARS

This wide, triangular headland that points south between Wigtown and Luce Bays is fine touring country, well served by small roads that meander past whitewashed cottages and through the central farmlands patched with heather and gorse.

Wigtown is a sleepy burgh with one very wide street and a little museum. The **Martyrs' Monument** (also known as Windyhill Monument) stands on a hill above town. It is dedicated to two Covenanters, Margaret McLachlan and Margaret Wilson, who were tied to a stake and allowed to drown in the rising tide.

Nineteen knee-to-waist-high granite boulders make up the Bronze Age **Torhouse Stone Circle**, which overlooks a hilly, windswept plain a few miles west of Wigtown. Three larger stones, the purpose of which defies archaeologists, stand in the middle.

A mile south of Wigtown at **Bladnoch** is the south-west's only distillery (open for half-hour guided tours Mon to Fri 10 to 4).

Further south, **Whithorn** is the birthplace of Scottish

Christianity, a part-seventeenth-century town with brightly painted houses and a handsome broad avenue dotted with statues and trees. The name comes from the old English, 'hwit erne', meaning white house. The Latin equivalent, 'candida casa', was the name given to the church founded by St Ninian, Scotland's first saint. Its location is unknown, though Isle of Whithorn and Whithorn both lay claim. The visitor centre in the middle of Whithorn marks the start of guided tours to the nearby **Whithorn Dig** (open Easter to Oct, daily 10.30 to 5). The first known Christian church in Britain was recently discovered here, as were numerous graves of early Christian settlers. You are likely to see archaeologists gingerly scraping away at the earth. Close by is a wattle and timber Viking house, reconstructed using evidence from the site. A small exhibition and audio-visual slide show tell of St Ninian's mission to convert the Picts.

You should also visit the **Priory** (open Easter to Oct, daily 10.30 to 5) next to the excavations, where Mary Queen of Scots once stayed. It has a finely carved Romanesque south doorway and the vaulted crypt dates from the mid-fifteenth century. In the small museum next door (open Easter to Oct, daily 10.30 to 5), are early Christian carved crosses and head-stones, including the Latinus Stone, a crudely incised pillar stone which is Scotland's earliest known Christian artefact.

Rispain Camp, high up and overlooking valleys in all directions, is off the A746 just over half a mile south-west of Whithorn. Park in the farmyard and walk 100 yards or so up the hill. The large, rectangular earthwork, surrounded by a deep ditch with one entrance 'bridge', is well defined by its covering of mown grass. Radio-carbon-dating has established it at around 60 BC.

Isle of Whithorn is not an island but a pretty town built around a harbour. A walk along the wild bluff that overlooks the bay will probably be remembered longer than a visit to the thirteenth-century St Ninian's Chapel, or St Ninian's Cave, on the beach along the south-west point.

The Luce Bay coast between Monreith and Glenluce is one of the south-west's most beautiful. The road curves past sandy or rocky bays and steep headlands, sometimes rising high, then sweeping down. To reach **Monreith Bay**, follow signs to St Medan's golf course; you will pass an otter sculpture, memorial to Gavin Maxwell, author of *Ring of Bright Water*, on the right of the road, which ends in a peaceful sandy bay. A little further north along the main A747 at Barsalloch Point is the grass-covered **Barsalloch Fort**, dating from the end of the first millennium BC. The view from the top is more impressive than the top itself. Thereafter the road hovers high over the rocky beaches of Luce Bay, then, in one dramatic sweep downwards, joins the shore just before the rather dour town of Portwilliam.

GLENLUCE TO STRANRAER

Glenluce Abbey (HS, standard times; weekends only in winter) stands in a fertile valley near the Water of Luce, a mile north of the village of Glenluce. One of Galloway's three Cistercian monasteries, it was founded by Roland, Lord of Galloway, around 1191 as daughter-house of Dundrennan. Not much is left of the abbey church, but the chapter house, rebuilt in the fifteenth century, is an elegant, centrally pillared and vaulted room. Of particular interest is the sophisticated, possibly unique, water supply system consisting of interlinking clay pipes and lidded junction boxes. Well-preserved remnants are displayed in the small museum, as are other finds such as cooking pots and coins.

Stranraer is a market town and Scotland's main port for ferries to Larne in Northern Ireland. It is also a holiday town, with a walled marine lake and leisure centre. The sixteenth-century **Castle** (the Old Castle of St John), on a square surrounded by shops, was a prison for Covenanters.

Just outside Stranraer, **Castle Kennedy Gardens** are amongst Scotland's finest. A tree-lined drive skirts the broad White Loch before arriving at the garden centre and tea-shop entrance to the monumental and formal gardens (open Easter to Sept, daily 10 to 5), set on an isthmus between Black and White Lochs. The castle was home to the Stair family in the seventeenth century; it was ravaged by fire in 1716 and never rebuilt. The ruin is now almost entirely covered in ivy, and rises out of a seemingly endless velvety lawn. The gardens were almost as overgrown 150 years ago, and it was only luck that turned up the original plans to which they have since been tailored. Great expanses of lawn are bounded by tall trees and flowering shrubs, in particular rhododendrons, of which there are around 35 varieties. A broad grass avenue is lined with 100-year-old, 70-foot-tall monkey puzzle trees. Special to Castle Kennedy Gardens are the wide views of flower-edged lawn or lochs. If you go as far as Stair family's current home, the Victorian Lochinch Castle (recommended for its pretty sunken garden), you will see both lochs at once.

Meadowsweet Herb Garden (open May to Aug, daily 12 to 5; closed Wed), on a promontory into Soulseat Loch, is only a little way south of Castle Kennedy but seems a world apart. A caravan acts as ticket booth, gift shop, even herbal tea bar. More than 100 herbs, organically grown, are compactly arranged. You are encouraged to rub the leaves and needles, so bring tissues to clean your fingers and keep scents distinct.

THE RINNS OF GALLOWAY

The narrow hammer-head protrusion off Scotland's extreme south-west corner is known as the Rinns of Galloway. As well as natural beauty, often turbulent seascapes and rocky, treeless headlands, the peninsula has several charming fishing villages and an excellent sub-tropical garden, yet is surprisingly uncommercialised.

Portpatrick

A likeable little harbour town, Portpatrick weathers its popularity well. Once a major port for importing Irish cattle (Northern Ireland is only 22 miles away), it lost out to Stranraer's larger and calmer waters in 1868. Fishing boats hide among the ranks of colourful craft. There are good boat trips, two golf courses, and the long-distance Southern Upland Way starts (or ends) here. **Little Wheels** (open July, Aug, daily; Easter to June, Sept, Oct, closed Fri), a few streets back from the harbour, houses working model (00-gauge) trains and miniature transport memorabilia which should enthral even the uninitiated.

The Southern Rinns

The southern half of the Rinns is bleaker than the north, but there is more to see. All the sights are within easy reach of the A716, which winds past small coves on the east coast. The turn-off to the **Kirkmadrine Stones** is signposted south of Sandhead. A dirt track leads to a late nineteenth-century burial chapel. The earliest known Christian monuments after those at Whithorn – several pillar stones incised with crosses and Latin inscriptions – were found near where it stands and are now on display in its glassed-in porch.

Ardwell Gardens (open Apr to Oct, daily 10 to 6) hold an impressive assortment of trees (including palms), a good rock garden, and, in spring, daffodils by the thousands. Better, however, is **Logan Botanic Garden** (open mid–Mar to Oct, daily 10 to 6), an annexe of the Royal Botanic Gardens in Edinburgh and study centre for the Department of Agriculture and Fisheries for Scotland. There is a woodland and a walled garden; both are large and beautifully arranged. Proximity to two coasts makes for a sub-tropical microclimate ideal for exotic flora; what started 100 years ago as a kitchen garden today boasts an enormous number of rare plants. Giant-leaved cabbage palms (actually of the lily family), tree ferns (palm tree shape, fern leaves) and Chusan palms with vast yellow flowers make a lovely jungle. Also commendable are the large salad bar/tearoom, and the low entrance fee.

Port Logan, like Portpatrick, is a small fishing village on the west coast, and was also a port for traffic from Ireland – witness the imposing jetty. At the natural but almost perfectly round fish pond, you can watch lunch being hand-fed to cod, pollack and plaice.

The **Mull of Galloway** is a narrow windswept headland with a car park and, at the edge of a 200-foot-high cliff, a lighthouse. Ireland and the Isle of Man are often visible.

The Northern Rinns

The northern part of the Rinns is largely pastureland, with more cows than trees. You can see Ireland and Ailsa Craig from its rocky shore on most days. Seabirds circle continuously, and the drive north from Stranraer along the western side of Loch Ryan is especially rewarding for bird-watching. The **Wig**, a wide, swooping bay, is a good viewing place, while **Lady Bay** a little further along is, by contrast, small and well protected, features that appealed to smugglers of the eighteenth century.

THE AYRSHIRE COAST

North of Stranraer

A favourite holiday destination for car-less Glaswegians once upon a time, this stretch of coast is now a weekenders' haunt. The A77 is also a major route linking the ferry ports of Stranraer and Cairnryan to Ayr and Glasgow. Consequently during the summer you can expect to be sandwiched between lorries as well as caravans.

The volcanic rock of **Ailsa Craig**, which lies ten miles

off the coast, comes into view soon after you pass the ferry terminal at Cairnryan. It is also known as Paddy's Milestone because it lies midway between Glasgow and Belfast, and its strategic position at the mouth of the Firth of Clyde made it a convenient tolbooth for foreign sea traffic in past centuries. Now it is a bird sanctuary and source of fine red granite for curling stones. It can be reached on boat trips from Girvan (early Apr to late Oct, phone 0465 3219 for details).

The Victorian town of **Girvan** was once a major landing site for herring, but nowadays fishing boats are outnumbered by pleasure craft. This is one of Ayrshire's most popular resorts, thanks to its long beach, golf courses and amusement arcades. Inland in a high valley is **Barr**, the area's most picturesque village. The narrow River Stinchar runs right through the middle and small, whitewashed cottages line its banks.

Culzean Castle

(NTS, castle and visitor centre open Apr to late Oct, daily 10.30 to 5; other times by appointment; country park open all year, daily 9 to sunset)

From **Turnberry**, five miles north of Girvan and home to one of Ayrshire's top two golf courses (the other is at Troon), take the coastal A719 to reach Culzean Castle. The Robert Adam castle, the sensational clifftop setting above three miles of coastline, the woodland park and acres of gardens add up to a superb half-day visit. Start beside the car park at the Home Farm (now the information centre, exhibition, gift shop and restaurant complex), which is also by Adam and faithfully restored to his original design. The huge crenellated castle was built between 1772 and 1792 around a fortified medieval house. The size and the detail of the exterior are typically Scottish baronial but proportions have a graceful Georgian quality. The interior is opulently furnished, but with taste rather than ostentation. Shapes and dimensions are pleasing, especially in the oval staircase with its Greek columns; bright rooms look over the Firth of Clyde with views of sea and islands that almost upstage the interior. Adam's intricate plaster ceilings have been restored to the cool and subtle tones he intended.

The country park by the castle includes woodland, successfully designed to give shelter from sea gales, and a huge walled garden filled with herbaceous borders. At the large swan pond, also colonised by seagulls and ducks, there is a snack bar and aviary. A deer park and adventure playground are additional treats.

Crossraguel Abbey

(HS, standard times; closed in winter)
A zigzag east from Culzean brings you to the noble ruins of Crossraguel Abbey. Founded in the early thirteenth century by Duncan, first Earl of Carrick, as a Cluniac monastery, it was plundered during the Wars of Independence and rebuilt in the fifteenth century. Its rich lands, a major prize during the Reformation, earned it more fame than its religious influence: probably no more than ten monks lived here in the fifteenth century. Little of the abbey still stands, but the chapter house, tower-house and dovecote are in fair shape.

Dunure

On the coast to the north is Dunure, a comely village with a miniature harbour and, near a cliff, the dilapidated **Dunure Castle**, one of the Kennedy family's residences. Mary Queen of Scots stopped here but the lay abbot of Crossraguel Abbey was a more noteworthy visitor, having been gently roasted on a spit by his host, the Earl of Cassillis, in 1570 to persuade him to hand over the abbey lands. (The coercion technique is said to have worked.)

On the A719 between Culzean Castle and Dunure, look for the sign marking the **Electric Brae**, an optical illusion best experienced travelling south: the road seems to slope downhill when in fact it climbs – an entertainingly jarring sensation.

Ayr and around

Ayr grew up around a castle which was destroyed by Robert the Bruce in 1298 to keep it from English hands. Today the town is important for commerce and tourism alike; a busy harbour, three golf courses and Scotland's foremost race course guarantee an unflagging pace of life. Three colourful parks are havens of peace and there are more than two miles of beach, looking out to Ailsa Craig and Arran. (Hope for clear weather: the sunsets are one of the town's unmissable sights.) However, modern Ayr has not made much of its sea and riverside setting. It might also frustrate Burns followers who come expecting the sights to match those in Dumfries. Robert Burns sights and memorabilia are neither as plentiful nor as rewarding, even if you include next-door Alloway; better are Mauchline and Tarbolton, not far inland. The Tam O'Shanter Museum, accepted starting point of Tam's epic ride and one of the major traditional ports of call for Burns enthusiasts, is closed until further notice. Nevertheless, souvenirs emblazoned with Burns' poems and portraits are everywhere. There is a good choice of places to stay, from cheap to expensive, a reasonable variety of restaurants, and plenty of craft and clothing shops.

On the south side of town is an accomplished statue of Burns by George Lawson, in pensive stance but with a whimsical expression; but its current setting is a disarray of modern buildings and noisy streets. In the centre of town, the Auld Kirk (parish church), at the end of Kirk Pont, is where the poet was baptised. Within the mellow stone archway at the entrance to the churchyard hang two huge iron mortsafes, once placed over coffins to thwart body snatchers. The cross-shaped church, built in 1653, was partly funded by Cromwell who dismantled its predecessor to build the armoury of his now mostly vanished fort. The churchyard, filled with several unusual sculpted bas-relief headstones, is wedged between the High Street and the river front, from where you can see all four bridges, including the thirteenth-century Auld Brig.

Loudoun Hall, in Boat Vennel near New Bridge, is one of Scotland's oldest houses, built by a wealthy merchant in 1503. It is one of the best examples of semi-fortified domestic architecture, and is nicely preserved. The balconies served for efficient slop hurling. Cromwell's fort is no longer, but a remnant of wall and turret stands at the corner of South Beach Road and South Harbour Street, giving an idea of its huge scale. Behind the Tourist Information Office, on Sandgate, is the compact **Queen's Court** shopping arcade, an ingenious restoration of Georgian and Victorian houses with old paving stones, lamp fittings and café tables.

On the northern side of Ayr, and merging with it, is **Prestwick**, as well known for its nearby airport as its resort facilities. **Troon**, not far beyond, is a much more appealing town. Off the main road, it has fine Edwardian and Victorian houses, quiet beaches and five 18-hole golf courses, including the Royal Troon, started in 1878.

Alloway

This small village, which blends into Ayr's leafy southern outskirts, is strictly for Robert Burns fans. The poet was born here and it was here that he set his epic poem, *Tam O'Shanter*. **Burns Cottage** makes a fitting first port of call (open June to Aug, Mon to Sat 9 to 7, Sun 10 to 7; Apr, May, Sept, Oct, Mon to Sat 10 to 5, Sun 2 to 5; Nov to Mar, Mon to Sat 10 to 4). William Burnes, the poet's father (his children dropped the 'e'), built the cottage and byre, now whitewashed and thatched, where Robert spent the first seven years of his life. The side-by-side rooms are as spartan today as they must have been then, unlike the gardens (dominated by four 100-year-old Irish yews) which have a pampered look. The first-rate small museum of manuscripts and ephemera accompanied by clear biographical panels has an original copy of the Kilmarnock edition of poems. The gift shop and tea-room are small but sufficient. More blatantly touristy is the **Land O'Burns Centre** (open July, Aug, daily 10 to 6; June, Sept, daily 10 to 5.30; Oct to May, daily 10 to 5), a single-storey, purpose-built complex with a car park the size of a football field on one side and lawn with picnic tables on the other.

The **Auld Kirk** is a small and roofless chapel in a simple graveyard, hardly a mystical setting, but the spot where Tam witnessed 'warlocks and witches in a dance'. Just above it is the nineteenth-century **Burns Monument** (opening times as for Burns Cottage), a neo-Classical, Corinthian-columned temple. Inside are a few oddments including a Bible owned by Burns' one-time fiancée, Highland Mary, and the wedding ring of his wife, Jean Armour. Come for a wander around the small garden packed with rare shrubs and lovely herbaceous borders, and for the view (best from the top of the Monument), which takes in the **Brig O'Doon**, the most picturesque of all stops on the Burns Heritage Trail. The small hump-backed bridge, which together with its reflection forms a neat O, spans a narrow river with lush banks and a backdrop of trees and fields. The bridge was Tam's means of escape, since witches, according to Burns' note to his poem, 'have no power to follow a poor wight any farther than the middle of the next running stream'.

INLAND FROM AYR

Robert Burns lived in and around **Mauchline** from when he was 18 until he was almost 30, and there is a plethora of sights – some with only vague associations – connected with

ROBERT BURNS (1759–1796)

Scotland's most famous poet was born in Alloway, a village just south of Ayr, on 25 January 1759. Hailed in his lifetime as 'ploughman-poet', Burns' agricultural antecedents appealed to the eighteenth-century idea that the well-springs of genius were the more intriguing for being found in a man of humble background.

In fact, Robert Burns, thanks to an intelligent and determined father, was an educated and well-read man. He read Ramsay, the Scottish poet, as well as Pope, Locke and Shakespeare. By the time he was 22, he had already worked in several agricultural jobs, without much success. Emigration to Jamaica seemed to be the solution to his problems. Though he had circulated manuscripts of his poems, none of his work was published until he was 27, but *Poems, Chiefly in the Scottish Dialect*, published in Kilmarnock in 1786, was an instant success.

He exchanged a pledge of marriage with Mary Campbell (Highland Mary), but in fact remained loyal (though far from faithful) to Jean Armour, whom he first declared his common-law wife at the age of 26. His womanising got him into trouble with the Presbyterian Kirk – a constant theme of Burns' best poetry is one of protest against the restrictions placed on mankind's freedom by artificial distinctions of birth, morals or custom.

He next published in Edinburgh, where he stayed and was fêted as literary hero for two winters, thereafter flinging himself into collecting, editing and writing the *Scottish Songs* which form such a large part of his work. In 1788, he moved, with his family, to Ellisland Farm north of Dumfries. A year later, after another failed attempt at agriculture, he moved to Dumfries and became a customs officer.

Burns hated hypocrisy and pomposity in all their forms, and there is little doubt that his most successful poems are the biting satirical pieces in Scots, such as *Holy Willie's Prayer*, though it is by such classic songs as *Auld Lang Syne* and the sanitised version of *Comin' Thro' the Rye* that he is often remembered. The cult of Burns – marked by Burns suppers held in his honour in Caledonian societies throughout the world – is often mawkish and sentimental. In fact, he was a tough, no-nonsense poet who loved sensual pleasures in the best tradition of his predecessors Ramsay and Fergusson.

He died at Dumfries in 1796 at the age of 37.

him. Burns' parents had several farms around Mauchline and he married Jean Armour in the town. Their cottage is now the **Burns Museum** (open Easter to Sept, Mon to Sat, 11.30 to 12.30 and 1.30 to 5.30, Sun 2 to 5), notable more for displays of curling stones and local boxware than Burns memorabilia. Around the corner is **Poosie Nansie's Tavern** used as a setting in *The Jolly Beggars* and still serving good ale. The small but almost Disneyesque **Burns Memorial Tower** (open Easter to Oct, Mon to Sat 9 to 1, 2 to 5; Nov to Easter, Mon to Fri only), to the north of the town, has had a facelift, and the poet's life and times are detailed on three floors.

A few miles west, in the centre of Tarbolton, the **Bachelors' Club** (NTS, open Apr to late Oct, daily 12 to 5, other times by appointment) is almost certain to intrigue. The top floor of this former inn was the meeting place for the debating society started by Burns in 1780. The first debate concerned the relative merits of a woman with fortune but neither looks nor personality, and a poor woman with both attributes. The guided tour is detailed and erudite but also entertaining, with plenty of anecdotes to fire the imagination and bring to life the décor, manuscripts and paintings.

Dean Castle

Burns' first major collection of poems was published in 1786 in **Kilmarnock**, a town 13 miles north-east of Ayr. However, the main sight here has no association with the poet. Dean Castle (open daily 12 to 5), the Boyd family's ancient home, stands on the northern outskirts of the town and, thanks to its variety, intimacy and informality, has high entertainment value for families. The compact fifteenth-century castle and fourteenth-century fortified keep are bursting both with fun and with worthy collections of musical instruments (lutes and small keyboards, in particular), medieval armour and tapestries. Children and brave adults will want to try out the *oubliette*, a cell just big enough to lie in, where prisoners were left and forgotten – try it in the dark if you dare. The guides, some of whom will even sing to demonstrate the acoustics of the minstrels' gallery, give an amusing and stimulating tour. The 200-acre country park, open year-round and free, has picnic areas, a duck pond, an adventure playground, nature trails, a riding centre and a small rare breeds farm.

THE NORTH AYRSHIRE COAST

The northern chunk of Ayrshire (called Cunninghame) suffers from its proximity to Glasgow, and industry tends to encroach on the holiday scene here. However, the views of offshore islands and landmasses are spectacular: Arran, Great Cumbrae, Bute and the tip of Kintyre. A couple of sights are worth seeking out around here, too, before you make for the ferries of Ardrossan (for Arran) or Largs (for Great Cumbrae).

Irvine

The horizon around Irvine is especially cluttered by factory smokestacks, and the town itself is a confusion of modern and old. **Glasgow Vennel**, near the intersection of the High Street and Townhead, is now a smart, renovated and pedestrianised street of stone and rendered cottages. It is home to one of the oldest **Burns Clubs**, as well as the thatched **Heckling Shop**, where Burns learned to dress flax. You can visit these year-round.

A short drive north, half-way between Kilwinning and Dalry, is the handsome stone **Dalgarven Mill** (open Mon to Sat 10 to 5, Sun 12.30 to 5.30). This wholesome renovation of a sixteenth-century corn mill is enthusiastically run by the great-grandson of the miller who rebuilt it in the last century, and houses a museum of country life and a first-rate costume gallery. In the milling area, the water wheel creaks and clatters and the millstones grind. Home-made snacks and baked goods are on sale in the coffee room.

Largs

As well as being the ferry terminal for the island of Great Cumbrae, Largs is a stop-off point for the world's last sea-going paddle steamer, the *Waverley*, which cruises the Firth of Clyde. The town is home to the huge Art Deco **Nardini's**, an ice-cream emporium, cafeteria and restaurant, originally founded in 1890.

Just south of Largs is the **Kelburn Country Centre**. The thirteenth-century castle, open during late April to May only, has been home to the Earls of Glasgow for nearly three centuries. The grounds, complete with babbling burn, overlook the Firth of Clyde and Great Cumbrae. The artfully reconstructed Home Farm (circa 1700), arranged around a courtyard, now houses an information office, café, restaurant and gift shop. Around it are garden walks and steepish trails up the glen. In a three-sided grotto, just beyond the castle, two waterfalls tumble over vertical cliffs into black pools.

ARRAN

Arran is one of the four Clyde islands (the others being Great Cumbrae, Little Cumbrae and Bute). Within its 20-mile length are several mountains of 2500 feet or more, glens, rivers, lochs, rocky coast, moorland, pine trees and colourful villages. Few islands with such variety are as easy and as inexpensive to reach: it takes only an hour by ferry from Ardrossan and half an hour from Claonaig on the Kintyre peninsula (seasonal sailings). Consequently, Arran has been a popular holiday retreat since the nineteenth century. It is not the place to come for peace and quiet, particularly in high season.

The main road circles the coast, hugging the rocky shore much of the way with uninterrupted sea views. Forestry plantations dominate the south-eastern side and mountains and foothills fill most of the north-eastern end; here is Goat Fell, the island's main destination for hill-walkers. Two roads cut through the middle of the island; prehistoric cairns are to be seen scattered near the lower road. From the coast road several short walks, with sea views as well as prehistoric sites, are signposted, though parking can be a problem. You may spot rare wildlife, including red squirrels and, increasingly, basking sharks, a large variety that comes close to land in warm weather. There are also red deer and seals.

Brodick Castle

Look to your right as you approach the pier at Brodick and you will see the bold, reddish form of Brodick Castle on a cliff against a backdrop of peaked mountains (NTS, castle open 1 to 18 Apr and 2 May to 30 Sept, daily, 19 Apr to 1 May and 2 to 23 Oct, Mon, Wed, Sat 1 to 5). To reach it, turn north past the hotels, guesthouses and gift shops that make up the town. Built in the thirteenth century on the site of a Viking fort, the castle has been home to the Hamiltons since 1503, when the earldom of Arran passed to the second Lord Hamilton. Restoration and extensions were carried out over the centuries (by Cromwell's men amongst others), and from most angles it now looks like a typical example of Victorian baronial architecture, incorporating Italian Renaissance elegance into defence structures such as turrets and corner towers. The interior is richly decorated and furnished, the porcelain and silver collections being particularly fine. In most of the rooms, dukes through the ages stare out of elaborate gilt frames; here also are landscape sketches by Gainsborough and paintings by Watteau. Do not miss the water-driven roasting spit in the huge, fully equipped kitchen. There are masses of rhododendrons in the surrounding woodland, and the early eighteenth-century walled garden is handsome, too.

Occupying several buildings of an eighteenth-century croft, the **Isle of Arran Heritage Museum** (open Easter to Oct, Mon to Sat 10 to 5), between Brodick Castle and the town, gives a rounded if uninspired glimpse into daily life of the past through period furnishings and old tools. The island's geology and archaeology are also explained and worth studying; you should bone up on the latter if you are planning to track down Arran's prehistoric monuments. The tea-room and picnic area are pleasant and the cakes home-made.

The coast road

Travelling clockwise saves the dramatic mountain scenery for last. The road south from Brodick leaves the coast for several miles before rejoining it at **Lamlash Bay**, with the green-peaked Holy Island guarding the harbour. At the southern end, at **Torrylin**, an 800-yard path leads to a chambered cairn of the fourth to third millennium BC. No more than half a dozen slabs are stuck into the side of a small grassy mound, but the walk through woodland and fields and the panoramic view of the sea and pastures from the site make the trip worthwile. Park at the shop.

The Kintyre peninsula, running parallel to the western coast, is in places only three or four miles across the Kilbrannan Sound, giving constant fine views. By the time you reach **Blackwaterfoot**, at the junction with the northern cross-island road (called 'the String'), the trees have given way to heather and bracken. Two miles north of Blackwaterfoot, by the golf course, a two-mile path leads along the shore to **King's Cave** where King Robert the Bruce supposedly watched the spider whose tenacious behaviour gave him courage for future battles against the English. The road rejoins the coast after a short stretch inland at **Machrie Moor**, a desolate and beautiful moor of heather and peat, framed by

Goat Fell and its neighbouring mountains in the distance. Here is a rich and most remarkable collection of Neolithic and Bronze Age monuments. The mile-and-a-half-long track in from the road dips then climbs slightly as it meanders through sheep pastures, by the abandoned Moss Farm, and past stone circle after stone circle. Short cyst burials and food vessels have been found in several sites and occasional signs offer explanations of the discoveries. Boulders are scattered everywhere. Then, suddenly, as you reach the summit of a small hill, an enormous moor rimmed by hills comes into view; standing in the middle are three widely spaced and stately rust-coloured stones over 15 feet tall. The full circle must have been awesome.

Lochranza

From Machrie Moor until Lochranza the road stays close by a narrow strip of rocky and pebbly beach. The **Twelve Apostles**, a string of colourful cottages, appears on your right just before you reach Lochranza. What was once a prosperous herring fishing village is now used for holiday cottages, but it is unaffected and tranquil; you may well encounter sheep wandering the town's streets. The (seasonal) car ferry to the Kintyre peninsula that leaves from outside town hardly disrupts the peace.

Lochranza's striking harbour and views out to sea are its main selling points. Small painted houses and cottages sit in a rather jumbled fashion around a deeply inset sea loch with the impregnable-looking **Lochranza Castle** on a gravel spit right in the middle of the harbour (ask at the post office opposite for the key). Before recent renovations it was reckoned to be a typical sixteenth-century tower-house, but has now been discovered to incorporate a medieval hall-house. These comparatively modest dwellings were precursors of tower-houses and consisted of two storeys only, with storage below and the lord's hall above.

On bright mornings, a stroll to the far end of the harbour may well repay you with a close-up view of seals sunning themselves on barely submerged rocks.

From Lochranza to Brodick

Shortly after heading inland from Lochranza the road begins winding up through bracken-covered moorland. The craggy summit of Goat Fell becomes an increasingly overwhelming presence; a good starting point for its ascent is by a two-mile path that starts at the sawmill, a few miles north of Brodick. This is fine walking country, with wide, reasonably gentle swathes of hillside. **Sannox Bay**, at the end of a short track near the point where the main road returns to the shore, is a very secluded and sheltered cove – a fine place for a picnic.

Rust–coloured, striated rocks slant into the sea around **Corrie**; the pastel–coloured cottages that line the road make it Arran's most photogenic village.

USEFUL DIRECTORY

Main tourist offices
Ayrshire Tourist Board
Suite 1005, Prestwick Airport
Ayrshire KA9 2PL
(0292) 79000

Dumfries and Galloway Tourist Board
Campbell House, Bankend Road
Dumfries DG1 4TH
(0387) 50434

Isle of Arran Tourist Board
Brodick, Isle of Arran KA27 8AU
(0770) 302140/302401

Tourist Board publications Useful: annual guides listing accommodation and main attractions (Ayrshire, Isle of Arran). Also *Exploring Dumfries and Galloway* – lists all attractions and activities with opening times. Special interest leaflets and factsheets include golf, fishing, cycling, walks.

Local tourist information centres
Ardrossan (0294) 601063 (Apr to Oct)
Ayr (0292) 284196
Brodick (0770) 302140/302401
Castle Douglas (0556) 502611 (Easter to Oct)
Culzean Castle (06556) 293 (Apr to Sept)
Dalbeattie (0556) 610117 (mid-May to Oct)
Dumfries (0387) 253862
Gatehouse of Fleet (0557) 814212 (Easter to Oct)
Girvan (0465) 4950 (Apr to Oct)

GREAT CUMBRAE

The Clyde island of Great Cumbrae is less than four miles from top to toe and only ten minutes from the mainland (by ferry from Largs). Its size makes bicycles and walking a sensible way of getting around, and the coast road offers wonderful seascapes of Arran, Bute and the Ayrshire coast along its ten miles or so. Cumbrae's longstanding popularity with day-trippers, weekenders and holidaying families means that you are unlikely to be alone on its beaches or trails.

Kilmarnock (0563) 39090
Kirkcudbright (0557) 330494 (Easter to Oct)
Largs (0475) 673765
Lochranza (0770) 830320 (May to Sept)
Mauchline (0290) 551916
Millport (0475) 530753 (Easter to Sept)
Newton Stewart (0671) 402431 (Easter to Oct)
Prestwick (0292) 79822
Sanquhar (0659) 50185 (mid-May to Oct)
Stranraer (0776) 702595 (Easter to Oct)
Troon (0292) 317696 (Easter to Oct)

Local transport
Dumfries Railway Station (0387) 55115
Stranraer Railway Station (0776) 706234
Ayr Railway Station (0292) 263364
Western Scottish Omnibus (0387) 53496
Caledonian MacBrayne Ferries (crossings all year from Ardrossan to Arran, Largs to Great Cumbrae, also seasonal service from Lochranza to Claonaig on the Mull of Kintyre) (0475) 650100
Stena Sealink Ferries (Stranraer to Larne, up to nine crossings daily) (0776) 702262
P&O European Ferries (Cairnryan to Larne, up to six crossings daily) (0581) 200276

Recreation
Galloway Forest Park (0671) 402420
Waverley paddle steamer cruises from Ayr and Firth of Clyde resorts 041-221 8152
Boat trips from Girvan to Ailsa Craig (0465) 3219

Millport, the island's only town, is a pleasing array of houses lining the gently curving harbour and long, sandy beach; the waters are fine for boating and sub-aqua diving. There are not many trees on Cumbrae, and from the **Glaid Stone**, marking the highest point, you have 360-degree views of the mountains and indented shores of the surrounding land masses and islands.

WHERE TO STAY

AUCHENCAIRN

Balcary Bay Hotel £££
Auchencairn, By Castle Douglas
Kirkcudbrightshire DG7 1QZ *Tel (055 664) 217/311*

Friendliness and a good location rather than outstanding character are the hallmarks of this good-value hotel. The old house has been modernised inside and bedrooms are plain and functional. Those overlooking Balcary Bay are the ones to go for.

Open: all year, exc mid-Nov to early Mar **Rooms**: 17
Facilities: fishing, water sports, snooker
Credit/charge cards: Access, Visa

KIRKCUDBRIGHT

Gladstone House £
48 High Street
Kirkcudbrightshire DG6 4JX *Tel (0557) 331734*

This is a lovely brown stone Georgian building in a quiet corner of town. The smart, cosy bedrooms have sloping ceilings and views over rooftops through massive dormer windows. Guests also have use of a comfortable sitting-room, full of books and records. Breakfast is served in a small but pleasant green and white room.

Open: all year **Rooms**: 3 **Credit/charge cards**: Access, Visa

LARGS

Brisbane House Hotel   ££
14 Greenock Road, Esplanade, Largs
Ayrshire KA30 8NF   Tel (0475) 687200

A sparkling seaside hotel, marbled throughout, with brass-railed staircases, and bedrooms furnished with mahogany, cherrywood and softly-coloured fabrics. High tea is available; otherwise, diners can choose from a seafood *table d'hôte* and extensive *à la carte*.

Open: all year **Rooms**: 23 **Credit/charge cards**: Access, Amex, Diners, Visa

PORTPATRICK

The Crown Hotel   £
North Crescent, Portpatrick
Wigtownshire DG9 8SX   Tel (0776) 810261

This quayside inn has plenty of character, with three bars, furnished with wooden-topped converted sewing tables, and a pretty, simple dining-room with a conservatory extension. The airy bedrooms, some with brass bedsteads, are well fitted out and have modern bathrooms. The menu includes steaks, grills, and some very fresh seafood. Good value.

Open: all year, exc 25 Dec **Rooms**: 12
Credit/charge cards: Access, Visa

Knockinaam Lodge   ££–£££
Portpatrick, Wigtownshire DG9 9AD   Tel (0776) 810471

Tucked away in its own little glen, this civilised Victorian house offers friendly and efficient service. The bar is slightly formal, but the rest of the house is prettily furnished with china lamps and sofas piled with cushions. Lawns run down to a small private beach. The dinners – jacket-and-tie affairs – are highly thought of and modern Gallic in style. The short set menu in French offers a choice at each course. Bedrooms vary in size but most are comfortably spacious, with period furnishings.

Open: all year, exc 4 Jan to 15 Mar **Rooms**: 10 **Facilities**: croquet **Credit/charge cards**: Access, Amex, Diners, Visa

STEWARTON

Chapeltoun House   £££–£££

Irvine Road, Stewarton
Ayrshire KA3 3ED   Tel (0560) 482696

Twenty acres of grounds surround this country-house hotel, which
provides a strong period atmosphere, plenty of comfort and
memorable food. The huge bedrooms have good-quality old
furniture and everything from sherry to shoe-cleaning kits. The
hall and dining-room are panelled and there's a fire for cold days,
as well as a comfortable lounge and bar.

Open: all year **Rooms**: 8 **Facilities**: fishing
Credit/charge cards: Access, Amex, Visa

TURNBERRY

Turnberry Hotel & Golf Courses   £££

Turnberry
Ayrshire KA26 9LT   Tel (0655) 31000

Here is a luxury hotel built in 1906, with two championship golf
courses on the doorstep and high standards of service. There are
several large public rooms to sit in and a restaurant with marbled
pillars, crystal chandeliers and views down to the sea. The bedrooms
are also luxurious and kitted out with all the extras. A piper plays
on the lawn every night.

Open: all year **Rooms**: 132 **Facilities**: golf, tennis, gym, squash,
spa treatment rooms, indoor swimming-pool, billiards, horseriding,
clay pigeon shooting **Credit/charge cards**: Access, Amex, Diners,
Visa

WHERE TO EAT

AYR

The Stables

Queen's Court
41 Sandgate, Ayr KA7 1BD   Tel (0292) 283704

This restaurant is in an eighteenth-century courtyard with shops. It
has a good-value daytime menu, with authentic Scottish dishes and
a vegetarian table d'hôte. The wine list includes wines from eight
English vineyards.

Open: daily 10 to 5; closed Xmas Day & Boxing Day
Credit/charge cards: Access, Amex, Visa

LARGS

Nardini's ★
Esplanade, Largs KA30 8NF *Tel (0475) 674555*

This cafeteria has been a Largs institution for over 100 years and caters for all meals throughout the day, starting with breakfast and including Scottish high teas of haddock, or liver, bacon and tomato, with home-made cakes and the outstanding Nardini ice-cream.

Open: daily 8 to 10.30; closed Xmas Day
Credit/charge cards: Access, Visa

TROON

Highgrove House
Old Loans Road, Troon KA10 7HL *Tel (0292) 312511*

Highgrove House offers solid creature comforts and large helpings of well-sauced food served by pleasant staff. Scottish salmon, langoustine and mussels feature, as well as plain grilled meats and excellent desserts.

Open: daily 12 to 2.30, 6.30 to 9.30 **Credit/charge cards**: Access, Amex, Visa

EDINBURGH

- A city in an outstanding natural setting, one of the most beautiful in Europe
- The best Georgian town-planning in Britain
- A wide variety of sights within a compact area
- The Edinburgh Festival

Houses in Charlotte Square

PLAN OF CENTRAL EDINBURGH

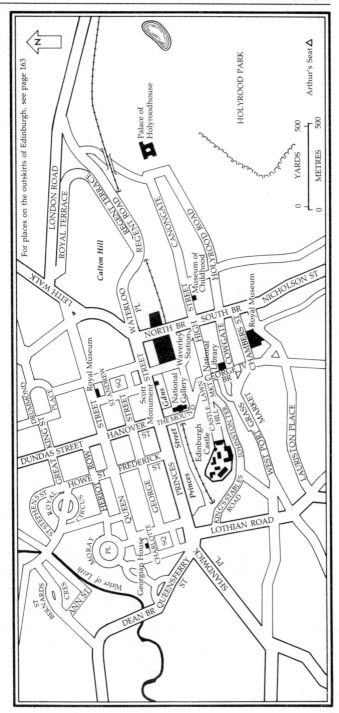

For places on the outskirts of Edinburgh, see page 163

N

Palace of Holyroodhouse

HOLYROOD PARK

Arthur's Seat △

YARDS 500

METRES 500

LONDON ROAD

ROYAL TERRACE

REGENT ROAD TERRACE

Calton Hill

LEITH WALK

CANONGATE

HOLYROOD ROAD

WATERLOO PL

HIGH STREET

Museum of Childhood

NORTH BR

SOUTH BR

NICHOLSON ST

DRUMMOND PLACE

KING ST

Royal Museum

ST ANDREW SQ

Scott Monument

Waverley Station

National Library

Royal Museum

CHAMBERS ST

COWGATE

GEORGE IV BR

National Gallery

Gdns

THE MOUND

HANOVER STREET

DUNDAS STREET

GREAT KING STREET

HOWE ST

HERIOT ROW

FREDERICK STREET

QUEEN STREET

GEORGE ST

PRINCES STREET

Princes Street

Edinburgh Castle

CASTLE HILL

LAWN MKT

JOHNSTON TER

KING'S STABLES ROAD

WEST PORT

GRASS MARKET

LAURISTON PLACE

LOTHIAN ROAD

STEPHEN'S ST

ROYAL CIRCUS

MORAY PL

CHARLOTTE SQ

Georgian House

SHANDWICK PL

QUEENSFERRY ST

DEAN BR

ANN ST

CRES

BERNARD'S ST

Water of Leith

EDINBURGH is the capital of Scotland and one of the most beautiful cities in Europe. Any catalogue of its virtues will include the lucky combination of crags and ridges on which it is built, the backdrop of the Firth of Forth, the hidden valley of the Water of Leith, the dominating castle and the contrast between the seventeenth-century warrens of the Old Town and the spacious neo-Classical architecture of the New. However, this list cannot begin to convey the experience of emerging from Waverley Station into the city centre for the first time. Princes Street, bounded by gardens all along one side, marks the beginning of the New Town, while the castle on its precipitous crag looms over the middle distance with the spires and jumbled roofscapes of the Old Town tumbling down from it. Few cities make such a strong first impression on the visitor.

Edinburgh is a city where there is almost always a view. In one direction there are the hills of Fife rising beyond the blue estuary of the Forth. In others there are the monuments on Calton Hill, or the great bulk of Arthur's Seat, or the castle. From Edinburgh's many high points – the Castle Esplanade, Calton Hill, the Scott Monument, or, further out, Arthur's Seat, the Braid Hills, Blackford Hill or Craiglockhart – there are panoramas to be had of the complete city, sprawling between the sea and the Pentland Hills.

It is a city that is compact enough to repay casual wandering – though you have to work at it, for the hills are many and steep. To explore the wynds and closes of the Old Town or the architectural details of the squares, streets and terraces of the New Town is to make constant discoveries, and there is a sufficient sprinkling of pubs, cafés and interesting shops to provide suitable breaks. Edinburgh is also a place for breaking away from the more obvious itineraries – exploring the half-hidden valley of the Water of Leith or the old harbour villages on the edge of the Forth, for example.

There are disadvantages. The wind is one, for every bitter breeze from the north or east is funnelled through the streets. Edinburgh citizens, despite their overcoats and furry hats, have a raw, stoical look to them from facing up to a lifetime of wind-chill. Fog is another hazard – the cold easterly haars (sea mists) can blanket Edinburgh while the country to the west is in bright sunshine. There is also Edinburgh's reputation for spending six months going to bed early to recover from its Festival, and the following five going to bed early to prepare for the next one. It is not quite justified, but the nightlife is inclined to be on the quiet side of respectable.

The New and the Old

The gun from the castle ramparts which shatters the peace of Edinburgh at one o'clock each day and leaves visitors in danger of heart failure does not herald the start of an invasion – it is merely a traditional time signal to shipping in the Forth. However, Edinburgh is close enough to the English border to have been on invasion routes many times.

Until the end of the eighteenth century the citizens remained huddled behind the walls of what is now the Old Town, a city whose buildings grew taller and more crowded as the population increased. Eighteenth-century visitors marvelled at the height of the tenements in much the same way as we now admire the skyscrapers of Manhattan, but at the same time had to suffer the insanitary conditions that went with them. The cry of 'gardy loo' warned passers-by that waste water (and worse) was about to descend from above, while Dr Johnson muttered to Boswell, 'I can smell you in the dark'. The old town of Edinburgh was a seething mix of people, with aristocrats, tradesmen and prostitutes living on different floors of the same buildings. Deacon Brodie, one of Edinburgh's folk heroes, could happily be a city councillor by day and a criminal by night, for his contacts in both worlds probably drank in the same taverns or 'howffs'. Throughout the constant crises of Mary Queen of Scots' reign, and throughout the religious and dynastic upheavals of the seventeenth century, the Edinburgh mob, boiling out of closes and wynds, could be relied on to take a hand in affairs, rioting at the attempted introduction of a new prayer book, stoning the coach of a commissioner, or lynching the unpopular captain of the town guard.

There could hardly be a greater contrast between this jostling muddle of a city and Edinburgh's New Town, started at the end of the eighteenth century. Beneath the castle, across the valley once filled by the swampy Nor' Loch, a Georgian town rose to a precise plan, with every street standing for order, harmony and reason. The great upsurge of intellectual and literary life at the end of the eighteenth century, which is now called the Scottish Enlightenment,

117

started in the warren of the Old Town but ended up here, in the elegant drawing-rooms and round the dinner tables of Princes Street, George Street and Charlotte Square. If the old Edinburgh was all squalor and fervency, the new Edinburgh was all self-confidence and reason.

If the Edinburgh of today seems less subject to change than any other Scottish city, it may be because it has never managed either to forget or to recapture these distinctive times. Comfortable in its much-parodied prosperous respectability, Edinburgh waits, a capital without a nation, for something to happen to bring it to centre-stage again. It is a city which is beautiful and enticing, but one which you know is unlikely to have changed when you next return.

Practical suggestions

The most important decision to make is whether or not to visit Edinburgh during the Festival. You should really visit twice, for the blanket of frenetic glamour which descends on the city during the weeks of the Festival turns it into a completely different place. Edinburgh is probably at its most beautiful and its most peaceful during autumn, when the slanting light of the evenings softens the stonework.

Arriving by train, or coming by car from east or south, gives you the best first impression of the city. However, if you fly, and are lucky enough to land at the airport from the east on a clear day (sit on the left-hand side of the aircraft), the view of Edinburgh is also superb. Buses run to the city centre half-hourly from the airport, which is around ten miles to the west.

While it is convenient to be based right in the middle of the city, Edinburgh's most central hotels are apt to be either pricey or in need of refurbishment. However, off-season or weekend breaks may be worth pursuing at the Sheraton, the Caledonian, the Balmoral or the Scandic Crown or in some of the smaller hotels in Princes Street, the Bridges or the New Town. There are few good guesthouses right in the centre, but large clusters exist among the Georgian terraces round Calton Hill, at Haymarket (west of the city centre but with frequent train connections to Waverley) and in the Victorian fringes to the north round Comely Bank and to the south, especially around Minto Street. There are good bus services from both.

THE OLD TOWN

When big as burns the gutters rin
Gin ye hae catcht a droukit skin
To Luckie Middlemist's loup in
And sit fu snug
O'er oysters and a dram o' gin,
Or haddock lug. (Robert Fergusson)

In the shelter of the plug of volcanic basalt which is now the Castle Rock a long tail of sloping land survived the scouring of the eastward-flowing glaciers of the last Ice Age. The two separate burghs which grew up around the castle at the top of this rocky spine and the abbey of Holyrood at the bottom

---

Getting around Edinburgh is easiest by using your feet to go downhill and buses (or taxis) to come back up again. Having your own car can be an advantage for visiting outlying areas, but parking in the city centre is very expensive and space is in short supply. Bus tours run from Waverley Bridge, just beside the station, and there are a number to choose from, complete city tours being especially good.

Edinburgh is well supplied with interesting shops, though Princes Street, the main shopping area, is largely given over to chain stores. For independent booksellers, try Thins (South Bridge), Bauermeisters (George IV Bridge) and Macnaughtan's (at the top of Leith Walk) for old books. Kinloch Anderson (Commercial Street, Leith) is a long-established kilt-maker. Jenners (Princes Street) is a stylish Victorian emporium, with the atmosphere of grander days. Dundas Street and the streets round the Grassmarket are the places to look for antiques, while Rose Street is stuffed with boutiques selling knick-knacks, clothes and crafts. Valvona and Crolla (Elm Row) is an Italian delicatessen with style, a shrine for Edinburgh gourmets and wine lovers. For haggis, make the trip to Macsweens in Bruntsfield Place – they also send them by post – and don't leave Edinburgh without trying some of the stickily sweet confectionery called Edinburgh Rock. Last-minute gifts can be found in the Waverley Market, a pleasant indoor mall by the station.

Edinburgh's Tourist Office is on top of Waverley Market, and has an excellent computer which can track down restaurants or hotels for you in the blink of an eye (though you may have to queue).

---

eventually merged, but it was not until 1767 that Edinburgh expanded much beyond the confines of the ridge and the streets immediately to the south – confines marked by the remains of the old wall built after Flodden (1513). This area is now the Old Town, and it is here that you will get a flavour of what sixteenth- and seventeenth-century Edinburgh was like – a cramped, impossibly crowded area of tall buildings on either side of the mile of road between the Castle and Holyrood. Here, many of the dramas of the time took place. John Knox, the Protestant firebrand, preached in St Giles, Montrose was taken to the gallows, the National Covenant was signed, the Treaty of Union debated and Cromwell's troops and Bonnie Prince Charlie's Highlanders paced the streets. Citizens kept pigs under their entrance stairs, drank in 'howffs,' patronised the stalls of the Grassmarket or the luckenbooths (lock-up shops) round St Giles and followed

THE EDINBURGH FESTIVAL

For three weeks every August/September the character of Edinburgh changes radically as performers and audiences pour into the city. The first Edinburgh Festival was held in 1947 and it has never looked back, although there are usually grumbles about funding and sometimes grumbles about quality. At a time when there is scarcely a large city without its International Arts Festival, Edinburgh manages to hang on to its premier position.

The Edinburgh Festival is broadly divided in two. There are the 'official' events, with invited companies or performers, and the famous 'Fringe', where a teeming horde of amateur and professional performers competes frantically for audiences in about 130 different venues ranging from graveyards to galleries. In addition there are separate film and jazz festivals, and a book fair every two years. There is now also a children's festival which is held at Easter. Then there is that perennial favourite, the tattoo on the Castle Esplanade.

During the Festival, Edinburgh's normal respectability vanishes under a sea of leaflets. Weirdly be-costumed performers tout their events, grassy spaces fill with floodlights, student groups bed down in any spare space they can find. The Fringe has its own legends: the overnight discovery that is wafted like magic to London's West End is a less common phenomenon than the traditional performance to two old ladies and a tramp, but it has happened.

the goings-on of the Scottish parliament in its new home at Parliament House.

The Old Town of Edinburgh has lost much of its life. It had more or less become a slum by the 1860s, the prosperous having long since moved out to the New Town or the spacious Victorian suburbs. Slum clearance programmes have left their mark on much of it, and genuinely antique buildings rub shoulders with restored or rebuilt houses. The cadies who could track down and deliver a message to anyone you cared to name in the taverns and coffee shops are long gone, as (probably) are the days when an English visitor could record standing by the Mercat Cross and taking, in a few minutes, 50 men of genius and learning by the hand. The Old Town is not quite a tourist enclave, for city administrators, bankers, booksellers and lawyers work here, and there are ancient pubs lurking between the tourist sights and the

---

Reviews in *The Scotsman* or the London papers are anxiously awaited.

For the first-time visitor, the Festival can be daunting. The best accommodation is booked months in advance, but if you arrive with no booking the Tourist Office can usually squeeze you in somewhere. Advance tickets for the big-name events of the official Festival, especially operas, sell out fast, and there will be a heavy demand for seats at any Fringe show that suddenly attracts attention. However, there is so much to choose from that it is unlikely you will be confined to an evening at home.

The energetic may visit exhibitions in the morning, take in one, or perhaps two, Fringe events in the afternoon, an official event in the evening, then as many more revues or late-night events as they have stamina for. A week at this pace and you will be suffering from severe culture shock, will have seen the inside of some very odd places and have sat through some very odd shows. You find out what is good and what is not by reading the *Scotsman* or the London press, watching the round-ups, previews and reviews on television, and, best of all, by talking to people on buses, in pubs or in your hotel.

If you are serious about Festival-visiting, it is best if you send off for programmes around March/April from the Festival addresses listed on page 152, and get your bookings (including accommodation) sent in plenty of time (bookings open from 12 April).

giftshops and any number of forbidding closes and wynds to explore.

Edinburgh Castle

(**HS**, open Apr to Sept, daily 9.30 to 5.15; Oct to Mar, daily 9.30 to 4.15; guided tours as and when required; castle closes 45 mins after sale of last ticket)

This is neither the most beautiful nor the most interesting castle in Scotland, yet its age and the magnificence of its setting make a visit here virtually compulsory. The rock it stands on dominates the city, and the views from its walls are superb. The approach over the sloping esplanade towards the toy gatehouse with the grim semi-circle of the Half Moon battery rising behind it is an experience in theatre best appreciated at the annual military tattoo.

This is not a simple fortification: the complex of buildings on top of the sheer-sided rock is more like a small military town, with a number of different things to see inside it. From the Iron Age to the twentieth century, Edinburgh Castle has been extended, altered, demolished and rebuilt to such an extent that it is hard to puzzle out the historical sequence, even armed with the guidebook. For those who enjoy this sort of detective work it is a satisfying place.

Edinburgh Castle once doubled as a royal residence but Scottish monarchs grew to prefer the greater comfort and space of Holyrood, leaving the castle's chief function as a military strong-point and, later, as barracks and prison. In the centuries since Randolph Murray scaled the rock and took the castle from the English in 1313 there have been many sieges. Although it is no longer a barracks, Edinburgh Castle is still a military headquarters, and there are two military museums within its walls as well as the Scottish National War Memorial.

Touring the castle is a matter of puffing up and down steep slopes or steps between buildings and ramparts and of pausing to look at the view. Guided tours are frequent in season and Historic Scotland's custodians have a good store of anecdotes. If you prefer to make your own way, the main points of interest are these.

● **St Margaret's Chapel** This tiny twelfth-century building is thought to have been built by David I in memory of his mother, Queen Margaret, who died in the castle in 1093. It was rediscovered in 1845 after being used as a powder magazine, and restored. A pretty Norman chancel arch divides the miniature nave from the apse. You will need to slip in during a gap between two tour groups to have any chance of appreciating its peace.

- **Mons Meg** A huge siege gun or bombard, manufactured in Flanders and given to James II in 1457. It used to stand on the battlements exposed to the elements and the depredations of schoolchildren, but has now been taken down into the vaults beneath the Great Hall and given its own audio-visual display (with suitable bangs and flashes), together with lucid descriptions of how it was manufactured and transported over medieval Scotland's boggy roads. The gun burst while firing a birthday salute to the Duke of York in 1680 and spent some years in the Tower of London before being returned to Edinburgh in 1829, after a petition by Sir Walter Scott. It was in these same vaults that French prisoners were confined: their graffiti are still visible.

- **The Great Hall** Built for James IV, this is the last of a series of medieval halls. Its use was probably entirely ceremonial. An earlier hall saw the notorious 'Black Dinner', when two Douglas scions were invited to dinner and casually slaughtered in front of the eight-year-old James II. The Great Hall was ignominiously turned into a barracks in the eighteenth century and only restored in the late nineteenth. The hammer-beam ceiling, despite being knocked about and restored, is outstanding, the rest of the restoration being rather gloomily Wagnerian. The Hall was the meeting place for the Scottish Parliament until 1639.

- **The Palace** The nineteenth-century clock-tower makes this building look more like a town hall than a royal residence. The two main points of interest are the room where Mary Queen of Scots gave birth to James VI and the walk-through display of the crown jewels of Scotland. James was born in a chamber not much larger than a cupboard, and the event became the subject of speculation in 1830 when what was said to be the body of an infant wrapped in a cloth with the initial J was discovered behind a panel, suggesting a last-minute substitution for a stillborn heir. 'Probably the legend will persist as meet fodder for trivial minds despite any attempt to dislodge it,' commented the historian George Scott-Moncrieff, and he was right.

The regalia of Scotland are also the stuff of legend. The crown which is on display may have been used by Robert the Bruce (though James V made it more imposing). It survived the Cromwellian melt-down (which is more than the English crown did) due to the cunning with which it was smuggled out of the besieged Dunottar Castle. The sword and the sceptre were given to James IV by different popes.

In 1707, after the Act of Union had been passed by the Scottish Parliament, the regalia were placed in a chest and walled up in the room where they now lie. Sir Walter Scott, who led the search which resulted in their rediscovery in 1818, thought this was done because such potent symbols were dangerous at a time when 'men's minds were agitated by the supposed degradation of Scotland beneath her ancient enemy'.

● **The Scottish National War Memorial** Sir Robert Lorimer transformed an old barracks block into a shrine to Scotland's war dead after World War I. Opinions of his architecture vary from enthusiastic to scathing, but there is much that is sombre and moving about the place. Douglas Strachan's windows are mystical and beautiful.

● **The Scottish United Services Museum** A scholarly foundation rather than a tourist attraction, the museum none the less has extensive displays tracing aspects of Scottish military history. It is a fascinating place for military history buffs, and a good spot to retreat to if it is raining. There is also the Regimental Museum of the Royal Scots and Royal Scots Dragoon Guards within the castle.

● **Mills Mount Battery** One o'clock is the time to be here, for that is when the gun is fired. Small crowds of children and camera-toting Japanese vie for position as soldiers time the explosion to the second.

THE ROYAL MILE

Four streets (Castlehill, Lawnmarket, High Street and Canongate) make up the long descent from the Castle to the Palace of Holyroodhouse. Together they form the so-called Royal Mile.

On either side of the streets, grey seventeenth-century stone houses rise, their frontages pierced by the dark mouths of closes, wynds and courts. Some of these lead into dank courtyards, some to restored or rebuilt houses, while others take you by way of steep steps or precipitous slopes through to the streets which run parallel to the Royal Mile in the glacier-gouged valleys on either side.

It makes sense to start at the top by the castle and work downwards. At least a day is needed for a respectable sample of the sights, and more if you want to see everything there is. What follows is a brief listing to indicate the main points of interest.

- **Outlook Tower, Castlehill** (open Apr to mid-Oct, Mon to Sat 9.30 to 6, Sun 10 to 6; end Oct to Mar, daily 10 to sunset) This is the home of one of Edinburgh's oldest attractions – a camera obscura built on the summit of a seventeenth-century house. The lower floors are a museum of optical knick-knacks such as holographs, but the camera obscura is much the best part. A periscope projects an image of the city outside on to a white table, round which enthralled children cluster, watching buses run up their arms. It is laughably simple, enthrallingly voyeuristic and enthusiastically explained. Go on a clear day – the system needs plenty of light to function at its best.

- **The Scotch Whisky Heritage Centre, Castlehill** (open all year, daily 10 to 5; extended hours mid-June to mid-Sept) A better sight than its title suggests: if you are not likely to be going distillery-visiting, this is the next best thing. The process of distilling is well set out, and it is interesting to find explanations of the role of grain whisky, which is often ignored in tours of single malt distilleries, and of the art of blending. There is, inevitably, a short audio-visual ride in a whisky cask past various historical tableaux, and a shop to end up in, with a good selection of whiskies on sale and admirable descriptions of their various qualities.

- **Milne's Court** and **James Court** These two courtyards on the north side of Lawnmarket are seventeenth- and eighteenth-century constructions designed to carve space out of the crowded closes. Hume and Boswell both lived in James Court and it was here that Dr Johnson stayed at the start of his tour to the Hebrides. Some of the buildings are original, but much has gone.

- **Gladstone's Land (NTS), Lawnmarket** (open Apr to Oct, Mon to Sat 10 to 5, Sun 2 to 5; closed in winter) The National Trust for Scotland has furnished this early seventeenth-century building to give a comprehensive idea of what life for a prosperous Edinburgh merchant might have been like in the closing decades of the seventeenth century. In the vocabulary of tenement life, a land means a house, while a house means a flat (see box, page 214). Thomas Gledstanes bought this land in 1617, added rooms to its street frontage and let out much of his property to various tenants. The house suffered the fate of many similar buildings in the Old Town, gradually degenerating into a slum as the better-off members of the population moved out to the New Town. It was rescued from demolition in 1934 and restored.

There would have been stalls under the arcades at street level, and a pig might have been kept beneath the stairway. Inside the house a good collection of seventeenth-century furniture has been put together, and there is a beautiful painted ceiling.

● **Lady Stair's House, Lady Stair's Close, Lawnmarket** (open June to Sept, Mon to Sat 10 to 6; Oct to May 10 to 5; also Suns in Festival 2 to 5) Another seventeenth-century building, which is now a museum to Sir Walter Scott, Robert Burns and Robert Louis Stevenson. It is a little old-fashioned but has some good portraits, some manuscripts and a few of the writers' personal possessions.

● **Brodie's Close, Lawnmarket** This was the home of the famous Deacon Brodie, respectable councillor by day and burglar by night, whose eventual execution in 1788 was watched by huge crowds. His daytime trade as carpenter allowed him into the houses of his victims (and also to take wax impressions of their keys), while at night he and his contacts conducted their robberies. He took flight for Holland after trying to rob the Excise Office but foolishly wrote to his mistress on his journey, and this led to his capture. Brodie is supposed to have become the model for Stevenson's tale of Dr Jekyll and Mr Hyde. There is a pub named after him opposite the close.

● **Parliament Square, High Street** This oasis of classical architecture in the middle of the Old Town's huddle is the result of early nineteenth-century rebuilding. A heart on the cobblestones marks the site of Edinburgh's Old Tolbooth, which was built in 1466 and served as council chamber, law court, meeting place for the General Assembly of the Reformed Kirk and as a prison. Montrose's head was displayed here after his execution. The ancient building was swept away in 1817, and Sir Walter Scott acquired the door (now built into Abbotsford). His description of the Old Tolbooth at the beginning of *The Heart of Midlothian* gives a good impression of what it may have been like.

It is worth going into **Parliament House** to see the Parliament Hall (open Mon to Fri 10 to 4), where the Scottish Parliament sat between 1639 and 1707. This splendidly roofed building dates from 1632 and is now the home of the Court of Session, Edinburgh's legal heart. In front of Parliament House, a statue of John Knox is a near neighbour to one of Charles II seated on a horse. Two more opposite temperaments can hardly be imagined.

Edinburgh's **Mercat Cross** stands close by with a few pieces of medieval stonework built into the nineteenth-century construction. The excuse for the demolition of the old cross in 1756 was that it held up the traffic, but there is a suspicion that it was destroyed because Bonnie Prince Charlie had his father proclaimed king here. The elegant Royal Exchange across the road was built to replace it as a bargaining spot for Edinburgh merchants, but it never appears to have caught on. The building is now the City Chambers. For a glimpse of the past far away from the tourist trail, try making an appointment at City Chambers to see the remains of Mary King's Close, preserved half-intact among the cellars of the newer building. It was closed for repairs in winter of 1993 with no fixed re-opening date; ring 031-529 4193 for information.

● **St Giles' Cathedral, High Street** The High Kirk of Edinburgh was only briefly a cathedral during the periods under Charles I and James VII when episcopacy was uneasily established, but its title has lingered on. John Knox was minister here in the time of Mary Queen of Scots, and this was the base from which he set out to confront the Queen in a series of stormy interviews at Holyrood. The old twelfth-century church was burnt by the English, and the present building dates from the fifteenth century. Before the rebuilding of Parliament Square, the church was virtually buried behind the Old and New Tolbooths and the luckenbooths and tiny stalls which traded in its shelter. The demolition of these revealed a much knocked-about church. Unfortunately, William Burn, who was commissioned to restore the fabric in 1826, drastically reshaped the exterior, so that it now looks antiseptic and bland. Only the tower, with its beautiful crown, survived the wholesale restoration.

Inside, various add-ons have turned the originally cruciform church into something closer to a square. It is rather a gloomy place, but worth exploring to see Sir Robert Lorimer's **Chapel of the Thistle** (1911) with an angel playing the bagpipes carved on the entrance arch. The scattered pieces of Montrose's body were buried in St Giles after his rehabilitation at the Restoration. There is also a memorial to his enemy, the covenanting Marquess of Argyll, who lost his head at the same time.

● **Tron Kirk, High Street** At New Year, Hogmanay revellers gather outside the old church. The spire, though a nineteenth-century replacement for one that was destroyed by fire, acts as a fine counterbalance to the crown of St Giles. The disused kirk will probably metamorphose into a visitor attraction of some kind.

● **Paisley Close, High Street** It was the collapse of a

tenement here in 1861, killing 35 and injuring many more, that brought the appalling conditions of those living in the Victorian Old Town to public attention and led to the appointment of Edinburgh's first Medical Officer. Widely known as 'Heave Awa' House, it has a scroll on the entrance recalling the words of a boy buried in the rubble: 'Heave awa' chaps, I'm no deid yet'.

• **Museum of Childhood, High Street** (open June to Sept, Mon to Sat 10 to 6; Oct to May, Mon to Sat 10 to 5; Suns in Festival 2 to 5)

The first of its kind in the world, and one of the noisiest museums going (more on account of music than of children), this is actually a serious-minded establishment. It was founded in 1955 by a man who claimed to have 'a rooted conviction that children are only tolerable after their baths and on their way to bed' and tried to set up a memorial window to 'Good'

THE UNION OF THE PARLIAMENTS, 1707

I had not been Long There but I heard a Great Noise and looking Out Saw a Terrible Multitude Come up the High Street with a drum at the head of them shouting and swearing and Cryeing Out all scotland would stand together, No Union, No Union, English Dogs and the like. (Daniel Defoe 1660–1731)

It is ironic that the union of the Scottish and English parliaments came at a time when the two nations were closer to war than had been the case for almost half a century.

Under King William, in the period between 1689 and 1702, relations between Scotland and England had been uneasy, partly because of William's vendetta against France – Scotland's oldest ally – but mostly as a result of the Darien venture. Frustrated (by English interests) in setting up Scottish trading companies to the East Indies or to Africa, the Scots had turned their minds to establishing a colony of their own, on the Darien peninsula of Central America. It was an ill-starred venture from the first, but active English hostility was held by many to be accountable for the failure of the colony. Scotland was bankrupt, for everyone with money to spare had invested in the scheme. A series of confrontational Acts of Parliament in England and Scotland over who should succeed to the British Crown worsened the situation, and in 1705 the Scots hanged a blatantly innocent English captain for alleged piracy.

King Herod. Joseph Murray's tongue-in-cheek humour is still to be found on many of the caption cards. Despite the supposed adult emphasis of the museum, the place fascinates children and parents alike. There are some splendid dolls' houses and unusual automata and slot-machines (including a gruesome execution), together with clothes, railways, dolls, board games, theatres, samplers, teddy bears and toy soldiers. The museum is housed in a steep and narrow old building, and it can sometimes be a bit of a squash.

● **John Knox House, High Street** (open all year, Mon to Sat 10 to 4.30) The oldest house on the Royal Mile (dating from 1490) looks suitably medieval as it juts out, slightly askew, into the High Street. The connection with Knox may be apocryphal, but it saved the house from demolition. The ground floor is a shop, but above it you will find a good painted ceiling and displays about the man

---

Yet, despite all this, active moves to create the Union were taking place. Under William's successor, Queen Anne, 31 commissioners from each country were appointed, and they managed to draft a treaty within nine weeks. In October 1706 the debate started in the Scottish Parliament to massive public hostility. There were riots in Glasgow and Dumfries, and the Lord High Commissioner's coach was stoned in Edinburgh. But the Scots had little choice: union offered freedom of trade and monetary compensation; independence meant probable bankruptcy and possible civil war. The treaty was approved by 110 votes to 69. The Scottish Parliament adjourned on 19 March 1707, and never met again.

The Act of Union preserved the Scottish church, the law, the judicial system, the rights of the Scottish nobles and the privileges of the Scottish burghs. It approved the Hanoverian succession and gave the English the security they needed in facing the French. The Scots were to receive £400,000 'Equivalent' to reimburse the Darien investors and to provide a boost for industry. Whether it was a fair settlement, whether Scottish parliamentarians were bribed, whether the English had broken the terms of the treaty, and whether Scotland could have survived as an independent nation are still matters for (often heated) debate.

who did more than anyone else to establish the Scottish Reformation.

The figure of Knox still provokes controversy. He had the bigot's inability to tolerate opposing views and the fanatic's zeal in propagating his own. Nor did he hesitate to blacken his opponents, Mary Queen of Scots in particular, whose tolerant religious policies were anathema to him. On the other hand he was courageous, inspiring to those who heard him, and he held a genuine vision of the spiritual regeneration of the country to which he belonged. Nevertheless, Knox turned the course of the Scottish Reformation towards that extremism which was eventually to plunge the country into a turmoil of suffering, truncate its artistic heritage and cut it off from its medieval roots.

- **Netherbow, High Street** A plaque marks the spot where the Netherbow gate stood until 1764, marking the eastern end of Edinburgh. The city fell to the Jacobites in 1745 when a raiding party under Cameron of Lochiel took advantage of the exit of a coach through this gate and stormed in – not that Edinburgh looked like organising much effective resistance anyway.
- **Morocco Land, Canongate** Look for the bust of a Moor outside the building (which itself is modern). It commemorates the pretty story of a persecuted Edinburgh student who fled abroad to Morocco, made his fortune and returned to exact his revenge on the city which had mistreated him. Instead he cured the Provost's daughter of the plague and married her, coming to live in the old building here.
- **Canongate Tolbooth, Canongate** (open Oct to end May, Mon to Sat 10 to 5; June to Sept, 10 to 6; Suns in Festival 2 to 5) Canongate kept its tolbooth when the Edinburgh one was swept away. The building, with its curious Germanic tower and turrets, dates from 1591; the clock, which looks as if it had just sprung from the front wall, like a cuckoo, is from 1884. Inside, the main attraction is an audio-visual exhibition with added smells, called the People's Story. It describes the everyday lives of Edinburgh people in the eighteenth and nineteenth centuries and, while a bit thin on exhibits and rather too worthily educational, it is a good counterbalance to the historical glamour of the Castle and Holyrood.
- **Huntly House, Canongate** (open June to Sept, Mon to Sat 10 to 6; Oct to May, Mon to Sat 10 to 5; Suns in Festival 2 to 5) Three old sixteenth-century houses contain this museum of the city of Edinburgh. It is like a huge antique shop, easy

to get lost in, and with embarrassingly squeaky floors if you wear rubber soles. Glass cases contain Roman remains from Cramond, medieval shards, pottery, glass, silver and plenty of civic memorabilia. There is an exhibition devoted to Field-Marshal Earl Haig, who was born in Charlotte Square, and a copy of the 1638 Covenant. It is a genial, old-fashioned kind of museum, concentrating on things rather than stories, and often undeservedly neglected by visitors in a hurry.

• **Site of Girth Cross and Holyrood Sanctuary** The circle of stones in the roadway is where Girth Cross stood at the foot of Canongate, marking the western boundary of the sanctuary of Holyrood Abbey. In a curious anachronism, this remained a sanctuary for debtors right up until 1880. Inside it they were safe from their creditors, and they were also allowed outside between Saturday and Sunday midnights. One of the most famous 'Abbey Lairds', as the debtors who sought shelter here were known, was Charles X of France, who abdicated in 1830, and was known in Edinburgh as 'Monsieur'. The Edinburgh historian E F Catford relates how he used to go snipe-shooting on the slopes of Arthur's Seat, with the Edinburgh children pursuing him, crying, 'Frenchy, Frenchy, dinna shoot the spruggies' (sparrows).

The Palace of Holyroodhouse

(Open Apr to Oct, Mon to Sat 9.30 to 5.15, Sun 10.30 to 4.30; Nov to Mar, Mon to Sat 9.30 to 5.45; closed when the Queen is in residence)

The Queen's official Edinburgh residence, site of garden parties and other royal occasions, Holyrood (for short) is, like the castle, firmly on the list of 'necessary' sights for visitors to Edinburgh. If you have little time for Scottish history, however, you can safely leave it alone, for as palaces go it is rather disappointing – the formal rooms that visitors see are scarcely luxurious, and the long period between the reigns of James VI and Queen Victoria when it was more or less neglected by British monarchs has left the place still feeling curiously untenanted. Nevertheless, the tour is well worthwhile for those curious about architecture or Mary Queen of Scots, and for the sake of one or two notable curiosities.

The Scottish kings grew to prefer Holyrood Abbey, whose remains are in the palace grounds, to Edinburgh Castle as a place to stay, and their lodgings gradually became a proper palace. James IV and V were responsible for most of the earliest building, but their work, with the exception of

131

one tower, was demolished when Holyrood was rebuilt for Charles II between 1671 and 1679. Sir William Bruce was the architect (see also Kinross House, page 282, and Hopetoun, page 177), and the elegantly classical façades of the central courtyard are considered to be one of his best achievements.

The tour, conducted by smartly uniformed guides with stentorian tones, leads you up the Great Stair, past a portrait of the Queen wearing the robes of the Order of the Thistle, through the royal dining-room, the throne room, the evening drawing-room and the morning drawing-room. The plasterwork of the ceilings is the best part of these. The private rooms designed for Charles and his Queen are more interesting because they are more intimate, though somehow the fact that Charles II never even saw them nor, indeed, any of Holyrood makes them rather sad places. The Great Gallery is much more cheerful; not only is it a splendid, bright corridor of a room, but it contains the palace's greatest folly – the series of paintings by Jacob de Wet. These, commissioned in 1684, show the complete line of Scottish kings. There were 111 paintings altogether (half of them of shadowy, half-legendary figures), of which 89 are still here. Poor De Wet finished the lot in two years, so it is hardly surprising that his imagination got a bit overstrained at times. Every portrait faithfully reproduces the prominent nose owned by Charles II – a quick way of proving the royal descent.

It is the two rooms in the old north-west tower where Mary Queen of Scots had her apartments that provide the climax of the tour. The outer chamber, with its marvellous ceiling (embellished for the brief homecoming of James VI), is where she argued over religion with John Knox, which left him impressed by her force of character, but unmoved in his opinions. This is also the scene of the murder of her secretary, Riccio, by a band of scheming nobles, her own husband Darnley among them. Riccio was left on the floor here with 56 dagger wounds in his body. In less scrupulous days not all that long ago visitors used to be shown an 'indelible bloodstain' on the floor, but this touch has been dropped, to the regret of many.

Of various exhibits in these rooms, the needlework by Mary and the Lennox jewel are particularly beautiful.

Holyrood Abbey

Only the nave of the abbey church remains, a small, blackened fragment of what was once a beautiful building. David I founded it, but what you see is largely thirteenth-century. The west door and the arcading in the aisle show what a richly decorated place it once was. Burnt by the English during the fifteenth-century Rough Wooing, and suffering further after the Reformation, the abbey church was used for the wedding of Mary and Darnley and for the Scottish coronation of Charles I (though the church needed a lot of repair before then). James VII's attempts to make it into a Catholic place of worship led to a sacking (and desecration of the royal graves) by the Edinburgh mob in 1688. The roof collapsed in 1768. Various proposals to rebuild the nave have come to nothing.

South of the Royal Mile

The Flodden wall, which for so long contained the entire city of Edinburgh, ran steeply downhill from the south side of the castle and roughly along the line of the ridge opposite. It enclosed the open area immediately beneath the castle known as the Grassmarket, the street called the Cowgate, and what is now Chambers Street. Parts of the wall can still be seen.

Grassmarket

This open rectangle surrounded by old houses and some modern intrusions used to be the haunt of Edinburgh's dossers, as was the Cowgate, which runs darkly eastward, parallel to the Royal Mile. Most of the area has been smartened up, but one or two mission houses remain as evidence of the way this old medieval marketplace degenerated into a nineteenth-century slum. With the smartening-up came clothing and antique shops, and several cheerful eating places, but one or two fascinating old shops survive amongst their more fashionable successors in West Bow, Victoria Street and Candlemaker Row. Keep a special watch for the one in Victoria Street selling every conceivable variety of brush.

The Grassmarket is probably best known as Edinburgh's place of public execution until 1784. Although some of the better-connected victims, such as Montrose, were executed by the Mercat Cross, hundreds of criminals or those condemned for their religion died in the Grassmarket, especially the hapless Covenanters who held out for their faith during the 'Killing Time' after the Restoration. The ex-Captain of the Town Guard, John Porteous, was lynched by a mob and strung up here in 1736. The most notorious inhabitants

THE COVENANTERS (1638–90)

The National Covenant, signed in Greyfriars churchyard in 1638, is the document which marks the start of a period in Scottish history which was triumphant, terrible and bitter. The Covenanting movement, which started as a proud, nationalistic and spiritual revolution, was to become an intolerant theocracy and eventually a pitiful remnant of stalwarts pursued and slaughtered by the forces of government. The events of these years are complicated, and intimately bound to the civil struggles going on in England, including the English Civil War.

1638 After riots in Edinburgh when King Charles I attempts to introduce an anglicised prayer book, the National Covenant is signed in Greyfriars. It makes no threats, merely rejects interference in the practice of the Reformed Kirk of Scotland. However, its appeal has to do with the symbolic nature of a covenant, drawn from the Old Testament; it is a bond between God and his chosen people. King Charles thinks it treason.

1638 In Glasgow, the Assembly of the Kirk becomes more radical. It abolishes bishops and disallows royal authority over the church. Charles attempts to raise an English army to curb this constitutional rebellion, but fails to invade. Subscription of the Covenant is made compulsory in Scotland.

1640 The Scots invade England to make Charles come to a settlement and force him, in 1641, to assent to the religious and constitutional changes. Splits now appear among the Covenanters, with some, Montrose in particular, unwilling to continue hostility to the King.

1643 Embroiled in a civil war they look like losing, the English Parliamentarians strike a deal whereby in return for Scottish military aid Presbyterianism will be established in England and Ireland. A Scottish army enters England.

1644–5 Montrose, now siding with the King, inflicts six defeats on the Covenanters in Scotland. Their confidence in their invincibility as God's chosen is severely dented.

1646–8 King Charles, defeated in war, surrenders himself to the Scottish Covenanting army, but refuses to sign the

Covenant. The Scots, unable to take an unregenerate King back to Scotland, are forced to hand him over to the English. The Covenanters split further, and eventually the extreme 'Kirk' party takes power, purging all those whose religious fervour does not measure up.

1649 Execution of Charles I. All the Scottish factions are horrified and Charles II is immediately proclaimed King in Scotland, while the English abolish the monarchy entirely. The rift between the two countries is complete.

1650 Oliver Cromwell invades Scotland and defeats the Covenanters at Dunbar.

1651 A Scottish invasion of England is defeated at Worcester. Charles II flees, leaving Cromwell to conquer Scotland and establish the Commonwealth. Scotland is under occupation for nine years.

1660 Charles II is restored. Over the next few years, the Covenants and all the acts passed by Covenanting parliaments in Scotland are repudiated. Bishops are reintroduced and kirk ministers from the previous regime must seek episcopal approval. Many ministers refuse to comply and become 'outers'. Despite increasingly repressive measures, congregations follow them to 'conventicles' in the hills rather than conform to the law.

1666 Covenanters from the west rebel and march on Edinburgh. They are defeated at Rullion Green. Executions in the Grassmarket follow.

1679 A further Covenanter rebellion is defeated at Bothwell Brig.

1680–1688 Continued persecution of increasingly small, extreme, Covenanting minorities; the period known as the 'Killing Times'.

1685 The accession of Catholic James VII is such a threat to the established Scottish church that Presbyterianism becomes respectable again.

1688 James VII deposed in an essentially English revolution.

1690 A mild version of Presbyterianism is re-established under William in a compromise between church and state. The Covenanting dream of establishing Christ's kingdom in Scotland is relegated to history.

of the Grassmarket were Burke and Hare, body-snatchers who turned to murder as a quick way of providing corpses for doctors to dissect. After Burke's execution, his skeleton was given to the Department of Anatomy at Edinburgh University, where it can still be seen.

St Cecilia's Hall (Cowgate)

(Open Wed and Sat 2 to 5; in Festival Mon to Sat 10.30 to 12.30)
Down at the brighter, eastern end of the Cowgate is an eighteenth-century music room (where concerts are occasionally held) which now contains the Russell Collection of early keyboard instruments, an unrivalled source of information for build-your-own harpsichord enthusiasts.

Greyfriars Kirk (George IV Bridge)

In 1638, the churchyard here was the scene of the signing of the National Covenant, an event which indirectly led to civil war in Scotland, England and Ireland (see the box on the Covenanters). Memorials to many of Edinburgh's worthies line the walls, but, sentiment being more interesting than history, most visitors make for the spot where Greyfriars Bobby, a Skye terrier, stood watch over his master's grave for 14 years. The church itself is rather uninteresting.

National Library of Scotland (George IV Bridge)

(Exhibition Room open Mon to Fri 9.30 to 5, Sat 2 to 5)
An oppressive building houses one of the largest libraries in Britain. Exhibitions, especially at Festival time, are usually worth a visit for bibliophiles, particularly if there is a display of characteristic Scottish bindings.

Royal Museum of Scotland (Chambers Street)

(Open Mon to Sat 10 to 5, Sun 2 to 5)
Dating from 1861, this magnificent building recalls the Crystal Palace. The dour, blackened exterior conceals a cathedral-like galleried main hall, which stretches skywards in a beautiful combination of iron and glass. A multitudinous collection of objects ranges from relics of ancient Egypt to a spruced-up evolution gallery. The most interesting section is the Hall of Power, which contains numerous scale models, many working,

of various types of steam engine, plus the oldest locomotive and oldest glider in existence. The Hall of Victorian Engineering is almost as good. The Natural History section is notable for the huge skeleton of a blue whale which overhangs it.

Edinburgh University old buildings (South Bridge)

The university was founded in 1582 (making it younger than Aberdeen, Glasgow or St Andrews). The Old College stands on the spot where Mary Queen of Scots' second husband Darnley was murdered after his house at Kirk o' Fields had been blown up. It is a Robert Adam/William Playfair building, interesting only for those keen on architecture or wishing to visit the **Talbot Rice Art Centre**, where a small collection of paintings is quietly exhibited in a lovely gallery designed by Playfair (open Tues to Sat 10 to 5).

A short way to the south lies George Square. This was laid out in 1770 as one of the first residential schemes outside the Old Town. The University has still not been forgiven in many quarters for demolishing much of the square and replacing the Georgian houses with modern, functional buildings.

The Meadows, to the south again, is a welcome patch of greenery for university students and for medical staff toiling in the complex of hospitals round Edinburgh's famous **Royal Infirmary**, whose first building was started in 1738.

THE NEW TOWN

Albert said he felt sure the Acropolis could not be finer.
(Queen Victoria)
The New Town of Edinburgh was the brainchild of George Drummond, six times Lord Provost, and not for nothing called Father of the City. His vision was of a new residential town rising on the fields beyond the Nor' Loch, and his energy eventually drove the town council to back it by getting an architectural competition under way. In 1767, a year after Drummond's death, the winning plan was chosen. It was by a virtually unknown architect, James Craig, and was simple but precise: two elegant squares linked by the three parallel streets now known as Princes Street, George Street and Queen Street.

No one seems to have wanted to be the first to move out of the familiar clutter of the Old Town. Incentives had to be offered before the initial house was built near St Andrew's

Square in 1769, but the new development rapidly became fashionable. The unity of design (which can still be seen beneath the Victorian and modern intrusions) was imposed by the council, and reaches its climax in the perfection of Charlotte Square (1791) – Robert Adam's finest achievement. One of Edinburgh's best features, the open valley between Princes Street and the Old Town, was saved from being built on, but only after an extensive lawsuit. The streets of Craig's New Town today form the commercial and financial heart of Edinburgh.

It was not long before new development started on the hill sloping down to the Forth beyond Queen Street. A second New Town, planned very much on the same lines as the first but with more uniformity of frontage, sprang up between the grand enclosures of Royal Circus and Drummond Place. During the first few decades of the nineteenth century, building went on apace. On the Moray Estate, immediately to the north of Charlotte Square, the grid-plan gave way to a series of linked circuses with some of the grandest architecture yet. Splendid terraces, designed for the wealthiest of Edinburgh's citizens, girdled the lower slopes of the Calton Hill, while further building went on to the west of Charlotte Square – the area now known as the West End.

The result of this frenzied, often speculative, building is an expanse of Georgian architecture unrivalled in Britain. The New Town is a treasure-house for lovers of architectural detail, for within the streets, terraces and squares there is endless variation of design and ornament. It is a pleasure to walk round even if you have little knowledge of the period, for much of the New Town remains residential, much has been well restored, and there are views, shops, pubs and constantly interesting corners to enjoy.

Exploring the New Town

Some of the best areas of the New Town to walk through are picked out here; there are plenty of others. The New Town Conservation Centre at 13a Dundas Street (031-557 5222) mounts exhibitions on the architecture of the area and also runs guided walks on request.

Princes Street

At the West End, where Lothian Road runs south towards the copper-roofed Usher Hall, scene of Edinburgh's large concerts, the restored red sandstone Caledonian Hotel is all that remains of the demolished Caledonian Station. It looks the length of Princes Street to its rival, the North British (now the Balmoral) above Waverley Station. Between these old competitors lies half a mile of shops on one side and Princes Street Gardens on the other. The gardens are the place to go statue-hunting, picnicking and strolling; in summer there are concerts at the bandstand in the centre. Slightly more than half-way down, the gardens are blocked by the Mound, up which a steeply curving road runs to link Old Town and New. The Mound was made from the earth scooped out from the excavations for the New Town, and started as a piece of private enterprise – a 'mud brig' across the marshy expanse beneath the Old Town where the waters of the Nor' Loch had been drained.

The two Greek temples lying at the foot of the hill (one Doric, the other Ionic) are both by William Playfair and date from the early nineteenth century; they house the Scottish National Gallery and the Royal Scottish Academy (see below). The impact of these temples on Princes Street is superb and, combined with the Calton Hill monuments, they go some way towards giving substance to Edinburgh's epithet, the Athens of the North. The Royal Scottish Academy, closest to Princes Street, has a statue of Queen Victoria lording it over the roof, easily mistaken for Athena.

The eastern end of Princes Street is dominated by the spire of the Scott Monument (see below), but the most beautiful building in this area is Robert Adam's Register House, with the Duke of Wellington on horseback before it. Don't miss the Café Royal tucked away in the narrow streets behind it – this excellent oyster bar and restaurant has opulent late-Victorian tiling and stained glass. The splendours of Waterloo Place, the eastern extension to Princes Street, are marred by two bureaucratic blots: the 1930s St Andrew's House in Regent Road, once described by Charles McKean as having 'the brooding, authoritarian characteristics of the secure head-quarters of an occupying power' and the universally derided St James Centre, a nasty bulwark housing civil servants and a shopping mall.

Calton Hill

This is the area where Edinburgh's obsession with Athens is most visible. The fragmentary Doric temple which you see from Princes Street is the **National Monument**, which was started in 1822 as a memorial to the dead of the Napoleonic Wars. It was intended to be a copy of the Parthenon in Athens, but funds ran out after only 12 columns. A more successful classical monument, by Playfair, is the little circular memorial to Dougald Stewart; among other striking buildings is the Nelson Monument (1807), a miniature battlemented tower in stark contrast to the classical work around it. Calton Hill provides one of the best panoramas of Edinburgh, but after dark it becomes inhabited by some pretty strange types and is probably best avoided.

Beneath the hill, beyond the magnificently processional exit from Princes Street through Waterloo Place, the Royal High School stands beside Regent Road. Built between 1825 and 1829, this is another Greek revival edifice of considerable ambition. Its modern history is a sad one, for it was totally converted internally between 1977 and 1980 in the hope that it would be used as the seat of the Scottish Assembly. The referendum of 1979 controversially failed to produce the necessary majority to establish this. The building remains in mothballs until the next attempt to give Scotland some degree of devolution.

A little further on, on the opposite side of the road, the Burns Monument (1830) hardly competes with the Scott Monument, and is much less visited.

Round the eastern spur of Calton Hill stretch two of the New Town's most magnificent terraces, Regent Terrace and Royal Terrace. These huge houses were designed to attract the wealthy because of their wonderful views and the spacious greenery at their back. Many are now hotels, where utilitarian subdivision of the interior has rather spoiled the effect.

Charlotte Square

Widely held to be one of the finest squares in Britain, this is the New Town's showpiece. The northern side, where Victorian alterations have been carefully suppressed, is especially beautiful in its regularity. The dome of St George's Church (1811) is the focal point for westward views along George Street. The church now houses part of the Scottish Record Office, and there is an exhibition of documents. Charlotte Square is at its best in spring, when the central garden blazes with crocuses. Traffic and parked cars spoil the tranquillity somewhat.

George Street

This was designed as the principal street of the first New Town and, with its breadth and its long vistas from Charlotte Square to St Andrew's Square, remains an impressive thoroughfare despite the cars which clutter its centre and the occasional intrusion of a modern building. Statues stand at street inter-sections, providing a headache for traffic planners. Several good shops are to be found in George Street, including Aitken and Niven for tweeds and Hamilton and Inches for silver and jewellery.

Moray Place

Development here started around 1822. Gillespie Graham drew up the two circuses and crescent, which for many are the most impressive sections of the New Town. Every last detail, down to the railings, is part of the design; the overall harmony is remarkable, even if there is a hint of the bombastic. In the 12-sided Moray Place the buildings are at their grandest, with Tuscan porticos gazing on the central garden. The backs of many of the houses hang sheer above the Water of Leith, best appreciated by walking down the valley from the Dean Bridge (page 146).

Dundas Street

A walk down this steep hill and through some of the streets on either side takes you through the best of the second New Town, with the elegant frontages of **Heriot Row** (much favoured by lawyers) and **Great King Street** contrasting with humbler but equally fascinating streets such as Northumberland Street and Nelson Street. Quirky shops selling antiques, fine arts and books rub shoulders with sandwich bars. If you get sated with Georgian houses, catch a bus back up Dundas Street to the High Street and the seventeenth century again.

New Town sights

• **The Georgian House (NTS), Charlotte Square** (open Apr to Oct, Mon to Sat 10 to 5, Sun 2 to 5; closed in winter) This is the National Trust for Scotland's figurehead property, and a recreation of gracious eighteenth-century living sufficiently infectious to make you long to have been

141

born 200 years ago. The drawing-room, with chairs arranged round the sides and paintings adorning the walls, stands ready for a formal soirée, while in the comfortable and casual parlour the imaginative may catch a hint of snuff or hear long-vanished voices debating the latest scathing piece from the *Edinburgh Review*. The dining-room too gives some idea of what an Edinburgh dinner party during the Enlightenment would have been like, with gleaming silver and heavy fabrics. However, it is probably the kitchen and the adjacent china cupboard and wine cellar which are most fascinating. Here you can sense the hectic activity round the open range and imagine the huge numbers of copper utensils being clattered from table top to scullery, while the bells in the passage jangled their summonses to attend on the drawing-room. The guides here are extremely knowledgeable, and there is a good, scene-setting audio-visual programme.

● **The National Gallery of Scotland, The Mound** (open Mon to Sat 10 to 5, Sun 2 to 5; in Festival, Mon to Sat 10 to 6, Sun 11 to 6)

The National Gallery has probably the finest collection of paintings outside London, and when the collection in the National Gallery of Modern Art (see page 147) is added in, there is scarcely a period or a movement left unrepresented. Internally, the National Gallery is arranged in a series of octagonal rooms, and their claret-and-green colour scheme is a copy of Playfair's original 1859 design. On the upper floor you will find the excellent collection of French Impressionists, and downstairs, in a modern extension, hangs the collection of Scottish painting. Lighting is somewhat on the dim side throughout the gallery, and the hanging – designed to be like a garden full of different views, architectural shapes and colour combinations – is fascinating, but may not please everyone.

Of the early paintings, the *Madonna and Child* by Verrocchio is the undoubted star. Five Titians compete for attention, the erotic *Diana and Actaeon* prominent among them. El Greco's *The Saviour of the World* gazes, icon-like, from the wall. Goya's *El Medico* in his vermilion cloak warms his hands over a brazier. Rubens' *Feast of Herod* shows John the Baptist's head being uncovered like a pork roast in front of a nauseated Herod, while all the guests scramble for a view. Gainsborough's *The Hon. Mrs Graham* is a lovely study of haughty beauty. Among the more modern works, Courbet's *Wave* is popular with visitors. Van Gogh is represented by his twisted olive trees, Monet by frosted haystacks, Cézanne by Mont St Victoire.

The Scottish collection, cramped in a room like an hotel foyer, has some fine portraits – many by Raeburn, (including his well-known *Rev. Robert Walker Skating on Duddingston Loch*), and by Allan Ramsay. William McTaggart's impressionistic landscapes form a radical contrast with Noel Paton's *The Quarrel of Oberon and Titania* – a biscuit-box fairy scene. David Wilkie's highly coloured scenes from Scottish rural life include *Distraining for Rent* – a real tearjerker.

● **The Scott Monument, Princes Street** Few, if any other, writers have a memorial like this. A huge Gothic spire, pinnacled, buttressed and loaded with crockets, finials and statuettes, rises 200 feet and 6 inches above Princes Street Gardens, and acts as a canopy for a statue of Sir Walter Scott, seated with a book in his hand and his dog by his side. The monument, designed by a previously unknown draughtsman, George Kemp, and inaugurated in 1846, was funded by private subscription, most of it raised in Edinburgh.

The monument is said to draw much of its inspiration from Melrose Abbey, Scott's favourite Gothic building. Its niches are filled with statuettes of Scottish poets and characters from Scott's works. At the level of the first gallery there is a small museum. Climbing the 287 steps of the narrow spiral stair to the top is an exercise in persistence, rewarded by views of central Edinburgh which beat even those from the castle walls.

This 'florid cenotaph' reflects the feeling of Scott's contemporaries that he, almost alone, had put Scotland back on the map after years of neglect, culminating in the triumphant visit of George IV to the city in 1822 which Scott stage-managed. The monument is currently closed for restoration but it can still be viewed from the outside.

● **The Royal Museum of Scotland, Queen Street** (open Mon to Sat 10 to 5, Sun 2 to 5) This is Scotland's premier historical and archaeological museum, with treasures from all over the country, including the Hilton of Cadboll Pictish stone, St Ninian's Treasure from Shetland, the Traprain Hoard of Roman silver and St Fillan's crosier and bell. It is a shame that there is an air of neglect about parts of this museum, as if it had lost energy in anticipation of its eventual amalgamation with its sister museum in Chambers Street. Many of its most famous pieces seem to spend a lot of their time on loan to various exhibitions, leaving rings in the dust of the glass cases which hold them.

The ground floor has a permanent exhibition about the House of Stewart, unhappily titled 'Dynasty'. Portraits of various royal Jameses look mournfully down on the visitor, and Prince Charles Edward's possessions glitter in a glass case. Upstairs, serried rows of glass cases with old-fashioned labelling contain prehistoric relics and Celtic artefacts, while on the top floor the Romans hold sway. The collection of Dark Age sculptured stones is very good, if the gallery is open. For all its faults, this museum should be visited, especially if you have already toured some of Scotland's archaeological sites.

• **Scottish National Portrait Gallery, Queen Street** (open Mon to Sat 10 to 5, Sun 2 to 5; in Festival, Mon to Sat 10 to 6, Sun 11 to 6)

The gallery shares the same building as the museum above, and provides a different slant on Scottish history. Many of the portraits you will find here are familiar from book covers or postcards. Montrose, Argyll, Dundee and General Monk glower down from the walls, as do any Stewart monarchs not being used for the Dynasty exhibition (see above). The chief figures of the eighteenth and nineteenth centuries are here, too – Scott, Burns, Hogg, Boswell and Hume – and the collection moves well into the twentieth century, keeping up to date with the great and the good of Scottish life.

THE SCOTTISH ENLIGHTENMENT

Scots are capable of waxing fairly tedious about the disproportionate number of men of genius, especially inventors, that the nation has produced, but the period known as the Scottish Enlightenment, when Scotland led Europe in ideas, is widely recognised as extraordinary. What provoked the sudden upsurge in Scottish intellectual and artistic life between 1760 and 1790 is a matter for social historians, but the result was a gathering of minds in clubs, howffs and later at New Town dinner parties, where arguments could be thrashed out and discoveries communicated. The men of the Enlightenment were humane, moderate, curious, rational and above all enjoyed conversation and the society of others.

Chief among them was the philosopher David Hume, whose religious scepticism shocked many of his contemporaries, but whose ideas, particularly about causation, had, and have, enormous influence. Adam Smith, whose *The Wealth of Nations* is the cornerstone of modern economics, was his friend. Then there was James Hutton, whose *Theory of the Earth* first proposed

THE WATER OF LEITH

You cannot yet walk all the way from the suburbs to the sea by the Water of Leith, but if you have a car, or use buses creatively to follow the course of Edinburgh's own trout stream, you will be taken into some interesting and unfrequented parts of Edinburgh. This is something of a do-it-yourself adventure, and will take the better part of a day.

On the far south-western fringe of Edinburgh, where the 'lang whang' road from Lanark (A70) enters the city through the smart suburbs of Balerno (visit Malleny Gardens – page 176 – while you are here), Currie and Juniper Green, a walkway of the *rus in urbe* variety runs by the river. Old mills and the remains of a railway show how important, even out here, the Water of Leith has been to Edinburgh's light industries, though it is now a semi-rural landscape, particularly beautiful at Colinton Dell and Craiglockhart Dell. The unspoilt village of Colinton lies tucked among some of Edinburgh's most palatial villas. A little further on, a detour east brings you to the whins and rocks of Craiglockhart hills (where the views are good).

Unless you want to make a pilgrimage to the Rugby ground

---

continuous erosion and uplift as the mechanism by which the Earth's surface was under constant change, and Joseph Black who discovered carbon dioxide. The interests of Lord Kames and Lord Monboddo extended beyond the law into linguistics, philosophy and history. The Adam family, the most famous architects of their age, Allan Ramsay and Henry Raeburn among the portrait painters and Robert Fergusson, whose vernacular poetry marked a new interest in Scots as a language, all lived during this period.

The 'second wave' of the Enlightenment came after the Napoleonic Wars, when, with figures such as Scott, Hogg, Cockburn and Jeffrey, and periodicals such as the *Edinburgh Review*, Edinburgh became a literary town *par excellence*. This pre-eminence was to last into the start of the Victorian period, when Edinburgh literary life went into a decline, with only Robert Louis Stevenson's affectionate and frustrated voice to give life to the city. Not until the 'Scottish Renaissance' of the 1930s, when writers such as Hugh Macdiarmid, Norman McCaig, Sidney Goodsir Smith and Robert Garioch started to reinject Edinburgh with political and literary life, was the Enlightenment to have any echo.

at Murrayfield, the best place to pick up the Water of Leith again as it nears the city centre is at Belford Bridge, west of Queensferry Street. The streets and crescents to the south of the river show how the Georgian pattern of the New Town was transformed into a Victorian version of the same idea. At the western end of Melville Street, St Mary's Cathedral (often unjustly ignored merely because it is Victorian) towers over the West End.

Downstream of Belford Bridge, the Water of Leith enters a steep gorge. If you come down Queensferry Street and over Telford's Dean Bridge (1829), you will hardly be aware of it. But just before the bridge plunge down Bell's Brae and you will arrive at the tiny Dean Village, an old milling centre now virtually lost among the cliff-like terraces of the New Town. It has been heavily restored where not demolished, and has become rather deliberately charming, but it remains a curious hidden enclave in the middle of the city.

Beneath the Dean Bridge, more greenery lines the banks of the river, hiding the little neo-Classical temple housing St Bernard's Well, whose sulphurous waters were once much favoured by New Town gentry. On the heights of the northern bank, and well worth seeking out, is Ann Street, one of Georgian Edinburgh's prettiest spots with long front gardens shielding the façades of the houses, and St Bernard's Crescent, an exercise in Doric grandeur.

At Stockbridge, further downstream, you will find plenty of curiosities in St Stephen Street and one of the least-known but best of Edinburgh's Georgian squares in the unfinished Saxe-Coburg Place. Further down the river you come across the Colonies, a collection of neat little cottage-lined streets designed as a worker's community, but now much sought after for their position and charm.

Apart from the semi-secret hideaway of Warriston Cemetery, there is now little to be said for the Water of Leith until you reach its junction with the sea at the old town which gives it its name. **Leith** was and is Edinburgh's port, and has seen almost as much history as the city behind it. Mary Queen of Scots returned to her kingdom here on a melancholy day of mist, and later George IV landed to cheering crowds. Fiercely independent of Edinburgh for years, Leith was eventually forced to capitulate for administrative convenience in 1920. The port has been much polished up of late and many of its old buildings have been restored, though heavy lorries still make strolling through it something of a hazard. The area called the Shore, where the river makes its final curve to the sea, is the most pleasantly nautical part, and there are thriving lunchtime bars and bistros.

Water of Leith sights

• **The National Gallery of Modern Art, Belford Road** (open Mon to Sat 10 to 5, Sun 2 to 5; in Festival, Mon to Sat 10 to 6, Sun 11 to 6) A reclining figure by Henry Moore takes its ease on the green lawns which front the long neo-Classical façade of John Watson's School, which now houses the National Gallery's modern art collection. Displays in the series of cool, sparse rooms inside frequently change, but most of the main periods of twentieth-century painting are represented, and there is an excellent shop of books to back up the paintings (though there is disappointingly little about the gallery's own collection). Although the collection was started only in 1960, there is a good core holding, with Picasso, Nash, a selection of Cubist paintings, some Surrealists and works by Hockney, Leger, Mondrian and others. The Scottish Colourists are well represented, but you may have to look hard to find samples of Glaswegian 'New Wave' painting on permanent display.

• **The Royal Botanic Garden** (open Mar, Apr, Sept and Oct, daily 10 to 6; May to Aug, daily 10 to 8; rest of year 10 to 4; plant houses open all year, daily 10 to 5) This is one of the best Botanic Gardens anywhere, and a spot well worth knowing about on a freezing day for its sequence of bright, warm and modern plant houses. The collections of ericaceous plants from the tropics are particularly unusual, but, on a fine day, there is much more to enchant the plant lover. The collection of rhododendrons and azaleas is renowned, and there is a splendid arboretum, as well as the first peat garden to be established in Britain. This is in no sense a formal garden – it is a large, wooded area that it is quite possible to get lost in.

FURTHER AFIELD

In its nineteenth- and twentieth-century expansions Edinburgh has absorbed a number of villages, many of which have retained their character in the middle of the surrounding streets. Those by the Forth make good lunching spots. If you are weary of the bustle of central Edinburgh, make for the following (the order is clockwise round the city, starting with Queensferry on the banks of the Forth).

Queensferry

The old village is now completely overshadowed by the two great Forth Bridges which sweep by it. Malcolm Canmore's queen, Margaret, used the crossing as early as 1070, but the first official ferry was not established until 1129. It ran for over 800 years before the opening of the Forth Road Bridge in 1964 made it obsolete. However, the village, with its lovely old terraced houses and small museum, is still worth wandering round, while readers of Robert Louis Stevenson's *Kidnapped* will want to visit the Hawes Inn, from where David Balfour was lured aboard the brig *Covenant*. Queensferry is also the best spot from which to admire the bridges, especially the Rail Bridge, which celebrated its centenary in 1990 and remains one of the finest cantilever structures in the world. Try the pedestrian walkway along the Road Bridge for splendid views over the Forth, though the swaying sensation as lorries rumble past can be alarming!

Boats run from Queensferry to the island of Inchcolm close to the Fife coast from Easter to the end of September (ring 031-331 4857 for details). The thirteenth-century abbey with its well-preserved monastic buildings and considerable restoration is the goal of this trip, made all the better for its isolated setting among the busy shipping lanes of the Forth.

Near Queensferry, the neat estate village of **Dalmeny** is a draw for church-lovers; the little Norman church here is one of the best-preserved in the country.

Dalmeny House

(Open May to Sept, Sun to Thur 2 to 5.30)
Home of the Earl of Rosebery, and the closest to Edinburgh of the sequence of stately homes along this bank of the Forth, this neo-Gothic house (1815) has splendid views over the Firth. The collection inside, including the library, owes much to the fifth Earl, who not only married the richest heiress in England but became Prime Minister in 1894 and had three Derby winners into the bargain. Many of the finest treasures from Mentmore, which the fifth Earl's wife inherited, are now at Dalmeny. There is much fine eighteenth-century French furniture and some very unusual tapestries designed by Goya. The fifth Earl was an expert on Napoleon, and his collection of relics of the Emperor is also here. Dalmeny is very much a family home, and all these treasures are offered for admiration in a setting which could hardly be less like a stuffy museum.

Cramond

Cramond, at the mouth of the River Almond, is where the Romans based themselves on this bank of the Forth (some of the finds in Huntly House and the Queen Street museum came from here). The remains of a fort are just visible. Romans apart, Cramond is a tranquil place, popular for weekend excursions from the city, and with small yachts and motor boats lying off the river mouth. Walk up the River Almond to see the seventeenth-century bridge where James V was rescued from footpads by the local miller. If beachside walks are more to your taste than leafy riverbanks, go across the small ferry to a fine stretch of shoreline leading westwards towards Queensferry or head back east along a rather tamer but breezy esplanade, trying to ignore the large storage silos which blot the shoreline.

Lauriston Castle (Cramond Road South)

(Open Apr to Oct, daily 11 to 4.20, closed Fri; Nov to Mar, Sat and Sun 2 to 3.20)

An old tower-house with a mansion added to it in 1827, this is a curious place, well worth seeking out among the quiet housing estates near Cramond. It is the interior that fascinates. The castle was given to the city in 1926 by its last owners, the Reids, who stipulated that as few changes as possible should be made to its contents. Mr Reid owned a firm of cabinet-makers which did a lot of work fitting out railway carriages, while his wife's family were sanitary engineers. The result is some fine panelling and remarkable plumbing, but Lauriston is especially interesting for the extraordinary collection of objects that the Reids assembled. They seem to have collected what they liked without regard for value or antiquity – huge numbers of commodes, masses of prints (some execrable), and a collection of 'wool mosaic' pictures, made by slicing longitudinally laid threads into a number of pictures, like a stick of rock. There is a sit-down weighing machine in Mrs Reid's bedroom, coconut shells in silver mounts, and a fine assembly of Derbyshire 'Blue John Ware'. The overall impression is of a homely clutter, full of things to gaze at.

Part of the charm of Lauriston lies in the enthusiasm of the guides, who genuinely love the house they look after and, this far away from the tourist trail, have time to spare.

Duddingston

Tucked under Arthur's Seat, Duddingston is the goal of countless walks across the expanse of Holyrood Park for lunch at what is thought to be the oldest pub in Scotland, the Sheep's Heid Inn. You can also get there by the lazier method of driving round the mountain-girdling road which runs under the columnar stratifications of Salisbury Crags and round the shoulder of the great volcanic plug which dominates the eastern side of Edinburgh. Arthur's Seat is easily climbed from Duddingston or from Dunsapie Loch (saving 300 feet of climbing) and the views of Edinburgh are worth the effort, though try to choose a day when the wind will allow you to enjoy them. Duddingston Loch is a bird sanctuary and enthusiasts with binoculars can be glimpsed among the reeds, while children throw bread to the more common species of duck and goose along the shore.

Craigmillar Castle (HS) (Craigmillar Castle Road)

(HS standard times, closed Thurs pm and Fri in winter; extended tours in summer Apr to Sept; contact the Castle on 031-661 4445 for details)
Driving southwards from Duddingston you quickly realise that the surrounding housing estates cannot improve Craigmillar's outlook, but once you arrive you see that they fail to diminish the impact of this substantial ruin. Two successive curtain walls rise in front of a fourteenth-century tower house, with later ranges added to it. The massive fortress was the place where the murder of Mary Queen of Scots' husband Darnley was planned, and where Maitland, Bothwell, Argyll, Huntly and Balfour probably signed a bond agreeing to his removal (though the bond, unsurprisingly, no longer exists). As a scene for the planning of an assassination, Craigmillar can hardly be bettered.

Blackford

A very fine viewpoint on Blackford Hill and the Royal Observatory, with an informative visitor centre, make a short expedition out to Blackford a pleasure, especially for astronomers. The pond is a famous toy boat-sailing spot.

Swanston

A favourite haunt of Robert Louis Stevenson and described in *St Ives*, Swanston's seventeenth-century cottages lie under the foot of the Pentland Hills, on the far side of the Edinburgh by-pass. Apart from the undisturbed old houses and the surrounding golf course there is nothing much to see, but paths lead into the Pentlands and across to the dry ski slope at Hillend. (See page 176 for description of the Pentlands.)

Corstorphine

Residents of Corstorphine are kept awake by the roar of lions, for Edinburgh Zoo (open Mon to Sat 9 to 6, Sun 9.30 to 6) lies on the bank of the hill. It is a steeply banked, fairly traditional zoo, good for a day out with children. The 'Penguin Parade' – a shuffle down the paths by the zoo's fine collection of the birds – is a high spot. If you are interested in agriculture, a short journey (follow signs to the airport) takes you to Ingliston and the **Scottish Agricultural Museum** (open Apr to end Sept, daily 10 to 5; Oct to Mar, Mon to Fri 10 to 5), where there is a large collection of implements from the past, reconstructed farm interiors and lots of photographs. Ingliston is also the scene of the Royal Highland Show in June each year, an agricultural show with distinctive Scottish tinges.

WHERE TO STAY

The Albany	£–££
39–43 Albany Street	
Edinburgh EH1 3QY	*031-556 0397*

A quiet, comfortable place to stay within easy reach of the town centre. Bedrooms vary from the high-windowed master rooms to the smaller rooms at the top. The drawing-room is pleasant to relax in, and there is a bright and airy basement restaurant.

Open: all year, exc 25, 26 Dec and 1, 2 Jan **Rooms**: 22
Credit/charge cards: Access, Visa

USEFUL DIRECTORY

Edinburgh Tourist Office, 3 Princes Street,
Waverley Market (031-557 1700)

Tourist Board Publications Very useful is the 'Welcome
to Edinburgh' brochure which has a small city centre
map with an outline of the history of the city, and a list
of tourist attractions and places to go. Useful newspapers
listing cinemas and places of interest are *The Scotsman* and
the *Edinburgh Evening News*.

Local transport
Edinburgh Airport Information 031-344 3212
Waverley Station (Scotrail) Passenger Information
Department 031-556 2451
St Andrews Square Bus Station Information 031-654 0707
Lothian Regional Transport Information and city tours
information 031-220 4111
Scottish Citylink Information (bus) 031-557 5717

City guides
Robin Sinton 031-661 0125
Scotline Bus Tours 031-557 0162

Entertainment
Royal Lyceum Theatre 031-229 9697
Playhouse Theatre 031-557 2590
Kings Theatre 031-228 5955
Usher Hall 031-228 1155
Queens Hall 031-668 2019
Edinburgh Filmhouse 031-228 6382

The Edinburgh Festival
Festival Offices: 21 Market Street 031-226 4001
Fringe Office: 180 High Street 031-226 5257
Tattoo Office: 22 Market Street 031-225 1188

Miscellaneous
The Royal Commonwealth Pool 031-667 7211
Meadowbank Stadium 031-661 5351
Hearts Football Club 031-337 6132

Caledonian Hotel £££
Princes Street
Edinburgh EH2 2AB   Tel 031-225 2433

This huge old station hotel has been completely renovated, but quite a lot of the old character remains; bedrooms are designed with care and interest. Prices are high.

Open: all year **Rooms**: 239 **Credit/charge cards**: Access, Amex, Diners, Visa

Channings £
South Learmonth Gardens
Edinburgh EH4 1EZ   Tel 031-315 2226

The hotel has high-quality (though somewhat impersonal) interior design, with well-conceived and comfortable bedrooms and rather small alcove lounges.

Open: all year, exc 24 to 28 Dec **Rooms**: 48 **Credit/charge cards**: Access, Amex, Diners, Visa

St Bernards Guesthouse £
22 St Bernards Crescent
Edinburgh EH4 1NS   Tel 031-332 2339

A bright, good-value Edinburgh guesthouse. It is now under new ownership and has been refurbished.

Open: all year **Rooms**: 8 **Credit/charge cards**: Access, Visa

Scandic Crown £££
80 High Street, The Royal Mile
Edinburgh EH1 1TH   031-557 9797

Sensitively designed to fit in with its prestigious surroundings, this is the best of Edinburgh's modern business hotels. Scandinavian influences include smorgasbord lunches, and the bedrooms have supremely comfortable beds and thoughtful extras like convenient plugs for computers. The food is extremely competent, and the private car park a massive advantage. Following a fire in 1992, the hotel has been completely refurbished, with a new restaurant and bistro-style 'Library'.

Open: all year **Rooms**: 238 **Facilities**: sauna, solarium, indoor swimming-pool, gym, private car park
Credit/charge cards: Access, Amex, Diners, Visa

Sibbet House £
26 Northumberland Street
Edinburgh EH3 6LS *031-556 1078*

First-class, medium-priced hotels are a rarity in the centre of Edinburgh, and Sibbet House gets booked up well in advance. A large house in the Georgian New Town, this is a cosy place, with antiques, family photographs and many lovely objects. The blue bedroom is the most attractive with its sofa and striped wallpaper. No evening meals, but a good choice of restaurants nearby.

Open: all year **Rooms**: 3 **Credit/charge cards**: Access, Visa

WHERE TO EAT

L'Auberge
56 St Mary Street EH1 1SX *Tel 031-556 5888*

A well-established restaurant in a street off the Royal mile that offers high-quality Scottish fare with a French influence.

Open: daily 12 to 2, 6.30 to 9.30
Credit/charge cards: Access, Amex, Diners, Visa

Bamboo Garden ★
57A Frederick Street EH2 1LH *Tel 031-225 2382*

This Chinese restaurant in a basement in Frederick Street offers a good range of dishes, including some reasonably priced set menus.

Open: daily 12 to 12; closed Chinese New Year
Credit/charge cards: Access, Amex, Visa

Cellar No 1 ★
1A Chambers Street EH1 1HR *Tel 031-220 4298*

Filled poppyseed buns are popular in the narrow cellar bar. Not surprisingly for a place beneath a wine shop wine is taken seriously here: about 30 are available by the glass.

Open: Mon to Sat 12 to 2.30, 6 to 10; closed Xmas, New Year
Credit/charge cards: Access, Visa

Chinese Home Cooking ★
21 Argyle Place EH9 1JJ   *Tel 031-229 4404*

As the name suggests, you can expect good, straightforward Chinese meals in this converted shop. The prices are kind to the pocket as well. Bring your own bottle.

Open: daily 5.30 to 11 **Credit/charge cards**: none accepted

---

Denzler's 121
121 Constitution Street EH6 7AE   *Tel 031-554 3268*

A new venture, specialising in Swiss cooking, for the Denzler family who have a long-standing reputation in Edinburgh.

Open: daily 12 to 2, 6.30 to 10; closed 2 weeks end July, first week Jan **Credit/charge cards**: Access, Amex, Visa

---

Doric Tavern ★
15 Market Street EH1 1DE   *Tel 031-225 1084*

Red walls might be a bit overwhelming but the Doric Tavern offers good, solid, unpretentious cooking. The set-price, three-course lunch is good value. There is a good wine bar upstairs.

Open: Mon to Sat 12 noon till late **Credit/charge cards**: Access, Amex, Visa

---

Indian Cavalry Club
3 Atholl Place EH3 8HP   *Tel 031-228 3282*

Don't be put off by the paramilitary uniform of the staff – this restaurant is a balance of brasserie and Indian restaurant. The wine list complements a good range of curries, many of which are mild.

Open: daily 12 to 2.30, 5.30 to 11.30; closed Xmas, New Year **Credit/charge cards**: Access, Amex, Diners, Visa

---

Loon Fung
32 Grindlay Street EH3 9AP   *Tel 031-229 5757*

You can choose from a wide range of noodle or rice one-plate dishes at this cheerful Cantonese restaurant.

Open: Mon to Thurs 12 to 11.30, Fri 12 to 12.30, Sat and Sun 2 to 12.30; closed Xmas and Chinese New Year **Credit/charge cards**: Access, Amex, Visa

Marché Noir
2–4 Eyre Place EH3 5EP   *Tel 031-558 1608*

Two set-price menus are offered daily at each meal. The food is mostly French, and the staff translate happily.

Open: daily 12 to 2, 7 to 10 (to 10.30 Fri and Sat); closed Xmas, New Year **Credit/charge cards**: Access, Amex, Visa

Marrakech
Marrakech Hotel
30 London Street EH3 6NA   *Tel 031-556 7293*

Below ground level, this hotel-restaurant is Moroccan-run, so naturally the food is Moroccan-influenced. You can bring your own alcohol.

Open: Mon to Sat 6.30 to 10; closed Nov
Credit/charge cards: Access, Diners, Visa

Martins
70 Rose Street North Lane EH2 3DX   *Tel 031-220 4062*

Lunches are fair value at Martins; the evening *carte* is more expensive but offers fresh, seasonal vegetables with perhaps a choice of two fish and two meat dishes. The restaurant is not easy to find, so check directions before you go.

Open: Tues to Fri 12 to 2, Tues to Sat 7 to 10; closed 1 week in June and Sept **Credit/charge cards**: Access, Amex, Diners, Visa

Pierre Victoire
10 Victoria Street EH1 2HG   *Tel 031-225 1721*

The three popular Pierre Victoire branches in Edinburgh all offer generous and imaginative food at very good value. The other two are at 38 Grassmarket and 8 Union Street. Be prepared for a squeeze.

Open: Mon to Sat 12 to 3, 6 to 11; closed Xmas, New Year
Credit/charge cards: Access, Visa

Seeds ★
53 West Nicholson Street EH8 9DB   *Tel 031-667 8673*

The cooking at this co-operative café is vegan and the menu changes constantly. Expect to share a table.

Open: Mon to Sat 10 to 9, Sun 11 to 8; closed 1st week Sept, 2 weeks Xmas **Credit/charge cards**: none accepted

Shamiana
14 Brougham Street EH3 9JH   *Tel 031-228 2265*

This smartly decorated restaurant is highly rated for its tandoori meals, curries and specialities from Kashmir and other parts of India.

Open: daily 12 to 2, 6 to 11.30 **Credit/charge cards**: Access, Amex, Diners, Visa

Shore
3 The Shore EH6 6QW   *Tel 031-553 5080*

This waterfront restaurant bases its menu on fish, but the blackboard menu offers other favourites too.

Open: daily 12 to 2.30, 6.30 to 10.15; closed Xmas and New Year
Credit/charge cards: none accepted

Singapore Sling   ★
503 Lawnmarket
The Royal Mile EH1 2PE   *Tel 031-226 2826*

Multi-cultural cooking and exotic cocktails are the thing at this Malaysian/Singaporean restaurant.

Open: Mon to Sat 12.30 to 3, Mon to Fri 6 to 11, Sat and Sun 5.30 to 11; closed Xmas **Credit/charge cards**: Access, Amex, Visa

Tinelli
139 Easter Road EH7 5QA   *Tel 031-652 1932*

Tinelli offers traditional Italian cooking and professional service to its customers.

Open: Tues to Sat 12 to 2, 6.30 to 11 **Credit/charge cards**:
Access, Visa

Vintners Rooms
87 Giles Street
Leith EH6 6BX   *Tel 031-554 6767*

There are two dining-rooms here, one – a former wine auction room – is small and formal, the other – larger and with a fire at one end – more welcoming. A good-quality daily menu includes several fish dishes as well as lighter lunches, although the prices are on the high side. No smoking.

Open: Mon to Sat from 12, 6.30 to 10.30; closed 1 week Xmas
Credit/charge cards: Access, Amex, Visa

Waterfront Wine Bar ★
1C Dock Place
Leith EH6 6LU   *Tel 031-554 7427*

A daily-changing menu features plenty of fish, with good alternatives for meat-eaters and vegetarians alike. Value for money extends to the wine list.

Open: daily 12 to 2.30, 6 to 9.30; closed Xmas and New Year
Credit/charge cards: Access, Visa

EAST LOTHIAN AND THE CENTRAL BELT

- A region of industrial relics, stately homes, interesting coastline and gentle hills
- Fine pastoral scenery in East Lothian and some excellent castles
- Plenty of history in the Clyde Valley and along the Forth coast

Chatelherault

TWO revolutions have left their mark on this swathe of country – the Agrarian and the Industrial. The fertile strip of East Lothian between the Lammermuir Hills and the beaches of North Berwick and Gullane became the proving ground for the late eighteenth-century transformation of Scottish agriculture from a virtually feudal system of strip-farming and common land into a productive and stable industry. Long leases were granted to tenant farmers and new crop varieties were bred; the threshing mill was invented and farming turned from a haphazard activity into something approaching a science. The neat villages, the enclosed fields, the solid farm-steadings, the woods and the pastureland which in many ways make East Lothian the most English of all the Scottish counties are the products of this revolution.

While the model for the Scottish Agrarian Revolution was largely taken from south of the Border, it may be argued that the Industrial Revolution really started in Scotland. For it was in Scotland that James Watt, by his invention of the separate condenser and the governor, turned the steam engine from an inefficient machine into an economical source of power for everything from pumps to locomotives.

Scotland's coalfields lie scattered in an arc around the Central Lowlands; her iron and steel industries were concentrated in the lower Clyde Valley, her spinning and weaving round Glasgow. It was in the Central Lowlands, too, that the petroleum industry was pioneered, at Bathgate and in Broxburn where paraffin and lubricating oils were distilled from coal and shale for the first time by 'Paraffin' Young, whose 1850 patent marks the start of commercial oil refining.

Today, the shale mines, the coal mines and the iron and steel works are extinct or moribund, and only their effects on the landscape remain. Even these are disappearing as the pink jelly-shaped 'bings' (slag-heaps) of waste shale are flattened and the old coal tips landscaped and planted under environmental improvement schemes. Even the sour old mining villages are slowly being given new leases of life as their housing is upgraded and commuters to Edinburgh or Glasgow settle in new estates on their fringes. Light industries are replacing the 'heavies' across the region, and there is a faint breath of regeneration which was non-existent 20 years ago.

Kings and Covenanters

Beneath the industrial débris lies a much older layer of Scotland. Stirling, Linlithgow and Edinburgh were the pivotal towns of the Scottish Court and it is hardly surprising that the country around them witnessed many of the power struggles that dogged medieval Scotland. The Central Lowlands were also the first stop for any invading army: the burghs of East Lothian at the end of the easiest route from the south were burnt almost as often as the Border towns. Everywhere in the region there are memories of the past – Sir James Douglas setting fire to his castle, the corpses of his enemies, his food, his wine and his horses to deny them to the English; James IV being warned of his death at Flodden by an apparition in Linlithgow church; Mary Queen of Scots surrendering to her enemies at Carberry Hill; George IV supping turtle soup at Hopetoun . . .

This region, together with neighbouring Dumfriesshire, has a tragic history for it was the battleground for the final struggle of the Covenanters against the doctrinal impositions of the restored Stewart kings. For almost 30 years, sustained by little more than faith, men and women deserted the churches where the law decreed they must worship and followed their outlawed ministers to the hills and bare moors to attend services known as conventicles. Every means of coercion was used against them and torture, on-the-spot execution, imprisonment or transportation to the colonies was often their fate. Yet they persisted.

EAST LOTHIAN

If you drive up the A1 from the south you will see the coast begin to flatten out as the Lammermuirs recede further from the sea. The huge bulk of Torness – Scotland's latest and most controversial nuclear power plant – and the Dunbar cement works beyond it are not a propitious beginning to East Lothian's pleasures, but if you have time a detour to the sea at Barn's Ness is worthwhile, especially for geologists – lumps of coal and fossil coral beds are two of the pleasures. Equally, a journey round the back roads past the villages of Oldhamstocks and Spott is more enjoyable than sticking to the main road. Two crucial battles were fought near Dunbar. The first, in 1296, marked the beginning of Edward I's ruthless conquest (he had already sacked Berwick), while

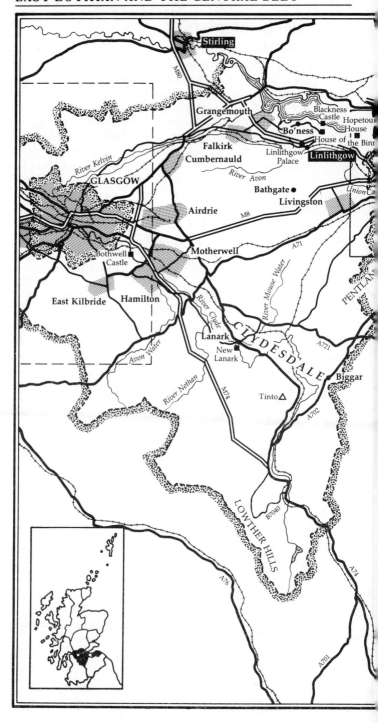

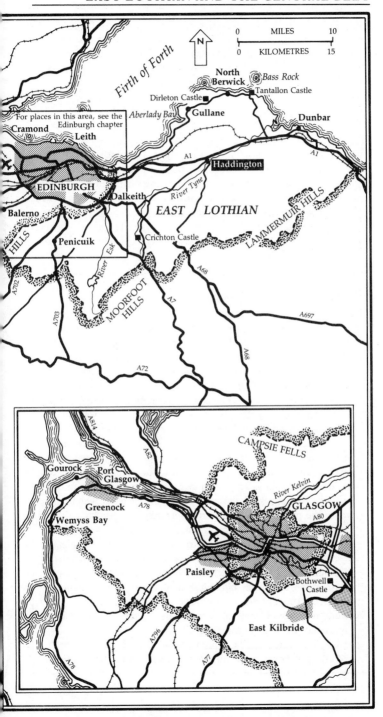

the second, in 1650, was the turning point of Cromwell's invasion of Scotland. 'The Lord has delivered them into our hands,' he is supposed to have said, watching the Covenanters leaving the high ground in the mistaken belief that they could overwhelm his army. The reverse was the case.

Dunbar

The decay of some of Dunbar's huge resort hotels suggests that as a seaside resort it is no longer as popular as it once was, and the town now seems to be realigning its image more towards heritage than sand. Interesting attempts are being made to slot modern housing into the vernacular tradition, continuing the work done by the architect Basil Spence, while some of the town's older buildings are being spruced up. The place to start (and maybe finish) exploring is down at

Practical suggestions

This urbanised region is not the first part of Scotland that springs to mind when planning a holiday. Most people take in a few of its sights on to a visit to Edinburgh or Glasgow, and this is probably the most sensible way of doing things. However, if you have a day or two spare and the weather forecast is too bad to venture further north, if you are tacking a weekend on to a business trip, if you want to play golf or build sandcastles, or if you want to do some walking on gentle hills, then this region is ideal.

The Forth coast and the Clyde Valley are the two most self-contained areas for touring, and both have some good scenery and sights. There is a lot to be said in favour of basing yourself for a day or two in East Lothian, where you can swing between seaside, golf course and moorland at whim, and where the towns and villages are interesting and attractive. The Pentland Hills provide some fine walks and are in easy reach of Edinburgh. Those who like industrial archaeology will find plenty of interest in the relics of the mines, canals, and industries of Mid and West Lothian which have been preserved and opened up to visitors, while the old ship-building towns on the bank of the Clyde west of Glasgow still have some atmosphere. No one should miss the old mills at New Lanark, scene of a remarkable experiment in social engineering.

Accommodation can be a problem, largely because Edinburgh and Glasgow are so close and tend to attract all the trade. In the

the **Victoria Harbour**, where the general picturesqueness of small fishing boats in a rocky enclave is enhanced by the red sandstone pillar which is all that remains of Dunbar Castle. The cacophony of the resident colony of kittiwakes adds to the nautical flavour. It is hard to imagine now, but Dunbar was once a major whaling and smuggling port.

Dunbar Castle, once one of the strongest fortresses on the coast, has had its moments. The castle's most famous piece of history occurred when Black Agnes, daughter of Robert the Bruce's companion Randolph, held out here against the English for five months in 1338, being relieved from the sea just when all hope seemed to be lost and promptly sending bread and wine to her besiegers to show that her supplies were better than theirs. The prophet True Thomas was here too, in 1286, telling the Earl of Dunbar that the following noon would bring a storm the like of which had never descended

---

country around both cities there are several plush hotels (often in venerable castles), and while these are used largely by business or sporting people and have correspondingly fat tariffs, you might find it worth ringing them on spec at weekends or off-season to see if you can pick up a bargain. East Lothian has a number of old inns in its towns and villages, and substantial numbers of seaside guesthouses and hotels in its coastal resorts. Elsewhere you are likely to find the scattered bed-and-breakfasts the best value – the biggest clutches are round Linlithgow and Lanark.

Good bases

● **Haddington** This old burgh makes an ideal base for exploring East Lothian. It is a small but lively town, the centre-piece for the prosperous farming countryside. Streets lined by elegant eighteenth-century houses run from its old triangular marketplace down to the River Tyne.

● **Linlithgow** The ruins of the royal palace and the loch behind its High Street dominate this old town, the most attractive in West Lothian. It has managed to retain a little of its market-town tranquillity despite the coming of the canal, the railway and the M9 motorway. It is well placed for exploration of the southern coast of the Firth of Forth, and also for picking through the industrial archaeology of the area.

● **Stirling** (page 265) also makes a good base for the north-western part of the area.

upon Scotland. A messenger arrived the next day bringing news of the death of Alexander III, the event which marked the beginning of the long agony of the Wars of Independence – a storm indeed.

The stump of the castle is all that remains of a building that appears once to have bridged several sea stacks outside what is now the harbour entrance: much was demolished in 1567 and yet more fell to Cromwell.

Elsewhere in Dunbar, the **Tolbooth** is early seventeenth-century and rather fine, while the imposing **Lauderdale House**, which stands at one end of the High Street, owes its current appearance to Robert Adam. The old promenade which fringes the cliffs between Dunbar and Belhaven Bay to the west makes a good walk. The **John Muir House** (open May to Sept, Mon to Sat 11 to 1 and 2 to 5.30, Sun 2 to 5.30; closed Wed) contains, among other pieces of domestic Victoriana, 'a midwifery potty for post-natal comfort'. The house and the nearby John Muir Country Park are memorials to the American pioneer of conservation, who was born here (though he moved next door when he was one and emigrated when he was ten). 'Country Park', with its suggestion of neatly ordered recreational landscape, is an unfortunate term for the wild sweep of Belhaven Bay, backed by dunes and a labyrinth of ancient tank-traps, with the saltmarshes and rocky outcrops of Tyninghame beyond. There are few better stretches of seashore south of Fife.

Dunbar to Gifford

This back route to Edinburgh (B6370) takes you along the fringe of the Lammermuir Hills and through some of East Lothian's prettiest villages. All over the countryside you will see the stone farm-steadings and rows of pantiled cottages which are reminders that East Lothian was in the forefront of the agricultural improvements of the late eighteenth century. The threshing machine was invented by an East Lothian man; new strains of wheat and oats were bred here; the editor of the first farming journal in Scotland came from East Linton.

Stenton is an extremely photogenic village, with its pan-tiled houses, its green, its medieval well and the remains of its old church. It once had a reputation for being in the forefront of the witch-burning craze. Now it has become rather gentrified, to the extent of having a small art gallery. Close to Stenton is the hidden valley of Pressmennan, where the nineteenth-century artificial Lake of Pressmennan lies concealed among the trees, now the setting for a secluded nature trail.

Further west, and a short way off the B6370, **Garvald** is a tiny place tucked into the shadow of the Lammermuirs with some lovely old cottages and a church going back to the twelfth century. Above the village on the edge of the moors is the modern **Nunraw Abbey**. The Cistercian community here has long links with the area, for Nunraw was originally a house belonging to the twelfth-century convent at Haddington, which was bought back by the Cistercians in 1946. It is possible to visit the chapel of the modern abbey, and you are quite likely to meet a white-habited monk on a tractor. The old tower-house is now a guesthouse. The narrow road winds up into the hills above Nunraw and eventually over into the valley of the Whiteadder. Back on the B6370, **Gifford** – another planned village from the eighteenth century, with a particularly harmonious church of Dutch appearance – makes a good centre for walks into the Lammermuirs and is a pleasant place to stop for lunch. Avoid weekends, though, when half of Edinburgh may join you.

Dunbar to Haddington

Neatly bypassed by the A1, **East Linton** is quiet and attractive, the sort of village where there is plenty of time for a gossip in the grocer's shop. The River Tyne pours through the centre in a rocky gorge, inhabited by fishermen optimistically loitering by dark pools and crossed by a fine old bridge – you will have to take to your feet to see it properly. A short distance downstream is the renowned **Preston Mill** (NTS, open Easter to end Sept, Mon to Sat 11 to 1, 2 to 5, Sun 2 to 5; Oct, Mon to Sat 11 to 1, 2 to 4, Sun 2 to 4). This red-tiled seventeeth-century watermill with its conical-roofed kiln is surrounded by the sort of ducks-and-placid-water scenery which has made it the subject of countless paintings and photographs from the nineteenth century onwards. The working machinery inside is not, in this age of restored water mills, as rare a sight as it once was, but the age of the place and the well-explained notices still make it essential visiting. **Phantassie Doocot** (NTS, times as Preston Mill) close by is perhaps not quite so deserving of notice but is nevertheless worth a look, especially if you have already remarked how well-sprinkled Lowland Scotland is with ancient *pigeonniers* (perhaps a lasting memento of the Auld Alliance with France). The dovecote at Phantassie has more than 500 pigeon nests and a revolving ladder to reach them by, plus a string course in the wall to stop the rats getting up.

Sticking up from the surrounding countryside south of East Linton, the rounded hill of **Traprain Law** is the plug of an ancient volcano. Traprain, despite being half quarried away, is an important archaeological site. It seems to have been the capital for local tribes from the Stone Age until the end of the Dark Ages and it was here that the famous Traprain Hoard of Roman silverware was found, now on display in the Royal Museum of Scotland (Queen Street) in Edinburgh. Views from the summit are hard to beat.

In the valley of the Tyne below Traprain Law stands **Hailes Castle** (HS, always open). Its position may seem odd until you realise how completely it blocks the strategic route of the Tyne and preys upon the road leading towards Edinburgh. For a castle on the main invasion route from England a lot remains, and some of it dates from before the Wars of Independence. The square *donjon*, the curtain walls and the remains of a sixteenth-century range are perhaps less memorable than the extremely unpleasant pit prisons and the peaceful setting on the banks of the river.

The old airfield at **East Fortune** is now the home of the Museum of Flight, an outstation of the Royal Museum of Scotland (open Easter to end Sept, daily 10.30 to 4.30). Its old hangar is crammed with aircraft ranging from the airship which made the first double crossing of the Atlantic to a Vulcan bomber. If you are in the area at the right time and are fond of aeroplanes, give it a try.

Haddington

Although most of its best buildings date from the seventeenth or eighteenth centuries, Haddington is a very old town, having been made a royal burgh in the twelfth century. Its position made it an obvious target for a spot of burning during the various English invasions of medieval times, and there was a period between 1548 and 1549 when the English actually occupied the town and defended it from the French troops sent against them by Mary of Guise. It was during this siege that the stone crown on the tower of St Mary's church was destroyed. John Knox the preacher was born here in 1505.

Haddington is a busy small town, acting as local shopping centre for much of prosperous East Lothian, so its central streets – where there was once a large, triangular market-place – are studded with parked Range Rovers and farmers stocking up on supplies. But there is more to the town than this, for the energy and enthusiasm of its inhabitants have brought about a careful programme of restoration and conservation, and there are many splendid old houses to gaze at while walking round the streets, following the *Historic Walks round Haddington* leaflet, available locally. Behind all the elegant eighteenth-century buildings, which culminate in William Adam's Town House, lies the street plan of the older burgh, and you can find fragments of the old town wall. If architecture palls, wander down to the banks of the River Tyne to look at the old bridges, photograph the occasional swan, or to take a stroll round **St Mary's Pleasance**, a beautifully restored garden.

Haddington is an ideal base from which to explore East Lothian, and is perfectly acceptable for day trips to Edinburgh too. There is often some cultural event or other going on, mounted by the Lamp of Lothian Collegiate Centre (062082 3738), the body responsible for so much of Haddington's conservation. The town-centre hotels lean more towards country trade than towards tourism, and are acceptable if uninspiring. The alternative is to stay in one of the guesthouses in or near the town – probably the best option.

In and near Haddington

• **St Mary's Collegiate Church** (open Easter to end Sept, Mon to Sat 10 to 4, Sun 1 to 4), down by the river, was built in the fourteenth century. A massive restoration programme, completed in 1973, re-roofed the chancel and transepts (which had been abandoned after the Reformation) and rebuilt much of the stonework of the eastern end of the church. The result, as at Dunblane Cathedral, is an inspiration, particularly when you look at the photographs of the work being carried out and realise what a mammoth task it was and how authentically it has been executed. Concerts are sometimes held in the old church – ask inside.

• **Lennoxlove House** (open Apr to Sept, Sat and Sun 2 to 5), a mile south of Haddington on the B6369, is worth making an effort to see (despite its limited opening hours) either if you are a Mary Queen of Scots follower or if you simply like stately homes. The seat of the Duke of Hamilton, the old extended and revamped tower–house, now contains much of the collection of portraits and chinaware which was removed from the huge Hamilton Palace before its demolition. The Hamiltons were the chief supporters of Mary Queen of Scots after her escape from Loch Leven and during the battle of

Langside that followed. Mary's death mask is at Lennoxlove, as is the silver casket which once contained the series of letters purporting to prove Mary's obsession with Bothwell and her part in the conspiracy to murder Darnley. They are likely to have been forged (Mary herself was never allowed to see them) but served their purpose in helping to keep her exiled in England.

North Berwick and the Forth coast

The semi-circle of land which juts northwards into the Forth contains East Lothian's best seaside and nature reserves, greatest number of golf courses and the remarkable Tantallon castle. It has long been the stamping ground for inhabitants of Edinburgh on fine weekends, but there is usually room to spare for everyone.

As you drive along the eastern coast towards Tantallon, keep an eye open for the sixteenth-century tithe barn at Whitekirk, which has survived more intact than Holyrood Abbey, whose monks used to store grain here.

Tantallon Castle

(HS, standard times, closed Thurs pm and Fri in winter)
The great red walls of Tantallon rise from red cliffs against which the sea lashes. 'Three sides of wall-like rock, and one side of rock-like wall' give the castle its superb defensive capabilities. A curtain wall with central keep/gatehouse and two flanking towers cuts the neck of a peninsula, which drops sheer to the sea on the other three sides. Although time, and the guns of Cromwell's general, Monk, have done their best to destroy it, Tantallon still overawes the visitor by its scale and setting. This was a Douglas stronghold, probably started in the late fourteenth century, and both a bargaining counter and a place of refuge for that powerful family when they were out of royal favour.

One and a half miles offshore, the **Bass Rock** floats in similar impregnability, streaked with white by its innumerable seabirds. Whatever the weather or time of day, the setting of castle, sea and cliff is one of the finest in the whole of lowland Scotland.

North Berwick

Popular seaside resort in Victorian and Edwardian times, North Berwick is still very much a going concern, with the necessary ingredients of golf courses, a pretty harbour and nearby sandy beaches. Just outside the town, a path leads to the top of **North Berwick Law**. It is well worth the short but steep climb to the top on a clear day – the views are magnificent. The curious arch on top turns out to be made from a pair of whale jawbones.

It was in North Berwick in 1591 that a well-known coven of witches were believed to have nearly caused the death of James VI by a storm. Their subsequent torture, trial and execution was a subject of much interest to the King, who not only wrote a book about witchcraft but may have let it be known to Shakespeare that *Macbeth* would be all the better received for having a touch of the occult in it. More prosaic grounds for the King's interest may have been the opportunity the North Berwick witches presented to discredit Francis, Earl of Bothwell, who was cited as the coven's devil. The Auld Kirk is the scene of the witches' arrest.

North Berwick is the place to look for a boat trip around the Bass Rock (see above), or perhaps to the other small islands of Fidra and Craigleith, which lie just offshore. A trip around the Bass, especially when the gannet colony is breeding, can be a deafening experience, but not one that you are likely to forget.

Dirleton

A few miles west of North Berwick, Dirleton is held by many to be the prettiest village in Scotland, but since English-style villages with houses clustered around a green are rare in Scotland, and pretty ones even rarer, there are none too many candidates. Certainly, for experts in domestic architecture, the cottages and houses clustered around the large green compose a remarkable collection of seventeenth- and eighteenth-century buildings. To the untutored eye, they are quaint or photogenic by turn.

However, Dirleton is so dwarfed by its castle that you are likely to be drawn to that massive building after no more than a cursory glance at the village. **Dirleton Castle** is older than Tantallon, and almost as colossal, even if its setting is not quite so fine. The gatehouse, where a modern wooden bridge replaces the old drawbridge, is just as imposing. As you walk up the long slope of the bridge, a round tower to your left is what remains of the thirteenth-century fortifications, and you need only compare the neat lines of ashlar masonry with the rubble work of much of the later building to see that the castle

171

was at its most formidable when it was first built. The interior of this tower, with its domed Lord's Chamber, is the most impressive part of the ruin. On the whole, you get a better feel for the place by walking round the outside under the looming walls. The interior is a bit of a muddle, the passages and chambers of the various periods of rebuilding all seeming to run together. Do not omit the beehive-shaped dovecote from your visit, and do not hurry through the garden either.

Gullane and Aberlady

Gullane has always been considered the posh resort of the peninsula, and a glance at the size of the villas on its fringes will go some way to proving the point. More importantly, it is probably second only to St Andrews in its reputation for golf. **Muirfield** is one of the best-known Scotland championship courses, and half the business deals of Edinburgh are said to be struck on its greens. Even if you cannot pull the strings which will get you on to the fairways here, Gullane has four other courses in the immediate vicinity.

For non-golfers, Gullane has sand in abundance – indeed, too much of it, for drifting sand was the original settlement's ruin. The last incumbent of the ruined twelfth-century church was dismissed from his post by James VI for smoking: the King was as intolerant of smokers as he was of witches.

The next bay down the coast is **Aberlady**, now a nature reserve of the mudflat and saltmarsh variety, good for migrant birds. The village here used to be the port for Haddington, but the silt that is good for birds was not so good for ships. The **Myreton Motor Museum** (open Easter to end Oct, daily 10 to 6, Nov to Easter 10 to 5), a short way inland, is an idiosyncratic collection of motoring memorabilia, going beyond vehicles to include posters, signs and general paraphernalia. West of Aberlady, church-lovers should visit **Seton Collegiate Church**, largely fifteenth-century, but going back further than that. Seton was one of the favourite haunts of Mary Queen of Scots.

Prestonpans

The ground between this ancient salt-panning centre and the ridge-top mining village of Tranent was the scene of the Jacobite victory of 1745 when the Hanoverian army under Sir John Cope was cut to pieces by Bonnie Prince Charlie's Highlanders in under 10 minutes. The victory put all of Scotland, apart from a few castles, into Jacobite hands, and came as a terrible shock to the Westminster government. It may also have instilled the fatal belief of invincibility into Prince Charles. It is difficult to see the shape of the battlefield under the modern development, and a good guide will be necessary if you want to pick out the course of events.

If you are exploring the area, the group of old houses in the centre of **Preston** is worth finding, as is the unspoilt and splendid mercat cross. On the edge of the sea, **Preston Grange** – part of the Scottish Mining Museum – is the bleak site of a former colliery with relics for industrial archaeology enthusiasts, notably a Cornish beam engine and a number of viciously toothed coal-cutting machines from different periods. A neat visitor centre, helpful custodians and a small collection of railway locomotives and cranes add interest.

Musselburgh

The Edinburgh bypass has removed the traffic which used to plague this old town at the mouth of the River Esk. The bridge which crosses the river is sixteenth-century, as is the tolbooth. Both are attractive. The extensive buildings of Loretto school stand on the grounds of an old pilgrim chapel. Pinkie House, part of the school, and open to the public on Tuesdays (2 to 4) during term-time, has fine plaster ceilings from the seventeenth century. South of the town, on the low Carberry Hill, Mary Queen of Scots and Bothwell drew up an army against the lords who had taken arms against her. Her troops melting away, Mary put herself into the hands of her opponents, who promptly whipped her off to Loch Leven and forced her to abdicate.

SOUTH OF EDINBURGH

For the visitor, the district of Midlothian is best described as good in parts. There is a lot of urban sprawl left from the days when the Midlothian coalfield was thriving. Now, places like Newtongrange and Penicuik have become dormitory towns for Edinburgh. However, hidden away in the valley between the Pentland Hills and the Moorfoot Hills, at the headwaters of the North Esk, South Esk and Tyne Rivers, there are stretches of attractive country, old houses and castles, and a few sights it would be a shame to miss.

On the A7 Galashiels road, **Newtongrange** is home to the

Lady Victoria Colliery, once the showpiece pit of the area and now part of the **Scottish Mining Museum** (open Apr to end Sept, daily 11 to 4). Only some of the actual colliery buildings are accessible but the museum is still worth finding, for it contains probably the best steam engine in Scotland – an enormous winding engine, gaily painted and still in full working order. There is also a very well put together display about the conditions of a miner's life, using voice-overs and models.

To the west, best reached from the A6094 or A703, is **Rosslyn Chapel** (open Apr to end Oct, Mon to Sat 10 to 5, Sun 12 to 4.45). Confusingly, the village is spelt Roslin. The chapel lies down a small track below it, and, for such a famous building, looks curiously neglected and ordinary from the outside. This impression is rapidly dispelled inside, for nowhere else in the country will you be confronted with such a superabundance of stone carving. Every surface which has lent itself to ornamentation has been covered in foliage, flowers, human figures and animals. Reactions vary, and many people find the chapel too over-decorated to be beautiful. The star piece of carving is the Apprentice Pillar, an even more elaborately encrusted piece of work than the rest, with its own (probably apocryphal) legend of the apprentice who carved it being murdered by the jealous master mason.

The chapel is fifteenth-century, though its style is early Gothic, and the aisle vaulting is very peculiar. It was the creation of William St Clair, who lived in Rosslyn Castle, and seems to have felt that founding a luxurious collegiate church was a suitable spiritual compensation for his sumptuous baronial life. After his death the project fell into abeyance, with only the choir complete.

It is well worth the hundred yards' stroll from the chapel to have a peek at **Rosslyn Castle**. A large notice by the gatehouse says 'Private' but the castle is surrounded by a country park, so you can gaze at its exterior. Its ruins are poised on a crag by the brink of Roslin Glen, where the ground drops sheer to the River Esk beneath. The crag can be reached only across a bridge; the ruins of the keep stand beyond, as does the intact sixteenth-century north range.

If you have come across Edinburgh Crystal glassware in the shops, the town of **Penicuik**, just south-west of Roslin, is the place to see it being manufactured. Guided tours run roughly every 15 minutes between 9 and 3.30 (Mon to Sat) from the visitor centre just off the A701 (children are discouraged for safety reasons). A walkway on the track of an old railway runs all the way from Penicuik to Bonnyrigg, passing through the remains of old industries and with some good woodland scenery along the way.

Crichton Castle

(HS, standard times; closed Oct to Mar)
This castle is a surprise. It is not until you actually arrive underneath its walls after walking along a short track that you realise that not a trace of modern development is visible. The ruin sits on a sharp promontory above a haugh (flat piece of land beside a river) where the River Tyne meanders between trees – a landscape which is easy to imagine unchanged for centuries. It inspired both Turner and Scott (in *Marmion*), and it was largely thanks to the interest they stimulated that the castle was preserved.

From the outside, the castle appears at first glance to be another of those uncompromising and probably uncomfortable Scottish fortresses, riddled with gun-loops. However, once in the courtyard, you are confronted with a façade which seems to have come straight from the Italian Renaissance. An arcade is crowned by a wall studded with diamond facets, looking like nothing so much as a huge bar of pale chocolate, while at one end there was once a balcony, worthy of Romeo and Juliet, overhanging the courtyard. A proper Renaissance staircase, with treads, risers and the remains of carved embellishments, leads upwards to what were once grand rooms lit by large windows.

This is the work of Francis Stuart, fifth Earl of Bothwell (nephew to Mary Queen of Scots' second husband), who had spent much of his life in Spain and Italy. Although he had his King to dinner in March 1586, he was too unstable a character to last long under the canny James VI – there was the affair of the North Berwick witches for a start (page 171). Eventually he fled abroad and never came back.

A path runs between Crichton and **Borthwick Castle**, two miles distant. Borthwick is a very tall (eight floors) fifteenth-century tower, with twin keeps, and is one of the best-preserved medieval castles in Scotland. It was to Borthwick that Mary Queen of Scots and Bothwell came shortly after their marriage. Now it is an hotel, but even if it is beyond your pocket to stay here the exterior is still well worth seeing.

THE PENTLAND HILLS

No peak in the Pentlands reaches 2000 feet, yet this small range of hills stretching away south-west of Edinburgh has some good wild country in an area which is in dire need of it. For the visitor, the Pentlands are hills where it is possible to walk to the heart's content without having to worry too much about precipices or getting lost on a trackless plateau. The hills are, however, wet and steep in places, so be prepared for adverse conditions. The closer to the Edinburgh end of the Pentlands you are the more fellow-humans you are likely to find, especially at weekends, but here are also the most shapely hills and the most scenic stretches of water. Some possible expeditions are described below.

Reached from the A702

• **Hillend Ski Centre** (open Mon to Sat 9.30 to 9, Sun 9.30 to 7) This used to be Britain's longest dry ski slope. If you enjoy skiing on upturned toothbrushes, the extensive network provides everything you need. Alternatively you could wait until winter and head for Aviemore. Non-skiers may find the chair-lift here a useful way of getting up into the Pentlands without effort.

• **Glencorse Reservoir** lies in a dog-legged valley under Turnhouse Hill, and the track up to it and beyond up the Logan Burn is probably the most popular walk in the area. This part of the Pentlands has been designated a Regional Park. It was on the southern slope of Turnhouse Hill that the battle of Rullion Green was fought in 1666. A pathetic army of probably fewer than a thousand Covenanters, mostly from the south-west, was defeated by General Tam Dalyell. Most of the prisoners were either executed or transported to the plantations of the West Indies (a favourite method of getting rid of stubborn religious dissenters).

Reached from the A70

• **Malleny Gardens, Balerno** (open daily 10 to sunset) Where the posh Edinburgh suburb of Balerno laps against the end of the Pentland Hills, these gardens surrounding a seventeenth-century house (private) hold an admirable collection of shrub roses. The garden is quite formally laid out, though there is a short woodland walk, and is well worth visiting if you are a rose enthusiast.

- **Threipmuir Reservoir** An extensive reservoir with plenty of bird-life in its thick reed-beds. Up the hill behind, paths lead in towards the waterfalls at the head of Logan Burn.
- **Cauld Stane Slap** The old drove road across the hills from the Harperrig Reservoir passes between the East and West Cairn Hills, through the slap (break in hills) to West Linton. This makes an excellent half-day's walk, though coordinating transport to and from either end can be difficult. Robert Louis Stevenson's *Weir of Hermiston* is the novel to take with you.

THE CENTRAL BELT

Between Edinburgh and Glasgow stretches a great Lowland valley of sour land, scarred by pit workings and dotted with mining towns and villages. Nor do the areas's new towns – Cumbernauld and Livingston – contribute much joy. Neither of them has a single modern building worth a detour to see.

Yet this is not the whole picture. There was life here before the Industrial Revolution – great houses by the Forth, prehistoric sites in the depth of the Bathgate Hills, the royal palace at Linlithgow and the cattle trysts of Falkirk. There are patches of fine country on the edge of the bleak mosses, or in the Bathgate Hills, which are all the more beautiful for being so unexpected. Finally, there are heartening signs of life, perhaps stimulated by the energetic resurgence of Glasgow, where communities have seized upon their past as an incentive to look forward, and are busy creating museums, dredging canals, bringing mines or railways back to life or constructing country parks.

Hopetoun House

(Open Easter to early Oct, daily 10 to 5.30)
This huge stately home is an amalgam of the work of Scotland's greatest architects. It was begun by William Bruce in 1699, extended and altered by William Adam in 1721, and finished off by his sons, the whole edifice not being completed until 1767. Bruce's interior work remains intact in several rooms, and it is interesting to compare his warm, homely style with the magnificent formality of the Adam state rooms. The most striking feature of Hopetoun is the pine-panelled front staircase, with intricate carvings, modern mural paintings (though you would never guess) and the recently uncovered and restored painted cupola where anxious

cherubs support a cracked globe – *At spes non fracta* is the Hope motto.

The Adam state apartments are on the stiff side, with an abundance of gilded stucco and rococo furniture, making an interesting comparison with some of the family's more relaxed interiors such as those at Mellerstain (page 62). Paintings abound, notably a specially commissioned series by Tideman, and there are portraits by Raeburn, Ramsay and Gainsborough.

Hopetoun's carefully landscaped grounds overlook the Forth Bridges, and are seen at their extensive best from the rooftop viewing platform of the house. Events at Hopetoun range from balls to antique fairs, but nothing is likely to come up to the splendour of George IV's visit here in 1822, when the portly monarch lunched on turtle soup and three glasses of wine. Four-horned St Kilda sheep inhabit the grounds along with red and fallow deer.

House of the Binns

(NTS, May to end Sept, Sat to Thurs 2 to 5; parkland all year, daily 10 to 7)

This is the next stately home westward along the banks of the Forth, and the contrast with Hopetoun could hardly be greater. The house is early seventeenth-century, and has gone firmly down the neo-Gothic road, helped by nineteenth-century embellishments. The guided tour is inclined to be slow but is worth enduring for the sake of the plasterwork in particular, and for the tall tales of General Tam Dalyell, the house's most notorious owner.

General Tam, nicknamed 'The Bluidy Muscovite', entered Covenanting demonology as one of their most dedicated enemies. A committed royalist who had fought with Charles II at Worcester, escaped from the tower of London and served the Tsar in Russia, he was recalled at the Restoration and was instrumental in the defeat of the Covenanting army at Rullion Green (1666) in the Pentland Hills. The General's prowess against the godly was logically attributed to his alliance with satanic power, and in the entrance hall of the Binns you can see the magnificent table which the Devil hurled into a nearby pond after losing to Tam at cards. It remained there for 200 years. You leave the Binns with tales of flagellation parties and of Tam's waist-length beard (he refused to shave in protest at the execution of Charles I). He also raised that most famous of Scottish Cavalry regiments, the Scots Greys.

Blackness Castle

(HS, standard times; closed Thurs pm and Fri in winter)
From a distance Blackness looks just like a small coaster
stranded on the rocks, and this impression is heightened
when you walk round the parapet to the sharpened 'prow'
of the walls, with the halyards of the flagstaff flapping in the
wind, the waves crashing on the shore directly beneath, and
the Firth of Forth stretching away in both directions.

The shape of Blackness was determined by the rocky spit on
which it was built in the fifteenth century. It started by acting
as guardian for the harbour which served as Linlithgow's
outlet to the sea, became a state prison for those out of favour
with the king, and ended as an ammunition store. A secret
passage is said to have linked it to the House of the Binns.

From the point of view of military history, Blackness is
a fascinating example of a fortification where the response
to the invention of siege artillery was simply to thicken the
walls and to go on thickening them until in places they became
a solid mass of stonework pierced by chambers for gunners.
The transformation of Blackness into this bulwark took place
between 1532 and 1567. In any event, the castle's fortifications
did not prove strong enough to resist Cromwell, whose siege
of 1650 did much damage (now repaired).

Bo'ness

Bo'ness is an old port on the shores of the Forth which has
seen better days but is now determinedly capitalising on its
past. A restored miner's cottage and a reawakened steam
railway are among the first stirrings of life. More unusual
is the nearby **Birkhill Clay Mine** (open Apr to Oct, Sat,
Sun 12 to 4; July and Aug, Mon to Sat 11.30 to 4, Sun 2.30
to 4) in the gorge of the Avon. You can travel direct on the
railway, reaching a tiny brown and white station beneath the
old mine buildings. These are still derelict, but the mine has
now been made safe enough for you to walk through the
old caverns where fire-clay was dug from the side of the
hill (it is a long stairway down to the mine entrance). The
firebricks produced from the mine were used as linings for
the locomotives and furnaces of the Industrial Revolution.

Nearby **Kinneil House** (HS, open Apr to Sept, Mon to Sat
9.30 to 5, Sun 11 to 5; Oct to Mar, Mon to Wed and Sat 9.30
to 4.20, Sun 12.30 to 3.30) has some ancient painted ceilings,
but its main claim to fame is that it was in an outhouse in the
grounds here that James Watt worked on his inventions.

A short way upstream from Bo'ness lies Grangemouth, Scotland's petro-chemical city, a mass of pipes, tanks and flares. From a distance its flames can create astonishing effects against the clouded Ochil Hills on the far side of the river.

Linlithgow

For a town which once ranked alongside Edinburgh and Stirling as the setting for a royal palace, time has not treated Linlithgow well. This is mostly the fault of the planners – of the Victorian era and of more modern times as well. Indeed, it would be hard to find a more crass ruination of an ancient burgh than that thrust upon Linlithgow in the late 1960s. The sawn-off, out-of-proportion monstrosities that break up the line of the old High Street can only make visitors shake their heads in baffled despair.

For all that, if you need a base in this area of the country, Linlithgow is the place to choose. It is free from the worst industrial scars and has managed to retain much of its gentle county-town atmosphere. The palace and St Michael's church on their mound above the town centre, the perfect loch-side setting (alas, the M9 motorway is too close to allow it to be called peaceful) and the remaining houses of the ancient royal burgh combine to make it an interesting town to explore, or even to relax in for a day or two. Bed-and-breakfasts provide the greatest choice of accommodation, and there are several in the pretty country round the River Avon outside town.

In and near Linlithgow

● **Linlithgow Palace** (HS, standard times; closes 6pm Apr to Sept) Windowless, roofless and weathering, the palace is still an outstanding *tour de force* of Scottish architecture over 200 years. Started by James I around 1425 and finished by James VI in 1624, the building silently demonstrates the level of luxury and functional magnificence which the Scottish kings expected of their palaces.

Standing in the central courtyard, in front of the elaborate fountain – said to be a wedding present from James V to Marie of Guise – you have James VI's plain and harmonious Renaissance façade in front of you, with James I's massive medieval hall in the range to your right, the state apartments of James IV to your left, and the English-style gallery of James V behind you. The cascades of reddish stone which make up the four frontages are vigorous and harmonious. Everything else inside the burnt-out shell, even the Great Hall, or the vaulting at the head of the stair to the royal apartments, is something of an anti-climax after the courtyard.

- **St Michael's Church** The curious spire which crowns the tower is not fifteenth-century like the rest of the church – it was lowered into position by helicopter in 1964. It is undeniably adventurous, but whether it is appropriate, or even elegant, is another matter. The window tracery – high Gothic, elaborate and yet simple – is the feature to admire inside the church, though some of the modern stained glass is worth a glance too. Spare a thought for James IV, who saw an apparition in the south transept which warned him of his doom at Flodden. Since he was too much the Renaissance man to pay heed, he went to war and died, leaving his Queen to wait in vain for his return in the topmost room of Linlithgow Palace (still known as Queen Margaret's bower).

- **Canal Museum** (open Easter to Sept, Sat and Sun 2 to 5) For canal enthusiasts, the museum has a good, if small, collection of memorabilia of the Union Canal. There are boat trips too along a reopened stretch of what was in 1822 the most comfortable means of travel between Edinburgh and Glasgow. Unfortunately the railway (1842) was just as comfortable, charged the same, and took two and a quarter hours instead of fourteen. Hence the museum.

- **Cairnpapple Hill** (HS, standard times; closed Oct to Mar) You hardly expect the low-slung Bathgate hills behind Linlithgow to produce the spectacular views they do. From this Bronze Age burial cairn you can gaze out over huge chunks of Lowland Scotland, bounded by the Ochil Hills and the Pentlands to north and south. Cairnpapple started as a Neolithic site and at one stage had a stone henge, but what is most visible today is the Bronze Age cairn (with modern roof). Descending a ladder out of the wind, you are confronted with the stones of the grave. The sepulchral voice from the shadowy corner turns out only to be Historic Scotland's tape-recorded commentary.

- **Torphichen Preceptory** (HS, standard times; closed Oct to Mar) The tall grey building rising above the houses of the small village on the B792 a few miles south of Linlithgow was once the headquarters in Scotland of the great monastic-military order, the Knights Hospitallers of the Order of St John of Jerusalem. What remains are the tower and two transepts of their church. Parts of it date from the twelfth century, but most is fourteenth- or fifteenth-century. The vaulting of the crossing and transepts is monumental,

181

and you can climb into the bell chamber above and look down on to the floor of the crossing. The rooms up here are used to tell you the history of the Order of St John, from its earliest beginnings down to its current role as the St John Ambulance Brigade (which is known in Scotland as St Andrew's Ambulance Association).

Falkirk

A fresh air of regeneration is blowing through Falkirk, evidenced by a new shopping precinct and the Marina Leisure Centre with its welcome swimming-pool. The **Falkirk Museum** (open Mon to Sat 10.30 to 1.30, 2.30 to 5) is not easily found but is well worth the effort of discovery, for there is interesting material here about local history from the Romans to the Carron ironworks, and the museum provides a good starting point for some do-it-yourself exploration.

Falkirk was the site of two major battles – first in 1298 when Wallace ran up against the English archers and lost, and later when Charles Edward Stuart's Highlanders attacked the Hanoverians and won. However, it is the Roman remains that most people visit Falkirk to explore, for the town stands on the line of the Antonine Wall which ran between the Forth and the Clyde and the most substantial remains of that fortification are in the area. It was built around AD 140, as a result of a decision to move the chief frontier defences forward from Hadrian's Wall. Unlike Hadrian's Wall, the Antonine Wall was constructed largely of turf, so there is a lot less of it left today. Nevertheless, at **Rough Castle** (HS, always open), signposted from Bonnybridge, west of Falkirk, there are the earthworks of a large fort and the remains of ditch and rampart in pleasantly wooded surroundings, while at **Callander Park** and at **Watling Lodge**, both in Falkirk, the old defensive ditch can be seen. Bits and pieces of the wall can be found all the way along its line as far as Bearsden near Glasgow, and trying to trace it among the clutter of modern development can provide an intriguing day's work.

Less easily traced are the remains of Falkirk's great days as a cattle fair for beasts from all over the Highlands. The driving of the black cattle south from the glens to the great Lowland trysts, where they were bought by dealers before continuing the journey towards England, is one of the little-known stories of Scotland. The practice began almost as soon as the frontier disappeared after the Union and continued for as long as cattle rather than sheep were raised in the hills. The drovers are gone, but their tracks across the hills remain, often used now by walkers.

Falkirk is the starting point for drives and walks into the Campsie Fells (page 273), and it is only a few minutes' drive from Stirling (page 265).

The Pineapple

(NTS, grounds open all year, 10 to sunset)
This is Scotland's most eccentric folly. It is a mile north-west of Airth on the A905. The Pineapple was in fact once a garden retreat on the Dunmore estate – a retreat in the shape of a 45-foot-tall stone pineapple, with a little domed room right at the top of the fruit, under the leaves. Each leaf is composed of cantilevered blocks of masonry which spring away from the dome with a realistic degree of spikiness. Built in 1761 by an unknown architect, the Pineapple is a reminder of the fact that eighteenth-century gentry expected exotic fruit along with their cabbages.

If you fancy a holiday inside the fruit, contact the Landmark Trust (0628 825925), which leases the building from the National Trust for Scotland – but be prepared to book two years in advance for peak times.

THE CLYDE VALLEY

The Clyde is probably the most celebrated of Scotland's rivers, though its popular image as a waterway surrounded by a hubbub of heavy industry is now outmoded. The industries are dead or dying and though weekend excursions for Glaswegians 'doon the watter' to the resorts of the Clyde estuary still linger these are well past their heyday. Increasingly, the Clyde in its lower reaches is becoming a recreational asset: walkways or country parks line its banks, and all is (nearly) tranquillity where once the night sky was lit by the glow of blast furnaces. The Clyde, especially in its upper reaches above Hamilton, is a beautiful river, and well worth a leisurely day's journey through its various sights.

If you have reason to go straight to Glasgow from Carlisle, the A74 (soon to be replaced by the M74) heads straight across the moors, past **Douglas**, the stronghold of the 'Black' branch of that remarkable family from the time of Robert the Bruce, but without much to see now except for **St Bride's Church**, where the tombs and effigies of such characters as 'Good

Sir James' (who was chosen to carry Bruce's heart to the Holy Land) and Archibald 'Bell-the-Cat' (who hanged the favourites of James III from a bridge in Lauder (page 58) are laid out as a kind of exhibition of the great and the grim.

Douglas Castle itself was a victim of a common form of destruction in this area – the opening up of a coal seam beneath ancient buildings and their consequent subsidence.

If you are in no hurry to reach Glasgow, take the A702 at Abington and follow the Clyde.

Biggar

This used to be a quiet agricultural town with a wide, tree-lined high street but without any great claim to fame, except that Wallace once crossed Cadger's Brig here while in disguise. In recent years, however, Biggar seems to have suffered a rush of blood to the head and has started spawning museums and a whole industry of leaflets, commemorative pencils and T-shirts to go with them (you can even find Biggar's motto – *London's London but Biggar's Biggar* – translated into Latin on the latter). They are exceptionally fine small museums, too, especially good for curious children but worth a day of anyone's time. Between them they will send you away thinking that Biggar is one of the most interesting places in Scotland (a huge compliment to the Biggar Museum Trust which runs three of them, plus the John Buchan Centre in nearby Broughton – page 49).

Gladstone Court (open Easter to end Oct, Mon to Sat 10 to 5, Sun 2 to 5), the oldest of the museums, is the result of one man's inability to leave anything from a demolished building unsalvaged. Here you can find Biggar's old manual telephone exchange with rows of jack plugs on wires and the nineteenth-century bank with its high wooden counter and air of Scottish financial integrity, together with the lovingly reconstructed interiors of many other shops and offices.

Moat Park Heritage Centre (open Easter to end Oct, Mon to Sat 10 to 5, Sun 2 to 5; winter by arrangement only), in an old church a few minutes away from Gladstone Court, is one of the best local museums in Scotland, with plenty of scale models and highly literate explanations. Imaginative touches abound – the geological section is fronted by poems from Hugh McDiarmid, while the Roman legionary in his glass case is far from being a sanitised model: he is covered in blood and carries the gory head of a vanquished tribesman.

Greenhill (open daily 2 to 5), in a small green dell below the town (near a good playground), is a rebuilt seventeenth-century farmhouse from the nearby countryside, turned into a Covenanting Museum. Relics are few, but the explanations of the conventicles and the persecutions of the Killing Time are as good as is possible with such a confusing period. Among the furniture, there is a fine old press bed (a bed in a cupboard).

Finally, there is **Biggar Gas Works** (HS, open end May to end Sept, daily 2 to 5) – a completely contrasting piece of history, dating from the time when many small towns like Biggar had their own local gas plant. Sheds contain various ovens and retorts, together with the machinery to ensure a good supply of light and heat to the town. All that is missing is the smell.

To complete the town's effervescent self-confidence, there is a small puppet theatre of renown which you can look round (Mon to Sat 10 to 5, Sun 1 to 5) even if there is no show on.

West of Biggar, the isolated bulk of Tinto Hill rises above the Clyde. Climbing it is easy, and the views from the top take in much of southern Scotland.

Lanark and New Lanark

This market town perched above the Clyde is a great deal older than it looks – it was made a royal burgh as early as 1140. It is famous as the place where Wallace first committed himself to open rebellion against the English by attacking the local garrison. The statue of the great man at the end of the High Street must be Scotland's most idiosyncratic: Wallace is adorned with a great woolly beard, which makes him look more like a genial pantomime character than a resistance hero. A few arches remain of the church where Wallace may have been married, but otherwise there is not much left of Lanark's past.

On the very banks of the Clyde at the bottom of a steep gorge behind Lanark lies **New Lanark** (open daily 11 to 5; closed Christmas and New Year), Scotland's most important memorial to the Industrial Revolution. It is nominated as a World Heritage Site and attracts more than 120,000 visitors a year, making it difficult to believe that the elegant eighteenth-century spinning mills and the village surrounding them were almost lost for good – only last-minute efforts in 1975 saved the virtually derelict buildings from the bulldozers.

New Lanark holds a unique place in social history, for this is the spot where Robert Owen, the son-in-law of the founder of the cotton mills, David Dale, put into action the unfashionable principle that the welfare of an industrial workforce was of fundamental importance to commercial success. Between 1814 and 1824 New Lanark became the scene of a pioneering social experiment. Education lay at the heart of this: no child under 10 was allowed to work in the mills (a revolutionary forgoing of labour), while in the company's school both punishment and reward were banned, and singing and dancing were taught to all. A sick fund, a co-operative village shop and the introduction of adult education classes were also part of 'Owenism'. Robert Owen's ideas were of great influence, not only on what we might now call benevolent capitalism, but on co-operative movements and on trade unionism.

New Lanark is also worth seeing for the beauty of its setting and for the fascination of its architecture. The Clyde, which flows under the walls of the grey stone mills, was the only river in central Scotland powerful enough to turn the water wheels from which thousands of cotton bobbins were powered. The three mills that remain were built between 1789 and 1826 with strong Palladian overtones, forcefully proving the point that industrial architecture does not have to be ugly. Around them cluster the other buildings of the community – the workers' housing mostly built by David Dale in the last years of the eighteenth century, Robert Owen's rounded Counting House, the classical-style Institute for the Formation of Character, and the impressively large School for Children. Most of the housing has been fully restored and is now privately owned or rented out by the New Lanark Conservation Trust, but you can look round one or two of the old tenement flats as well as the Institute and the industrial buildings.

Because so much effort has had to go into the preservation of the buildings, New Lanark is some way behind other industrial museums in terms of working machinery or other exhibits, but a good start is being made in bringing back some equipment – a steam engine and a spinning mule are being set up. On the floor of one of the mills a theme-park-style ride carries you gently through New Lanark's history, guided by the spirit of one of the children who worked and played and learned as part of Robert Owen's remarkable experiment. There are also several craft workshops, a shop and a café.

Falls of Clyde

Immediately above New Lanark, the Falls of Clyde Nature Reserve stretches along the bank. After about half a mile's slightly muddy walk upstream, you reach **Corra Linn**, the most famous and the best of the three falls where the Clyde plunges into its gorge. Corra Linn has lost much of its muscle to hydro-electricity since the days when it was a port of call for every landscape-lover in the district, but the situation, where the river tumbles into a huge rock cauldron, is still impressive enough to be worth the walk. If you are there during a spate, or on one of the days when the flow of water is fully restored (call Scottish Power on 041-637 7177), the waterfall is magnificent.

Lanark to Hamilton

Below Lanark, almost as far as Glasgow, the Clyde is sunk in a deep valley, well sheltered from the winds that blast the barren moors above it. As you descend from the bogs round Forth or Carluke into the micro-climate of the valley, trees grow without being wind-shorn, fruit is on sale at the roadside, and rows of glasshouses grow chrysanthemums, pot plants and bedding plants to be sold in the many garden centres. The Clyde's tributaries here are also pretty – the Nethan is good for aimless pottering, while more strenuous efforts need to be made to trace the Mouse Water through its narrow gorge. The valley of the Avon is the most accessible, running as it does through Chatelherault Country Park.

Craignethan Castle

(HS, standard times; closed all winter)
Two miles west of Crossford, this fifteenth-century castle is well preserved and under-visited. The approach road across a desolate, scrub-covered land suddenly reveals the ruins on their high spur above the Nethan. Enthusiasts of military architecture go to see its *caponier* – a dank, vaulted chamber built across the moat to help defend the place against artillery – but the ruins are worth a stop if you are at all fond of castles, or of Walter Scott, for Craignethan features in *Old Mortality* in the guise of Tillietudlem.

Chatelherault Country Park

(Open daily to sunset; visitor centre Apr to Aug, daily 10.30 to 5; Sept to Mar 10.30 to 4.30; closed Christmas and New Year)
This French-style name in the middle of the Clyde landscape

goes back to the time of Mary Queen of Scots' childhood, when the French title of Duke of Chatelherault was given to James Hamilton, second Earl of Arran, partly to make up for losing the regency to Mary of Guise, the young Queen's mother. The Hamiltons were heavily involved in the confused civil struggle following Mary's flight to England, and were eventually defeated. In a later century, the exploitation of the rich coal seams of this area brought huge prosperity to the Dukes of Hamilton, though the effect on the landscape was less pleasing.

The **Chatelherault Hunting Lodge** (open Apr to Aug, daily 11 to 4.30; Sept to Mar, daily 11 to 3.45), which stands in the middle of what is now the country park, is a William Adam building dating from 1740. Two pavilions flank an expanse of curtain wall in Adam's usual harmonious symmetry. Its recent restoration from a state of near-total dereliction has been a remarkable success; only the curious lean of the building remains to show the dire effect that coal extraction had on the structure. The lodge is not large, but the magnificence of the various rooms leaves you in no doubt that splendour is more important than size. Much of the plasterwork that adorns walls and ceilings has had to be re-created from photographs and the few fragments left by vandals, fire and weather, while the urns and finials on the roof are also modern copies of the missing originals. Even the formal garden behind one of the pavilions has been lovingly put back. A visitor centre built in the kennel yard, where the dukes' hounds once jostled, gives you some idea of how the lodge was built and how it was restored.

Elsewhere in the park, you come across the remains of old Cadzow Castle, the Cadzow herd of wild white cattle, and the memorial monument to the eleventh Duke. A fitting climax to the tour of the remnants of Hamilton grandeur is a visit to the nearby mausoleum (tours June to Aug, daily at 3 and 7; Easter to June at 3; Sept to Easter, Sat and Sun at 2). Its curious acoustics have given it the longest echo in Europe, and so have prevented it from ever being used as a chapel.

Hamilton to Bothwell

Near Hamilton the landscape changes abruptly from rural to urban as the Clyde passes beside the towns which were once the centre of Scotland's coal, iron and steel industry. The sprawl of towns like Motherwell and Wishaw may not look very inviting, but there are one or two places worth knowing about – notably, for a wet day, the modern Aquatec Leisure Centre (0698 276464) at **Motherwell** with its tropical swimming-pool and adjacent ice-rink. At **Blantyre**, the David Livingstone Centre (open early Mar to early Nov, Mon to Sat 10 to 6, Sun 2 to 6) is worth visiting not only for an insight into the explorer's life but also for a look at the cramped tenement where he was brought up. Through imaginative use of pictures and exhibits, the African Pavilion takes you into the continent which Livingstone explored.

Where the A74 crosses the Clyde below Hamilton is the site of the battle at Bothwell Brig, where the Covenanters were routed by the Duke of Monmouth in 1679. This was more or less the final convulsion of the Covenanting movement – an unequal battle between a government determined to impose at least some kind of order on religious affairs in Scotland and an army whose fervency was almost their only weapon, but which was fatally riven by sectarian debate. Walter Scott gives a clear, if cynical, picture of the battle in *Old Mortality*.

Bothwell Castle

(HS, standard times; closed Thurs pm and Fri in winter)
This red sandstone ruin in its pleasant park above the Clyde was once one of the most strategically important strongholds in Scotland, and a crucial point in the Wars of Independence. Its most notable feature is the ruined *donjon*, a great circular tower of enormous strength, which may have been almost all that existed of the castle in the thirteenth century. Held at first by the English after the ill-fated resurgence of courage on the part of 'Toom Tabard' John Balliol, then taken by the Scots in 1290, the castle became the object of an expert piece of siege warfare when Edward I of England came hastening to take his revenge in 1301. He commissioned an enormous siege tower as high as the parapet and this monstrous machine forced the surrender of the castle in less than a month.

After changing hands several more times until 1377 the castle had a relatively peaceful existence before being largely cannibalised for a new mansion, demolished (subsidence again) in 1926. Not surprisingly, the ruins are complicated to sort out, but the remains of the massive *donjon* with its first-class masonry are unbeatable. A small heap of round stones – precursors of cannon balls – salvaged during excavation bear witness to the various sieges in the castle's history.

PAISLEY/THE CLYDESIDE TOWNS

Paisley

For many people, Paisley means the curious swollen comma shape used to decorate shawls, dressing-gowns and now duvet covers. The pattern in fact came from Kashmir, but Paisley rapidly gained a monopoly of it. The place to learn everything there is to know about it is the **Paisley Museum and Art Gallery** (open Mon to Sat 10 to 5), where there is an exhibition of about 500 different shawls. You should also come to Paisley

---

USEFUL DIRECTORY

Main tourist offices
East Lothian Tourist Board
Granada Services, A1
Old Craighall, by Musselburgh
East Lothian EH21 8RE
031-653 6172

Mid Lothian Tourism
1 Whiteheart Street, Dalkeith
Mid Lothian EH22 1AE
031-663 2083

Linlithgow Tourist Board
Burgh Hall, The Cross
Linlithgow, West Lothian EH49 7EJ
(0506) 844600

Clyde Valley Tourist Board
Horsemarket, Ladyacre Road
Lanark, Lanarkshire ML11 7LQ
(0555) 662544/665709

Greater Glasgow Tourist Board
35–39 St Vincent Place
Glasgow G1 2ER
041-204 4400

Tourist board publications: useful booklets for practical listings include the annual *Greater Glasgow Quick Guide* and the *Clyde Valley Handbook*. All the above boards publish accommodation listings and a variety of special interest leaflets (including golf and fishing).

---

for the sake of its abbey, a twelfth-century foundation, rebuilt in the fourteenth and fifteenth centuries and subjected to the usual neglect at the time of the Reformation. Restoration was begun in 1897, and, thanks to Sir Robert Lorimer, has resulted in a very beautiful church (do not be put off by the bland exterior). Keep an eye open for the very rare twelfth-century panels showing scenes from the life of St Mirren.

Paisley seems to be almost swamped with churches, for the town's weavers participated enthusiastically in all the various

---

Local tourist information centres
Abington (08642) 436
Biggar (0899) 21066 (Apr to Oct)
Bo'ness (0506) 826626 (Apr to Sept)
Dalkeith 031-663 2083
Dunbar (0368) 863353
Falkirk (0324) 620244
Hamilton (0698) 285590
Lanark (0555) 661661
Linlithgow (0506) 844600
Motherwell (0698) 373989
North Berwick (0620) 2197
Old Craig Hall, nr Musselburgh 031-653 6172
Penicuik (0968) 672340

Local transport
Edinburgh Airport Information Desk 031-344 3212
Glasgow Airport Information desk 041-887 1111
Scotrail Information, Edinburgh 031-556 2451
Scotrail Information, Glasgow 041-204 2844
A large number of bus companies serve this area; route information and timetables are available from all the tourist offices listed above.

Ferries
Gourock–Dunoon (Caledonian MacBrayne) 0475 650100; (Western Ferries) 041-332 9766
Gourock–Kilchreggan–Helensburgh (Clyde Marine Motoring Co Ltd) 0475 721281
Wemyss Bay–Rothesay (Caledonian MacBrayne) (0475) 650100

---

secessions and schisms of the Scottish Kirk. Many are now vacant or put to other uses, but a quick count will prove the depth of religious feeling that once existed here. Paisley is a pleasing industrial town, once important in the manufacture of cotton thread. The weaving industry, which thread-making replaced, is recalled at the small Weaver's Cottage at **Kilbarchan**, west of Paisley, where there are relics, a loom and weaving demonstrations (NTS, open early Apr to May and early Sept to Oct, Tues, Thurs, Sat and Sun 1 to 5; June to Aug, daily 1 to 5).

The Clyde coast

West of Glasgow, on the southern bank of the Clyde, a succession of bleak industrial towns lie squeezed between the river and the steepening moorland behind them (much of this is now a Regional Park, with visitor centres, nature reserves, views and walks). The things to see here are limited in number but provide a happy variety, and a trip down here will be worth the effort.

At **Finlaystone House** (grounds open all year, daily 10.30 to 5; house Apr to Aug, Sun 2.30 to 4), west of Langbank, the garden should please most visitors with its imaginative design and its series of garden 'rooms'. The house (when open) is worth visiting to see the collection of dolls. John Knox may well have held the first reformed communion in Scotland in the grounds, and a yew tree commemorates him. There is also a Burns signature – scratched on a window, as usual. At **Port Glasgow**, an otherwise unlovely town, the sixteenth-century Newark Castle (HS, standard times, closed all winter) is an elegant building, fairly intact, though its setting is now ugly. **Greenock** is the birthplace of James Watt, and you can find some relics in the McLean Museum and Art Gallery (open Mon to Sat 10 to 12, 1 to 5) as well as a small collection of paintings by James Guthrie and others. On a hill behind Greenock stands a memorial to the Free French of World War II from which the views are wonderful. **Gourock** is a resort rather than an industrial town, and the place to catch ferries heading across the Clyde for Dunoon on the Cowal Peninsula, Kilchreggan and Helensburgh. Round the corner of the coast, and heading south, you will come to **Wemyss Bay**, the ferry port for Bute, and the site of a beautiful station.

WHERE TO STAY

GIFFORD

Forbes Lodge £
Gifford, East Lothian EH41 4JE *(062 081) 212*

A tranquil Wolsey Lodge tucked away in beautiful gardens beside a small river. Inside, the house is a mix of elegance and informality: family portraits line the walls and there is a cosy drawing-room and library. The bedrooms, some with bathroom, are spacious and comfortable with interesting features. Dinners, by arrangement only, are good value.

Open: all year, exc Xmas Day and Boxing Day **Rooms**: 3
Credit/charge cards: none accepted

GULLANE

Greywalls £££
Muirfield, Gullane
East Lothian EH31 2EG *(0620) 842144*

A beautiful, rambling Lutyens house which offers quiet good taste and views over Muirfield championship golf course. Bedrooms in the main house are decorated with colourful birds, trees and flowers; those in the new wing feel more functional. The cooking is modern and unfussy, with hearty breakfasts. There is a library, and the gardens are sheltered from sea breezes.

Open: all year, exc Nov to Mar **Rooms**: 18, plus lodge (4 rooms) and 3 gatehouses **Facilities**: tennis, croquet
Credit/charge cards: Access, Amex, Diners, Visa

UPHALL

Houston House ££
Uphall, West Lothian EH5 6JS *(0506) 853831*

This elegant old house with its peaceful gardens has survived untouched on the fringes of Livingston. Bathrooms have had to be squeezed into the older bedrooms, which are on the dark side but nicer than the somewhat soulless rooms in the old steading. There is a formal dining-room serving ambitious food, and a lively cocktail bar, though nowhere really comfortable to relax.

Open: all year **Rooms**: 30
Credit/charge cards: Access, Amex, Diners, Visa

WHERE TO EAT

BIGGAR

Shieldhill Hotel
Quothquan, Biggar
ML12 6NA   *Tel (0899) 20035*

The menu changes daily, with four choices at each course. The food is usually cooked from Scottish produce and you can expect ambition and adventure to have gone into the dishes. Reservations are required.

Open: daily 7 to 9, Fri to Sun 12 to 2
Credit/charge cards: Access, Amex, Diners, Visa

GULLANE

La Potinière
Main Street
Gullane EH31 2AA   *Tel (0620) 843214*

To mark the quality of Hilary Brown's cooking, La Potinière was named 'County Restaurant of the Year' by *The Good Food Guide 1994*; the restaurant also has an outstanding wine cellar.

Open: Sun to Tues and Thurs lunch at 1; Fri, Sat lunch at 1 and dinner at 8; closed Oct, 1 week in June **Credit/charge cards**: none accepted

HADDINGTON

Browns Hotel
1 West Road
Haddington EH1 3RD   *Tel (062 082) 2254*

Browns have a policy of serving all diners at the same time, which some can find restricting. However, the atmosphere is congenial and the food, by using only the best produce, a success.

Open: 7.30 for 8 (dinner); Sun lunch 12.30 for 1
Credit/charge cards: Access, Amex, Diners, Visa

LANARK

East India Company
32 Wellgate
Lanark ML11 6DT *Tel (0555) 663827*

The East India Company is a simple but pleasantly decorated Indian restaurant that specialises mainly in North Indian cooking.

Open: daily 12 to 2, 5 to 11.30 **Credit/charge cards**: Access, Amex, Visa

LINLITHGOW

Champany Inn
Linlithgow EH49 7LU *Tel (050 683) 4532/4388*

The luxurious Champany Inn has been awarded a symbol for an outstanding wine cellar by *The Good Food Guide 1994*. You can expect to choose your steak raw, pick your own lobster or crayfish and select from a salad bar or cheese table. Housed in the same building, the Champany Inn Chop and Ale House offers simpler food in plainer surroundings.

Open: Mon to Fri 12.30 to 2, Mon to Sat 7 to 10; closed 1 week from Dec 24 **Credit/charge cards**: Access, Amex, Diners, Visa

NORTH BERWICK

Harding's
2 Station Road
North Berwick EH39 4AU *Tel (0620) 4737*

Harding's serves good food in neat surroundings in a building between a station and housing estate. The menu changes daily and is complemented by an above-average wine list, as noted by the wine glass symbol awarded by *The Good Food Guide 1994*. No smoking.

Open: Wed to Sat 10.30 to 11.45, 12.15 to 2, 7.30 to 9; closed 1 week in Oct, 3 weeks at Xmas **Credit/charge cards**: none accepted

GLASGOW

- Scotland's largest city, famous for its industrial past and for its resurrection as a modern cultural capital
- The home town of architect Charles Rennie Mackintosh, and the site of some magnificent nineteenth-century architecture too
- A city with some of the best museums and galleries in Britain

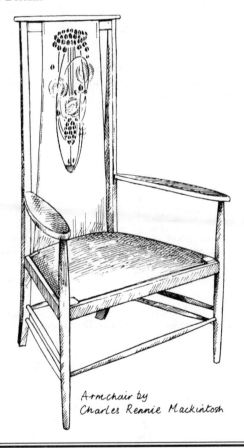

Armchair by
Charles Rennie Mackintosh

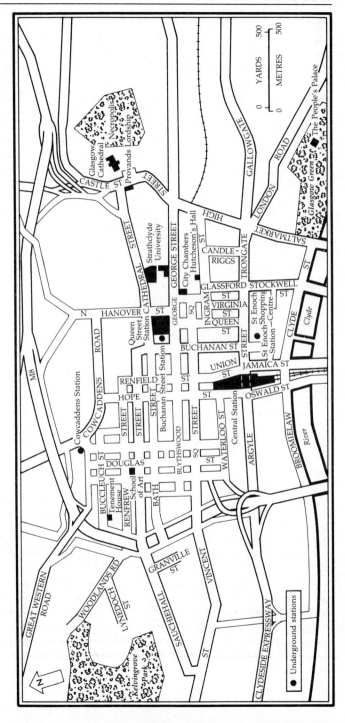

THE days are long gone when visitors to Scotland could ignore Glasgow. The city is now essential visiting, if only to discover what lies behind all the extensive hype with which it has been promoting itself to the outside world. Surprisingly enough, the transformation of Glasgow from decaying industrial dead-end to a spruced-up, revamped cultural and media capital is worthy of all the marketing razzmatazz, for it is extraordinary. It is all the more ironic that such a successful inner-city revival should have happened in this most traditionally fervent of Socialist cities, with money spent on high-profile marketing campaigns, festivals and large-scale prestige projects rather than on more traditional left-wing causes. The bewildering changes seem to have left many Glaswegians torn between pride in what has been achieved and a certain ruefulness at what they feel may be a betrayal of principle. One opinion is constant – Glasgow has done it by itself, and you will not be thanked for muttering about Thatcherite principles in action.

The signs of Glasgow's rebirth are all around. The extensive stone-cleaning programme has freed whole streets of Victorian buildings from black grime and left them basking in their warm sandstone. The rebuilding has studded the skyline with cranes, while street hoardings announce yet another mega-development. Urban renewal projects are gradually bringing life to the decaying East End, with buildings being dusted down or renovated and turned into offices or yet another arts centre. For an immediate entry into the new Glasgow, make straight for St Enoch shopping centre, where, under the largest glass roof in the whole of Europe, you can wander for hours, surrounded by greenery and Muzak, ignoring the grey drizzle outside.

Worries that the old Glasgow spirit has been smothered by glass and concrete seem to be unfounded. Take a 'refreshment' in one of the legion of pubs, go to the fitba', wander about the Barras or Paddy's Market and you will not have to look far for the raucous, humorous, argumentative and slightly inebriated Glasgow made famous by its comics from Harry Lauder to Billy Connolly.

Apart from the fun of exploring the city centre and trying to calculate how much money is being poured into it, Glasgow's greatest attractions are its capacity to provide entertainment and its nineteenth-century architecture. The galleries and museums are superb. The city is home to the Scottish Opera, the Scottish Ballet and the Royal Scottish

Orchestra, not to mention the renowned Citizens' Theatre and the BBC Scottish Symphony Orchestra, so opportunities for highbrow culture abound. However, you only have to be in Glasgow for the Mayfest – the trade-union-inspired festival which is now Britain's second biggest arts festival – to realise that it does not stop there. June/July has a mammoth jazz festival as well as a folk festival, and the world pipe band competitions take place in August. Glasgow's long love affair with popular theatre is far from dead – the Christmas pantomimes are a sell-out, and appearances by hypnotists, variety acts and comedians hugely popular. Try being among a Friday night audience for atmosphere. Even away from the theatres and concert halls, there is always something going on, right down to the round of folk evenings in the pubs, the flourishing nightclubs, or the pavement artists at work in Buchanan Street. The city bounces with energy – the reason why New Yorkers claim to feel more at home here than anywhere else in Britain.

As for Glaswegian architecture, it is the work of Charles Rennie Mackintosh (1868–1928) that people most want to see; his most accessible buildings are the School of Art, Willow Tea Rooms and nearby Hill House. The other great Glasgow architect, 'Greek' Thomson (1817–75), is less well known outside the city, but is being enthusiastically promoted.

Throughout the streets of the Merchant City, and westward from it, impressive, sometimes self-important, nineteenth-century warehouses and offices rear above the streets. Almost every style, from Palladian through Venetian to Egyptian, can be found, sometimes cleaned up and pristine, sometimes still covered in industrial grime.

Not everything about Glasgow is appealing. It is a big, sprawling, superficially ugly city, with great gaps in its centre where motorways, railways and slum clearance programmes have torn out chunks of the old town. It has suffered, especially in its outlying housing estates, from some of the worst planning mistakes of the 1960s, and is virtually split in half by expressways. The contrast with elegant, compact Edinburgh could hardly be greater. That contrast extends to the character of the two cities, and it is hardly surprising that each of them is subject to outrageous stereotyping – often propagated by the inhabitants of the other. Part of the enjoyment of visiting Glasgow and Edinburgh in sequence is to test whether their citizens really are warm-hearted, humorous, drunk and violent on the one hand or dignified, clean-living, stuck-up and offhand on the other.

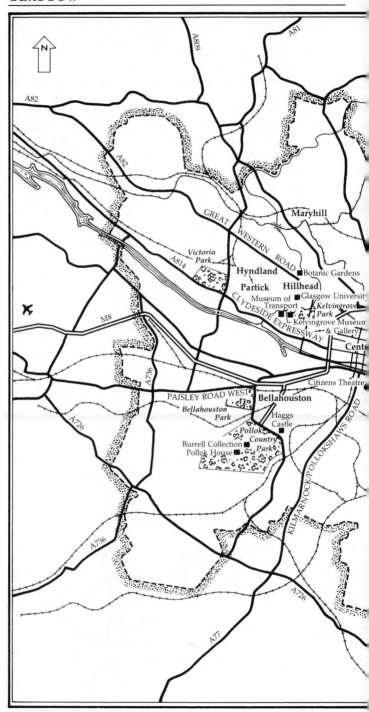

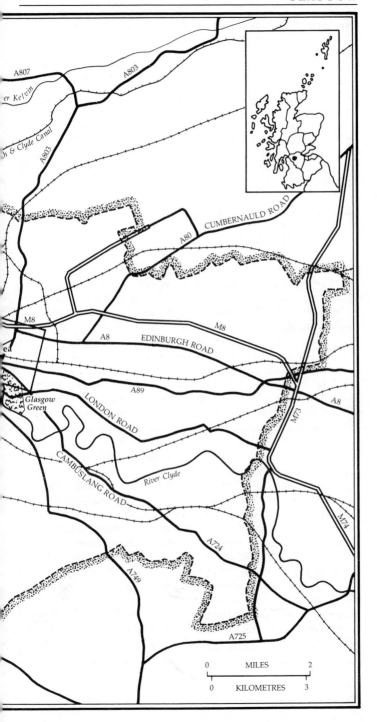

Second City of Empire

This was the name Glasgow adopted for itself in its manufacturing heyday. Since the union with England first opened up the opportunity to trade with America, Glasgow has been a city of merchants and industrialists. Tobacco brought the first wave of prosperity, followed by cotton, followed by engineering. Ship-building is probably Glasgow's most famous industry, but building locomotives for half the railways of the British Empire came only a short way behind. Heavy industry of every kind made Glasgow into a nineteenth-century boom town, and made it desperately vulnerable in the lean years of the twentieth.

Practical suggestions

In some respects, Glasgow has yet to catch up with itself in terms of providing infrastructure for visitors. The city is too big to see on foot, and the routes of the colourful horde of buses and the extensive suburban railway network can seem baffling at first. The circular subway – dubbed the Clockwork Orange because of the colour of its carriages – trundles round the periphery of the city centre, and is useful for sights on the western side of the city (but not the eastern). You can get a one-day unlimited-travel ticket called a Heritage Trail which comes with a booklet listing places of interest at each stop. City-centre parking is expensive and the traffic lights on the grid of streets are reputed to have the slowest changes in Europe. Travelling by taxi is certainly the quickest and liveliest way of getting around (Glaswegian taxi drivers are the chattiest, wittiest, kindest and perhaps the least comprehensible in Britain), but costs mount up. To solve travel problems, start at the **St Enoch Square Travel Centre** (open Mon to Sat 9.30 to 5.30). Inner city transport guides do exist but it is advisable to check details first as bus routes are constantly changing. Much the best way of orientating yourself in Glasgow is to take a city bus tour, a mammoth and comprehensive round trip from George Square (running everyday between the end of April and the end of September).

The two obvious areas to base yourself in are the city centre with its numerous chain hotels (some of which offer short break or weekend bargains) or the area round the University of Glasgow at Hillhead and Hyndland on the western side of the city. Here the hotels have more character and are

The population in 1800 was around 50,000; by 1870 it was half a million. Refugees from the Highland Clearances and from the Irish potato famines of the 1840s poured into the town. In their wake came the urban poverty and disease which were to dog Glasgow for the better part of a century. They were the reverse side of the civic pomp and commercial rivalry which stocked Glasgow with so many fine buildings and endowed its galleries and museums. The infant mortality rate was appalling.

The slump which followed World War I was bad every-where but especially so in Glasgow, with its dependence on ships and heavy engineering. It was around this time that the

---

supplemented by guesthouses, but the city centre is not within walking distance.

There is about three days' worth of solid sightseeing before you exhaust Glasgow's attractions, and much more if you are interested in architecture, or want to explore some of the less obvious corners, or share the city's shop-until-you-drop mentality. Many of the best museums are free – a great incentive. Another of Glasgow's advantages is an enviable location within range of splendid countryside – from the popular attractions of Loch Lomond to the gentler Campsie Fells. For entertainment listings, consult the *Herald* or the *Evening Times* or arm yourself with *The List*, published every fortnight and available from newsagents, bookshops and the Tourist Information Centre. The Ticket Centre in City Hall (Candleriggs) sells tickets for most of the theatres in Glasgow.

The chief shopping streets are Argyle Street, Buchanan Street and Sauchiehall Street. Most chain stores have branches here. Among the specialist shops, try: Cooper Hay Rare Books (Bath Street) for antiquarian books and prints; the Victorian Village (West Regent Street) for a series of antique stalls; the Whisky Shop (Princes Square) for whisky; James Begg (Renfield Street) for bagpipes; the Glasgow Style Gallery (487 Great Western Road) for Mackintosh, Art Deco, Art Nouveau and Glasgow-style furniture.

To get to grips with the Glasgow dialect, you can do no better than to buy *The Patter* by Michael Munro (Glasgow District Libraries, 1985), which gives a glossary of most local expressions, including the vulgar ones.

'Red Clydeside' epithet was coined, confirming Glasgow's working-class radicalism, which started as early as 1787 when the hand-loom weavers went on strike rather than suffer a 25 per cent pay cut, resulting in the death of three of them. In 1848, the year of the Communist Manifesto, six more people died in riots. Ten members of the Independent Labour Party were elected from Glasgow in 1922, and in 1972 the famous sit-in took place in defence of the threatened yards of Upper Clyde Shipbuilders. This long tradition of political awareness and action is still an inspiration to many of Glasgow's writers and artists, even now that so many of the old industries have gone painfully to the wall and are rapidly being superseded by the bright offices of computer software specialists and graphic designers.

THE EAST END

This was the medieval part of the city, though nothing much of that period remains now. The High Street, once at its centre, is now on the eastern fringe of all the activity, and is a fairly dismal place, with old railway yards at its top and crumbling shops and houses where the Gallowgate and London Road meet at Glasgow Cross. However, the urban renewal project here has saved several of the best buildings and there are several good things to see within walking distance of Glasgow Cross.

Medieval Glasgow

Glasgow's origins are lost in the legends surrounding St Kentigern (or Mungo as he came to be known), who came to Glasgow on a cart yoked to two wild bulls somewhere towards the end of the seventh century, and founded his monastery on the banks of the Molendinar burn. To him, Glasgow owes its motto, 'Let Glasgow flourish by preaching of the word' (the last five words have been dropped by a more secular age).

Glasgow Cathedral, started in 1136, is the best relic of the medieval city. It is the only cathedral in Scotland to have survived the Reformation virtually intact, being saved from the mob by local craftsmen, and is a first-class, if rather gloomy, example of mid-thirteenth-century Gothic. As Scott's character Andrew Fairservice describes it, it has 'nane o' yere whigmaleeries and curliewurlies and opensteek hems about it', and the exterior is very plain. The interior, though, is fascinating – especially in the choir, where the outgrowth of mouldings create a waterfall of stone pouring downwards from the clerestory to the forceful chutes of the aisle columns. The vaulted lower church made necessary because of the fall of the land underneath the choir is more forest-like, its massive piers sprouting springers in all directions. Here is to be found the tomb of St Kentigern. Other good parts of the cathedral are the Lady Chapel, with magnificent vaulting, and the unique rood screen. The last archbishop, James Beaton, brother of the more famous cardinal who was murdered at St Andrews, fled to France at the Reformation, taking the cathedral's relics and many of its treasures with him. The building of a new visitor centre is underway; it should be open by the autumn of 1992.

East of the cathedral, the **Necropolis** is a magnificent graveyard on a hill, covered with the elaborate tombs of rich industrialists and merchants. The figure of John Knox stands on top of a huge pillar, glowering down on the city and the cathedral below. Views of the city are very good.

Opposite the cathedral, across Castle Street, you will find **Provand's Lordship** (open Mon to Sat 10 to 5, Sun 12 to 6), which is Glasgow's oldest house, dating from 1471. It was once the home of the Canon of Barlanark, and later became a sweet-shop, a pub and a furniture-maker's workshop. Now it is a museum, with mementoes of its later roles (the sweeties are especially welcome), but particularly interesting for the reconstruction of a pre-Reformation room, with appropriately uncomfortable furniture.

The **Royal Infirmary** overshadows the cathedral and stands on the site of the Bishop's Palace. Here Joseph Lister introduced the concept of an antiseptic surgical environment. Many of the other buildings a little to the west are part of Glasgow's second university, the University of Strathclyde. They occupy some of the site of the original Glasgow University, founded in 1451 and Scotland's second oldest. Don't miss the equestrian statue of King William at the edge of the High Street below the cathedral. As tour guides will happily relate, many a Glaswegian has questioned his own sobriety on seeing the horse's tail move. But it does – it is jointed on.

Around Glasgow Cross

The mercat cross is a replica of the original, but the **Tolbooth Tower**, all that is left of the original building, is seventeenth-century, and dominates the area which was once Glasgow's heart, especially in the days of the tobacco merchants who gathered nearby. The other tower in view is the **Tron Steeple**, once part of a church but now the home of the Tron Theatre, scene of many locally written productions and with a popular bar. Trongate merges into Argyle Street, Glasgow's most populous shopping street, crammed with buses for most of its length, but with a curiously isolated pedestrian area at the Trongate end.

East of Glasgow Cross, between Gallowgate and London Road, is the market universally known as the **Barras**. Everything from junk to fresh fruit can be found here, but it is not so much what is sold as the way it is sold that draws visitors. This is the place to hear the inimitable Glasgow patter – a flow of earthy wit and shameless come-on lines – with which the traders assail and entertain their customers. Weekends are the time to go; the market opens between 9 and 5 and it's always busy.

Saltmarket, running south towards the Clyde, was once an appalling warren of slums (an estimated 200 brothels lined it), and is still fairly tatty. To the east of it lies the beautiful eighteenth-century **St Andrews Parish Church**, with a portico like a Greek temple, rescued in the nick of time from decay. Another interesting eighteenth-century church, just to the south, is **St Andrews-by-the-Green**, a Georgian building, now the headquarters of a housing association.

If you explore round the railway arches to the west of the **Briggait**, which was once a fish-market and more recently a shopping centre, you will find **Paddy's Market**, where the goods are extremely second-hand. It makes a contrast to the glamour of the New Glasgow, and there seems to be a creeping conspiracy to get rid of it – something strongly resisted by those who see it as a popular Glasgow institution.

Glasgow Green

Officially adopted as a public park in the seventeenth century, this large, open patch of greenery by the Clyde has long been the focus of all kinds of open-air activity, from football to political meetings. Freemen of Glasgow still have the right to graze a flock of sheep here. Nelson stands on a column at the western side, and a ceramic version of Queen Victoria is nearby. Glasgow Green is where James Watt hit on the idea of a separate condensing cylinder for the steam engine, thus sparking off the Industrial Revolution. A boulder marks the site where he had his brain-wave.

The **People's Palace** (open Mon to Sat 10 to 5, Sun 12 to 6), on the north-east edge of the Green, started as a late-Victorian piece of cultural do-goodery for the people of East Glasgow. Now it is a splendid and idiosyncratic museum of the city, one of the most fascinating places in Glasgow. It is a popular and populist place, full of schoolchildren and family groups gazing at the ephemera of Glasgow of old, gathered in a warren of glass cases, reconstructed shops and tableaux. There are salvaged bits from old houses and churches, fragments of the medieval city dug out of holes, newspaper cuttings about the blitz, football memorabilia, weapons confiscated from suffragettes, and much more. The People's Palace was busy salvaging what it could of Glasgow long before the first yuppies arrived on the scene, and it has plenty of stories to tell. Do not leave without having a cup of tea in the Winter Gardens at the rear, where the glass roof covers neat arrays of flowers, and do not miss the murals by Ken Currie (one of Glasgow's latest generation of excellent painters), which adorn the ceilings of the top floor and are peopled by idealised muscular figures from Glasgow's working-class history.

Almost opposite the People's Palace, the **Templeton Business Centre** is an extraordinary orange (in some lights) replica of the Doges' Palace in Venice, built as a carpet factory in 1889. The story goes that the architect was asked to name his favourite building – this was the result.

THE CLYDE

The famous 'Song of the Clyde' would be different if it were written today. Sanitised, smartened and with barely a boat to be seen on it, the Clyde, where it flows through Glasgow, now looks more like a municipal pond than a great waterway. The docks and the warehouses on its banks have gone. So has the great fleet of paddle-steamers which used to throng Broomielaw long ago, ready to take passengers 'doon the watter' to the resorts of the Firth of Clyde.

Now the **Clyde Walkway** runs beside the river from the bottom of Saltmarket as far as the Scottish Exhibition Centre two miles away. It can be a windy walk, and an interesting one in places. Look out for the statue of 'La Pasionaria' close to Glasgow Bridge on the north side of the Clyde, set up to commemorate those Glaswegians who joined the International Brigade in the Spanish Civil War, and for the two rotundas of the old **Clyde Tunnel**, one now a complex of restaurants and the other a hands-on technology museum, good for children. The **Finnieston Crane**, once the largest in Europe, forms a distant landmark. It was used for loading locomotives on to ships, and in 1988 a locomotive made entirely from straw was hung from it – a good example of Glasgow sculptors' love of large-scale humour.

The *Waverley* down by Anderson Quay is the last ocean-going paddle-steamer in the world, and makes regular excursions down to the Clyde coast in summer, if her boilers are in order (phone 041-221 8152 for details).

CENTRAL GLASGOW

The Merchant City

After the Union of Parliaments in 1707 the Scots were suddenly free to trade with America, and Glasgow was ideally positioned to take advantage of this. The merchants who traded in the tobacco, sugar and cotton of the New World built their houses and warehouses to the west of the High Street, in the area roughly bounded by George Street to the north and Buchanan Street to the west, the area now known as the Merchant City. After falling on lean times, like much of the centre of Glasgow, the Merchant City has now filled with the wine-bar and bistro culture of the New Glasgow, and is being much touted as a place for the visitor to explore.

It is certainly worth doing this, for the sake of the buildings (though few remain from the eighteenth century). This is an area to wander through or to eat in rather than to shop in. Worth looking out for are:
• **Hutchesons' Hall, Ingram Street** (NTS, open Mon to Sat 9.30 to 5) This was the site of a hospital founded in the seventeenth century. The statues of its founders, made in 1649, now occupy niches in the pretty early nineteenth-century building, with its neat white clock tower and spire. It now acts as offices for the National Trust for Scotland, but the hall on the first floor is open, and well worth seeing for its rich decoration.
• **Trades House, Glassford Street** A Robert Adam building from 1794, still fulfilling its original function as a home for Glasgow's 14 guilds. Go in here to see the banqueting hall and the saloon.
• **Virginia Galleries, 33 Virginia Street** This is where Glasgow merchants once haggled over cargoes of tobacco

or sugar. Now it is more likely to be Glasgow shoppers bargaining for antiques.

• **Royal Exchange (Stirling Library), Royal Exchange Square** The mansion hidden at the heart of this porticoed building once belonged to a tobacco merchant. It is now the oldest and largest lending library in Glasgow, having also been the Royal Exchange, where dealings in sugar, rum, cotton and other commodities went on. The old hall – a massive Byzantine construction with a lovely roof – is full of neat shelves of books.

• **Royal Bank of Scotland, Royal Exchange Square** This is a wonderfully positioned building, flanked by arches and columns and with an elegant Ionic portico. The interior is worth a look, too, even if you do not want to cash a cheque. The well-known **Rogano** seafood restaurant is just round the corner, with exuberant Art Deco design.

George Square and Buchanan Street

This was the heart of Victorian Glasgow, and is the heart of the New Glasgow too. You will step straight into it if you have just arrived by train at Queen Street Station. George Square is a welcome open space in the grid of streets, with small areas of green and a liberal sprinkling of statues. Sir Walter Scott is at the centre of things, on top of a Doric column. George III, after whom the square is named, has no statue – his failure to preserve the American colonies, and hence Glasgow's tobacco trade, saw to that. However, Queen Victoria, Robert Burns and James Watt are all there, flanked by Glaswegians of varying degrees of fame.

The square is dominated by the lavishly ostentatious **City Chambers**, erected in 1888 in best Italian Renaissance style. No building says more about Glasgow's self-confidence and civic pride in its Victorian heyday, particularly if you take a tour of its magnificently (if sometimes excessively) decorated interior. (Tours normally run Mon to Fri at 10.30 and 2.30, and last about one hour. It is best to call first on 041-227 4017.) Granite columns, marble capitals, mosaic upon mosaic, a massive staircase adorned with arches, more pillars and more purple and red marble culminate in a cupola of tinted glass. The council hall has carved mahogany in abundance, while the banqueting hall, with murals and arched ceilings, just stuns. The guides who take you round are out-and-out enthusiasts for this extraordinary piece of wedding-cakery.

At the corner of West George Street, **Merchant's House** (open Mon to Fri 9 to 5) is a further lavish memorial to Glasgow's trade. Amazons support the windows and a sailing ship tops the dome. The banqueting hall is yet another *pièce de résistance*.

A block to the west of George Square, Buchanan Street is the city's smartest shopping area. Towards the bottom of it, Argyle Arcade houses jewellers by the score. Further up, the Princes Square shopping mall is a piece of 1980s chic, where whispering escalators carry you up from a central courtyard to an array of eating places and fashionable shops. This is the place for conspicuous consumption. Where Buchanan Street crosses St Vincent Street, the Clydesdale Bank is almost as conspicuous. Roman emperors line an astonishing black and gold hall. Victorian Venetian architecture breaks out again at the Stock Exchange and the Royal Faculty of Procurators.

At the very top, without warning, Buchanan Street suddenly starts to go seedy. Just where it begins to peter out to the desolate expanse of the Buchanan Street Bus Station stands the 1990 **International Concert Hall**, a squat sandy building, of which many rude things have been said. If you cannot go to a concert here (few people are rude about the acoustics), there are guided tours. (Tours run Mon to Fri at 2; call 041-332 6633 for details.)

The city centre

The grid of streets which lie between Buchanan Street and the M8 to the west makes up the heart of Glasgow's shopping and office districts, with residential streets on the edges. It is, in best American style, a separate downtown area, and feels, after a hard day's footslogging, about as big as Manhattan.

In pauses between the shops (Sauchiehall Street, partly pedestrianised, is the chief shopping street here), look out for:

- **Gardner's Building, Jamaica Street** The first building in Europe built of cast iron and glass, and a very elegant one.
- **Ca'd'oro, Union Street** Another cast-iron and glass building in lavish Venetian style, restored after fire caused a great deal of damage.
- **St Vincent Church, St Vincent Street** An extraordinary building by Alexander 'Greek' Thomson – a mixture of ancient Egypt, ancient Greece and smatterings of India.

- **Blythswood Square** A beautiful neo-Classical square – the nearest Glasgow comes to approaching the elegance of Edinburgh's Charlotte Square.
- **Willow Tea Rooms, Sauchiehall Street** Reconstruction though it is, this is a must for all fans of Charles Rennie Mackintosh. It is one of four tearooms he was commissioned to design, and is to be found above a jeweller's shop. Typical Mackintosh high-backed chairs pierced with little squares are grouped round the tables; mirrors and painted glass decorate the walls. The effect Mackintosh had on ordinary Glaswegians is caught by Neil Munro: '. . . the chairs is no' like ony ither chairs ever I clapped eyes on, but you could easy guess they were chairs; and a' roond the place there's a lump of lookin'-gless wi' purple leeks pented onit every noo and then . . .' You may have to queue for some time.
- **The McLellan Galleries, Sauchiehall Street** (open Mon to Sat 10 to 5, Sun 12 to 6) Refurbished and reopened in 1990, the Galleries now contain the largest temporary exhibition space in the country outside London, hosting half a dozen major exhibitions a year.
- **The Glasgow School of Art, Renfrew Street** This, the most famous of Mackintosh's buildings, was built in two stages between 1897 and 1909, and shows the architect at his most adventurous. Each façade is different, and enthusiasts will be able to trace Mackintosh's influences, from Elizabethan mansion to Scottish baronial. The oriel windows, stretching over several floors, are the most eye-catching part of the exterior. Tours of the interior are usually run three times daily in summer and twice a day in winter, but it's best to call first to check details (041-353 4526). The interior of the building is even more fantastical than the outside. The two-storey library has lamps like miniature ziggurats, and wood carved into endless fascinating shapes, while the top-floor gallery contains many splendid examples of Mackintosh furniture. The Glasgow School of Art has had, and still has, an inestimable influence on the success of generation upon generation of Glasgow painters.
- **The Tenement House, Buccleuch Street** (NTS, open Mar to Oct, daily 1.30 to 5, and you may book in advance; call 041-333 0183 for details) This museum is a time-capsule, where the way of life of a previous generation has been preserved intact. The Glasgow tenement (see box) is still the city centre's most typical form of housing, and this is your chance to see what life used to be like for the inhabitants. The flat ('house' in tenement terminology) belonged to Miss Agnes Toward, who

moved here in 1911 and died in hospital in 1975. Apparently unimpressed by modernity, this ordinary Glasgow woman lived in a way almost unchanged from Edwardian times, rarely disposing of anything. Now you see her hall, parlour, bedroom, bathroom and kitchen with everything in place, from the box beds carefully tucked away in the walls to the great black kitchen range. Pots of jam stand in the cupboard and the mangle and washboard remain by the sink.

THE UNIVERSITY AND THE WEST END

At one time the M8 and the Clydeside Expressway were not going to be alone in carving through Glasgow – the whole of the Great Western road was also going to be remodelled in favour of the car. Luckily, motorway developments came to a halt, but only after the 'bridge to nowhere' over the M8 had been built (you can see it standing forlornly near the end of Waterloo Street). The change of plan has left central Glasgow linked to the West End by only the most tenuous of threads across the gulf of the motorway. You will rapidly discover just how tenuous it is if you attempt to drive from the centre to the university area without consulting a street map first: you may find yourself swept out to the airport before you know it.

Kelvingrove

The **Mitchell Library** (open Mon to Fri 9.30 to 9, Sat 9.30 to 5), on the edge of the motorway and reached from Granville Street, is best seen at night, when the domed building is lit up by floodlights. It is the biggest reference library in Europe, and has collections devoted to Glasgow and to Burns.

North of the library, make for Woodlands Road and Lynedoch Street, for this is the way to reach the **Park Conservation Area**. This cloistered little enclave of houses and towers draws superlatives, such as 'the most perfect piece of mid-nineteenth-century planning'. It has also been likened to an Italian hilltop town, and when you see the towers of Trinity College rising over the curving crescents of sandstone houses you can see why. However, the genius of the planners ran out when it came to naming the streets: Park Circus, Park Gate, Park Gardens, Park Quadrant, Park Street and Park Terrace. Even if you are not an architecture fan, it is worth finding your way here for the views of Kelvingrove Park and of the city.

A MACKINTOSH CHECKLIST

Born in Glasgow in 1868, and hailed in Europe in his own day, Charles Rennie Mackintosh was largely ignored at home except by the few visionaries, such as Kate Cranston, who loved his work and were prepared to put up with his unpredictable temper. Despairing of success, Mackintosh left Glasgow in 1913. He died in 1928. Today, his sparse but distinctive style has become something of a cult, and you will find postcards, posters or reproductions of his designs throughout Glasgow and the world.

• **Queen's Cross** Mackintosh's only church. Now head-quarters of the Charles Rennie Mackintosh Society. Information centre and an exhibition. Open Mon to Fri 10 to 5, they can help arrange tours and give up-to-date details of opening times (see page 219).

• **Glasgow School of Art, Renfrew Street** His best-known building. The interior is remarkable. For information on tours, see page 211.

• **Willow Tea Rooms, Sauchiehall Street** Exact reconstruction of one of the four tearooms built for Kate Cranston.

• **Ruchill Church Hall, Ruchill Street** The Church Hall was designed by Mackintosh in 1898.

• **Hunterian Art Gallery, University Avenue** Has a reconstruction of three floors of the Mackintosh's own home (home closed 1.30 to 2.30 daily).

• **House for the Art Lover, Bellahouston Park** Built from Mackintosh's entry for an architecture competition.

• **Scotland Street School, Scotland Street** Now a museum of education.

• **Martyrs' Public School, Parson Street** Difficult to reach because of motorways and generally not open to the public.

• **Former Daily Record Building, Renfield Lane**

• **Former Glasgow Herald Building, Mitchell Street**

• **Craigie Hall, Drumbreck Avenue** Mackintosh helped to extend the house in 1893. It contains furniture and decorative fittings completed for the interior of the House for the Art Lover. (Craigie Hall is currently closed, possibly till 1995 – for details ring 041–427 6884.)

• **The Hill House, Helensburgh** Reached by train from Glasgow Queen Street. Mackintosh built this house for the publisher William Blackie. Now run by the NTS (see Argyll chapter).

Museum of Transport

(Open Mon to Sat 10 to 5, Sun 12 to 6)

Sited in part of the immense interior of **Kelvin Hall**, this is a transport museum to beat all others in the size and range of its collection. Fleets of bicycles and motor-bikes, early cars – especially from the Scottish builders – and, of course, the famous Glasgow trams make up a large part of the display. There are also steam locomotives to remind you that Springburn was once the largest locomotive building centre in the world. Yet it is the Clyde Room, with its display of model ships, which probably draws most people. The majority of models are of ships built on the Clyde, the *Queen Mary* and the *Queen Elizabeth* among them. This museum is a good place for children for there is almost bound to be something that will catch their eyes and, though most of the exhibits are out of bounds as far as climbing over them is concerned, it is a cheerful and friendly place.

Kelvingrove Art Gallery and Museum

(Open Mon to Sat 10 to 5, Sun 12 to 6)

Opposite the Kelvin Hall, on the edge of Kelvingrove Park, this turn-of-the-century spiked and turreted building seems to have its rear facing the road. The story goes that the architect built it the wrong way round and was so mortified

THE TENEMENT

Long before Glasgow's nineteenth-century expansion, tenements were a common form of Scottish urban existence, especially in Edinburgh. However, the best nineteenth-century examples are to be found in Glasgow. Tenements are essentially blocks of flats joined together to form a unified frontage which is pierced at intervals by narrow passageways, called closes, leading to the back of the building. The flats (called houses) open on to a single staircase which leads up from the close. In Edinburgh's old seventeenth-century tenements, there would have been a social mix within one building, the gentry occupying the first floor, and increasingly poorer families in the flats and rooms higher up. Today, tenements are becoming the province of the refurbishing middle classes. At their best, they are magnificent dwellings, and some of Glasgow's splendid red sandstone that he leapt to his death from the topmost floor when it was complete. Alas, road alterations provide the more prosaic explanation. Inside, it is easy to be waylaid by the museum on the ground floor, which has a superb collection of arms and armour, but most visitors come to see the paintings. These form one of the best collections in Britain.

The star of the modern collection is undoubtedly Dali's *Christ of St John of the Cross*. Rembrandt's *Man in Armour* also draws the crowds, as does Whistler's *Portrait of Thomas Carlyle*. Among Scottish painting, you will find the Glasgow Boys of the 1880s and the Scottish Colourists – Peploe, Cadell, Hunter and Fergusson. An extensive collection of Dutch works, French painting, prints, sculpture and the decorative arts rounds it off.

If you are in need of a refreshment afterwards, try the Exchequer Bar at 59 Dumbarton Road – a big, interesting pub full of paintings.

Kelvingrove Park

This park, between the Kelvingrove Art Gallery and Museum and the University of Glasgow, is the most pleasant open space in the city – well worth strolling through. It is dominated by the long Victorian Gothic frontage of the university at the top of the hill. You can easily get diverted up the Kelvin walkway beside the river of that name, which will lead you

terraces contain flats with five or six high-ceilinged rooms, many with elaborate plasterwork and spacious halls, putting the housing estates of most English towns firmly in the shade.

Yet the tenement could also become a slum. The 'single-ends' or one-room flats of the Gorbals, where sometimes a dozen people would live with no plumbing and lavatories shared between the whole building, were awful. It was the massive overcrowding of the inner-city tenements – even though the buildings themselves were often substantial – that gave rise to Glasgow's terrible nineteenth- and twentieth-century housing problems. The wholesale demolition of the worst tenements and the rehousing of their inhabitants in high-rise blocks within the city or on satellite estates nearby is now acknowledged to have been an inadequate solution to the problems of urban deprivation. These days, Glasgow's tenements are preserved wherever possible.

up through Kelvinside towards the Forth and Clyde canal. The massive fountain standing in the park commemorates the Lord Provost under whom the waters of Loch Katrine were piped into Glasgow to form the water supply. This enlightened piece of civil engineering did much to reduce the awful statistics of death from cholera and typhus in Glasgow's Victorian slums.

The University of Glasgow

Founded in 1451, the university moved to this site in 1870, away from its old position on the High Street. It now forms a complex of buildings around its Victorian Gothic centrepiece, with the quiet streets of Hillhead behind it, and the lively shops and eateries of Byres Road immediately to the west. Once through the 1951 memorial gates, you will find the visitor centre. If you do not have time or inclination to tour everything, try to see the splendidly Gothic **Bute Hall** and the **Hunterian Museum** with its geological, numismatic and archaeological collections. On no account miss the **Hunterian Art Gallery** (open Mon to Sat 9.30 to 5).

The doors, by Eduardo Paolozzi, are the first indication of the gallery's style. They are cast-aluminium, and burnished like some precision piece of aerospace engineering. Inside them, the impression is of brightness and space – the paintings are hung to splendid effect. The collection is small but surprisingly comprehensive, and, for followers of Whistler, unrivalled outside Washington. There are further examples of Glasgow painters and a superb collection of prints, including some by Hockney, Picasso and Dürer.

At one end of the gallery is a reconstruction of Mackintosh's home. There are three floors' worth of his fascinating furniture, and plenty of ideas for budding cabinet-makers and interior designers alike. One of the peculiarities of the reconstruction, which you can see from the outside, is the entrance door built several feet off the ground.

In close proximity to the University is the Halt Bar (Woodlands Road). The décor is minimal but the atmosphere more than makes up for that – you may even be treated to an impromptu folk song.

Great Western Road

A drive or a bus ride down this long ruler-straight avenue reveals more of Glasgow's best planning. The terraces and crescents along the road were laid out in the 1830s, and some are superb. Keep your eye open for Grosvenor Terrace, with its massively long uniform frontage, and for Great Western Terrace, by 'Greek' Thomson. On the opposite side of the road from Grosvenor Terrace lie the **Botanic Gardens**. The gardens themselves, lovely though they are, are rather put in the shade by the huge glasshouse of **Kibble Palace**, brought here on a boat from Loch Long in the late nineteenth century and now filled with ferns to provide a warm green atmosphere. Elsewhere there is a rock garden and a herb garden and plenty of space to sit. By following the walkway up the River Kelvin or by driving up Maryhill Road, you reach the **Forth and Clyde Canal**. For canal-lovers, the Kelvin Aqueduct (1790) and the Maryhill Locks are the things to see. Much renewal is in progress on the canal and it may soon be open again.

SOUTH OF THE CLYDE

To explore down here you will need a car, or else to have grown accustomed to the buses, for the sights are scattered and few are within walking distance of the city centre. The Clockwork Orange subway helps for some. The district of the **Gorbals** lies south of the river from the High Street. The name's association with slum living and razor-wielding gangs is largely the responsibility of Alexander MacArthur, who wrote the novel called *No Mean City* (published by Corgi). The days of the slums are only to be seen in old photographs now, for the Gorbals has been cleared in favour of tower blocks. These days you go through the Gorbals to visit the Citizens' Theatre or the Tramway Theatre, with its huge space for epic productions, or to admire the lines of the modern Glasgow Central Mosque. Mackintosh fans make for the Scotland Street School, now a museum of education.

At **Ibrox**, with its own subway station, is the stadium which is home to Glasgow Rangers, and a shrine for football-lovers, while in **Bellahouston Park**, the House for the Art Lover was constructed from plans submitted by Mackintosh for a German competition. (The outside is complete and merits a visit to have a look but the incomplete interior has delayed the opening.)

In St Andrews Drive stands the baronial **Haggs Castle** (open Mon to Sat 10 to 5, Sun 12 to 6), a historical museum designed with children in mind, with restored kitchen and Victorian nursery. The castle lies close to Pollok Park, with its two famous sights.

The Burrell Collection

(Open Mon to Fri 10 to 5, Sat 12 to 6)
A decade since the Burrell Collection opened to the public, it is still difficult to divorce its symbolic value from its actual worth as a collection to visit and admire – for some would say that it was the opening of the Burrell

---

USEFUL DIRECTORY

Main tourist office
Greater Glasgow Tourist Board and Convention Bureau
35–39 St Vincent Place
Glasgow G1 2ER
041-204 4400

Tourist Board publications Useful brochures, all available free from the Tourist Board, are *Greater Glasgow Quick Guide, Where to Stay in Greater Glasgow* and *Greater Glasgow Short Breaks.*

Local transport
Glasgow Airport enquiry desk 041-887 1111
Prestwick Airport enquiries (0292) 79822
Bus to Glasgow or Prestwick – enquiries 041-332 9191
Glasgow Central Station (for trains to/from the south) and Glasgow Queen Street (for fast trains to Edinburgh, and trains north) 041-204 2844
Scottish Citylink bus services 041-332 9191
Travel Centre (St Enoch Square) 041-226 4826
Discovering Glasgow Tours (bus) 041-942 6453
Helicopter trips 041-226 4261 (Clyde Helicopters)

City walks
For details of City Walks contact Iris Sommerville
041-942 7929

---

in 1983 and the 'Glasgow's Miles Better' campaign of the same year that together succeeded in putting the city back in the minds of the art, media and subsequently business worlds.

The story of the Burrell Collection is also, in its way, symbolic. It is the collection of one man, a Glasgow ship-owner, who bought throughout his long life (he died in 1958 at the age of 97), using the fortune amassed from the shrewd timing of the sale of his fleet. He donated the collection to Glasgow in 1944, but surrounded the gift with restrictions, notably that the collection should be exhibited

---

Entertainment
City Hall (ticket centre) 041-227 5511
New Atheneum Theatre 041-332 5057
Citizens' Theatre 041-429 0022
King's Theatre 041-227 5511 (ticket centre)
Mitchell Theatre 041-227 5511 (ticket centre)
Old Atheneum Theatre 041-332 2333
Pavilion Theatre 041-332 1846
Theatre Royal (Scottish Opera) 041-332 9000
Tramway Theatre 041-227 5511 (ticket centre)
Tron Theatre 041-552 4267
Year-round Mayfest information 041-552 8000
Glasgow International Concert Hall 041-227 5511
(ticket centre)
Henry Wood Hall (Royal Scottish Orchestra) 041-226 3868
Stevenson Hall 041-332 5057

Glasgow Film Theatre 041-332 6535
Salon (Hillhead) 041-339 4256

Football
Glasgow Rangers FC 041-427 8500
Glasgow Celtic FC 041-556 2611

Miscellaneous
Trips on the Clyde, July and August (Waverley Excursions)
041-221 8152
Headquarters of Charles Rennie Mackintosh Society
041-946 6600

---

in a purpose-built gallery, and that it should be in a rural setting removed from Glasgow's pollution. It took almost 40 years before Glasgow was able to comply, first finding a site in the Pollok estate (donated in 1966) and then running an architectural competition to come up with a building that could best display the diversity of the collection.

The result is something of a triumph, for the building is remarkable, its glass walls in one place allowing the shady woodland against which it is built to merge with the objects inside, and in another acting as the setting for medieval stained glass. Medieval ceilings and gateways are built into it, and the Hutton Rooms – from Burrell's castle near Berwick – form a kind of medieval house within a house.

The collection's strongest point is the medieval European collection of furnishings, tapestry, woodcarving and stained glass, but the range of objects from the ancient Mesopotamian and Egyptian civilisations and the Chinese ceramics, bronzes and jades are also remarkable. Then there is the glass, the silver and the needlework, and finally of course the paintings. These are chiefly nineteenth-century French, and include some fine examples of Degas and Cézanne. Works of the Hague School were also among Burrell's favourites.

Burrell's taste, especially in paintings, is seen by some as ultra-conservative. This is perhaps a little unfair. If the collection as a whole can give an insight into his preferences, it would seem that he avoided the florid and enjoyed simplicity of line. This is best seen in the collection of silver and glassware, but is also reflected in the German woodcarving and the objects from the ancient civilisations.

Pollok Country Park and House

The estate of Pollok was held by the Maxwell family from 1269 to 1966, when it was donated to Glasgow. It has now been turned into a country park in the middle of the city, and a most tranquil place it is, with a herd of Highland cattle mournfully surveying the strollers and the golfers.

At the centre of the park lies **Pollok House** (open Mon to Sat 10 to 5, Sun 2 to 5). This is an excellent counterpoint to the Burrell Collection, for here, in contrast to the purpose-built modernity of the Burrell building, is a neo-Classical house whose homely interior acts as the setting for a superb collection of Spanish, Dutch and British paintings. In particular, there are fine works by William Blake, Hogarth, Goya, El Greco and Murillo. There are also many portraits – often of the Maxwell family. The setting of these paintings among the furniture and plasterwork of the airy rooms is part of the charm. It is foolish to traipse hotfoot to the Burrell and neglect Pollok, though all too many do. Apart from anything else, the formal gardens round the house are beautiful.

WHERE TO STAY

Babbity Bowster   £
16–18 Blackfriars Street
Glasgow G1 1PE   *Tel 041-552 5055*

The simple pine bedrooms may be too spartan for some tastes, but this lively café/bar/restaurant offers a crash course in modern Glasgow culture. The cheerful bar is popular with the locals, and folk and jazz artists make regular appearances. All-day food ranges from filled rolls to lamb stovies; there is more choice but less atmosphere in the upstairs restaurant.

Open: all year **Rooms**: 6 **Facilities**: private car park
Credit/charge cards: Access, Amex, Visa

One Devonshire Gardens   £££
1 Devonshire Gardens
Glasgow G12 0UX   *Tel 041-334 9494/339 2001*

These days the hotel spans three houses, each displaying the flair that makes this one of Britain's most memorable hotels. Bedrooms are individual and opulent: all have magnificent fireplaces and sofas, and a TV and CD player tucked away. Bathrooms are similarly grand (three have shower only). The drawing-rooms are huge and bright, and the menu in the dramatic dining-room uses plenty of fresh Scottish ingredients. (See also Where to eat.)

Open: all year **Rooms**: 27 **Credit/charge cards**: Access, Amex, Diners, Visa

---

The Town House   £
4 Hughenden Terrace
Glasgow G12 9XR   *Tel 041-357 0862*

An elegant, carefully restored late-Victorian house offering good value in a smart West End location. The top-floor gallery is restful and conservatory-like, and the lounge has an impressive fireplace and comfy leather sofas. Several of the bedrooms are huge and some have views of the garden; all rooms have showers. The short dinner menu sticks to standards like lasagne and steak.

Open: all year **Rooms**: 10
Credit/charge cards: Access, Visa

Town House   ££
54 West George Street
Glasgow G2 1NG   *Tel 041-332 3320*

In a splendid Victorian building close to Queen Street Station this comfortable new business hotel has a sense of style and flair. Bedrooms are bright with modern soft furnishings and plenty of pampering extras, as well as glitzy bathrooms. The public rooms still have some of their original character, and the French-influenced menu is strong on fish and seafood. The weekend breaks are good value.

Open: all year, exc Xmas Day **Rooms**: 34 **Credit/charge cards**:
Access, Amex, Diners, Visa

WHERE TO EAT

Amber Regent
50 West Regent Street G2 2RA   *Tel 041-331 1655/1677*

Part of a popular trio of Chinese restaurants under the 'Amber' banner, the Amber Regent is run by Andy Chung. The menu offers a mix of Cantonese, Pekinese and Szechuan with satays and grilled and barbecued specialities.

Open: Mon to Sat 12 to 2.15, 6 to 11.30
Credit/charge cards: Access, Amex, Diners, Visa

La Bavarde   ★
19 New Kirk Road, Bearsden G61 3SJ   *Tel 041-942 2202*

Bread is baked daily at La Bavarde and there are also home-made pastas and chutneys. The three-course lunch menu is particularly good value.

Open: Tues to Sat 12 to 1.30, 6.30 to 9.30; closed 3 weeks end July, 2 weeks Xmas **Credit/charge cards**: Access, Amex, Diners, Visa

Buttery
652 Argyle Street G3 8UF   *Tel 041-221 8188*

The Buttery was awarded 'County Restaurant of the Year' by *The Good Food Guide 1992*, and you can expect modern cooking at fair prices with professional service.

Open: Mon to Fri 12 to 2.30, Mon to Sat 7 to 10.30; closed public hols **Credit/charge cards**: Access, Amex, Diners, Visa

Café Gandolfi   ★
64 Albion Street G1 1NY   *Tel 041-552 6813*

What was once a study, wood-panelled Victorian pub is now a bistro-type café serving food all day. Salads and light meals are appealing to vegetarians and meat-eaters alike and can be washed down with Czech Budweiser.

Open: Mon to Sat 9 am to 11.30, Sun 12 to 11.30; closed public hols, Xmas and New Year **Credit/charge cards**: none accepted

Caffé Qui   ★
Cochrane Street G1 1HP   *Tel 041-552 6099*

The Italian Centre in Glasgow contains this superbly decorated and spacious restaurant with a wide range of popular Italian dishes. The café upstairs is more informal with a shorter menu.

Open: daily 10 to midnight, Sun 11 to 11; closed Xmas
Credit/charge cards: Access, Amex, Diners, Visa

Colonial India   ★
25 High Street GL 1LX   *Tel 041-552 1923/6782*

The décor and service are in colonial style, and the cooking and baking are Karahi and good, with choices for vegetarians. The wine list is above average and there is a variety of beers.

Open: Mon to Sat 12 to 11.30 or midnight, Sun 2 to 11.30; closed Xmas **Credit/charge cards**: Access, Amex, Diners, Visa

Loon Fung   ★
417 Sauchiehall Street G2 3JD   *Tel 041-332 1240*

Loon Fung is a spacious Chinese restaurant at the top of Sauchiehall Street. Among more familiar items on the menu are some Cantonese specialities. Helpings are very generous.

Open: daily 12 to 12
Credit/charge cards: Access, Amex, Visa

Mitchell's ★
157 North Street G3 7DA *Tel 041-204 4312*

Fresh fish, game and organic vegetables from an Arran freeholding make up the ingredients for dishes in Mitchell's, which has a restaurant and a separate bistro.

Open: Restaurant: Tues to Fri 12 to 2, 7 to 10, Sat and Mon 7 to 10; bistro: Mon to Sat 11.30 to midnight, Sun 12 to 4
Credit/charge cards: Access, Amex, Diners, Visa

October Café ★
The Rooftop, Princes Square
Buchanan Street G1 3JN *Tel 041-221 0303*

This is the place to go in Princes Square where quality is high and price is not. A glass-fronted lift will take you up to the bar and brasserie; the former serves simple food until early evening, while the brasserie has an all-day à la carte menu.

Open: Mon to Sat 11 to midnight, Sun 12 to 5; closed Xmas
Credit/charge cards: Access, Amex, Visa

One Devonshire Gardens
1 Devonshire Gardens, G12 0UX *Tel 041-339 2001*

Fine food made from fine Scottish ingredients is on offer in the darkly luxurious interior of One Devonshire Gardens, a notable entry in both *The Good Food Guide 1994* and *The Which? Hotel Guide 1994*. A good wine list, with plenty of carefully selected half-bottles, completes the picture.

Open: all week 12.30 to 2 (exc Sat) and 7 to 10.15
Credit/charge cards: Access, Amex, Diners, Visa

Rogano
11 Exchange Place G1 3AN *Tel 041-248 4055*

This lively art deco ground-floor restaurant and basement café has become an institution in Glasgow. The menu offers a fair range with the emphasis on fish and seafood. Café Rogano, in the basement, is an all-day cheaper alternative. The overall ambience is of comfortable enjoyment.

Open: Restaurant: Mon to Sat 12 to 2.30, 7 to 10.30; café: Mon to Thurs 12 to 11, Fri and Sat 12 to midnight; closed public hols
Credit/charge cards: Access, Amex, Diners, Visa

Ubiquitous Chip
12 Ashton Lane G12 8SJ   *Tel 041-334 5007*

The Ubiquitous Chip, or UB Chip, as the locals call it, is a converted warehouse, in a trendy lane next to Glasgow University, with an abundance of greenery inside. It has been open for more than 20 years, and the atmosphere is very informal and the food decidedly Scottish, even providing vegetarian haggis. This restaurant has an outstanding wine award from *The Good Food Guide 1994* for its cellar.

Open: Restaurant: Mon to Sat 12 to 2.30, 5.30 to 11, Sun 6.30 to 11; bistro: Mon to Sat 12 to 11, Sun 12.30 to 11; closed Xmas
Credit/charge cards: Access, Amex, Diners, Visa

ARGYLL AND AROUND

- A ragged coastline hiding unruffled sea lochs
- St Columba's sacred island of Iona
- Islands to suit all tastes from tiny Gigha to the wilds of Mull

Iona Abbey

DEEPLY indented coastlines and a web of offshore islands make Argyll at once distinct and enticing. The view across lochs and firths is almost always decorated by close or distant land masses of overlapping hills or mountains, misty or sharp contours and shapes that are forever changing as you drive along. Long and low-lying Kintyre, for instance, is more memorable for views across water than for inland scenery. Reflections of hills or mountains, castles or sheep-dotted slopes are true and sharp in this land of narrow and mirror-smooth bands of water.

Most sights in Argyll are minor, but there is a fair variety. Popular spots include Inverary, home to one of Scotland's most famous castles, and Oban, busy fishing port and tourist centre. Close to Glasgow is Charles Rennie Mackintosh's Hill House – not to be missed. The hill fort of Dunadd, the capital of the ancient kingdom of Dalriada, gets its fair share of visitors; it is surrounded by one of the highest concentrations of prehistoric monuments anywhere in Scotland. Amongst the castles, many of which are in advanced stages of ruin, are Kilchurn on Loch Awe, and Castle Stalker – both with atmospheric settings. Other sights include an underground power station, a couple of wildlife centres, a clutch of woodland gardens, and a reconstructed old Highland township. Finally, there is Iona, the sacred heart of old Scotland and still the centre of popular pilgrimage.

The Inner Hebridean islands included in the chapter – Mull, Colonsay, Islay, Jura, Coll and Tiree among them – vary from very small to very large, and from flat and fertile to mountainous and desolate. In many cases the smaller they are the more interesting: consider the religiously important Iona, the freakish geology of Staffa, or the lush and untrampled Colonsay. But if you are after total seclusion, look further north. Above all, be warned that the loch-pierced mainland and erratic ferry schedules are not designed for time-conscious travellers; do not assume that you can slip in a quick island tour to top up your Scottish experience. Yet you should not exclude the islands from your itinerary if you do have time. The rich endowment of hill forts, burial cairns and Celtic remains are rewarding even if you have only the faintest knowledge of pre- or ancient history.

Bureaucratically speaking, Argyll ceased to exist in 1975 when the giant new Strathclyde region scooped it up along

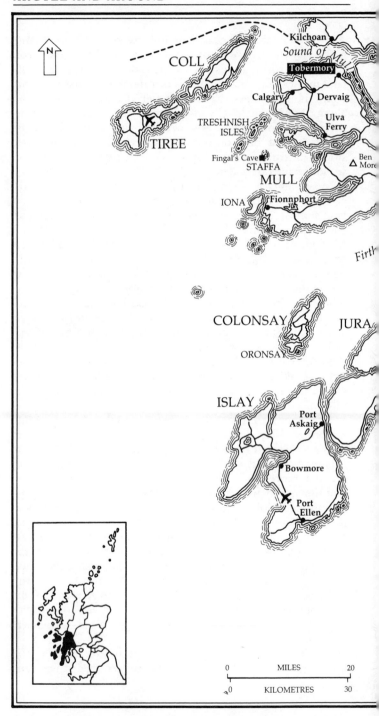

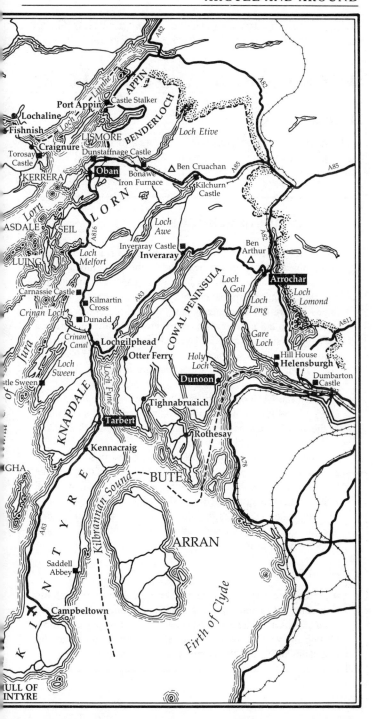

with a multiplicity of unrelated areas, including Glasgow itself. But the name and spirit of Argyll live on.

LOCH LOMOND AND LOCH LONG

Dumbarton Castle

(HS, standard times; closed Thurs pm and Fri in winter)
The grey town of Dumbarton, capital of the old kingdom of Strathclyde before Norse raiders seized it in AD 877,

---

Practical suggestions

Although this part of the country boasts virtually as much geographical variety as can be found in the whole of Scotland, you should not assume that a holiday in Argyll will provide the complete Scottish experience. For a start, main roads (though improved) are few and narrow lanes the norm. Popping over to the islands is not necessarily a simple business either, unless you are happy to stick to Gigha and Mull: ferries go far less frequently to Jura, and only a few times a week to Coll, Tiree and Colonsay. You cannot just arrive and expect to find a bed for the night, either – Colonsay has just one hotel, for instance.

Prime tourist spots such as Oban, Inveraray Castle, Loch Lomond and Bute can get unpleasantly touristy, but since much of the area is often passed through rather than visited, in much of Argyll you are unlikely to feel crowded.

Common holiday activities include fishing and walking, as well as boating, which is ideal in the protected water round the myriad islands. From Oban south to Kintyre, marinas swell with yachts. You don't need to bring your own boat or spend all your time on water, of course. Charter and cruise boats line the quays of lochs and harbours such as Loch Fyne and Loch Lomond, as well as Oban itself.

Good bases

• **Arrochar** Small but stretching over more than a mile of shore, with many B&Bs looking out across Loch Long to uninhabited mountains. Good facilities, especially at the cheaper end. Fine boating and walking area and central for the high moorland and mountains north and the Dunoon peninsula to the south.

---

appears almost as soon as you have crossed the Erskine Bridge.

The castle sits on a high, steep-sided rock near where the River Leven flows into the Clyde. There is an eighteenth-century, box-shaped, windowless magazine, but apart from some ramparts and a few gun batteries little else is left of the fortress which once defended all of western Scotland. During the Wars of Independence, the governor of Dumbarton, Sir John Monteith, turned traitor against William Wallace (see page 272) and may have imprisoned him here before sending him to his gruesome execution in London.

- **Dunoon** The best place to stay if you are visiting the Cowal peninsula, especially if you arrive there on the ferry from Gourock. A good town for strolling in, with four miles of promenade and a large harbourside park complete with castle ruin. Plenty of B&Bs in Kirn, a suburb a little to the north. You are unlikely to find accommodation on the last Friday and Saturday in August, when the Cowal Highland Gathering takes over the town.
- **Tarbert** Halfway along the Kintyre peninsula and handy for catching ferries: Claonaig to Arran (during the summer), Tayinloan to Gigha, Kennacraig to Islay and Jura. Small, with no sights to speak of, but pleasant and not often inundated by tourists. The main part of town, facing west, curves round a very deep harbour. Average restaurants and accommodation.
- **Oban** Oban is easy to like for the quick pace of life as well as its broad and handsome harbour. It is perfectly placed for day trips up and down the coast, and a primary port that links the mainland with Mull, Coll and Tiree. Smaller ferries to many of the little islands in and around its harbour leave from landings just outside town. A wide choice of sights in and around town, and a plethora of small, carless islands to explore means that you are unlikely to get bored. No shortage of accommodation, and the best range of restaurants and shops for miles around.
- **Tobermory** Mull's capital, near the north-east tip, can be reached via ferry from Oban. The town consists of one great swoop of harbour street, with some houses raked up the hill behind: colourful and unassuming guesthouses are scattered around outside of town, but there are a few mid-range hotels on the harbour.

If you climb the long staircase up the White Tower rock you will be rewarded with an intriguing panorama over the industrial lower Clyde. Long views of moors and mountains to the north are also revealed.

Loch Lomond

Twenty-three miles long and five miles across at the widest point, Loch Lomond's 18,000 acres cover the largest area of any lake in Britain. Although it sits right at Glasgow's doorstep, it is remarkably clean and very much less spoilt than you might expect. Its tree-lined shores and mountainous backdrop are not seen at their best from a car – you must get out and walk down to the shore.

Open farmlands and wooded islands mark the southern end. There are good facilities, especially for boating: the recently developed **Duck Bay Marina**, near the south-western tip, is a pleasant, if touristy, spot with a sizeable stretch of beach and a playground as well as a marina and hotel.

As the lake starts to narrow halfway up, so trees close in on you and Ben Lomond comes into view; by the time you reach Tarbet, the road is almost lost between a bank of thick pines and the water's edge. Stop at the observation site at the northern tip for a splendid view that extends far down the loch.

The problem with this side of Loch Lomond is Highland-bound traffic; Loch Lomond's western shore is never entirely peaceful and is often exasperatingly crowded, particularly at weekends. If you want to escape the A82, the B831 to Glen Fruin makes a good trip, the narrow road rising through a broad, gentle valley to high moorland and an eventual view of Gare Loch. But the best way to appreciate the virtues of Loch Lomond is by boat – hire your own or take a cruise.

Helensburgh

The less direct route to Arrochar along the A814 leads you to this sedate but stylish seaside resort. Victorian houses flank wide avenues that are tidily arranged on a grid. As you move up the hillside, views of the Firth of Clyde and Gare Loch get bigger and better and so do the properties. Helensburgh is both a popular spot for day-tripping Glaswegians and a desirable residence. John Logie Baird, inventor of the television, lived here, but most people associate Helensburgh with Charles Rennie Mackintosh. **The Hill House** (NTS, open Apr to Dec exc Xmas, daily 1 to 5), which he built in 1902 for publisher Walter Blackie, is a delight. Outside the gates are six large street lamps, constructed from recently discovered Mackintosh sketches; inside the house, bold, angular shapes are mixed with jubilant, decorative patterns of sinuous, swirling lines. The colour scheme of black, pinks and purples is equally self-confident. Restrained by cost and by Blackie's taste, Mackintosh had to forgo designing every bit of furniture and decoration, but you have to look hard to find a single hinge or nail at odds with his grand scheme. The dining-room shows how clever he was at integrating Blackie's old furniture with Art Nouveau. The house is essential visiting for Mackintosh fans, and nearly everyone will find pleasure in the harmonious design. You can stock up on Mackintosh motif tea towels, mugs and books at the gift shop, and there is also a tea-room.

As you leave Helensburgh and travel north you drive along the shore of **Gare Loch**, a Combined Operations base during World War II.

Then the road takes you up the eastern shore of **Loch Long**, a narrow, deep and sheltered sea loch. Its name comes not from its shape but from the Gaelic 'loch of the ships', harking back to Viking times when longships were dragged across the narrow strip between Arrochar and Tarbet to Loch Lomond. Tankers are often moored along its southern shores, but recreational sailing takes over in the north.

Arrochar

A popular tourist centre and stepping-off point for the nearby mountains, the so-called 'Arrochar Alps', Arrochar makes the most of its position at the head of Loch Long. The town spreads along more than a mile of the eastern shore with its houses and hotels looking over the water to the much-climbed Ben Arthur, known as 'the Cobbler'.

From Arrochar the A83 heads west past the Argyll Forest Park and up Glen Croe. The Cobbler remains in view for the first few miles and is then replaced by craggy Beinn Ime and Beinn an Lochain, which soar upwards from a valley choked with bracken and populated by sheep and trees. The **Rest and Be Thankful** pass at the watershed between Lochs Long and Fyne is a good place to breathe the air and gaze at mountains. The narrow road (B828) that runs along the west side of Loch Goil eventually reaches

Carrick Castle, a privately owned, unblemished ruin from the fifteenth century.

COWAL AND BUTE

The deeply indented, lobster-claw-shaped Cowal Peninsula is easy to reach from Glasgow (by ferry from Gourock), and in summer walkers and boating types, fond of its gentle hills and calm inlets, come here in droves. However, there is plenty of undeveloped wilderness and many miles of lightly populated coast. The **Argyll Forest Park** covers much of north-east Cowal, but not all of it is plantation, and there is a reasonable variety of vegetation. It is criss-crossed by woodland and hill trails and forest roads, popular with walkers but hardly overrun.

Dunoon

The regular car ferries from Gourock to Dunoon connect with the train from Glasgow, while cruises on the Clyde also stop here. So the place really buzzes in the summer, especially on the last Friday and Saturday in August, when the Cowal Highland Gathering overtakes the town.

Dunoon is the largest town on the peninsula, with many fine houses remaining from Victorian and Edwardian days when wealthy Glaswegians came on holiday. The four miles of promenade are as popular for evening strolls now as they were then. **Castle Hill**, a spacious green park above the pier, rises steeply to the few remaining fragments of a thirteenth-century castle from where you can see many miles of shore and sea. A statue of Highland Mary, whom Burns almost married, stands just below.

The waters have not always been entirely the province of pleasure craft. **Holy Loch**, an inlet on Dunoon's northern side, was a base for American nuclear submarines from the early 1960s to late in 1991. For the best loch views, travel north up the A880 to the little holiday village of Ardentinny.

Younger Botanic Garden

(Open mid-Mar to Oct, daily 10 to 6)
The entrance to these wonderful gardens is just north of Ardbeg on the A815. They were planted by James Duncan

between 1870 and 1880, later owned by Younger (of brewery fame) and in 1928 were handed over to the nation. They are naturally laid out and sheltered by tall trees. A striking grass avenue, planted with Californian redwoods, channels you into undulating parkland, dotted with flowering shrubs (some say Younger has the best collection of rhododendrons in the world), enormous Scots pines, little ponds and occasional formal flower beds. You can also climb into the wooded hillside.

South-west Cowal

This is the most peaceful part of Cowal. The A886, the new Strachur–Tighnabruaich road, runs through green fields; the B8000 hugs the shores of Loch Fyne. At Otter Ferry (from the Gaelic 'oiter' for sandbank) a single-track road connects the two, crossing a high, craggy moor from which you have several good vantage points.

South of Otter Ferry the road veers inland through quiet farmland. **Kilfinan** consists of a few buildings, one of which is an excellent inn, and a good beach. The small Victorian village and yachting centre of **Tighnabruaich** lies on the shore of the Kyles of Bute and makes a good goal for a trip, with fine views from the A8003 north.

Bute

Fifteen miles long and no more than five across, Bute has long been a popular holiday island. Previous generations stuck to Rothesay, but now that more people bring cars, the island's remoter shores have sprouted camping and riding centres, and there are three golf courses. Much of Bute is pasture and farmland, tame and undemanding but memorable when seen against the far-off, stark mountain ranges of Arran. The north-western side offers uncrowded, sandy and rocky bays.

Rothesay

The old resort has an endearingly buoyant air during the summer months, and has recently had a face-lift: the cast-iron Winter Garden Pavilion has been returned to its former exuberant glory and yachts, sea birds and bathers populate the wide harbour.

- **Rothesay Castle** (open daily 9.30 to 6.30), one of the

best-preserved early castles in Scotland, is in itself a justification for joining the ferry queues. It was probably first
built in the late twelfth century, though the earliest confirmed
date is 1230, when Norsemen stormed it. There are no
other circular core castles in Britain, and Rothesay's round
silhouette is startling. Its solid, ivy-covered walls are more
than 130 feet in diameter. Of the four great drum towers,
one is still standing. Cottages once filled the middle, as
demonstrated by a small but illuminating model in the Great
Hall, with its large window seats and high arched fireplace. A
reconstructed wooden ceiling hung with Gothic-style wheel
lamps shows how the principal chamber might once have
looked.

• **Bute Museum** (open Easter to Oct, daily 10.30 to 4.30;
Nov to Easter 2.30 to 4.30), behind the castle on Stuart Street,
has two small but well-arranged skylit rooms devoted to geology, archaeology, old Clyde steamer models and photographs
of old Rothesay.

• **Ardencraig Gardens** (open May to Sept, Mon to Fri 9.30
to 4.30, Sat, Sun 1.30 to 4.30), on the southern outskirts of
town, has a stunning show garden and several spectacular
fuchsia greenhouses. It also does a fair line in cactuses and
has a tea-room, too.

St Mary's Chapel

Also known as Lady Kirk, the chapel is possibly 800 years old.
It stands about half a mile south of Rothesay next to the parish
church. It is small and roofless but two recessed canopy tombs
and the effigy of a man in armour have survived remarkably
well. The tomb on the north wall, possibly that of Alice,
stepmother of Robert II, consists of a flat, nearly formless
figure and baby, and, carved on its base, a row of female
figures in heavily pleated robes.

St Blane's Chapel

This chapel is older and more handsome than St Mary's,
but its setting, a fertile dip near the southern windswept tip
of the island that gets the best view of Arran's blue-grey
mountains, is its most memorable attribute. St Blane was
born on Bute in the sixth century and a monastery dedicated
to him was built here. The narrow, roofless chapel is worth
seeing for the delicately carved columned Romanesque arch
of the chancel.

LORN AND OBAN

Inveraray

In the heart of Campbell country, the Georgian town of Inveraray sits near the northern tip of Loch Fyne. The town is debonair and well kept, but it can sometimes feel like an open-air gift emporium for Inveraray Castle: the handsome façades of the houses lining Main Street East are hard to appreciate amongst the array of tartans flowing from giftshop doorways. A stroll around is unlikely to be boring even so, for the town is photogenic, especially down by the harbour. It is here, within a wall right by the water's edge, that you will find **Inveraray Jail** (open Easter to Oct, daily 9.30 to 6, July, Aug 9.30 to 7; Nov to Easter 10 to 5), a clever reconstruction of prison buildings that have life-sized models of inmates sleeping, making herring nets or, in one case, nursing a baby. Try out the hammocks (or the bare wood floor) and crank the hard labour machine as you listen to grim tales of prisoners' fates. The courtroom (1920) is always in session, and you can sit amongst the grey-clad models and listen to the trial of a farmer accused of an insurance fraud. The Crime and Punishment exhibition, relating cases of benighted suspects and evil criminals, rounds out the visit.

Walk directly inland from the jail to find the **Episcopal Church of All Saints**, from the bell tower of which you get an especially good all-round survey of town, castle, mountains and loch, as well as a close-up glimpse of the ten bells which together weigh eight tons.

Inveraray Castle

(Open early Apr to mid-Oct, Mon to Thurs, Sat 10 to 1, 2 to 6, Sun 1 to 6; open Fri in July, Aug)
This, the seat of the Duke of Argyll, is one of Scotland's grandest stately homes. It was planned in 1745 by the third Duke, who wanted to build it on the elevated site then occupied by the town, so the town was rebuilt in its present position. The solid, square bulk of the Gothic-revival castle has crenellated turrets at each corner; witch-hat tops were added in 1877. Inside, hardly a surface remains ungilded. The state dining-room is a French *tour de force*, with delicate flower garlands painted within panels defined by gilt mouldings. Much of the fine period furniture is also French. The spectacular arms room and large, stone-floored kitchen

237

are other highlights. Portraits of Campbells hang throughout the building, and their lives are documented in exhaustive detail. In the grounds, a Combined Operations Museum commemorates through photographs, models and posters Inveraray's role as a training centre during the last war.

Loch Fyne

Argyll Wildlife Park (open Apr to Oct, daily 9 to 6.30; Nov to Mar, daylight hours) shows off pens and enclosures filled with wildcats, badgers, rare birds of prey, foxes and wild boar. Tame roe deer, goats, sheep and ducks of every description follow you along the paths, especially if you are carrying a bag of feed.

Auchindrain Old West Highland Township (open Apr to Sept, daily 10 to 5; closed Sat in Apr, May, Sept), three-and-a-half miles south of Argyll Wildlife Park, was a working farm until the middle of this century, and the last to be run on communal-tenancy terms. Twelve tenants paid a single rent to the Duke of Argyll and worked plots of land, annually reallocated (by lot) to give every farmer a turn at the best. Houses and barns, a few thatched but most with red corrugated roofs, are spread out beside a narrow burn. A few are ruined shells; the rest are furnished in different period styles, with the minutiae of daily life on display.

Crarae Garden (open Apr to Oct, daily 9 to 6; Nov to Mar, daylight hours) has been described as the closest Scotland comes to a Himalayan gorge. Azaleas and rhododendrons grow from niches in the rocks which fringe a steep torrent, and drop flame-coloured petals into the peaty water. Huge specimen conifers tower above the rapids and there are groves of acer and eucalyptus. Three colour-coded walks, lasting from half an hour to two hours, criss-cross their way up the glen, leading you through a landscape which intrigues in its combination of inspired planting and natural grandeur. The plant sales area is expertly run.

Lochgilphead, curving around the head of Loch Gilp, has pleasant wide streets and plenty of guesthouses. At the beginning of the nineteenth century, a developer tried to attract people and industry; the town mustered a few mills and a gasworks, but they had closed by the end of the century. That left fishing, but the herring in Loch Fyne vanished suddenly before World War I. Nowadays, Lochgilphead is a market town and tourist centre.

Loch Awe

Loch Awe is a 23-mile sliver of prime trout-fishing water running parallel with the upper reaches of Loch Fyne.

Its most dramatic scenery and its best sights are at its northern end, but a long round trip on the minor roads beside the loch is also rewarding. The ruined but still substantial and renovated **Kilchurn Castle**, on a shingle tongue at the northern tip, has an especially magnificent approach. As you walk the 500 yards from the road, the hills and mountains give way to a view of the loch with the silhouette of the castle looming centre stage. The original tower was built by Colin Campbell, first Earl of Argyll, in 1440, and was a crucial stronghold of the Campbells of Glenorchy. At the end of the seventeenth century, barracks that included the two round corner towers were added, turning it into a formidable castle. It was never conquered; the enormous fallen turret that dominates the courtyard was the victim of a gale. An information board at the top of the five-storeyed tower identifies the glorious range of mountains to the north. Boat trips on the loch leave from a pier beside Loch Awe Hotel.

Ben Cruachan, rising steeply above the **Pass of Brander**, bars the passage westward, apart from the narrow channel forced by the river. Here Robert the Bruce won a battle against the MacDougalls before taking Dunstaffnage Castle. Under the mountain is a hydro-electric plant with a difference, for it is buried in the guts of the mountain (open Easter to Oct, daily 9 to 4.30). A half-mile ride under the mountain delivers you to the turbine hall, where the guides explain the pumped storage system.

Turn on to the B84 at the foot of the pass to visit **Ardanaiseig Gardens** (open Apr to Oct, daily 8am to 9pm), which are at their best during the spring and summer when the rhododendrons, azaleas and wild flowers are out.

Crinan Canal

By driving down Loch Awe to the sea-coast of Lorn, you reach an area of low hills, jagged rocks, heavily indented shoreline and offshore islets. The canal cuts across the peninsula between Loch Fyne and Loch Crinan, the short cut saving boats the long and dangerous journey around the Mull of Kintyre. The Crinan Canal, opened in 1801, is nine miles long and has 15 locks. Its engineer was Sir John Rennie, but Thomas Telford was called in to sort out early snags and often gets all the credit.

You need not come in a boat to enjoy the Crinan Canal – a walk along the towpath watching boats of all shapes and sizes jockeying for position and negotiating the locks has plenty to recommend it.

Dunadd and Kilmartin

The strange flat basin of land fringing the Crinan Canal to the north has a dense collection of ancient settlements. The Iron Age hill fort of **Dunadd** is recognised as the capital of the ancient kingdom of Dalriada and the site of its monarchs' investiture. Unfortunately, knowing its historical significance ahead of time can spoil your visit, because there is not much left to see on the steep-sided hill rising abruptly from the great Moss of Crinan. Just below the grassy peak is a footprint, and a shallow dip in a rock – from which collected rainwater may have been used to bless newly-crowned monarchs. You have to use a lot of imagination to visualise the scene – not easy in high season, because Dunadd is very popular.

Older fragments of the past litter the valley just to the north and many are more satisfying than Dunadd with more to see and fewer people to get in the way. **Dunchraigaig Cairn** dates from the second millennium BC, and consists of sea-worn boulders piled above several stone coffins (cists). It is typical of several other burial cairns, though with a diameter of 98 feet, it is larger than most. Tongue-and-groove carving on the slabs at **Ri Cruin** cairn suggests good woodworking skills. Grave robbers were active in these parts, but **Nether Largie** was left intact. **Nether Largie South** is the most remarkable cairn in the district, chambered, large enough to enter, and left in its natural state. Across the road the upright stones of **Templewood Circle** form an incomplete circle around a burial cairn. Look for the double spiral carving on an orange-coloured stone, thought to have been connected with sun worship. **Kilmartin** itself has a castle of little interest, but in the church the Celtic **Kilmartin Cross** has what is thought to be one of the oldest images of Christ in Britain and the pretty churchyard has a wealth of medieval crosses and gravestones, with informative signs to help you appreciate the carvings.

Kilmartin to Oban

Carnasserie Castle (open at all reasonable times) is an imposing and strategically sited tower-house built in the sixteenth century by John Carswell, who translated the first book to be printed in Gaelic, *The Book of Common Order* (1567). The five-storeyed castle is in fair shape, and important because it was transitional between castle and mansion house. Given that the fireplace on the first floor is made of hard schist, its detail is remarkable. Carnasserie sits well above the A816, two miles north of Kilmartin, but a track brings you quite close.

From Carnasserie Castle to Oban you are in the thick of boating and riding country. **Ardfern** is a good place to watch yachts and powerboats, or you could drop into **Craobh Haven** on the Craignish peninsula's northern coast to see a wonderfully sited eighteenth-century Scottish fishing village which turns out, on closer inspection, to be reproduction, its modest size making it all the more realistic.

The B844, which leaves the main road halfway between Loch Melfort and Oban, leads to the islands of **Seil** and **Luing**. Seil is connected to the mainland by the splendid humpbacked **Clachan Bridge** (1791), referred to as the Bridge over the Atlantic. Where the road ends you look across to Easdale, a little island off Seil's western coast, which gives a vivid glimpse into a slice of Scotland's heritage. This is slate-quarrying land, and the life and times of the once large population of Easdale is displayed at the **Easdale Island Folk Museum** (open Apr to Sept, Mon to Sat 10.30 to 5.30, Sun 10.30 to 4.30). Nearby abandoned quarries serve as an outdoor exhibition. A little ferry goes from Seil to the pier of the touristy hamlet of Easdale. Luing, whose slate was used on the roof of Iona's Abbey, can be reached by car ferry from Seil.

Oban

The tourist centre and ferry port of Oban is a likeable place, its energy generated by townsfolk, fishing boats, visitors and pleasure craft alike. The broad harbour, lined by shops, restaurants and large, old-fashioned hotels, is nearly cut off from the sea by the island of Kerrera, and houses are closely packed on the hillside.

Oban offers a standard diet of tourist sights and events, but if you have only a few hours here, forget them all and just savour the town, the harbour and perhaps a woollen shop or two. Pick up a smoked salmon sandwich or a dish of cockles at any of the seafood snack bars near the terminal on Railway Quay and watch ferries arriving and departing. Climb up to **McCaig's Folly**, a nineteenth-century coliseum crowning Oban's hillside. The view of town, harbour and islands from its park is superb, even if the folly itself falls short of expectations. McCaig was a local banker, but his attempt to immortalise himself while providing employment for hard-up townsfolk bankrupted him.

Of the more conventional things to see, the **World in Miniature** (open Easter to Nov, Mon to Sat 10 to 5, Sun 2 to 5), on one arm of the harbour, is more British than universal; its 50 miniature rooms and dioramas are intricately worked, but if it is crowded you cannot appreciate it fully. This and a tour of **Oban Distillery** (open Mon to Fri, 9.30 to 5, also Sat Easter to Oct) are the town's best rainy day activities.

Oban Rare Breeds Farm Park (open late Mar to Sept/Oct, daily 10 to 5.30; mid-June to Aug, 10 to 7.30), a few miles north of the town, is blessed with a lovely hilltop location. It is good fun, too, and well organised, with farm animals, common and uncommon, enclosed in pens (which you may enter) or roaming free.

A bewildering collection of islands lies in the Firth of Lorn and Loch Linnhe near Oban, many little more than rocks poking out of the sea. Ferries go to **Lismore** and **Kerrera**, the most popular destinations for walking. Lismore is nine miles long, very green, with the occasional farm-steading and with excellent shore walks. Kerrera, opposite Oban and reached from a jetty at Gallanach, south of the town, is slightly hillier. Two circular walks begin at the jetty. The northern loop is longer but defined by a track; go south and you walk over grass and along the rocky shore. Views from **Gylen Castle**, built in 1587 by the MacDougalls, justify the trek.

BENDERLOCH AND APPIN

The imposing **Dunstaffnage Castle** (open Easter to Oct, daily 9 to 6), three-and-a-half miles north of Oban, grows from a rock foundation at the entrance to Loch Etive. The MacDougalls founded the castle in the thirteenth century, since when it has changed little. Robert the Bruce took the castle from the MacDougalls in 1309, and by the late fifteenth century it was in Campbell hands (the Duke of Argyll owns it today). Flora Macdonald was imprisoned here in 1746 on her way to brief confinement in London. A seventeenth-century tower-house and three towers are integrated with the curtain wall, within which stands an early eighteenth-century dwelling. The chapel, a short distance away in a wood, is also thirteenth century and is most notable for the dog-tooth carving on its Gothic windows.

At the mouth of **Loch Etive**, which plunges deep into the hills, the **Falls of Lora** are a fierce tide-race created by this sea-loch's narrow mouth and the broad reef that spans more than half of it. Water flow is so restricted that the loch cannot empty and fill at the same rate as the tide comes and goes. The result is a rushing and swirling of angry water. Stand in the middle of the long, cantilevered Connel Bridge to get a bird's-eye view or walk down to the shore in the village of Connel.

Five miles east of Connel Bridge, on the north shore of the loch, **Ardchattan Gardens** surround a mansion by the ruins of a priory built in 1230 (open Apr to early Nov, daily 9 to 9). Robert the Bruce convened a parliament here in 1308. The gardens, specialising in shrub roses, potentillas and herbaceous borders, were planted to be at their best between July and September, but the spring flowers can be just as gratifying. The ruins are worth exploring too: medieval tombstones with carvings of skeletons, skulls and cross-bones abound.

On the south side of the loch is **Bonawe** (HS, standard times; closed in winter), Britain's most complete charcoal-fuelled, iron ore smelting furnace. It was founded in 1753 and worked for just under a century, cannon balls being one of its main products. The Cumbrian ironmasters who built Bonawe have been accused of exploiting the region, denuding it of nearly all its original forests, but it is hard not to admire the handsome, solid stone furnace building and storage rooms. Maps suggest a route and plaques describe the buildings. A little of the oak forest that fuelled Bonawe remains in the **Glen Nant Nature Reserve**, two miles south of Taynuilt.

Port Appin

From Connel Bridge, the A828 runs north through peaceful countryside. A turn south after doubling round the Loch Creran brings you to a flat, half-hidden peninsula, a country of marshy fields, oak and rocky shore. Port Appin is the place to stop for a walk, or to cross to Lismore, or to watch the yachts.

After leaving Loch Creran, look out for **Castle Stalker** rising out of the sea. Almost as much a favourite for photographers as Eilean Donan Castle on Loch Duich, this grey keep, lapped by the sea and with a background of islands and hills, makes a magical image of Scotland – the more so since the castle is usually inaccessible to the public.

KNAPDALE AND KINTYRE

Knapdale, south of the Crinan Canal, is a forested, hilly area with many walking trails, few inland roads and some exciting coastal drives. The western side has the most sights and views over to the mountains of Jura – unforgettable with a sunset behind them.

Both shores of **Loch Sween** are worth touring, the roads winding through bracken and trees, with the opposite shore reflected in the water. A few small islands sit at the mouth, but beyond is nothing but the Sound of Jura. **Castle Sween** (always open) is on the eastern arm and your first glimpse of its setting is bound to make an impact, whether to exclaim at the beautiful loch and its surrounding landscape, or to groan at the caravan park by the ruin. The castle dates from the middle of the twelfth century, with towers added in the thirteenth. Robert the Bruce attacked it twice during his western campaigns. Things to note are the shallow buttresses, the 7-foot thick, 40-foot high curtain walls, and the round tower at the north-west angle which had a prison and sophisticated plumbing.

Three miles south is the ruined thirteenth-century **Kilmory Knap Chapel**, as gaunt as its scrubland surroundings. Its roof is now glass, to protect the carved stones within. Most notable is the tall, fifteenth-century MacMillan's Cross which has a crucifix on one side and a hunting scene on the other.

The land now narrows into the **Kintyre** peninsula. Were it not for a one-mile strip of land at **Tarbert**, Kintyre would be an island. The town is a cluster of Victorian houses surrounding the tip of the deep West Loch Tarbert. Fishing boats and yachts vie for space along the harbour piers; above them stands the small, ivy-cloaked ruin of Bruce's Castle (renovated rather than built by Bruce). Kennacraig, the main ferry port for Islay and Jura, is six miles to the south.

Gigha

Gigha, connected by ferry from Tayinloan, lies just three miles off the west coast of Kintyre. It is a tiny island, criss-crossed with dry stone dykes and with everything in miniature, from the trout loch to the golf course. Gigha has one road so a bicycle is the best transport (especially since space for cars on the ferry is limited). You can hire a bike at the post office or the Gigha Hotel. Head for the lush **Achamore House Gardens** (open dawn to dusk): created by Sir James Horlick (of hot drink fame) who owned the island, they make the most of Gigha's mild climate and acid soil. Azaleas, rhododendrons, camellias, palms and palm lilies all thrive in the almost frost-free conditions.

Campbeltown and south

In the nineteenth century, Kintyre's main town boasted a large herring fishing fleet and over 30 distilleries. It now survives on tourism, local commerce and just two distilleries. Despite an attractive harbour, the town is neither quaint nor beautiful. The late fourteenth-century, disc-headed **Campbeltown Cross** is unfortunately placed in the centre of a roundabout, but it is superb, both in its design and the delicacy of carving, including a mermaid and a sea monster. **Campbeltown Museum** (open all year, Mon, Tues, Thurs, Fri 10 to 1, 2 to 5, 6 to 8, Wed and Sat 10 to 1, 2 to 5), on Hall Street, has many archaeological specimens, and the eighteenth-century **Town House** on Main Street has a surprising but stylish octagonal steeple. **Davaar Island**, at the mouth of Campbeltown Loch, can be reached on foot at low tide, via a long shingle causeway. In 1887, Archibald MacKinnon painted a crucifixion on the wall of a large cave on the island's south side. It is sometimes hard to see, as the only light comes from a hole in the rock, but it is a novel sightseeing experience all the same.

As you head west towards Keil Point, an overgrown medieval chapel, possibly the successor to the original chapel of St Columba, is easily mistaken for a large hedge. **St Columba's Footprints**, at the top of a grassy knoll just beyond the chapel, are the supposed proof that the saint first entered Scotland through southern Kintyre.

The **Mull of Kintyre** is the southernmost point of the peninsula. A narrow road snakes from Southend through rich farmland, and delivers you to a scraggy headland. The road ends by a lighthouse, only 12 miles from Ireland.

The east coast of Kintyre

The B842 which runs down the east side of Kintyre gives you superb views of Arran across the Kilbrannan Sound. **Saddell Abbey** sits by a burn in a tranquil glen shielded from the road by a thick copse. A Cistercian abbey was founded here in the late twelfth century either by Somerled, the first king of Scotland, or his son, Reginald. Today it is a tumbledown ruin, with gravestones dating from the fourteenth to sixteenth centuries, protected under a shelter. Their artistic merit is admirable and their condition variable. Among the carvings, look for the galleon, the priest holding a chalice and the deer hunt.

Carradale, at the foot of a steep, hairpin-bend road, is a holiday village with a tiny, working fishing harbour – unpretentious, pleasantly isolated and with a sandy beach and caravan park. **Grogport Tannery** sells sheepskins and the process is explained in the small adjoining workshop.

Skipness Castle (always open), the Campbells' southern-most stronghold, is two-and-a-half miles north of Claonaig (ferries to Arran) on a dead-end road. A short walk through a wood brings you to a huge fortress built around a thirteenth-century hall and sixteenth-century tower-house.

ISLE OF MULL

Of the Scottish islands, Mull comes closest to Skye in popularity, though many visitors are really bound for Iona. Mull is large and bleak, with mountains of respectable size at the southern end but elsewhere largely covered by moorland or plantations. The real draw is Mull's wild coast, much of it accessible only on foot. Walking is the way to get the most out of the island; see Olive Brown and Jean Whittaker's *Walking in North Mull* and its companion, covering South Mull and Iona, for a wide choice of routes.

Getting to Mull is easy. Car ferries run from Oban to Craignure and Tobermory, from Lochaline to Fishnish and, in season, from Kilchoan on Ardnamurchan to Tobermory.

If you take a car, arrive with a full tank and keep topping up: petrol stations are few and far between.

Torosay and Duart Castles

Close to the ferry port of Craignure are two distinctly different castles, each within sight of the other. The A849 south from Craignure terminal brings you first to **Torosay Castle** (open Easter to mid-Oct, daily 10.30 to 5; gardens open daylight hours in winter, 9 to 7 in summer), a nineteenth-century Baronial stately home. Inside, there are fine Edwardian furnishings, but everything is informal and approachable. There are no 'do not touch' signs, and you are encouraged to look through giant scrap-books full of clippings and photos of the family's ventures. Among the paintings and drawings are works by Landseer and Sargent. The formal gardens are especially fine, with a walk bordered by eighteenth-century Italian statuary. In converted stone barns you can watch Isle of Mull weavers in full production. An anecdotal, informative and refreshingly modest guide book is a further plus point. You can walk to Torosay along a forest path starting just south of Craignure, or take the narrow-gauge **Mull and West Highland Railway**, which chugs along sedately for 20 minutes (under steam and diesel) through gorse and woodland.

Duart Castle (open May to Sept, daily 10.30 to 6), perched at the end of a promontory overlooking Loch Linnhe and the Sound of Mull, has the best view on Mull. The castle, seat of Maclean chiefs, goes back to 1250, but most of the present building is a reconstruction, the achievement of Sir Fitzroy Maclean in 1912. Several rooms display sea, war and scouting memorabilia.

North Mull

The north-east coast is Mull's tamest and smoothest and is separated from the mainland by the narrow Sound of Mull. **Pennygown Chapel**, nine miles north of Craignure, is a good example of a pre-Reformation chapel, more than a dozen of which were built on Mull by missionaries from Iona. Note the thick walls and carved gravestones.

Tobermory is Mull's small capital, and lies tucked into the shore at the island's sparsely populated northern end. Its sheltered harbour is lined by smart Georgian houses

247

painted in bold colours; shop windows display fishing tackle and walking gear more prominently than souvenirs. **Mull Museum** (open Apr to Oct, Mon to Sat 10 to 1, 2 to 5), in an old baker's shop on the harbour front, is small and old-fashioned, a good place to learn about Mull's history and to read about the galleon from the Spanish Armada (the *San Juan de Sicilia* or *Florencia*), which sank in mysterious circumstances in Tobermory harbour. Its treasure of doubloons, now well buried in silt, has eluded salvage crews ever since.

West of Tobermory, **Dervaig**, a little hamlet with paired whitewashed cottages and a pencil-spired church, sits at the head of Loch Cuin. Stop at **Coffee & Books** for old and new books, wines and spirits, cheeses and vegetables as well as information, local lore and first-rate coffee.

Two sights are within a few miles of town. The **Old Byre Heritage Centre**, on the hill road to Torloisk, has an audio-visual show above the gift shop and licensed tea-room, but the stone buildings are the best feature. Once the smallest professional theatre in the world, the **Little Theatre of Mull**, on the Salen Road, has expanded to 43 seats. Plays written or adapted for a cast of two are performed through the summer and seats should be booked in advance at Cottage Crafts or Druimard Country House Hotel in Dervaig, or by phone (see page 258).

A major Canadian city took its name from the small fishing village of **Calgary**, whose grand sandy beach, ringed by old trees and cliffs, is the island's most alluring. **Kilninian Church** deserves a look for its imposing medieval gravestones where Maclean, Chief of Torloisk, is shown with pointed helmet, kilt and broadsword, his elaborately carved wife at his side. Tours to the terraced **Treshnish Isles** off the north-west coast of Mull, sanctuary to birds and grey seals, run from Ulva Ferry and Dervaig in calm conditions.

Ben More and Ardmeanach

Ben More, at 3,267 feet, is one of the highest mountains in the Hebrides, yet the ascent is gentle. Start at Dishaig, four miles past Knock on the B8035.

MacKinnon's Cave on the coast west of the point where the B8035 turns south towards Loch Scridain, is one of Mull's best-known sights, but accessible only on foot. The track to Balmeanach Farm takes you to a path leading to a magnificent clifftop and then steeply down to a beach of large boulders. Various theories, one concerning an abbot, another a piper, explain the cave's name. It is huge and very deep, with a wide interior chamber. Keep to the path, make sure to arrive at half tide on a falling tide, and take a torch.

The Ardmeanach peninsula has another famous destination, more out-of-the-way but more unusual than MacKinnon's Cave. **MacCulloch's Fossil Tree** has suffered more damage since the famous geologist discovered it in 1819 than during the previous 50 million years, but it is now protected from souvenir hunters and geology students. The cast of the large pine tree, 40-feet tall, five across, and hollow, is still a fascinating sight. You can walk the 10-mile round trip of the peninsula, but plan to reach the tree on a falling tide.

South Mull

Pilgrims en route to Iona once trudged along a narrow track from Glen More to Fionnphort, the route now followed by the A8490, and south Mull is still a country for energetic walkers. There are basalt arches, a stone circle and several deserted lochs to see, but they are all well away from the road. **Bunessan**, the largest village for miles around, is now a base for holidaying families rather than a fishing village, though lobster boats still operate. At **Fionnphort**, less a town than a car park, the road ends. Iona lies offshore and regular passenger ferries connect the two islands.

IONA

'The morning star of Scotland's faith' is small (three miles by one-and-a-half) and mostly flat and windswept, but its importance to Christianity is great. Christian roots go back before St Ninian, but Columba usually gets the credit for sanctifying this ancient isle. The missionary-saint arrived from Ireland in AD 563 with 12 companions, founded a monastery (now destroyed), and began his long journeys to convert the pagan Picts. Scottish kings (48 in all) were buried here until the eleventh century. Reginald, son of Somerled, founded a Benedictine monastery and Augustinian nunnery at the beginning of the thirteenth century, but both were vandalised during the Reformation. The Iona

Cathedral Trust now owns the sacred precincts; the rest of the island belongs mostly to the National Trust for Scotland.

The small medieval **nunnery** is a well-maintained ruin; the church and chapter house are original, while the cloister and refectory were built around 1500. **MacLean's Cross** is one of Iona's best medieval religious carvings, decorated with Celtic motifs. The **Abbey**, near the site of the original monastery and stark and severe against the flat expanse of green, has been massively restored, but the north transept and arcade of the north wall of the choir, along with some elaborate carvings, are original. The **Abbey Museum** has a rich collection of cross-marked gravestones. The eighth-century **St Martin's Cross** is remarkably complete, with serpent-and-boss ornament on the east face and holy figures on the other. The restored twelfth-century **St Oran's Chapel** is the island's oldest building, and arguably the most handsome. Of pinky-grey stone, it is unadorned save for its one splendid Norman doorway with bold chevron and beak-head decoration on three round arches. To take in the abbey, cross, chapel and graveyard, with the sea and Mull beyond, stand on the small knoll directly opposite the entrance. This is **Torr an Aba**, where Columba's cell is said to have been.

Few will remain unmoved by Iona's spiritual peace. Despite throngs of day-trippers in and around the main sights, finding tranquil spots is easy. Beaches of white sand or colourful pebbles distinguish the coast. At the **Bay at the Back of the Ocean** on the western coast, there is a golf course, tended by sheep, and a spouting cave. The **marble quarry**, last active around 1915, has a rock-cut reservoir, and crude, rusted remains of the cutting frame. It is near the southern tip of the island and just around the corner from **St Columba's Bay**, yet another fine sandy beach, and the saint's supposed landing site.

Staffa

Staffa is one of the most popular excursions from Mull and Iona. Its covering of grass and orchids over a shiny black base of hexagonal basaltic pillars gives it the look of a not altogether successful soufflé rising above a misshapen fluted dish. **Fingal's Cave**, or, as locals often refer to it, 'Musical Cave', inspired Mendelssohn's overture and John Keats' remark: 'For solemnity and grandeur it far surpasses the finest cathedral'. Individuals run trips to Staffa from Dervaig, Ulva and Iona. A new pier now makes landing easier, but the Atlantic swell is often fierce around Staffa unless conditions are good.

THE OTHER ISLANDS

Islay

Islay is among the most populous and fertile of the Hebrides. The trim villages have simple, unadorned houses and the landscape is often spartan, though peat bogs, fertile farmland, low heather-clad hills and stone outcroppings provide variety. Some visitors come just for the golf, others for the wildlife, the monuments or the whisky.

From the ferry at Port Ellen it is a short walk (past three distilleries) to the island's most highly prized artefact, the **Kildalton Cross**, carved (probably by a sculptor from Iona) 1200 years ago. The blue-grey stone cross is impressively large and neatly decorated with Celtic motifs and stylised figures. It seems odd that, although it has survived the elements well enough so far, it is still left outside. The fierceness of the elements on Islay is easy to appreciate on the **Oa**, a little rounded peninsula of hillocks, machair, cow and sheep pastures to the west of Port Ellen. On the **Mull of Oa** stands a bulbous, rocket-shaped monument to the Americans lost when the *Tuscania*, bound for France during World War I, rammed the rocks. It is a short walk from the end of the paved road.

Bowmore is reached from Port Ellen on a ruler-straight road originally designed to take a railway. On either side stretch miles of peat bog scarred by angular cuts and grooves where it has been harvested to fuel home and distillery fires. Bowmore has an intriguing round church designed to ward off evil spirits, who can hide only in corners. The village also has the island's most tourist-friendly distillery (founded in 1779), should you fancy a tour and a nip.

On the **Rinns of Islay**, a hammer-head protrusion in the west of the island, stone walls and a few abandoned home-steads decorate a desolate land. Surf booms along the whole of the western shore. The cliffs at **Sanaigmore** offer prime viewing. A track off the B8018 leads to the calmer waters of **Loch Gorm**, seasonal home to over 20,000 barnacle geese. The village of **Port Charlotte**, stretched along a wide bay, is known for its cheeses and its beaches (good for shell-hunting and bathing) as well as the **Islay Field Centre** (for serious or occasional naturalists), and the compact **Museum of Islay Life**. **Portnahaven**, at the southern tip of the Rinns, is a pretty, steeply raked village with a deeply indented, angular harbour which provides a sanctuary for seals and a mooring for fishing boats.

The A846 Bridgend to Port Askaig road cuts through the island's least populous, more forested eastern side. The **Islay Woollen Mill**, a mile and a half beyond Bridgend, has a well-stocked gift and clothing shop. The mill was established in 1883 on the site of an earlier seventeenth-century enterprise. You are free to walk around the antiquated and dusty workshop and inspect the rare Spinning Jenny and Slubbing Billy (for twisting and knobbling yarn). The clatter and rumble now emanates from modern warping and power weaving machines. **Finlaggan**, a few miles short of Port Askaig, has a loch, castle ruins and a helpful new visitor centre which displays archaeological remains. **Port Askaig**, huddling at the base of a steep, wooded hillside, is little more than dock and car park.

Jura

Jura's cone-shaped peaks, the **Paps of Jura**, have been landmarks for passing ships down the ages. Nothing else on Jura can hold a candle to their beauty, although they are less easy to appreciate from the island itself than from the Kintyre peninsula. Wildlife, remote moor and timeless seascapes are Jura's finest assets. Red deer graze nonchalantly beside Highland cattle. Wild goats are commonplace. Views out to sea from the island's one road are especially rewarding because of the height from which you look over the water. Jura has only one true village (Craighouse), which would almost fit into the shadow of its distillery. Otherwise, crofts, some abandoned, are the only sign of habitation. **Barnhill**, a rambling stone house where George Orwell wrote *Nineteen Eighty Four*, stands in forlorn isolation at the end of a bumpy track that continues where the main road stops. From here a path winds north along the shore to reach the **Gulf of Corryvreckan**, which divides Jura from Scarba. Arrive one hour after low tide to see and hear the whirlpool, notoriously hard to navigate but wonderful to behold, at its best. Corryvreckan, whose roar can be heard long before you reach it, is the most dangerous tide race in Scotland. It is named after the legendary Breacan who anchored his boat here by a rope of maidens' hair. One maiden had been untrue so the rope parted and Breacan was drowned.

Jura is large enough to accommodate the most reclusive walker, but pause for thought before taking a car over. The island is a popular excursion from Islay, so its narrow road sometimes chokes with day trippers. The uninhabited west coast is hard to reach, but raised beaches of smooth pebbles and a series of huge caves are incentive enough for trekkers.

Colonsay and Oronsay

Colonsay lies 25 miles from the mainland and, with Oronsay, is only 10 miles long from tip to toe. It has several historical and archaeological sites, but you will probably remember it best for its tranquillity. Quiet, undemanding, with only three ferries per week, it is the perfect retreat, though in danger of becoming an island with more holiday homes than permanent residents. Apart from one hotel and a couple of bed and breakfasts, all accommodation is self-catering.

Colonsay is an island of green pastures, fine beaches, cliffs, rocky coves, woodlands, moors, and lochans covered in water-lilies. Five hundred varieties of local flora and 150 species of birds have been recorded. **Colonsay House Garden**, a small but concentrated woodland of rhododendrons, giant palms, and exotic shrubs, is worth a stroll. The curved **Kiloran Bay**, not far to the north, has a magnificent half-mile-long beach of honey-gold sands, just right for surfing after strong Atlantic winds. Of the island's various standing stones, those at Kilchattan, **Fingal's Limpet Hammers**, are most imposing but you cannot get very close because they are enclosed in a fenced-off field. Near Kilchattan is **Port Mor**, a pebbly beach with large rocks, chattering seabirds and good surf. Bronze Age forts or duns are plentiful on Colonsay; **Dun Eibhinn**, a dramatic hump next to the hotel, is an easy climb.

Some say the name of **Oronsay** comes from the Norse for ebb-tide island, which is a just description of Colonsay's near-appendage. At low tide the Strand is easy to cross on foot. St Columba first set foot in Scotland on Oronsay but did not settle because he could still see his native Ireland. The present, fourteenth-century **Priory**, sitting within sight of the sea in surprisingly lush pasture, supposedly occupies the site

USEFUL DIRECTORY

Main tourist offices
Bute and Cowal Tourist Board
Tourist Information Centre
7 Alexandra Parade
Dunoon
Argyll PA23 8AB
(0369) 3785

Bute and Cowal Tourist Board
Tourist Information Centre
15 Victoria Street
Rothesay
Isle of Bute PA20 0AJ
(0700) 502151

Loch Lomond, Stirling & Trossachs Tourist Board
41 Dumbarton Road
Stirling FK8 2QQ
(0786) 475019

West Highlands and Islands of Argyll Tourist Board
Area Tourist Office
Mackinnon House
The Pier, Campbeltown
Argyll PA28 6EF
(0586) 552056

West Highlands and Islands of Argyll Tourist Board
Boswell House
Argyll Square, Oban
Argyll PA34 4AN
(0631) 63122

Tourist Board publications: annual visitor's guides
listing main sights and accommodation (all five tourist
boards). Special interest: forest and hill walks (Dunoon),
Islay and Jura Whisky Tour (Mid-Argyll), *What to do in
a Day/Afternoon* (Bute), birdwatching (Oban), plus leaflets
on fishing, walks. Order by post or phone from above
addresses.

Local tourist information centres
Balloch (0389) 53533 (Mar to Nov)
Bowmore (0496) 810254

Campbeltown (0586) 552056
Craignure (06802) 377 (Apr to Oct)
Dumbarton (0389) 42306 (Apr to Oct)
Dunoon (0369) 3785
Helensburgh (0436) 72642 (Apr to Oct)
Inveraray (0499) 2063
Lochgilphead (0546) 602344 (Easter to Oct)
Oban (0631) 63122
Rothesay (0700) 502151
Tarbert (0880) 820429 (Easter to Oct)
Tobermory (0688) 2182

Local transport
Loganair (direct air services from Glasgow to Islay,
Campbeltown and Tiree) 041-889 1311
West Coast Motors/Scottish City Link (runs bus service
from Glasgow to Lochgilphead and Campbeltown)
(0586) 552319 or 041-332 9191

Ferries

All run by Caledonian MacBrayne, (0475) 650100, ask for
information, except where other numbers are given.

Car ferries
Wemyss Bay–Rothesay, Bute (up to 20 sailings daily)
Colintraive–Rhubodach, Bute (frequent sailings daily)
Claonaig–Lochranza, Arran (mid-Apr to mid-Oct, up to
ten sailings daily)
Tayinloan–Gigha (up to nine sailings daily Mon to Sat, also
Sun from Mar to mid-Oct)
Oban–Lismore (Mon to Sat, up to four sailings daily)
Lochaline–Fishnish, Mull (frequent daily service Mon to
Sat, also Sun early May to Aug)
Oban–Craignure, Mull (up to six sailings daily)
Kilchoan–Tobermory, Mull (Mon to Sat mid-Apr to
mid-Oct, up to seven sailings daily)
Oban–Colonsay (three sailings a week)
Kennacraig–Port Ellen, Islay (one to three sailings daily)
Kennacraig–Port Askaig, Islay (one or two sailings daily
Mon to Sat, also Sun Apr to Oct)
Oban–Tobermory–Coll–Tiree (three to five sailings a week)

Oban–Castlebay–Lochboisdale (three to five sailings a week)
Seil–Luing (frequent daily sailings, passenger only Sun)
(08523) 252
Port Askaig, Islay–Jura (frequent sailings daily, reduced
service Sun), (0496) 840472/840388

Passenger ferries
Fionnphort–Iona (frequent sailings every day, reduced
service Sun and out of season) (0475) 650100
Port Appin–Lismore (several sailings daily) (0631) 73217
Seil–Easdale (frequent sailings daily, reduced service Sun)
(08523) 370
Gallanach, Oban–Kerrera (several sailings daily, reduced
service Sun) (0631) 63665

Boat trips
Trips out of Rothesay, Bute 041-221 8152; (0475) 650100;
(0475) 21281
Loch Lomond cruises from Balloch (0389) 52376/51610
and (0389) 51481; and from Tarbet by Arrochar
(03012) 356
Loch Etive cruises from Taynuilt (08662) 430
Loch Awe cruises from Loch Awe station (0838)
200440
Trips from Dervaig to Staffa, the Treshnish Isles and Coll
(06884) 223
Trips from Iona and Fionnphort to Staffa (06817) 358
Trips from Ulva Ferry on Mull to Staffa, the Treshnish
Isles and Iona (06884) 242

Other
Information and tickets for the Little Theatre, Mull
(06884) 245
Bus trips from Oban to Mull and Iona (06802) 313 or
(0631) 62133
For cruises on the Clyde, see under Glasgow.

of his original monastery. Oronsay's new American owner
has tidied up the mellow stone ruins and created a museum
of ancient carved gravestones within the old **Prior's House**.
For many people, the two-and-a-half-mile walk from the car
park, almost half of which takes you over wet sand scattered
with seaweed and crab shells, remains the high point of a visit
to the island.

Coll and Tiree

Coll and Tiree are both quiet, gentle islands, whose attractions for visitors are undisturbed peace, bird-life, views, coastal scenery and gentle walking. They lie to the west of Mull and can be reached by ferry from Oban, or, in the case of Tiree, by plane from Glasgow.

Both islands are flat, but where Tiree is fertile and sprinkled with crofts Coll is more conventionally Highland, with hard rock and peat hags, and has a much smaller population. Both islands have magnificent, deserted beaches – those on Tiree are likely to be populated by surfers, for the island's waves are reputed to be excellent. Sunshine is common out here away from the rain-attracting hills, but so too are strong Atlantic winds.

There is little point in using a car – hiring a bicycle is cheaper and a more sensible way of getting around. There are a number of small sights – prehistoric remains and a ruined castle or two. There are guesthouses and self-catering accommodation on both islands. You should be able to buy enough for picnics locally, but do not expect anything sophisticated in the islands' shops.

WHERE TO STAY

ARDRISHAIG

Fascadale House £
Tarbert Road, Ardrishaig
By Lochgilphead, Argyll PA30 8EP *Tel (0546) 603845*

An elegant Victorian villa with views over Loch Fyne. Standards are more in keeping with a country-house hotel than a bed and breakfast, and the bedrooms are big and comfortable with excellent bathrooms. Good value.

Open: all year, exc Nov to Feb **Rooms**: 3, plus 3 cottages
Credit/charge cards: none accepted

ARDUAINE

Loch Melfort Hotel £
Arduaine, By Oban
Argyll PA34 4XG *Tel (085 22) 233*

Set at the foot of Loch Melfort, this is a good-value base. The dignity of the solid white house is slightly undermined by the

1960s chalet-style extension, but the hotel is warm and comfortable, especially the bar and panelled library. Bedrooms are being upgraded with pine and fresh fabrics, and the cooking makes the most of the local seafood.

Open: all year, exc 3 Jan to 1 Mar **Rooms**: 27
Credit/charge cards: Access, Visa

COLONSAY

Isle of Colonsay Hotel	**£–££**
Colonsay PA61 7YP	*Tel (095 12) 316*

The 2-hour crossing from Oban makes this eighteenth-century hotel one of the most isolated in Britain. The friendly owners provide lots of perks, such as free use of bicycles and, for those staying more than five days, free trout-fishing, golf and use of a dinghy. Most of the bedrooms have private facilities. Dinner is part of the package, with good seafood; simple bar lunches.

Open: all year, exc Nov to Feb (open for New Year)
Rooms: 11   **Credit/charge cards**: Access, Amex, Diners, Visa

CRINAN

Crinan Hotel	**£**
Crinan, Argyll PA31 8SR	*Tel (0546 83) 261*

Bright bedrooms decorated with pine and vivid fabrics all have a view of the sea or of the Crinan Canal. There is plenty of space in the sitting-rooms, and a choice of two good restaurants.

Open: all year, exc Xmas **Rooms**: 22 **Facilities**: watersports
Credit/charge cards: Access, Visa

DERVAIG

Druimard Country House	**£**
Dervaig, Isle of Mull	
Argyll PA75 6QW	*Tel (068 84) 345*

New confident and friendly owners for this small hotel next to the UK's smallest professional theatre – the Mull Little Theatre. Bedrooms are well equipped with sensible, solid furnishings. The residents' lounge is on the small side; a pleasant conservatory doubles as bar and breakfast room where people gather for pre-performance dinners.

Open: Mar to Oct **Rooms**: 7
Credit/charge cards: Access, Visa

Druimnacroish Country House £
Druimnacroish, Dervaig
Isle of Mull, Argyll PA75 6QW *Tel (068 84) 274*

There are flowers everywhere at this comfortable, old stone
farmhouse a mile outside Dervaig. There is a conservatory and
two lounges, and the spacious bedrooms are well equipped,
with bathrooms well up to country-house standards. Dinners are
traditional and a touch formal, with everyone sitting down at the
same time.

Open: mid-Apr to mid-Oct **Rooms**: 6
Credit/charge cards: Access, Amex, Diners, Visa

ERISKA

Isle of Eriska £££
Ledaig, By Oban, Argyll PA37 1SD *Tel (063 172) 371*

Peace and quiet reign in this civilised island outpost. The bedrooms,
all with showers and reached by the staircase from the panelled hall,
vary in size and have a mix of furnishings and views. The library
has an equally interesting variety of books, and there are plenty of
deep sofas to read them in. Dinner is a formal six-course affair.

Open: all year, exc Nov to Feb **Rooms**: 16 **Facilities**: tennis,
riding, croquet, putting green, water sports, clay pigeon shooting
Credit/charge cards: Access, Visa

IONA

Argyll House £
Isle of Iona, Argyll PA76 6SJ *Tel (068 17) 334*

Close to Iona's ferry pier, this simple nineteenth-century hotel is
much more than a convenient overnight stop. Homely touches
include coal fires in the lounges, interesting paintings and a bright
sun lounge, with pot plants and Lloyd Loom furniture. The food
is well-thought-out, with organic produce and always a vegetarian
choice. Bedrooms, most with bathroom, are small, though they are
pretty in pine and reproduction wood.

Open: Easter to early Oct **Rooms**: 19
Credit/charge cards: Access, Visa

KENTALLEN

Ardsheal House	**££–£££**
Kentallen, Appin	
Argyll PA38 4BX	*Tel (063 174) 227*

A pretty and fascinating eighteenth-century West Highland mansion on the edge of Loch Linnhe, given lots of character by its American owners. Local watercolours decorate the walls and there are some massive pieces of old furniture. A tiny panelled bar was once the butler's pantry and a magnificent brass lamp hangs over the table in the pine-panelled snooker room. The dining-room, half in the conservatory, half in a more formal room, serves excellent food.

Open: Feb to Dec **Rooms**: 13 **Facilities**: tennis, billiards, games room **Credit/charge cards**: Access, Visa

The Holly Tree	**££**
Kentallen, Appin	
Argyll PA38 4BY	*Tel (063 174) 292*

The old railway station is now a popular hotel. The station tea-room is the bar, while the dining-room with its central enclosed fire inhabits what were once the platforms. Bedrooms have superb views over Loch Linnhe and are modern and comfortable with just about enough space to relax in; those downstairs without the view may be cheaper. Under new management.

Open: Mar to Dec, and by arrangement Jan and Feb **Rooms**: 10 **Facilities**: fishing **Credit/charge cards**: Access, Amex, Visa

KILFINAN

Kilfinan Hotel	**£**
Kilfinan, Nr Tighnabruaich	
Argyll PA21 2EP	*Tel (070 082) 201*

The dining-room of this old coaching-inn in the middle of tiny Kilfinan has huge fireplaces and beams, but the rest of the hotel is bright and modern. Although it is short on places to relax, there is a pleasant paved area outside, and the pretty bedrooms with sprigged wallpaper. Under new management.

Open: all year, exc Feb **Rooms**: 11 **Facilities**: fishing, games room **Credit/charge cards**: Access, Amex, Visa

KIRN

Enmore Hotel £–££
Marine Parade, Kirn
Dunoon, Argyll PA23 8HH *Tel (0369) 2230*

A pleasant Victorian resort hotel with a friendly welcome and unexpected luxuries. There is a large residents' lounge with plenty of relaxing sofas, a small bar and a formal dining-room. Bedrooms are individual and pretty – one has a queen-sized waterbed, another a four-poster. Food is fresh and well presented.

Open: all year, exc 2 weeks in Jan **Rooms**: 12 **Facilities**: games room, squash **Credit/charge cards**: Access, Visa

OBAN

Knipoch Hotel ££
Oban, Argyll PA34 4QT *Tel (085 26) 251*

Knipoch looks out over Loch Feochan, with an old house buried inside the modern extensions and conversions. The décor is a bit stark, and the identical bedrooms have small bathrooms, but the standard of welcome and very good dinners are more in keeping with a country-house hotel.

Open: mid-Feb to mid-Nov **Rooms**: 17
Credit/charge cards: Access, Amex, Diners, Visa

PORT APPIN

The Airds Hotel £££
Port Appin, Appin
Argyll PA38 4DF *Tel (063 173) 236*

A charming old inn on the edge of Loch Linnhe. Bedrooms vary considerably in size but all are comfortable, with bright floral fabrics in the newly redecorated ones. There is a sunny conservatory and two sitting-rooms with fires and comfortable armchairs. The food is always interesting.

Open: all year, exc 6 Jan to 6 Mar **Rooms**: 14
Credit/charge cards: Access, Visa

STRACHUR

Creggans Inn £
Strachur, Argyll PA27 8BX *Tel (036 986) 279*

A West Highland inn on the shores of Loch Fyne, fizzing with life and style. The sun lounge at the front has views across the loch, and there is a popular bar which serves food. The dining-room is more sober with a menu that includes haggis and oyster stew. Bedrooms are peaceful and elegant, with relaxing bathrooms. Good value.

Open: all year **Rooms**: 21 **Facilities**: games room
Credit/charge cards: Access, Amex, Diners, Visa

TARBERT

West Loch Hotel £
Tarbert, Argyll PA29 6YF *Tel (0880) 820283*

This modest but comfortable old inn, close to the ferry pier, makes an excellent overnight stop if you don't mind the occasional lorry passing during the night. Fresh, bright and newly furnished inside, the bedrooms make the most of their limited space, with electric blankets, duvets and efficient showers. Hearty food.

Open: all year, exc Jan **Rooms**: 7
Credit/charge cards: Access, Visa

WHERE TO EAT

CAIRNDOW

Loch Fyne Oyster Bar ★
Clachan Farm, Cairndow PA26 8BH *Tel (049 96) 236*

A simple café-cum-restaurant and produce shop at the end of the Loch serves local oysters, shellfish and smoked meats throughout the day.

Open: daily 9 to 9 **Credit/charge cards**: Access, Amex, Visa

TIRORAN

Tiroran House
Tiroran, Isle of Mull PA69 6ES *Tel (068 15) 232*

There is a house-party atmosphere in this small shooting-lodge with water and hills to one side, and plantations to the other. There is a set-price dinner, with a no-choice main course, at a single sitting, offering local produce including venison and island-smoked fish with good desserts.

Open: daily 7.45; closed Oct to mid-May
Credit/charge cards: none accepted

STIRLING AND PERTH

- Boundary country between Lowlands and Highlands, with landscapes from raspberry fields to mountains
- Outstandingly beautiful rivers
- Historic towns in Stirling and Perth, shapely mountains such as Schiehallion and Ben Lawers, and the lovely Glen Lyon
- Heather, good castles, skiing, Picts, Pontius Pilate and Mary Queen of Scots

Caledonian pine

THIS large area of central Scotland has enough variety for several holidays. The geological boundary separating the Lowlands from the Highlands runs diagonally across it from the south-west, so wherever you go you are in easy reach of both mountain scenery and the attractions of the Lowland valleys. Historically, it is one of the most intriguing parts of the country. The Picts and the Romans both left traces here, while many of the most critical moments in Scotland's history were witnessed by the old towns and castles of the area.

Although the cities of Edinburgh and Glasgow have moved Scotland's centre of gravity south of the River Forth, it was the fertile lands beyond that natural river barrier which were the strategic heartland of the kingdom in medieval times. The chief battles of the Wars of Independence – Stirling Bridge (1297), Falkirk (1298) and Bannockburn (1314) – were fought here, while it was to the quiet priory of Inchmahome that Mary Queen of Scots was taken in 1547 to keep her out of English clutches. Crossing the River Forth northwards can still feel like entering a sanctuary. Southern Scotland is left behind.

However, while the River Forth formed a barrier to invaders from the south, trouble has not always come from that direction. It was from the mountains that the royalist forces of Montrose emerged to inflict two terrible defeats on the Covenanters at Tippermuir (1644) and Kilsyth (1645), and it was from the same direction that Dundee led his Highlanders to the Jacobite victory at Killiecrankie in 1689. Half a century later, the troops of Prince Charles Edward Stuart descended from the mountains to take Perth at the start of the last of the Jacobite uprisings – that of 1745.

So there is an ambiguity about the fertile countryside round Perth and Stirling, with its magnificent, spate-heavy rivers, its sunny fields and its chains of low hills: it is at once the centre of old Scotland and its vulnerable edge.

Beyond the Highland line

Like many another vanishing tribal society, the Highlanders of Scotland started to become the subjects of romantic legend the moment they ceased to be a threat. This happened early in the nineteenth century, and nearly two centuries-worth of tartanry, bagpipes, clan gatherings and other images carefully fostered to this day by the tourist industry have totally obscured the suspicion or fear with which the Highlands were once regarded – as late as 1773, Dr Johnson provided himself with a pair of pistols before venturing into the mountains, though Boswell managed to persuade him to leave them behind.

Before 1746, the Highlands posed a degree of threat to the government of Lowland Scotland which was the more incalculable and the more feared because the allegiances, the language, and the way of life of the Highland clans bore little relationship to those of their Lowland compatriots. In the age of Classicism, coffee-shops and taffeta gowns, it is perhaps hardly surprising that when a Highland army erupted into England, reaching Derby and causing George II to make plans to flee the country, its final defeat at Culloden should have been followed by savage suppression of the Highland way of life. Highland dress was banned, the carrying of weapons forbidden, and the jurisdiction of the chiefs removed.

The breaking up of Highland society, begun in 1746, was to continue through the eighteenth and nineteenth centuries. Poverty, emigration, famine, eviction, Anglicisation, absentee-landlordism, unemployment and neglect were to play their parts in breaking the clan system and in depopulating the land. When you enjoy the emptiness and solitude of a Highland glen, remember that it was not always so.

What is happening to the Highlands today remains controversial. The commercial foresters, the marketing men, the sporting agents, the second-home buyers and the humble tourists in their bed-and-breakfasts may all be part of a continuing process of degradation – or they may not. This is not an argument for this book but you will not understand the Highlands better by ignoring it.

STIRLING

Stirling stands on about the only piece of firm ground in the marshy flatlands round the tidal River Forth. For hundreds of years it was the lowest point at which the Forth could be bridged, so the town commanded all routes northwards. That it overlooks seven battlefields is hardly surprising.

Like Edinburgh, which it uncannily resembles in miniature, Stirling has a grey castle on a crag and a warren of old buildings ranging down the steep slope to its east. It is a friendly, carefree town, less dignified than Edinburgh, but ready to remind you that its place in Scotland's history is just as important.

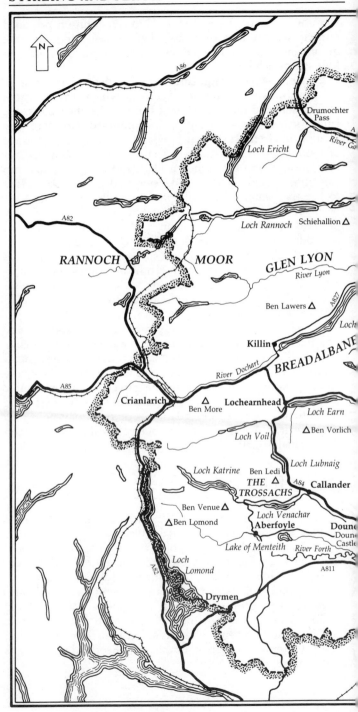

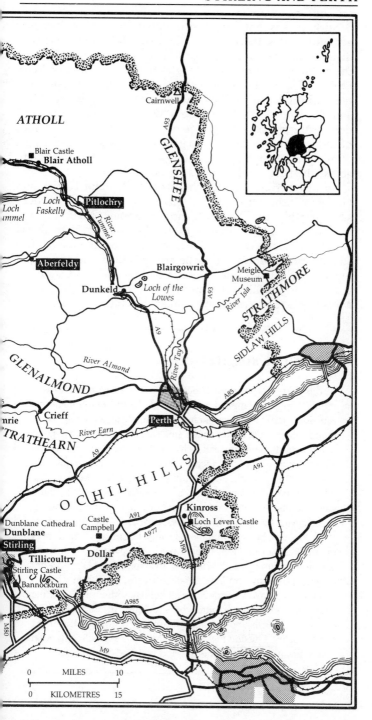

Stirling was not just a stronghold to prevent invading armies crossing the Forth; it was also a favoured royal residence – and there are plenty of stories connected with it, from the stabbing of the Black Douglas to the crowning of Mary Queen of Scots. The town has some fine buildings, especially the **Guildhall** (1634), the **Church of the Holy Rude** (1415) and the eroded façade of **Mar's Wark**, a Renaissance-style demonstration of wealth, set off by the plain competence of the seventeenth-century **Argyll's Lodging** opposite. Best of all, perhaps, is the low, multi-arched **Old Bridge** (1400) across the Forth, still in use as a footbridge.

Stirling lies close to the industrial belt round Falkirk and Grangemouth, but is barely affected by it. It has its modern side (notably the Thistle Centre Shopping Mall) but the atmosphere of the town is more Victorian with medieval and Renaissance overtones – a pleasant combination. The streets leading up to the castle are sprinkled with cafés and pubs, of which Whistlebinkies in St Mary's Wynd is one of the most atmospheric. Chain stores cluster in Port Street and Murray Place; you can enjoy colourful swimming at Rainbow

Practical suggestions

In this part of Scotland it is better to get to know one area well rather than going on great tours through the scenery (though that is possible too). **The Trossachs**, sometimes called the Highlands in miniature, is the most popular small area – perhaps too popular in high season – full of small lochs, medium-sized mountains and a network of walks. The **Ochil Hills** are much less frequented, and there is a scatter of interesting sights along their fringes. The Lowlands of **Strathearn** and **Strathmore** are for those who like their scenery constantly interesting but not necessarily spectacular. The glens leading westward from the A9 north of Perth are each blessed with more history, legend and fine scenery than this book can cover. **Glen Lyon** is the prettiest, with **Loch Rannoch** running it a close second. Everyone should spend a day or two in **Stirling** and have a look at **Perth**, in both of which it is possible to have a happy Scottish holiday without once getting your feet wet or being bitten by a midge. Accommodation is plentiful in Perth and Stirling and in the resorts of Callander and Pitlochry. Outside these places there is a sprinkling of good hotels and plenty of guesthouses and bed-and-breakfasts.

Slides in Goosecroft Road and explore odd crannies down by the Forth. Nearby Stirling University has the MacRobert Arts Centre, with a variety of exhibitions and performances.

Stirling's forte, so far as the visitor is concerned, is live performance. In summer, the town is alive with actors, dancers and fiddlers, and there are set-piece displays such as a medieval market, Beating the Retreat (with fireworks), and a tartan festival. You are likely to be assailed by a gruff James IV or a forceful Mary Queen of Scots on a street corner, or else urged to go on a ghost walk, take part in a ceilidh or watch Highland dancing. Stirling has also unilaterally shifted Burns Night (normally 25 January) to the height of summer.

Good bases

- **Stirling** If you want to meet James IV wandering the streets or join in some Scottish dancing, this is the place to do both: there is a constant round of live performances and street activities in summer. Stirling is a fine and important town, its castle alone being worth the better part of a day's exploration. There is no difficulty about getting to Stirling or finding somewhere to stay, and it is in the best possible position for exploring the Trossachs and the Ochils.
- **Perth** The town does not have much left by way of old buildings, but there are a few curiosities and some fine green spaces. Perth is large, bustling and not at all touristy, with good shopping and a fair range of places to stay. Getting there by road or rail is easy, and the town makes an excellent touring base for Strathearn, the Angus glens and the Highlands which bound it to the north.
- **Pitlochry** This has been the tourist resort for the southern Highlands since the coming of the railway in 1863, and it retains something of the atmosphere of a Victorian holiday spot. It is extremely busy in season but manages to remain unspoilt. There is a superabundance of places to stay, and it is worth having a good look round before deciding. Pitlochry's strong point is the large number of gentle walks in the area, and it is also a good place from which to explore the valleys of the Tay and the Tummel.
- **Aberfeldy** Smaller and quieter than Pitlochry, Aberfeldy is an attractive town where it is possible to feel part of the local life even in high season. While it lacks a huge choice of places to stay it is well situated on the banks of the Tay, right in the centre of the best mountain country in the region.

All this could easily have turned the town into a theme-park of Scottish kitsch, but the effect (so far) is to inject energy into a place that might otherwise be too comfortably normal.

Stirling's further advantage is its position for touring. The Trossachs are half an hour distant; there are good day trips to the Campsie Fells, Crieff, Aberfeldy and Loch Tay or to Kinross and Perth, and it is easy to reach the sights south of the Forth, such as Linlithgow Palace or Cairnpapple Hill.

In and near Stirling

Stirling Castle

(HS, summer: Mon to Sun 9.30 to 6; winter: Mon to Sun 9.30 to 5)

Whisper it who dares, this is a more interesting castle to visit than Edinburgh. It takes some getting into, for you must first escape from the National Trust Visitor Centre (open daily, closed Jan) by the Esplanade and then penetrate the grossly thick Outer Defences (built against artillery in fear of a Jacobite uprising) and the further wall of the Forework (built by James IV but much chopped about later). A sunny former bowling-green with a good view over the parapet delays you further. Below the cliff, the grass-covered earthworks are the remains of what was once a formal garden where kings and courtiers would wander.

Eventually you arrive at the two buildings at the heart of the castle, the Palace and the Great Hall. Start with the Great Hall and do not be put off by the fact that it seems to be a building site, for this is one of the most stimulating restoration programmes in Scotland. The hall (probably built around 1500) was divided and sub-divided when it was later used as barracks, and all the windows were altered. Now the original room, complete with massive fireplaces, is re-emerging, with new mouldings being dovetailed into the medieval stonework. The final stage will be the rebuilding of the hammer-beam roof. Meanwhile, a corner of the hall has been turned into a medieval building site with rope scaffolding and model labourers in amongst the real craftsmen, so that for a second you are caught in a time-warp.

The Palace next door has one of the earliest classical façades in Britain. The niches, statues, gargoyles, string courses and pediments are French in inspiration, Scottish in craftsmanship, and were instituted by James V. Inside, the royal apartments are now bare except for the grand fireplaces, and are used for displaying the Stirling Heads, a series of beautifully carved wooden bosses which once adorned the ceilings. The figures are emblematic, from a king to a cook, from Venus to Lust, but carved with such verve that they are more like character-portraits.

The King's Old Buildings now house the regimental museum of the Argyll and Sutherland Highlanders, with medals, paintings, uniforms and silver. In 1542, James II stabbed the Earl of Douglas here, whom he suspected of treachery, and threw him out of the window. A skeleton was conveniently found underneath the window in 1797 to prove it.

There is more, though these are the best parts. The view from the walls westwards to the peak of Ben Lomond and north-east to the Ochils rising vertically out of the plain is still marvellous. To the south and east the ravages of the twentieth century have made it harder to be appreciative.

Cambuskenneth Abbey

(HS, always open)
This was once an important Augustinian foundation, but there is little left of it today for the builders of the seventeenth-century houses in Stirling had scant respect for their old abbey and used it as a stone quarry. From the top of the twelfth-century bell-tower you can see the foundations of the abbey church and enjoy a peaceful view of the custodian's immaculate lawn and of Stirling beyond. Trying to find the road to the abbey among the windings of the Forth can be half the fun of a visit, but even so this is a place for enthusiasts only.

The Wallace Monument

(Open Feb to Oct, daily 10 to 4 [Feb, Mar, Oct], to 5 [Apr, Sept], to 6 [May to Aug])
Sticking up like a kind of Gothic candle from Abbey Craig to the north of Stirling, and almost as prominent in the landscape as Stirling Castle, the Wallace Monument is a Victorian folly. The view from the top is not as good as from Stirling Castle, but you have the compensation of standing where Wallace once stood watching the English army winding its way over the Forth before the battle of Stirling Brig in 1297.

Wallace's massive sword awaits you inside the Monument, as do two separate audio-visual displays. One describes the

271

district while the other does its best to bring to life the Hall of Heroes, an unpleasantly Teutonic collection of white marble busts of famous Scots, including a sour Argyll, a bristly John Knox, Adam Smith and David Livingston.

Bannockburn Heritage Centre

(NTS, open Apr to Oct, daily 10 to 6)
Don't look for this in the village of Bannockburn (though there is a short town trail for battlefield seekers gone astray – leaflet from Stirling Information Office). The Heritage Centre is actually a mile to the west, separately signposted from the M80.

Robert the Bruce's victory over the English at Bannockburn

WILLIAM WALLACE

By the end of 1296 Edward I of England had thoroughly conquered Scotland, deposing John Balliol (known as 'toom tabard' – empty coat) and turning the country into an occupied province. Yet, by the very next year, Scotland was stirring with revolt against English rule. This movement was less inspired by the Scottish nobility (many of whom had lands in England which they stood to lose) than by the small landowners, among whom was William Wallace, the son of a Renfrewshire knight.

Wallace, despite the many statues of him up and down the country, is a shadowy figure but his achievement in crystallising the resistance to English occupation was extraordinary. The nobles, including Robert the Bruce, were fickle or timorous by turns, and more inclined to put store by rank than ability. Nevertheless, Wallace succeeded in conducting successful guerrilla warfare against the English and, together with Andrew de Moray, inflicted a major defeat on an English army at Stirling Brig in 1297. After this, he was knighted and elected Guardian of Scotland in the name of the exiled King John.

However, guerrilla tactics did not save the Scots at Falkirk in 1298, when Edward appeared on the scene with another army. The Scottish pikes were no match for the English archers, and the battle became a rout. Wallace was forced to flee and shortly after resigned the Guardianship. He was eventually captured – perhaps betrayed – in 1305, and executed in London with the barbarity reserved for traitors, on the command of a king whose sovereignty he never acknowledged.

---

carries so much symbolism in Scotland that a Heritage Centre was probably unavoidable, although the correspondingly devastating English victory at Flodden is marked only by a simple and sad memorial. Even so, the National Trust's strictly neutral presentation may seem timid to fervent Scottish patriots, while outsiders may wonder why there is so much fuss about a battle fought in 1314.

No one seems to be certain precisely where the action took place and housing estates cover the area anyway, so this is not the most interesting of battlefields. The audio-visual display in the Heritage Centre goes a long way to make up for this, and there is a statue of Robert the Bruce and the remains of the stone where he may have grounded his standard. Nevertheless, it is a difficult place in which to be overcome by elation or despair.

The Campsie Fells and East Loch Lomond

To the south-west of Stirling, the Campsie Fells conveniently separate the industrial unpleasantness of the western Central Belt from the upper Forth Valley. Unless you climb to the top of the range, you may not suspect that the suburbs of Glasgow lie on the far side. The hills provide a breath of fresh air and some rural peace and quiet for many people, and the A818 road which runs beside the River Carron through the pretty village of Fintry and on to the equally attractive Drymen is unspoilt and makes a gentle outing.

East Loch Lomond is much prettier. This is the quiet shore of the loch, for the road running along it ends at Rowardennan and only campers, caravanners and picnickers use it. From near Balmaha you can look out over the wooded islands which stud the southern half of the loch and watch the pleasure boats pottering round them. There are numerous coves, walks and picnic places and energetic souls set out here to walk the long-distance **West Highland Way**, which runs up Loch Lomond, eventually to finish at Fort William. Ben Lomond, which rises over 3000 feet above the loch on this shore, is easily climbed from Rowardennan. On a clear day you can see the coast of Ireland and the peak of Ben Nevis.

Dunblane Cathedral

(HS, standard times; closed Thurs pm and Fri in winter)
North of Stirling, the small town of Dunblane, lying in a hollow and by-passed by the A9, is the kind of pleasant place

you might stop at for a cup of coffee but otherwise ignore. This would be a mistake for the cathedral here is not to be missed, even if church-visiting normally leaves you cold.

After 300 years of ruin, a restoration programme, started in 1889, re-roofed the nave and lavishly re-crafted the interior. The period of restoration coincided with the revival of craftsmanship in stained glass and wood around the turn of the century, and continued to embrace the finer agonies of expression which came during and after World War I. The result is an ancient, weather-beaten building containing some of the finest modern wood-carving and stained glass in the country.

The windows, with austere, beautiful faces subtly worked in lilacs and palest blue, shine behind the eroded pillars of the nave, with contributions by the artists Kempe, Strachan, Davis (the lovely *Nunc Dimittis* windows) and Webster. The carving of the pews, the screen and the choir stalls was mostly designed by Sir Robert Lorimer, and repays close scrutiny by revealing a Noah's ark-full of animals crouching in the choir stalls, while every single pew in the nave is carved with a different flower.

THE BATTLE OF BANNOCKBURN

The eight-year campaign fought by Robert the Bruce not only to drive the English from Scotland but also to have himself recognised as king inside his own country reached its climax at Bannockburn in June 1314. For a leader who understood the virtues of guerrilla warfare and recognised the danger of confronting the English in pitched battle, the prospect of fighting the enormous force brought to Scotland by Edward II must have been a dreadful one. He was forced into it by the rash bargain made between his brother, Edward, and the English garrison of Stirling Castle: if the castle were not relieved by mid-summer it would surrender. The English rose to the challenge, and Bruce had to confront them to retain any credibility.

The dispositions made by Bruce, including skilful choice of ground and the digging of pits, would have been unlikely to have saved the Scots but for a terrible tactical mistake on the part of the English. Following preliminary skirmishing in the evening of 23 June, during which Bruce killed the heavily armed De Bohun with a blow of his battle-axe, the English appear to

The modern work fits well into the simple Gothic fabric of the building, which is seen at its best from the outside, especially if you look at the west front (which Ruskin adored) and the south side, where a pinkish Norman bell-tower seems grafted on to the thirteenth-century walls behind.

Doune Castle

(HS, standard times; closed Thurs pm and Fri in winter)
From Dunblane you can veer west to join the A84, the main route to the Trossachs, at **Doune**. This village was once a centre for the manufacture of pistols and produced beautifully crafted weapons which are now museum pieces. Nearby, the late fourteenth-century stronghold of Doune Castle stands above the River Teith. It was built by one of the most powerful and unscrupulous men in medieval Scotland, Robert Stewart, first Duke of Albany.

As the younger son of one weak king (Robert II) and brother of another (Robert III), it did not take Albany, elected as Guardian of Scotland in 1388, long to achieve

---

have withdrawn for the night into the boggy ground near the bank of the Forth, the worst possible terrain for the English heavy cavalry.

On seeing this the next day, Bruce went over to the attack, using his few cavalry to neutralise the opposing archers and his infantry to confine the English within a constricted and marshy space. The sheer size of the English army, and its inability to manoeuvre in such unfavourable conditions, caused chaos. The battle, hard fought for most of the day, seems to have reached a turning point with the appearance of Scottish reinforcements – traditionally thought to be only the camp-followers – who appeared over the skyline at a moment critical for English morale. The battle turned to rout. Edward II fled, first to Stirling and then, hotly pursued, to Dunbar and Berwick.

The spoils of Bannockburn were huge, enabling Bruce to ransom members of his family whom Edward had been holding hostage in England. Yet the battle did not lead at once to English recognition of Scotland as an independent kingdom, as Bruce had hoped. That had to wait until the treaty of Northampton in 1328, just before the death of King Robert the Bruce.

---

something approaching supreme power. Only the two sons of Robert III, David and James, stood between him and the throne. David died in Albany's 'safe keeping' at Falkland in 1402, and is widely believed to have been deliberately starved to death. Then the 11-year-old James, on his way to France for his own safety, was conveniently waylaid by English 'pirates' and taken to the English court, where he was to remain for 18 years. Albany, on the other hand, died in his bed in his eighties. Whatever history's assessment of him, there is no doubt what the captured James felt: on his eventual return to Scotland as king, one of his first acts was to eradicate the Albany family for high treason. Four of them were beheaded at Stirling, and Doune castle was forfeited to the crown.

Doune Castle was designed to be both strong and imposing, and, since a lot of it remains, it is an awe-inspiring place, with severe curtain walls and a massive gate-tower. Domestic arrangements are quite sophisticated, with corbelled 'free drop' latrines, three different halls, extensive kitchens and enough enormous fireplaces to remove at least some of the chill from the air. Extensive restoration in 1883 led to some rather peculiar refurbishing of the biggest rooms (banners, heavy dark wood and flagstoned floors).

Near Doune

Just to the north of Doune is the **Doune Motor Museum** (open Apr to Oct, daily 10 to 5), a collection for the enthusiast rather than for the whole family. The Earl of Moray's assembly of polished thoroughbreds stands in gleaming ranks, with all the famous names represented. The museum is also a centre for motor-racing hill climbs and other events.

To the south of Doune, **Blair Drummond Safari and Leisure Park** (open early Apr to early Oct, daily 10 to 5.30) is the only conventional safari park in Scotland.

THE TROSSACHS

Strictly speaking the Trossachs is the short, rocky pass between Loch Achray and Loch Katrine, but the name now generally refers to the rugged country lying between Callander and Loch Lomond. It is easy enough to see why the Trossachs sprang to fame, for in the days before luxury coaches and double-track roads visitors could reach this part of the Highlands without difficulty, while the legends and the scenery were given a huge puff by Sir Walter Scott in *The Lady of the Lake* and were everything that Romantic taste might desire.

It is harder to see why the Trossachs remains so popular. Much of the scenery has been swathed in conifer plantations; Loch Katrine has been raised 17 feet and turned into a reservoir for Glasgow, and Scott's poetry is no longer in fashion. Yet the coaches and caravans go on rolling in. True, the Trossachs has the advantage of being easily accessible to much of Scotland's population and there is plenty of fine scenery left, despite the afforestation, especially if you take to your feet. For an extended holiday you will probably be better off elsewhere, but for a day-trip taste of the Highlands in miniature the Trossachs is a reasonably good bet.

Callander

On the road here from Doune, the views become more extensive, the hillsides barer, the ground gradually rockier. But any idea of wild desolation is rapidly dispelled once you reach Callander itself, for the town fairly seethes on summer weekends. It is far from being the quiet rural community pictured in that most famous of Scottish soap-operas, *Dr Finlay's Casebook*, for which it acted as the setting. Dr Cameron and Janet would be lost among the gift shops and tea rooms.

Among all the activity, you will find the **Trossachs and Rob Roy Visitor Centre**. This purpose-built attraction is set up in an old kirk, well placed to pull in the crowds. In lists of genuinely heritage-worthy Scots Rob Roy McGregor must rank pretty low but – thanks largely to Sir Walter Scott – he found a place in the myth of Romantic Scotland, and Callander is exploiting it. Consequently, there are two separate exhibitions devoted to the exploits of this glorified cattle-thief, of which one has a model cow to greet you and, crouching behind a rock, a model clansman whose face, by a trick of projection, comes to a semblance of life as he mutters to himself about the joys of cattle-stealing. Next, in a small theatre, slide projectors and loudspeakers have been set up to ask, 'Rob Roy, hero or villain?', but the script is so banal you may quickly lose interest.

The Trossachs proper

A laugh was on every face when William said we were come to see the Trossachs; no doubt they thought we had better have stayed at our own homes. (Dorothy Wordsworth, 1803)

It is a short run beside Loch Venacher and Loch Achray (both very attractive in autumn when the rowan-berries are at their best) to the branch road which leads off to the foot of Loch Katrine. The road plunges briefly through a gorge and emerges at a large car park and a pier. All the most scenic parts of Loch Katrine are out of sight, so you will need either to walk or else wait for the next sailing of the *Sir Walter Scott*, which runs from here up to Stronachlachar on the west bank, in order to see much. Notices forbidding any pollution of Glasgow's water supply add an unwelcome touch of officialdom to the scenery, but this is made up for by a fine, small exhibition about the construction of the Loch Katrine aqueducts in 1859 and the importance of this newly piped-in water in helping to alleviate Glasgow's terrifying infant mortality.

Aberfoyle

As it climbs over the Duke's Pass, the A821 runs mostly through conifers. The forests have been amalgamated into the **Queen Elizabeth Forest Park**, and the Forestry Commission is doing its best to suggest they are attractive by widespread provision of walks, picnic places and even the **Loch Achray Forest Drive** (for which there is a charge). However, one spruce is much like another, and better walks are to be had by striking out for the summits of Ben Venue or Ben Ledi, both relatively gentle mountains (though you will still need proper equipment) or by seeking out a low-level walk by a river or loch, such as the path to the Bracklinn Falls just to the north of Callander.

On the far side of the Duke's Pass you come down to Aberfoyle, a quieter centre than Callander, but busy in summer all the same. From here, the narrow B829 past Loch Ard towards Loch Arklet and the east bank of Loch Lomond is worth exploring, its only disadvantage being that you must return the way you went. Queen Victoria was luckier; she climbed on board the *Prince Consort* for a sail on Loch Lomond: 'A pleasant idea that that dear name should have carried his poor little wife, alas! a widow, and children on their first sail on the beautiful lake.'

From Aberfoyle you can return to Stirling on the A873,

which flanks the old marshes of **Flanders Moss**. Most of them have been transformed into fertile farmland, but for many years they were part of Stirling's natural defences.

Inchmahome Priory

(HS, standard times; closed winter)

The ruins stand a short distance south of the A873 on an island in the middle of the Lake of Menteith, one of the few expanses of water in Scotland that are not called lochs. There is no arcane tradition behind the name, merely a mistake by a Dutch surveyor helping to drain Flanders Moss. To get to the island you must embark on Historic Scotland's ferry, which is summoned by turning a semaphore board on the end of the jetty.

Inchmahome is an important place for followers of Mary Queen of Scots, for it was here that the young Queen came in 1547. Like many other Scottish religious houses before the Reformation, the priory had passed into the hands of commendators, who were royal appointees usually more interested in income than in religion. In this case, the commendators were the Erskine family, and Lord Erskine was the guardian of the young Mary. She was hidden here briefly after the Scots had been defeated by the English at the battle of Pinkie. The following year she set sail for France and marriage to the Dauphin. She was not to return for 12 years.

The priory ruins are simple and reasonably well preserved, especially the east window of the church with its five lancets. In the old Chapter House lie the heavily weathered remains of a double effigy of a thirteenth-century Earl and Countess of Menteith. It is an affectionate memorial: she rests her hand on his shoulder and they lie turned towards each other. Around the ruins and the careful lawns, paths wander over the island under redoubtable old trees. Mary's Bower, Mary's Garden and Mary's Tree remain as memories of the island's most famous visitor, but since the Queen was only four, and spent only three weeks here, she probably did not do much gardening. The custodian's hut is roomy enough to shelter in on a wet day while you are waiting for the return boat.

THE OCHIL HILLS

Stirling to Dollar

The A91 runs eastward from Stirling, close underneath the steep escarpment of the Ochil Hills. These rounded, grassy half-mountains run north-eastward to Newburgh on the Tay, diminishing gradually in size as they go, with fine views north and south to reward those few visitors who climb to explore their tops. Small mill towns (collectively called the Hillfoots) were built to take advantage of the water rushing down the steep glens on their southern side and the road passes through this old industrial landscape, which is more attractive than the clutter of power stations and refineries which fringe the banks of the Firth of Forth. The Hillfoots were once an important weaving centre and there are still a few mills nearby where you can hunt for tweed or tartan, though the recent creation of a 'Mill Trail' is perhaps over-egging the pudding. There are a few curiosities here but nothing to compare with Culross down on the banks of the Forth, and that is where you should go first if you are short of time.

As you travel east from Stirling, **Blairlogie** is pretty, **Menstrie** has a restored but undistinguished sixteenth-century tower-house with connections to Nova Scotia, while **Alva** has the beautiful Strude Mill (now put to other uses). At **Tillicoultry**, the Clock Mill Heritage Centre is thin on exhibits but the staff are most friendly. These last two villages both have steep glens rising behind them, with old sluices and dams to discover.

A detour south on the A908 to **Clackmannan** reveals the remains of a sixteenth-century tolbooth and a fourteenth-century tower on the outskirts of the little town. The chief curiosity here is the Clach of Mannan, by the tolbooth. This is a large stone on a modern plinth, which may or may not be sacred to a pre-Christian sea-god, and may or may not be very old indeed. It sits contentedly with lorries rumbling past, and may well outlast everything round about it.

Castle Campbell and Dollar Glen

Dollar is a comfortable residential town and a good place to seek out lunch before tackling Castle Campbell (HS, standard times; closed Thurs pm and Fri in winter). From the car park up in the hills behind the town, a path descends into Dollar Glen (NTS, open all year). If you are not fit enough for this steep and sometimes slippery route there is a more straightforward but very narrow and steep road leading on from the car park.

At the bottom of Dollar Glen, the Burn of Care and the Burn of Sorrow meet in a tangle of rock faces and tumbled slabs. Cleverly engineered walkways lead through impossibly narrow gaps between lichen-encrusted slabs while the water hisses beneath. Few gorges have such a fascinating labyrinth at their bottom. Eventually, steep steps lead you from the depths of the Burn of Care and you see the walls of Castle Campbell above you.

Many things have been said about the Campbells, most of them bad, but at least they changed the name of their castle, which, in keeping with all the Care and the Sorrow, used to be called Castle Gloom. Gloomy it is not. It has splendid views across the Forth Valley to the Pentland Hills, and the custodian has planted flowers wherever there is room. The grim fifteenth-century tower at the castle's centre is virtually intact, with its four rooms on four floors linked by a wheel stair. Around it, the remains of later buildings are less overtly designed for defence, and there is even a tiny two-arched loggia tucked into a sunny corner of the courtyard where you can imagine it may occasionally have been pleasant to sit.

The castle was the Lowland stronghold of the Earls (later Dukes) of Argyll, and a symbol of the increasing Campbell influence which was at its greatest during Scotland's long conflict with Charles I, Charles II and James VII. John Knox stayed and preached here, though he probably never used the rock called Knox's Pulpit.

Rumbling Bridge

A small compensation for days of rain is that Scotland's waterfalls and gorges are at their best. The gorge at Rumbling Bridge is one of the most magnificent, though you might never guess it was there, since the road (A823 south, beyond Dollar) leaps it without a dip. Keep a sharp look-out for the signposted car park just to the north of the bridge, and walk to the edge of the chasm which the River Devon has carved from a fault in the rock. This was a favourite sight for visitors in the last century, and recently all the walkways and balconies down the precipitous sides have been restored. The Deil's Mill, where a horrible rumbling rises out of the depths, is especially worth stopping at. The nineteenth-century bridge which now carries the road over the gorge was built directly above its predecessor, which remains slung underneath it, creating a peculiar effect. The old bridge had no parapet, and must have taken steely nerves to cross on horseback.

Kinross

Although the town's Tourist Information Centre has been banished to a wooden chalet in the middle of a motorway service area (at Junction 6 of the M90 – there is a good butterfly farm here too), this does not mean Kinross has nothing worth looking at.

If you come in summer, on no account miss the gardens of **Kinross House** (open May to Sept, daily 10 to 6). The house was built by the architect Sir William Bruce in 1686 and it is one of his best, for he built it for himself. It is not open but you can admire the grey classical frontages, which are perfectly complemented by the gardens. At their centre, a formal design directs the eye towards Loch Leven Castle seeming to float on the loch beyond, while the scents and colours of the herbaceous border and shrubbery fill the air under the enclosing walls.

Green-jacketed anglers in deerstalker hats are a common sight where the waters of Loch Leven lap at the lower edge of the town for the wild, pink-fleshed trout that inhabit the loch are famous for their number and their flavour. It is relatively easy to find space in one of the dozens of boats lined up by the shore (ring 0577 863407 as far in advance as possible).

The bird-watchers you meet will have been to **Vane Farm** on the south side of the loch, where the RSPB has a visitor centre. Telescopes have been set up for visitors, through which you can gaze at geese and duck foraging among the clumps of rushes by the shore. The best time to see the thousands of autumn migrants is from mid-October onwards.

Fishermen and bird-watchers are few in number compared to those who visit Loch Leven because of Mary Queen of Scots. To follow her trail, you need to find the pier where two cheerful custodians take turns in ferrying you out to Loch Leven Castle.

Loch Leven Castle

(HS, standard times; closed in winter)
Here, under a load of misery which might have staggered a mind more masculine than hers, Mary exerted the potent witchery of her charms upon the heart of young Douglas, who, intoxicated with a romantic passion and ambitious hopes, sacrificed his duty and family interests at the shrine of all-powerful love. (The Scottish Tourist, 1827)

The first thing worth noting is that the trees, the carefully cut grass, the wooden benches and the overall air of pastoral contentment that pervades the island on which the castle stands would not have been what Mary Queen of Scots experienced here during her 11 months' imprisonment. The level of the loch was higher, the island smaller, the castle damp and old-fashioned and, in contrast to Historic Scotland's patient custodians, Mary's gaolers seem to have been coldly hostile to the point of cruelty.

By the time Mary came here as a prisoner in 1567 the castle already had a long history. The island may have been fortified during the English occupation under Edward I and captured by Wallace and/or Robert the Bruce, later resisting renewed attempts by the English to take it. As a place to isolate an important prisoner from her supporters and to wring from her an enforced abdication, Loch Leven was perfect. On top of this, Mary suffered a miscarriage here, and she was far from well afterwards. Yet she escaped. The manner in which she did so has all the elements of a good thriller – the loyalty of the orphan Willie Douglas, whom she persuaded to help her, the careful stealing of the keys, the holing of all the boats except the one needed for escape, and finally the moment of highest drama as the Queen crossed the courtyard in disguise, fearing last-minute discovery.

The thriller has no happy ending. In spite of the fact that supporters flocked to her, Mary's army was fatally beaten at Langside 11 days after her escape in May 1568. She fled south and decided to cross the Solway and seek help in England. Instead she was to find further imprisonment and eventual execution, 19 years later.

Come to Loch Leven Castle on a day without much wind (boats do not run if it is rough), and preferably with some sun, for there is nowhere much to shelter. Arm yourself with Antonia Fraser's *Mary Queen of Scots* but don't be lulled by the peace of the island – it was not always this way.

Kinross to Perth

The M90 swings over the eastern end of the Ochils into Strathearn. Castle-lovers should break at Junction 7 to see **Burleigh Castle**, a beautiful tower-house in two sections, built a century apart. Sir James Balfour, who built the later of the towers, had a hand in the nastier events of the sixteenth century. He helped murder Cardinal Beaton in 1546, served on the French galleys with John Knox, and was one of those who is thought to have signed the bond agreeing to the murder of Darnley, Mary Queen of Scots' second husband.

MARY QUEEN OF SCOTS

It is hardly surprising that tragedians have found inspiration in the reign of Scotland's most famous queen: her life seems to belong more to the stage than to the pages of history. Widowed by the death of her husband François II of France, she returned to Scotland in 1561 at a time when the country was poised between France and England (which was nothing new), and between the forces of Roman Catholicism and Protestantism.

Her very existence posed threats or offered opportunities to half of Europe. Her marriage to a Catholic prince would be a blow struck for the Counter-Reformation and would help to isolate Protestant England. She was, in the eyes of many Catholics, already the legitimate Queen of England, and certainly had a strong claim to the succession should Queen Elizabeth I die childless. Within Scotland, the Protestant lords and ministers (especially John Knox) regarded her with deep suspicion, while the Catholics expected her to reinstate the old church and reverse the Scottish Parliament's decision to adopt Protestantism. Moreover, the young queen found no substitute among the self-interested Scottish nobility for the steady counsel she had become used to from her Guise relatives in France.

It is Mary's tolerance and humanity in the midst of this political mire which have so appealed to nineteenth- and twentieth-century sensibilities. Yet they were inappropriate qualities in a sixteenth-century ruler. Mary's far more ruthless and devious cousin, Elizabeth of England, was a less likeable person but a more successful Queen.

The beginning of Mary's reign in Scotland was a success. It was her marriage to the featherbrained Lord Darnley in 1565 that sealed her fate. An immediate rebellion against the couple was put down, but as Mary herself became disillusioned with Darnley the opportunities for those who desired to de-stabilise her rule increased. The murder of her secretary, Riccio, with Darnley at the head of the killers, is one of the many distasteful episodes of Mary's reign. Darnley, arrogant, foolish and resentful that he had not been granted the crown matrimonial, was provoked into an attempted coup through an easy arousal of his jealous suspicions of Riccio. Whether or not there was also a direct intent to murder the Queen, or at least pose a threat to her unborn child, is less clear, though the purpose of the conspiracy seems to have been to hold her powerless at

Stirling. The coup might well have succeeded if Mary had not managed to swing the unstable Darnley behind her again in the course of a night and to escape from Holyrood.

The murder of Darnley in Edinburgh in 1567, when the house in which he was sleeping was blown up (though Darnley himself was found strangled in the garden), cast a taint of suspicion on the Queen from which she was never to recover. Her marriage to the Earl of Bothwell, who was closely involved in the plot to kill Darnley, took place a bare three months later – a scandalous union.

Many of the nobles who immediately took up arms against Bothwell and the Queen had given Bothwell their secret approval only a month before. This may have helped him persuade the Queen into marriage, but it did him no good now. At Carberry Hill near Edinburgh the rebellious nobles outfaced the smaller army of Bothwell and the Queen. Mary submitted herself to the safe conduct of the nobles, who included many of the conspirators in the murder of Riccio.

Safe conduct turned out to mean imprisonment at Loch Leven and an enforced abdication in favour of the infant James. When the Queen escaped, the speed with which she gathered an army showed her support still to be strong. Her defeat at Langside was followed by the rash decision to seek shelter in England. Mary seems always to have hoped for Elizabeth's friendship, but the latter perceived her as a threat and so held the Scottish Queen in detention in England. Meanwhile, Scotland was split into further factions. During the 19 years that Mary was an exile in England, four separate regencies governed in the name of the young King James VI.

The threat posed by Mary as a centrepiece of Catholic plotting eventually became too great for the English government to bear. In 1586 she was secretly tried on the charge of conspiring to assassinate Elizabeth. The evidence against her seems largely to have been fabricated. Her inevitable execution – at Fotheringhay Castle in Northamptonshire – followed, despite Elizabeth's initial hesitation in signing the death warrant.

The questions which remain are numerous. How closely was Mary implicated in Darnley's murder? Was her marriage to Bothwell a matter of policy or a matter of the heart? Why did she flee to England after Langside? Did she really plot against Elizabeth? The life of Mary Queen of Scots continues to fascinate those who love historical puzzles.

Abernethy (Junction 9) is only a small village now, but it was once the hub of a Pictish kingdom and an important centre for the Celtic church. A ninth-century round tower standing by the churchyard is the only reminder of this long-vanished importance, but it is a lofty and impressive one none the less. At Abernethy, Malcolm Canmore (the same Malcolm who ends as King of Scots in Shakespeare's *Macbeth*) paid homage to William the Conqueror in 1072. This unfortunate act was to give birth to the perennial English idea that Scotland was part of the English feudal domain, and led indirectly to all the agonies of the Wars of Independence.

You can buy Abernethy biscuits in the village, but they actually originate from the parish of Abernethy on Speyside. They are certainly palatable, if not local.

PERTH

Ecce Tiber! Ecce Campus Martius! shouted Agricola's Roman soldiers on first seeing the green hollow in the hills by the dark River Tay where Perth was to be founded. The resemblance to Rome is not that close, but it makes a good story. The Romans built a camp near here and Perth has not looked back since. It gained from being close to Scone Abbey, the traditional coronation spot of Scottish kings, and had several religious houses of its own until John Knox's fiery sermons of 1559 inflamed the mob to pillage them all. In one of the monasteries, Blackfriars, James I came to a grisly end at the hand of an assassin in 1437. He had made one enemy too many among his powerful relatives.

In 1396 North Inch, by the bank of the Tay, was the scene of a ritual combat between Clan Chattan and Clan Kay, with 30 champions on each side bloodily settling their differences in front of King Robert III. This battle is the centre-piece of Sir Walter Scott's novel *The Fair Maid of Perth*. At the edge of this park today you will find the **Black Watch Museum** a comprehensive regimental museum with a strong family feeling to it, situated in a much-reconstructed tower-house.

Perth is not short of places to stay, though they are scattered. There are several guesthouses and small hotels on the east side of the Tay and numerous hotels in the town centre, one of which, the Salutation, accommodated Charles Edward Stuart. The green spaces of North and South Inch beside the Tay are ideal for a stroll and for watching Perth's citizens taking the air, while the grid pattern of shopping streets – perhaps an inheritance from the Romans – allows for a convenient morning's browsing.

In and near Perth

Perth Art Gallery and Museum

(Open Mon to Sat 10 to 5, also Sun in May Arts Festival)
Crowds flock to see the heavily touted **Fair Maid's House**, which is a glorified craft shop with some medieval parts, but they virtually ignore this museum, which lies a few yards away and is far more interesting. It is a splendid, no-nonsense town museum with some good ideas about presentation, and interesting displays, notably the local Perth silverwork.

Church of St John

The church is small and plain, but it has witnessed plenty of history. Edward I worshipped in it during his 1296 campaign of conquest, while John Knox preached here the inflammatory sermons of 1559 which were to lead to so much destruction. The most recent remodelling was in 1926, by Sir Robert Lorimer, whose gentle touch softens the fifteenth-century stonework. There is a beautiful window by Strachan at the east end.

Branklyn Garden

(NTS, open Mar to Oct, daily 9.30 to sunset)
Essential visiting for keen gardeners, this is a large town garden with peat-loving plants. It lies on the east side of the Tay at the end of a street of large villas, and it is signposted from the A85 towards Dundee. The garden is made to feel larger than it is by clever design; wandering round the beds of primula and meconopsis can take much longer than you might imagine. The newly replanted rock garden and the small alpine house contain some rarities. Get to the garden early; it can become overcrowded by mid-morning.

Huntingtower Castle

(HS, standard times; winter closed Thurs pm and Fri)
A bland castle in an uninspiring setting on the very edge of the A85 to Crieff, Huntingtower has a curious structure of two fifteenth-century towers linked by a seventeenth-century

wing. It is worth stopping there to see some of the earliest painted ceilings to be found in Scotland.

In the sixteenth century Huntingtower was in the possession of the Ruthvens (Earls of Gowrie), who were notorious and unpleasant conspirators. They were at the forefront of the plot to murder Riccio, Mary Queen of Scots' secretary, helped with the imprisonment of Mary on Loch Leven, and here at Ruthven Castle (as it was then called) kidnapped the young James VI in 1582 and held him for ten months. He got his revenge in 1600 when another plot involving the Gowries seems to have gone wrong. Two members of the family died in a fracas at Perth, and the King hunted the others ruthlessly.

The castle does have a romantic legend too: the 'maiden's leap' between the two towers refers to the action of the first Earl's daughter, who was forced to leave her lover's bed in a hurry on hearing her mother's approach and made this perilous jump.

Scone Palace

(Open Easter to mid-Oct, Mon to Sat 9.30 to 5, Sun 1.30 to 5; July and Aug, daily 10 to 5)

Approached from the A93 north of Perth, this huge mansion has ample space for tour coaches and hence gets more attention than it warrants. The neo-Gothic architecture may be described as restrained, but it is not restrained enough. Experts on ivories and French furniture will enjoy the interior, but for others the grounds will be the best part. The site of Scone Abbey, where so many Scottish Kings were crowned, can be seen, although there is nothing left of it. The Stone of Destiny on which the King sat for the ceremony was removed by Edward I to Westminster Abbey in 1296 – though you will doubtless hear that he was fobbed off with an imitation – and there it remains despite a brief outing in 1950–51 when it was taken by Scottish Nationalists and brought to Arbroath Abbey.

David Douglas, who discovered the Douglas fir, worked at Scone Palace as gardener. For a botanist, he suffered a sticky end – while in America he fell into a pit dug to catch bison. Unfortunately, a bison was already inside.

WEST OF PERTH

Strathearn

The wide valley of the Earn is gentle, arable land, with blue hills always lining the distance. The small sights of its eastern end cover a long period of time and a variety of interests. The Romans recognised the virtues of Strathearn as a line on which to establish military outposts. The chief of these was **Ardoch Roman Camp**, just outside Braco, which guarded the road south through Strathallan. Its extensive earthworks remain.

The Picts have left their mark too, in the shape of a weathered cross-slab outside St Bean's Church at **Foulis Wester**, east of Crieff. Inside the church there is a piece of MacBean tartan which went on an Apollo mission to the moon and another Pictish stone showing Jonah and the whale, a story which obviously much pleased the Picts, as it is a common theme. At **Muthill**, the pointed arches of a fifteenth-century church are attached to a square twelfth-century tower, while **Tulliebardine Chapel**, an easily overlooked barn-like building on the corner of a minor road off the A823 near Auchterarder, is actually a fifteenth-century collegiate chapel with an interior almost unaltered.

In summer the formal Italian gardens of **Drummond Castle**, where you can see one of the huge ornate sundials much fancied by the Scottish nobility, are open every afternoon. If you are fond of books you should visit **Innerpeffray Library** (open Mon to Sat 10 to 12.45 and 2 to 4.45, Sun 2 to 4; closed Thurs), south of Crieff on the B8062; the oldest library in Scotland, it houses a collection of rare books which is the more astonishing for being in such a tiny place. On the southern edge of Strathearn, the 'long town' of **Auchterarder** has a polished steam engine in working order at the Great Scots Visitor Centre (open daily, Easter to May 1 to 5; June to Oct 10 to 5), round which is built a portrayal of Scottish innovators.

Crieff and the Sma' Glen

Crieff used to hold one of the biggest trysts (cattle fairs) in Scotland until Falkirk became the centre for these long-vanished events. Today it is an easy-going little market town taking advantage of its position on the very edge of the Highlands to gather tourists into its shops and its tiny museum. The visitor centre just to the south of town is really a sales pitch for locally made products, including pottery and paperweights.

There are a number of hotels in Crieff which date from its days as a nineteenth-century resort, among them the massive Crieff Hydro. Numerous guesthouses are also to be found if you want to stay for a night or two.

The **Sma' Glen** is the usual name given to the route which runs northwards from Crieff to Amulree at the foot of Glen Quaich, though the glen itself is only a short stretch beside the River Almond. There is a salmon leap a little further downstream at **Buchanty Spout**, and a good, long walk westwards up towards the head of Glenalmond. In August the bell heather on the moors round Amulree turns the whole landscape rosy lilac.

Comrie

'The Shakey Toun' lies right on the edge of the Highland Boundary Fault, and owes its nickname to the earth tremors which occasionally rattle teacups. The world's first ever seismometers were set up here and you can still visit Earthquake House and look at the equipment.

However, Comrie's main sight is the **Scottish Tartans Museum** (open Apr to Oct, Mon to Sat 10 to 6 [9.30 to 6.30 in summer months], Sun 11 to 5; Nov to Mar, Mon to Fri 10 to 1 and 2 to 5, Sat 10 to 1). The atmosphere at this headquarters of the Scottish Tartans Society is academic rather than gift-shoppy. Displays explain the history of tartan and show examples of how the patterns are built up in weaving. There are fragments of early tartan, and human figures in glass cases are clothed in various forms of Highland dress. You are told how to put on the belted plaid (the precursor of today's kilts) by putting belt and plaid on the ground and lying down to do up the belt. A small garden grows those plant species which were used to dye the cloth. The real work of the centre is on computer, where records of clans, surnames and tartans from all over the world are stored.

For an attractive drive or walk, try nearby **Glen Lednock**.

St Fillans

The village is named after the sixth-century missionary from Ireland, who is associated not only with Loch Earnside but with Glen Dochart and Strath Fillan as well (see Killin later in this chapter). Robert the Bruce insisted that the relics of the saint were carried into battle at Bannockburn. St Fillans is lucky in its setting at the gentle eastern end of Loch Earn, and is a centre for watersports, with a comfortable hotel. There are some good short walks on the hillsides near the village, particularly around Glen Tarken (get hold of a leaflet about it from Crieff Tourist Information Office).

At the western end of the loch you reach **Lochearnhead**, which is largely a water-skiing and water sports centre, much busier than St Fillans. Here you join the A84 which runs northwards from the Trossachs towards Killin.

THE ROAD NORTH TO PITLOCHRY

North of Perth the main A9 to Pitlochry passes through the rugged scenery of the Tay and Tummel valleys. Unfortunately, the terrible design of this road, with short stretches of dual carriageway alternating with long curves where it is never quite safe to overtake slow lorries or caravans, is at its worst here, and trying to split your time between watching the traffic and watching the scenery is not sensible. The Tummel is not quite the river it was before the huge hydro-electric network of tunnels and dams was built, but the Tay – deep, black and swirling in the strath where it sweeps past Birnam and Dunkeld – is the sort of river to haunt dreams and inspire legend.

For once the forests here improve rather than spoil the landscape; much is the result of careful work by various Dukes of Atholl. Many of the plantings are venerable, especially the larches of Dunkeld and the trees of Birnam Wood, though the latter will not be the same ones that Shakespeare wrote about. Fragments of mixed woodland break up the conifers, while the craggy hills rising above the trees give fresh texture and colour to the scenery. Bright blue lupins have established themselves on shingle banks by the Tay.

Dunkeld

When the Vikings drove St Columba's monks from Iona in about 729, it was to Dunkeld that they came. Its religious importance was further established by the cathedral, which dates from the twelfth century. After the battle of Killiecrankie in 1689, Dunkeld was the scene of a further battle, in which the Highland forces, dispirited by the death of their leader, Dundee, were defeated. In the process, medieval Dunkeld was thoroughly burnt.

What you see today, apart from the remains of the cathedral, is therefore eighteenth-century at its oldest, and very attractive it is too, for the short Cathedral Street, very like a cathedral close, is lined by harled cottages restored by the National Trust for Scotland. One of them is now the Tourist Information

Centre, while another contains the military Museum of the Scottish Horse.

Behind the houses lie the remnants of the cathedral – the nave roofless, the choir still serving as parish church. Take a wander round the outside to look at the fifteenth-century windows with their elaborate tracery. At the back of the building, the huge scraggy larch tree is the 'parent larch', possibly the first grown in Scotland. It was planted in 1737 and is the ancestor, no doubt, of millions more. If you are fond of larches, drive up the east bank of the Tay to Dunkeld House and persuade someone at the hotel to show you the pot-grown larch in the grounds. This huge specimen started life in an eighteenth-century greenhouse before being planted out, and its enormous roots still faithfully reproduce the shape of the pot in which it was grown.

Loch of Lowes

This is one of a series of glacial lochs east of Dunkeld which run in a chain towards Blairgowrie and are known as the Stormont lochs after the district they lie in. Loch of Lowes is the largest, and is a nature reserve. From a hide you may be able to watch the ospreys which spend part of the year here. Even if there are none, the visitor centre will have information on what other kinds of bird you are likely to see.

The Hermitage

(NTS; open all year)
A mile-long walk by the River Braan, west of Dunkeld and signposted from the A9, is ideal for stretching your legs after too long in a car. It runs through ancient woodland to a folly, built in 1758, called Ossian's Hall or the Hermitage. Beyond lies Ossian's Cave – another piece of artifice. The whole walk, with its waterfall, gorge and little bridge, reflects the late eighteenth-century taste for the picturesque. It is still utterly charming, with only a faint hint of the ridiculous.

NORTH-EAST OF PERTH

Glenshee

Whether you travel up Glen Isla on the B954 (the pleasanter road), or stick to the A93 north from Blairgowrie, you rapidly leave the fertile Lowlands behind and drive into increasingly wild country. The hills on either side of the Glenshee road are unshapely great mounds which become higher and more barren as you penetrate deeper into them, with scree streaking the upper slopes of Creag Leacach and the Cairnwell at the head of the pass.

Spittal of Glenshee, a watering hole for skiers (with the isolated and comfortable Dalmunzie House to stay in close by), is the last village you pass before heading up the steep stretch of road to the Cairnwell pass. This road used to be notorious for the Devil's Elbow – a steep hairpin bend which was the bane of buses and was frequently blocked by snow. Now the road is straight, graded and anonymous, though the disintegrating remains of the old hazard lie just beyond the fence.

At the lip of the pass, the **Cairwell Chairlift** will take you effortlessly up the mountain, summer or winter. Beyond the pass, the road drops rapidly towards Braemar and Deeside (see the chapter on the North-East).

Strathmore

This fertile valley runs from the junction of the Rivers Isla and Tay right over to the east coast. Strathmore is Scotland's soft fruit country, responsible for the best raspberries in the world. Tractors here look like giant insects from a horror film, built tall and narrow for straddling rows of canes. There are many pick-your-own farms.

Blairgowrie is the centre for the western end of the valley, a place somewhat bedevilled by traffic. Three miles south, at **Meikleour**, stands one of those useless curiosities which brighten the traveller's day: a beech hedge planted in 1746 and now 85 feet high. It is trimmed every 10 years.

Meigle Museum

(HS, standard times; closed winter)

Long before raspberries were domesticated, the Picts had made Strathmore a centre of population. At the village of Meigle, the old school has been converted into a museum to house 30 Pictish carved stones and four fragments, dating from the seventh to the tenth centuries. The custodian needs to open the building for you, but a visit is worthwhile.

The room is dominated by three great stone cross-slabs, almost entirely covered in intricate carving. One shows Daniel in the lions' den, the lions pawing at him like overgrown cats while Daniel pats their heads. Beautiful interlaced patterns shroud the edges of another slab, and on the rear are examples of most of the enigmatic symbols – disc, Z-rod, 'swimming elephant' and mirror and comb – which appear on many Pictish stones, and whose meaning is lost to us. The stones are full of movement, curves and knots, and obviously belong to a culture very different from the Anglo–Norman society which was to become dominant in Lowland Scotland.

PITLOCHRY

At first sight, Pitlochry is a place which appears to have bred hotels, gift shops and tour coaches to the exclusion of all else. It is nevertheless a mistake to write the town off as a ghastly tourist trap and move on without delay. It is certainly crowded, and neither beautiful nor historic, but it has managed somehow to retain the leisurely atmosphere of the old-fashioned mountain resort which it has been since the coming of the railway in 1863. There is no shortage of places to stay, ranging from large Victorian hotels in spa style to simple guesthouses. Prowl until you find a place to suit you and remember to check the menu, for the town is short of decent restaurants if your hotel disappoints.

Pitlochry is an excellent place for gentle walks, especially along the banks of **Loch Faskally**. Many other Scottish lochs have suffered from the raising of their levels for hydro-electric needs, but this entirely man-made stretch of water is a resounding success in the landscape. You can walk as far as the pass of Killiecrankie should you wish, but there are plenty of shorter round trips. Boats can also be hired. The old village of **Moulin** on the outskirts of Pitlochry makes another good stroll, with a pleasant pub at its end, while a stiffer walk beyond the golf course up the hill of **Craigower** (NTS) rewards you with fine views.

At the **Pitlochry Festival Theatre** you can now see eight plays in six days in season. The tent-like interior of the foyer recalls the marquee in which the theatre started in 1951. A short distance upstream, beneath the massive dam and power station, thick glass windows allow you to peer into the swirling waters of the **Fish Pass**, a series of ascending pools by the side of the dam allowing salmon upstream to spawn. Although there is often nothing but an empty tank to look at, a random visit will occasionally find a salmon or sea trout poised inside the glass. An electronic recorder counts the fish passing up the ladder but none exists to count the visitors, who must far outnumber them.

While at the dam, don't miss the **Hydro-Electric Visitor Centre** (open Apr to late Oct, daily 9.40 to 5.30) – not so much to see the power station, which just hums away without any visible action, but the series of excellent exhibitions, films and electronic displays which show the workings of the station, describe the Tummel Valley Hydro-Electric scheme, or tell you about the life-cycle of the salmon.

Edradour Distillery, up the hill to the east of Pitlochry, is the smallest distillery in Scotland, but there seems to be enough room for all the visitors. It is free and friendly but a little plagued by wasps.

LOCH TAY

Ballinluig to Aberfeldy

Five miles south of Pitlochry, the A827 strikes across the Tummel and points you in the direction of Aberfeldy, Crianlarich, Oban and the sea. By following the south bank you pass the minor road to **St Mary's Church** at Grandtully. The church, dating back at least to 1533, looks like a barn attached to the neighbouring farm. Inside, however, there is a ceiling richly decorated with medallions and heraldic crests, probably done around 1636. It is the pleasure of finding a small hidden treasure which makes a visit here rewarding.

Aberfeldy

Aberfeldy is an unrushed place, little more than a large village with an attractive square and a few shops. If you do not want to stay in the bustle of Pitlochry, Aberfeldy is just as well situated for touring and a great deal more peaceful.

Aberfeldy is distinguished by General Wade's bridge across the Tay. This is widely seen as the road-building General's *tour de force*. He brought in William Adam to design it, and it took two years to build. With its pinnacles and steep arches, it is certainly the most imposing bridge in the Highlands. Beside it stands the **Black Watch Monument**, a memorial to that most famous of Highland regiments, which was raised in 1739.

Aberfeldy Water Mill is a carefully restored oatmeal mill, driven by the waters of the Moness Burn. The process looks simple, but as you listen to the technical details it becomes obvious that there is more to milling than meets the eye. Porridge-freaks and oatcake-addicts will travel miles for stone-ground oatmeal of different grades such as is sold here.

The local beauty spot, the **Birks (birches) o' Aberfeldy**, owes its fame to a poem by Burns and the walk up the miniature glen behind the town to the Falls of Moness is pretty enough if you feel like a stroll.

Castle Menzies

(Open Apr to mid-Oct, Mon to Sat 10.30 to 5, Sun 2 to 5)
This creepy-looking pile across the Tay from Aberfeldy and beyond the tiny village of Weem was derelict for years. Clan Menzies got hold of it in the nick of time and it is now being restored as a Clan Centre, but also as rather more than that, for it is a splendid example of a 'Z-plan' fortification (a castle with a tower on diagonally opposite sides of the main wing). Clan Menzies have a stupendous task on their hands for the castle had almost rotted to pieces, but the work is progressing fast and there are now few parts that are inaccessible, although there is not a great deal to see inside. The most intriguing objects are the items the restorers found behind the old walls, which include a single green satin eighteenth-century lady's shoe.

Fortingall

Follow the River Lyon up behind Drummond Hill and you reach this cluster of houses – an unlikely place to find the oldest living thing in Europe and the alleged birthplace of one of the most vilified characters in history.

The former is a yew tree. It does not look 3000 years old at first glance, but once you have peered over the railings that keep you away from it and have seen that all the fragments of wood were once one huge trunk, whose circumference in 1776 was 65 feet, the timescale begins to sink in. The poor old tree has suffered much, from souvenir hunters, bow-makers and festival bonfires, but it still lives on.

The vilified character was Pontius Pilate. The story goes that he was the son of a local woman (maybe a Menzies) and a Roman envoy sent by Caesar Augustus, who went back to Rome with the baby once his mission was completed. How true the tradition is is anybody's guess, and the village does not exactly celebrate its infamous son, even now.

Taymouth Castle

This mammoth nineteenth-century folly of a mock castle stands hidden by trees at Kenmore, by the foot of Loch Tay. It was completed just in time for Queen Victoria's visit, and she was thrilled: 'The firing of the guns, the cheering of the great crowd, the picturesqueness of the dresses . . . formed one of the finest scenes imaginable. . . . It was princely and romantic.' It is all very different now, for the castle stands empty and the yellow flags of the local golf course flutter on the lawn. You cannot go inside the castle, but it makes a pleasant diversion to peer at it from the outside and imagine Queen Victoria's enjoyment.

Glen Lyon

This is the longest glen in Scotland, running almost across to Glenorchy. It is not quite a cul-de-sac, since a road winds out across the shoulder of Ben Lawers down to Loch Tay, making one of the best round trips from Aberfeldy. A copy of the *Tamdhu Guide to Aberfeldy and Glenlyon*, available from local tourist information centres, will bring the landscape to life. Glen Lyon was populous Campbell territory for many years; now it is almost deserted, apart from the odd 'big hoose' or large farm. The outlawed Macgregors were here too, persecuted by the Campbells of Glenorchy and Lawers (who bred a bloodhound suckled by a Macgregor woman, so that the dog would know the smell of its enemy).

The entrance to the glen beyond Fortingall is half-hidden and dramatically steep. Then the scenery relaxes, the river broadens and becomes good for picnics and the glen opens up into an attractive valley between the steep slope of Ben Lawers on the left and Carn Gorm on the right.

As you penetrate to the end of the road the glen becomes wilder and the encroaching mountains more persistent, until finally you come to the dam which doubled the size of Loch Lyon behind it. Beyond, all is pathless wilderness.

Ben Lawers

A road runs on either side of Loch Tay to Killin. The main A827 is fast and undemanding, with good views of the loch, but of little else. The back road on the southern shore is narrow and slow, but you have the advantage of being able to look across the water to the peak of Ben Lawers.

For a closer look at Ben Lawers (which has been a National Nature Reserve since 1975), head for the road which runs over its shoulder to Glen Lyon (see above). On the flank of the mountain you will find a visitor centre (NTS, open Apr to Sept, daily 10 to 5), with the usual facilities and information – quite a good introduction to the hill. Various walks are suggested, but your chances of spotting the rare alpines for which Ben Lawers is famous are remote unless you know exactly what you are looking for. Ben Lawers is a friendly sort of mountain for a hill walk, and correspondingly popular. If you want mountainous solitude, go somewhere else.

Killin

A small village at the head of Loch Tay, Killin is busy with walkers and those who have stopped to look at the **Falls of Dochart**. These rather tame rapids are easily visible from the road, so more photographs are taken of them than they actually deserve. At Killin are to be found the healing stones of St Fillan, the only relics of his that remain in their original position (ask at the local Tourist Office if you want to see them); his bell and crosier, originally under the guardianship of hereditary 'dewars' (keepers of holy relics) have now ended up in the Royal Museum of Scotland in Edinburgh. In Killin, Shutters restaurant makes a valuable lunchtime halt, especially in the rain. Otherwise, try driving up Glen Lochay to get away from the crowds, though unless the weather is perfect it is inclined to be a melancholy spot.

LOCHS TUMMEL AND RANNOCH

The B8019 branches west from the A9 three miles north of Pitlochry to take you into the glacial gouge which holds these two lochs. You can also get here over the hill from Aberfeldy. The beauty spot of **Queen's View** at the foot of Loch Tummel, with its long vista over the water to the pyramid peak of Schiehallion on the opposite shore, remains unspoilt but the rest of Loch Tummel has been ruined by the dense conifers clothing the hills on its northern shore. All colours other than spruce green have been expunged.

Luckily, Loch Rannoch beyond is a different story. Beyond

Kinloch Rannoch, the last evidence of tourism is a time-share enterprise, but then you are alone with the loch. The drive round is excellent. On the northern shore, birch forest comes down to the lake edge, dusty gold in autumn, silver-green in spring, with the aquamarine or slate grey of the water seen through the trunks.

On the Southern shore, and worth all the drive to see, is the **Black Wood of Rannoch**. This pine forest contains some of the few gnarled survivors of the great Caledonian forest, and a beautiful place of light and air it is, with great lumps of moss and heather as its floor, and pines of all ages, alder and birch growing in profusion.

If you continue west beyond Bridge of Gaur towards Rannoch Station, the landscape changes. The woodland of Loch Rannoch lies behind as the road climbs towards Rannoch Moor, that great seed-bed of Ice-Age glaciers. At this eastern end the land is not beautiful, for the glacial rubble is like a gargantuan overgrown building site and hydro-electric man has not disguised his work very carefully. Push on to **Rannoch Station**, where, beside the isolated railway at the end of the road, under suddenly wide skies, you will find a single white hotel, a cottage, and a silence such as you have seldom heard before.

PITLOCHRY TO DRUMOCHTER

Killiecrankie

(NTS Visitor Centre, open Apr, May, Sept, Oct, daily 10 to 5; June to Aug, daily 9.30 to 6)

The tourist enters the celebrated Pass of Killiecrankie with a feeling approaching to terror. (The Scottish Tourist, 1827)

Killiecrankie lost much of its wild grandeur when the River Garry gave up most of its water for the sake of electricity. The **Soldier's Leap** across the narrowest part of the gorge, where a fleeing Englishman jumped to save his skin from the Highlanders hard on his heels, does not now look quite such a desperate feat. However, the steepness of the pass, its link with a famous battle won by an all-out charge of the clans and the general loveliness of the surrounding woodlands make Killiecrankie much-visited.

The battle of Killiecrankie was the climax of the Jacobite uprising of 1689. James Graham of Claverhouse, objecting to the way in which James VII had been forced into exile and the Scottish crown offered to William of Orange, had gathered a Highland army to dispute the cause. The charge of the clans at the head of this narrow gorge put the Williamite army to flight. Dundee, however, was fatally wounded in the battle, and without his leadership the uprising fizzled out after the Highland army was blocked at Dunkeld (page 291). Dundee (Bonnie Dundee of the song) owes his romantic reputation to Killiecrankie, but is the same man whose ruthless persecution of the Covenanters after the restoration of Charles II gave 'The Killing Times' to Scottish history.

The visitor centre (undergoing major alterations till May 1994, ring 0796 473233) has a detailed account of the battle and is signposted from the A9.

Blair Atholl

This is a modest village, by-passed by the new A9, and is the place to look for somewhere to stay (although there is not too much choice) if you want to do some of the long walks that thread through the lumpy mountains of the district of Atholl to the east. The restored **Blair Atholl Mill**, like the one at Aberfeldy, will grind the oatmeal for your porridge with a great rumbling of grindstones and rattle of boxed-in elevators carrying the oats or cracked grain to the floor above.

The next stretch of the A9 northwards will serve to introduce General Wade, who chose this route for one of his many roads. Sent to Scotland in 1724 after the 1715 Jacobite rising, he built roads and bridges through the Highlands which, to a great extent, still define what you can see from your car today and what you cannot. These roads, a network of military communication where none had previously existed, were built to keep the Highlands pacified. Ironically, they were put to use by Charles Edward Stuart during his campaign in 1746. Now they are mostly hidden beneath tarmac, though many of his bridges remain, notably at Aberfeldy. Some stretches (marked 'military road' on OS maps) are left where modern road-makers have chosen a different route. Perhaps the most remarkable is at the Corrieyarrick pass (built 1735), which runs between Laggan and Fort Augustus. 'If you had seen these roads before they were made, you would get down on your knees and bless General Wade', runs the old saying.

Before the coming of the General, two alternative routes northwards ran up **Glen Tilt** over to the River Dee and up **Glen Bruar** over the pass called Minigaig down as far as Glen Feshie and Speyside. These old routes now make two of the finest medium-distance walks in Scotland, through country which is about as remote from modern life (and from rescue) as it is possible to get in Britain. Even if you do not want to make the full crossing, for which you must be adequately prepared, exploring the start of both walks is enjoyable. Although this country is deserted now, it was not always so; you will find the remains of shielings up both glens, where cattle used to be pastured in summer before the days of depopulation.

Blair Castle

(Open Apr to Oct, daily 10 to 6; Apr, May, Oct, Sun 2 to 6)
Home of the Duke of Atholl, Blair Castle is the mustering ground of his private army, the only one allowed in Britain. The Atholl Highlanders were the product of a moment's romantic weakness by Queen Victoria, who visited the castle in 1844.

The panelled entrance hall to this pleasing mixture of castle and stately home is garnished by pretty patterns of of muskets, bayonets and swords – unusual wall-coverings. Unusual too was the practice of keeping large stags in the grounds and glueing their shed antlers on to the skulls of dead deer to make the estate's trophies look outstanding (there are ranks of them in the ballroom).

Blair Castle is old, turreted and white, and there is a lot of it. It is not easy to tell from the outside what is thirteenth-century and what is Victorian, though the castellations most certainly are the latter. The best parts of the interior are the Georgian conversions of older rooms, the drawing-room ceiling being especially elaborate and beautiful. Rank upon rank of family portraits cover the walls and there is often an accompanying family tree to show you who was who. The most eccentric and fascinating collection in the castle is the Victorian miscellany on the lowest floor, which has everything from old ball dresses and reticules to mourning brooches. Innocuous-looking walking canes conceal a sword, an airgun, a blowpipe and a collapsible fishing rod.

There is a family connection to the 1745 rising, for Lord George Murray, Prince Charles' one competent commander, was brother to the Duke of Atholl. Consequently, there are a number of Jacobite relics, including the Chevalier's gloves and lockets with his miniature inside. Knotty, hoary seventeenth-century furniture is scattered around, and objects in glass cases, from snuff-boxes to fragments of flag, are everywhere; by the time you progress to the collection of china, you are beginning to wonder whether you will ever reach the end. A gift shop rounds off the experience.

The castle grounds are both ducal and welcoming, which means specimen trees, picnic benches, few restrictions on where you walk and a car park which, for once, is not a half mile trudge in the drizzle. This is primarily a stately home for lovers of odds and ends; you cannot help wondering where all the junk was kept through the years before it went on display.

Drumochter

After Blair Atholl the A9 leaves the southward-flowing river valleys and heads up Glen Garry to this bleak pass at the top of a great barrier of peat bog and sour hillside which separates the districts of Atholl and Badenoch and marks the boundary between Tayside and Highland regions. On one side lies the mountainous hump of the Sow of Atholl,

---

USEFUL DIRECTORY

Main tourist offices
Loch Lomond, Stirling & Trossachs Tourist Board
41 Dumbarton Road
Stirling FK8 2QQ
(0786) 475019

Perthshire Tourist Board
45 High Street, Perth PH1 5TJ
(0738) 38353

Tourist Board publications Annual *Visitor's Guide* (Loch Lomond, Stirling & Trossachs – lists everything from sight opening times to boat trips and crafts; Perthshire), quarterly events guides. Special interest: guides on fishing, golf, walking, cycling. Postal or phone orders from the above addresses.

---

mirrored by the Boar of Badenoch on the other. It always seems to be raining on Drumochter, no matter how clear the skies are elsewhere.

In the fourteenth century this would have been a long, wet journey on horseback, with the followers of the Wolf of Badenoch lying in wait. The Wolf was Alexander, Earl of Buchan and Ross, a bastard son of King Robert II, who struck fear into Lowland hearts. Nominally justiciary of the north, he made the central Highlands into a fastness, whence his predatory raids, notably that on Elgin, gave him, and this part of the world, an unenviable reputation.

Local tourist information centres
Aberfeldy (0887) 820276
Aberfoyle (0877) 382352 (Apr to Oct)
Auchterarder (0764) 663450
Blairgowrie (0250) 872960/873701
Callander (0877) 330342
Crieff (0764) 652578
Dunblane (0786) 824428 (May to Sept)
Dunkeld (0350) 727688 (Mar to Oct)
Killin (0567) 820254 (Apr to Sept)
Kinross (0577) 863680
Pitlochry (0796) 472215/472751
Tillicoultry (0259) 752176 (Apr to Oct)
Tyndrum (0838) 400246 (Apr to Oct)

Local transport
Scotrail Stirling (0786) 464754
Midland Bluebird Bus Services (0786) 473763
Tayside Transport (0382) 201121

Ferries and cruises
Loch Katrine 041–355 5333
East Loch Lomond (Balmaha) (036087) 214
(Inversnaid) (0877) 386223
(Rowardennan) (036087) 273

Watersports
Loch Tay (0887) 830291
(0887) 830236

WHERE TO STAY

ABERFELDY

Farleyer House   £–££
Aberfeldy, Perthshire PH15 2JE   *Tel (0887) 820332*

A spot of luxury in the middle of the Perthshire Highlands, surrounded by wood and parkland. The sitting-rooms are upstairs, in best Scottish tradition, to take advantage of the light, while downstairs the formal dining-room serves modern, appetising food. Bedrooms are furnished with attractive antiques, like most of the rest of the house.

Open: all year, exc first 3 weeks in Dec and Feb **Rooms**: 11
Facilities: golf **Credit/charge cards**: Access, Amex, Diners, Visa

AUCHTERARDER

Auchterarder House   £££
Auchterarder, Perthshire PH3 1DZ   *Tel (0764) 663646*

A grand Victorian building with panelling, high ceilings and spacious rooms. The atmosphere is relaxed and comfortable, and encourages you to take advantage of the warm conservatory or the cosy bar. The food is traditional but excellently presented, while bedrooms vary from the cosy to the grand.

Open: all year **Rooms**: 15 **Credit/charge cards**: Access, Amex, Diners, Visa

BLAIRGOWRIE

Kinloch House   ££–£££
By Blairgowrie, Perthshire PH10 6SG   *Tel (0250) 884237*

A very relaxing family-run hotel in a splendid ivy-covered baronial house. There's a large conservatory in which to sit and enjoy the sun, and a flickering fire and comfortable old armchairs in the hall. The food is beautifully presented, majoring on fish and game. Bedrooms are cosy with pine and antique furniture.

Open: all year, exc 15 to 30 Dec **Rooms**: 21 **Facilities**: fishing
Credit/charge cards: Access, Amex, Diners, Visa

CALLANDER

Roman Camp   **££–£££**
Callander
Perthshire FK17 8BG   *Tel (0877) 330003*

Built as a shooting lodge and set in beautiful grounds, the Roman Camp provides a quiet hideaway from the tourist throngs at Callander. Inside the pretty pink building, the sitting-room and panelled library exude peace. The dining-room is not so romantic, but bedrooms are comfortable with plenty of extras.

Open: all year **Rooms**: 14 **Facilities**: fishing
Credit/charge cards: Access, Amex, Diners, Visa

DUNKELD

Kinnaird   **£££**
Kinnaird Estate,
By Dunkeld
Perthshire PH8 0LB   *Tel (0796) 482440*

This luxury sporting hotel on Tayside doubles as a country-house retreat. Bedrooms have huge triple beds, comfortable chairs before the fire, and a decanter of sherry among the trimmings. Bathrooms are even better. The food is nouvelle cuisine and beautifully presented. Drinks are brought to you with the menu in the drawing-room, where there are deep sofas and a crackling fire.

Open: all year, exc Feb **Rooms**: 9 **Facilities**: billiards, fishing, tennis, shooting **Credit/charge cards**: Access, Amex, Visa

KILLIECRANKIE

Killiecrankie Hotel   **££**
Killiecrankie
by Pitlochry
Perthshire PH16 5LG   *Tel (0796) 473220*

A good base for exploration of the Highlands and also for good Highland food. The bar area produces some excellent dishes in a comfortable setting – like a homely, yet smart, inn.

Open: all year, exc Jan, Feb **Rooms**: 11
Credit/charge cards: Access, Amex, Visa

ST FILLANS

Four Seasons Hotel   **£–££**
St Fillans
Perthshire PH6 2NF   *Tel (0764) 685333*

A simple, friendly and good-value hotel in a lovely village at the eastern end of Loch Earn. There are open fires in the library and bar, a comfortable sitting-room and fine views down the loch. Bedrooms have plain wooden furniture and adequate bathrooms, but are comfortable, and there are family rooms in the annexe.

Open: all year, exc mid-Dec to Feb **Rooms**: 12 plus 6 chalets
Credit/charge cards: Access, Visa

SPITTAL OF GLENSHEE

Dalmunzie House   **£–££**
Spittal of Glenshee
Blairgowrie, Perthshire PH10 7QG   *Tel (0250) 885224*

A family-run hotel in a turreted mansion near the top of Glenshee, right in the middle of the hills. The atmosphere is pleasantly relaxed; there's a peaceful sitting-room, and the bedrooms, most with bathroom, are extremely comfortable. The food comes in ample quantities, with no fanciness. Good value.

Open: all year, exc Nov to 27 Dec **Rooms**: 16 **Facilities**: fishing, tennis, golf, games room **Credit/charge cards**: Access, Visa

STIRLING

The Heritage   **£**
16 Allan Park
Stirling, Stirlingshire FK8 2QG   *Tel (0786) 473660*

The atmosphere inside this central hotel is distinctly provincial French, with its long thin bar, soft velvet cushions and flock wallpaper in the dining-room. Bedrooms are spacious and crisply furnished – some bathrooms are on the small side.

Open: all year, exc Xmas and New Year **Rooms**: 4
Credit/charge cards: Access, Visa

Park Lodge Hotel ££
32 Park Terrace
Stirling FK8 2JS *Tel (0786) 474862*

If you don't look too carefully, you could be in a French country château. The Marquetty family, who also own the Heritage (opposite), have transformed their Stirling townhouse with baroque panels and gilded mouldings, heavy curtains and high brass beds. The salon feels designed for a drink before the opera, and there's a conservatory, a dining-room and a small walled garden.

Open: all year **Rooms**: 9 **Credit/charge cards**: Access, Visa

TUMMEL BRIDGE

Kynachan Lodge £
Tummel Bridge, By Pitlochry
Perthshire PH16 5SB *Tel (0882) 634214*

This pleasant, small hotel makes a good base for exploring Perthshire, though Loch Tummel itself nowadays is spoilt by hydro-electric clutter. The wooden staircase and hall are distinctly grand, bedrooms are well designed, and the five-course dinners have Scottish overtones. Excellent value.

Open: all year, exc Nov to Easter **Rooms**: 6 **Facilities**: fishing
Credit/charge cards: Access, Visa

WHERE TO EAT

ABERFOYLE

Braeval Old Mill
By Aberfoyle
Stirling FK8 3UY *Tel (0877) 382711*

People return repeatedly to this lovingly restored mill for a choice of four dishes at dinner and two or three at lunch. The mill also has a fine wine list and has been awarded a wine symbol for an outstanding wine cellar by the 1994 *Good Food Guide*.

Open: Tues to Sat 7.30 to 9.30, Sun 12.30 to 1.30; closed 1 week Nov, Feb and end May **Credit/charge cards**: Access, Visa

DUNKELD

Tappit Hen
7 Atholl Street
Dunkeld PH8 0AR   *Tel (0350) 727472*

With the emphasis on home baking the Tappit Hen produces light scones, sponges and cakes as well as filled rolls and sandwiches in a charming coffee-shop.

Open: summer, daily 10.30 to 5; winter, daily 10.30 to 4.30; closed 1 week early Jan **Credit/charge cards**: Visa

KINROSS

Croft Bank House Hotel
30 Station Road
Kinross KY13 7TG   *Tel (0577) 863819*

The restaurant, like the rest of the hotel, is Victorian in style and has an extravagant menu that benefits from fresh ingredients and a flourish of frills.

Open: Tues to Sun 12 to 2, 7 to 9
Credit/charge cards: Access, Visa

PERTH

Betty's Coffee Parlour
67 George Street
Perth PH1 5LB   *Tel (0738) 32693*

Betty's serves huge cups of strong espresso, as well as cake, and light snacks, which makes it popular with shoppers.

Open: daily 10 to 6; closed Xmas and New Year
Credit/charge cards: none accepted

Timothy's
24 St John Street
Perth PH1 5SP   *Tel (0738) 26641*

Timothy's has been around for over twenty years, and attracts its customers with a blend of Danish-inspired starters and open sandwiches; daily specials, too.

Open: Tues to Sat 12 to 2.30, 7 to 10
Credit/charge cards: Access, Visa

FIFE AND ANGUS

- Golfing country – Carnoustie and St Andrews
- Ancient ports and fishing villages, a royal palace and some fine stately homes
- Gentle, fertile landscapes, with the isolation and grandeur of the Angus glens to the north as well

St. Andrews Cathedral

THE peninsula of Fife lies between the twin firths of Forth and Tay. North of the Tay, the Grampian mountains rise above the fertile countryside of Strathmore, bounding the district of Angus. Fife and Angus are rich farming country for the most part, and the inland scenery, except where the Angus glens penetrate the Grampian massif, is unspectacular, though wherever you find a hill you will usually find first-class views to go with it. It is the coast which draws most visitors – either to see the ancient trading ports and fishing villages along the coast of Fife, or else to play the renowned golf courses on the links.

Before the Forth and Tay bridges were built, Fife was effectively cut off from the rest of Scotland by the long estuaries. In the Dark Ages it may have had its own king – locals still like to refer to the Kingdom of Fife. In 1975, Fife was the only part of Scotland to mount a successful resistance against plans to partition it between neighbouring regional authorities. Even today, most of the visitors who arrive by car must pay to get into the region, for both Forth and Tay bridges carry tolls. St Andrews, on the eastern fringe, was once the religious and academic centre of pre-Reformation Scotland. Modern-day pilgrims go there to see the spot thought of as the home of golf.

Dundee, on the north bank of the Tay, is the fourth largest

THE PICTS

The *picti*, or painted ones, was the name given by the Romans to the inhabitants of the land beyond Hadrian's Wall. In the third centry AD, most of what is now Scotland was under Pictish rule, but 700 years later, after the unification of Picts and Scots under Kenneth MacAlpine in AD 843, they appear to have been either absorbed or subjugated.

For a race which left behind it such graphic monuments in stone and silver, frustratingly little is known about the Picts. Although Pictish kings began to be converted to Christianity as early as the sixth century, during St Columba's lifetime, we have no identifiable manuscripts from Pictish monasteries to rank with those from Anglo-Saxon England (though the famous *Book of Kells* may be a Pictish manuscript). We have no knowledge of what town in Scotland. Famous today for the three Js of jute, jam and journalism, it also has a long history as a trading, ship-building and whaling port. It is not a beautiful town but gives life and energy to the agricultural surroundings of both Fife and Angus.

The Eastward look

The ports up and down this coastline (especially after the loss of Berwick to the English) provided Scotland's trading link with the rest of Europe. Before the trade with America from Glasgow shifted Scotland's industrial energies towards the west, merchants from the coasts of Fife and Angus were busy importing and exporting to the Baltic, to the Hanseatic ports and to the Low Countries. Timber, cloth, fish and wool were the staples of this trade, and the long history of weaving in the small towns of Angus is linked to it. You can also find echoes in the Baltic timber that lines the rooms of old houses, and in the distinctive domestic architecture of places like Culross, Pittenweem or Crail, with hints of Holland or Lübeck. Whaling was an important industry in the nineteenth century, the oil used to soften jute. It was in Dundee, too, that the ship was built which took Captain Scott to the Antarctic for the first time.

language the Picts spoke – where we find the Ogam script carved on stones it is unintelligible – while Latin records are confined to a list of Pictish kings and a few inscriptions. Nor, apart from what we can see on their carved monuments or interpret from the remains of their houses, do we know much about what they looked like (at one time they were thought to have been pigmies but evidence from burials shows otherwise), how they lived, or how their society worked, although the historian Bede claimed that they practised matrilineal succession.

What we do have are the symbol stones which once must have existed in hundreds or even thousands over the land. These enigmatic and elaborately beautiful works of art (see later in the chapter) show us glimpses of a culture of which it would be a joy to know more.

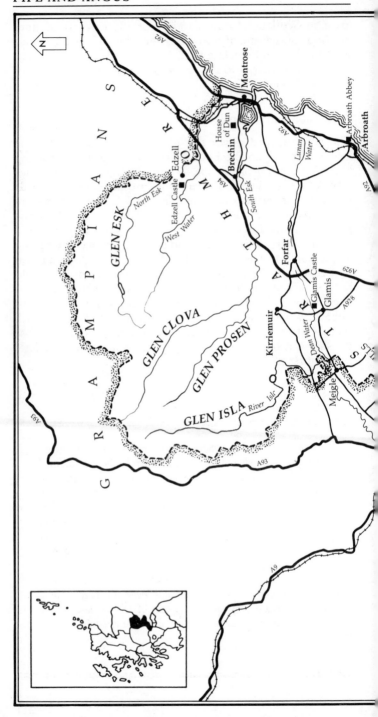

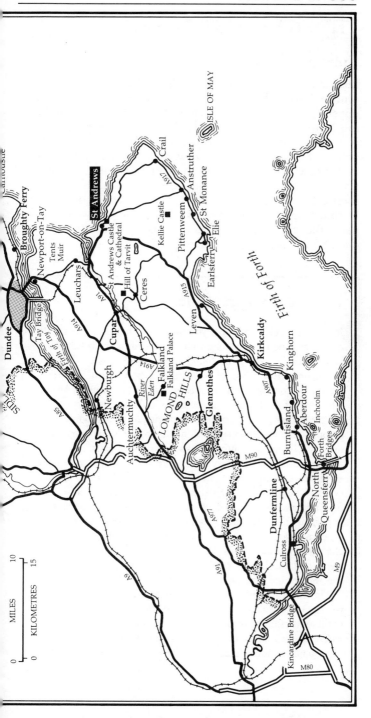

THE FIFE COAST TO CRAIL

Culross

Lost among a landscape of cooling towers, the sixteenth-century burgh of Culross survives intact in the industrialised upper estuary of the Forth. It was rescued and restored by the National Trust for Scotland over a 50-year period. It is a showpiece and, like other showpieces, gets crowded. Four or five steep cobbled streets are lined with pantiled and harled cottages; a small square has a replica mercat cross and a seventeenth-century tolbooth which now acts as the visitor centre. Luckily, there is nothing twee about the old village. Despite its photogenic qualities it has the air of a well lived-in place, though there is little now to suggest that this was once one of Scotland's major trading ports.

Practical suggestions

If you are a golf fiend, or if you want to be beside the sea, Fife and Angus should be among your choices for a Scottish holiday. Lovely beaches are to be found round these coasts, while the golf courses rival those of Ayrshire or East Lothian. A further reason for coming to this area is to explore the glens of Angus. They are off the tourist trail and there is plenty of variety among them, whether you are driving or exploring on foot. Finding good accommodation there may be difficult – many of the people you meet will be the self-sufficient type who prefer tents.

The most rewarding way to see Fife and Angus is to wander slowly through the area from the south, with Aberdeen as your eventual goal. Culross, Falkland, the East Neuk of Fife and St Andrews are the obvious stopping points. St Andrews is important and attractive enough to be worth the effort of getting to, even if you do not wish to spend longer in Fife. If you do, climb the Lomond Hills for views, go to the folk museum at Ceres and the Deer Centre near Cupar, visit Falkland Palace and wander the long sandy coastline at Tents Muir.

The Tay road bridge takes you straight to Dundee, from where you can either go up the coast to Arbroath with its abbey, or head north to Strathmore to visit the Iron Age and Pictish remains, the pick-your-own farms and the old weaving towns.

Accommodation is plentiful in the coastal towns and villages

At the top of the steep hill behind the village are the remains of **Culross Abbey** (HS, access from keykeeper; details at site). The old choir and tower are now the site of the Parish Church, and there is little left of the rest. Nevertheless, it is worth the climb for the peaceful surroundings and the views over the Forth.

Even if you are not there on the occasions when the **Study** (NTS, open Easter, early May to end Sept, Sat and Sun 2 to 4), with its panelling and painted ceiling is open, do not miss the **Palace** (due to open spring 1994 after restoration; phone 031-226 5922 for information), the grandest house in the village and the best place in Scotland to see how prosperous merchants of the seventeenth century lived. Sir George Bruce made his money from coal and salt panning. He also had fingers in foreign trade, for he used Baltic timber and Dutch tiles to decorate his palace. You wander through the three different

---

of both Fife and Angus, though you may have very much less selection inland.

Good bases

- **St Andrews** has few rivals in the region. The ruins of its cathedral and its castle mark its previous importance, while the Royal and Ancient golf club on the sandy links is the symbol of its modern claim to fame. It has the oldest university in Scotland to lend life to the streets, a wide choice of hotels and guesthouses to stay in, and some magnificent beaches within easy striking distance.

- **Earlsferry and Elie** These two burghs form the nicest resort on the north Forth coast. They are blessed with a long sea front with rocks, golf and caravans at one end and sand and a lighthouse at the other. The burghs are old, and there are attractive houses to see. Earlsferry and Elie do not draw quite the same crowds as the more picturesque villages of Anstruther and Pittenweem to the east. Accommodation is mostly of the seaside guesthouse type, but there is plenty of it.

- In **Angus**, Arbroath, though less interesting than St Andrews, is a possible seaside base for a night or two. Inland, the small towns of Angus – Forfar, Kirriemuir and Brechin – are not especially lively places to stay. There is more to be said for staying briefly in Dundee – it may seem like many another industrial city, but it has a humour and accent all its own.

ranges of the palace by a circuitous route which makes you feel it is much larger than it is. There are spiral stairs and corner rooms, views of the neat garden, old fireplaces and a fireproof and burglar-proof strongroom. The panelling and the decorative painting are the high points. The Allegory ceiling has 16 worthy scenes, each with a motto, painted on the pine barrel-vaulting. 'Mens pleasures fond do promeis only joyes. Bot he that yeldes at lengthe him self destroyes' reads one – a suitable reflection if you are tempted into the village pub for lunch. The National Trust for Scotland recently took over the running of the Palace from Historic Scotland, so there may be changes.

East of Culross, **Charlestown** and **Limekilns** are also ancient, though very much less compact than Culross; they do not receive the same flood of visitors.

Dunfermline

Back in the reign of Malcolm Canmore (1005–1034), Dunfermline was the site of a royal palace. The abbey was founded by David I, and the royal burgh remained a favourite among Scottish kings. The old ballad *Sir Patrick Spens* starts with the King sitting 'in Dunfermline toun, drinking the bluid-red wine', before despatching Patrick Spens on an ill-fated voyage to Norway.

Edward I of England found an excuse for burning the abbey in 1303; the Scots, he said, had turned it into a den of thieves by holding their rebellious parliaments there. The zealots of the Reformation who destroyed more of it required no such justification. Yet the abbey (HS, standard times) is enjoyable as much for its history as for its beauty, for this is where the Scottish kings were buried after Iona had become vulnerable to Norse raiders. This is where Scotland's saintly Queen Margaret, fleeing from the Norman Conquest of England, married Malcolm Canmore, and proceeded to establish a priory on the site of an old Celtic church. This too is where she was buried, her shrine in the old Lady Chapel becoming a place of pilgrimage.

Dunfermline's most famous burial is signalled from afar. The words 'King Robert the Bruce' are woven in stone on the balustrade of the tower of the nineteenth-century parish church, which was built on the site of the abbey's choir. In 1818, while the foundations for the church were being dug, the remains of the Bruce were unearthed. A plaster cast was taken of his skull, and he was left to lie in peace.

The magnificent Norman nave is really the only part of the old abbey church worth careful study. There are huge pillars and a substantial west door flanked by towers. Most of the domestic buildings of the monastery were pillaged long ago, but the remains of the refectory are palatial – you can see why a thirteenth-century chronicler stated that two monarchs with all their retinue would have room and some to spare. Even less is left of the old royal palace – one wall only.

Dunfermline was the birthplace of Andrew Carnegie, the American steel magnate whose philanthropic bequests ran into millions. There is a museum about his life at the cottage where he was born (open Apr to Oct, Mon to Sat 11 to 5, Sun 2 to 5; Nov to Mar, daily 2 to 4), but his most eloquent memorial here is the beautiful park of **Pittencrief Glen**, which he bought and gave to the town. Dunfermline's linen industry is remembered in the **Dunfermline Museum** (open Mon to Sat 11 to 5), which has samples of fine damask and a hand-loom.

Aberdour

The town's castle stands almost next door to the sunny old-fashioned railway station with its beds of flowers, where families once poured off the train (most now come by car) and headed for the Silver Sands beach – perhaps the same beach where Sir Patrick Spens was walking when he got the King's fatal letter telling him to put to sea. Aberdour is the nicest resort on this part of the coast – a solid, dignified-looking place with views over the Forth to Edinburgh.

Aberdour Castle (HS, standard times, closed Thurs pm and Fri in winter) was a Douglas stronghold, and for a crucial period the residence of the Earls of Morton. When Mary Queen of Scots' secretary, Riccio, was murdered in Holyrood Palace (see box, page 284) in 1566, the Earl of Morton was one of the principal conspirators and had to leave for England in a hurry. He was soon back, however, helped to force Mary to abdicate, and eventually became Regent, before being executed on the charge of having had a hand in the death of Darnley, Mary's second husband.

The castle's heart is a very ancient tower – possibly the earliest remains are eleventh-century. This part is badly ruined, so the sixteenth- and seventeenth-century extensions are more interesting to wander around. The gardens are by far the best part of the castle – the seventeenth-century walled garden is filled with colour, and the terraces beneath the castle, which are still being restored, are also delightful.

East of Aberdour lie **Burntisland** and **Kinghorn** – the former with extensive sand, the latter notable as the place where Alexander III, the last of Scotland's Celtic kings, was thrown off a cliff by his horse in 1286. He was apparently hurrying, heedless of advice to the contrary, to rejoin his second bride, the sensuous Yolande of Dreux. His death marked the end of Scotland's golden age.

His successor was his grand-daughter, Margaret, the Maid of Norway, who was declared Queen at the age of three. For a moment all seemed to be going well, for a treaty was signed in 1290 which agreed to marry Margaret to the son of Edward I of England, thus solving at a stroke the problems which existed between Scotland and Norway and Scotland and England. But the little girl, sent from Norway when she was only eight, died in Orkney – from seasickness, it is said. With her went Scotland's last hope, for there were now 13 claimants to the throne; the only person in a position to adjudicate was Edward I of England, and he – as became clear – expected feudal obedience in return for his decision.

Kirkcaldy

The curious scent of linseed oil and twine which used to hang over Kirkcaldy came from the manufacture of linoleum, for which this town was famous. Kirkcaldy is not attractive – traffic schemes ruin its dignity and its modern architecture is undistinguished – but it may be worth running the gauntlet of the town centre if you want to see the collection of paintings by McTaggart and Peploe, who are particularly well represented in the Museum and Art Gallery here (open Mon to Sat 11 to 5, Sun 2 to 5), along with the pottery for which the town was also known. The industrial section will initiate you into the secrets of linoleum-making.

Elie and Earlsferry

Strung out around a bay between a rocky headland and a sandy one, these two burghs have gradually merged into one large seafront village – although when walking or driving from one end to the other, you pass through two distinctively different old centres. Elie, at the eastern end of the bay, is where the sand is and where the harbour lies tucked under the lighthouse. Earlsferry has a rocky headland and some prosperous and substantial houses.

Although it fills up on fine weekends, the resort seldom

gets really crowded. It is a gentle, respectable sort of place, where you can play on the sands or go golfing or sailing, but where there are not many opportunities for raucous self-indulgence. Elie's best-known bather was Lady Janet Anstruther, who used to make her servants ring a bell when she was about to go in for a dip, so that the populace would know to keep away. Earlsferry is said to be the place where Macduff, in flight from Macbeth, was ferried across the Forth. He managed to get the town made a royal burgh as a result, with the stipulation that the inhabitants should always convey any fleeing criminal over the Firth, and should not allow any other vessels to put to sea until the fugitive had got halfway across. All the town's charters were burnt in an Edinburgh fire, so it is not worth putting this to the test.

St Monans and Pittenweem

From the west, St Monans' T-shaped fourteenth-century church seems to be standing on its own. However, steep wynds leading down to the cottage-lined harbour lie beyond it and there is more modern housing on top of the hill. The church's tower and short spire give it a solid, reassuring appearance; inside the church, a model ship hanging from the roof emphasises the community's reliance on the sea, and you can even hear the waves on the rocks outside.

Pittenweem, the next fishing town to the east along the stretch of coast known as the East Neuk, is a more substantial place. The 'weem' part of the name refers to the cave in the village (Cove Wynd, key from the Gingerbread Horse shop), said to have been the retreat of St Fillan. The cave is still a shrine, though the entry is through a building that looks more like a harled public convenience. A stone altar stands on one side, and there is a blocked-off staircase once used by smugglers. Pittenweem was once the twelfth richest town in Scotland, and the substantial seventeenth-century houses are a mark of that prosperity. The prettiest part is down by the harbour, where piles of orange or green nets dry in the sun, and seagulls wheel above the fishing boats. Many of the red pantiled cottages with their crow-step gables bear small National Trust markers, for the towns of the East Neuk are where the National Trust for Scotland's 'Little Houses' restoration scheme has probably had its greatest impact.

Kellie Castle

(NTS, castle open Easter, May to end Sept, daily 2 to 6; early to mid-Apr, Sat and Sun 2 to 6; garden and grounds open all year, daily 10 to sunset)

This castle is well worth the short diversion from the coast, even if you only have time to look at the exterior. Two fifteenth-century towers are linked by a later sixteenth-century building, and the result is a curious T shape. A walk round the outside reveals contrasting architecture, from the four-square simplicity of the eastern tower to the turrets, corbelling and crow-step gables of the south-west one.

The story of its nineteenth- and twentieth-century 'rediscovery' and restoration by one of Scotland's most talented families gives Kellie a touch of romance lacking in its previously prosaic history. Professor Lorimer, father of the architect Robert Lorimer, took over the tenancy of what was becoming a crumbling ruin in 1878, and the preservation and revitalising of the house is largely as a result of the efforts of three generations of a family who loved the place. You can sense this as you wander through the interior, for it is adorned by their work and governed by their taste. The ancient painted panelling and the fine seventeenth-century plaster ceilings are complemented by paintings, fabrics and furniture which are often Lorimer in inspiration or design. One room is given over to the work of Robert Lorimer, but it is mostly the achievements of his daughter-in-law, Louise, that have turned Kellie Castle into a genuinely homely place. The garden too is largely a Lorimer production.

Also close to Pittenweem, **Balcaskie House and Gardens** (open June to Aug, Sat to Wed 2 to 6) provide an elegant break from the fishing towns. The house owes much to the architect Bruce, and contains various curiosities linked to the Anstruther family who own the place (the fetters worn by General Philip Anstruther while a prisoner of the Chinese, for example). Look out too for the table made from the sounding board of a pulpit and for the painted ceiling where Icarus appears to be tumbling from the clouds as you walk around the room beneath him. This is a gently-paced, informal house, where the guides seem to have plenty of time to satisfy your curiosity.

Anstruther

This is the biggest and the most touristy of the East Neuk towns. People come here for the Scottish Fisheries Museum (open Apr to Oct, Mon to Sat 10 to 5, Sun 11 to 5; Nov to Mar, Mon to Sat 10 to 4.30), which has an extensive collection of creels, models and old photographs, some lovely paintings by local artist John McGhie, the reconstructed sitting-room of a fisherman's house, and a mini-aquarium whose contents provoke squeals from visiting school parties.

In the strung-out harbour, the red *North Carr Lightship* (open Mon to Fri 9 to 3, Sun 12 to 4) lies by the pier. A visit brings home just now cramped were the conditions in which the crew had to live and work. Families dodge amongst the cars along the harbour-front, gazing into the gift shops and licking ice-creams. There is also a small sandy beach.

Anstruther is the starting point for trips to the **Isle of May**, which lies some six (often choppy) miles out into the Forth. Birds are the draw here, especially the puffins. Boats run between May and September, and depend on the tide; the trip takes four or five hours, and warm clothes and a picnic are essential – call (0333) 310103 for information.

Crail

The most compact and the prettiest of the East Neuk towns has a winning combination of a broad High Street, a delicate golden-brown harbour with steep wynds running down to it, a crescent of sand backed by cliffs and a strong smell of fish to prove authenticity. There is a tiny town museum (open Easter week, June to early Sept, Mon to Sat 10 to 12.30, 2.30 to 5, Sun 2.30 to 5; Apr, May, late Sept, weekends only 2.30 to 5) and a harbour-master with a forceful personality ('To steal this life-belt shows your own value of human life'). A short walk along the coastal path will give you the best of the views of the Bass Rock and North Berwick Law on the far side of the Forth. The church goes back to the thirteenth century and has an earlier Pictish cross slab. While there is nothing particularly special to pick out Crail from the other towns on the coast, it is the best to see if you have time only for one.

ST ANDREWS

If you stand in the middle of the scanty remains of the cathedral of St Andrews, you are at medieval Scotland's spiritual heart. What is now an unassuming university town and seaside resort was once as influential as Edinburgh or Stirling, while the men who ruled here as bishop or archbishop – Lamberton, Beaton, Sharp – were often as powerful as Scotland's kings. St Andrews owed its ecclesiastical pre-eminence to the tradition that the Greek monk Regulus landed here with relics of the apostle Andrew in the year 345. St Andrew became patron saint of Scotland, and his relics remained here until they were lost at the Reformation.

In fact, the earliest Christian settlement at St Andrews is more likely to date from the eighth century, and to have been more closely connected to Northumbria than to Greece. Whatever the case, St Andrews grew increasingly important, and became an archbishopric in 1472.

It is hardly surprising that the cruellest dramas of the Scottish Reformation were played out here. The reformer Wishart was burnt beneath the castle walls, and his persecutor, Cardinal Beaton, was murdered in his turn (his body thrown into the castle's dungeon and covered in salt to preserve it). John Knox studied and preached here and was taken forcibly from the castle after a year's siege to serve on the French galleys. In the seventeenth-century religious convulsions, the Archbishop of St Andrews was waylaid and butchered by Covenanters a few miles away.

St Andrews has the third oldest university in the United Kingdom, founded in 1411, where three of Scotland's fifteenth-century poets – Dunbar, Douglas and Lindsay – studied, where the reflector telescope was invented, and where Mary Queen of Scots planted a thorn tree. Its students wear red gowns – legend has it that they could be more easily recognised entering brothels if thus clad. The best way of seeing the university's ancient buildings is to take one of the organised tours, which run twice daily from July to September.

Most foreign visitors come to St Andrews because of golf, for, although it is not the oldest golf club in the country, the Royal and Ancient Golf Club is now recognised as the ruling body of the sport, and St Andrews, with its four courses draws enthusiasts from all over the world. Almost all the golfing activity takes place at the north-western corner of the town, where the Royal and Ancient club house stands. Here are the big (and pricey) golfing hotels, and the museum of golf.

However, if your interest lies elsewhere, you can ignore the sport entirely and still find much to please you. The burgh has an untouched medieval street pattern, with North, South and Market Streets fanning out from the cathedral; it is a pleasing combination of university town, classy resort and shopping centre for a large rural area. Very little architectural vandalism has taken place, and there are many buildings from the eighteenth century and earlier. If you come to the town during the Lammas Fair on the second Monday and Tuesday in August (a medieval survival), you will find the centre packed with stalls and amusements.

To the north of the town lies the West Beach, a long, dune-backed stretch of sand pounded and furrowed by the breakers of the North Sea. The further you venture along here, the more you will have it to yourself. A second beach, less attractive but more accessible, lies just to the east of the town, and there is the old harbour (built from the stones of the cathedral and castle) to fish in as an alternative. St Andrews still thrives as a family seaside resort, of the gentle, slightly old-fashioned, donkey-riding kind, and if you are lucky enough to hit a spell of fine weather you are unlikely to be disappointed by it.

As far as accommodation goes, you have a choice between the big hotels, where there will be golf balls on sale at reception, and the large numbers of guesthouses, many of which are well used to sandy children. The Byre Theatre is one source of evening entertainment, but if you visit the city in term time you will find a wide range of events.

The main sights

● **St Andrews Cathedral and Precinct** (HS, standard times) Not much remains of what was once the greatest church in Scotland, but luckily what the Reformation mob and the stone-quarriers left behind is striking. The great east front stands alone and unsupported by prop or buttress, looking as though the next gale will blow it flat like a domino. At the opposite end of what was once the nave, the single remaining spike of the western front hangs above the small houses of Market Street like a spiritual lightning conductor. Round these, the foundations, sections of arcaded wall, a few thirteenth-century windows and the stumps of great pillars are all that remain of a building which was started in 1160 and consecrated in 1318 in the presence of Robert the Bruce.

Although it must once have been dwarfed into insignificance by the cathedral which stood beside it, the twelfth-century **Church of St Regulus**, or St Rule, has re-emerged into the light with the cathedral's ruin. A single square tower, over 100 feet high, rises almost alone from a forest of gravestones, with a small Saxon choir at its base. This was the predecessor of the cathedral. Climbing the tower in the

323

constrictions of the tiny spiral stair can be claustrophobic and dizzying, but the view of the town from the top is worth the effort. From here you can see how all the cathedral precinct was enclosed by a strong wall (the fourteenth-century gateway into it called the Pends is now traversed by cars rather than canons). Outside the wall lie the foundations of the even earlier Celtic church, **St Mary of the Rock**, whose clergy were gradually displaced in favour of Augustinian canons under the remodelling of the Scottish church on Roman Catholic lines carried out by Queen Margaret and Malcolm Canmore.

Do not leave the cathedral precinct without looking at the **museum**, where among the collection of early Christian sculptured stones is a sarcophagus, a blend of Pictish and Anglian work, with David killing a lion, surrounded by all kinds of vividly carved animals running full pelt.

● **St Andrews Castle** (HS, standard times) The castle, strikingly poised on the sea's edge, was in fact the bishop's palace – and a notable prison for reformers. It was from here that Cardinal Beaton watched Wishart being burnt beneath the walls, and from here that his own murdered body was displayed to the crowd. Although there is not much left of the building, two fascinating features remain. One is the bottle dungeon, carved 24 feet down into the rock and narrowing towards the trap-door at the top, through which prisoners and food were dropped alike. Of all Scotland's nasty dungeons, this is the one in which it would be easiest to despair. The other relic of the castle's history is the mine and counter-mine. When the reformers (disguised as masons) broke into the castle and murdered Beaton in 1546, they held the place for a year against all efforts to take them. One such effort was a mine – a tunnel from outside the walls – against which the chosen defence was an opposing tunnel – the counter-mine – driven to meet it. You stumble down the narrow counter-mine to the spot where besieged and besiegers met in an underground clash, pedestrians scurrying along the pavement above your head.

● **British Golf Museum** (open Easter to Oct, daily 10 to 5.30; Nov, 11 to 3, closed Wed; Dec to Feb, 11 to 3, closed Tues and Wed; Mar to Easter, daily 10 to 5) This high-tech venture will tell you all you ever wanted to know about golf. As well as exhibits of golfing memorabilia, there are endless audio-visual gadgets – including tapes, touch-screen computers and videos – that allow you to test your own knowledge of the game or to watch the winning shot of the 1974 Open. Enthusiasts will happily spend a day here, while there are curiosities to interest the non-golfer too, such as the history of golf ball making, from the days of the leather-and-feather ball onwards, or the fact that James II banned the game – it was keeping people from archery practice.

Other things to see

Of the university buildings, **St Salvator's College**, founded in 1450, retains its fifteenth-century church and tower, **St Mary's College** has a sixteenth-century range, and **St Leonard's Chapel** has been well restored to recreate its old medieval lay-out. **St Andrews Preservation Trust Museum** (open July, Aug, Mon to Sat 10 to 5) in North Street has relics of old St Andrews, mostly from Victorian times. The **West Port**, at the head of South Street, is a rare survival of an old burgh gateway, still holding up the traffic. The **Burgh Kirk** – Holy Trinity – is fifteenth-century in origin, but heavily restored. Inside is a grotesquely decorated marble memorial to the slaughtered Archbishop Sharp. Only scanty fragments of **Blackfriar's Chapel** remain from another of St Andrews' once-thriving religious foundations.

In College Street, spare a thought for one of Scotland's more peculiar lovers, Pierre de Châtelard. This French gallant seems to have contracted a passionate obsession for Mary Queen of Scots, to the extent of twice intruding into her bed-chamber. The second occasion was once too many – the cross in the street marks the spot of his execution. His last words were 'Adieu the most beautiful and most cruel princess of the world'.

Round St Andrews

If you are keen on church architecture, drive up the unattractive estuary of the Eden, past the smelly paper mill at Guardbridge and through the outskirts of the huge base at RAF Leuchars to **Leuchars Church**, where the chancel and apse are outstanding in twelfth-century Norman style. It is a pity that the surroundings are not more attractive, but the church is certainly worth discovering. If you are travelling by train you will have the chance to test the platforms at Leuchars station, which are said to be the windiest in Scotland.

North of Leuchars, reached from the B945, the great stretch of beach, dunes and pine forest called **Tents Muir** reaches from the northern bank of the Eden estuary almost as far as Tayport at the mouth of the Tay. Two nature reserves are to be found here, as well as networks of coastal or inland walks and picnic sites. Although a very popular spot for fine weekends, Tents Muir is too big for you to feel cramped by over-organisation, and is thoroughly recommendable for a day by the sea (though swimming may be hazardous because of currents).

INLAND FIFE AND
THE NORTH COAST

Falkland Palace

(NTS, open Apr to Sept, Mon to Sat 10 to 6, Sun 2 to 6; Oct, Mon to Sat 10 to 5, Sun 2 to 5)

This was once the favourite hunting lodge of the Stewart kings. At one time there was to have been a courtyard surrounded by buildings, but there was never a west range and only the south and east ranges remain. It was James IV and James V who were responsible for most of what you see today, and the result is a Renaissance building, owing much to the French. The frontages are decorated with pillar buttresses, medallions and ornate dormer windows, and some crafty work has been done on the south range to give an impression of a symmetry which does not in fact exist.

Falkland was the scene of James V's death. Afflicted by despairing melancholy after the defeat at Solway Moss in 1542 (see page 36), he was not consoled by the news of his daughter's birth. 'It came wi' a lass and it'll gang wi' a lass,' he exclaimed, referring to the Stewart dynasty, but his daughter, Mary Queen of Scots, enjoyed the hunting here.

The restoration of the interior of the south range is entirely thanks to the efforts of the Crichton Stuart family, who became hereditary keepers of the palace in 1887. The rooms here are done as far as possible in the style of the seventeenth century, with exact reproductions of furniture and painted ceilings. Among many ancient pieces, look out for the ornate James VI bed and the magnificent tapestries. Two rooms in the east range have also been restored as bed-chambers, one as the 'King's Room' containing the seventeenth-century Golden Bed of Brahan, made in the East Indies.

Falkland Palace has two further points of interest – the tennis court and the garden. The tennis court (royal or 'real' tennis, of course) is the oldest in Britain. Unless you are lucky enough to see a game being played (a local club plays on summer weekends), you will probably be left unenlightened about exactly what happens, despite the efforts of the guidebook to explain the obscure rules. The garden is easier to appreciate. Laid out after World War II to complement the frontage of the palace rising behind it, it is a mass of herbaceous colour from May onwards, while its subtle design only gradually reveals itself as you walk round. Do not leave Falkland without wandering round the old burgh, where there are some well-preserved and photogenic old houses.

Ceres and around

Ceres, midway between Falkland and St Andrews, is a small, quiet, attractive village, worth going to for the sake of the **Fife Folk Museum** (open Apr to Oct, daily 2.15 to 5; closed Tues), which is housed in the old Weigh House and a couple of weavers' cottages. What raises this folk museum above the many similar ones is the strong sense of community involvement demonstrated by the book of donations – some items even come from Canadian emigrants. This manages to give life and unity to the collection of domestic utensils, scales, milk churns and relics of the weaving industry. Ceres is just about large enough for an hotel and an antique shop or two. If you want a really quiet village to stay in, you might consider this one.

Not far north, **Hill of Tarvit** (NTS, house open Easter, May to Oct, daily 2 to 6; early to late Apr, Sat and Sun 2 to 6; garden and grounds open all year, daily 10 to sunset) forms a fascinating comparison with Hill House near Helensburgh, and it is almost worth the drive across central Scotland to see the two in sequence. Both houses were designed by renowned Scottish architects – Lorimer and Mackintosh respectively – for wealthy industrialists. In 1902, at Hill House, Mackintosh had to compromise with his client's taste; in 1906, at Hill of Tarvit, Lorimer had to design (or, strictly, remodel) a house round the collection of paintings, furniture and porcelain amassed by the Dundee jute manufacturer Frederick Sharp. In both houses, the smallest details of design are governed by the imagination of the architect.

At Hill of Tarvit, Lorimer's public rooms provide 'correct' settings for the collections they were designed to hold, without descending into pastiche. Thus the entrance hall, panelled in oak, looks baronial enough to show off the Flemish tapestries which hang there, but is none the less original.

327

The drawing-room, filled with French furniture, is, in its plasterwork and woodwork, pure eighteenth-century France, while the magnificence of the Palladian-style dining-room sets off the Georgian furniture which fills it.

Of the many things to look at, the collection of Dutch paintings, the silverwork and the Chinese porcelain are all good. Do not ignore the more modern side to the house with its Wizard vacuum cleaner with continuous suction and the shower with its ascending spray. Do not miss the gardens either – another Lorimer design.

Finally, a few miles away, the **Scottish Deer Centre** (open Apr to Oct, daily 10 to 5; Nov to Christmas weekends only) is much less tacky than the initial impression of souvenir shop, restaurant and ice-cream kiosk might suggest. In fact, once you have seen the excellent audio-visual, and taken a tour round the fields to look at and learn about deer, you come away both well informed and well satisfied.

DUNDEE

Of the three Js that made Dundee, it was jute that turned it into a flourishing industrial town (look for the chimney known as Cox's Stack which is said to be wide enough for a taxi to drive round the top). The jam and the journalism have had more influence on the rest of the country, however, for Dundee is where marmalade, using Seville oranges, was first invented, and it is the home of the *Beano* and other publications from the D C Thomson stable.

One of the most idiosyncratic is the *Sunday Post*, a newspaper with a curious stuck-in-the-1950s mixture of homely gossip and sentimental patriotism which has become a staple of popular Scottish culture. All Scots will recognise 'Oor Wullie' – the spiky-haired comic-strip urchin whose seat is an upturned bucket. The *Sunday Post* is heartily loathed by those trying to awaken Scotland to the modern world, but many a Scot in exile will fall upon a chance copy with cries of joy all the same.

Dundee is not a pretty place, but equally it is a city without artifice, with plenty of humour and plenty of life. It suffered from constant sackings during Scotland's many wars, from Edward I's burning in 1296 to Monck's effective pillaging during the Cromwellian invasion of 1651. It may be that the habit of rebuilding their town became so ingrained in Dundonians that they could not give it up. Little survives from before the nineteenth century, and much of the city centre is entirely modern, though sculptures and murals brighten it up. Dundee is busy sprucing up its tourist attractions – a new visitor centre down by the docks is one example. Don't leave town without buying a Dundee cake.

Drive up to the top of **Dundee Law**, a volcanic plug sticking out of the city centre. Beneath you, the Tay road bridge runs apparently diagonally across the estuary. The rail bridge lies a little further upstream, and you may be able to pick out the stumps of its predecessor beside it – a reminder of the disaster of 1879 when it collapsed as a train was crossing it. The famous elegist of the disaster is the poet William McGonagall, who lived in Dundee for much of his life. Widely hailed as the worst poet in Scotland if not the world, and subject of endless parodies, McGonagall has now become something of a cult figure:

> So the train mov'd slowly along the Bridge of Tay
> Until it was about midway,
> Then the central girders with a crash gave way
> And down went the train and passengers into the Tay
> The Storm Fiend did loudly bray
> Because ninety lives had been taken away
> On the last Sabbath day of 1879,
> Which will be remembered for a very long time.

Sights in Dundee

- **Discovery and Unicorn** The ship in which Captain Scott voyaged to the Antarctic in 1901 returned to Dundee, where she was built, in 1986. Now *Discovery* (open June to Aug, daily 10 to 5; late Mar to May, Sept to mid-Oct, Mon to Fri 1 to 5, Sat and Sun 11 to 5) has been fully restored and populated with realistic models. The expert guides rapidly draw you into the minutiae of arranging an Antarctic expedition: $1^1/2$ tons of mustard are laid in, 330 tons of coal are stored beneath the officers' mess. And the ship itself gleams with brass and polished wood, looking as good as if newly launched. Ask lots of questions. The *Unicorn* (open daily 10 to 5) berthed nearby, looks more of a hulk than a warship from the outside, for she has no masts. Launched in 1824, she is one of the oldest warships still afloat. Below decks, long rows of guns sit on their carriages, and there are various exhibits about nineteenth-century naval life.
- **McManus Art Gallery and Museum** (open Mon to Sat 10 to 5) Recently renovated, and much less gloomily Victorian

than it once was, this is the place to come to for an introduction to Dundee's history and to absorb detail about the whaling and the jute industries. Upstairs, the collection of Victorian paintings is important, and well hung in bright rooms.

THE COAST TO MONTROSE

East of Dundee, you arrive at **Broughty Ferry**, a fishing village which developed into a suburb of Dundee when the 'jute princes' built their houses here. Castle enthusiasts should delve into the estates on the north-western side of the town to find **Claypotts Castle** (HS, standard times; closed in winter), which is a complete example of a sixteenth-century Z-plan castle. The practice of squaring off and corbelling a tower to provide an extra room at the top is here carried to such extremes that the whole castle seems in danger of overbalancing.

On the far side of Buddon Ness, which juts sandily into the Tay but is mostly occupied by the military, **Carnoustie** is renowned for its championship golf course, but is also a small seaside resort, with fine sand. East Haven, a little further along the coast, is a much smaller beach, half-hidden by the cliffs on both sides.

Arbroath

It is difficult to know whether Arbroath is more famous for its 'smokies', its abbey, or the declaration of Scotland's freedom from English overlordship which was signed here in 1320. It is a solid red sandstone town with the ruins of the abbey squarely at the centre and a working harbour and rows of fishermen's cottages beneath. Down by the harbour, every second house has a sign offering fresh smokies, and it is senseless not to sample this smoked haddock while you are here. Boat trips run from the harbour to visit local caves and cliffs or to go sea fishing.

The Signal Tower Museum was reopened in October 1991 after major renovation and gives an insight into the local fishing and jute industries.

Arbroath Abbey

(HS, standard times)
A satisfactory amount is left of the great red thirteenth-century abbey church – certainly enough to see that it must once have been a splendid place, lit by the huge round window in the

western gable – of which only the lower half remains – and the remarkable lancets in the transepts. There is plenty for architecture enthusiasts – notably the variety of the patterns of the arcades – while the fifteenth-century sacristy and abbot's house are sufficiently complete to give a good impression of at least a part of the monastic life. The gatehouse which once led into the walled precinct of the monastery remains intact.

The Declaration of Arbroath, which was signed here on 6 April 1320, confirmed the Scottish nobility's support for the kingship of Robert the Bruce, and was taken to the Pope at Avignon. It was an important step in Scotland's intense diplomatic effort after Bannockburn to gain international recognition for the independence won on the battlefield. The declaration was probably drafted by the abbot of the time, Bernard de Linton. If so, he had a good line in rhetoric, as the ringing phrases of the document's most famous passage (in translation from the Latin) prove: 'For, so long as one hundred remain alive, we will never in any degree be subject to the dominion of the English. Since not for glory, riches or honours do we fight, but for freedom alone, which no good man loses but with his life . . .'

St Vigeans

By driving past an industrial estate on the northern outskirts of Arbroath, you arrive at a cul de sac where a small red church stands on a high mound, surrounded by low cottages. The tiny village is named after a seventh-century Irish saint, and has the atmosphere of an ancient sacred site. In one of the cottages you can see the collection of Pictish stones found (HS, access from keykeeper; details at site). Although not quite so inspiring as the collection at Meigle they are more than worth the brief excursion.

Lunan Bay

The cliffs north of Arbroath are suddenly broken by the sweep of this classically beautiful beach, found on many a postcard but often deserted for all that. Above the sand there is the gaunt ruin of a red sandstone castle, while at either end of the bay rocky headlands jut into the sea.

Montrose

With its tidal basin behind it and the sea to its front, Montrose seems almost cut off by the sea; it looks like a town from a

Dutch painting as you approach it from the south. Apart from being the birthplace of the famous Marquess of Montrose, it has had remarkably little share in Scottish history, and remains a peaceful, rather sleepy place, with a broad High Street. The museum – purpose-built in 1842 – has prints, paintings, boxes of shells and stones and curious pieces of historical flotsam, such as a bicorn hat, said to be Napoleon's. There is also an evocative message found in a bottle: 'No water on board, provisions all gone. Ate the dog yesterday, 3 men left alive . . .'

Behind the town, **Montrose Basin** is almost landlocked, and at low tide it becomes a great pool of mud. Attractive it is not, but for naturalists it is one of the best places to see duck and waders in huge numbers.

INLAND ANGUS

Reekie Linn

Follow the B954 north from near Alyth to **Bridge of Craigisla** for Reekie Linn, one of Scotland's best waterfalls: the river plunges suddenly into a deep gorge. From the car park there is little warning of what is to come, but a very

PICTISH STONES

The majority of carved Pictish stones are concentrated in eastern Scotland, especially around Strathmore in Tayside, the fertile areas of Moray, Banff and Aberdeenshire, and the Tain and Dornoch peninsulas. A couple of hundred have survived, and many more may lie buried or built into houses. These stones seem to have been carved between the sixth and ninth centuries, and vary from unshaped slabs of stone with designs incised into them, to elaborate monuments or Christian cross-slabs with intricate patterns and figures carved in relief. The stones are remarkable enough for the scale and beauty of their carving, but what must intrigue even the most casual onlooker is the meaning of the symbols with which many of them are embellished. Mirror and comb, double disc, Z-rod, serpent, crescent and the curious beast known as the 'swimming elephant' are the most common, and they appear on their own, as part of a secular scene, or on a short walk brings you to the top of this 'smoking fall'. There is an even better viewpoint on top of a jutting cliff a little further on. Wild broom clouds the whole place yellow in early summer. The urgent warnings to take care are justified – there is no protection.

Glamis Castle

(Open Easter to mid-Oct, daily 12 to 5.30)

Royal and literary connections draw the crowds here. The multi-turreted pinkish pile of Glamis Castle is not only the traditional scene of Macbeth's murder of Duncan, but also the home of the Queen Mother's family – the Bowes-Lyons, Earls of Strathmore and Kinghorne. The grounds surrounding the castle were remodelled in best eighteenth-century style: as you approach down a long, straight avenue flanked by trees, the conical turret caps reveal themselves, followed by a village-worth of chimneys and towers. Although the core of the castle is fifteenth-century or earlier, its present appearance is largely a result of late seventeenth-century work.

At the busiest times, tours through the sequence of grand rooms turn into one of those delicately balanced affairs whereby as soon as one group leaves a room, another files in behind it. This puts pressure on the time-keeping

---

Christian cross-slab alike. Furthermore, they are common to all of Pictland, their use cutting across boundaries between tribes or kingdoms.

What these symbols meant to the people who used them (and they were not just carved on stones but on humbler objects too) is unknown. One theory is that the stones are memorials to people or events denoted by the symbols. Another is that they are property markers, with the symbols representing different genealogies. Neither of these interpretations seems entirely satisfactory when you are confronted by the detail of the carved symbols themselves.

Pictish stones were mostly free-standing uprights. Many remain in their original positions in open countryside, and it can be quite a job to track them down. Others are to be found in churchyards to which they have been moved. The best indoor collections are at Meigle in Tayside, St Vigeans in Angus, St Andrews in Fife, Dunrobin Castle in Sutherland and in the Royal Museum of Scotland (Queen Street) in Edinburgh.

of the guides, who none the less manage to sustain a serious and thorough commentary. The highlights are the painting of the third Earl dressed in what looks like see-through armour, the jester's outfit (he got the sack for making a pass at a lady in waiting) and the plaster ceilings of the drawing-room and billiard-room. The chapel is decorated with seventeenth-century painted panels by Jacob de Wet (see also Holyrood) on walls and ceiling. It is said he was so outraged by his low pay (£90 for four years' work) that the night before he finished, he endowed his 'Christ mistaken for a gardener' with a floppy hat and gave St Simon a pair of spectacles. Look too for the gloomy St Andrew obviously wondering how the two fishes he carries can possibly feed five thousand. The chapel has a ghost – that of Lady Janet Douglas, burnt for witchcraft. The royal apartments, arranged as a suite after the present Queen Mother's marriage into the royal family, are simultaneously homely and ornate. From the comfort of these rooms you come to Duncan's Hall, in the oldest part of the castle, where, standing beneath a large stuffed bear, the guide explains the Shakespeare connection. The family exhibition contains a wide variety of curiosities from a violin-playing monkey to the Old Pretender's watch (stolen by the maidservant who cleaned his room when he stayed here in 1715).

Glamis has a noticeably relaxed and pleasant restaurant to end up in, and plenty of space in the grounds to stroll through. An extremely complicated sundial stands beside the castle, precisely three degrees west of Greenwich.

Angus Folk Museum

(NTS, open Easter, May to Sept, daily 11 to 5)
In the village of Glamis, and making a very good counterpoint to the splendours of the castle, this museum is housed in a number of old cottages and stuffed with artefacts from the everyday life of the nineteenth and early twentieth centuries. The cottages are themed so that you move from a laundry to a weaving room, kitchen, schoolroom and nursery. A well-put-together and well-laid-out place.

Kirriemuir, Forfar and Brechin

J M Barrie, creator of Peter Pan, was born in Kirriemuir. His birthplace, 9 Brechin Road (NTS, open Easter, May to Sept, Mon to Sat 11 to 5.30, Sun 2 to 5.30), is easily missed if you are not keeping a close watch. Exhibits in this small museum are a mixture of furnishings such as Barrie's writing desk, accounts of theatrical performances, photographs and newspaper cuttings. For our salacious era, the various cuttings suggesting that Barrie was more than just a friend to the Llewellyn boys he eventually adopted make intriguing reading.

Forfar, an old weaving town, lies six miles south-east of Kirriemuir. Go into the town if you want to see the horrible Forfar bridle, used to restrain witches as they were burnt. It is in the local museum (has been closed for restoration; call 0307 465101 for information). Otherwise, take the B9113 eastward to see the remains of the twelfth-century **Restenneth Priory** (HS, access from keykeeper; details at site), or follow the B9134 to **Aberlemno** to see the Pictish carved stones here. There are four of them, the best, with its entwined beasts and its battle scene, being in the churchyard.

On top of the nearby **Finavon Hill** are the remains of one of the most accessible vitrified forts in the country. There are still wrangles over whether the fused stonework of these Iron Age defences was created by deliberate burning of fires round them, or whether it was the result of enemy assault. If you wish to see more of the Iron Age remains, head north-east for the twin Iron Age forts at **Caterthun** up behind Brechin, which are again very accessible. A lot of stonework can still be seen, and the outline is clear.

Most people pause in the steep little town of Brechin to look at the round tower (HS, access from keykeeper; details at site), which, like the one at Abernethy dates from the tenth century and is similar to those found in Ireland. It stands beside the little cathedral, much of which was either restored or rebuilt at the beginning of the century, although parts are thirteenth-century.

The Angus glens

The glens running north from Strathmore into the Grampians make an attractive contrast to the lowlands of Angus. The hills surrounding them are not of the dramatic, craggy kind, but are high, rounded lumps, often heather-covered, which merge into the high plateaux which separate Strathmore from Deeside. It is not until you get further east into Grampian region that roads manage to penetrate through the massif, though a network of old tracks and drove roads radiates from the head of the Angus glens, notably from **Glen Clova** and

Glen Doll. For exploring by car, both **Glen Clova** and **Glen Prosen**, with roads on either side, allow round trips, while you can travel furthest into the mountains up **Glen Esk**.

At the westward side of the district, the upper stretches of Glen Isla and the tributaries of Glen Finlet and Glen Taitney can all be explored easily enough on foot, though there are a lot of trees about. Glen Prosen is more open, and the woods more attractive. Glen Clova is where Scott planned his expedition to the Antarctic, and a memorial stands by the foot of the glen. This is probably the most popular of the Angus glens – if you want more solitude, try the road which runs up beside West Water behind Brechin, from Bridgend to

---

USEFUL DIRECTORY

Main tourist offices
Kirkcaldy District Council Tourist Information Centre
The Beehive, 14–16 Durie Street
Leven KY8 4HE
(0333) 429464

St Andrews & NE Fife Tourist Board
70 Market Street
St Andrews KY16 9NU
(0334) 72021

City of Dundee Tourist Board
Tourist Information Centre
4 City Square
Dundee DD1 3BA
(0382) 27723

Angus Tourist Board
Tourist Information Centre
Market Place
Arbroath DD11 1HR
(0241) 77883

Tourist Board publications: annual *Visitor's Guide* (Kirkcaldy, St Andrews & NE Fife, Dundee, Angus) – listings include main sights, sports, plus *What's On Guide*. Special interest: *North East Scotland Coastal Trail* (entire NE coastline), guides on golf (St Andrews & NE Fife, Kirkcaldy). Postal or phone orders from the above addresses.

Waterhead. Glen Esk, up behind Edzell, is a long haul through rolling scenery. Loch Lee, at the head of the glen, is a good spot for walking if you like a watery backdrop. **Glenesk Folk Museum** (open Easter to May, Sat and Mon 2 to 6, Sun 1 to 6; June to Sept, Mon to Sat 2 to 6, Sun 1 to 6) diverts you en route.

Unless you are bent on doing some strenuous walking through to Deeside or across the tops, the Angus glens are best sampled as slow excursions on a fine day, with time to stop beside the rivers or just to look at the views. The midges may, as usual, put paid to any idea of evening picnics – otherwise the country looks its best at this time of day.

Local tourist information centres
Anstruther (0333) 311073 (Easter, May to Sept)
Arbroath (0241) 72609/76680
Brechin (0356) 623050 (June to Sept)
Burntisland (0592) 872667
Carnoustie (0241) 52258 (Apr to Sept)
Crail (0333) 50869 (June to Sept)
Cupar (0334) 52874 (mid-June to Sept)
Forfar (0307) 467876 (June to Sept)
Kirriemuir (0575) 574097 (June to Sept)
Kirkcaldy (0592) 267775
Montrose (0674) 672000 (Apr to Sept)

Local transport
Dundee Railway Station (0382) 28046
Kirkcaldy Railway Station (0592) 204771
Leuchars Railway Station (0334) 839206
Fife Scottish Omnibuses (0334) 74238
Moffat & Williamson Bus Co (0382) 22155
Strathtay Scottish Omnibuses (0382) 28054

Other useful information
Boat Trips to Isle of May daily from Anstruther Harbour, May to Sept (0333) 310103
For information about playing golf at St Andrews, phone the Links Management Committee (0334) 75757
For weather conditions in the Angus Glens area of the Grampians, phone (0891) 500442 (pre-recorded information)

Edzell Castle

(HS, standard times, closed Thurs pm and Fri in winter)
On a warm day there are few more pleasant spots than
this. Historic Scotland's curator will be mowing the grass
or planting seedlings in the grounds of the ruined red castle,
an elegant affair built by the Lindsays in the sixteenth century.
However, it is not so much the ruins as the castle's pleasance
which charms. This is a tiny walled garden, created in 1604
in that short period between the union of the crowns and the
outbreak of the civil and religious wars when it seemed that
Scotland had time at last for a few luxuries. The walls are set
with bas reliefs of improving subjects such as the Cardinal
Virtues and the Liberal Arts, and the niches between them
spill white and blue flowers over the red stone. In the centre,
formal parterres are surrounded by a box hedge which picks
out the Lindsay motto. In one corner stands a summer house
(there used to be a bath house in another). The best view of
the garden is to be had from the upper floors of the castle:
here you can best see the perfection of the lay-out.

House of Dun

(NTS, house open Easter, May to mid-Oct, daily 11 to 5.30;
garden and grounds open all year, daily 10 to sunset)
Newly restored by the National Trust for Scotland, this
William Adam mansion is primarily for lovers of elaborate
plasterwork, for the huge trophies and emblems by Joseph
Enzer which decorate the public rooms are extraordinary.
Dun was an Erskine holding from the fourteenth century,
though the house itself dates from 1730. The Earl of Mar
(called 'Bobbing John' after his political vacillations) was in
exile after his failed Jacobite rising in 1715 but seems to
have influenced the design of the place nevertheless, for he
was always writing to his kinsman, David Erskine, with
suggestions for the new house, and the elaborate plasterwork
certainly contains cryptic Jacobite symbolism. However, the
design of the house is unmistakeably Adam, with its slightly
severe façade, its first-floor library and its chimney-pieces and
fireplaces.

The second character of influence to the house, as becomes
plain from the awe in which the guides seem to hold her, was
Lady Augusta, an illegitimate daughter of King William IV,
who married into the family in 1827. She was responsible
for most of the fine needlework, including that on the
huge four-poster given to her as a wedding present by her

father. She also did a lot of work in the gardens, collecting plants from the countryside on outings in her yellow carriage.

One of the best curiosities at Dun (though it does not belong to the house) is 'Mr Riach's Performing Theatre of Arts', a miniature child's theatre, with about 200 cut-out characters. A video shows how it was used. Even if nothing else in the house charms you, this will.

WHERE TO STAY

AUCHTERHOUSE

Old Mansion House £££
Auchterhouse, By Dundee
Angus DD3 0QN   Tel (082 626) 366

A beautiful, very old house surrounded by even more beautiful gardens. The spacious, comfortable bedrooms have a mixture of furnishings and many antiques, and bathrooms are anything but antiquated. Dinners are à la carte and lavish – one dining-room is especially magnificent with an ornate ceiling and ancient fireplace.

Open: all year, exc Xmas to 4 Jan **Rooms**: 6 **Facilities**: tennis, croquet, swimming-pool, squash **Credit/charge cards**: Access, Amex, Diners, Visa

EASSIE

Castleton House ££
By Glamis, Forfar
Angus DD8 1SJ   Tel (0307) 840340

The interior of this grey Edwardian house close to Glamis Castle is cheerful and warmly welcoming. All of the spacious bedrooms are different and furnished with flowery or patterned modern fabrics, while bathrooms have good showers. The friendly owners serve up ambitious food; even the bar lunch allows a three-course blow-out. There is a new conservatory restaurant with brasserie-style food.

Open: all year **Rooms**: 6 **Credit/charge cards**: Access, Amex, Visa

PEAT INN

The Peat Inn £££
Peat Inn, By Cupar
Fife KY15 5LH   Tel (033 484) 206

The restaurant is the most important feature but the accommodation is luxurious – bedrooms are really split-level suites with masses of space and marble bathrooms. The food is excellent and superbly presented, and you can eat à la carte or from a four- or six-course set menu. Breakfast is brought to your sitting-room.

Open: Tues to Sat; closed Xmas Day **Rooms**: 8
Credit/charge cards: Access, Amex, Diners, Visa

ST ANDREWS

Rufflets   £££
Strathkinness Low Road
St Andrews
Fife KY16 9TX   *Tel (0334) 72594*

An impressive and informal country-house hotel set in 10 acres of beautiful gardens. The best bedrooms are those in the older part of the house, especially the two turret rooms, though newer rooms are comfortable and smart. The restaurant has lovely views, and the good-value menu offers traditional regional dishes.

Open: all year **Rooms**: 25
Credit/charge cards: Access, Amex, Diners, Visa

Rusacks Hotel   £££
Pilmour Links
St Andrews
Fife KY16 9JQ   *Tel (0334) 74321*

Rooms at the back face the old golf course and the sea, and the views are spectacular. There is a bar decorated on a 1920s golfing theme, grand reception rooms with marble pillars, and massive windows in the pretty sun-lounge and elegant sitting-room. Bedrooms vary in size, views and price, but all have luxurious bathrooms. The food is a treat.

Open: all year **Rooms**: 50 **Facilities**: golf, sauna, solarium
Credit/charge cards: Access, Amex, Diners, Visa

St Andrews Old Course Hotel   £££
St Andrews
Fife KY16 9SP   *Tel (0334) 74371*

The hotel was completely refurbished in 1989 and the interior is now grand, extremely luxurious and imaginatively designed. There is a lovely conservatory with views over the seventeenth hole, and a hand-painted frieze in the library. Bedrooms have stylish marble bathrooms and every possible comfort. You can eat in the formal restaurant, in the rôtisserie, or have snacks in the conservatory.

Open: all year, exc Xmas week **Rooms**: 125 **Facilities**: gym, health spa, solarium, heated swimming-pool **Credit/charge cards**: Access, Amex, Diners, Visa

WHERE TO EAT

ANSTRUTHER

Cellar
24 East Green
Anstruther
Fife KY10 3AA   *Tel (0333) 310378*

The Cellar is a rough-stone and tiled restaurant with exposed beams and low ceilings. The chef, Peter Jukes, cooks very fresh fish and the restaurant has an award for an outstanding wine cellar from *The Good Food Guide 1994*.

Open: Tues to Sat 12.30 to 1.30, 7 to 9.30; closed Mon in Winter
Credit/charge cards: Access, Amex, Visa

ARBROATH

Gordon's   ★
32 Main Street
Inverkeilor, By Arbroath
Angus DD11 5RN   *Tel (0241) 830364*

You can expect fresh fish and seafood in Gordon's, as well as friendly service. Arbroath is home to the smokie, so it naturally features on the menu.

Open: Tues to Sun 12 to 2.30, 4.30 to 9.15; closed 2 weeks mid-Jan
Credit/charge cards: Access, Visa

AUCHMITHIE

But 'n' Ben   ★
Auchmithie, By Arbroath
Angus DD11 5SQ   *Tel (0241) 77223*

The local speciality is Arbroath smokie served hot and buttered. Lunch, high tea and dinner unite the best local produce: Arbroath fish, vegetables and garden herbs and seasonal game.

Open: daily 11 to 9.30; closed Tues
Credit/charge cards: Access, Visa

CUPAR

Ostlers Close
25 Bonnygate, Cupar
Fife KY15 4BU   *Tel (0334) 55574*

Flavours are more important than fussy presentation at Ostlers Close. There is an abundant output from the kitchen of home-made breads, pasta, ice-creams, herbs, jellies and chutneys and a seasonal supply of fish and game.

Open: Tues to Sat 12.15 to 2, 7 to 9.30; closed 2 weeks June
Credit/charge cards: Access, Amex, Visa

DUNDEE

Raffles
18 Perth Road
Dundee DD1 4LN   *Tel (0382) 26344*

Raffles overlooks the River Tay and offers well-judged, carefully prepared food at reasonable prices. Vegetarians catered for.

Open: Tues to Fri 12 to 2, 5.30 to 9.30, Fri 5.30 to 10.30, Sat 11.30 to 10.30 **Credit/charge cards**: none accepted

FALKLAND

Kind Kyttock's Kitchen
Cross Wynd, Falkland, Cupar
Fife KY7 7BE   *Tel (0337) 57477*

After a visit to Falkland Palace, this simple restaurant can look after your hunger pangs. Expect pleasant, efficient service, good, plain food and low prices. Try the pancakes.

Open: Tues to Sun 10.30 to 5.30; closed 2 weeks Xmas
Credit/charge cards: Access, Visa

THE
NORTH-EAST

- A country of contrasts – flat lowlands, rocky coastline and desolate mountains
- The most rewarding area of Scotland for castle-visiting
- The ancient, oil-prosperous city of Aberdeen

Whisky Distillery

T HE Grampian mountains, rising to their highest and most desolate in the Cairngorm range, form a largely impassable massif in the centre of Scotland. Round them on three sides run the lowlands of Kincardine, Aberdeenshire, Buchan, Banff and Moray. In the past, some of the most powerful men in the country – the Earls of Moray, Huntly, Buchan and Mar – had their power base here. Too far north to be within easy reach of Edinburgh or Stirling, the great families up here were inclined to go their own way and did not always take kindly to events further south. In the eleventh century, the men of Moray were in constant rebellion against the king; 300 years later Robert the Bruce had to break the power of the Comyn Earls of Buchan. Mary Queen of Scots fought against the Earl of Huntly in the sixteenth century, while in 1715, the Earl of Mar raised the country for the Jacobites.

The traditional industries of this corner of Scotland – farming, fishing and whisky-distilling – have been supplemented in the last decades by oil. This turned Aberdeen into a boom town and brought much-needed business to the east coast. Three things draw visitors: the whisky distillery country of lower Speyside, the scenery and the romance of 'Royal Deeside' and the great castles of Aberdeenshire. However, there is more to enjoy than these, including two coastlines and a several secret corners, such as the valleys of the River Findhorn and the River Don.

The castles

The north-east has a superabundance of castles and fine country houses. There are ruins of great fortresses (Kildrummy, Huntly) and Georgian mansions (Haddo, Duff), but the area is renowned for its beautiful tower-houses. The Scottish tower-house developed from the defensive fortress by building upwards and outwards from a thick-walled core. The medieval habit of placing rooms one above the other and linking them by a spiral stair was retained, but lateral space was created by corbelling out the upper storeys and adding turrets, towers or gabled rooms, so the houses grow larger and more intricate as you climb up through them.

Several reasons for the appearance of this style of architecture in the late sixteenth century are given, from the continuing need for a castle that could be defended to the relative abundance of stone and the expense of good wood. The beauty of these fortress houses was recognised by the Victorians, and the nineteenth-century revival of Scottish baronial style can be seen everywhere, but there is no comparison with the originals, and the north-east is the place to see the best of them.

To avoid a surfeit, it is sensible to be selective. Our first choices would be Crathes (superb combination of house and garden), Fyvie (extravagant architecture and fine paintings), Craigievar (perfect architecture, but apt to be crowded), Huntly (romantic ruin with good architecture), Corgaff (for setting and good restoration), and Fasque (untouched Victoriana, and a different experience from all the above).

SOUTH OF ABERDEEN

Fasque

(Open May to Sept, daily 1.30 to 5.30; closed Fri)

The Grampian mountains gradually pinch the valley of Strathmore into a narrow strip of countryside between the sea and the hills. This is the Howe of the Mearns, a stretch of difficult farming land, made famous as the setting for Lewis Grassic Gibbon's trilogy of rural life, *A Scots Quair*. Where the B974 breaks north through the declining hump of the mountains you come to the village of **Fettercairn**, marked by a triumphal arch in memory of a visit by Queen Victoria, and then to Fasque, the family home of W E Gladstone, four times prime minister before retiring in 1894.

Fasque is a neglected, damp-ridden, rotting white elephant of a house, abandoned – or so it seems – at the height of its splendour around 1914, and left undisturbed ever since. As such, it is a welcome antidote to the carefully restored and highly polished castles further north. In the servants' hall, ranks of chairs stand covered in dust, waiting for domestic staff who will never return. Cupboards open on heaps of rust-covered candlesticks and boot-trees; in the laundry, ranks of flat irons stand on the long-unkindled stove. A double staircase of wonderful proportions leads you up from the quiet hallway to the drawing-room above, where again, everything – portraits, furniture, china – waits suspended in its slow decay. The only moving things are the deer cropping the grass beyond the windows. One small room holds relics of the great prime minister – a collection of cuttings, small gifts from constituencies, addresses from admirers.

Despite the damp, the closed-off rooms, the weak light-bulbs and the smudged handwritten notices that guide you

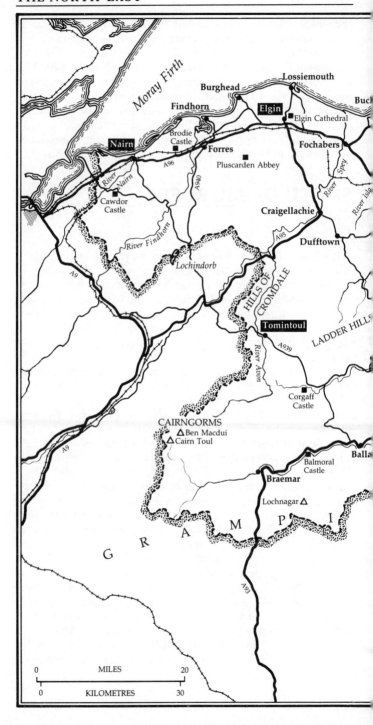

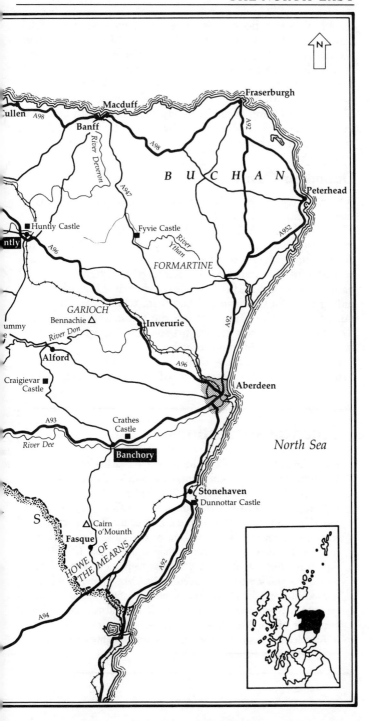

round, this is a house which recalls a bygone way of life more potently than any of the burnished Victorian kitchens elsewhere in the country. Reason says it cannot continue – it will either decay completely or else be restored – so see it before it is lost.

North of Fasque, the road continues up the side of Cairn o' Mount, running through lonely moorland with extensive views before descending into the valley of the Feugh and arriving at Banchory.

Dunnottar Castle

(Open Easter to Oct, Mon to Sat 9 to 6, Sun 2 to 5; Nov to Easter, Mon to Fri 9 to dusk)

The coastal road (A92) from Montrose to Stonehaven is more interesting than the dual carriageway which links Dundee and Aberdeen, with good views out to sea and small villages tucked into the steep shore. There is an extensive coastal nature reserve at **St Cyrus**, while the church at **Kineff** was the hiding place for the regalia of Scotland, which were smuggled out of Dunnottar Castle during the Cromwellian invasion. The ruin of this great castle, just south of Stonehaven, is the most important stopping point.

In about 1382 Sir William Keith, Great Marischal of Scotland, came into possession of the massive crag which

Practical suggestions

For a family seaside holiday, head for the beaches of Nairn or Lossiemouth; for Highland scenery and tough walking, Braemar and Deeside are the best areas. For gentler but still strenuous walking, try the area round Tomintoul. For fishing, unless you can afford to pursue salmon on the Dee or the Spey, start your researches with the Avon, the Don or the Ythan. For touring, head for the valley of the Don, although the coastal trail along the Moray Firth would be a good alternative. For castles, the area north and west of Aberdeen is the place to start. Golfing is good all along the north coast; naturalists should head for the east coast. If you want to bury yourself in local life, go to the farmlands of the Mearns or of Buchan. Spend at least a day in Aberdeen. A taste of all of these would probably provide the most satisfactory holiday of the lot.

is almost split from the mainland. It is hardly surprising that he considered the site more suited to a castle than to the church which shared it with earlier fortifications. In demolishing the church he got himself excommunicated, but in exchange built himself a virtually impregnable fortress, for it is a steep climb over the narrow neck of land which is the castle's only point of approach.

A litter of buildings from different periods covers the crag, dominated by the fifteenth-century keep. When living conditions there came to be regarded as too primitive, a large, comfortable mansion was built in the sixteenth and seventeenth centuries. The restored drawing-room here allows superbly contrasting views of angry sea and peaceful courtyard.

Dunnottar was especially important in the period of the Scottish civil and religious wars. It was from here that the seventh Earl Marischal watched his land being burnt in 1645 by his one-time ally, Montrose, while Andrew Cant, one of the Covenanting ministers to whom he had given refuge, told him: 'Trouble not, for the reek will be a sweet-smelling incense in the nostrils of the Lord'. It was here too that the Scottish regalia were sent for safety during Cromwell's

---

Good bases

- **Tomintoul** A small village high on the edge of the Grampians, very well placed for walking in the hills, for dropping down to visit the Speyside distilleries or for touring the valley of the Don.
- **Nairn** A friendly, quiet seaside town on the Moray Firth, with sandy seashore close by and the wooded Findhorn valley to explore. Inverness is within easy reach.
- **Elgin** An old town which grew up around its medieval cathedral and is now the shopping centre for the rich countryside around. The beach at Lossiemouth is close, as are the distilleries of Speyside, and there are a number of historic sights nearby.
- **Huntly** An elegant town with a ducal atmosphere, thanks to the remains of Huntly Castle which dominate the place. It is very quiet and off the tourist trail, but a good place from which to explore the north-east corner of the region.
- **Banchory** Of the small towns on the River Dee, Banchory is best placed for castle-visiting and is within easy reach of Aberdeen. It is a smart place, with enough business trade from Aberdeen to push accommodation prices up a little, and it is also a popular stopping place on tours of the Dee valley.

---

invasion and occupation, to be smuggled out again during the eight months' siege in 1651 which ended in the castle's final capitulation; and in the sorry chapter of persecution which followed the restoration of Charles II, 167 Covenanters were crammed into a dungeon (the Whig's Vault) at Dunnottar.

Stonehaven and beyond

The old fishing town of Stonehaven, despite the fact that its beach is more shingle than sand, remains a popular resort. The oldest part is by the harbour, with the newer, predominantly Victorian town stretching up the hill behind. It is a gentle, old-fashioned sort of place – douce rather than raucous, and more suited to brisk strolls around the harbour than to getting a suntan on the beach. It comes to life on Hogmanay, with a fire festival all of its own. The old Tolbooth on the harbour's edge is Stonehaven's most venerable building, now a small museum and tearoom.

Beyond Stonehaven, a series of fishing villages lie squeezed into crannies in the cliffs, reached by short detours from the dual carriageway road. Where herring boats were once hauled bodily out of the water and the fish loaded into creels, Aberdeen commuters now return from a hard day in the office. **Findon**, one of these tiny places, has given its name to the ubiquitous Finnan haddie – the smoked haddock (which should really be peat-smoked, but seldom is) found on most Scottish hotel menus.

DEESIDE

If Queen Victoria had not bought Balmoral and turned it from a pleasant country house into a monstrosity, the River Dee and its valley would not have half the draw they do today, for 'Royal Deeside' is where the monarch has her very own self-catering property, and half the fun of travelling along the river is being able to cast an eye over the boundary fence. Balmoral apart, a trip over Glenshee and down the Dee with lunch at Braemar and tea at Banchory provides a worthwhile taste of Highland country. There is, however, something slightly packaged about the Deeside scenery, as if Nature had deliberately produced an assemblage of heather, pine forest and mountainside designed to appeal to manufacturers of biscuit boxes and picture postcards. The River Don, to the north, has a more subtle attraction.

The waterfall (more a series of rapids and a narrow gut) at **Linn of Dee** is as far up the river as you can get by road, and is the starting point for a series of medium-distance walks through the heart of the Grampians. The best-known of these is the one through the mountain trench of the Lairig Ghru to Rothiemurchus and the Spey Valley. Another route runs southwards to Glen Tilt with a branch to Glen Feshie. All these walks take you deep into the wilderness and should not be undertaken without suitable preparation, but you can explore a little further up the Dee without trouble.

Braemar

This small town lies at the bottom of the road descending from the Cairnwell pass. Because of its position it is a centre for walkers, climbers and skiers, though at 1100 feet above sea level it is scarcely a balmy resort. It is also a popular stop for coach tours, so there are plenty of shops and places for tea. The Braemar Gathering, held in September, has the highest snob-value of all Highland Games, since the royal family usually put in an appearance. The Gathering is also one of the largest and best, noted for the piping.

Balmoral

Between Braemar and Balmoral the Deeside scenery is at its best, with the river plunging along beside the road and Scots pines outlined against the ridges of hills rising towards the lovely mountain of Lochnagar. From May to July the grounds of **Balmoral Castle** are open to the public (provided the royal family is not in residence). Walking here, you can appreciate (or not) Prince Albert's talent as castle-designer, for there seems little doubt that he played a large part in the rebuilding that went on after the royal family bought the estate in 1852.

Ballater

The town started its life as a spa when an old woman bathing in a nearby peat bog cured herself of scrofula and her discovery was exploited by the local Jacobite laird, who had just been reprieved from execution. If this does not sound auspicious, Ballater is nevertheless quite a good stopping point on the road downstream, being less crowded than Braemar and not quite so refined as Banchory. It is also the place from which to explore the road up Glen Muick – a favourite for those on the trail of Queen Victoria, but also worth a detour in its own right. One good reason for coming up here is to climb Lochnagar: it is a relatively easy ascent, but quite a dangerous mountain, with numerous vertical cliffs dropping abruptly from its summit. Views from the top on a clear day are the best in the eastern Highlands. Various walks also lead from near Ballater over the Mounth to Glen Esk in Angus. Arranging some way of getting back is usually the hardest part of such expeditions.

Five miles downstream of Ballater, the flat expanse of **Dinnet Moor** is peppered with lochans, scrub birch and Scots pine. The landscape was formed after the last Ice Age, and is now a nature reserve.

Banchory

Banchory is sufficiently close to Aberdeen to be commutable, as well as making an excellent place for the entertaining of business clients. Consequently, you are apt to find that the posher hotels have helicopter pads and plenty of room for salmon rods. The fishing on the Dee in this area is renowned (and correspondingly pricey). Even if you are not in the helicopter league, Banchory's shops and tearooms are worth a stroll. An exploration of the valley of the **River Feugh**, which joins the Dee here, takes you into peaceful woodland, where in autumn the crimson rowan, russet bracken and pale yellow birch are as well coordinated as if an interior designer had arranged them.

Crathes Castle

(NTS, castle opens Easter to Oct, daily 11 to 6; other times by appointment; garden and grounds open all year, daily 9.30 to sunset)

This is the very best of the Aberdeenshire sights, combining as it does a sixteenth-century tower-house, which is second only to Craigievar in the balanced elegance of its architecture, with a twentieth-century garden which will be enthralling to keen gardeners. Leave yourself at least two hours to explore.

The main part of the house was finished in 1596. Its heart is an L-shaped building with narrow slits of windows. At about third-floor level the house starts growing outwards. A smooth wall bulges and throws out a half-column, which rises for a further two floors until a sudden lateral corbelling allows space for a tiny rectangular room before a further forward corbel supports the battlemented parapet. Elsewhere the sequence is reversed, with the rounded corners of the main walls abruptly squared off, corbelled, and crowned with a round pepper-pot turret or a square gabled tower. The word organic could be applied to this architecture – its shape is reminiscent of a huge beech tree.

Crathes is famous for its painted ceilings, which are among the best in Scotland. Three remain, with a whole gallery of characters, emblems, mottoes, grotesques and patterns taking up every cranny of the awkward spaces around the beams. Unfortunately, little of the decoration in the vaulted High Hall has survived, though there is enough to show how pretty it must have been. The ghost at Crathes is well documented (a good ghost apparently adds to visitor numbers), while a more tangible relic of the castle's antiquity is the Horn of Leys, given by Robert the Bruce to an early member of the Burnetts, the family who owned and lived in Crathes for more than 350 years. The finest room in the castle is the Long Gallery right at the top, which has a beautiful oak-panelled ceiling and views over the gardens below.

The gardens at Crathes are the work of the thirteenth baronet and his wife, Sybil. In the walled garden and among the venerable eighteenth-century yew hedges in front of the castle they planted a remarkable series of colour gardens, by and large following the designer Gertrude Jekyll's principles, but with the addition of their own considerable originality. The current gardens were started around 1926. The most unusual border is the Colour Garden, where yellow, red and bronze combine superbly. The Golden Garden, developed by the National Trust after Lady Burnett's idea, is another inspiring section. Among the shrubs, keep an eye open for the *Eucryphia glutinosa* which covers itself in white flowers in the shelter of the great yews, and for the many interesting viburnum, cornus and berberis varieties. If you still have the energy, there is a further wild garden among the trees beyond the old wall. The plant sales area is good evidence of the skill and interest of the gardening staff.

Drum Castle

(NTS, house open May to Sept, daily 2 to 6; early to late Apr and Oct, Sat and Sun 2 to 5; grounds open all year, daily 9.30 to sunset)

This castle stands about five miles downstream of Crathes and is a very different building, for here an early seventeenth-century mansion has been tacked on to a square thirteenth-century keep. This old tower is actually the more interesting part for it survives almost intact, with the exception of the former Great Hall of the keep, which was turned into a library and incorporated into the newer house. The storeroom, the upper hall and the battlements demonstrate what an impregnable (if uncomfortable) fortress Drum used to be. Views from the battlements are worth the steep climb. The interior of the mansion house has been heavily Victorianised, but a few of the older features remain. There are good portraits of, and plenty of detail about, the Irvine family, who held Drum from the time of Robert the Bruce. A small arboretum in the grounds provides a pleasant short walk.

THE LECHT AND THE RIVER DON

Tomintoul

Tomintoul squats on the very edge of inhabitable country at the top of Strath Avon. The rolling plateaux of the Ladder Hills start just beyond the village, while the great tops of the Cairngorms lie to the south. Despite its height of 1160 feet, this is not the highest village in Scotland – that honour goes to Wanlockhead in Dumfries and Galloway. Tomintoul looks strange in its isolated setting, for it is a planned village, created from scratch in 1779 with its long street and central square. The main road east jinks sideways out of the village – if you do what comes naturally and follow the main street to its end, you end up on a track.

In the country round Tomintoul there is a choice of medium-distance highish-level walks, while the Glenlivet Estate (owned by the Crown) to the north of the village has an abundance of waymarked routes, some of which are suitable for mountain biking. Pony-trekking is available in summer and cross-country skiing in winter (the ski slopes of the Lecht are also in easy reach). Accommodation is not abundant, but it should be possible to find somewhere to stay. Tomintoul has a small **museum** of local life (open Easter to Oct, Mon to Fri 9.30 to 6, Sat 9.30 to 1, 2 to 5; also June, July and Aug), with a well-conceived reconstruction of an old smithy.

The Lecht Road (A939) running between Tomintoul and

Strath Don is a splendid piece of eighteenth-century engineering; it was largely built by the military after the 1745 rising. It is still one of the first roads in Scotland to be blocked by snow and as you travel over the pass through the Ladder Hills it is easy to see why, for expanses of windswept moorland stretch in all directions, a blaze of purple when the heather is in bloom. The climb up the pass from Tomintoul is relatively gentle but the road rushes in recently improved sweeps down the other side until, in a suddenly green strath just beyond the few scattered houses of Cock Bridge, you reach the River Don and Corgaff Castle.

Corgaff Castle

(HS, standard times; closed in winter)
Thanks to an enthusiastic curator and an excellent restoration by Historic Scotland, a visit to Corgaff Castle is well worth the short climb up from the car park. It is a miniature sixteenth-century white tower surrounded by a curious star-shaped wall and, despite its isolation, has an eventful history. This started with a nasty massacre during a patch of local rivalry when King James VI was a child, and continued with an occupation by Montrose in 1645. At the time of the Jacobite uprisings, Corgaff, thanks to its isolated position, acted as rallying point and weapon store. After Culloden, the Hanoverians turned it into a stronghold – part of the network of watch-posts on the Highlands – and it is this period that produced the exterior fortification against musketry and that the interior restoration represents. Life for the garrison was not exactly comfortable – five or six double beds fill the small rooms. Corgaff lingered on as a military post until 1831, although by then the soldiers were watching for illicit stills rather than Jacobites.

Glenbuchat Castle

(HS, access at all reasonable times)
Follow the River Don along the A944 and A97 for the next two castles. Glenbuchat is easily missed, for it stands directly above the road, but the ruined, unfrequented, sixteenth-century Z-plan castle is worth a stop. There is easily enough left to give you a good impression of what it was like to live here – rather comfortable by the look of things. The last laird, 'Old Glenbucket', is one of the tragic figures of the Jacobite years. Having already fought in the rising of 1715, he returned

to the field at the age of 68 to take part in the desperate retreat from Derby and was with Prince Charles at Culloden in 1746. Thereafter, with a price on his head, he was forced, like so many others, to spend months living rough and dodging the redcoats before eventually escaping from Scotland by sea. He died in poverty in Boulogne in 1750.

Kildrummy Castle

(HS, standard times; weekends only in winter)
Only a few miles beyond Glenbuchat, Kildrummy is a very different kettle of fish. It was once a huge medieval fortress, seat of the Earls of Mar, and symbolic of that noble family's power and status.

Edward I of England may have supervised some of the building work which raised Kildrummy's four towers and produced its imposing gatehouse. He no doubt regretted this during the Wars of Independence, for Kildrummy became a Bruce stronghold, and held out against the English until the garrison was betrayed from inside – in this case a treacherous blacksmith set fire to the store of grain in return for as much gold as he could carry. His reward was paid in the form of molten metal poured down his throat. Kildrummy's second claim to fame is as the place where much of the plotting for the 1715 Jacobite uprising occurred, for it was the sixth Earl of Mar who raised the standard for that revolt.

Kildrummy is now ruined – only the foundations of the gatehouse and of the Snow Tower remain, and the rest has been much used as a stone quarry. However, enough remains to show how strong the place must once have been.

Kildrummy Gardens

(Open Apr to late Oct, daily 10 to 5)
A certain Colonel Ogston bought Kildrummy Castle in 1898 and built a new castle (now an hotel) nearby. Needing a garden to go with it, he commissioned a Japanese firm to make a water garden in the 'Back Den', the ravine which provided the defensive cover for the back of the old castle. Among the rocks of the old quarry on the fringes of the Den, an alpine garden was constructed. Since the colonel's time the gardens have gone through periods of neglect, but are now well re-established under a trust. The primary appeal of the planting is in the old quarry, where acers and rhododendrons are blended skilfully in the tumbled rock.

The water garden, apart from some magnificent gunneras and a good collection of *Primula florindae*, is less interesting. There are some fine specimen trees. This is less a garden for specialists than Crathes but is a stimulating example of naturalistic planting, and, especially in autumn, makes for a colourful and peaceful stroll.

Craigievar Castle

(NTS, open May to end Sept, daily 2 to 6; grounds all year 9.30 to sunset)

From Mossat the A944 follows the Don eastward to Alford, the landscape becoming flatter but dominated by the shapely peak of **Bennachie**, a mountain of no great height yet visible from every quarter. Four miles to the south of Alford on the A980 stands Craigievar, a castle widely held to be the apotheosis of the tower-house.

Craigievar was not built for the convenient shepherding of bus-loads of visitors, and you can sometimes sense that the castle's guides wish that 'Danzig Willie' had shown a little more foresight when building his home in 1626. A certain amount of desperate shuffling on staircases, of peering over other people's heads, and a feeling of being squeezed slowly towards the exit is likely to be your lot if you hit Craigievar at peak visiting time. The popularity of the castle and the fact that National Trust for Scotland has removed it from its publicity should not put you off going, however, for the architecture is fascinating. The solid L-shaped trunk of the house blossoms effortlessly into a whole village-worth of gables, balustrades and bartizans. It is worth walking slowly round the outside looking at the constantly changing perspectives of the roofs.

Internally, Craigievar is very different from Crathes. William Forbes of Menie, who had 'made a goodly pile merchandising at Danzig' was obviously keen to impress. Quite what his contemporaries made of his taste is unrecorded, but time has dulled the excesses and it is possible to admire Danzig Willie's medieval-style hall, complete with its vaulted ceiling, musicians' gallery and massive coat of arms, without suffering the temptation to giggle. Decorative plasterwork is Craigievar's forte: there is scarcely a room without a superb moulded ceiling. The one in the Queen's Room (apparently named in hope of a visit rather than as the result of one) is the best of these. At the very top of the house, the Long Room runs the entire width of the castle and is plain and beautiful with its small alcoves.

Alford

Montrose won a victory over the Covenanters near this large village, which is now home to the **Grampian Transport Museum** (open late Mar to late Oct, daily 10 to 5), a large, if antiseptically displayed, collection of ancient vehicles. A narrow-gauge steam railway is part of the set-up. From Alford, side roads follow the Don through the Garioch district, dotted with small havens like the villages of Monymusk and Oldmeldrum, as well as less attractive spots, such as Inverurie. Seek out the **Maiden Stone** near the hamlet of Chapel of Garioch – this is the best of the many Pictish stones in the area and shows Jonah and two whales along with a Z-rod symbol and the 'swimming elephant'. If what you are looking at does not have these carvings, but is instead shaped like a nubile girl, you have been sidetracked by a rival maiden – a modern sculpture of Primavera, who stands almost opposite.

Castle Fraser

(NTS, castle open May to June, Sept, daily 2 to 6; July and August 11 to 6; early to late Apr and Oct, Sat and Sun 2 to 5; grounds all year, daily 9.30 to sunset)
The appearance of the castle at the end of its avenue is distinctly French, thanks largely to the conical turrets which grace the corners of the Z-plan structure and the wings of the courtyard with their capped half-dormer windows. Although the central tower is really quite small, Castle Fraser looks a lot less compact than Crathes and less graceful than Craigievar. Nevertheless, it is actually a subtle, harmonious building, despite numerous alterations and rebuildings.

Most of the furnishings are nineteenth-century and on the scanty side, though they give an excellent idea of how such a castle was lived in at that time. The grounds of the castle (best appreciated from the roof) have more antiquity about them – they bear the stamp of eighteenth-century landscaping. The walled garden is certainly worth a look on the way back to your car, for it is sheltered and colourful.

ABERDEEN

The Silver City has come in for a lot of flak over the past decades for having become the poodle of the oil industry – the Houston of the north – with accusations of high prices, a brash attitude and a generally unpleasant boom-town atmosphere. This is a gross exaggeration, though the city looks and feels prosperous, and some prices are geared more to expense accounts than to humble tourists. However, to avoid the city would be foolish, especially since it contains a first-class art gallery. The granite from which much of it is built really does glisten silver in the sun, though on a cloudy day, Aberdeen looks as grey as anywhere else.

Aberdeen is a mixture of St Andrews and Glasgow, with the academic atmosphere and the seascapes of the former and the bustle and some of the planning mistakes of the latter. It lies spreadeagled between the mouths of the Don and the Dee, without seeming quite certain whether its heart is the tranquil, academic area round the former or the busy seaport of the latter. Although it has a magnificent stretch of curving shoreline, Aberdeen is a riverside, not a seaside, city. The links behind the beach and the esplanade remain undeveloped, providing an open aspect in the heart of the city and a good blow of sea air for the inhabitants.

Aberdeen is also renowned for its parks. You are most likely to go to Seaton Park near the cathedral, or Duthie Park with its Winter Gardens and its beds of roses, but there are plenty more to discover.

The centre is a mixture of architecture – a few elegant Georgian buildings, plenty of Victorian, one or two hideous pieces of Post-War Municipal and modern buildings dating from the oil boom, all rather haphazardly scattered along streets which are longer than they seem to be before you start walking; a bus map will be useful. Most of the activity happens on or around the ruler-straight Union Street, especially at its eastern end by Castle Street, where the seventeenth-century mercat cross stands. The modern Bon Accord Centre has chain stores under cover, Tourist information is to be found in Broad Street, and the streets running towards and round the harbour make the best area for casual wandering. Aberdeen has a relaxed attitude to people who enjoy watching ships, and you can poke around the quays without being harassed. There is usually something going on: sea-going barges laden with drilling pipes, supply vessels for the rigs, fishing boats, and the 'North Boats' to Kirkwall and Lerwick coming or going. The fish market is already stirring into life at about 4.30am.

Walk along the northern edge of the quays towards the sea to discover the tiny planned fishing village of Footdee (or Fittie) clustered at the tip of Aberdeen harbour, with the esplanade and Aberdeen beach stretching away north of it. Fittie consists of three little squares of cottages, and is still a self-contained living community, so there is some excitement in discovering it, counteracted by the sensation that you are intruding.

Old Aberdeen

This is the area of the city up by the mouth of the River Don, containing the city's most venerable buildings. Start by wandering across the **Brig o'Balgownie**, unless you happen to be an only son riding a mare's only foal (Thomas the Rhymer predicted the bridge would fall in these circumstances, and Lord Byron – as an only son – remembered the 'awful proverb which made me pause to cross it'). This is Scotland's oldest bridge, built in the early fourteenth century, and a very beautiful single-arched structure it is.

Walk back through Seaton Park to **St Machar's Cathedral**. Only the nave and aisles remain of this largely fifteenth-century building, so it appears unbalanced from every angle except at the west front. It is imposing all the same, with twin spires and a magnificent heraldic roof in the interior, which dates from 1520. The 48 shields that compose the ceiling provide a kind of visual guide to the spiritual and secular hierarchies of sixteenth-century Scotland and Europe.

Once you have dodged the traffic on St Machar Drive, you come to a section of pedestrianised tranquillity in the High Street. This is the university quarter of Aberdeen, and is dominated by the crowned tower of **King's College** – founded in 1495 – which is worth exploring to have a glimpse of the chapel. The High Street has a veneer of ancient houses on either side, behind which the modern university buildings rear their heads.

Central Aberdeen

Make your way from Union Street to Schoolhill to visit the excellent **Aberdeen Art Gallery** (open Mon to Sat 10 to 5, Thurs 10 to 8, Sun 2 to 5). The collection is magnificent and beautifully displayed; the slight austerity of the building is countered by a lively shop and café, and the tone varies from the formal melancholy of the War Memorial Court to the bright spaciousness of the upper rooms.

The gallery's strength lies primarily in its collection of

British painting through three centuries, but the decorative arts section is almost as good – the collection of locally worked silver and of modern enamel and ceramic work on the ground floor is full of gleaming objects whose placing and juxtaposition have been carefully thought out.

The wide range of paintings and drawings includes Blake's *Raising of Lazarus*, Piper's *Dunnottar Castle*, Millais' wonderful portrait of a self-confident young girl, entitled *Bright Eyes*, Paul Nash's windswept *Wood on the Downs*, Augustus John's sensuous *The Blue Pool*, and, among local painters, James Cowie's *Two Schoolgirls* and James McBey's simple and precise capturing of *Ythan Mouth*. Look out also for the ridiculously melodramatic *Flood in the Highlands* by Landseer.

Close to the tourist office in Broad Street stands **Provost Skene's House** (open Mon to Sat 10 to 5), the oldest domestic house in Aberdeen with title deeds dating from 1545, although most of the building is seventeenth-century. It has been restored and turned into a museum of domestic life from Cromwellian to Victorian times; as you move from room to room, you shift from one period to the next. This allows you to compare furnishings and standards of comfort, and to decide which period you would most have enjoyed living in. One room has a seventeenth-century painted ceiling, overflowing with religious imagery, showing how slow the full force of the Reformation was to catch on in these parts. To counteract the silent furniture, a rather well-acted audio-visual brings to life some of the characters who made their mark on the house over the years.

You cannot miss **Marischal College**, also in Broad Street, for its frontage is a rippling maze of granite ribs, like a complicated root system or a fishing net. The college was founded in 1593, but the frontage was built in 1906 and the buildings behind are only slightly earlier.

In Shiprow, a street running down to the harbour, **Aberdeen Maritime Museum** (open Mon to Sat 10 to 5) is housed in another ancient building – Provost Ross's House. The museum traces Aberdeen's history as a port, from the building of the harbours to the advent of the oil industry. There are plenty of pictures, photographs and models to look at (and a National Trust for Scotland shop), and you can glean information about what is going on in the North Sea (although there is disappointingly little about the modern fishing industry).

DUFFTOWN AND HUNTLY

There are names on the map in this area which ring bells, notably Glen Livet and Glen Fiddich. For this is Speyside whisky country, and the characteristic pagoda caps and breath of malty steam of the distillery are an inescapable part of the scenery.

The landscape, where the Grampians peter out towards the coast of the Moray Firth, consists of low heather-covered hills, which flatten out towards the east into the plains of Buchan. **Strath Avon** is the prettiest of the tributary valleys of the Spey, with peaty water pouring through steep stretches under the Hills of Cromdale. **Glen Livet**, which joins it a short distance before it reaches the main river, is smaller and gentler. The first distillery here was founded in 1824, replacing an estimated 200 illicit stills.

Below Bridge of Avon the Spey is at its most beautiful, with dark swirling pools haunted by oystercatchers and by salmon fishermen, whose cars with attached rod-clips stand outside the hotels of **Aberlour** and **Craigellachie**. The road running down Strathspey towards Elgin is apt to be busy, and to see the river you really need to take to your feet. The long-distance **Speyside Way** runs by the river from Spey Bay to Ballindalloch (leaflet from tourist offices), and sections of this make excellent short walks.

Dufftown and around

This is another of the many planned villages in the area, laid out in 1817 in the form of a cross, at the very centre of distillery country. The **Glenfiddich Distillery** (open Easter to mid-Oct, Mon to Sat 9.30 to 4.30; Sun 12 to 4.30) on the edge of the village has an extremely popular and extremely slick visitor centre and tour, and this is Dufftown's main attraction. If you like ruins, however, visit **Balvenie Castle** (HS, standard times; closed in winter), which is half-hidden by the steam from the distilleries. This was once the seat of Robert the Bruce's rivals, the Comyn Earls of Buchan, but most of what remains dates from the sixteenth century.

Half a mile south of Dufftown, **Mortlach Church** is thought to be one of the earliest places of Christian worship in the north of Scotland. The building itself has some twelfth-century work, but tradition has it that an existing church was extended in 1010, after Malcolm II won a battle against Norse invaders. Two very old carved stones – the

Battle Stone and the Elephant Stone, with inscribed Christian symbols – suggest that there may be something to the story that the church was founded by St Moluag in AD 566. The stones and the peaceful setting are worth seeing, but the church is not especially beautiful.

Huntly

The broad square, the great archway spanning the street to the north and the careful layout all speak of an eighteenth- and nineteenth-century town deliberately designed to reflect the magnificence of the local magnate. In this case, the local magnates were the Gordon family – Earls and later Marquesses of Huntly before they became Dukes of Gordon.

Huntly is a quiet agricultural town in the middle of wooded countryside, safely by-passed by the main A96. Its convenient position for touring Speyside and the Banff coast makes it a good place to stop for a night or two. For recreation there is a newly refurbished swimming-pool, a golf course, and opportunities to fish the Bogie, the Isla and the Deveron.

Huntly Castle

(HS, standard times; closed Thurs pm and Fri in winter)
This is a magnificent ruin of a sixteenth-century palace, but the fortifications on the steep bank of the River Deveron go back much further than that and it is easy enough to see the motte and bailey of the first timber castle that stood here in the time of Robert the Bruce. The fragmentary remains of the tower-house which succeeded it are also visible, though little is left other than a few courses of stone. However, the palace, with its round tower, oriel windows and unique heraldic doorway, remains reasonably intact. The doorway still achieves its purpose: as you approach it, you are confronted by the arms of Huntly, the royal arms of Scotland, the five wounds of Christ and finally the risen Christ in Glory – all mounting in sequence above your head and instilling a proper sense of your own lowliness. The Covenanters who occupied the castle during the Civil War studiously defaced the more 'popish' elements, but the rest remains untouched.

The castle is at its most impressive from the outside, for the oriel windows, French in inspiration and probably craftsmanship too, jut out high over the south front. Above and beneath them runs a giant frieze, inscribed – with what you will be beginning to recognise as a characteristic lack of modesty – with the names of the first Marquess and his wife in letters a couple of feet high.

The interior of the castle has some further examples of heraldry – this time it is the mantelpieces above the elaborate fireplaces which remind you firmly whose home you are in. The wall walk on top of the great round tower gives you a bird's-eye view of Huntly and the Deveron valley beneath. Up here you find the most human feature of the palace – a tiny turret room built above the main staircase where the first Marquess liked to escape from all his magnificence and enjoy the view.

Leith Hall

(NTS, house open May to Sept, daily 2 to 6; early to late Oct, Sat and Sun 2 to 5; grounds all year, daily 9.30 to sunset)

South of Huntly, off the A97, Leith Hall makes a interesting contrast to the great castles such as Crathes or Castle Fraser. It started life as a simple laird's house, its oldest section dating from 1650, and was gradually extended around its courtyard

WHISKY DISTILLERIES

Of all Scottish industries, the whisky industry flaunts itself most openly to the public. In almost every region covered by this book there is at least one distillery you can visit. Whisky – 'the water of life' in the Gaelic – has been made to seem as typically Scottish as tartan or the bagpipes, and distillery-visiting is often promoted as an unmissable part of the Scottish experience. This is nonsense, for you can perfectly well appreciate Scotland without knowing anything about whisky.

That said, visiting distilleries can be great fun, and, while the process is the same in all of them, there is a lot of variety in the way they present themselves to visitors. In the distilleries of the more famous brands there may be kilted guides and batteries of audio-visuals. In smaller and more out-of-the-way places you are likely to be taken round by someone in overalls. At Dallas Dhu (page 376) you go round by yourself. Take your pick, but remember that if you are asked to pay for anything, plenty of competitors will show you round free.

The process of distilling is simple – one of the reasons illegal over the following centuries until it reached substantial proportions. The Leith (later Leith-Hay) family lived in the house right up to the time it was given to the National Trust for Scotland, and the history of the house is really the history of the family who lived there. There are fine parts of the house – notably the Georgian rooms, with lots of family portraits and one or two good pieces of furniture – but nothing of exceptional interest. The garden is good (at its best when the long herbaceous border is full of colour).

BUCHAN AND FORMARTINE

East of Huntly, the land suddenly flattens. This is Buchan – an isolated countryside consisting of small farms, winding back roads and big skies. As you approach the sea, the trees dwindle away and the wind rises. It is a countryside which can seem bleak, especially in the dead winter months; it seems far removed from the forests and moors which lie only a few dozen miles westward. The best area to explore is round the valley of the Ythan, a river famed for its sea trout and whose

---

stills existed for so long in the Highlands. Barley is allowed to germinate and is then dried over a peat fire (malted) before being ground and added to hot water in a huge vessel called a mash tun. Here yeast is added and the mixture is left to ferment. Malt whisky, made from malted barley alone, is then distilled twice in huge copper stills, and put into oak casks to mature. Grain whisky, which includes other cereals, is continuously distilled, and is much less dependent on geographical location for its flavour. The best-known brands of Scotch are blends, containing many different malt and grain whiskies. The more expensive 'single malts' are the product of a single distillery. Their distinctively different flavours depend on a number of factors, including the source of the water, the shape of the stills and the nature of the casks used for maturing. You will hear plenty about what makes each whisky unique as you visit the distilleries.

All the best distillery tours offer you a free dram at the end. If you are driving, some will give you a miniature bottle instead, but you may have to put up with orange juice. The *Scotch Whisky Association* (071-629 4384), produces a useful map of distilleries which welcome visitors.

deep estuary is a relic of a past geological era, when a much larger stream poured over what is now the North Sea to meet the Rhine.

Fyvie Castle

(NTS, castle open May, Sept, daily 2 to 6; June to Aug, daily 11 to 6; early to late Apr and Oct, Sat and Sun 2 to 5; grounds all year, daily 9.30 to sunset)

No one can accuse Fyvie of lacking character, though whether you love it or hate it depends on your taste. It is a Z-shaped mixture of palace and castle, which straggles across its surrounding lawns like a snake which has swallowed a carpenter's rule. It has five towers (rather too many), each named after a family that owned Fyvie – Preston, Seton, Meldrum, Gordon and Leith. The fantastic roofscape of turrets, dormers and finials is largely the responsibility of Sir Alexander Seton, who bought the place in 1596. The south front, where the original gatehouse with its drum towers (perhaps going back to the time of Edward I) has been modified into a five-storey archway with flanking turrets, shows off the architecture at its grandest.

Internally, the castle bears the stamp of Alexander Forbes-Leith (who became Lord Leith in 1905). Having married an American heiress and made a fortune in the Illinois Steel Company, he bought Fyvie in 1889 and proceeded to pour money into refurbishing and extending it in his own inimitable style. This is seen to best effect in the astonishing Gallery, a room in the 'modern antique' mode. One end of it is taken up by a gargantuan self-playing organ, installed in 1906, while seventeenth-century tapestries clothe the walls, a massive French Renaissance fireplace juts out into the room and a Tiffany lamp sits by the leaded window.

Not all of Fyvie was Edwardianised. Several magnificent plaster ceilings remain from earlier periods, as does Fyvie's most beautiful feature, the great wheel stair. Its ten-foot-wide pinkish stone steps rise for four floors.

Whatever you think of Lord Leith's taste in armour, tapestry or furniture, there is no doubt about the quality of the pictures, especially the portraits, that he assembled at Fyvie. In this he was building on a collection established by the previous Gordon owners, which included Fyvie's most famous painting, Batoni's portrait of William Gordon, a Byronic figure poised with drawn sword against a classical background. Yet it is the Raeburn portraits which are the most striking in number

and quality, and these were almost all acquired by Lord Leith
– he was especially fond of tracking down portraits of his
Aberdeenshire connections. The portraits of Mrs Gregory and
of John Stirling of Kippendavie and his daughter are worth the
whole journey to Fyvie to see.

Fyvie has its mysteries – notably the secret vault below
the Charter Room, which has never been opened because of
an unpleasant curse. Attempts to gain entry are supposed to
result in the death of the laird and the blindness of his wife –
and this has twice occurred.

Haddo House

(NTS, house open May, Sept, daily 2 to 6; June to Aug, daily
11 to 6; early to late Apr and Oct, Sat and Sun 2 to 5; grounds
open all year)

A little further down the Ythan, off the B9005, Haddo House
was another Gordon property, and makes a good contrast to
Fyvie (with which there appears to be a little quiet rivalry
– Haddo has a Batoni portrait, which according to the
guides is 'rather more natural' than the one at Fyvie, for
example). Haddo is an Adam mansion, its Palladian style
and austere, symmetrical façade very different from the spikes
and turrets of older tower-houses. Unfortunately, much of the
interior is Adam revival from 1880 rather than the real thing
(papier-mâché ceiling mouldings and 'Adam-style' fireplaces,
for example), but the effect is still splendid. Haddo House has
a guided tour, and you can get pretty befuddled by the Gordon
family tree after hearing about the activities of the owners of
Haddo for almost an hour. One of them was prime minister in
1852, but the others tend to become a blur, despite the guides'
best efforts.

Haddo is furnished with comfortable clutter rather than
suits of armour. There is a chapel, with some Burne-Jones
designs. The nineteenth-century library at the end of one
of the wings is too like a gentlemen's club to be very
interesting, but tempts you to take down the odd volume and sink into one of the old leather armchairs. Keep
an eye open too for the Queen's Bedroom, which contains a portrait of Queen Victoria aged four, where she
looks even more like a large plum than she did in her
old age.

Haddo is well established as a cultural centre for the
neighbourhood. Operas, choral concerts and plays take place
in a Canadian-style hall built near the house, and there are

usually other activities throughout the season. (Call the Arts Trust Office, tel 0651 851770, for information.)

Pitmedden Garden

(NTS, open May to Sept, daily 10 to 6)
If you like intricate seventeenth-century formal gardens in French style, then Pitmedden, east of Oldmeldrum, is unmissable. It was created by Sir Alexander Seton around 1675, but had to be re-created from scratch in the 1950s – it had become a kitchen garden. This has been done with some panache, with the planting of four great parterres, three of which follow seventeenth-century designs for the gardens at Holyrood in Edinburgh.

The garden is surrounded by a retaining wall and is sunk beneath the level of the ground to the west, for it is essential to see all the patterns from above. Two small pavilions and a double stone staircase break up the smooth expanse of terrace. Beneath you, there is a maze of box hedges and 40,000 colourful annuals, from which the designs and lettering are created. The sound of rooks in the nearby trees fills the garden, and all is elegance and peace.

A small agricultural museum is here too – largely a collection of farm implements, but with an interesting example of an Aberdeenshire farm-worker's bothy. The museum still has a long way to go in other respects.

THE COAST NORTH OF ABERDEEN

The east coast of Aberdeenshire alternates between swathes of sandy beach and rocky headlands. It is an exposed seashore, with nothing much to restrict the wind as it scours inland. Small fishing villages with inadequate harbours dot the shore. You can be alone as much as you want here – and on the rare still day of sunshine it can be very beautiful. However, if your time is limited the coast of the Moray Firth is more scenic.

Among the dunes and rough heath of the Ythan estuary is the **Sands of Forvie Nature Reserve**, a stopping point for both bird-watchers and botanists. Huge numbers of eider duck concentrate here in the breeding season. **Cruden Bay** is the next place worth a halt. Although a major oil pipeline runs ashore here, the bay – with its high dunes and semi-circle of sand – is unspoilt. At the northern end a tiny harbour and a few cottages make it positively photogenic. An enormous hotel was once built here, with tennis courts, croquet lawns and a golf course, for in the railway age Cruden Bay was to be the resort to beat them all. Alas, it was just too far away for people to come to, and the project was a mammoth flop; nothing remains save the golf course, which is still going strong.

The ruins you see against the horizon just north of Cruden Bay are the remains of **New Slains Castle**. A short puddle-strewn walk from the road takes you into its tumbledown, labyrinthine interior. The castle dates from 1598 and, although most of the best stonework has been robbed, some fine pieces of granite remain to show how well constructed it must have been. The cliff-edge situation impressed Dr Johnson in 1773, and the waves still slap against the cliff foot with suitably dramatic force.

At the **Bullers of Buchan**, two miles further north, a car park by the edge of the road signals that this is a beauty spot. In fact it is more of a terror spot, for the Bullers (boiler) is a collapsed sea cave, with a chasm over 200 feet deep. A narrow arch of rock separates it from the sea. A legend goes that a local laird, when drunk, won a bet by galloping around the chasm on horseback, but contemplation of this feat, once he had sobered up, was enough to make him die of shock. The Bullers is at its best in rough weather, but worth the short walk at any time. Dr Johnson insisted on exploring the place by boat. It is unlikely that you will want to imitate him.

Peterhead

This is a big, rather grim, fishing town built largely of granite. Peterhead's harbour and fish market bustle, and, if you like watching fishing boats come and go, or getting up at 4 in the morning to watch boxes of fish being haggled over, this is an excellent place. A small museum (open Mon to Sat, 10 to 12, 2 to 5) takes you back to Peterhead's heyday as a whaling and then a herring port.

If you prefer country matters, the **Aden Country Park and North East of Scotland Agricultural Heritage Centre**, a few miles west of the town, is not quite as impressive as its title, but makes a good introduction to the old Aberdeenshire farming life for all that (park open daily dawn to dusk; centre Apr, Oct, weekends 12 to 5; May to Sept, daily 11 to 5; also first 2 Suns in Nov 12 to 4). **Deer Abbey** (HS, access at all reasonable times) close by is famous as the source of a ninth-century manuscript with twelfth-century Gaelic annotations – the earliest example of written Gaelic. Now the abbey is reduced to scanty ruins, only of interest to the enthusiast.

North of Peterhead, the sand starts again. On this shifting, exposed section of coast, the villages are huddled against the elements. One (Rattray, by the Loch of Strathbeg) has vanished altogether. There are golf courses round here, and some attempts to suggest that holiday-makers come – they must be a hardy breed. Finally, where the coastline turns abruptly west, the fishing town of Fraserburgh stands, offering a haven from the wind, but not much else.

THE MORAY COAST

If Scotland were Cornwall this coast would be crowded throughout the season, for its combination of cliff scenery, sandy beaches and ancient towns is just as attractive as that of the West Country. Since Scotland is not Cornwall it is largely neglected, despite its well-signed coastal trail, by all except golfers and those Scots who discovered its charms some time ago. For those who love wild seashores, two or three days spent near this coast are likely to pay dividends.

Nairn

Nairn is a small, genteel seaside resort, though to call itself the Brighton of the North may be stretching things. Certainly its sandy beach is more comfortable to lie on. It is a restrained town, where the back streets are lined with substantial stone villas, each with its own rose garden, and where every second house does bed and breakfast. There are also a substantial number of hotels (plus plenty of farmhouse accommodation in the surrounding country), so you are unlikely to have difficulty in finding somewhere to stay. If it is a day or two by the seaside you are looking for, Nairn is more sheltered and better set up for families than its competitors (though Findhorn is better for small boats, and Lossiemouth has the best beach).

South of Nairn
Cawdor Castle

(Open May to early Oct, daily 10 to 5)
Lord Cawdor runs away with the prize for the wittiest and

most instructive guidebook to any sight in Scotland. Not only that, his castle is a joy to visit: its history is leavened with homeliness, its dignity modified by mild eccentricity. To add to the bargain, the garden is a delight. Forget *Macbeth* – this is a place well worth travelling to for its own sake.

It starts with a legend. An early Thane of Cawdor, wanting a new castle, had a dream in which he was told to load a donkey with gold, let it wander around for a day and watch where it lay down, for this would be the best spot for his new castle. He did this, and the donkey proceeded to lie down under a thorn tree. The tree still stands (long defunct) in the middle of the vaulted guardroom of the fourteenth-century tower and carbon-dating has shown it to be older than the surrounding castle (although holly rather than thorn). This same room contains a dungeon which was discovered only in 1979. It is typical of Lord Cawdor's tongue-in-cheek approach that everything found in this dungeon is displayed without regard to its worthiness – there are sawn-off bits of moulding, bones of chicken and horse, pieces of crab and lead.

On a more cultivated level, the paintings are especially worth looking at – both the portraits (brought to life by Lord Cawdor's notes: '. . . the handsome lady in the saucy brown hat is Mrs Jane Philips, affectionately nicknamed Aunt Glum . . .') and the more serious pieces such as several by John Piper and a Stanley Spencer, not to mention some fine watercolours. The tapestries are also good, helped again by suitable (or unsuitable) notes on their subjects.

It is hard to know what to pick out from the rest. The tour takes you through the Modern Kitchen ('the object on the table is not a thumbscrew, it is a French duck-press') as well as the old one, past the collections of Victoriana, the Pet's Corner ('Albert passed away untimely after drinking a gallon of red-lead paint primer'), the Stones, the Eastern Promise ('To your left is the present Lord Cawdor's aikido black belt'), a model of the castle, a model of a man-o'-war, not to mention the drawing-room, several bedrooms and various cubby-holes. After all this, the garden may seem a haven of normality. It is, and very colourful with it.

The Findhorn Valley and Lochindorb

The River Findhorn drains the wilderness of the Monadhliath Mountains south of Inverness. Where it runs south of Nairn it flows black and powerful in the confines of its wooded gorges. To drive on the minor roads round the villages of

Ferness, Dulsie and Relugas is to enter a secret countryside, hidden in the pines of the Darnaway Forest. There are walks, rides and one or two things to see, such as **Ardclach Bell Tower** (HS, access at all reasonable times), a fortified belfry of 1665, perched high above the church it served.

The A939 to Grantown-on-Spey climbs from the Findhorn river over the ridge of a stony moor which separates Strathspey from the fertile lands round Nairn – one of the most attractive routes in this part of Scotland. At the top (a short diversion from the road) is the bleak expanse of **Lochindorb**, a stretch of water notable for having been the strategic lair of the Wolf of Badenoch (see page 303) around 1372, from which he mounted his raid to burn Elgin Cathedral. His old castle, taking up every spare foot of an island in the loch, was demolished on James II's orders (the old yett can be seen in Cawdor Castle), but you can still make out the walls. Lochindorb is a grim place to this day.

Nairn to Elgin

At **Auldearn**, the site of one of Montrose's victories over the Covenanters in 1645, you can climb up to Boath Doocot, where a plan shows how the battle was fought in and around the small village below you. It is worth the short diversion from the main road as a viewpoint rather than a battlefield site.

Brodie Castle

(NTS, castle open Apr to Sept, Mon to Sat 11 to 6, Sun 2 to 6; early to mid-Oct, Sat 11 to 5, Sun 2 to 5; other times by appointment; grounds all year, daily 9.30 to sunset)
There have been 25 Brodies of Brodie since the thirteenth century, and Brodies have been living at Brodie Castle since 1567. Today they share it with the National Trust for Scotland.

With care you can disentangle the outline of the original sixteenth-century Z-plan tower-house from the later additions. Internally it is not so easy, for much of the old house was 'improved' in Victorian times and the Renaissance pillars in the entrance hall turn out to have been carved in the 1840s. The same period produced the cosy library and the spectacularly successful Gothic fireplace in the red drawing-room. The other star piece in the interior is the seventeenth-century plasterwork on the ceiling of the dining-room – a riot of mermaids, fruit and flowers. The collection of twentieth-century paintings (notably watercolours) assembled by the twenty-fourth Brodie should be seen, while the same laird's interest in daffodils turns the well-landscaped grounds into a picture in spring.

Forres

If civic pride is measured in colourful flowerbeds Forres is the peacock of the region, and the list of awards won for its floral displays must daunt less dedicated municipalities. On the outskirts of this otherwise unremarkable town, and perilously close to the by-pass, stands Sueno's Stone, one of the best Pictish stones in Scotland. It is over 20 feet high and is covered on one side with a huge battle scene, dotted with footmen, cavalry and headless bodies.

Findhorn

The B9011 past RAF Kinloss takes you to this exposed village on the edge of Findhorn Bay, a stretch of water which is attractive when the tide is in, but not when it is out. It is almost the only refuge for small sailing boats on this coast, however, so there are dinghies to lend colour, and a small water-sports centre beside the few cottages sufficiently far out of the wind to look relaxed. Behind the village, the dunes reach aridly into the hinterland.

Findhorn has achieved notoriety as the place where 'they grow giant cabbages' – 'they' being the Findhorn Foundation, a community founded in 1962, dedicated to building 'a spiritually based, holistic planetary culture'. In so far as it anticipated the popularity of Gaian theories by half a generation, the Findhorn Foundation has some reason to feel pleased with itself; it reveals itself to visitors as a stable, slightly self-conscious place. If you hang about looking lost for long enough, someone will show you around the palatial community centre, though not many giant cabbages are in evidence.

On the far side of the mouth of Findhorn Bay, a forest now covers the famous Culbin Sands – huge dunes six miles long and two miles wide, known as the Scottish Sahara. These sands are supposed to have buried a whole estate in 1694, and it is said that the steeple of the old church occasionally emerged from the dunes as they shifted. Now the whole area has been stabilised by tree-planting – a triumph for the Forestry Commission, but less romantic for the rest of us.

Burghead

This is a substantial nineteenth-century town of single-storey fishermen's cottages laid out in a grid plan over a blunt peninsula. It is a place that has been battered by generations of winds, and has, metaphorically speaking, all its hatches permanently battened down. Do not dismiss it for its superficial unattractiveness, for this unlikely spot appears to have been the centre of a large Pictish settlement, of which one remarkable relic remains. This is **Burghead Well** (HS, access at all reasonable times), and you find it by squeezing round the gable ends of grey cottages on the sea's edge and seeking out the custodian. A flight of steps leads you down into a chamber hewn out of solid rock, where a still pool of water lies. The well may have been some kind of ritual centre, perhaps even built by followers of St Columba in the sixth century. Burghead is one of three Scottish towns

JAMES GRAHAM, MARQUESS OF MONTROSE (1612–1650)

In the confused tangle of the Scottish civil wars of the seventeenth century, the figure of Montrose stands out as the single personality whom it has been possible to cast in a romantic light, thanks to his loyalty to his king, Charles I, his abilities as a leader of men in the tradition of Wallace or Bruce, and his death in the hands of his Covenanting enemies.

Montrose was among the first to sign the 1638 Covenant, and for the first years of the confrontation between King Charles and the Scots was firmly on the Covenanting side. However, as the Covenanters increasingly began to demand the subordination of king to kirk and parliament, Montrose, who perceived only anarchy in this course of events, became increasingly alienated. It was the signing of the Solemn League and Covenant in 1643, by which the Scots agreed to join the English armed rebellion against King Charles, which seems to have made up Montrose's mind for him. In early 1644 King Charles commissioned him lieutenant-general of the royal forces in Scotland – not that there were any at that time. Montrose's entry into Scotland, with two companions and no troops, was not auspicious.

(see also Lerwick and Stonehaven) which has a New Year fire ceremony – in this case the Burning of the Clavie (a tar barrel) on 11 January. West of Burghead, a beautiful creamy bay of sand and wild seas fades into the spume, and reaches almost as far as Findhorn.

Lossiemouth

Until you see the beach, it is hard to imagine that this grey, grid-plan fishing town can be a much-loved holiday resort, for Lossiemouth, like other towns and villages along this coast, bears the utilitarian stamp of a place that expanded in a hurry to cope with a boom industry – in this case the nineteenth-century herring rush. Apart from some of the quainter cottages with gable ends facing the sea and a half-buried look about them, Lossiemouth is ugly. Its attractions are not enhanced by the rumble of aircraft from the nearby RAF base.

Yet the beach redeems the place, as does the golf course, the flourishing harbour where seine-netters lumber out on

His luck turned when he met Alasdair Macdonnell, who had come with a small force from Antrim in the King's cause. Montrose won his first victory against the Covenanters at Tippermuir in August 1644, sacked Aberdeen and disappeared into the Highlands. In the winter, he descended on Argyll with a force of clansmen happy to pillage the lands of Clan Campbell. In January 1645, by an astonishing flank march through the snow-bound glens beside Loch Ness, he took the pursuing force of Campbells by surprise at Inverlochy. Throughout the spring of 1645 Montrose was in Aberdeenshire, beating the Covenanters at Auldearn and Alford, and, when he finally descended on the Lowlands, he shattered another Covenanting army at Kilsyth. But it could not last. The Scottish troops in England hurried home, yet Montrose got no support from the weakened King. In September he was outmanoeuvred for the first time, and his army routed at Philiphaugh. At the beginning of 1646 Montrose was still trying to continue his campaign, but on 25 April King Charles surrendered to his enemies and Montrose was forced abroad.

He returned in 1650, commissioned by King Charles II, raised troops in Orkney, but was soundly defeated at Carbisdale in Sutherland and captured a few days later. Taken to Edinburgh, Montrose was tried, condemned and executed on 21 May.

the tide, and the cram-full little **museum** (open May to Sept, Mon to Sat 11 to 5) down by the piers, complete with a reconstruction of Ramsay Macdonald's study – for Lossiemouth has produced a British prime minister. If you hit a fine spell and want to build sand-castles, this place is worth remembering.

Dallas Dhu

(HS, standard times; closed Thurs pm and Fri in winter)
Deep in the country to the south of the A96 – you may need a good map to find it – lies a distillery which has been turned into a museum by Historic Scotland, allowing visitors more time than they would have on a guided tour, and also allowing children under eight (not allowed by law into some parts of working distilleries) to see what happens.

The distillery has been very well arranged to let you poke and prod at your leisure, with a clear leaflet to explain the process, a trail of painted footmarks to follow, and some good human models which suddenly come to life and start explaining their job (keep an eye open for the customs officer). It comes as close to the real thing as a museum possibly could, and would make either an excellent introduction to distillery-visiting or a fitting finale.

Pluscarden Abbey

(Open daily at all reasonable times)
In bald terms, this is a thirteenth-century monastery which is now owned and being restored by a community of Benedictine monks. Yet Pluscarden is more than this: it is an ancient piece of Scotland's religious tradition which has been resurrected from decay, and is being made beautiful once more.

Parts of the abbey do look like a building site for the monks have a long way to go, though what has been achieved since 1948 when the fraternity took up residence is impressive. The choir, the transepts and the tower of the old church have been fully restored. The nave exists merely at foundation level.

Pluscarden is a mish-mash of architectural styles and of rejiggings of existing work. One side of the choir, for example, is lit by large windows with fine tracery, while the other has only a few small lights, the outline of the larger arches being firmly blocked in. Curious half-arches are to be seen on the exterior walls too, as if the architect had changed his mind half-way up. The glory of the place lies in its modern stained glass, much of it done in the abbey workshops. It is difficult to forget the searing reds which illuminate the chancel, setting the ancient walls alight all over again. The abbey is lucky in its setting – nothing disturbs the peace of the valley it sits in, apart from the birdsong.

Elgin

A self-confident, ancient royal burgh, Elgin acts as the natural market-town for the fertile coastal strip of Moray. It has a High Street which contains some ancient arcaded houses, a municipal park of some splendour, suitable shops and monuments, a small museum, and a good scattering of hotels and guesthouses – nothing exceptional perhaps, but everything in the right proportions and the right place. It is a larger and livelier place than either Nairn or Huntly, and makes an ideal base in which to stay for exploring both coastal and inland regions.

All the same it is a far cry from the days when Elgin was the cathedral city of the north, rivalled only by St Andrews. The story of Elgin's thirteenth-century **cathedral** (HS, standard times; winter closed Thurs pm and Fri) shows Scotland at its best and at its worst – on the one hand the raising of a building which in scale, elaboration and beauty could compete with any in medieval Europe; on the other, the wanton destruction by piracy, religious fervour, avarice and neglect which left the building a wreck.

For all this, it is still possible to catch something of the scale and magnificence of what used to be the 'Lanthorn of the North', either by contemplating the well-preserved chapter house with its jerky vaulting and ceiling bosses (look for the dragon with folded wings) or by gazing at the splendour of the western doorway. In the middle of the ruin, a single Pictish cross-slab stands, older by far than all this folly.

East of Elgin

Seven miles beyond Elgin lies **Fochabers**, which owes its position beside the road to the desire of the Dukes of Gordon to have some privacy at their nearby castle – the village was shifted wholesale in the eighteenth century. It still has the look of an estate village, and many of the houses are attractive. The **Fochabers Folk Museum** (open daily 9.30 to 1, 2 to 6; closes at 5 Nov to Mar) is well worth a look, not just for its collection of old coaches but for the heaps of ancient domestic objects which clutter the place. However, the main attraction near Fochabers is a factory: **Baxters Visitor Centre** (open Mon to Fri 9.30 to 4.30; also Sat and Sun 11 to 4.30 from early May to end Sept). The story of Baxters – producers of fine Scottish foods to the gentry – is a folksy tale to bring tears of joy to the eyes of the marketing department. George Baxter, gardener to His Grace the Duke of Gordon in the nineteenth century, had a wife whose home-made jams found favour with all who sampled them. From grocery shop to factory by the banks of the Spey, helped on its way by the philanthropic Duke, the Baxter enterprise expanded, and continues to expand.

Tours of the factory (weekdays only) are slickly handled and fun, though you may have to wait on busy days. The inevitable audio-visual is followed by a visit to the canning line, where thousands of the silvery objects rattle round conveyor belts at high speed. The day's 'menu' is chalked up, so that you know what delicacies are in production (though if it is beetroot, you will be able to tell the moment you arrive). Is there any truth in the old story that the choicest raspberries are picked out with a reverential murmur of 'The Queen', before being packed off to Balmoral?

The fishing towns

From Spey Bay, where the river joins the Moray Firth amongst great shingle banks, the coast begins to change character. Gone are the sand dunes and inland woods; in their place rise cliffs of reddish rock. In every indentation lie fishing villages and towns – often surprisingly large for such a difficult coast. Some are jammed with fishing boats and container lorries; others lie quiet. Almost all have their 'seatown', a cluster of the oldest cottages, gable end to the sea and the street, which was the heart of the fishing community.

The Scottish fishing industry remains poised on the edge of precipitous decline and you are likely to hear bitter words about quotas and the arbitrary rules about who can fish where and for what – while you can sense, all along the coast, that times are hard. The following is just a choice of the towns and villages worth exploring; there are more.

● **Buckie** is a grey, industrious fishing town, full of sea-food processing factories, fish-selling agencies, container lorries, ice-factories, ship chandlers and repair yards. All the action is down by the harbour, although you might take a break in the **museum** (open Mon to Fri 10 to 8, Sat 10 to 12) by the public library, where there are plaster models of fish if you are too late for the real thing.

- **Findochty and Portknockie** are typical of the quiet fishing burghs whose inhabitants now work out of Buckie. Look for the rather fine modern statue of the fisherman in Findochty. There is dramatic cliff scenery between the two.
- **Cullen** gave its name to an excellent smoked haddock soup. It is not an attractive town but it is blessed with a long stretch of sand and a fine golf course, both of which draw visitors. The old church is fourteenth-century.
- **Portsoy** exudes a greater air of antiquity down by its harbour than neighbouring villages, with some of the houses going back to the early eighteenth century. There is a leaflet to guide you round. Portsoy marble is a species of locally quarried serpentine. It once provided two chimneypieces for the palace at Versailles; now it provides pretty souvenirs, on sale by the harbour.

Banff

For lovers of eighteenth-century architecture, Banff is something of a treasure trove. In those days, the landed gentry from much of the surrounding country were accustomed to abandon their draughty seats in the winter and congregate somewhere where they could enjoy each other's company. Banff was the chosen spot, and the result is a number of substantial houses. The town retains much of the dignity of earlier centuries, and is a complete contrast to the raucous hive of maritime activity in **Macduff**, across the Deveron estuary. The silting up of its harbour put a stop to Banff's days as a fishing town, though old fishers' cottages remain.

Dr Johnson, who had already eaten 'a vile meal' in Elgin, found the Black Bull Inn here 'indifferent'. Standards have changed for the better, and you should find a choice of reasonable places to stay.

Duff House

This great baroque mansion which dominates the outskirts of Banff is slowly being rescued from its decay. Polish and Norwegian troops, the Kings Own Scottish Borderers, German prisoners of war, the staff and guests of an hotel and sanatorium and even a bomb have all left their mark

USEFUL DIRECTORY

Main tourist offices
Grampian Highlands & Aberdeen Tourist Board
St Nicholas House, Broad Street
Aberdeen AB9 1DE
(0224) 632727

Aberdeen & Gordon Tourist Board
St Nicholas House, Broad Street
Aberdeen AB9 1DE
(0224) 632727

Banff & Buchan Tourist Board
Collie Lodge, Banff AB45 1AU
(0261) 812789

Kincardine & Deeside Tourist Board
Bridge Street, Banchory AB31 3SX
(0330) 822066

Moray and Elgin District Tourist Board
17 High Street, Elgin IV30 1EG
(0343) 542666

Inverness, Loch Ness and Nairn Tourist Board
Castle Wynd, Inverness IV2 3BJ
(0463) 234353

Tourist Board publications Very useful: *What to See and Where to Go in Grampian Highlands and Aberdeen*; also annually updated *Visitor's Guide*. Special interest booklets include ones on the Castle Trail, the Malt Whisky Trail and the Victorian Heritage Trail, and cover activities such as fishing, hillwalking and golf. The *In and Around* series of leaflets are also useful.

on it, and it has nearly, but not quite, collapsed under the strain.

William Adam started building Duff House for the first Earl of Fife in 1735, and, although their relationship degenerated into a legal wrangle and the second Earl avoided all contact with the Adam family as he continued the house, William left behind a magnificent block with a façade ornamented by Corinthian capitals to the pilasters, and a wealth of

Local tourist information centres
Aboyne (03398) 86060 (Easter to Sept)
Aden (0771) 623037 (April to Oct)
Alford (09755) 62052 (late Mar to Sept/weekends in Oct)
Ballater (03397) 55306 (Easter to late Oct)
Banchory (0330) 822000
Banff (0261) 812419 (Apr to Oct)
Braemar (03397) 41600
Buckie (0542) 834853 (May to Sept)
Cullen (0542) 840757 (May to Sept)
Dufftown (0340) 820501 (Easter to Oct)
Forres (0309) 672938 (mid-May to Oct)
Fraserburgh (0346) 518315 (Apr to Oct)
Huntly (0466) 792255 (late Apr to Sept)
Inverurie (0467) 620600 (late Apr to Sept)
Keith (0542) 882634 (May to Sept)
Nairn (0667) 452753 (Apr to Oct)
Peterhead (0779) 71904 (Apr to Oct)
Stonehaven (0569) 762806 (Easter to Oct)
Tomintoul (0807) 580285 (Easter to Oct)

Local transport
Aberdeen Airport Information (0224) 722331
Inverness Airport Information (0463) 232471
Scotrail Aberdeen (0224) 594222
Scotrail Elgin (0343) 543407
National and Caledonian Express bus and coaches
041–332 4100
Bluebird Northern bus and coaches (0224) 212266

Other useful numbers
P&O Aberdeen for information on boats to Orkney &
Shetland (0224) 572615
Aberdeen 'What's On Line' (0224) 636363

detail. The interior of Duff House is closed, but will reopen in 1993 as an art gallery, heralded as 'The Tate of the North'.

Gardenstown and Pennan

Gardenstown is squeezed on to what is almost a cliff face, and the road down is on the precipitous side of steep. The cottages at the bottom are so jammed together that there is scarcely room for two cars to pass on the street. If you survive the descent, spare a minute or two to wander round the harbour and observe how many modern facilities this place manages to cram into its tiny space. Further round the bay, tucked under the cliffs of Troup Head, lies the even more dramatically situated **Crovie**. Don't even think of trying to get your car there – walk instead. Beyond the headland lies **Pennan**, the one village on the coast that starts tourist literature off on superlatives. If you saw the film *Local Hero* you will immediately recognise the red telephone box and the pub. Pennan is not so much a village as a single row of cottages squeezed on to a shelf between a gnarled, overhanging cliff and the sea, leaving so little room that washing has to be dried on the very edge of the breakwater. There is absolutely nothing to do here except walk from one end of the street to the other and to take photographs, though if you do want to spend a romantic night in the inn listening to the beat of the waves on the shingle you will find that prices have been inflated only a little by celluloid fame.

WHERE TO STAY

ABOYNE

Hazlehurst Lodge	£
Aboyne	
Grampian AB34 5HY	*Tel (033 98) 86921*

A mixture of guesthouse and restaurant in an old stone villa. Bedrooms are comfortable and warm, and the atmosphere is arty.

Open: all year, exc Jan **Rooms**: 5 **Credit/charge cards**: Access, Amex, Visa

BALLATER

Craigendarroch Hotel	£££
Braemar Road	
Ballater, Deeside AB35 5XA	*Tel (033 97) 55858*

This comfortable hotel and timeshare complex just outside Ballater makes up in facilities what it lacks in atmosphere. The complex is based around an old house but most of it is modern. Three restaurants cater for most pockets, and there's a quiet little study and bar. Bedrooms are bland but have all the extras, and there is masses to do.

Open: all year **Rooms**: 50 **Facilities**: tennis, sauna, solarium, dri-ski slope, squash, swimming-pool, gym, snooker, crèche, adventure playground **Credit/charge cards**: Access, Amex, Diners, Visa

---

Tullich Lodge   **£££**
By Ballater, Aberdeenshire AB35 5SB   *Tel (033 97) 55406*

The owners of this granite baronial house have stamped their love of the Victorian period throughout, from the furniture to the bath taps and the heavy draping of the curtains. The public rooms are spacious and the bedrooms, again Victorian in tone, are pretty and comfortable. Four-course dinners use plenty of local fish and game.

Open: Apr to Nov **Rooms**: 10 **Credit/charge cards**: Access, Amex, Diners, Visa

---

BANCHORY

Banchory Lodge   **££**
Banchory
Kincardine & Deeside AB31 3HS   *Tel (033 02) 82625*

This rambling Georgian house attracts many regulars, most of whom come for the fishing and the friendly atmosphere. Some of the bedrooms are rather heavily decorated in Edwardian-style, some brightly modern. The nicest ones overlook the Dee, and there are several family rooms. Hearty Scottish food.

Open: all year, exc first week Jan **Rooms**: 24
Facilities: fishing, sauna, games-room
Credit/charge cards: Access, Amex, Diners, Visa

ELGIN

Mansion House Hotel   **£££**
The Haugh
Elgin, Morayshire IV30 1AW   *Tel (0343) 548811*

The dark Victorian building is staple country-house fare, with elegant furnishings in the piano lounge and restaurant and a fine selection of malts in the still room. Bedrooms have bright designs and good quality furniture, though some are a little cramped. There is also a smart leisure complex. A wide selection of food is available from the bar menu and the à la carte restaurant menu.

Open: all year **Rooms**: 20 **Facilities**: games room, sauna, heated pool, gym **Credit/charge cards**: Access, Amex, Diners, Visa

FETTERCAIRN

Ramsay Arms   £
Fettercairn, Kincardine and Deeside AB30 1XY   Tel (0561) 340334

Queen Victoria once stayed at this village pub. Now it has a fine panelled dining-room, a sauna and Jacuzzi, and very well refurbished bedrooms. There's a lively public bar and more genteel lounge bar, welcoming staff, and decent food.

Open: all year **Rooms**: 12 **Facilities**: sauna, gym, Jacuzzi
Credit/charge cards: Access, Diners, Visa

KILDRUMMY

Kildrummy Castle   £££
Kildrummy, By Alford
Aberdeenshire AB3 8RA   Tel (097 55) 71288

The hotel is set in a 'new' castle (built in 1901) beside the ruins of a much older one in a pretty part of the Don Valley. There's a stone porch and panelled hall, and a spacious and bright drawing-room. Bedrooms contain a mix of old and new furniture and vary in size, with modern, neat bathrooms.

Open: all year, exc Jan **Rooms**: 15 **Facilities**: billiards, clay pigeon shooting, fishing **Credit/charge cards**: Access, Amex, Visa

KINGUSSIE

The Cross   ££
Tweed Hill Brae, Ardbroilach Road
Kingussie, Inverness-shire PH21 1TC   Tel (0540) 661166

The Hadleys have relocated their restaurant and hotel into a converted tweed mill overlooking the riverside. Bedrooms are peaceful with magnificent half-tester beds and imaginative use of pine and soft fabrics.

Open: all year, exc 3 weeks in May and 5 weeks Nov/Dec; restaurant closed Sun, Mon eves **Rooms**: 3
Credit/charge cards: Access, Visa

LESLIE

Leslie Castle ££–£££
Leslie, By Insch
Aberdeenshire AB52 6NX Tel (0464) 20869

The owners have restored the castle from a ruin to create a homely guesthouse full of interest. The breakfast room has a flagstoned floor and huge fireplace, while the old great hall and living quarters upstairs are turned into comfortable rooms with dark oak furniture. The bedrooms are spacious, modern and extremely comfortable – two have four-posters.

Open: all year **Rooms**: 4 **Credit/charge cards**: Access, Amex, Visa

NAIRN

Clifton House ££
Viewfield Street, Nairn
Nairnshire IV12 4HW Tel (0667) 53119

A comfortable and unusual outpost for theatrical types on the shores of the Moray Firth. The owner's talents in stage direction have been put to good use, and pictures and mirrors, crimsons and reds have transformed what is a rather ordinary building into a place with a hint of decadence. Good food with plenty of very fresh seafood.

Open: Feb to Nov **Rooms**: 12 **Credit/charge cards**: Access, Amex, Diners, Visa

PETERHEAD

Waterside Inn ££
Fraserburgh Road, Peterhead
Aberdeenshire AB42 7BN Tel (0779) 71121

A comfortable business hotel in the coastal wilderness of Aberdeenshire, fresh and clean on the outside, and cheerfully warm within. Rooms are in two large blocks and there's a swimming-pool, a sauna, a grill-room and restaurant, two bars and snooker tables.

Open: all year **Rooms**: 110 **Facilities**: snooker, sauna, solarium, swimming-pool, gym **Credit/charge cards**: Access, Amex, Diners, Visa

WHERE TO EAT

ABERDEEN

Faraday's
2 Kirk Brae
Cults, Aberdeen AB1 9FQ   *Tel (0224) 869666*

Faraday's is a converted nineteenth-century hydro-electric sub-station. The exterior is stark but inside is pure Victoriana, and has an intimate feel, with fresh flowers and candles on the attractively laid out tables. There is a good selection of Scottish dishes among a global choice. The wine list is quite expensive but offers variety across the range.

Open: Tues to Sat 12.30 to 1.30, Mon to Sat 7.30 to 9.30
Credit/charge cards: Access, Visa

Megna Tandoori   ★
11 Dee Street
Aberdeen AB1 2DY   *Tel (0224) 572065*

The Megna is a superior curry house with a reputation for good-value, high-quality Indian food.

Open: Mon to Sat 12 to 2, 5 to 11, Sun 3 to midnight
Credit/charge cards: Access, Amex, Diners, Visa

Silver Darling
Pocra Quay
Northpier, Aberdeen AB2 1DQ   *Tel (0224) 576229*

This restaurant is right on the quay and has spectacular views of the sea and the comings and goings of fishing boats. Run by a Frenchman, Didier Dejean, the dining-room is equally French and Aberdonian. The menu makes use of the local catch and is often cooked in the style of M Dejean's native Provence.

Open: Mon to Fri 12 to 2, daily 7 to 9.30; closed 2 weeks
Xmas   **Credit/charge cards**: Access, Amex, Diners, Visa

DRYBRIDGE

Old Monastery
Drybridge, Buckie, Banffshire AB56 2YB   *Tel (0542) 32660*

The views and the position of the Old Monastery are sensational.
The restaurant is sited in the chapel and the bar in the cloisters. The
Grays are welcoming hosts and the emphasis is on the materials –
good venison, salmon, beef and lamb. No smoking.

Open: Tues to Sat 12 to 1.30, 7 to 9.30
Credit/charge cards: Access, Amex, Visa

THE CENTRAL AND NORTHERN HIGHLANDS

- Mountain scenery and empty wilderness in abundance
- The outdoor holiday centres of Strathspey and the Great Glen

Urquhart Castle

For many visitors, the real Scotland begins beyond Drumochter Pass or Rannoch Moor. Further south, it seems, the landscape is tame, the way of life effete and the midges mere shadows of the great biters of the Great Glen. The central and northern Highlands are marked by a change of scale – mountainous country becomes more extensive, roads fewer, the glens longer and the population sparser. It can be a mysterious, sometimes awesome country: wild, bleak and beautiful in fine weather, a dismal hell in the rain. Parts of this landscape are tamed – Speyside and the Great Glen bustle with holiday-makers. Parts are not – the rust-coloured bogs of Sutherland contain scarcely a house. Parts – the gentle country of Easter Ross, for example – are outposts of Lowland countryside in the middle of the Highlands.

The emptiness of the countryside is comparatively recent. The glens were once full of settlements, whose crumbled remains are marked by heaps of bracken-covered stone. The Clearances, when people were evicted from their houses to be replaced by sheep, were only a part of the long-running process of depopulation which swelled the Lowland cities and forced so many families on to the emigrant ships. Over 22,000 Scots went to Nova Scotia between 1815 and 1838; by 1840, Glasgow had absorbed more than 30,000 Highlanders.

The sheep that replaced the Highlanders in the glens eventually proved equally unprofitable. The sheep farms gave way to the deer forests, and huge tracts of once-populated land became the province of the deer, the ghillie, and the gentleman with the rifle. Much of the Highlands remains divided into sporting estates covering several thousand acres and the big Edwardian shooting-lodges still stand, surrounded by sheltering trees and game larders. The subject of land ownership in the Highlands is a touchy one, and you get drawn into an argument about it at your peril.

Another characteristic building of the northern Highlands is the croft house. A croft, famously defined as a piece of land surrounded by legislation, is a smallholding, the house usually ringed by a couple of fields. Few crofters have enough land from which to make a full-time living, and most supplement their income by fishing, forestry or from tourism.

Stamping ground of the clans

Before the coming of the sheep or the shooting-lodge, Highland life, deep in the mountains, centred around the extended family – the clan. The chieftain was father to his clansmen, possessing a power over them verging on the absolute, but with an equally absolute responsibility for their welfare. Where the hierarchies of Lowland society were defined by rank or wealth, the clansman defined himself by his genealogy. He might acknowledge a difference in seniority to others in his clan, but none in quality.

The truth of what clan life was like has become so obscured by romance that it is difficult to gain a clear picture. It was certainly bloody: feuds between clans were continuous, and the 'tail' of fighting men that a chieftain could raise was the most important measure of his power. Life was also pastoral, revolving around the rearing of black cattle, but there was always poverty, and raiding the neighbouring clan or joining a Lowland struggle in the hope of plunder were popular ways of relieving it. The clansman was always his own man, and one of the frustrations of generals from Montrose to Prince Charles Edward was the tendency of their Highland allies to return home when they had amassed enough loot or when it was time for the harvest.

Highland culture was, and in a few places still is, subtler than the bagpipes-and-Highland-games spectacular which is happily thrust at tourists. The history of the clan was in the custody of bards who transmitted it orally from one generation to the next, and of the piper whose duty it was to inspire the clan to battle or recall its dead in sonorous laments. Before the Battle of Culloden in 1746 there were few outsiders to record this Gaelic culture, and afterwards its mainspring had been broken. It lives on in the work of modern Gaelic poets, of whom Sorley Maclean is the most renowned, in the expertise of pipers, and in the festivals of song and music called 'Mods'.

After two centuries of emigration, the clans are now dispersed in a worldwide diaspora. Yet beneath the fashion for clan gatherings, clan museums, clan tartans, or tracing ancestors – which a cynic may see as an attempt to glue together something which is irrevocably broken – there are echoes of old loyalties which refuse to die away.

SPEYSIDE

As you travel north over the Drumochter Pass from Glen Garry and Blair Atholl, the network of glens and lochs making up the Tay river system is replaced by the single broad strath of the Spey, bleak here in its upper stretches, with two great mountain massifs – the Monadhliath to the west and the Cairngorms to the east – on the horizons. The Monadhliath are a featureless jumble of hills little frequented by visitors, but the Cairngorms, with many of the highest tops in Scotland among them, are beautiful. They are a constant presence beside the Spey valley, sometimes sinister in the lurid light preceding a blizzard, sometimes alluring in the purples and greens of summer.

The tourist industry has expanded over the 30-odd years since Lord Fraser conceived a purpose-built resort at Aviemore, and now covers most of Speyside from Newtonmore to Grantown. Thanks to the ski slopes on Cairn Gorm, to the opportunities for sailing and wind-surfing on Loch Insh and Loch Morlich, and to the endless tough or easy walks in the area, this is one of the few parts of Scotland to have a genuine year-round tourist season.

At **Dalwhinnie**, whose lonely distillery is the first sign of the great whisky industry of Speyside, there is a glimpse of the top of Loch Ericht, a deep trench scooped out by glaciers running north-east from Rannoch Moor, with the gloomy shoulder of Ben Alder hanging over it. The A889 branches off here to join the A86 which runs down Glen Spean to Fort William.

Newtonmore is the first of the series of small towns lining Speyside to have been given a new lease of life by tourism, and is one of the more peaceful. This is Macpherson territory (the clan museum is here) and also a stronghold of shinty – a game like hockey but even more vicious – which has fanatical adherents throughout the Highlands, but especially on Speyside.

Like so many of the planned villages in the Highlands, **Kingussie** consists of a single long street with a few side streets off it. Busier than Newtonmore, Kingussie's major attraction is the **Highland Folk Museum** (open Apr to Oct, Mon to Sat 10 to 6, Sun 2 to 6; Nov to Mar, Mon to Fri 10 to 3). A visit will make you see both the ingenuity of the people living in a land with few resources and uncertain climate, and the grinding poverty which so many of them endured. With a little effort you can imagine the squalor and the malnutrition which led the poet Southey to call the old black houses of the Highlands 'men-styes'.

Across the A9 are the shattered remains of Ruthven barracks (HS, always open), built by the Hanoverians after the Jacobite rising of 1715, taken by the Jacobites in 1746, and blown up by them after the defeat at Culloden.

391

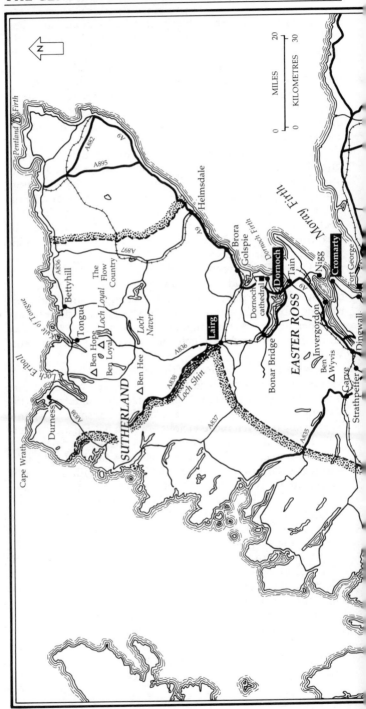

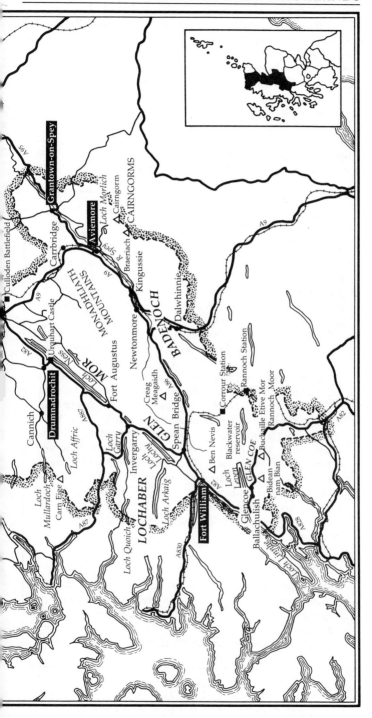

All the animals at the **Highland Wildlife Park** near Kincraig (open Mar to Sept, daily 10 to 5, Oct to early Nov, daily 10 to 4; well signposted from the A9) are, or once were, indigenous to the Highlands, including wolves, deer and wildcats. Part of the park is drive-through, part walk-through, and it is informative and sensibly organised (there is a free kennel for your dog, for example).

Nearby **Loch Insh** is a pretty, round loch – really a widening of the Spey. It is a good place to watch birds (there is an RSPB reserve at Insh marshes) and you may see an osprey if you are fortunate. Gardeners should head

---

Practical suggestions

A holiday this far north makes sense only if you enjoy being outdoors, and do not mind too much about the weather. For botanists, geologists, hill-walkers, naturalists, anglers and photographers, this region is tailor-made. The further north you explore, the less you will see of your fellow man and the fewer facilities you will have at your command. Shops tend to sell staples only, petrol becomes more expensive and television reception may be fuzzy. However, for real isolation you will have to go to the islands, for you will not find it here.

The two great valleys of Speyside and Glen More (the Great Glen) at the southern end of the region are the focus for most of the area's tourism. Speyside has Scotland's first purpose-built resort at Aviemore and some of the finest scenery in the land. It is ideal for a family holiday, both summer and winter. The Great Glen, with Loch Ness at its heart, is less scenic, but has plenty of facilities. The Loch Ness Monster draws crowds though it is possible to escape them. For deserted moorland, central Sutherland is matchless. Easter Ross is the place for golf and for gentle walks. The north coast has its own stark beauty of cliffs, knobbly headlands and bays of silvery sand.

Good bases

• **Aviemore** Speyside's 1960s purpose-built resort, Aviemore is bustling, sometimes vulgar, usually lively, and with plenty of activities. It is not for everyone, but is a genuine year-round family resort.

• **Grantown-on-Spey** Grantown is sedate and Victorian in

for Jack Drake's Inshriach Nursery, on the back road (B970) to Aviemore, which is famous for alpines.

Aviemore

The bones of a small, grim railway town are buried in what is now almost entirely a tourist resort. The Aviemore Centre, a complex of hotels, ice-rink, cinema, shops and arcades lies at its heart. These buildings, despite being firmly 1960s in style, have worn well, thanks to the good sense of the original design. Nevertheless, it is a shock to come across what might

---

tone, elegant in layout and well placed for exploration of Speyside. It has a number of solid hotels.

- **Fort William** The excellence of the location and the proximity of first-class mountain country go some way to counteract this town's fundamental dreariness. There is a large range of guesthouse accommodation and reasonable facilities.
- **Drumnadrochit** The village itself is bedevilled by traffic and by 'Nessie' souvenir tat, but it is centrally placed for touring round Loch Ness and for penetrating the glens to the west. Staying in one of several smaller communities spread up Glen Urquhart will shield you from the worst of the main road.
- **Beauly** This very small, red sandstone town to the west of Inverness is ideal if you do not want to get bogged down in the city itself. The position is good for exploration of Glen Affric and Easter Ross. There is not a huge choice of accommodation.
- **Cromarty** Isolated on the tip of the Black Isle, Cromarty is a handsome burgh which has so far avoided the worst effects of tourism, while managing to provide a choice of places to stay. It is too far away from the through-routes to be a sensible centre for touring, but would be ideal if you wanted a few days in a small town by the sea.
- **Dornoch** This is a very pretty small town, famous for its golf course and for its good sands. The old cathedral in its centre is beautiful. Dornoch is a seaside resort of a quiet and restrained kind. It is ideal in a spell of good weather, and not badly placed for touring either.
- **Lairg** The position of Lairg makes it the obvious place from which to wander the desolate expanses of Sutherland. It lies at the foot of Loch Shin and is the centre of a network of bus routes. Not a great deal happens in the village itself, but there is a fair choice of accommodation.

---

well be a package-holiday resort on a Mediterranean coast in the middle of the Scottish Highlands, and it is certainly no place for those who hate lively and occasionally noisy entertainment. Aviemore also has plenty of accommodation outside the Centre.

The resort's huge advantage is that there is always something going on, even on the wettest of days. In winter, the ski shops are crowded, and mini-buses covered in ski racks fill the car parks. In summer the same shops sell rucksacks and anti-midge cream, while the mini-buses are full of families setting off on ranger-led walks. In both seasons mountaineers abound, though the high tops of the Cairngorms can be Arctic in temperament and climate. They should deter all but the expert in winter, and will punish the foolhardy at any time of year.

Most outdoor activities take place in nearby Glen More. Loch Morlich is home to sailing and windsurfing; you can fish the Spey (not one of its best stretches) or the various stocked lochs set up to cater for learners. You can visit Scotland's reindeer herd, learn rock-climbing, or go cross-country skiing. Information about all these activities and more can be found at the Tourist Information Centre in Aviemore, the Forestry Commission Centre by Loch Morlich or the Rothiemurchus Visitor Centre at Inverdruie.

Glen More

The great bowl which extends eastwards from Aviemore to the foot of Cairn Gorm is part forest park and part nature reserve (the reserve extends over much of the Cairngorm range). At its heart lies Loch Morlich, fringed by beaches of coarse granite sand. The pines of Rothiemurchus form one of the largest remaining fragments of the old Caledonian forest to be found in Scotland, and are now being carefully husbanded. It is one of the last strongholds of the rarer species of Scottish wildlife – the capercaillie, the blackcock, the pine marten, the red squirrel and the wild cat.

The walks range from gentle strolls through the silence of the forest – perhaps round **Loch an Eilein** to strenuous expeditions. The most famous of these is through the **Lairig Ghru** pass down to Linn of Dee, and leads you under the shoulders of Braeriach and Ben Macdui (whose summit is haunted by a dimly perceived grey man) right through the heart of the Cairngorms. If you insist on standing on top of a mountain without too much effort, the Cairn Gorm chair-lift (reached by the road up to the ski slopes of Coire na Ciste and Coire Cas) will get you within striking range. In winter, the slopes here are dotted with figures weaving their way downhill, the car parks are full, and you must go elsewhere for wilderness.

Boat of Garten and Carrbridge

Boat of Garten is the terminus for the small steam railway which runs in season from Aviemore. Nearby is Loch Garten, one of the most popular nature reserves in Scotland, made

---

THE GLENCOE MASSACRE

In the 'Glorious Revolution' of 1688, the Catholic James VII of Scotland and II of England fled the country to avoid being deposed. The English Parliament offered the crown of England to the Protestant William of Orange. The Scots, after some hesitation, offered the Scottish crown too. The rising in support of James, started by Graham of Claverhouse (Bonnie Dundee), petered out after Dundee's death at the Battle of Killiecrankie but certain clans remained in opposition. All chiefs were required to take an oath of loyalty to King William by 1 January 1692, but it was not until the last minute that the chief of the MacDonalds of Glencoe went to sign at Fort William. No one there was authorised to receive his oath, and he had to go to Inveraray, which put him technically in breach of the deadline.

The purpose of the orders which were thereafter issued to Campbell of Glenlyon, telling him to 'fall upon the Rebells, the McDonalds of Glenco, and putt all to the sword under seventy' was simply 'pour encourager les autres'. The orders reached Campbell on 12 February 1692, after he and his 128 men had been billeted on the MacDonalds for two weeks, and the massacre began at five the following morning. Some 40 MacDonalds were slain.

Queen Victoria piously hoped that King William had known nothing about it. This seems unlikely, although the chief agent in the massacre was Sir John Dalrymple, Master of Stair. There was an inquiry, but although the Scottish parliament agreed that the killing had been murder, Stair suffered only dismissal and King William's involvement was glossed over.

---

famous as the breeding site of the first ospreys to begin the recolonisation of the Highlands.

Carrbridge lies where the road to Inverness curves out of the Spey Valley and begins its climb up the Monadhliath to the Slochd summit. The village is almost as full of guesthouses and ski schools as Aviemore, but is a more peaceful place. The **Landmark Highland Heritage and Adventure Park** (open Apr to June, Sept, Oct, daily 9.30 to 6; July, Aug 9.30 to 8; Nov to Mar 9.30 to 5) provides visitors with a carefully tended stretch of old pine forest, equipped with boardwalks to stop your feet getting wet and a treetop trail to carry you to the upper storeys of the pines. There is a small nature trail, an adventure playground, and an audio-visual about the history of man in the Highlands, if it is wet.

Grantown-on-Spey

Grantown has the air of a place that was a well-established holiday town when Aviemore was a collection of shacks. It is a little too far from the slopes of Cairn Gorm to be able to capitalise on the skiing boom, so has to make do with its traditional clientele – those who come to fish on the Spey and those who prefer gentle walks by the river to flogging through the mountains. Grantown is staid and Victorian in its architecture, with a large central square and a long street of shops. If you intend to explore the Spey, Grantown is better placed than Aviemore, and the immediate surroundings are more enticing.

RANNOCH MOOR TO FORT WILLIAM

From Tyndrum the A82 to Fort William runs north-west into the hills, flanked by the scree-littered cone of Ben Dorain. Across the expanse of Loch Tulla you look at the mountains which run down the south-eastern side of Glen Etive. A lonely path runs through Glen Kinglass to Loch Etive; otherwise the hills are trackless. Here, as you approach the West Highlands, there is a stepping up in the scales of grandeur and roughness of the scenery.

Most travellers get their first glimpse of **Rannoch Moor** after driving up the steep ascent above Loch Tulla. The overwhelming impression is of a watery desolation – mile upon mile of peat hag, cut by networks of small burns and lochans, with cotton grass ruffling in the wind. This hollow among the hills was filled with ice as recently as 10,000 years ago.

Nowadays, it is Scottish bog at its most uncompromising – trying to walk across its squelchy expanse without a compass in bad conditions is potentially lethal. The most sensible track, sticking to dry ground, runs along the shore of Loch Laidon and eventually ends up at Rannoch Station (catch a train back to Bridge of Orchy). Great stumps jutting from the peat hags like the bones of dinosaurs show that this area, like so much of what is now treeless wilderness, once carried a forest.

Rannoch Moor is best seen from the train. Between 2,000 and 5,000 men took almost five years to build the railway which crosses the very heart of the wilderness – it runs for miles without sight of house or road. Corrour Station, near the foot of Loch Ossian, lies entirely on its own – you can walk from here back to Rannoch Station.

Glen Coe

At the head of Glen Coe stands one of Scotland's best-known mountains, **Buachaille Etive Mor**, the Great Shepherd of Etive. For rock-climbers, it is a landscape of beloved gullies and buttresses; for the rest, it is a shapely triangle of precipitous rock, gleaming with ice in winter, pearly grey in summer, which stands like a lighthouse on the western extremity of Rannoch Moor.

Behind it the road begins to drop into Glen Coe. The glen is famous for its notorious massacre, which, unlike the many massacres which took place in the ceaseless feuds between clans, was inspired by politics, and it is this, and the abuse of hospitality that went with it, that has made it notorious.

The road runs parallel with the jagged height of the Aonach Eagach ridge on one side and passes the three massive buttresses of Bidean nam Bian, known as the Three Sisters, on the other. When cloud hangs on the tops and the serried slabs of the buttresses are glistening with rain, Glen Coe is at its most sinister and oppressive.

Most of the mountains here are the province of the experienced walker only, but a summer expedition into the 'Lost Valley' of Coire Gabhail is demanding but less dangerous. The hanging valley between two of the Three Sisters is approached by a steep path up from the River Coe, which winds among great tangles of boulders and trees. The open expanse at the top comes as a welcome surprise after the constricted path;

on a still day, this is a sheltered spot, with only echoes from the surrounding cliffs to disturb the peace.

Glen Etive, which branches off south-west just before Glen Coe, is a greener, brighter and less threatening glen to explore if you have time. The narrow road winds beside the River Etive down to a lonely pier at the head of the loch. There are plenty of grassy spaces for picnics (though beware midges). A fine day's ridge walking is to be had along the great nose of Aonach Mór to the peak of Stob Ghabhar overlooking Loch Tulla, but the usual precautions about map and compass apply stringently.

At the foot of Glen Coe, the **National Trust Visitor Centre** (NTS, open Apr to late May and early Sept to mid-Oct, daily 10 to 5; late May to early Sept, daily 9.30 to 6) has information about flora, fauna and history, plus ranger-led walks in summer, while **Glencoe** village has a simple memorial to the massacre and a small museum. Beyond **Ballachulish**, once famous for its slate quarries, the road north swings over Loch Leven towards Fort William.

Fort William

Squashed between Loch Linnhe and the mass of Ben Nevis, Fort William's location at the crossroads of the only through-routes in this part of the world, together with its easy access to Glen Nevis and Loch Ness, has turned the town from a military outpost into a holiday resort. Fort William is neither attractive nor particularly historic, and is often drenching wet into the bargain. Even so, the gift shops and tea-rooms do a thriving trade in summer, while model 'Nessies' of every shape and size line the shop windows.

There are two good reasons for basing yourself here. The first is that, short of Oban, Inverness, Aviemore or Portree, you will not find anywhere else with as many shops or so much choice of places to stay or eat. The second reason is that Fort William makes an obvious base for exploring the Ben Nevis range, which has some of the best hill-walking in the country, and now skiing at the developing Aonach Mór complex nearby (the gondola system will take you up the mountain in summer too).

Much the most interesting sight in Fort William is the **West Highland Museum** (open Nov to Easter, Tues to Sat 10 to 5; May to June and Sept to Oct Mon to Sat 10 to 5; July, Aug, Mon to Sat 9.30 to 5.30 and Sun, 2 to 5). It is serious, modest and rather old-fashioned. The Jacobite section's star offering is a secret portrait of Charles Edward Stuart, which looks like a splodge of paint until you hold a curved mirror to it. There are also many local stories, including one describing the first ascent of Ben Nevis by car in 1911.

Ben Nevis

The great hump-backed mountain rising behind Fort William is, at 4406 feet, Britain's highest. Streams of visitors have been making their way up it since the nineteenth century, and nowadays its top is the object of an annual race. The views are wonderful, but the summit is rather bleak. The great precipice which rings the mountain's north-eastern flank provides some of the finest rock-climbing ground in Britain, and for the experienced walker there is wonderful ridge walking on the Mamores, the Aonachs and the range known as the Grey Corries. These hills have some of the heaviest rainfall in Scotland, so go well prepared.

Glen Nevis

Because it is so close to Fort William this glen sees a lot of visitors. It is worth persisting along the road to the car park at the end, from where the walk beside a deep gorge to the Steall waterfall is relatively easy, if rough. The track continues beyond the falls right through to Corrour Station in the middle of Rannoch Moor, about 14 miles from the car park.

GLEN SPEAN

Glen Spean is the only route to link Speyside with the southern part of the Great Glen. It is not the prettiest of glens, for fluctuating water levels caused by the dam below Loch Laggan often leave exposed patches of shingle or mud.

Spean Bridge, at the foot of the glen, is a popular stopping point because of the large woollen mill shop here and the memorial to the Commandos who trained in the nearby mountains during the World War II. This aggressive monument, with three stern figures gazing over the hills, is much photographed. At Roy Bridge a narrow road with scanty passing places winds northwards up the hill into **Glen Roy**. This otherwise ordinary, lonely glen has been made famous by the 'Parallel Roads of Glen Roy', a geological freak which you see clearly as the road turns into the upper glen. Three level stripes follow the contours of the hills about 600 feet above the floor of the glen, looking exactly as if someone had carved roads in the side of the mountains. These were once the shorelines of the deep loch that filled Glen Roy at the end of the last Ice Age; the water was unable to escape because of a ice dam in Glen Spean. The three levels reflect different stages in the melting of the ice.

Glen Roy was also the scene of the forced march by Montrose over the hills in the depths of winter. During his 1645 campaign in support of King Charles I, Montrose found his tired troops pinned in the Great Glen between an army of Campbells near Fort William and other hostile troops at Inverness. With about 1500 men and little food apart from oatmeal, he marched south-east up Glen Tarff from the shore of Loch Ness, over passes choked by snow and down Glen Roy before inflicting a terrible defeat on Argyll and his Campbells at Inverlochy.

Creag Meagaidh, the mountain which rises on the northern shore of Loch Laggan, is not shapely, but has a corrie of considerable grandeur. The path leads in from Aberarder (boggy but not difficult) to the depths of Corie Ardair, surrounded by cliffs and with a calm lochan in the middle. The whole area is a nature reserve and it is well worth the walk to see.

At Laggan, close by the junction of the A86 and the A889, the minor road heading west is General Wade's old road (1735) over the Corrieyairack pass to the Great Glen. The road peters out into a track fairly rapidly, and makes a good walk.

THE GREAT GLEN

Glen More, also known as Glen Albyn or the Great Glen, is the remarkable geological fault which almost severs Scotland. Running from Loch Linnhe in the south-west to Inverness in the north-east, this ruler-straight declivity is filled by deep lochs, linked by Telford's Caledonian Canal. The glen has long been the most important through-route in the north of Scotland, and inspiring or shameful things have happened in its depths. But it is the supposed presence of a monster in the dark profundities of Loch Ness that draws visitors here. A whole branch of the tourist industry thrives on this legend (or as-yet-unproven fact), which was first voiced by St Columba's biographer.

Looked at dispassionately, the Great Glen is monotonously straight, its hillsides tree-clad and uniform, and its lochs interchangeably similar in the mind's eye. Military strategy, not beauty of setting, lies behind the location of its small towns. Yet the Great Glen has advantages. It is a fine place for watery activity, from sailing to boat trips; the glens off it to the west are beautiful and distinct, and Strath Errick and Strath Nairn behind the hills to the east contain further good landscape.

North from Spean Bridge

The A82 rushes you to Inverness if you are in a hurry. Roads branch into the westward-leading glens, all of which carry you into the isolated mountainous territory lying between Loch Ness and the sea, though forestry blights the scenery in places. What would otherwise be excellent walking country west of **Loch Arkaig** is especially badly affected, and both here and at the eastern end of **Glen Garry** you need to get up above the trees to see the views. The road running along **Loch Quoich** is recommended for its isolation and its views of distant mountains. It eventually brings you to Kinloch Hourn, where you have the satisfaction of being on the edge of nowhere before making the 21-mile return trip.

A shorter expedition involves taking the A87 up to Loch Cluanie and returning down **Glen Moriston**. A viewpoint on the way up allows you a marvellous panorama of Loch Garry and the hills beyond, while Glen Moriston, with its brawling river running beneath wooded banks, is beautiful. A memorial beside the A887 commemorates Roderick Mackenzie, who drew pursuit away from Prince Charles Edward Stuart after Culloden and was shot in mistake for him.

Seven miles north of Invergarry at the foot of Loch Ness is **Fort Augustus**, built after the rising of 1715 and named after William Augustus, Duke of Cumberland – later to be called 'Butcher' after the Battle of Culloden. What remains of the fort is incorporated into the buildings of the Benedictine Abbey, a foundation set up in 1867 by monks from Ratisbon. Fort Augustus is a sleepy sort of place today.

Just south of Drumnadrochit, the ruins of **Urquhart Castle**

(HS, standard times), the most substantial fortress on Loch Ness, are essential viewing for most passers-by, as much for the drama of the site as for the interest of the castle. The ruin stands on a promontory jutting into the loch, and its walls drop sheer into the water. This stretch of the loch is where numerous sightings of the monster have been made, so the walls are manned by hopeful monster-gazers. For much of the castle's history it figured as a bastion against the western clans, especially Macdonald Lords of the Isles. During the period of the Jacobite troubles, some of the castle was blown up to prevent it from falling into 'rebel' hands. Thereafter, stone robbers and the weather continued the destruction.

Drumnadrochit

If you are not put off by the traffic and the 'monster' tat which fills the place, Drumnadrochit is excellently situated for exploration of Loch Ness, Inverness, and the glens of Cannich and Affric. The main village stands at the head of a sheltered inlet of Loch Ness but scattered houses extend up Glen Urquhart, which rises gently behind, and if you can find somewhere to stay here it is far enough away from the loch shore to be peaceful.

By the main road, the **Loch Ness Monster Exhibition Centre** (open Easter to May, daily 9.30 to 5.30; June 9 to 8; July to early Sept 9 to 9.30; early Sept to mid-Oct 9.30 to 8; mid- to late Oct 9.30 to 5.30; Nov to Easter 10 to 4) is housed in a substantial building. Forget any forebodings for the exhibition is well presented, and almost dispassionate. It is a walk-through audio-visual experience – rooms come to life in turn, with lights and commentary to highlight the photographs, statistics and scientific gadgets used in the hunt for the monster. A lot of money has been spent to this end – a whole fleet of boats making a sonar trawl, for example – but nothing has been proved. While the technology is impressive, it seems even more impressive that all the electronic wizardry of the twentieth century has been unable to penetrate the murky depths of Loch Ness precisely enough to reveal more (or less) than a few ambiguous traces.

In Glen Urquhart, the heap of stones which forms the prehistoric **Corrimony Chambered Cairn** (HS, always open) is surrounded by 11 standing stones. A passage, part of which is still roofed, leads to the central chamber.

Glen Affric, Glen Cannich and Strathfarrar

The road up Glen Urquhart to the modern village of Cannich is the quickest way into the scenery of these lengthy westward-running glens. The return trip down Strath Glass and round by Beauly makes a good outing. This is large-scale landscape: the glens stretch for miles to the west, with high mountains bunched in an untidy tangle around their heads. For the hill-walker, this is an area for long, hard days alone with the deer.

Strathfarrar is the northernmost of the three glens, and is accessible only on foot. It is a long 14-mile plod to Loch Monar at the top. Glen Cannich is more enclosed and not so beautiful as Glen Affric, the road up it winding over hummocks of rough ground and through woods of birch and alder to arrive at the dam behind which toss the waters of Loch Mullardoch. Glen Affric, despite hydro-electric works, has that particular combination of water, hillside and ancient pine forest which is unmatchable on a fine day. The road up is narrow and winding, but there are parking places, often with walks striking off from them into the old pine woods. Dog Fall is a popular spot – it got its name after a shepherd tried to dispose of his old dog here, but was later woken by her pathetic scratching at his door. Remorse overcame him and he allowed her to live out her days in peace. Loch Affric has been left in its natural state, and is a suitably beautiful climax to the drive.

Strath Errick and Strath Nairn

This hidden piece of country lies between the slopes of the hills bordering the eastern edge of Loch Ness and the western edge of the Monadhliath mountains. It is the country of Clan Fraser. The watershed between the two straths is barely noticeable, and the whole area forms a single open upland valley, dotted with craggy outcrops and small lochs. Away from the narrow horizons of the Great Glen, this seems a light and airy region, though the heavy afforestation will spoil much of it when the trees are taller.

Down on the shores of Loch Ness itself runs General Wade's old military road, the B852. It is much quieter than the A82 on the opposite bank, and has picnic spots along the shore. At **Foyers** the waterfall used to be a great draw (a spot praised by Burns), but it is now emasculated by hydro-electric needs, except in spates. It is still worth stopping for, though, as is the narrow gorge at **Inverfarigaig** a little further north.

INVERNESS

All the main routes through the Highlands pass through Inverness sooner or later, making it almost impossible to avoid. For the inhabitants of Sutherland, Caithness and the Northern Isles, Inverness is the great southern metropolis. If you come from anywhere else, you will find it a small, rather ordinary town – a bit of industry here and there, quiet residential estates and a compact centre with unexceptional shops (apart from Melvens, one of the best bookshops north of Edinburgh, and a good example of a covered market). The influx of summer visitors colours the streets, but Inverness can be dull off-season, while on Sundays nothing stirs.

Like Dundee, Inverness has not treated its older buildings with respect, and a number of vile modern buildings intrude into the Victorian architecture. The oldest houses are to be found in **Church Street**, notably Abertarff House, which dates from 1592. The Victorian Gothic cathedral of St Andrew is worth a glance on a wet day, while the modern Eden Court contains a theatre and gallery. In the battlemented nineteenth-century mock castle, **Inverness Museum** (open Mon to Sat 9 to 5; also Sun 2 to 5 July, Aug) has a

THE BATTLE OF CULLODEN

The aura of tragedy which surrounds Culloden is the result of the inevitability of the Jacobite defeat. After its long and dispiriting retreat from Derby, a half-starved, under-strength army, exhausted after an abortive night march on Nairn, faced a body of disciplined troops on ground which its most experienced officer considered utterly unsuitable.

In such circumstances, the charge of the clans was a gamble almost bound to end in failure. For half an hour they had suffered under an artillery bombardment to which they were powerless to reply. The charge, when it came, was an ill-coordinated act of courage, its only chance of success being to break the opposing troops by its ferocity. At Prestonpans and Falkirk, the Hanoverians had broken; at Culloden, sustained by their artillery and by their three ranks of bayonets, they held. At times the clansmen, powerless to reach the redcoats with their broadswords, were reduced to throwing stones.

comprehensive regional collection – the silver is especially worth seeing.

Culloden Battlefield

The ground where the 1745 Jacobite rising was snuffed out is well signposted from all the southern and eastern approaches to Inverness. The National Trust has restored Drumossie Moor to something nearing its state on 16 April 1746. With flags fluttering above the barren ground, and the wind whipping over the heather, the field of Culloden is by far the most evocative of Scotland's battlefields.

The visitor centre (NTS, open Apr to Oct, daily 9 to 6; Feb, Mar, Nov, Dec, daily 10 to 4) is the obvious starting point and has an audio-visual introduction to the battle which is both beautifully scripted and movingly narrated. Thereafter, paths lead over the moor to the headstones which bear the names of all the clans who fought in the battle. Over 1000 of the Jacobite Highlanders fell on this ground, and few of the wounded were spared. The restored cottage of Old Leanach marks the spot where 30 Highlanders were burnt alive.

Culloden is at its best on a day of cold sleet carried on the wind – the conditions under which the battle was fought.

All along the line, the Jacobite front rank was thrown back – the Macdonalds on the left, Clan Chattan, Frasers, Camerons and Stewarts of Appin on the right. Hanoverian casualties were given as 50 dead; well over 1000 of the Highland army died and Prince Charles Edward was led from the field to begin months of fugitive existence before he made his final escape to France.

The aftermath was savage – most of the wounded were killed where they lay, and the prisoners, being 'rebels', were ill-treated. But the real savagery was to come. The victorious Duke of Cumberland, recognising, perhaps rightly, that this military defeat was not enough to put an end to Jacobite dreams, resolved to make an example of the Highlands. Burnings and summary arrests were followed by the banning of Highland dress. For his deeds, it is said that the English named the garden flower Sweet William after him – the Scots equivalent is the weed called Stinking Willie.

Clava Cairns

Three stone chambered cairns stand in a wood not far from Culloden. Although they are open to the skies, their size and the huge number of stones used to build them show what impressive structures they were in the third millennium BC. Standing stones ring them. Oddly enough their setting adds to their air of mystery – if your experience of prehistoric monuments is linked to open barren moorland, try these cairns for a contrast.

Fort George

No enthusiast of military architecture can afford to miss this completely intact example of an eighteenth-century stronghold (HS, standard times). Fort George was started in 1748, with the aim, after Culloden, of ensuring an impregnable base in the Highlands (earlier forts had proved too vulnerable to attack). The result is a network of glacis, ditches, ravelins and bastions on the neck of a small peninsula jutting into the Moray Firth by Ardersier to the east of Inverness. You can test its impregnability by walking round the outside and imagining how you might get in under fire.

Through the gateway, the eighteenth-century barracks with their parade ground in front look much like an upmarket housing estate. There was room for two battalions. Some rooms have been reconstructed to show standards of accommodation in 1780 and 1868. Fort George is now the HQ of the Queen's Own Highlanders, and the regimental museum is filled with some fine displays.

EASTER ROSS

North of Inverness, three firths push inland towards the mountains, enclosing two isolated peninsulas. The countryside at their heads where the Rivers Beauly, Conon and Oykel flow down from the glens is hilly and wooded. It seems a manageable, tame landscape, yet the bulk of Ben Wyvis rising above it is a reminder that you are still in the Highlands.

Oil has wrought changes here, visible in the platform fabrication yards of Nigg. On the whole, the changes are for the better, injecting some much-needed prosperity into the small towns and villages, and leaving few unsightly messes behind.

Beauly

'Quel beau lieu', Mary Queen of Scots is reputed to have said, looking at this small russet town 14 miles west of Inverness. Beauly has a couple of hotels, an old-fashioned woollen and tweed shop (Campbell and Company) with a country-wide reputation, and a pleasant, wide main street. It also has the ruins of a beautiful thirteenth-century priory, with notable windows.

The Black Isle

This used to be secret country before the Beauly Firth was bridged and the A9 driven through its centre. Few people stop to explore, even now. Much of the Black Isle is farmland or forest, though some patches of oakwood and bog remain. It is on the coast that the most interesting places are found.

Drive east on the A832 and look out for a flash of garish colour by the side of the road. This is a clootie well, a spring whose waters have healing or magic properties. Those who drink hang pieces of bright cloth (or the occasional plastic bag) from nearby branches to mark their visit. There is another such well near the village of **Avoch**, a pronunciation trap (the 'a' and 'v' are silent) with a pretty harbour.

The A832 brings you to **Fortrose**, where copper beeches and yew trees stand by the fragmentary remains of the cathedral, and substantial Victorian villas with ball and spike finials on their gables line the quiet streets. The cathedral (HS, always open) dates from the thirteenth century but now only the south aisle and the sacristy remain. Still, the warm, buttery sandstone and the simplicity of the early Gothic vaulting are exceptional.

On the eastern side of the small headland of Chanonry Point (the result of a glacial moraine) lies the little resort of **Rosemarkie**. The beach is not appealing. Go instead to the museum at **Groam House** (open May to Sept, Mon to Sat 11 to 5, Sun 2.30 to 4.30; Oct to Apr, open weekends only), which has a fine Pictish symbol stone as well as videos about the Black Isle and the Brahan Seer. This famous local came to a sticky end in a barrel of boiling tar on Chanonry Point for being rather too frank with the Countess of Seaforth about what her absent husband was up to. Chanonry Point is also the place to try to see the Moray Firth's school of bottle-nosed dolphins.

Cromarty

The ancient royal burgh at the tip of the Black Isle is still not much larger than a village, but contains some of the most beautiful late eighteenth-century buildings in Scotland. Cromarty's prosperity was due to the imagination of George Ross, who bought the town in 1772 and supplemented the Scandinavian trade with a variety of small industries. Substantial red sandstone houses line some of the streets and old fishermen's cottages cling to the shore. There is a quiet little church with three separate lofts, and the restored buildings of an old rope works. The new **Cromarty Courthouse** (open Easter to Oct, daily 10 to 6; Oct to Easter, 12 to 4) explains the history of the town.

Two men from Cromarty achieved renown in very different fields. One, Sir Thomas Urquhart, is remembered for his translation of Rabelais, for his eccentricity, and for the fact that he died laughing when he heard of Charles II's restoration in 1660. The other, Hugh Miller, early nineteenth-century stonemason, naturalist, philosopher and writer, is little read now, but his researches into the local old red sandstone still bring geologists to trace his footsteps. His house is now open as a simple museum (NTS, open Easter, May to late Sept, daily 10 to 1, 2 to 5.30).

Beyond the town, a narrow lane leads up to the top of **South Sutor**, one of the twin precipitous headlands guarding the narrow entrance to the Cromarty Firth. From the rubble of old military emplacements here, the view stuns. Northward, white-streaked cliffs and a green sea; southward, on a clear day, the whole of the Moray coast stretching into the haze.

Dingwall and around

The Munros hold much of the land round here, on condition that they furnish a snowball in mid-summer to their overlord if required to do so, some poor retainer being despatched to the northern corries of Ben Wyvis for the purpose. Dingwall itself is a small town, by-passed by the traffic, and a place to stock up on necessities if you are venturing into the wild. The **museum** (open May to Sept, Mon to Sat 10 to 5) contains a good selection of local relics, including a monstrous clock mechanism.

Not far west, on the A834, **Strathpeffer** is said to be Scotland's answer to Bavarian mountain resorts. Its outcrop of Germanic-looking hotels and villas denotes that the place was once a spa, with a branch railway line from Dingwall (the restored station is now a craft centre). In keeping with the spa atmosphere there are plenty of undemanding walks in the surrounding countryside. One such leads to the **Eagle Stone**, a Pictish monument on the outskirts of the town. It is said (by the Brahan Seer) that ships will moor to it if it falls three times. It has fallen twice so far.

Garve, on the A832, is barely more than a hamlet by a road junction, but there are plenty of parking places and picnic spots in the woods nearby, while the **Falls of Rogie** are popular, largely because they are close to the road. The railway running through Garve towards Kyle of Lochalsh (the subject of many a closure scare) is lauded as one of the most attractive lines in Britain. So it is, in its last few miles by Loch Carron, but the long run down Strath Bran and Glen Carron cannot hold a candle to the line from Fort William to Mallaig.

The Tain Peninsula

More people have heard of Glenmorangie than of Tain, for that whisky is certainly the best-known product of the area. Flat and unlovely in parts, and with the industry of Invergordon and Nigg on its southern shore, the hammer-headed peninsula sandwiched between Dornoch and Cromarty firths is not immediately appealing but retains the capacity to surprise, occasionally.

One such surprise is the **Black Rock Gorge**. With its inauspicious beginning near the caravan site at the back of Evanton, this takes a bit of finding among the trees which fringe it (try the third track to your left). The cleft is so deep and narrow that it is almost impossible to see the bottom without taking foolish risks, and there are no paths or barriers. Mosses and ferns dangle in the chasm like a hairy fringe, and the River Glass hisses in the depths.

Take the B9175 towards the North Sutor headland and explore the minor road behind Nigg for its views. At Nigg, see the fine Pictish cross-slab in the church. A further Pictish stone stands near the roadside by the coastal village of Shandwick, covered with hunting and battle scenes.

Near the tip of Tarbat Ness, **Portmahomack** is one of the oldest planned villages in Scotland, dating from the early eighteenth century. It is a tiny seaside resort with a little golf course, a semi-circle of sand, some rocks to climb over and a couple of streets of cottages. On a fine day, it is perfect. The old church here has a slightly oriental-looking dome instead of a spire – it was possibly once used as a lighthouse.

The solid, self-confident sandstone town of **Tain** is a burgh of great antiquity, but of no great beauty. The turreted tolbooth dominating the High Street looks like a product of Victorian baronial, but is early eighteenth-century. Elizabeth de Burgh, wife of Robert the Bruce, fled to St Duthus Chapel for sanctuary in 1307. The Earl of Ross did not give a fig for such niceties and handed her over to Bruce's enemies.

Strathcarron

Not to be confused with the better known Glen Carron to the west, this gentle valley runs down to join the Kyle of Sutherland opposite Bonar Bridge. Roads run on either side of the light, open strath, while fragments of old pine forest remain up towards its head. The combination of river and heathery scenery is very fine.

In the churchyard of **Croik**, where the road ends, people from neighbouring Glencalvie took shelter after being evicted from their homes in May 1845. Scratched on the glass of the church windows are the graffiti which are their only memorial.

SUTHERLAND

North of the Dornoch Firth lies Sutherland, a huge tract of the bleakest wilderness in Scotland. Only a few tour coaches battle their way up the east coast to Dunrobin Castle and John O' Groats. The west coast is a jumble of rock; the straths of the centre are empty of people and the small settlements of the east and north cling to the rough coasts. Sutherland is the province of the angler, the bird-watcher and the forester.

Strath Oykel

Flocks of wading birds feed on the mudflats of the Dornoch Firth, and salmon fishermen line the Kyle of Sutherland above the cheerful village of Bonar Bridge. The River Oykel, which empties into this estuary, has its source by Ben More Assynt close to the west coast, and its valley forms a convenient route to Ullapool.

Drive up the Oykel from Bonar Bridge and turn up **Glen Cassley** to see the Cassley Waterfall, which plunges into a rocky pool surrounded by pine trees and boulders. There will probably be salmon fishermen, up to their chests in waders, to watch for entertainment. Just beneath the falls lies an old graveyard with tombstones under the pines.

As far as Oykel Bridge, the road dips in and out of conifer plantations, and there is not much to be said for it, but as it climbs over the watershed, towards Ledmore, the eastern peak of **Suilven** rears into view. This is far the best way to approach Scotland's most remarkable mountain, for it appears like an unscalable alpine peak over the horizon.

Lairg and Loch Shin

The River Shin pours into the Oykel by the power station at Inveran. Take the B864 from here through Achanay Glen to visit the **Falls of Shin**. These form the best salmon leap in the country, and there is a large car park for visitors and a well-maintained path down through the trees to a platform above the falls. The river plunges in a peat-coloured chute into a black pool, from which the salmon hurl themselves upwards into the force of water. An early evening in summer when there is plenty of water is said to give you the best chance of seeing them – take anti-midge precautions.

Lambs from all over the north are brought to the sales at **Lairg**, a sunny village by the foot of Loch Shin which is also the connecting point between the railway and the network of post buses which wind over Sutherland's isolated roads. For its size, Lairg has a reasonable sprinkling of hotels and guesthouses, a network of gentle walks, and a number of hill lochs containing trout.

The A838 beside the long, narrow **Loch Shin** is monotonous at first, but eventually emerges into bleak and mountainous terrain by Loch Merkland and Loch More, where the broken quartzite on the tops of Foinaven and Arkle is easily mistaken for the shimmer of ice. Beyond, the scenery changes to the fragmented, knobbly country typical of Sutherland's west coast. When the rain is lashing down, this is the sort of landscape where you hope your car was properly serviced; even on fine summer days it seems stark and primeval.

The northern routes from Lairg

From Lairg, the A836 to **Altnaharra** emerges gradually from the spruce forests which suffocate the views for the first few miles. From now on, the forests – always present and always spreading – are merely irritating patches on the great tawny blankets of bog which stretch in all directions, except where the rounded humps of Ben Klibreck heave themselves skywards. Altnaharra is little more than a few cottages, but a renowned centre for anglers. The salmon rivers flowing northwards are famous – getting a day on one of them is nearly impossible – but there is trout fishing in abundance in the isolated lochs or burns.

From Altnaharra, the route that takes you through the most isolated country is the B873 down Loch Naver to Syre and on the B871 to Kinbrace on the River Helmsdale. This skirts patches of the **Flow Country** – that quaking blanket bog, half-water, half-land, which is (or was, before the tree-planting started) an untouched quagmire whose intact community of plants, birds and animals is unique. If your interest in natural history extends to a day up to your knees in peat mire, try striking eastward from Kinbrace over the low tops to the plateau of marsh and *dubh* lochans which runs along the Caithness/Sutherland boundary. Another, unsurpassable, way of seeing the Flow Country is to take the train, for the railway which runs up the Strath of Kildonan loops eastward from Forsinard towards Wick, running over mile after mile of wilderness.

A more mountainous round trip from Altnaharra involves driving down Strath More under the shadow of Ben Hope and returning via Tongue past Lettermore and Loch Loyal. One attraction en route is the well-preserved broch of Dun Dornaig.

The shallow valley of Strath Naver running down to Bettyhill is a less attractive route, but interesting for its relics of the Clearances. At **Rossal**, just before you emerge from the forest at Syre, the remnants of a pre-Clearance village lie in a clearing. Here you can see the layout of a typical settlement, from which the inhabitants were summarily turfed out and told to start making their living at Bettyhill.

The East Coast

Dornoch

Golf is the biggest draw here, but Dornoch is also blessed with an excellent sandy beach. There are a number of golfing hotels fronting the links, as well as one or two in the town itself and plenty of guesthouse accommodation. Dornoch is a handsome old burgh, with a little cruciform cathedral, greenery and flowers. The **cathedral** (open dawn to dusk) was started in

1224 by Gilbert de Moravia, and the bishop's palace (now an hotel) rose alongside. The cathedral was burnt in 1570 during a clan feud and restored (with much butchering) by William Burn in 1835. A better restoration in 1924 has left it a very beautiful church indeed: the thirteenth-century work at the crossing – all in deep red sandstone – is wonderful. Do not miss the gargoyles peering from the eaves.

Dunrobin Castle

(Open Easter, May to mid-Oct, Mon to Sat 10.30 to 4.30, Sun 1 to 4.30; June to Sept 10.30 to 5.30, Sun 1 to 5.30)
As the only stately home north of Inverness regularly open to the public, and as one of the very few sights in Sutherland or Caithness, Dunrobin Castle gets more attention than it really warrants. The castle, to which the 'fairy-tale' epithet is often attached, is in fact a ponderous nineteenth-century version of a French château with Scottish baronial overtones, and something not quite right about the proportions of the Renaissance-style windows. Buried in the depths of Sir Charles Barry's work are the remains of a much older castle, while Sir Robert Lorimer remodelled much of the interior following a fire in 1915.

Dunrobin has passed through hard times since the days when the wealth of the Dukes of Sutherland drove the railway north (the Duke's private station can still be seen). Few traces remain of its period as a school, but the furniture has that aura of having been stored away and not used for years. The best things are the paintings – some fine portraits of diaphanously clad duchesses and some Canalettos. Wander down to the gardens for the best view of the castle, and go to the museum to see the Pictish stones.

Helmsdale and Kildonan

Helmsdale, at the foot of a steep ravine, was a fishing settlement for displaced crofters which boomed during the herring years in the second half of the nineteenth century. A new bridge sweeps you through the town, but it is worth turning off and exploring the old harbour, with buildings going back to the heyday of the herring fleet. Helmsdale also has the **Timespan Heritage Centre** (open Easter to Oct, Mon to Sat 10 to 5, Sun 2 to 5) where, among a well-mounted display of local history (including the Clearances), you will also find the Barbara Cartland room – for the romantic novelist is a regular visitor. If your taste for incongruity needs further sharpening, have a snack in 'La Mirage', a café with a difference.

The River Helmsdale, one of the best and most exclusive salmon rivers in Scotland, runs down the **Strath of Kildonan**. This is well known for its prehistoric remains, and as the scene of the 'Kildonan gold rush', when a whole shanty town sprung up at Baile an or, the town of the gold.

The North coast

The north coast of Scotland, confronting the turbulent waters of the Pentland Firth, is a remote place, and the narrow road skirting it is slow, winding and unfrequented. The steep cliffs are broken here and there by perfect beaches, and by the long fingers of sea – the Kyles of Durness and Tongue, and Loch Eriboll – that reach inland. Those who come

---

THE HIGHLAND CLEARANCES

'... the entire population were then compressed into a space of three thousand acres of the most barren land in the parish, and the remaining one hundred and thirty thousand acres were divided among six sheep farmers.' (Evidence to the Napier Commission, 1883)

There are few corners of Scottish history as emotionally and politically charged as the Clearances. Throughout the nineteenth century, landlords evicted Highland tenants from their homes, replacing the pattern of marginal smallholdings with extensive sheep farms. It was not until 1886, in the face of growing civil disobedience such as the Battle of the Braes on Skye, that the Napier Commission's report resulted in the passing of the Crofting Act. This gave crofters security of tenure and brought the Clearances to an end, but did nothing to restore land already cleared.

The methods of eviction were often harsh, in some cases involving violence, and certainly the burning of croft houses. Some of those evicted from their homes were resettled by the sea to work in the kelp industry, to take up fishing, or to try to wrest a new living from even more marginal land. But many thousands more emigrated. The Clearances were the most significant factor in the depopulation of the Highlands, but not the only one. Not

---

here are rewarded by the summer nights, the wildness of the sea and the dunes, and the relaxed pace of life in the small communities.

Cape Wrath

Getting to the most north-westerly tip of mainland Britain is an adventure. There is no road from the south, and no bridge across the Kyle of Durness. Instead, a ferry shuttles across, connecting with a minibus on the far side (to no particular timetable). When the Kyle is too rough, the operation comes to a halt. Once across the Kyle, the minibus bumps along 10 miles of deserted track – the whole of this area is a naval bombardment range – until the lighthouse at Cape Wrath comes into view. You look at the cliffs to the east and the cliffs to the south, and at the skerries of the Pentland Firth being creamed by the waves. If it rains you take

---

every ruin you see has an eviction behind it.

The left-wing view of the Clearances is to see them as part of a capitalist drive to maximise gain at the expense of the people. Much the best popular expression of this interpretation remains John McGrath's 1973 play *The Cheviot, the Stag and the Black, Black Oil*. The right-wing view sees the Clearances as an unnecessarily harsh but inevitable process, justified at the time by the fashionable theory of political economy (satirised by Dickens in *Hard Times*) and in retrospect by the success of many of the emigrants' descendants. The view today's visitor gets is most likely to be the fashionable 'heritage' approach to the topic, which concentrates clearly on the dispersed communities and their lifestyle, but is apt to simplify the underlying issues.

The first Duke of Sutherland is a key figure in the demonology of the Clearances. Sir Ian Moncrieff (quoted in the guide to Dunrobin Castle) sums him up as a man willing 'to dedicate his life and fortune to making other folk do something they found desperately disagreeable for the sake of what he believed to be their future good'. On the other hand, Rob Donn, the Gaelic poet (quoted by John McGrath in *As an Fhearann*) wrote: 'First Duke of Sutherland, for your deviousness and collusion with the Lowlanders, the depths of hell are what you deserve. I would rather have Judas by my side than you.' The Duke's statue stands on Ben Vraggie; its subscribers include his 'grateful tenants'.

USEFUL DIRECTORY

Main tourist offices
Aviemore and Spey Valley Tourist Board
Grampian Road, Aviemore PH22 1PP
(0479) 810363

Fort William and Lochaber Tourist Board
Cameron Centre, Cameron Square
Fort William PH33 6AJ
(0397) 703781

Inverness, Loch Ness and Nairn Tourist Board
Castle Wynd, Inverness IV2 3BJ
(0463) 234353

Ross and Cromarty Tourist Board
North Kessock, Black Isle IV1 1XB
(0463 73) 505

Sutherland Tourist Board
The Square, Dornoch, Sutherland IV25 3SD
(0862) 810400

Tourist office publications: annual visitor's guides.
Special interest leaflets include Loch Ness Monster Trail
(Inverness), A9 Trail (Ross and Cromarty), Ski Scotland
(Aviemore and Spey Valley).

Local tourist information centres
Aviemore (0479) 810363
Ballachulish (08552) 296 (Apr to Oct)
Bettyhill (06412) 342 (late Mar to Sept)
Carrbridge (0479) 841360 (May to Sept)
Dornoch (0862) 810400
Durness (0971) 511259 (late Mar to Oct)
Fort Augustus (0320) 6367 (Apr to Oct)
Fort William (0397) 703781
Grantown-on-Spey (0479) 872773 (Mar to Oct)
Helmsdale (04312) 640 (Apr to Sept)
Inverness (0463) 234353
Kingussie (0540) 661297 (May to Sept)
Lairg (0549) 2160 (Mar to Sept)
North Kessock (0463) 73505
Ralia (Newtonmore) (0540) 673253 (Mar to Oct)
Spean Bridge (0397) 712576 (Apr to Oct)
Strathpeffer (0997) 421415 (Easter to Nov)

Public transport
Inverness Railway Station (0463) 238924
Fort William Railway Station (0397) 703791
Aviemore Railway Station (0479) 810221
Inverness Airport (0463) 232471
Wick Airport (0955) 2215
Highland Bus and Coach (0463) 237575/233371
Cromarty–Nigg ferry (regular daily summer service,
weekdays only winter, check) (086 285) 324/(0374) 179732
Corran ferry, Loch Linnhe (frequent crossings) (08555) 243
Durness–Cape Wrath ferry (0971) 511376

Aviemore information
Rothiemurchus Estate (farm tours, estate safaris, fishing,
clay pigeon shooting) (0479) 810858
Forestry Commission Centre, Loch Morlich (0479) 861220
Aviemore–Boat of Garten steam railway (0479) 810725
Cairngorm ski information (0479) 861261
Local mountain weather information: East Highlands
(0898) 654668, West Highlands (0898) 654669
Glen More area mountain rescue (0479) 810222
Aviemore Centre (0479) 810624

Recreation
Boat trips on Loch Ness (04562) 395, Loch Ness and
Caledonian Canal (0463) 233999
Nevis Range Aonach Mor information (skiing, gondola
cable cars, walks, mountain bikes) (0397) 705825
Glencoe mountain rescue (08552) 258
Glencoe chairlift (08552) 303

shelter in the old engine room of the lighthouse among
some ancient diesels. And that is it – a far cry from the
tourist trappings of John O' Groats.

Durness

There is a café and gift shop in Durness called 'The Last
Resort', which sums the place up. Hardy caravanners come
here, and others drawn by the magnificent beaches and
sand dunes around Faraid Head; regulars will tell you of
the pleasure of swimming from Balnakeil sands with only
seals for company. A limestone outcrop at Durness turns

the country green, and explains the quality of the local trout lochs. The geology, and much else, is explained in the excellent visitor centre (open June to Sept, Mon to Sat 9.30 to 6, Sun 11.30 to 5.30; Mar, Apr, Oct, Mon to Sat 10 to 5; May 10 to 6), with liberal illustrations by local schoolchildren. **Balnakeil Craft Village** is a group of vile concrete blocks, marked on windy days by colourful kites, where you can buy candles, knitwear and so on. The buildings were once an early warning station; later an enterprising council let them to craftspeople at peppercorn rents.

Smoo Cave

This cavern, east of Durness, is another result of the limestone. A steep path leads down to the entrance, out of which rushes a small burn. The cave's outer chamber is massive, and the drips fall at speed. The roar of a waterfall comes from an inner chamber, which you penetrate on a neat wooden bridge, deafened by noise and blinded by spray where the burn plunges 70 feet from the sinkhole above. If there is not too much water, a rubber inflatable will take you into a further chamber. An unusual form of graffiti is the rule here: visitors leave their messages picked out in stones on the slope in front of the cave.

Loch Eriboll to Bettyhill

Loch Eriboll is a very beautiful sea loch, which you have plenty of time to admire as the road winds round it. It was here that the Norse ships gathered before sailing south to their defeat at Largs in 1263 and here, in 1945, that the remnants of the German U-boat fleet surfaced to surrender.

As you come over the rise beyond Loch Eriboll, the multi-peaked Ben Loyal lies before you, and will dominate the view henceforth.

A causeway crosses the **Kyle of Tongue**, which is pleasant when the tide is in, but very muddy when it is out. Just before you cross it, a road northwards takes you to the small township of Melness. This area of indented coastline, with a little pier, offshore rocky islets and rumours of Jacobite gold, may tempt you into staying. Tongue itself, a semi-rural town with a ruined castle rising above it, is a good alternative.

The settlement of **Bettyhill**, 12 miles east, was established for evicted crofters at the time of the Clearances, and was named after the first Duchess of Sutherland. It is windblown, but there is beautiful seashore nearby. Part of Torrisdale Bay is a nature reserve, especially good for botanists, while Farr Bay to the east has a lovely beach. The **Strathnaver Museum** (open Easter to Sept, Mon to Sat 10 to 1, 2 to 5) is in the old church at Bettyhill, and is the place to absorb the history of the locality. The sections on the Clearances and on post–Clearance life are particularly strong.

WHERE TO STAY

CROMARTY

Royal Hotel £
Marine Terrace, Cromarty, Ross-shire IV11 8YN   Tel (0381) 600217

At the front of this friendly, comfortable seashore hotel a glass verandah looks straight over the Cromarty Firth. Most of the spacious bedrooms share the view; all are well maintained. There is a restaurant, but the bar meals are ample. Good value.

Open: all year **Rooms**: 10 **Credit/charge cards**: Access, Amex, Visa

DRUMNADROCHIT

Polmaily House £–££
Drumnadrochit, Inverness-shire IV3 6XT   Tel (0456) 450343

This comfortable, unelaborate country hotel near Loch Ness is well away from the hubbub of Drumnadrochit. The white-painted house is filled with books, rugs and old furniture. There is a games, books and TV room, pretty bedrooms (most with bathroom), and the food is excellent.

Open: all year, exc Nov to Easter **Rooms**: 11
Facilities: tennis, croquet, unheated pool
Credit/charge cards: Access, Visa

FORT WILLIAM

The Factor's House   ££
Torlundy, Fort William
Inverness-shire PH33 6SN   *Tel (0397) 705767*

If Inverlochy Castle (below) is beyond your purse, try this hotel, run by the son of Inverlochy's owners. A modern-looking building at the foot of one of the avenues which lead to Inverlochy, this is a small, unpretentious place with a friendly atmosphere.

Open: mid-Mar to mid-Nov **Rooms**: 7
Credit/charge cards: Access, Visa

Inverlochy Castle   £££
Torlundy, Fort William
Inverness-shire PH33 6SN   *Tel (0397) 702177*

One of Scotland's premier hotels, which successfully manages to recreate a world of elegant country luxury. Carefully chosen period pieces furnish the hall, lounge and billiard room, and the comfortable drawing-room overlooks the loch. Luxurious bedrooms have superb bathrooms. The grounds are extensive, and the food makes the most of local fish and game.

Open: Mar to end Nov **Rooms**: 17 **Facilities**: billiards, fishing, tennis **Credit/charge cards**: Access, Amex, Visa

---

GARVE

Inchbae Lodge   £
By Garve, Ross-shire IV23 2PH   *Tel (09975) 269*

An isolated Victorian hunting lodge, six miles west of Garve on the A835 Inverness to Ullapool road. Locals drop in at the cosy little bar for a drink and a natter, and the bedrooms are light with pine furniture. There are also chalet rooms, used only in summer, and good for people with dogs.

Open: all year, exc Xmas **Rooms**: 12 **Facilities**: fishing, stalking, clay pigeon shooting **Credit/charge cards**: none accepted

---

INVERNESS

Dunain Park   £££
Nr Inverness, Inverness-shire IV3 6JN   *Tel (0463) 230512*

A comfortable hotel near Inverness with friendly staff and a warm welcome. Two large sitting-rooms have views across the hills, and furnishings are a mixture of the new and the old. There are plenty of books in the light bedrooms, and the food is good.

Open: all year **Rooms**: 12 plus 2 cottages **Facilities**: sauna, heated indoor swimming-pool **Credit/charge cards**: Access, Amex, Diners, Visa

LAIRG

Achany House	££
By Lairg, Sutherland IV27 4EE	*Tel (0549) 2172/2433*

This towered mansion has been restored to its glory and turned into an exceptional guesthouse. Bedrooms are spacious and beautiful, dinners are five-course affairs, and there is a genuine unforced house-party atmosphere. Good value. Check opening times in 1994, for they may be restricted.

Open: Apr to early Nov **Rooms**: 3
Credit/charge cards: Access, Amex, Visa

Sutherland Arms Hotel	££
Lairg, Sutherland IV27 4AT	*Tel (0549) 2291*

A simple, traditional fishing hotel, and a lively centre for the locals. The hotel gets the essentials right, with cosy lounges, reasonable food, and bedrooms which have everything you need.

Open: Apr to end Oct **Rooms**: 26
Credit/charge cards: Access, Amex, Visa

NEWTONMORE

Ard-na-Coille	££
Kingussie Road, Newtonmore	
Inverness-shire PH20 1AY	*Tel (0540) 673214*

This good-value, fairly plain hotel is well-placed for exploring the Spey Valley. The bedrooms, many of which have wonderful views towards the Cairngorms, are bright, modern and comfortable. Downstairs, the dining-room is rather stark but the food is good, and there is a comfortable sitting-room.

Open: all year, exc mid-Nov to late Dec **Rooms**: 7
Credit/charge cards: Access, Visa

WHERE TO EAT

FORT WILLIAM

Crannog ★
Town Pier, Fort William PH33 7NG   *Tel (0397) 705589*

This restaurant at the end of the pier overlooking Loch Linnhe serves huge platefuls of langoustines with garlic butter and superb bouillabaisse packed with good things. The owners cure salmon, eels, mussels and Cheddar cheese in their own smokehouse.

Open: daily 12 to 2.30, 6 to 10 **Credit/charge cards**: Access, Visa

HELMSDALE

La Mirage ★
7–9 Dunrobin Street, Helmsdale KW8 6JA   *Tel (043 12) 615*

An eccentric Romantic oasis in this fishing port, with white garden furniture and fake greenery under a slowly revolving fan. Food includes many deep-fried dishes, home-baked scones and shortbreads; there is also a high tea menu on Sundays.

Open: daily 12 to 8.45; 12 to 7 Dec to Easter
Credit/charge cards: none accepted

INVERMORISTON

Glenmoriston Arms ★
Invermoriston IV3 6YA   *Tel (0320) 51206*

After failing to see the Loch Ness Monster, this is the place to go for malt whisky sampling before tackling some toothsome bar snacks: haggis, poached wild salmon, venison in red wine or steak pie with chips or baked potato. The restaurant serves more expensive meals.

Open: daily 12 to 2, 6.30 to 8.30
Credit/charge cards: Access, Visa

INVERNESS

Nico's Bistro ★
Glen Mhor Hotel
9–12 Ness Bank Road, Inverness IV2 4SG   *Tel (0463) 234308*

This is a bistro within a traditional hotel on the river bank beneath the castle. The restaurant has river views and serves a Taste of Scotland menu concentrating on local fish, shellfish and game. The bar serves authentic Highland dishes, plus grills and pasta.

Open: daily 12 to 2.15, 5 to 9.30 **Credit/charge cards**: Access, Amex, Diners, Visa

MUIR OF ORD

Dower House
Muir of Ord IV6 7XN   *Tel (0463) 870090*

An eighteenth-century dower house hotel whose food is widely praised for its presentation. The menu includes turbot in sorrel sauce, langoustines or venison in a juniper sauce, followed by sticky toffee pudding. The wine list has been given an award by the 1994 *Good Food Guide*.

Open: daily 7.30 for 8 (one sitting); closed 2 weeks Mar, 3rd week Oct, Xmas Day **Credit/charge cards**: Access, Visa

RHICONICH

Old School Restaurant   ★
Inshegra, Rhiconich IV27 4RH   *Tel (0971) 521383*

A former Victorian schoolhouse fills a culinary gap in this far-flung corner of the mainland. The homely food includes locally caught fish, roasts and casseroles. There is a separate vegetarian menu and delicious bread and butter pudding.

Open: daily 12 to 2, 6 to 8; closed Xmas
Credit/charge cards: Access, Visa

THE
NORTH-WEST

- The best that Scotland has to offer in mountains and sea lochs
- Skye and the Small Isles
- Inverewe Gardens

Suilven

IN a spell of clear, warm weather, the beauty of Scotland's north-western coastline is unrivalled. The interlacing of mountains, islands and sea becomes a study in blues and greens, picked out in a pure, northern light. Geological upheavals have left the coast broken by sea lochs from Mull to Kinlochbervie, and have created mountains unlike any others in Scotland. From the map, it might seem laborious or monotonous country for touring, but this is not so: the complexities of the geology have left a landscape where vegetation and rocks change radically between one area and the next, from oak woods where mosses and lichens proliferate, to the bare gneiss desert of Sutherland, where bog myrtle, coarse grass and bell heather are all that grow. The shapely peaks of the Five Sisters of Kintail and the humped, isolated masses of Suilven or Cul Mór are mountains from different geological eras, utterly distinct. Even the sea lochs have individual characters, from the gloomy waters of Loch Hourn to the sunny openness of Loch Torridon. Many are dotted with the rafts of salmon farms, which slightly spoil their appearance, but are of vital importance to the local economy.

For many people, the charm of the north-west lies in the remote places where single-track roads wind round stony outcrops to end in tiny crofting townships on rocky shores or in the wilderness altogether untouched by the car, where you must still carry all that you need to survive on your back. It is in the north-west that you are most aware of how thinly populated the Highlands now are. With the exception of Ullapool there are no towns, and even the larger villages seldom run to more than a few rows of houses and a simple shop or two.

Then there is Skye. This is the most popular of all the Scottish islands, sold as heavily for its romantic connections with Flora Macdonald and Bonnie Prince Charlie as for its scenery of mountain and sea. The romance is overdone but the scenery is hard to beat, for the serrated peaks of the Cuillins, black and bare against a blue sky, are unforgettable. To experience Scotland at its best, you should travel on a steam train from Fort William to Mallaig, and then cross the Sound of Sleat to Armadale, with the mountains of Knoydart blue on one side and the outlines of Eigg and Rum rising from the sea on the other.

The weather is not always good, for the mountains on this coast attract the heaviest rainfall in the British Isles. When the clouds close in and the midges come out, the whole area descends into a kind of grey misery in which even the most

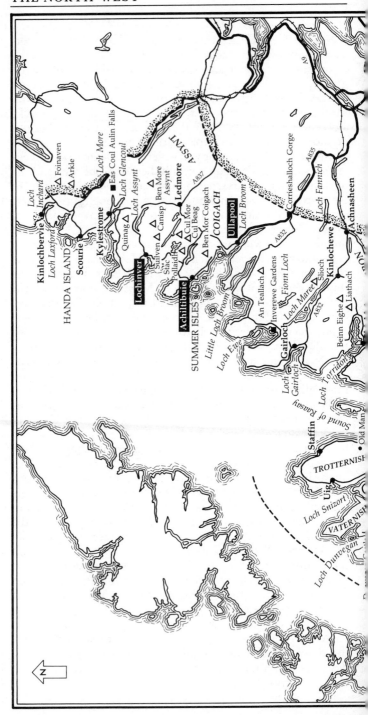

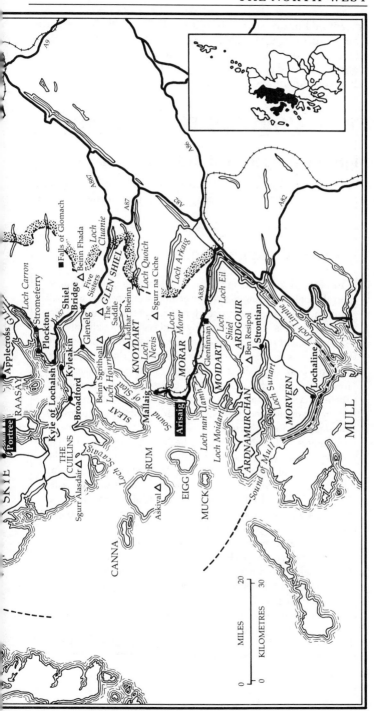

determined optimists can find it hard to keep their spirits up. Then you need to be able to scrap your plans for outdoor expeditions and turn to books or indoor games instead. When planning a holiday up here, it is vital to think how you will stay happy if the weather turns against you.

FROM MORVERN TO KNOYDART

Morvern, Ardgour and Ardnamurchan

The barrier of Loch Linnhe leaves the districts of Morvern, Ardgour and Ardnamurchan isolated. Few visitors come;

Practical suggestions

The best way to explore the north-west is to take a long, leisurely tour through it, leaving time for expeditions to Skye or the Small Isles, and being prepared to stop for a night or two in any area that you like. This is also a particularly good region for self-catering – your chances of having good scenery beyond the windows are high, there is masses of space for children to roam in and few main roads to worry about. If you want to stay put in a particular area there is much to be said for choosing Skye, Kintail, the Torridon area, Ullapool or Achiltibuie, all of which are within easy reach of outstanding scenery and are relatively well provided with facilities for visitors.

Climbers will probably make a beeline for the Black Cuillin on Skye, while experienced hill-walkers are embarrassed by the choice here, and merely have to decide whether the mountains of Kintail, of Torridon or of Sutherland are most to their taste. The inexperienced hill-walker is better off elsewhere, for most of the mountains are precipitous, but there are plenty of tough, low-level walks as compensation.

This is great country for the angler who is happy to pursue wild 'brownies' in remote lochs. Sea-trout fishing is often available too, though opportunities to catch salmon are limited. There is plenty of sea-fishing, with expeditions easily arranged from most of the harbours.

If you are interested in natural history, the nature reserve at Beinn Eighe should be your starting point. Bird-watchers make for Handa Island in the breeding season. Geologists are drawn those who do mostly travel to Lochaline for the ferry to Mull through inland scenery desolate except where patches of scrub oak and birch woodland add splashes of colour. All the beauty is to be found on the coasts. On the eastern side you look across to the hump of Ben Nevis with the blue spikes of the Glencoe hills rising behind, while to the west there are wave-lashed rocks and a string of the white sandy beaches for which the coast is renowned.

Morvern is bounded by Loch Sunart to the north and the Sound of Mull to the South. The prettiest road here is the B8043, which leads you down a rocky stretch of coast to sudden greenery round Camasnacroise. **Lochaline** is the only village of any size, with some pleasant greenery round it and

---

to the Moine Thrust. Perhaps the most interesting area of this convulsive pressure zone is Assynt, north of Ullapool.

Island-lovers may be disappointed in Skye, which has none of the remoteness they may seek. But isolation is possible on Eigg, Muck, Rum, Canna and Raasay. Mallaig is the crossroads for ferry traffic, and a particularly useful place for those relying on public transport.

Good bases

• **Portree** Skye's 'capital' is a neat little town built around its sheltered harbour. It can get busy with visitors, but never quite loses its peacefulness. Well located for touring Skye, it has plenty of accommodation and is very much the centre of the island's life.

• **Ullapool** This friendly fishing town was planned in the eighteenth century and has worn well. Boat trips and fishing expeditions are popular and there is plenty of accommodation.

• **Achiltibuie** This straggling township is blessed with superb views, a nearby sandy beach, some fishing, and easy access to the Sutherland mountains. It is a slow drive to or from it and there are few facilities, so it is especially suited to stay-put self-catering holidays.

• **Lochinver** The village itself is rather ordinary, but the surrounding country is splendid, with sandy beaches to the north and mountains to the east.

• **Arisaig** Good beaches and a variety of boat trips make this small village worth considering.

two ancient castles at Ardtornish Point and Kinlochaline, the former once belonging to the Lord of the Isles, and the latter (a MacInnes stronghold) in a good state of preservation.

Ardtornish gave its name to the unlikely-sounding Treaty of Ardtornish-Westminster (1461). This was a plot to divide Scotland between the Lord of the Isles and the exiled Earl of Douglas, under the overlordship of Edward IV of England – a fairly typical example of the sort of conspiracy faced by the medieval Stewarts.

Ardgour is more rugged than Morvern, its fastnesses penetrated by three long glens. It is bounded by Loch Shiel, Loch Linnhe and Loch Sunart. **Strontian** is the main settlement, a tiny village which gave its name to the element strontium, which was isolated from ore found here. The old mines behind the village are sited above a vein of mineral-rich rock running down from Ben Resipol. This beautifully isolated peak dominates the western fringe of Ardgour, and the views of the Hebrides from its top are wonderful. Moss and lichen flourish in Ariundle Wood in Strontian Glen, where the humidity and the purity of the air make for a riot of unlikely growths.

Ardnamurchan is a low, bare peninsula of blue-white skies, ochre ground and the vestigial remains of volcanoes, with the westernmost point of mainland Britain at its end. It is blessed with some beautiful beaches but is otherwise an exposed and windswept place, wonderful if you like wind on your face, but not everyone's cup of tea.

The drive along the shore of Loch Sunart beyond Salen, on a typical West Highland road pinned between hill and seashore, shows this peaceful loch at its best, rippled by flotillas of duck. A short way beyond Glen Beg, a walk will take you to a pillar of great age, carved with a cross and a dog, thought to be in memory of St Ciarin and possibly dedicated by St Columba.

Mingary Castle, a thirteenth-century stronghold that is more impressive from a distance than close to, rises out of the sea near Kilchoan. In 1588, a Spanish galleon from the Armada was wrecked on Mull, and its crew was enlisted by Maclean of Duart for an attack on Mingary. Even with this help he did not succeed in taking it. A car ferry runs between Kilchoan and Tobermory on Mull, making a very pleasant day trip if the sea is calm.

Sanna Bay is the most renowned of Ardnamurchan's beaches (so not the most deserted). Further pretty coves lie along the northern coast, the grassy areas round the shore a feast of clover, buttercup and thyme.

Moidart

Moidart is almost cut off from its neighbours by the great trench of Loch Shiel, best seen from the monument at Glenfinnan. Those intent on following Charles Edward Stuart's footsteps should go to Dalilea at the southern end. From here he was rowed up to Glenfinnan to meet the gathering clansmen.

Loch Moidart, cutting inland from the sea, is island-studded, heavily wooded and may have seals lying on its skerries. It is a picture of loveliness at high tide in fine weather, and desolate at low tide in the rain. The best way to see it is to branch left beyond Acharacle to the little township of Cul Doirlinn. On a small island (accessible except at very high tide) are the ruins of **Castle Tioram**. This, the impregnable stronghold of Macdonald of Clanranald, survived for four centuries until it was burnt by the fourteenth chief, as he set off for the 1715 uprising, to prevent his Campbell enemies from occupying it.

Glenfinnan

The monument at the head of Loch Shiel commemorates the raising of Prince Charles Edward Stuart's standard on 19 August 1745. The monument, which looks like a lighthouse from a distance, is cared for by the National Trust for Scotland, and in the visitor centre (NTS, open Apr to late May, early Sept to mid-Oct, Mon to Sat 10 to 1, 2 to 5, Sun 10.30 to 1; late May to early Sept, Mon to Sat 9.30 to 6, Sun 10.30 to 6) there is a first-class explanation of the complex events leading to the '45, including a clear chart of Stewart genealogy which makes it plain why the 'Old Pretender' was the legitimate claimant to the throne of Britain. Once you have grasped the background, climb the tower for the view.

Loch nan Uamh

This sea loch on the way to Arisaig is where the French ship *Du Teillay* landed Prince Charles Edward and his seven companions on 25 July 1745 to start their attempt to raise the Jacobite clans. On the 20 September 1746, the fugitive prince, his army shattered and with a price of £30,000 on his head, embarked from this same loch on another French ship. Diligence will lead you to the beach where he landed (by the Glen Borrodale burn) and to the cairn which marks the spot where he re-embarked.

Arisaig

A small cluttered harbour and a small village at the head of Loch nan Ceall, a knobbly peninsula to the south and a lather of reefs and skerries offshore make up this ill-defined district. The village of Arisaig itself has a number of places to stay, and there are further guesthouses in nearby crofting townships. The area makes a good base for two reasons: the lovely (though exposed) silver sand beaches to the north and the variety of boat trips, especially to the Small Isles, which run from the harbour here and from Mallaig to the north.

Many of the beaches near Arisaig have caravan sites beside them, but there is no lack of space. The best views are seaward, where the Cuillins of Skye and Rum puncture sunsets with jagged outlines. The bay by the township of Back of Keppoch is particularly well situated for this view. By walking a short distance away from the beaches closest to the road, you should find peace and quiet. **Loch Morar** is a geological freak, for it is far deeper than the sea which lies a quarter of a mile distant, a tribute to the erosive power of ice channelled between mountains. The Loch is said to have a monster whose appearance foretells the death of a Macdonald of Clanranald. The western end of the loch is studded with wooded islands. The scenery gets bleaker if you walk eastward along its northern shore towards Tarbet, on the southern shore of Loch Nevis (roughish going). Careful study of the timetable may enable you to catch the thrice-weekly mail ferry from Tarbet to Mallaig.

Mallaig

This is a utilitarian ferry and fishing port, with little charm as a place to stay in but plenty as a place to visit. In summer, Mallaig is crowded with cars waiting for ferries, passengers from steam excursions on the railway, fish lorries, and tourists who have simply arrived at the end of the road and are wondering what to do next.

On a fine day, wandering around Mallaig's quay watching the cosmopolitan traffic or perhaps trying to pick up a bucketful of prawns cheaply from one of the small fishing boats is a pleasant way of passing an hour or two. On a wet day, Mallaig is dismal, and there are barely enough pubs and cafés to contain the crowds seeking shelter. Raucous seagulls seem to mock their discomfort.

Mallaig is a natural junction for island-hoppers, hikers

and those using public transport. Motorists wishing to go further north must cross to Skye, or return all the way to Fort William. Foot passengers, juggling the complexities of crossings from Mallaig and Arisaig, can reach Eigg, Rum, Muck and Canna, Skye or Kyle of Lochalsh. Those bent on getting into the wilds of Knoydart without having to trek over the mountains can catch the thrice-weekly mail ferry to Inverie. It gives you a little time ashore without having to rough it overnight. Both Mallaig and Arisaig have boats available for charter, allowing you either to supplement the official timetables, cruise the coasts or go fishing.

Knoydart

The mass of rugged country lying between Loch Nevis and Loch Hourn was once home to over 1000 people. Now its population is minuscule. Few visitors penetrate through the 'rough bounds' of the mass of craggy peaks which fringe the heads of the lochs. To get into Knoydart you must abandon wheeled transport and be self-sufficient, for apart from a small hostel at the tiny settlement of Inverie, the only accommodation is mountain bothies. For hill-walkers, the ridges of Ladhar Bheinn make excellent walking, with marvellous seaward views to the Small Isles and Skye when the rain holds off.

KINTAIL AND GLENELG

Glen Shiel

The great trench running westward from Loch Cluanie is the smoothest and fastest route west from the Great Glen to Skye, and thunders with tour coaches bound for the Kyle of Lochalsh ferry. The glen is hemmed in on either side by high ridges and peaks, and the modern road plunges between them towards the glitter of Loch Duich at the foot. The mountains themselves are better seen from further away, but their steep, grass-clad slopes, silvered with rocky outcrops and spouting rivulets after rain, are enough to make the hill-walker itch to pull on boots.

Glen Shiel was the scene of the culminating battle of one of the lesser Jacobite uprisings – that of 1719. It was little more than a nuisance raid, mounted by a force of Spaniards in alliance with the local Mackenzies. The Jacobites' base at Eilean Donan Castle was bombarded by English frigates, and the Spaniards and the Mackenzies were rapidly defeated by a force from Inverness.

At the foot of Glen Shiel, the river widens into a small loch, and here the tiny village of **Shiel Bridge** acts as a base for campers and caravanners, sells chocolate and gives out information to visitors stretching their legs before the drive down Loch Duich.

Glenelg

The steep zigzag pass of **Mam Ratachan** from Shiel Bridge is the course of the old military road to the Hanoverian barracks at Glenelg. It was also the drove road for the cattle crossing from Skye by the Kyle Rhea narrows. Once spectacular, the road is now blighted by forestry but the viewpoint near the summit is still first-class. You look back up Glen Shiel with the peaks of the **Five Sisters of Kintail** rising on the northern side in sequence. Owned by the National Trust for Scotland, these mountains are marvellous for hill-walkers, being easily reached from all sides and allowing expeditions of varying length and complexity.

Beyond the pass, the road drops to **Glen More**, a sheltered valley studded with small farms. At its foot, you turn right to reach the Kyle Rhea ferry to Skye. This summer crossing is worth knowing about to avoid long queues at Kyle of Lochalsh, but telephone (059 981 302) to make sure it is operating, or ask at Shiel Bridge.

The houses of Glenelg stand close to Bernera Barracks, a utilitarian ruin. A short distance south, **Gleann Beag** hides two of the best-preserved brochs on the mainland – **Dun Telve** standing on flat ground on the right of the road, and **Dun Troddan**, rather more fragmentary, on a hillside a little further up the glen. The walls of the former rise to 33 feet, and the double skin of the wall and the series of galleries passing between the two skins are clearly visible. If you have been disappointed in making the trek to brochs which turn out to be little more than rubble, these two come as a revelation.

The house Gavin Maxwell wrote about as 'Camusfearna' was at **Sandaig**, on the coast a mile or two south of Glenelg village. Many of those who have read *Ring of Bright Water* and its sequels attempt to make their way here, only to be frustrated by the dense conifer plantations which line the road and make the place difficult to get to. If you do persist through the trees down to the shore, you will find a bay of the haunting loveliness that Maxwell describes. However, it is a melancholy place – nothing remains of the house but rubble.

By continuing south to the end of the road you penetrate the fastness of **Loch Hourn**, a brooding, shadowy sea loch, at its best when silvered by the evening sun. Behind the pretty lochside village of Arnisdale, the scree slopes of Beinn Sgritheall rise into the mists that usually crown its top.

Loch Duich

The most peaceful way to watch this loch is to take the road along the southern shore. It is a dead end, but if you explore along it you are rewarded by the remains of a broch, hidden among the trees beyond Totaig. From Totaig, the view out over the meeting of three lochs (Duich, Long and Alsh) is splendid – Eilean Donan Castle lies almost opposite, and tide races churn the waters into swirls of colour.

BROCHS

Brochs are a type of fortress unique to Scotland. They were tall, circular towers, not unlike modern cooling towers in shape. They had no windows and the walls were double to allow galleries and stairways to run between the inner and outer skins. The interior of the broch was open to the sky, but roofed galleries probably ran round the walls, allowing the inhabitants some shelter.

The remains of about 500 brochs are visible, many of them close to the sea. For many years arguments raged about who built them and what they were used for. The Picts were popular candidates at first, but it now seems certain that brochs are Iron Age constructions, dating from around 100 BC. The skill of the construction can be seen in the better-preserved examples: the inner and outer walls are pinned together by stone cross-slabs, stairways run up towards vanished parapets, and doorways have impressive lintels. The need for such fortresses seems to have disappeared by about AD 200. Thereafter, old brochs often became the centre of a small settlement, perhaps with little houses being built inside. The best-preserved broch of all is to be found at Mousa on Shetland (page 507); those in Glenelg come a close second.

The A87 beyond Shiel Bridge bends round the head of Loch Duich. If you want to walk, turn off to Morvich. The most popular low-level walk from here is to the **Falls of Glomach**, the second highest waterfall in Britain. The start – through conifers – is not attractive, but the views improve as you approach the saddle of Bealach na Sroine. From here it is a quick downhill lope to the falls. Unless you are blessed with a head for heights, you will have to make do with the view of the upper part of the falls as they plunge 500 feet into a narrow ravine.

If you are not hooked on waterfalls, try the path up Gleann Choinneachain to the windswept pass of Bealach an Sgairne, from which you look down on the boggy beginnings of Glen Affric.

Eilean Donan Castle

(Open Easter to Sept, daily 10 to 6)
The subject of countless photographs and paintings, Eilean Donan Castle has been used so extensively to sell Scotland that you are bound to recognise its familiar outline. It is ironic that the building is a total restoration, completed only in 1932, though a very successful one. It is an obligatory stop on the road to Skye, its setting being the main attraction, for only two rooms and an extensive souvenir shop are open to visitors.

The castle's history goes back to the thirteenth century. Its Mackenzie owners entrusted it to the Macraes (a clan who proudly styled themselves 'Mackenzie's shirt of mail'), and it was a Macrae who undertook the restoration two centuries after the castle had been destroyed by Hanoverian bombardment during the 1719 uprising.

Eilean Donan's modern incarnation as the film director's ideal backdrop is actually more interesting than its history. Chat to the custodians on a quiet day and you will hear gossip about who came to advertise what, and how the rain and the midges drove everyone crazy.

LOCH ALSH AND LOCH CARRON

The main focus of activity in **Kyle of Lochalsh** is the ferry pier. Two small ferries shuttle back and forwards to Kyleakin on Skye, usually managing to cope adequately with the queues, though you should be prepared for a bit of a wait until the toll bridge, currently under construction, is opened in the late summer of 1995.

Loch Carron marks a divide in the landscape. North of here the tangles of rhododendron thickets become sparser and the land harsher. The mountains change radically: the jumbled peaks and ridges give way to isolated mountains of red sandstone, often topped with shining quartzite, whose sides drop in precipitous terraces gouged with gullies. The damp, quasi-tropical lushness turns to a starker and less fertile seaboard where outcrops of grey-white gneiss, scraped clean by glaciers, thrust through thin coverings of peat and grass.

Built on the edge of a sheltered bay of Loch Carron, and with spindly palm trees to prove that Scotland is sub-tropical after all, **Plockton** is the kind of village that artists settle down to paint. Here they wear midge-repellent. Plockton is tranquil and beautiful of an evening; during the day its craft shops can get crowded.

East of Plockton a road wide enough for three tour coaches whisks you up the southern shore of the loch, with various viewpoints from which to look over to the tangle of low hills on the far side. If you are continuing north, double round the head of Loch Carron and down to the village of the same name, where there is a nature reserve in a dangerous and spectacular gorge.

From here the road crosses a low neck of land to **Loch Kishorn**, once the scene of oil-platform construction, and with a certain amount of industrial clutter still visible. You then have the choice of heading across moorland to Shieldaig, or of taking the long diversion round the Applecross peninsula.

APPLECROSS AND TORRIDON

The road that runs west from Loch Kishorn into Applecross is the closest thing to an alpine pass in Britain. It wriggles up a corrie between walls of rock and scree to a series of hairpins beneath the col at Bealach na Ba. The black cliffs of Beinn Bhàn and Sgurr a' Chaorachain loom over the approach, suggesting a rugged wilderness beyond the pass, but at the top there is only undulating moor, sloping gently down to the sea.

Applecross was once a monastery, founded in 673 by St Maelrubha, and second only to Iona in importance. It was destroyed by the Norsemen, and virtually nothing remains.

The village has a pub, a telephone box and a few houses. Southward, a lonely cul-de-sac road runs to Toscaig, with coves to explore and clear views to Skye.

Northward, the road was opened only in 1976, too late to save many of the tiny townships along the shore. The landscape of Applecross itself is uninspiring – all the interest lies in the views seaward, where the islands of Raasay and Rona half-hide the hills of Skye behind.

Shieldaig, where the road across Applecross rejoins the main route, is an early nineteenth-century planned village, as lovely as Plockton but less obviously postcard material. Offshore views are blocked by an island which is a sanctuary for a stand of ancient Caledonian pines. Sheep munch grass on Shieldaig's little waterfront.

Eastward from Shieldaig, a modernised road speeds you to the head of Loch Torridon. An older road, now a quiet track, runs beneath it by the water's edge, making a gentle walk with views over the loch and surrounded by venerable trees. Now the scale of the Torridon mountains makes itself felt. Three great mountains tower above **Glen Torridon** – Beinn Alligin, Liathach and Beinn Eighe. Liathach is the queen, its castellated ridge running parallel to the glen 3,400 feet beneath, dwarfing the cottages of Torridon into insignificance. On a grey day, with the clouds hiding the battlements of the ridge, Liathach loses little, for then the layered terraces of stone and grass disappear into the grey swirl, to unguessable heights.

Drop into the **visitor centre** (NTS, May to late Sept, Mon to Sat 10 to 5, Sun 2 to 5) at the head of Loch Torridon to learn the extent and nature of the Torridon estate.

Do not ignore the **deer museum** (NTS, open all year) here either – it was set up by a local man with a lifetime's experience of deer management, and explains, with little sentimentality but much sympathy, the life of the red deer on the Scottish hills. There are also gruesome photographs of what can be done to deer by poachers or careless visitors.

Bordering the Torridon estate to the east lies the **Beinn Eighe National Nature Reserve**. Beinn Eighe does not loom above the road as menacingly as Liathach, but its southern face, streaked with quartzite screes, is forbidding enough to deter thoughts of a casual climb. However, an exceptional low-level walk strikes up the cleft of the Coire Duibh Mhoir burn between Liathach and Beinn Eighe. On reaching the northern side of these mountains, you see them in a different aspect – hollowed by enormous, echoing corries. You can make for Loch Coire na Caime under the highest tops of the Liathach ridge, which is spectacular enough, or you can contour round the flank of Beinn Eighe to Loch Coire Mhic Fhearchair. This corrie is second only to the Toll an Lochan beneath An Teallach (page 443) in drama. Screes rise steeply above the dark lochan, and a sheer triple buttress, split by dark gullies, looms above the far end.

LOCH MAREE AND GAIRLOCH

Loch Maree, with the peak of Slioch reflected in its silver-blue, island-dotted waters, is rivalled for beauty only by Loch Lomond. The A832 runs along the south-western shore; much of the north-eastern shore can be explored on the path leading through Letterewe Forest. North of Slioch lies a tract of remote deer forest, bog and precipitous mountain, empty of human habitation and savage in bad weather.

Just north-west of Kinlochewe village is the **visitor centre** for the Beinn Eighe National Nature Reserve (open May to Sept, daily 10 to 5), a vital port of call if you want to learn about the natural history of the area. Further west, you arrive at the parking place for two nature trails on the lower slopes of Beinn Eighe. The low-level walk leads you through the old pine forest around which the reserve was established. The mountain trail is extremely steep, and quite beautifully crafted, with a minimum disturbance of the land. If you do not want to penetrate the remote hinterland of the reserve, these walks are an excellent alternative. Useful 'breathing points' are spaced along the trail, each with a feature of natural history picked out for you to contemplate.

Boats containing intent fishermen drift on Loch Maree, for it is a renowned sea-trout loch. Ask at the Loch Maree Hotel about fishing possibilities.

At the western end of the loch, the road runs down to the River Kerry to the coast. Turn left on the minor road to Redpoint through a secluded landscape of water, birch and oak. **Badachro** is a tiny village by the shore, its pub ideally situated on the sea's edge, with views of rocky islets in the bay. Continue south to get to three beaches of reddish sand (one accessible only on foot). They are all fairly exposed, so do not expect to do much basking in the sun.

After miles of sparsely populated country, the holiday resort of **Gairloch** comes as a surprise. The Mackenzies of Gairloch resisted the fashionable nineteenth-century trend for turfing people off the land, and this has left the coasts of Gair Loch sprinkled with cottages. Gairloch is popular because of the sandy beaches in the area, and there are numerous guesthouses and caravan sites. Stop here to see the **Gairloch Heritage Museum** (open Easter to Sept, Mon to Sat 10 to 5) which has a splendid collection of objects salvaged from houses and cottages in the area, including an illicit still. It gives an excellent impression of West Highland life.

LOCH EWE TO LOCH BROOM

Inverewe Gardens

(NTS, gardens open all year, daily 9.30 to sunset; visitor centre and shop open Apr to late May, early Sept to mid-Oct, Mon to Sat 10 to 5, Sun 10.30 to 5, late May to early Sept, Mon to Sat 9.30 to 5.30, Sun 10.30 to 5).

That a sub-tropical garden exists on the same latitude as Siberia is thanks to the mild climate created by the North Atlantic Drift, and to the efforts of one man – Osgood Mackenzie – to transform a barren patch of ground on which only a single stunted willow grew. The project was started in 1862 with shelter belts to protect the site from the salt-laden gales. Estate workers carried in soil in creels and the first plantings were made. By the time Inverewe was given to the National Trust for Scotland in 1952 by Osgood Mackenzie's daughter, it was already famous. The size of the coach and car park testifies to its popularity.

Inverewe is a woodland garden, its winding paths dotted with rarities from the southern hemisphere and China. It has an enormous *Magnolia stellata*, superb rhododendrons, primulas and azaleas. At its heart lies a sheltered rockery full of interesting plants. All the time you sense what a fragile place this is, for its luxuriance is surrounded by boggy moorland and distant mountains. Inverewe is at its most colourful in spring, but also has superb autumn colouring. July and August do not find it at its best, except for the hydrangeas, but there is always something to admire. Plant lovers should aim to spend the better part of a day here. Seeds are on sale.

Gruinard Bay

Over the neck of the Rubha Mór peninsula, Gruinard Bay, with its famous pink sands, forms a shallow bite out of the coast. If you are in search of a peaceful spot in the sun, take the minor road up the western side to Mellon Udrigle, where there is a sandy beach, a cluster of cottages, a campsite and a lovely view. Even if the mountains to the east are being rained on, it may well be fine out here and on other coastal peninsulas.

Gruinard Island, a heather-clad lump in the bay, was used during the Second World War to conduct experiments in biological warfare, and was infected with anthrax. For years after the war the island remained contaminated – something of a local scandal. However, a massive decontamination programme was put into effect a few years ago, and Gruinard is now pure once again.

Little Loch Broom and Loch Broom

A further neck of land separates Gruinard Bay from the tranquil waters of Little Loch Broom. At its top, you gaze out to the scattered **Summer Isles** in the sea to the north-west. Up Little Loch Broom, the A832 runs wide and straight along the shore, putting the local sheep in hazard of their lives. Once past the sudden spout of the waterfall at Ardessie and the hotel at Dundonnell you can stop for a strenuous walk up to Loch Toll an Lochain underneath the peaks of **An Teallach**. The precipices and tumbled screes of the mountain are faithfully reflected in the black water cupped under its cliffs. It is an awesome place, surrounded on three sides by bare rock or steep grass.

From the head of Little Loch Broom, the A832 winds up the narrow valley of the peaty-yellow Dundonnell River and debouches on to bare open moorland at the top – a spectacular and lonely drive, at its best from west to east – where you gaze into the tangle of mountains above Loch Fannich. This is the best-known of several Destitution roads in the West Highlands, built at the time of the potato famines in the mid-nineteenth century by the labour of those whose only alternative was starvation. They were financed from a Destitution Fund – hence their name – and it is worth remembering the road's origin as you stop to tuck into a picnic. Just when this road seems to be running straight into the mountains it takes a dog-leg north-east along a small glen scented with bog myrtle and joins the A835 from Garve to Ullapool at the head of the Corrieshalloch Gorge.

Corrieshalloch Gorge

This is among the most accessible of Scotland's gorges, and purist gorge-lovers may sneer at its slightly touristy atmosphere. A torrent pouring from a melting ice-cap on the Fannich mountains cut the Corrieshalloch at the end of the last Ice Age. Now a quick walk down a wooded path takes you to the chasm, spanned by a bouncy suspension bridge. There is a nasty drop to today's rather pathetic little river enclosed between vertical walls of black rock, on which ranks of exotic ferns thrive in such footholds as they can find. The Falls of Measach at the head of the gorge are more a chute than a waterfall proper and provide appropriate thunder only in heavy spate. The trout at the bottom of the ravine are reputed to be of grand size and fearsome fighters.

On the road to Ullapool, **Lael Forest Gardens** are actually a scruffy plantation of conifers, not worth your time.

ULLAPOOL

A real town, and a genuinely pleasant one, Ullapool was established in 1788 by the British Fisheries Society to take advantage of the huge catches of herring which were taken in Loch Broom. The rectangular grid plan of streets lined by cottages and the neat lochside frontage show the benefits of eighteenth-century town planning, ruined in some places by the less inspired ideas of the twentieth century. The huge shoals of herring are long gone but fishing is still important to Ullapool, although in summer the town seems entirely given over to tourism. Europeans of all nationalities wander the streets and, on a warm evening, an informal procession of Italian and French couples can give the town's little promenade in front of the harbour a Mediterranean atmosphere. This is about the only place north of Stirling where you can enjoy watching the street life. Much of it centres round the excellent Ceilidh Place – a combination of coffee shop, folk club, bookshop and hotel – but it extends down to the sea front, where groups gather to study the posters advertising boat trips to the Summer Isles or sea-fishing expeditions. A heavy smell of fish and chips occasionally drifts over the streets if the wind is wrong. The car park for the ferry to Stornoway is sometimes used by a pipe band or Highland dancers when not occupied by queues for the Western Isles.

The local **museum** (open Easter to Oct, Mon to Sat 9 to 6) occupies a split site – half in the old kirk, where photographs and histories of the town are lovingly brought together, and half in a room behind a bookshop, where geological specimens vie for pride of place with scruffy stuffed birds and a curious collection of historical flotsam. This includes Lord Nelson's razor and a scented pastille found in the pocket of Charles I's coat after his execution.

ULLAPOOL TO KINLOCHBERVIE

North of Ullapool, the west-coast scenery becomes even more the stuff of fantasy. Isolated dull red or silvery mountains rear out of a wilderness of grey-white tumbled rock. Cotton grass, bog myrtle and bell heather cover the peat, except where it has been trenched for drainage or dug for fuel. On still evenings, you can scent the peat-smoke from the tiny communities clinging to the coastline.

This land is too much of a desert for some visitors, for walking through the hummocks of bare rock and picking your way around the boggy lochans can be work rather than pleasure, while the steepness of the mountains may deter thoughts of casual hill-walking. For others, the far north-west corner of Scotland is pure magic.

Coigach

This is the district between Loch Broom and Cam Loch, which marks the boundary between the old counties of Ross and Sutherland. The fast A835 runs through it to the Ledmore junction, where the A838 provides an escape route back to Lairg and the east coast, but these are boring routes. Instead, once you are past the severe bulk of **Ben Mor Coigach**, take the minor road at Drumrunie and head west to the **Inverpolly National Nature Reserve**. Two of the reserve's three peaks, **Cul Beag** and **Stac Pollaidh**, hide the inner sanctuary from the road. Cul Beag is not easy to admire from close quarters, but Stac Pollaidh, as it comes into view by Loch Lurgainn, is one of the most remarkable sights in the area. At just over 2000 feet it is barely a mountain, but its ridge, eroded into a fantasy of sandstone pinnacles and towers, belongs to some airy alpine peak. The mountain is reflected photogenically in

Loch Lurgainn, but this is not a good road for stopping on, and it is better to persist to the car park underneath the path up to the ridge.

To penetrate the interior of Inverpolly forest, go back a mile to the cottage at Linneraineach and take the track north a short way beyond. This is a wonderful low-level walk, leading you into a cirque of peaks, floored by lochs with sandy beaches. **Cul Mor** rises above Loch an Doire Duibh, round which you can walk before returning. Climbing Cul Mor, either from here or from the duller approach from Knockan, back on the main road, reveals the full beauty of the pattern of lochs, notably Loch Sionascaig and Loch Veyatie. You can gaze southward to the peaks of An Teallach and westward across the Minch to the mountains of Harris.

Achiltibuie

Beyond Inverpolly the road continues west past Loch Osgaig (which is likely to be sprinkled with anglers) and the stunning sandy beach at Achnahaird to arrive at the straggling crofting township of Achiltibuie. It is not the immediate surroundings but the wonderful views south and south-west to all the tangled mountains of Ross, with the Summer Isles lying on the sea in the foreground, that make Achiltibuie popular.

If the weather is fine there are few better places on the coast for an outdoor family holiday, with trout in the lochs, the beach at Achnahaird, the mountains of Inverpolly, and the rocky coastline along to Reiff to explore. There are sea-fishing opportunities, and trips to the Summer Isles. Achiltibuie is well supplied with self-catering properties, some bed-and-breakfasts, and the Summer Isles Hotel, whose bar is a refuge even if you do not stay there.

Achiltibuie's chief curiosity is the **Hydroponicum** (open late Mar to early Oct, daily, 90-minute tours at 10, 12, 2, 5). This huge greenhouse surrounded by clutter lies beneath the Summer Isles Hotel. Careful ventilation and control of the light create several different sub-tropical zones and a variety of exotic plants are grown without the aid of soil. Liquid nutrient trickles along channels filled with strawberry plants or drips on to the roots of banana trees. Oranges, lemons and figs compete with maidenhair ferns for space on the upper floor. Downstairs, apples and peaches ripen, and courgettes grow in fat ranks. The Hydroponicum still has to solve pest and algae problems, but the sight of what can be grown is enough to tempt you to buy the miniature jars, pots and packets of nutrient on sale.

Assynt

The coastal road north from Achiltibuie winds tortuously through a labyrinth of rocky hummocks and river valleys. It is not a road to take a caravan on, nor is it a road for careless drivers. By the time you arrive at **Inverkirkaig**, you are in need of a break. The tiny village fronts a broad, seaweedy bay, with the River Kirkaig running into it.

Assynt's chief village, **Lochinver**, is a mixture of grubby fishing harbour and clean, cottage-lined street. Tucked into a sheltered inlet, Lochinver suffers from lack of views but is the only place for miles with a decent choice of accommodation or anywhere much to eat. It is also the best place from which to climb Suilven and Canisp. You reach these mountains by the long walk past Glencanisp Lodge, which is made less wearisome by the increasingly spectacular sight of Suilven's western peak rearing above the intervening ridges.

As well as mountains, the Lochinver area has beaches. These are to be found on the Stoer peninsula where the best sand is at Achmelvich, Clachtoll and Clashnessie. There are also small coves to explore, while a boggy walk will take you to the sea-stack of the Old Man of Stoer at the northernmost tip of the peninsula. Campsites and bed-and-breakfast accommodation are to be found by the main beaches. On the north coast, **Drumbeg**, with its loch and its view, is worth pausing at, and **Nedd**, a little further on, is also attractive.

The stubby ruins of **Ardvreck Castle** sit on a little headland in Loch Assynt, easily reached from the A894. There is not much of it left, but it has gone down in history as the place where Montrose was finally captured after his defeat at Invershin. A small beach nearby on the loch shore makes a good spot from which to contemplate the ruin.

A bridge now sweeps the road over the Kylesku narrows, replacing the last ferry crossing on the road north. The old village of **Kylestrome** on the far bank is colourful with flowers, and lobster boats putter around in Loch Cairnbawn. The favourite occupation for visitors here is to take boat trip up Loch Glencoul to see the highest waterfall in Britain. The **Eas Coul Aulin** is four times higher than Niagara, but somehow has not managed to achieve the same reputation.

Scourie

This sheltered village at the head of a cove is the centre for trout fishermen who like nothing better than to pursue their quarry through the myriad lochans that dot the gneiss desert inland. Scourie is nothing much, but it has an hotel, a rocky coastline to explore, and is generally a haven in a wilderness. Off the coast to the north lies **Handa Island**. This is the north-west coast's seabird city, though after early August you may not see much. Ornithologists are drawn to Handa in considerable numbers, and information about boat trips is to be found by the cottage at Tarbet. The 350-foot Stack of Handa stands 80 feet from the cliff's edge.

Kinlochbervie

North of Laxford Bridge the road from Lairg joins the route north, after traversing the length of Loch Shin. The scenery here is bleak in the extreme, for the mountains of Ben Stack, Arkle and Foinaven are massive lumps of inhospitable scree and rock, glimmering in the sunshine like snow. Do not be surprised to meet the odd fish lorry (though the heaviest traffic is at night), for Kinlochbervie has now become one of Scotland's chief fishing ports. The town sits in the middle of bleak scenery, with its little housing estate looking extremely incongruous. The modern port is enthralling if you are around when the catch is being landed.

Holidaymakers come for the sake of the beaches rather than the fish. The most famous of these is Sandwood Bay – everyone's ideal beach, with its long curve of empty white sand, a small river and a loch. It is empty because access is difficult. Even if you subject your car to three miles of extremely rough track, you will still have to walk a mile or so to reach it. In fine weather it is worth every step. Other, more frequented but still beautiful, beaches lie under the small township of Oldshore More. Beyond Sandwood Bay the coast is trackless right up to Cape Wrath (page 417).

SKYE

Skye exerts a hypnotic appeal, reflected in the number of coach tours that have the island as their destination. On a clear windy day, with the ridges of the Black Cuillin exposed under the sun in all their starkness and the Sound of Raasay dotted with white combers, the island is magical. However, few parts of Scotland are so disappointing in the rain or sea mist, when the mountains vanish, the treeless moors become soggily hostile and the sea turns a sullen grey. If the weather turns against you on your way to Skye (and the island has a notoriously fickle climate), change your plans if possible and try again later. This is an island which needs fair weather to be enjoyed.

As Scottish islands go, Skye is well endowed with facilities for visitors and, although there are few tourist sights as such, they are all sold hard. The island has plenty of places to stay, and you even have a choice of shops and places at which to eat. So, while Skye only occasionally feels overcrowded, do not expect to find yourself alone. If you need some solitude, you only have to make the short crossing to Raasay.

The best walks are long, difficult, or both, while the Black Cuillin is the preserve of the rock-climber or experienced rock-scrambler. However, if you are neither fit nor experienced, there are several enjoyable short walks, usually by the coast. The tourist office in Portree has a first-class selection of leaflets on walks.

Many visitors come to Skye because of its associations with the flight of Charles Edward Stuart after Culloden, and in particular because of Flora Macdonald, the girl who brought him, disguised as her maid, from Benbecula in the Western Isles to Portree. From there he went to Raasay, back to Skye, and eventually to a cave near Elgol where the Mackinnons gave him a banquet and a boat to Mallaig. It is easy enough to visit the scenes of these adventures, less easy perhaps to avoid the retrospective sentimentality that turned Flora Macdonald into a legend even in her own lifetime.

Sleat

If you cross to Skye from Mallaig, your first impression of the island will be of a richly wooded, sheltered shore. Close to the ferry pier at Armadale, the **Clan Donald Centre** (open early Apr to Oct, daily 9.30 to 5.30, limited winter opening) is more than just another clan centre, for there is an excellent exhibition and audio-visual outlining the history of the Lordship of the Isles. The loose confederation of clans under the Clan Donald Lords of the Isles took over from their Norse predecessors in ruling the Hebrides more or less independently of the Scottish kings. Their ambitious attempts to extend their power eastward reached their climax in the drawn Battle of Harlaw in 1411, but it was not until 1493 that the power of the Lords of the Isles was broken, and 'Without Clan Donald, there is no joy' turned from motto to lament. Armadale Castle, where the exhibition is mounted, is surrounded by fine woodland, and there are ranger-led walks further afield.

Sleat has numerous hotels and guesthouses lining its eastern coast, most of them with fine views over to the mainland. By driving over to the west coast from Kilbeg, you pass immediately into a bleaker and less frequented landscape.

Kyleakin to Portree

Kyleakin is where you land if you come over on the ferry from Kyle of Lochalsh. It is a nondescript village, but studded with tearooms and craft shops, which will prove invaluable if the rain has set in. There is a small creeper-covered ruin of a castle to look at while you wait for the ferry back.

After the straggling village of **Broadford** the road to Portree negotiates the fringes of the Red Hills. These mountains lie adjacent to the Black Cuillin but they are entirely different, being large, rounded mounds of pinkish granite with scree-covered flanks. Both are the product of the ancient volcanic activity which makes the scenery of Skye so different from the neighbouring mainland.

At **Luib**, by the side of the main road, there is the first of the Skye folk museums (open Apr to Oct, daily 9 to 6). This one – just an old croft house with a few utensils and a smoky peat fire – is atmospheric and well worth a halt if there are not too many visitors there already. Of particular interest is the collection of fading newspaper cuttings about crofters' grievances – Skye was the setting for some of the most intense fight-backs by crofters threatened with eviction during the Clearances. A cairn on the B883 commemorates the 'Battle of the Braes', when police were confronted by stone-throwing crofters, and there is a memorial to the Glendale Land League at Colbost. Government over-reaction (troops and marines were stationed on Skye) eventually led to the enquiry which resulted in the Crofting Act of 1886.

Portree

Skye's little capital bustles with visitors on a hot summer's day, to the extent that you begin to wonder whether there are any local people left. It is an attractive place, set above the shore of a perfect blue-green inlet of the sea, and the row of painted cottages by the harbour beautifully offsets the elegant main square. Apart from the Royal Hotel where Prince Charles Edward Stuart said goodbye to Flora Macdonald, there is not much to see. However, with its pubs, shops, banks and selection of places to eat, Portree is a natural hub if you are in need of some facilities. It is also the starting point for many of the island's bus services and for most of its bus tours.

Elgol and Loch Coruisk

At Broadford, the road to Elgol branches off. This is a cul-de-sac well worth exploring for the combination of sea and mountain scenery on the way, and with the added attraction of a boat trip into the heart of the Black Cuillin at its end. The boats to Loch Coruisk run from Elgol in season (ring 04716 244). As you cross Loch Scavaig, the black basalt and gabbro of the mountains closes in on either side, while the main ridge reveals itself as a great jagged circuit of teeth and pinnacles. A short walk from the boat brings you to Loch Coruisk. Enthralled nineteenth-century painters, inspired by Scott's *Lord of the Isles*, came to Coruisk and left impressions of a gloomy Gothic sanctuary whose overwhelming scale diminished man to a mere speck. It is not quite like that, though the wilderness of tumbled scree and layers of bare glaciated slabs beneath sheer cliffs cut by gullies leave an indelible impression.

Loch Harport and Glen Brittle

The drive down Glen Brittle gives you another excellent view of the Black Cuillin on the western side of their semi-circle. Emerging from forestry plantations, you gaze straight into the black recesses of Coire a' Mhadaidh. The road runs on down the glen, with splendid views of the mountains until you reach the campsite and shore at the bottom. This is a hive of activity for climbing expeditions, and there is a lot of entertainment to be had from watching the climbers loading up.

Further west, off the B8009, the **Talisker Distillery** runs very slick and informative tours during the summer season. At **Bracadale**, near the foot of Loch Harport, Skye's best preserved broch – Dun Beag – is on a hillside above the main road. From Bracadale, the B885 crosses Skye's lonely and boggy interior back to Portree.

Dunvegan Castle

(Open late Mar to Oct, Mon to Sat 10 to 5.30, Sun 1 to 5.30; other months by appointment)

The large car park and the numerous coaches signal that this, Skye's only substantial tourist sight, is extremely popular. It is pricey if all you want to do is visit the castle, but if you take advantage of the fine gardens and grounds for a walk it becomes better value. The castle is the seat of Macleod of Macleod and has been continuously inhabited for about 750 years.

The castle's exterior belies its age, for the Victorians added pepper-pot turrets and a battlemented gatehouse. The antiquity reveals itself in the interior, where the old barrel-vaulted kitchen goes back to 1360, and where there is an unpleasant dungeon. The various stages in the building are well explained in the leaflet. The castle just about manages to retain the atmosphere of a lived-in home; the ancestral portraits in the dining-room and the drawing-room are comprehensive and rather fascinating. There are Jacobite relics which once belonged to Flora Macdonald, a portrait of Dr Johnson, who stayed here, and a very beautiful fifteenth-century silver cup. There is also Rory Mor's horn, a massive drinking vessel, which the chief's heir must drink to the dregs 'without setting down or falling down', when it is filled with claret (about one and a half bottles).

The greatest curiosity in Dunvegan is the 'Fairy Flag'. Enclosed in protective glass, this almost colourless piece of fabric looks like a dishcloth in the last stages of decay. It has been dated to between the fourth and seventh centuries, while its silk is of Near-Eastern origin. This banner, Am Bratach Sith, was given to a MacLeod chief by a fairy and it has the power to ensure victory for the clan in battle. It is known to have been used twice successfully. Popular boat trips to see seals run from near the castle.

Glendale and Vaternish

A 'visitor route' is signposted westward from just before Dunvegan village, and leads along the shores of Loch Dunvegan and over the neck of the peninsula beyond. The small sights include a crofting museum at Colbost, a restored watermill built into a steep rocky cleft, the memorial to the Land Leaguers who fought back against the Clearances, and even a toy museum. The most unusual, though, is the tiny **Piping Centre** (open daily in season, check times with tourist office) at Boreraig, which is something of a shrine to the famous Macrimmons, who were traditionally pipers to the Chief of the MacLeods. This is a serious place, where you will receive an enthusiastic reception.

The peninsula of Vaternish beyond Dunvegan is the place to go to watch the sun setting in a blaze of red over the Outer Hebrides, which line the horizon like dream islands. If there is no sunset, there is Skye's oldest pub at Stein to enjoy.

Trotternish

The north-east peninsula of Skye provides one of the best round trips from Portree, with a few sights worth stopping for and some amazing rock scenery. **Uig** is the attractive ferry port for North Uist and Harris, and most of the town's business revolves round ferry timetables.

At **Kingsburgh**, the refugee Prince Charles Edward sought shelter, and Dr Johnson not only slept in his bed (rather later on) but met Flora Macdonald here. The house where all this happened is long gone. In the cemetery north of **Kilmuir**, there is an austere memorial to Flora Macdonald, inscribed with Dr Johnson's tribute: 'A name that will be mentioned in history, and if courage and fidelity be virtues, mentioned with honour.' Nearby is the **Skye Museum of Island Life** (open Easter to Oct, Mon to Sat 9 to 5.30), another folk museum, this time in a cluster of restored cottages and buildings, with the usual collection of domestic artefacts.

The east coast of Trotternish is where the rock scenery for which the peninsula is famous is to be found. A slow-motion landslip, caused by basalt lava on top of less stable rock sliding gradually downhill, has resulted in an escarpment of sheer cliffs, with broken-off fragments as outriders. The **Quiraing** is the best known of the strange formations, and is easily reached by a path from the minor road which crosses from Uig to Staffin. The various rock features of the Quiraing – the Prison, the Table and the Needle – can be appreciated only on foot. Eroded to curious squares and pinnacles, these rocks farrowed from the main cliffs lie in picturesque confusion.

Kilt Rock, a sea cliff nearby, gets its name from the vertical columnar basalt strata overlying horizontal ones beneath, the result bearing only the most fanciful relationship to tartan. The sea-cliffs in this area of Staffin are especially spectacular, as is the nearby waterfall which plunges vertically over them into the sea. Further south, the **Old Man of Storr** is a cigar-shaped pinnacle which has detached itself from the cliffs of the Storr behind. It is a laborious, though short, trek up to its base, but unless you are a first-class rock-climber you will not make much further progress.

It is worth noting that the inhabitants of this corner of Skye observe Sundays very strictly, and some guesthouses will not take weekend guests for that reason. Check with the tourist office before booking.

RAASAY

The island of Raasay lies off Skye's eastern coast. It is secluded and gentle, even when Skye is bustling, but has a comfortable and friendly hotel. Its lack of mountains is made up for by the excellent sea views and there are coastal walks, some quite strenuous, with the cliff scenery of the east coast rivalling that of Trotternish. The curious flat-topped Dun Caan is a volcanic hill, made famous as the place where Boswell danced a 'Highland Dance', while visiting the island with Dr Johnson in 1773. Raasay was the birthplace of Scotland's best-known modern Gaelic poet, Sorley Maclean. His poems (many of which he translated into English himself) contain many references to Raasay.

There are many small curiosities to be found on the island: the old iron ore mine at Suisnish that was worked by German prisoners during World War I, and the mermaids lying outside the perilously dilapidated Raasay House (now an outdoor centre), whose cost drove the last MacLeod chief into bankruptcy. Brochel Castle, a vegetatious ruin, stands picturesquely on the east coast, and makes a good goal for a short drive. Beyond, the road to Arnish was built single-handedly by a local crofter over 10 years from 1966, after the local authority declined to do the job itself.

THE SMALL ISLES

The Small Isles, part of the Inner Hebrides group, fill the sea between Skye and the Peninsula of Ardnamurchan. Of all the islands clustered around Scotland these four are the most tempting to visit, for the jagged outline of Rum and the curious profile of Eigg seen over an aquamarine sea from the Moidart coast suggest places of almost tropical beauty. However, these islands, with their small and precarious populations and difficult communications, are not for people who need extensive facilities, and accommodation is limited. Short visits are possible, especially in the summer months when the year-round ferry service from Mallaig is supplemented by cruises from Arisaig, but the timetables are apt to leave you with either too little time on each island, or else too much.

Rum and Canna

Often spelt Rhum to avoid alcoholic associations, Rum is a wet, mountainous island and is at its most attractive from a distance for all except the naturalist and the walker, although those who enjoy eccentric hotels should make a special pilgrimage here. The island's population was unceremoniously forced off to Canada during the nineteenth century, and Rum became an uninhabited deer forest for sporting millionaires. It was the last of these, the Lancastrian industrialist George Bullough, who built the extravagant fantasy of Kinloch Castle, importing stone from Arran and craftsmen from Lancashire to create a bizarre combination of Scottish castle, Tudor mansion and Italian palazzo. This gross but charming folly is now an hotel; its interior remains as it was – a memorial to conspicuous consumption in an unlikely setting. Apart from this hotel, accommodation on Rum is limited to bothies and a campsite in Kinloch.

Rum is owned and managed by Scottish Natural Heritage as a huge outdoor research centre. Red deer form one of the most important areas of their work, but the island is also the scene of the experimental reintroduction of the sea eagle to Scotland. Access to parts of the island is restricted – ask the warden before exploring away from the marked nature trails. One interesting walk runs across the island to Harris Bay, where the Bullough family's mausoleum – a Doric temple surmounted by crosses – stands incongruously beside the sea. Rum's midges are notorious.

Canna is owned by the National Trust for Scotland, after years of benevolent stewardship by the Gaelic scholar Dr John Lorne Campbell. It is a small island, only five miles long, bounded by cliffs and with bright fertile patches fringing its rugged interior – a good place for birdwatchers and botanists and a very quiet refuge. Accommodation is extremely limited.

USEFUL DIRECTORY

Main tourist offices
Fort William and Lochaber Tourist Board
Cameron Centre, Cameron Square
Fort William PH33 6AJ
(0397) 703781

Isle of Skye & South West Ross Tourist Board
Meall House, Portree, Isle of Skye IV51 5VZ
(0478) 612137

Ross and Cromarty Tourist Board
Achtercairn, Gairloch, Ross-shire IV21 2DN
(0445) 2130

Sutherland Tourist Board
The Square, Dornoch, Sutherland IV25 3SD
(0862) 810400

Tourist Board special interest publications: guides on
fishing include *Where to fish in Ross & Cromarty*, factsheets
on river fishing and trout lochs on Skye, and *Fishing in
Sutherland*; walks and drives, including Wester Ross coastal
route; pony trekking; golf.

Local tourist information centres
Broadford (0471) 822361 (Apr to Oct)
Gairloch (0445) 2130
Glenshiel (059981) 264 (Apr to Sept)
Kyle of Lochalsh (0599) 4276 (Apr to Oct)
Lochcarron (05202) 357 (May to Oct)
Lochinver (05714) 330 (late Mar to Oct)
Mallaig (0687) 2170 (Apr to Oct)
Portree (0478) 612137
Strontian (0967) 2131 (May to Sept)
Ullapool (0854) 612135 (Easter to Oct)

Local transport
Mallaig Railway Station (0687) 2227
Fort William Railway Station (0397) 703791
Kyle of Lochalsh Railway Station (0599) 4205
Highland Bus and Coach (covers region) (0463) 233371
Skyeways buses (Skye and mainland routes) (0599) 4328
Wester Bus (Gairloch area) (0445) 2255

Car ferries

Lochaline–Fishnish (frequent service Mon to Sat, also Sun late May to Aug) (0475) 650100

Kilchoan–Tobermory (mid-Apr to mid-Oct, Mon to Sat, up to seven sailings daily) (0475) 650100

Inchree–Corran (frequent daily crossings) (08555) 243

Mallaig–Armadale (Note, passenger service only Oct to mid-Apr) (0475) 650100

Glenelg–Kylerhea (Easter to Sept, Mon to Sat, frequent service) (059981) 302

Kyle of Lochalsh–Kyleakin (frequent service) (0475) 650100

Sconser–Raasay (Mon to Sat, up to six sailings daily) (0475) 650100

Ullapool–Stornoway (Mon to Sat, up to three sailings daily) (0475) 650100

Uig–Tarbet (Mon to Sat, one or two sailings daily) (0475) 650100

Uig–Lochmaddy (Mon to Sat, also Sun late Apr to mid-Oct, one or two sailings daily) (0475) 650100

Passenger ferries

Mallaig–Eigg–Muck–Rum–Canna (four to five sailings a week) (0475) 650100

Mallaig–Kyle of Lochalsh (Apr to Oct, Fri only) (0475) 650100

Mallaig–Tarbet, Loch Nevis (two to three sailings a week) (0687) 2320

Mallaig–Inverie (two sailings three days/week) (0687) 2320

Arisaig–Eigg–Muck–Rum–Canna (daily service May to mid-Sept) (06875) 224/678

Other boat trips

Elgol–Loch Coruisk (04716) 244

Mallaig–Loch Coruisk (0687) 2320

Dunvegan–seal islands (047022) 206

Kylesku–Eas Coul Aulin waterfalls (05714) 446

Trips out of Arisaig (06875) 224/678

Mountains

Kintail mountain rescue (0599) 4299

Skye mountain rescue (0478) 612888

Cuillin Guides, Skye (0471) 14239

Eigg and Muck

In recent years Eigg has been sensitively steered towards quiet tourism, so there is more accommodation here than on the other islands and a genuine welcome for people who are happy to enjoy the island's peace. Eigg is dominated by the strange peak of An Sgurr, a flat-topped volcanic outcrop with precipitous sides. There are also singing sands at the Bay of Laig, which whisper underfoot in the right conditions. The most gruesome sight on Eigg is Macdonald's Cave, where 400 members of that clan were summarily suffocated by raiding MacLeods, who lit a fire at the entrance.

Flat and fertile, tiny **Muck** has just over a mile of road and a beautiful shell beach. It is really too small to stay on for long (there are two small hotels, camping and holiday cottages), but the ferry from Arisaig allows you to explore it inside a day on three days a week.

WHERE TO STAY

ACHILTIBUIE

Summer Isles   ££
Achiltibuie, By Ullapool
Ross-shire IV26 2YG   *Tel (085 482) 282*

A simple hotel in an extended crofting township, with fine views of sea and islands. The public bar is usually full of chatty locals; there is a small lounge and fresh, well-appointed bedrooms, most with bathroom. The food excels with fresh fish a strong point.

Open: Easter to mid-Oct **Rooms**: 12 (most in annexe), plus cottage **Credit/charge cards**: none accepted

ARISAIG

Arisaig Hotel   £–££
Arisaig, Inverness-shire PH39 4NH   *Tel (068 75) 210*

This unpretentious, friendly hotel in the centre of Arisaig doubles as the local pub. The food is more important than luxury, with seafood and breakfasts particularly good. The bedrooms vary in size and views, but are perfectly adequate. Most have bathrooms, and some are in a modern annexe. Under new ownership from February 1994.

Open: all year **Rooms**: 15 **Credit/charge cards**: Access, Visa

Arisaig House £££

Beasdale, By Arisaig
Inverness-shire PH39 4NR   *Tel (068 75) 622*

A grand Victorian mansion surrounded by woodland and rhododendrons, three miles east of Arisaig. Bedrooms are light and spacious,
with those overlooking Loch nan Uamh by far the nicest. Flowers
bedeck the magnificent sitting-rooms, and the gardens make for
pleasant strolls.

Open: early Mar to end Nov **Rooms**: 14 **Facilities**: billiard room
Credit/charge cards: Access, Visa

GLENCRIPESDALE

Glencripesdale House ££–£££

Loch Sunart, Acharacle
Argyll PH36 4JH   *Tel (096 785) 263*

For absolute isolation, few hotels beat Glencripesdale, a converted
farmhouse on the shores of Loch Sunart. The bedrooms are full of
character and the sitting-room full of books, and there's a separate
children's playroom in the outbuildings. The tariff, which includes
dinner, packed lunch and afternoon tea, is excellent value. The
current owners were intending to sell at the time of going to press
– check before you book.

Open: all year, exc Nov to Feb (open Xmas and New Year)
Rooms: 4 **Facilities**: fishing, table tennis, games room,
water sports   **Credit/charge cards**: none accepted

GLENELG

Glenelg Inn £–££

Glenelg, By Kyle of Lochalsh
Ross-shire IV40 8AG   *Tel (059 982) 273*

Glenelg looks like a typical pub, with a large, warm bar and
fine views out towards Skye. But stay overnight and you will
be impressed by the furnishings, the charming host, and the
straightforward but excellently cooked food. Bedrooms are quiet
and simple but elegantly put together, and there is a small
morning room.

Open: Easter to end Oct (inn open all year) **Rooms**: 6
Facilities: solarium, two boats
Credit/charge cards: none accepted

GLENSHIEL

Kintail Lodge ££
Glenshiel, By Kyle of Lochalsh
Ross-shire IV40 8HL *Tel (059 981) 275*

A welcoming base at the foot of Glenshiel. Bedrooms are mostly
light and comfortable and priced according to size and view. Some
of the furniture is dated, but the conservatory and sitting-room are
relaxing, with splendid views of Loch Duich.

Open: all year, exc 24 Dec to 2 Jan **Rooms**: 12
Credit/charge cards: Access, Visa

KINLOCHBERVIE

Kinlochbervie Hotel ££
Kinlochbervie, By Lairg
Sutherland IV27 4RP *Tel (0971) 521275*

On a hill above the busy fishing harbour, Kinlochbervie is a mix
of genteel hotel and restaurant, jolly pub and bistro, as well as
hostel – the cheap rooms in the annexe are fairly basic. In the main
hotel, bedrooms are comfortable rather than pretty. The food is
well cooked, with plenty of seafood, and the residents' lounge and
dining-room have fine views of the harbour.

Open: all year (restricted services Nov to Mar) **Rooms**: 22
Credit/charge cards: Access, Amex, Diners, Visa

LOCHINVER

Inver Lodge Hotel ££–£££
Lochinver, Sutherland IV27 4LU *Tel (057 14) 496*

A modern purpose-built hotel, Inver Lodge is short on character
but is comfortably furnished and set in an area of starkly beautiful
countryside. Facilities are good, with access to fishing on nearby
rivers and lochs, and dinners are set five-course affairs. The views
are tremendous.

Open: Apr to end Oct **Rooms**: 20 **Facilities**: sauna, solarium,
billiard room **Credit/charge cards**: Access, Amex, Diners, Visa

PORTREE

Viewfield House £
Portree, Skye IV51 9EU *Tel (0478) 612217*

Seemingly untouched since Edwardian times, the charm of Viewfield House makes up for what it lacks in modern comforts. The hall contains what may be the finest collection of taxidermy in a UK hotel. The bright bedrooms are furnished with antiques here and there and the biggest rooms, one and three, are massive. Guests gather for drinks in front of the fire before moving into the dining-room for a five-course dinner. Good value.

Open: Apr to mid-Oct **Rooms**: 11
Credit/charge cards: Access, Visa

RAASAY

Isle of Raasay £
Raasay, By Kyle of Lochalsh IV40 8PB *Tel (0478) 660222/660226*

This neat and friendly little hotel provides a perfect base on an under-visited island. Bedrooms are simply furnished, as is the whole hotel, and have good bathrooms. Dinner is served early (at 7pm) and may include some choice among its four courses. The owners were intending to sell as we went to press – check before you book.

Open: Apr to mid-Oct **Rooms**: 12
Credit/charge cards: none accepted

RUM

Kinloch Castle £££
Rum, Inverness-shire PH43 4RR *Tel (0687) 2037*

An industrialist's folly on an isolated island, Kinloch Castle is an exceptional hotel in a time-warp, from the balconied Great Hall with its stags' heads to the bedrooms with their old but comfortable beds and amazing showers in the public bathrooms. The smoking room contains a full-size billiard table. The food is also excellent, and a house-party atmosphere quickly develops as guests take dinner round a large polished table.

Open: Mar to Oct **Rooms**: 9, plus 13 hostel rooms
Facilities: fishing, billiards **Credit/charge cards**: none accepted

SCOURIE

Scourie Hotel £
Scourie, Sutherland IV27 4SX   *Tel (0971) 502396*

A fishing hotel through and through, but non-anglers are made to feel welcome and there is enough space in the two lounges and bars to escape fishy conversations. The public rooms are tartan-carpeted and cosy, while the modernised bedrooms, most with bathroom, are simple but comfortable. Food is plain and reasonably priced.

Open: mid-Mar to Oct   **Rooms**: 20
Credit/charge cards: Access, Amex, Diners, Visa

SHIELDAIG

Tigh an Eilean ££
Shieldaig, By Strathcarron
Ross-shire IV54 8XN   *Tel (052 05) 251*

This small hotel is gloriously situated on the loch's edge in a beautiful Highland village. But the real charm of Tigh an Eilean is the neatness and freshness with which everything is done. The food is its other strong point – traditional country cooking. Good value.

Open: Easter to end Oct   **Rooms**: 11   **Facilities**: fishing
Credit/charge cards: Access, Visa

TALLADALE

Loch Maree Hotel £–££
Talladale, By Achnasheen
Wester Ross IV22 2HL   *Tel (044 584) 288*

One of Scotland's best-known fishing hotels, friendly and not overpriced, which has benefited from recent renovations. There are two bars, a smart dining-room and small sitting-room, and the scenery on the loch side is wonderful. The food is straightforward and filling. Beware the poor sound insulation in some rooms.

Open: all year   **Rooms**: 31   **Facilities**: fishing (10 boats)
Credit/charge cards: Access, Visa

ULLAPOOL

Altnaharrie Inn £££
Ullapool, Ross-shire IV26 2SS   *Tel (085 483) 230*

Guests are ferried over from Ullapool to the isolated house on the far shore of Loch Broom. Altnaharrie is a friendly, pampering hotel which draws people back time and again. The five-course dinners get rave reviews, and there are two lounges, a good library, comfortable bedrooms with excellent views, and acres of moorland to walk in. No smoking.

Open: late Mar to Nov   **Rooms**: 8
Credit/charge cards: Access, Amex, Visa

Ceilidh Place   ££
14 West Argyll Street
Ullapool, Ross-shire IV26 2TY   *Tel (0854) 612103*

With a bookshop, café, restaurant and concert hall, the Ceilidh Place is the cultural centre of Ullapool, and an excellent hotel into the bargain. From a collection of cottages passages ramble off in all directions to the bedrooms, some small, others more spacious, and some with bathroom. Good, fresh bistro-style food.

Open: all year   **Rooms**: 13, plus 11 annexe rooms with bunk-beds   **Credit/charge cards**: Access, Amex, Diners, Visa

WHERE TO EAT

DUNVEGAN

Harlosh House
By Dunvegan, Skye IV55 8ZG   *Tel (047 022) 367*

A small but cosy place, in a very isolated position, offering a modern menu containing strong soups, faggots, and local langoustines with ginger and coriander, as well as good ice-creams.

Open: daily 7 to 8.30; closed end Oct to Easter
Credit/charge cards: Access, Visa

ULLAPOOL

Morefield Motel   ★
Ullapool IV2 2TS   *Tel (0854) 612161*

The motel consists of a pub serving good-value meals all the year round, with a more expensive restaurant open from Easter to the end of October. The Motel's share in a trawler means wonderfully fresh fish, and a good selection of seafood is caught locally.

Open: daily 12 to 2, 5.30 to 9.30; restaurant closed Nov to Easter
Credit/charge cards: Access, Amex, Visa

THE WESTERN ISLES

- Remote islands which are the last stronghold of the old Highland way of life
- Superb beaches and wild flowers
- Excellent fishing

Harris tweed loom

THE islands of the Outer Hebrides (or Western Isles), which run for 130 miles parallel to Scotland's north-west coast, are unlike anywhere else in the country. Superficially they share many of the features of the north-west mainland – there are mountains, fertile coastal strips, magnificent beaches, desolate peat bog and endless lochans. However, the Western Isles, despite the aircraft and the ferries which serve them, are remote, and for the inhabitants to climb into a car and head for the bright lights is easier said than done. Because of this, they remain in many ways the last stronghold of old Highland life. Communities are closely bound to the sea and to the soil; Gaelic is widely spoken; religious faith is strong, and hospitality is as genuine as you can hope to find in a tourist-infested world.

It is, however, a grave mistake to think that you are venturing into some unsophisticated outpost of Britain. The inhabitants of the Western Isles have seen many attempts to 'modernise' them, from those efforts by James VI to set up a colony of Fife men on Lewis in 1598 to the twentieth-century efforts of Lord Leverhulme to turn Lewis and Harris into the base for a huge fishing industry, so they are wary of outsiders' grandiose schemes to transform their way of life. They are equally aware of how easy it is for the islands to be neglected – the Western Isles did not even have their own local government until 1974. Consequently, opinions are strongly held out here. The most recent crisis that the outside world has inflicted on the Western Isles has been the failure of the Bank of Credit & Commerce International. The Western Isles Council had £23 million deposited in the bank – no one knows how it can ever be replaced.

In religion, the islands are split between the Presbyterian Lewis, Harris and North Uist, and the predominantly Roman Catholic South Uist and Barra. Benbecula has adherents of both doctrines. On Lewis and Harris, the Free Presbyterian Church of Scotland and the Free Church of Scotland (the Wee Frees) are both strong, and Sundays are very strictly observed. It is worth remembering that public transport will not be running and shops and petrol stations will not be open. On the Roman Catholic islands, things are more relaxed.

Fishing and crofting are the islanders' main occupations, and island life outside Stornoway revolves around the rhythm of the seasons and of the tides. Almost every islander will have more than one occupation – work on the croft may be supplemented by lobster-fishing, weaving of Harris tweed,

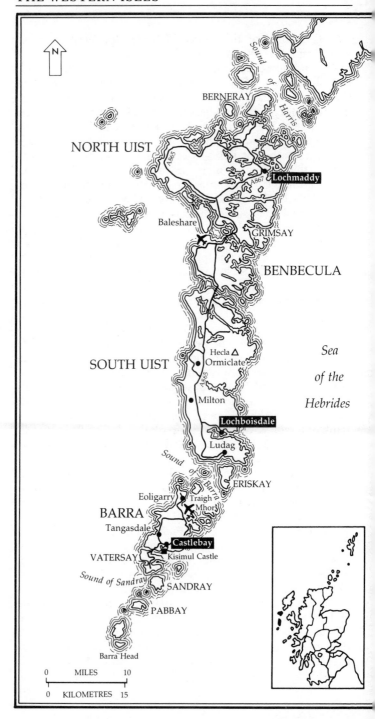

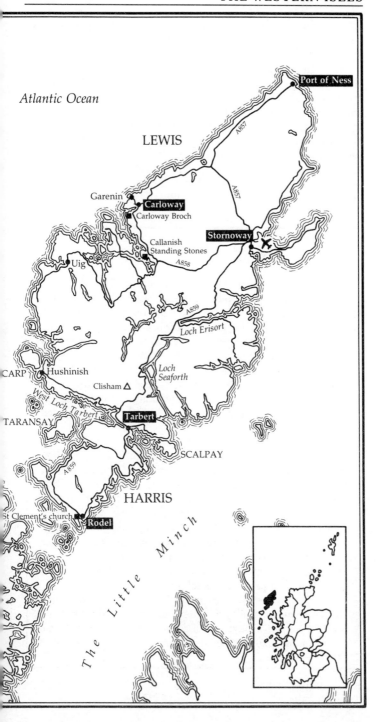

Atlantic Ocean

LEWIS

Port of Ness

A857

Garenin
Carloway
Carloway Broch

Callanish
Standing Stones

Stornoway

A857

A858

Uig

A859

Loch Erisort

CARP
Hushinish

Clisham △

Loch
Seaforth

West Loch Tarbert

TARANSAY

Tarbert

SCALPAY

A859

HARRIS

St Clement's church **Rodel**

The Little Minch

driving the post-bus, running a guesthouse or any number of other money-spinning activities. This makes for a network of relationships where everyone knows everyone else.

For visitors, especially those who have roots in the islands, the Western Isles exert a fascination which is difficult to justify to those who have not yet been there. The landscape of the interiors is mostly unrelenting rock, bog or water, and the long, straggling, crofting communities by the shore, where the functional croft houses are linked by wires and telephone poles, have no similarity to conventionally pretty villages. Even the superb beaches have their drawbacks, smelly sea-weed being the commonest. Yet these are not the images that endure. Instead, it may be the blanket of wild flowers on a Uist

Practical suggestions

It is possible, if you have time, to make your way from one end of the Western Isles to the other with your car, but you will need to master CalMac's ferry timetables and be prepared for some early starts or late arrivals. Leaving your car behind, hiring locally, and taking advantage of air services between Stornoway, Benbecula and Barra is an easier option. If you have plenty of time and a spirit of adventure, a combination of local buses, taxis and small pas-senger ferries will also get you from one end to the other. If you find yourself stranded, asking around locally will often unearth people willing to help get you from A to B where no formal transport exists.

If you do not want to spend time on ferries, stick to the linked islands of Lewis and Harris, Benbecula and the Uists, or Barra and Vatersay. Lewis and Harris – not separate islands, but always quirkily treated as such – are for wilderness-lovers and hill-walkers. Benbecula and the Uists are for anglers, naturalists and beachcombers. Barra and Vatersay are for those who like small island communities with a bit of everything. Guesthouses are the most popular and usually the best form of accommodation, though there are a number of hotels in Stornoway, the ferry ports, and on Benbecula and Barra. There are self-catering properties on all the main islands.

Conventional sights are few and far between. The most famous are the stones of Callanish. Most other prehistoric sights (of which there are plenty) are disappointing unless you are an expert. Of the castles, Kisimul on Barra is the best preserved.

machair, a shower clearing over the hills of Harris, a riotous evening in a Stornoway bar or simply the scent of burning peat drifting over the islands that you will remember.

LEWIS

The interior of Lewis is bare of people and bare of trees. The northern half is a flat, deserted moorland of rain-washed skies and distant horizons, where the only signs of human activity are the trenches and embankments of peat-cuttings, often marked by piles of plastic sacks. These excavations are everywhere, for peat is the universal fuel of the island and

The Western Isles Island Council has adopted a policy of using Gaelic place names on road signs, except in Stornoway and Benbecula, where they are bilingual. Most maps still use the English names, however. To help you find your way round, we recommend using a map (such as the one available from the Western Isles Tourist Board) which shows both names.

Place names

Lewis	Eilean Leodhais
Stornoway	Steornabhagh
Butt of Lewis	Rubha Robhanais
Ness	Nis
Carloway	Carlabhagh
Harris	Na Hearadh
Tarbert	Tairbeart
Rodel	Roghadal
North Uist	Uibhist a Tuath
Lochmaddy	Loch nam Madadh
Newtonferry	Port nan Long
Benbecula	Beinn na Faoghla
Balivanich	Baile a Mhanaich
South Uist	Uibhist a Deas
Lochboisdale	Loch Baghasdail
Eriskay	Eiriosgaigh
Barra	Barraigh
Castlebay	Bagh a Chaisteil
Vatersay	Bhatarsaigh

every croft house will have its peat stack, where the neat piles of dried black turf stand ready for the fire. The scent of peat smoke hangs over Lewis, an aroma which seems compounded of whisky, grass bonfires and a hint of coffee.

All the inhabitants of Lewis live by the sea, approximately 8,000 of them in Stornoway on the east coast, the only town on the islands. On the west coast, a long string of crofting townships runs the 34 miles from Ness to Carloway. Further south, settlements become sparse as rocky hills bulge out of the moor and long sea-lochs cut into the coast.

Lewis was once dominated by the MacLeods, said to be descendants of early settlers from Iceland. During the reign of James VI, when attempts to colonise Lewis with 'civilised' Lowlanders took place, Mackenzies managed to gain possession of the island. Cromwell demolished Stornoway Castle during a punitive expedition in 1653. In 1844, Lewis was sold to Sir James Matheson, who built Lews Castle in Stornoway and began to develop the infrastructure of the island. He also set up a short-lived industry to extract tar from peat. The man who really had ambitions for the island, however, was Lord Leverhulme, founder of Lever Brothers, who bought it in 1918. He planned to turn Lewis into the base for a major fishing industry, with its own railway system, and he poured money into developing the infrastructure. Conflict between Leverhulme and local men returning from the war who wanted land of their own, as well as the decline of the fishing industry, eventually led to the abandoning of his plans. The magnate's parting gesture, in which he offered Lewis to the islanders themselves, was turned down by all except the Stornoway Council. The island was split into estates and sold, and almost 1,000 people emigrated.

Stornoway

Clustered at the end of an eastward-thrusting peninsula, Stornoway is a small fishing town which also happens to be the only settlement of any size in the Western Isles – hence it is the administrative centre. There is not a great deal to see once you have bought any necessities you need (opportunities to do this will be limited elsewhere on the island), but a walk around the harbour will prove worthwhile if fishing boats are unloading. The **Museum nan Eilean** (currently closed for restoration) offers background on local history, or you could perhaps walk in the grounds of **Lews Castle** (now a college), where the woods and shrubs would be unremarkable elsewhere, but, in the Western Isles, are exceptional. The tiny art gallery of **An Lanntair** is the most rewarding of Stornoway's places to visit. Exhibitions here are refreshing and radical.

The west coast of Lewis

From Stornoway, the A859 and A858 carry you westward across the interior of Lewis to the road junction at Garynahine. From here, the B8011 leads to the south-west corner, a country of gneiss and granite with a tiny population. The best beach on Lewis is here, at **Uig**, where in 1831, a crofter dug up the Lewis Chessmen, 78 pieces of Scandinavian origin, carved from walrus ivory and dating from the twelfth century. The kings glower, the queens look as if they are suffering an attack of the vapours, and the pawn-warriors bite their shields in frustration. You can buy reproductions on Lewis; the originals are split between museums in Edinburgh and London.

By continuing on the A858, you arrive at the **Callanish Standing Stones** (HS, always open). Set on a lonely small peninsula that is unlikely to be spoilt by crowds, the 53 stones form a pattern like a Celtic cross, with an inner circle and four arms. They date from 3000 BC and are thus older than Stonehenge. Their function is unknown, but a lunar observatory is a popular explanation.

A short distance north, the remains of **Carloway Broch** stand close to the road on a hillside overlooking the sea. The broch is very well preserved; part of the wall is still 30 feet high. Collapsing stonework has exposed the interior galleries and stairs. At **Garenin**, a little further on, detour from the main road to see the ruins of a village of 'Black Houses' (see below).

The next place to stop is **Shawbost** (open Mon to Sat at all reasonable times), where a folk museum, started as a project by local schoolchildren, has blossomed into a fascinating, if ramshackle, collection of artefacts and junk collected from all walks of Hebridean life.

Arnol is the place to see how the people of Lewis used to live. The **Black House Museum** (HS, standard times; closed Sun) is a conserved example of a type of housing once common throughout the Highlands and Islands. Thick, low, double walls packed with peat for insulation support a roof thatched with heather and straw and weighed down with stones. Often there is only one door, used by both cattle and humans, and the interior is split between byre and living quarters. A peat fire smoulders on a central hearth. There is no chimney and the smoke filters out through the thatch. At first glance such living conditions may seem unbearably primitive but, in a land desperately short of everything but stone and heathery peat, and with a vile climate, the black house represented an extremely effective use of available material. It was energy-efficient in the best modern tradition: the double walls for insulation, the cattle for a renewable source of heat, the soot-impregnated roof to be used as fertiliser on the fields, and the absence of heat loss through windows. Black houses were inhabited until the 1960s (some modernised ones still are).

From Barvas, the A857 returns across the moors of Lewis to Stornoway, but if you are determined to explore further, a 15-mile drive on the coast road will bring you to the district of Ness and the Butt of Lewis. The tiny Port of Ness will provide you with tea before you make your way to the lighthouse on the very tip of Lewis, a wild and windy spot. Glance at the tiny twelfth-century **St Moluag's Church**.

HARRIS

Where Lewis is predominately flat moorland, Harris is largely mountain and rock. As you drive south from Stornoway on the A859, you will see the mountains rising in a barrier before you, with cloud probably hanging over their peaks. On the left, the narrow ribbon of Loch Seaforth eats deep into the coast; the land to its east is without road or habitation. At Tarbert, beyond the mountain barrier, Harris is almost split by the sea. On the west coast, south of here, wonderful sandy beaches suddenly turn the desolation silver.

The separation of Harris from Lewis goes right back to Norse times, when the island was divided between the two sons of Leod. Harris remained in MacLeod hands until 1834. Lord Leverhulme (see Lewis) also hoped to make Harris part of his ambitious schemes, and he concentrated his energies here when his plans for Lewis came to nothing. His death in 1925 brought an end to his plans for Harris also, and little remains of his work apart from the roads and the small harbour at Leverburgh.

North Harris, the land lying north of Tarbert, is the country for hill-walkers. None of the mountains here are as high as those on the Scottish mainland, but they are steep, rocky in places, and views from them can be marvellous. **Clisham**, the highest peak, is relatively easy to get to from the A859. The B887 runs along the coast westward to a dead end in Husinish Bay (with a small sandy beach), passing the turreted shooting lodge of Amhuinnsuidh Castle on the way.

Tarbert is a tiny place, but as it is the ferry port for Harris it has more facilities (such as a bank and a restaurant) than anywhere else. Ask at the Tourist Information Centre or the Harris Hotel if you want to fish for sea trout. East of the village, a 10-mile drive takes you through scattered communities to Carnach, where a car ferry crosses to **Scalpay**. Fishing keeps the population going on this remote piece of land, which makes a good destination for an expedition from Tarbert.

You should certainly drive right round **South Harris**, for the change in landscape between east and west is fascinating. The road down the west coast passes the firm sandy beaches of Luskentyre and Scarista, and everywhere there are patches

---

MACHAIR

Machair is the name given to the strips of land lying behind the beaches of west Scotland and the islands. These strips are notable for their fertility, in contrast to the poor, acid peat of the interior. In summer they are a blaze of wild flowers, and provide good grazing. The explanation lies in the shell sand, with its rich content of calcium, which is carried inshore from the beaches by the wind and neutralises the acidity of the peaty soil. The very best land lies a little inland from the beaches, where the soil is neither too sandy nor too peaty, and this area will be where the crofters have their small fields. During the Clearances, many families were forced off this good land and were given plots of infertile peat instead. Their only way to grow crops was then to create the so-called 'lazy beds', patches which were made fertile by laborious application of seaweed, and raised slightly above the surrounding ground to give some drainage. The machair, meanwhile, was given over to sheep. The machair today is prized for the variety of flowers it produces – primroses, buttercup, vetch, orchid and gentian. In damper patches (wet machair) clumps of wild iris provide favoured shelter for corncrakes. Rabbits are the greatest menace to the machair, for their burrowings allow the wind to get at the sandy soil beneath the surface.

473

of fertile machair. At **Leverburgh** you can see the remains of Lord Leverhulme's building works for his projected fishing port, but the village itself is just a row of houses. The passenger ferry for North Uist runs from here. Carry on to **Rodel**, at the very end of the A859, to see **St Clement's Church** (HS, always open). This beautifully crafted twelfth-century church is a remarkable find in such a far-away spot. Inside, the tomb of Alexander MacLeod, who died in 1547, is even more remarkable. Its carvings, showing a hunting scene, a castle and many religious images, repay a close look.

The single-track road up the east coast of Harris winds amongst outcrops of rock, bare of any vegetation. Crofts cling to tiny patches of level ground by the shore and boats are tied up in the many inlets. Along the road, especially near the township of **Plocrapool**, are several places where you can stop to watch Harris tweed being woven. The crofters are sent materials and patterns from Stornoway, and make up the lengths of tweed on clattering looms in small sheds beside their houses. You can sometimes see packets of cloth left by cottage gateways for collection, where it will be taken to Stornoway for finishing. If the tweed is not hand-woven, dyed and finished in the Western Isles, it cannot be stamped with the orb symbol which marks Harris tweed.

It was thanks to the Countess of Dunmore, who started the fashion for it in 1842, that Harris tweed became sought after. It was given its trademark in 1909. About five million yards of Harris tweed are produced annually by about 750 weavers.

BENBECULA AND THE UISTS

These three islands are linked by causeways which cross the shallow inlets of the sea between them. The sea creeps inland in so many arms and there are so many fresh-water lochs that it is difficult to know which island you are on. In fact, there is almost as much water as land on these islands, and one of the delights of flying over them on Loganair's services from Benbecula is to watch the light reflected back at you from the hundreds of lochs, as if someone had shattered mirrors over a green and brown carpet. Sit on the east-facing side of the aircraft for the best view.

These are the islands to come to for sandy beaches, for sand runs almost the full length of their west coasts. Magnificent beaches they are too, catching the full force of the Atlantic as it piles on to the shore, haunted by crying seabirds and backed by sheets of wild flowers in early summer. The eastern side of the islands is where the lochs are – you can fish for trout and sea-trout until your arm drops off, but still fail to cover more than a fraction of the available water. The only respectable hills are on the east of North and South Uist – worth climbing to have your feet on dry ground or to catch new views of this bizarre landscape of rock and water (especially fine from **Eaval** on North Uist if you can ever pick your way across to it).

North Uist

The ferry docks at **Lochmaddy**, a village so girdled with lochs that it almost floats. Again, the Tourist Information Centre here is the place to ask about fishing, or try at the Lochmaddy Hotel. Lochmaddy makes a good base for anglers, and is the largest settlement on the island.

There is not much by way of sights on North Uist – the numerous prehistoric remains are fun to track down, but there is usually little to see when you reach them. The charms of the island lie in its beaches, especially those on its north coast, and in its birds. The **Balranald Nature Reserve** is a breeding site for duck and waders and an RSPB reserve. This is one of the places in Scotland where you really do have a chance of seeing an otter, and in summer you may hear the call of the corncrake, a bird that is now extremely rare everywhere in Britain except among the crofts of the Western Isles, where traditional agricultural methods provide shelter for it.

Benbecula

Benbecula was linked to North Uist by causeway only in 1960. Before that, the only way to pass between the islands on foot was by fording the tidal sands between the islands. It is a relatively fertile island, and less beautiful than its neighbours, being flat and dotted with rather ugly crofts.

At **Balivanich** the army base adds to the utilitarian feeling, but compensation is to be found in the relatively large number of shops and other amenities. Here, too, is the airport.

Benbecula's sandy beaches are lovely, but subject, like other westward-facing beaches, to having malodorous piles of seaweed deposited on them by storms. A huge forest of kelp grows off the west coast of the islands; it was once extensively used in making glass and provided income for numerous communities. It is still occasionally collected and dried, as a valuable source of fertiliser.

At **Liniclett**, in the south of the island, the community school has extensive facilities, including a library and small museum. It is also the site of various entertainments which are open to visitors. The school was the subject of a rare spat between the religious communities when it opened, the Presbyterians wishing it to be closed on Sundays and the Catholics seeing no reason why it should be.

It was from Benbecula that the refugee Prince Charles Edward set off with Flora Macdonald over the sea to Skye.

BONNIE PRINCE CHARLIE (1720–1788)

When Charles Edward Stuart, the son of 'The Old Pretender', or James VIII as his Scottish supporters knew him, set foot on the Hebridean island of Eriskay on 23 July 1745, his attempt to restore his father to the throne of Britain seemed doomed. Three previous efforts (1707, 1715 and 1719) had come to nothing; French support was lukewarm at best, while the strength of Scottish and English support was uncertain. The young prince persisted in the face of initial discouragement, sailing to the mainland and raising his father's standard at Glenfinnan on 19 August. If he had not personally persuaded Cameron of Lochiel to raise his clan, little might have come of his effort, for many of the Highland chiefs on whom he relied had refused to join him.

Despite its initial success in defeating the Hanoverian troops at Prestonpans and in occupying Edinburgh, the rising of 1745 was faced with failure from the moment it became clear that there was going to be no general uprising in England. Prince Charles' youth, optimism and charm created devoted followers for him, but a distrust of his father's Catholicism and an unwillingness to hazard life and limb in an uncertain cause deterred many others, even if they had no love for the Hanoverian kings.

The Jacobite army had reached Derby before military discretion caused its leaders to choose withdrawal. The Prince was outraged, but could do nothing. The recall of seasoned Hanoverian troops from the war against France diminished the hopes of success,

He was disguised as her maid, a fact that the famous song does not mention.

South Uist

The history of South Uist, like that of its neighbours to the north, has been a turbulent one. The Norsemen were succeeded by the Lords of the Isles (this is Macdonald territory), and after them, on the forfeiture of the Lord of the Isles, the Campbell Earl of Argyll was made King's Lieutenant. After the Battle of Culloden, Prince Charles Edward spent much time hiding in the islands before his escape to Skye and France. The introduction of the potato increased the population, but the failure of the crop in 1846 brought famine. Clearance and emigration followed,

and the Battle of Culloden in 1746 put an end to them. Some have judged Prince Charles' decision to return to France after that battle as premature, if not a betrayal, but it was little more than a recognition of reality.

After Culloden, the story of the charming, headstrong Prince takes on a tinge of genuine heroism. With a price of £30,000 on his head, and with soldiers combing Scotland for him, the royal refugee wandered the Highlands and Islands for five months. Sleeping rough or in crude bothies and in constant fear of discovery, he dodged from Arisaig to the Western Isles, guided and supplied by men and women who never dreamed of betraying him. Disguised as a maidservant, he was brought back over the sea to Skye by Flora Macdonald and eventually reached Mallaig and the hills above Loch Quoich and Loch Arkaig, where he was sheltered by the 'Seven men of Glenmoriston', who may have been brigands, but were devoted to the Prince. On 19 September, in company with Cameron of Lochiel with whom he had begun the whole desperate venture, he finally boarded a French ship in Loch nan Uamh and returned to exile.

His plea to Louis XV for 20,000 men went unheard, and eventually he was expelled from France. Wandering Europe, still in search of support, the Prince increasingly gave way to stubborn despair and to drink. He died in Italy in 1788. His marble tomb in Rome was partly paid for by the Hanoverian George III. With the deal of his brother, the line of the exiled Stuart kings came to an end.

and the population of South Uist dropped by 2,000 in 20 years.

You are welcomed into South Uist from the north by the statue (1957) of Our Lady of the Isles, which stands on the side of a low hill above the road. **Loch Bee**, which you cross just before reaching the statue, is the haunt of mute swans, while the next large loch, **Loch Druidibeg**, is a nature reserve, with a large colony of greylag geese, many breeding waders and some stretches of machair too. Beyond, the A865 runs

---

USEFUL DIRECTORY

Main tourist office
Western Isles Tourist Board
26 Cromwell Street
Stornoway, Lewis PA87 2DD
(0851) 703088

Tourist Board publications: annual Western Isles accommodation and tourist guide (sights, boat trips, crafts, cycle hire etc.); also *Failte Gazetteer* (places of interest, shops, restaurants); bilingual English/Gaelic *Western Isles Tourist Map*; angling leaflet. Order by post or phone from address above.

Local tourist information centres
Harris, Tarbert (0859) 502011 (Easter to Oct)
North Uist, Lochmaddy (08763) 321 (Easter to Oct)
South Uist, Lochboisdale (0878) 700286 (Easter to Oct)
Barra, Castlebay (0871) 810336 (Easter to Oct)

Public transport
Stornoway airport (0851) 702256
Loganair enquiries (flights from Glasgow, and inter-island services between Stornoway, Barra and Benbecula)
(0851) 703067
British Airways enquiries (flights to Stornoway from Inverness and Glasgow, and to Benbecula from Glasgow)
(0851) 703240
Stornoway bus station (0851) 704327
Post-bus timetables available from tourist information centres or Inverness post office (0463) 234111

---

down the spine of the island, with lochs and hills to the east, crofts, machair and Atlantic beaches to the west. You can divert to **Ormiclete** to see the ruins of a castle, or to **Milton**, where a cairn marks Flora Macdonald's birthplace. **Lochboisdale**, South Uist's ferry port and chief settlement, is set on a sea-loch of singular beauty whose imposing entrance between two sloping hills opens out into an island-dotted bay. There is even a ruined castle on an island to greet you if you arrive by ferry.

Mainland ferries

Car ferries from the mainland to the Western Isles are run by Caledonian MacBrayne (0475) 650100:

Ullapool–Stornoway (3 hrs 30 mins, Mon to Sat, up to three sailings daily)

Uig–Tarbert (1 hr 45 mins, Mon to Sat, one or two sailings daily)

Uig–Lochmaddy (1 hr 45 mins, Mon to Sat, also Sun late Apr to mid-Oct, one or two sailings daily)

Oban–Lochboisdale (5 hrs, up to six sailings a week)

Oban–Castlebay (5 hrs, up to four sailings a week)

Inter-island ferries

Harris–Scalpay car ferry (Mon to Sat, frequent service) (0475) 650100

Harris–North Uist car ferry (one or two sailings a week) (0475) 650100

North Uist–Berneray car ferry (Mon to Sat) (08767) 230

South Uist–Eriskay car ferry (Mon to Sat) (08786) 261

South Uist–Barra car ferry (up to four sailings a week) (0475) 650100

Harris–North Uist passenger ferry (Mon to Sat in summer, three days a week in winter) (08767) 230

Eriskay–South Uist–Barra passenger ferry (Mon to Sat) (0878) 700233

Other

National Trust for Scotland boat cruises to St Kilda, also conservation working parties on the island; ring 031-226 5922, or write to NTS, 5 Charlotte Square, Edinburgh EH2 4DU.

BARRA AND VATERSAY

From the map, Barra may look too small to be worth bothering with, but this is a mistake. On this self-contained island you will find a compendium of all the best parts of the Western Isles – beaches, machair, small crofting communities, and peat-smothered hills. Only the lochans are missing down here – otherwise Barra makes a perfect taster for Hebridean life.

Castlebay is a sheltered harbour with, right in its centre, a castle on a rocky shoal. **Kisimul Castle** (open Apr to Sept, Wed, Fri and Sat afternoons) is the ancient home of the MacNeil chief. On days when it is open, you are rowed out to it for a close-up of the fifteenth-century walls, but it is just as rewarding to gaze at it from the harbour-front of Castlebay.

Barra has one circular road (A888), and driving or bicycling slowly round this is one of the island's two diversions. The west coast is the nicest area, with the best beach (at Tangusdale) and a small valley of crofts – good for a gentle stroll – at Borve.

Detour north from the main road to see the beach of **Tràigh Mhór**, the 'cockle strand' which once provided 100 to 200 cartloads of the shellfish a day. This beach is also Barra's airport – a small shelter stands by it where families wait to pick up relatives who have been shopping in Glasgow. At low tide, the aircraft buzzes in, its wheels kicking up a fine spray from the sand as it touches down.

By the beach, and quite unmistakable, for it is a shell-crushing works, stands the house that was once the home of Compton Mackenzie, author of *Whisky Galore*, among other novels. He spent much of his later middle-age on Barra, and briefly made the island a literary centre.

The second of the island's diversions is to drive across the new causeway to the island of **Vatersay**. There is nothing here apart from crofts, two beautiful beaches and some superb machair full of wild flowers, but on a clear day you can see the string of now uninhabited islands to the south – Sandray, Pabbay, Mingulay and Berneray.

Other islands

- **Berneray** The island is reached by ferry from Harris or North Uist. Its chief attraction are the beaches on the western side, their machair a wonderful place for wild flowers.
- **Eriskay** Reached by ferry from South Uist, this tiny island supports about 200 people. Most visitors come to see the place

where Prince Charles Edward first set foot in Scotland in 1745, or to catch a glimpse of the wreck of the *Politician*, which went down in 1941 carrying 20,000 cases of whisky. Compton Mackenzie's novel *Whisky Galore* and the subsequent film did much to make Eriskay famous.

• **St Kilda** Forty miles west of the Western Isles, the stark rocks of St Kilda rear from the Atlantic. The community was evacuated in 1930, and only the army maintains an occasional presence here.

WHERE TO STAY

LICKISTO

Two Waters Guesthouse £
Lickisto, Isle of Harris
Outer Hebrides PA8 3EL *Tel (085 983) 246*

An excellent, friendly guesthouse in an extremely remote spot. It is hard to avoid fellow guests in the cosy sitting-room or at the communal table, and the pretty, flowery bedrooms (most with shower) are small too. But you can feast on the seafood, home baking and home-grown vegetables, and potter about in the owners' boat. Good value.

Open: all year, exc Oct to Apr **Rooms**: 4 **Facilities**: boat, fishing **Credit/charge cards**: none accepted

SCARISTA

Scarista House £–££
Isle of Harris
Western Isles PA85 3HX *Tel (0859) 550277*

This converted manse stands at the edge of a deserted beach. Bedrooms are individually designed, including those in the annexe, and there is a well-stocked library and a comfortable sitting-room. The generous, straightforward dinners (no choice) make use of excellent fresh food; breakfasts are superb.

Open: all year, exc mid-Oct to Easter **Rooms**: 8
Credit/charge cards: none accepted

UIG

Baile-na-Cille £
Timsgarry, Uig
Isle of Lewis PA86 9JD *Tel (085 175) 242*

A refuge with a reputation for high-spirited fun. The old manse is modern and comfortable with plenty of space for children and dogs. Bedrooms, most with bathroom, are spacious, and everyone eats the good home-cooked dinners at communal tables (give your preferences when you book). Good for families, and good value.

Open: 1 Mar to 1 Oct **Rooms**: 14, 5 cottages **Facilities**: fishing, dinghy **Credit/charge cards**: Access, Visa

WHERE TO EAT

CARNAN

Orasay Inn ★
Loch Carnan
South Uist PA81 5PD *Tel (087 04) 298*

Fifteen minutes from Benbecula airport lies this remote modern inn in barren surroundings. On offer are good seafood platters, grills, curries and Chinese dishes, with a vegetarian selection. Take-away available.

Open: daily 9 to 11pm (1am at weekends) **Credit/charge cards**: Access, Diners, Visa

LOCHMADDY

Langass Lodge
Langass, By Lochmaddy
North Uist PA82 5HA *Tel (087 64) 285*

This was once a fishing lodge. Local Uist brown trout mousse, Uist salmon and meat dishes such as fillets of pork and lamb cutlets all feature on the menu.

Open: daily 12 to 2, 5 to 10; closed Feb and Mar
Credit/charge cards: Access, Visa

CAITHNESS, ORKNEY AND SHETLAND

- Scotland's far north: gales, cliffs, seas and islands
- Superb prehistoric sights
- Seabird cities and endless other birds

Puffins

A GLANCE at a map will show the link between Caithness and the island groups to the north. The Gaelic place names of the Highlands are replaced by a new vocabulary – peerie, geo, wick and voe. These names are relics of the time when Caithness, Orkney and Shetland were part of Norway, not of Scotland.

The Norse jarldom based on Orkney lasted more than 500 years (rather less in Caithness), and it was only in the nineteenth century that the last Norse-speaking inhabitant of Shetland died. The Scandinavian influence is still strong but the Norsemen were far from the first inhabitants of the islands. Nowhere else in Britain is there such a density of prehistoric sites, many dating from 3500 BC. Their remains survive together with the settlements of the Bronze Age, the brochs of the Iron Age, the houses of the Picts and the occasional Norse long house. At Jarlshof in Shetland the remains of houses spanning 2500 years lie exposed.

History is not all that these areas have in common. In Caithness, Orkney and especially Shetland, the sensation that parts of Scotland are closer to the Arctic than to the south of England becomes inescapable. This has little to do with the temperature, which is mild for a part of the world on the same latitude as southern Greenland and Alaska. It has more to do with the absence of trees, the short summer nights, the teeming birdlife, the hissing gales and the feeling that you are on the edge of the unbridled north.

Caithness

Most visitors pass through Caithness on their way to John o'Groats, or to the Orkney ferry from Scrabster. Yet the district has a distinctive character, worth a little exploration. After the sodden moors of Sutherland, the green fields of the north-eastern tip of Scotland seem strange and exotic, the more so since there are no trees to block the views. Instead of trees, you see flagstones. Beneath the soil lie layers of horizontally bedded sedimentary rock, which splits perfectly into thin slabs. Roofs, walls, fences and floors are made from this stone (so are the pavements of many of Britain's cities), and where the sea washes against cliffs of it you find extraordinary effects, from half-finished flights of giant stairs to sea-stacks like carefully balanced towers of biscuits.

The moors lap all around. The blanket bogs of Sutherland extend into Caithness, their unique bird life and desolate beauty threatened by afforestation. The controversy over the spread of the trees has been well publicised, but until you have stood by the Grey Cairns of Camster and seen how the conifers wash up to them like an algae-ridden tide, you are unlikely to appreciate the full extent of the tragedy.

Orkney

It is Orkney's good fortune to be prosperous, beautiful and endowed with world-class sights at the same time as being far enough away from major population centres for there to be little threat from the unpleasant side-effects of mass tourism. Deserted beaches are two-a-penny, custodians have time to chat to you, the wildlife is undisturbed and tour coaches are rarely bigger than minibuses.

Mostly flat and mostly fertile, the Orkney islands are cattle-farming country. Neat fields run down to rocky or sandy beaches; offshore skerries are populated by seals and birds; small boats weave between the islands to set lobster pots. In Orkney, evidence of the far-distant past lies everywhere. The standing stones of Stenness and Brodgar, the chambered cairn of Maes Howe and the Neolithic village of Skara Brae would be worth journeying to see anywhere, but their setting against the stark sea or sky of Orkney adds hugely to their appeal.

Shetland

According to Tacitus, the Romans sighted Shetland on their expedition round Britain and named it Thule after the mythical island on the edge of the world. And this is what it feels like. Shetland is an acquired taste, for to spend money coming to a climate that is, at best, uncertain and to a landscape which has little of the welcoming fertility of Orkney may seem an act of sheer folly. Yet Shetland can be addictive in much the same way as strong black coffee. A draught composed of Arctic wind, luminous skies and tearing seas can stimulate and revivify when you are feeling creative, or misanthropic, or overdosed on stress. If all you want is to relax in comfort in the sun, leave it well alone.

In early summer Shetland's cliffs teem with seabirds, while rare waders breed on its lochs and desolate moorlands. To come to Shetland without doing a spot of birdwatching is a waste, even for those whose closest contact with feathers is normally their duvet. The seabird colonies in the full

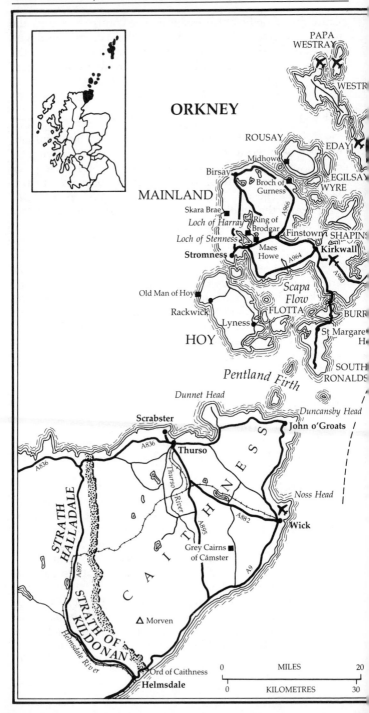

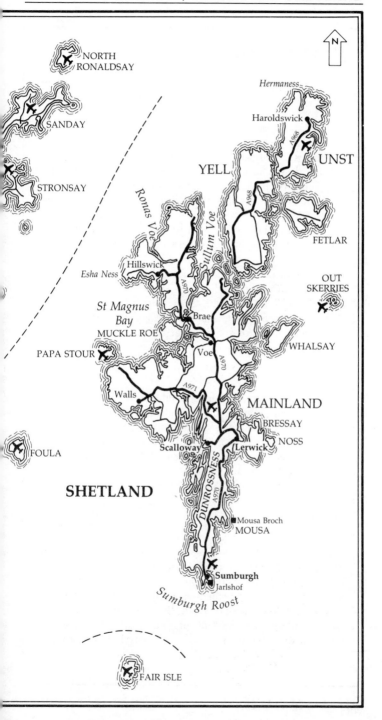

NORTH
RONALDSAY

SANDAY

STRONSAY

Hermaness

Haroldswick

A968

YELL

UNST

Ronas Voe

Sullum Voe

A968

FETLAR

Hillswick

Esha Ness

A970

OUT
SKERRIES

A78

*St Magnus
Bay*

MUCKLE ROE

Brae

PAPA STOUR

Voe

A970

WHALSAY

Walls

A971

MAINLAND

BRESSAY

NOSS

Scalloway

Lerwick

FOULA

SHETLAND

DUNROSSNESS

A970

A971

■ Mousa Broch
MOUSA

Sumburgh

Jarlshof

Sumburgh Roost

FAIR ISLE

Practical suggestions

You can combine Orkney, Shetland and Caithness into one holiday, but both Orkney and Shetland really deserve more than a brief visit. Flying between the islands and the mainland is the quickest and most convenient way of travel, but you can journey between Caithness, Orkney and Shetland by car ferry too.

Wind is a constant feature of life here, and the knitwear industry thrives on tourists who have packed one sweater too few. You are not likely to regret buying locally – there are excellent bargains. Wellies are indispensable: ankle-deep peat sludge or a minefield of cowpats may lie between you and what you want to explore. Waterproof trousers are a good idea, too: many chambered tombs have large puddles in their entrance passages, and you may have to crawl. Be cautious of strong winds on cliff-edges and crumbling rock.

Getting to Orkney, Shetland or Caithness from further south is easy, though it may not be cheap. Flights from Glasgow and Edinburgh are frequent, and you can come via Inverness or Aberdeen too. There are daily car ferries from Aberdeen to Orkney and Shetland.

Caithness

Most of the accommodation in Caithness is clustered around the chief towns of Wick and Thurso, neither of them desperately attractive. A couple of good hotels make up for the rest. Bed-and-breakfast is your best bet. Wick has air connections north and south, and a railway station, while car ferries run from Scrabster to Orkney and on to Shetland and a passenger ferry crosses to Orkney from John o' Groats in summer.

Orkney

You can happily spend all your time on Mainland (Orkney's largest island), but we recommend visiting some of the outlying islands too. All can be reached by sea (some of the crossings can be pretty bouncy) and there are so-so services to all but two (book a week in advance), but nothing can compare with island-hopping on Loganair's eight-seater aircraft. Buzzing over the translucent sea and touching down on miniature grass airstrips makes for wry reflection on more usual forms of air travel. If you are not fussy about which islands you go to, Loganair have good-value three-flight deals on a stand-by basis. Flights run to the minute: do not get stranded.

Kirkwall is Orkney's capital and makes a convenient base for exploration and for shopping. The most renowned prehistoric sights are on Mainland, but enthusiasts should plan to visit Rousay, Hoy, Sanday and Papa Westray too. Anglers should base themselves near the lochs of Stenness and Harray, which are the most famous fishing waters, while birdwatchers make for Westray, Papa Westray or North Ronaldsay (for migrants). Sub-aqua enthusiasts dive to see the remains of the scuttled German High Seas Fleet in Scapa Flow. Other wartime relics are to be found on Hoy.

There is a reasonable choice of accommodation on Mainland, Hoy and Rousay, farmhouse bed-and-breakfasts being especially common, and you can just about get around Mainland by bus. On outlying islands there is no public transport, and accommodation is much sparser. However, thanks to the entrepreneurial inhabitants, you will usually be able to find a car or bicycle to hire and somewhere to stay, even in spots which the Kirkwall tourist office claims are bare of facilities. Telephone the local community centres (some of which double as guesthouses) on the islands to be pointed in the right direction.

Shetland

In Shetland there is little need to stray from Mainland (again the largest island), though you should visit Fair Isle if you possibly can. A car is almost essential on Shetland, though there are coach outings to some remote spots and the bus network is reasonable. Fly-drive deals are available or you can bring your own car from Caithness via Orkney, or from Aberdeen. Roads on Shetland are excellent. **Lerwick**, the capital, has good shops and plenty of atmosphere; the finest scenery is in the north and west of Mainland, the best sights in the south. The seabird cities on the islands of Unst or Noss are relatively easy to reach and worth seeing, while Fair Isle and Fetlar also draw birdwatchers. For really remote island communities to visit, Foula and Out Skerries have few rivals.

All the outlying islands can be reached by sea, but you cannot take your car to Foula, Fair Isle or Papa Stour (nor would you want to). Frequent car ferries run to Yell, Unst, Fetlar, Whalsay and Bressay. You should book in advance in summer. Loganair operates regular flights from Tingwall airport, slightly north of Lerwick, to Unst and Fair Isle. During the summer Loganair runs reasonably regular flights and day trips to Foula, Out Skerries, Papa Stour and Fair Isle.

Many of Shetland's hotels leave rather a lot to be desired; some were built rápidly at the beginning of the oil boom and are now decaying equally rapidly, while others act as staging posts for oil workers, sailors or helicopter pilots rather than as havens for the holidaymaker. Do not book without seeing what you are getting. In general, you are likely to find better value and be better looked after in bed-and-breakfast places. If you are bent on self-catering base yourself within striking distance of Lerwick, so that you can stock up on essentials without having to drive too far.

cacophony of the breeding season are not lightly forgotten. Nor is being dive-bombed by skuas, harassed by aggravated terns, or simply sitting watching the puffins at their burrows. Bring binoculars.

CAITHNESS

The East Coast

. . . the inciville and barbrous behaviour of the most part of oure subjectis in Caithness . . . (James VI, 1611)
Beyond Helmsdale, a ridge of hills which form part of the massif of Scaraben runs to the coast, providing a barrier between Caithness and Sutherland. The coastal road now climbs easily over the **Ord of Caithness**, but it used to be quite a motoring adventure. Caithness Sinclairs still avoid crossing the Ord on a Monday, for it was on this day that 300 men set out under Earl William to take part in the Battle of Flodden, where they were wiped out.

A little way beyond the Ord, signs point over a heathery ridge to the Clearance village of **Badbea**. The few humps of bracken-covered stone at the far end of the short path drive home the human suffering of the Clearances with great clarity. This was the sort of place where communities were forced to settle after being evicted from inland straths. Right on the edge of the cliffs (legend goes that the village children had to be tethered, like goats), with no shelter and little fertile land, people eked out some sort of living. The village was finally deserted when the last of its folk emigrated to New Zealand. It is hard to imagine, picking among the ruins of the crofts, or looking at the names inscribed on the memorial that stands over them, how anyone managed to exist in such a place.

By the side of the road a few miles further north **Lhaidhay Croft Museum** (open Easter to Oct, daily 10 to 6) is a well-preserved long croft house, furnished as it might have been in the nineteenth century. This is an excellent small museum, full of curiosities, most of them donated by local people. There are box beds, beautiful linen night-shirts and even a primitive washing machine. The lasting impression is of a snug comfort, both for the inhabitants and their beasts in the adjacent byre – quite a contrast to Badbea.

If you turn north on the minor road out of Clyth, the three huge stone piles of the **Grey Cairns of Camster** become visible among the young trees which surround them. These chambered cairns date from around 2500 BC. The three entrance passages are each guarded by a little gate to keep the sheep out, and it is worth the damp crawl into the biggest cairn at least, for the interior chamber is a spacious and sombre place (despite its concrete roof).

Back on the main road, the **Hill O' Many Stanes** is a very peculiar prehistoric site. On a patch of level ground on a hillside just off the main road, 22 rows of small upright stones form a fan shape. They are mostly under knee height, and there are more than 200 of them. No one is sure of their purpose.

By the village of **Ulbster** is Whaligoe harbour, the most unlikely landing place on the fierce east coast of Caithness. Almost 365 vertiginous steps are needed to climb down the cliff to the pier beneath. Not surprisingly, the harbour has long gone out of use, but its very existence is testimony to the wealth to be had from the herring boom; 24 boats once operated from this harbour, and the catch was carried up those terrible steps on the backs of the fishermen's wives.

Wick

In 1589, when Wick became a royal burgh, it was a small village with a harbour scarcely worth the name. By 1862, 1122 boats were fishing for herring from Wick and a whole new town and harbour had been built for the industry.

The town was packed with the seasonal workers – gutters, packers and coopers – needed to get the fish from boat to barrel as quickly as possible. Today, Wick is quiet again, the herring gone, the fishing fleet much reduced in number. The herring industry comes to life again in the **Wick Heritage Centre** (open Easter to mid-Oct, Mon to Sat 10 to 5), one of the most detailed fishing museums on the whole Scottish coast.

Wick is a grey stone town – stark, like many another Scottish fishing port, as if its energies were focused entirely on the sea beyond the harbour wall. If you are interested in town planning, a stroll across the river brings you to 'Poltney' or Pultneytown, sponsored by the British Fisheries Society in the early nineteenth century, and planned and laid out by Thomas Telford.

A port of call for most visitors is **Caithness Glass** (for glassblowing, open Mon to Fri 9 to 4.30; shop open Mon to Fri 9 to 5, Sat 9 to 1; June to Sept, Sat 9 to 4, Sun 11 to 5), where, in a remarkably informal factory where furnaces roar and red-hot glassware is carried back and forth, you can follow the making of glass from ingredients to finished article. Among other things the factory produces the annual *Mastermind* trophy.

North of Wick

Out beyond Wick airport (beware, the road crosses the runway), on the edge of Noss head, the remaining masonry of **Castle Sinclair** and **Castle Girnigoe** (one is a later extension of the other) rises out of the haze like a factory chimney. A very muddy walk takes you down to the cliff edge, and reveals the work of a mad or inspired builder. The castles stand on the narrowest of promontories, with the sea sucking at stacked layers of flagstone beneath. George Sinclair, fourth Earl of Caithness, threw his son into a dungeon here on suspicion of treachery, first starved him, then fed him on all the salt beef he could eat, and finally left him to die of thirst.

After this grisly tale, there is no better place to go than nearby **Duncansby Head**. This is the true north-eastern tip of Scotland, and is adorned by the Stacks of Duncansby – rock spires which rise straight out of the sea. There is also a lighthouse, two long geos, a cave, the Rispie tide-race, wheeling seabirds and short turf full of wild flowers.

The North coast

John o' Groats

Rainy rainy rattlestanes, dinna rain on me. Rain on Johnny Groats hoose, far across the sea. (Nursery rhyme)

John o' Groats is a curious place for a tourist trap, for there is nothing here apart from an hotel and a scattering of gift shops. This may change with the advent of yet another heritage centre and the redevelopment of the hotel. Still, it is being here that counts, and for as long as John o' Groats is considered to be 'opposite' Land's End in Cornwall, long-distance walkers, cyclists or fund-raising bed-pushers will continue to make it their starting or finishing point, and the coaches will fill the car park.

Jan de Groot was a Dutchman, whom James IV employed in 1496 to start a ferry to the recently acquired territory of Orkney. He is said to have built an octagonal house with eight internal doors to solve problems of family precedence. The house is long gone, but the hotel sports an octagonal tower in its memory.

John o' Groats is not the northernmost point of mainland Britain. For that you must visit **Dunnet Head** to the west, a peninsula of humpy moorland, with good views of Orkney and the Pentland Firth on a clear day.

Thurso

This town used to be Scotland's chief trading port with Scandinavia, though you would never think so today. It is still the largest town on the mainland north of Inverness, its economy considerably boosted by the nearby Dounreay nuclear research station, now being run down. Much of the town was planned by Sir John Sinclair ('Agricultural Sir John'), one of the best-known 'Improvers' of the eighteenth century. Thurso is a slightly scruffy place with little to linger for, apart from the **Thurso Folk Museum** (open Easter to Sept, Mon to Sat 10 to 5), where there are Pictish stones and the collection left by the Victorian naturalist Robert Dick, whom the locals thought to be daft.

Just north of Thurso lies **Scrabster**, the terminal for the car ferry to Stromness in Orkney, and a good place to arrange sea angling.

The road west runs past the attractive River Forss to **Dounreay**, where the dome of Britain's prototype fast reactor stands out against the blue of the sea. The clutter of buildings round it mars the striking effect. In summer you may be able to see inside (ring 084780 2701/2235 to check).

ORKNEY

Kirkwall

Orkney's capital has been in existence since the eleventh century, so has the restrained dignity of a small town with a lot of history under its belt. Beside the magnificent red sandstone twelfth-century cathedral old houses line the single main street, while the ruined Bishop's Palace and Earl's Palace add Renaissance grandeur. Pottering around the shops and looking at the silverwork inspired by Norse designs does not take long, and a day will serve to cover the sights. Nevertheless, Kirkwall makes a congenial base. Roads radiate from it all over Mainland, and there is a distillery to visit, a small theatre and a swimming-pool.

Sights in Kirkwall

●**St Magnus Cathedral** (HS, Mon to Sat 9 to 1, 2 to 5) That a building of such size and splendour should exist so far out on the periphery of Scotland may seem surprising until you remember that when it was built, Orkney was the seat of a powerful Norse earldom. By the twelfth century, Orkney's inhabitants had stopped pillaging monasteries on the coasts of Britain and had turned Christian themselves. The cathedral bears the name of Orkney's own martyr, St Magnus.

Magnus was co-Earl of Orkney with his cousin, Haakon. After a series of disputes, the two met in 1117 on the island of Egilsay for a reconciliation. Haakon, however, broke the agreed terms and arrived with a large body of men, making it apparent that execution, not negotiation, was on the agenda. After Haakon's standard-bearer had refused to kill Magnus, his cook, Lifolf, eventually did the deed. The skull of Magnus, found in the cathedral in 1919, bears a great gash, very much as the fatal axe blow is described in the verse chronicle of early Orcadian history, the *Orkneyinga Saga*. The cathedral was founded by Magnus' nephew, Rognvald in 1137. It is constructed of a lucent red sandstone with occasional interleavings of yellow, and propped by massive nave columns like sea stacks. The Gothic clerestory pours light into the building, so that on sunny days it seems to glow throughout its interior.

●**Earl's Palace** (HS, standard times; closed in winter) This is the ruin of a magnificent Renaissance building which speaks of power and luxury. Huge oriel windows once flooded it with light, and enormous fireplaces held promise of roaring warmth. Yet its owner was a ruthless tyrant who needed a bodyguard of 50 men when he went to the cathedral only a few yards away, and whose eventual execution had to be postponed until he had been taught the Lord's Prayer. This was Patrick Stewart, Earl of Orkney, the son of one of James V's bastards. His palace was constructed by what amounted to slave labour. The ground floor is evidence of the Earl's priorities, for it consists of a series of enormous vaulted storerooms, and a giant kitchen. Upstairs, the hall's beautiful windows are complemented by some severely practical loopholes for muskets.

●**The Bishop's Palace** (HS, standard times; closed in winter) This building, just over the road from the Earl's Palace, is in places contemporary with the cathedral, though it was remodelled a number of times. It is a much more complicated building than the Earl's Palace, and a less obviously beautiful one, though there is plenty to interest those who like tracing architectural developments.

●**Tankerness House Museum** (open all year, Mon to Sat 10.30 to 12.30, 1.30 to 5; also Sun 2 to 5, May to Sept) Close to the cathedral, this museum makes a good starting point for learning about prehistoric Orkney, best seen before visiting the sites. The permanent exhibition leads you round the life and times of Orkney's earliest settlers, via pottery, carved stones, reconstructions of stone furniture and rows of skulls. Tankerness House has many of Orkney's best finds; keep an eye open for the delicate and beautiful bone combs, and do not be so distracted by the exhibits that you fail to notice the age and elegance of the house itself.

Deerness and the Gloup

The eastern side of Mainland, willow-green, open and bathed in a pearly light, does not have the abundance of archaeological sights to be found west of Kirkwall, so few visitors travel much further than the airport. The area is good for isolated seaside or clifftop wandering, however. An expedition to the **Gloup**, right out on the eastern side of the Deerness peninsula, will not reveal something from a horror film, but a collapsed sea cave – its outer arch still intact – where waves suck and gurgle at the bottom of a chasm.

The Churchill Barriers and Lamb Holm

On top of a foundation of giant, haphazardly piled concrete blocks, a ribbon of road links Mainland to the islands of Lamb Holm, Glimps Holm, Burray and South Ronaldsay. The rusting remnants of sunken ships poke from the water beside the causeway. The concrete and the wrecks are the results of attempts to block the entrances from the North Sea to **Scapa Flow**, the sheltered anchorage which became a major naval base in two world wars. The blockships proved unable to prevent an enterprising German U-boat from slipping into Scapa Flow on 14 October 1939 and torpedoing the battleship *Royal Oak* with the loss of 800 lives, so the concrete Churchill Barriers were installed with the labour of 550 Italian POWs.

The prisoners left a reminder of their stay in the shape of the **Italian Chapel** (always open) on Lamb Holm. The Mediterranean façade of this tiny church, with its columned portico and surmounting belfry, seems incongruous in the steely northern light. The prisoners put it together from two Nissen huts, moulded concrete and whatever scrap came to hand. Inside, a Madonna and Child is painted on concrete above the altar, and there is an elaborate wrought-iron rood screen.

Isbister Chambered Cairn

(Open Apr to Sept, daily 10 to 8; out-of-season visitors should ring 085683 339)
Past the peaceful village of St Margaret's Hope and hidden among the hilltop farmsteads of the island of South Ronaldsay lies the Neolithic chambered cairn popularly known as the Tomb of the Eagles, from the many bird carcasses found in the 4000-year-old burial chamber. The site is family-run (a most unusual occurrence), for the tomb lies on land belonging to farmer Ronald Simison. Even more unusually, he excavated the site himself. At Liddel Farm, you are taken on a most entrancing journey back in time. You are handed a prehistoric axe, which moulds perfectly into your hand, then

a shiny black ring (the two halves found 10 years apart) and then the cool, smooth skulls of a woman and a man, dead at 35 and 26. You will also encounter a row of wellies ready for visitors on the porch, and a trolley, knee patches and torch by the tomb entrance.

The north coast of Mainland

There are prehistoric remains to whet your appetite as you head west from Kirkwall, notably the chambered cairn on Wideford Hill, but unless you are keen on a roughish walk it is probably better to save your energies for the **Broch of Gurness** (HS, standard times; closed in winter) on the shore opposite the island of Rousay. The broch lies beyond the Sands of Evie, where oystercatchers and curlews strut in the shallows, at the narrowest part of the Eynhallow Sound. It is a complicated site (though much of it has vanished into the sea) with a jumble of Iron Age houses surrounding the substantial remains of the broch at their centre, a surrounding ditch and rampart and the relocated remains of a Pictish house and what may have been a Norse hall. Explanations are clear and convincing, and artists' impressions help to give you an idea of what it was once like.

Birsay

The ecclesiastical centre of the islands before St Magnus Cathedral was built, Birsay is now an exposed straggle of a village. It is dominated by the austere remains of the **Earl's Palace** (HS, always open), another work of the deplorable Stewart earls. Off the coast lies the **Brough of Birsay**. Brough is the word for tidal island, and this one is reached across a slippery causeway. The sea can sneak up behind you, so pay heed to the custodian on the island, or keep your eyes peeled. Check the tide tables in the *Orcadian* before coming: Birsay is one hour before Kirkwall.

Much of the ancient settlement on the brough has been lost to the sea, but what is left is the most substantial complex of Norse buildings on the islands. The Norsemen were not the first inhabitants, for the shattered remains of a Pictish stone were found scattered over the graveyard of the little twelfth-century church. A copy is now in place, showing two dignified warriors marching behind their chief.

Maes Howe

(HS, standard times)

Of the four great prehistoric sights grouped by the Loch of Stenness, Maes Howe is the most fabulous. It is a giant chambered cairn standing on a levelled platform with a rock-cut ditch running round it. The entrance passage and much of the interior of the tomb are built from gigantic slabs of stone, slotted together with the neatness of a Lego building.

A long stooping shuffle through the entrance passage takes you into the dim central chamber, where the custodian gradually brings up the lights to show you the details of the ceiling corbelling, the three side-cells and the massive block-stones which would have closed upon the last remains of the deceased. You are told how, on the shortest night of the year, a shaft of light from the setting sun will turn the entrance passage to gold and throw a splash of light on to the back wall of the chamber.

Attention then shifts to the graffiti. These were left in the twelfth century by Norsemen who seem to have broken into the tomb more than once (the *Orkneyinga Saga* records that two men went mad here while sheltering from a snowstorm). The scratchings of the Norsemen's runes show up under the custodian's torch: there is a lion and what could be a walrus. In translation, the runes are generally no more interesting than modern graffiti, but some talk of 'a great treasure', an idea sniffily dismissed by archaeologists. Maes Howe was empty when excavated. It is curious to think of those Norse warriors scratching on the walls only 800 years ago, while the time that separated them from the people who dragged the massive slabs over the moors to build this astonishing place was closer to 4000 years.

The Stones of Stenness and the Ring of Brodgar

Only four great monoliths survive out of the original 12 which made up the stone circle of Stenness, poised where the Loch of Harray flows into the Loch of Stenness. Grey, gaunt and lonely in the middle of farmland, the huge slabs seem to have been frozen in place. It is easy to imagine them lumbering down to drink at the loch on some midsummer's night, and indeed one seems to have been caught in the act, for as you cross the causeway between the two lochs, a single menhir – the Watch Stone – stands on the very edge of the water.

The time to be at the nearby Ring of Brodgar is at sunset, preferably when the sky boils with cloud and burning light. The 27 stones (there were once 60) stand still and lonely in a perfect circle silhouetted against the hills of Hoy, with water on both sides and a great sweep of sky above.

The lochs on each side of the ring, Stenness and Harray, are the best-known fishing lochs of Orkney. Stenness is unusual in that you can catch sea fish as well as fresh-water fish. This is because of the loch's narrow outlet to the sea, which leaves the water sufficiently fresh to hold trout, but which can bring in pollock, herring, plaice and, of course, sea trout.

Corrigall and Kirkbister Farm Museums

(Open Mar to Oct, Mon to Sat 10.30 to 1, 2 to 5, Sun 2 to 7)
Between them, these old Orkney farms give a clear impression of life in the last century. While conditions were less spartan than in one of the black houses of the Hebrides, they were hardly luxurious. At Kirkbister, you will find an unaltered example of an old Orkney kitchen, with its free-standing hearth, smoke hole in the roof and tiny bed built into the thickness of the wall. Corrigall is more fully restored, complete with implements, hens and cheese but, while there is more to see, it is rather less evocative.

Skara Brae

(HS, standard times)
This is Orkney's second extraordinary prehistoric sight. It is a complete Neolithic village, buried for millennia in the sand until unearthed by a freak storm in 1850. It is hard to see until you are standing almost on top of it, for the village was semi-subterranean, built deliberately in the middle of a great heap of decayed household refuse – the midden. Skara Brae is 5000 years old, yet its state of preservation, right down to the furniture and the drainage system, is such that a great effort is needed to realise that it is older than the Egyptian pyramids or Stonehenge.

Skara Brae lies right at the edge of the sea, where the Bay of Skaill takes a great bite out of Mainland's rugged west coast. The waves lash the edge of the site, and much of it may have been lost to erosion in previous centuries. This curious little community, where cramped, tortuous passages lead between spacious houses, with the local stone-working workshop set a little apart, irresistibly recalls a suburban housing estate. All the houses have the same design, with little cupboards, stone-sided beds and central hearths, and all have stone dressers arranged opposite the doorways, perhaps so that *objets d'art* could be displayed with maximum effect to the neighbours. All that is missing is the television.

Current theories suggest that Skara Brae was a self-sufficient, egalitarian community of farmers and fishermen. Everything they had was made from stone, bone, wood or skin – there is no evidence of metal or cloth. Yet some of the things they produced – especially the intricately carved and decorated stone objects of unknown purpose – and some of their building techniques – notably the strong possibility that the village had a sanitation system flushed by running water – make it impossible to dismiss the inhabitants of Skara Brae as primitive. For six centuries or so they lived in their village, then abandoned it – no one knows why.

When you have gazed enough, the foreshore of the Bay of Skaill is good for a gentle stroll. On the other hand, if there is a wind blowing, travel down the coast to **Yesnaby**, where the sea beats against cliffs and shelves of flagstone and cormorants perch on half-submerged rocks, their outstretched wings giving them the appearance of scarecrows.

Stromness

Only the gulls and the arrival of the ferry from Scrabster disturb the quiet of this town. It was once a far livelier place, for the Hudson Bay Company's ships called in regularly on their fur-trading run to northern Canada, and Stromness supplied both men and stores for the Davis Strait whalers. The main street meanders for a mile between the seafront and the steep slope of Brinkie's Brae. At the start of Victoria Street, the complex of buildings by the pier has been converted into the **Pier Arts Centre** (open Tues to Sat 10.30 to 12.30, 1.30 to 5; July, Aug also Sun 2 to 5). Displayed here is a permanent collection of twentieth-century works by Barbara Hepworth, Ben Nicholson, Naum Gabo and Eduardo Paolozzi which was donated to Orkney by Margaret Gardiner; there are also temporary exhibitions, children's workshops, lectures and poetry readings.

Stromness Museum (open Mon to Sat 10.30 to 5; closed 12.30 to 1.30) was founded in 1837 and is showing its age, but the wonderful clutter of photographs and objects, mostly donated by local people, can absorb you for hours.

The most fascinating story told here is that of the scuttling of the German fleet in Scapa Flow in 1919. The fleet had been interned at the end of World War I to await the terms of the peace treaty, its sailors cold and dispirited. On 21 June a group of children from Stromness went on a cruise which turned out to be the most exciting school outing ever: all around them huge warships suddenly started to sink, deliberately scuttled in a final act of defiance. Seventy-four ships went to the bottom. The subsequent salvage operation was extremely complicated. Three battleships and four battle-cruisers remain on the sea bed and they form an excellent sight, in clear waters, for scuba-divers.

Hoy

The island of Hoy is unlike the rest of Orkney, being hilly, peat-covered and sparsely populated. It has the finest cliff scenery in the islands, culminating in the huge precipices of St John's Head, and in the Old Man of Hoy, the most famous of Scotland's sea-stacks. This is also the place to see relics of Orkney's wartime base, which is in the south of the island.

Lyness

The car ferry from Houton docks under the shadow of the rusting naval guns which stand watch over the visitor centre (open mid-Apr to mid-Oct, Mon to Fri 9 to 4, Sun 10.30 to 3.30; mid-Oct to mid-Apr, Mon to Fri 9 to 4) at the end of the pier. Much of the display has been salvaged from the depths of Scapa Flow, including an old aircraft engine, and there is a mass of information about wartime Orkney. The place is still in its early days, but shows every sign of becoming good. The enormous propellor and drive shaft of *HMS Hampshire*, which went down off Marwick Head in 1916 taking Lord Kitchener with her, is the largest exhibit.

The hillsides are studded with the rotting foundations of bunkers, hutments and emplacements, but little else is left of a base that once held more than 60,000 personnel. If you explore the crumbling road that leads up the hillside, you come to the mouth of a tunnel leading deep into the rock where fuel oil was stored out of reach of the bombs, and the area still smells of it. At the base of the hill lies a windswept cemetery, containing the dead of two world wars.

The Dwarfie Stane and Rackwick

Hoy's only chambered tomb, and a remarkable one, lies off the road that leads across the north of the island to Rackwick. The neat path that leads away from the road rapidly disappears, and unless you have wellies you will be ankle-deep in peat mire by the time you reach the huge block of sandstone that contains the tomb. This, complete with two side cells, has been hollowed out of the solid rock. Only stone tools were used and there cannot have been room for more than two people to work at a time. Why did they go to this enormous effort? No one knows.

At the end of the road lies **Rackwick**, held by some to be the most beautiful spot on Orkney. It is also the starting point for the walk to the **Old Man of Hoy**. Rackwick is a sheltered green breach in a rampart of red sea-cliffs. It would be perfect if it had a sandy beach, but alas there are only boulders.

The path to the Old Man of Hoy goes uphill round the headland east of Rackwick. At first you see only the green top of the Old Man level with the cliff edge, but as you draw near the plunging layers of rock which make up the stack become apparent. It is a substantial walk to reach the cliffs of St John's Head further along the coast, and the view from the Stromness to Scrabster ferry is just as good.

Rousay

Next to Mainland, this is the best island for prehistoric remains, and there is some accommodation if you want to take more than a day over them. The single road runs around the perimeter and the chief sights are close to it, so hiring a bicycle is probably the best way of getting around.

The **Midhowe Chambered Cairn** (HS, always open), like Maes Howe, is about 5000 years old, but of a very different design. Whereas Maes Howe has a central chamber with cells built into the walls, Midhowe has a long passage partitioned by pairs of upright slabs, resembling a byre as much as anything, and known as a stalled cairn. It is housed in a modern hangar, which has a gantry allowing you to walk above the tomb and look down into it. Deep silence hangs over this age-old burial ground, and it can be a relief to get out into the wind again.

Only a short walk away is one of the best brochs in Orkney. Much of the surrounding settlement has dissolved into the ocean, but **Midhowe Broch** still stands 13 feet high. One of the interesting features is the ground-level gallery (most brochs have their galleries higher up), and if you have a torch you may be tempted to explore the dark, narrow passage. Two smaller stalled cairns, **Knowe of Yarso** and **Blackhammer**, lie on the way to Midhowe. Neither lives up to Midhowe in scale. Even if you ignore these, the chambered cairn called **Traversoe Tuick** is worth a visit, for here two separate tombs were built one on top of the other and you can explore both.

Westray

Westray is a large, solid island with a long flat tail stretching to the south-east, a range of low hills to the west, the bird cliffs of **Noup Head** to the north-west and an area of sand dunes and machair in the north. **Pierowall**, quite a substantial village, is strung out round the edge of an attractive bay, and it is here that you will arrive if you have come by boat or hitched a ride in from the airstrip. Birdwatchers will probably set out for Noup Head without delay (it is a longish walk), but the first sight for most visitors will be **Noltland Castle** (HS, access from keykeeper; details at site), half a mile's stroll from the village. This splendid sixteenth-century Z-plan fortress is studded with gunloops, and is a place of extraordinary strength for such a remote location. It was built by an incomer from Fife, of dubious reputation, called Gilbert Balfour. It is not just a grim, damp fortress, for the main staircase with its great stone newel at its head is a spacious and beautiful piece of building (take a torch to see it at its best). North of Noltland, Westray's golf course lies on the flat links leading down to the sea. A walk across the sandy turf reveals wild flowers – and hosts of rabbits (many of them black), for there are no ground predators. By making a few inquiries in Pierowall, you should be able to see the holding tanks full of lobsters (usually with some gigantic specimens) in the centre of the village.

Papa Westray

You can get here by boat, but if you are coming from Westray it may prove irresistible to splash out on the shortest scheduled flight in the world. It takes two minutes. Papa Westray is small, and uninhabited at its northern end, where the fields give way to maritime heath. This is **North Hill**, now a nature reserve inhabited by bonxies (skuas) and thousands of arctic terns. The former will buzz you ferociously if you intrude. A stout hat is a good idea for protecting your head against skua strikes.

More or less in the centre of the island, through an extremely muddy farmyard, a track leads you down to the **Knap of Howar**, the oldest standing house in north-west Europe. If you have visited Skara Brae, you will recognise the structure you find here – a semi-subterranean house built into a midden. Unlike Skara Brae, this is not a village but an independent farmhouse, complete with a barn next door.

The east coast is a good place to see seals, both common and grey, which haul themselves up on to the reefs at low tide and bask with head and flippers in the air, looking as if they were doing an aerobics exercise. This is also the side of the island to make for in order to get a boat to the islet **Holm of Papa**, which has an excellent chambered cairn. You may be able to arrange this on the spot by asking at the island's shop, or ask at the tourist office at Kirkwall.

Sanday

This is a big, low-lying island, shaped like a pterodactyl in flight. If you want to explore it thoroughly you will need a car, unless you are a very fit cyclist. Arriving off the ferry brings you straight to the village of Kettletoft, where someone will give you advice. Sanday's other village is charmingly called Lady.

Sanday is ideal for beach-lovers. The coastline is indented with one bay after another – sandy, weedy, rocky, calm or full of hissing waves. They face enough different directions for you to be certain of finding shelter. The **Bay of Lopness** with miles of dunes is one of the best, and the beaches on either side of the Els Ness peninsula are also good. You are certain to see seals somewhere as you prowl the coastline. The views from the small hill in the south-west of the island – prosaically called the Wart – encompass much of Sanday, Stronsay to the south and the cliffs of Calf of Eday.

Sanday is good for birds, especially terns, and the marshy areas round the Loch of Langamay and North Loch in the north-east tip of the island are the places to look. At Tafts Ness, one of the biggest prehistoric sites in Europe remains unexcavated. Over 500 burial mounds dot the landscape. However, the best prehistoric sight on Sanday is **Quoyness chambered cairn** (HS, access from keykeeper; details at site).

This is the same type of tomb as Maes Howe, and, although not on the same scale, it is an impressive piece of work. Part of the attraction is its isolation – you need not worry about crowds here. The tomb lies near the extremity of Els Ness, half a mile beyond the end of a sand-covered track.

Other islands

●**Eday** has much more heather moorland than most of the islands, and used to export peat widely. The outstanding monument is the prehistoric Stone of Setter, a standing stone fully 15 feet high, superbly situated.

●**Egilsay** If you look over Rousay Sound towards Egilsay, the prominent round tower on the church could easily be mistaken for a factory chimney. It in fact belongs to the twelfth-century St Magnus Church, which stands on the site where St Magnus is supposed to have prayed the night before his murder.

●**Flotta** Orkney's oil island is dominated by the oil terminal, and best viewed from a distance.

●**North Ronaldsay** This is the smallest and most remote of the northern islands. The seaweed-fed sheep are a unique breed and roam the shore in a communal flock, confined by a dry-stone dyke. There is the much-ruined Broch of Burrian by the shore to visit and rare migrant birds to spot.

●**Shapinsay** Shapinsay is a flat, gentle island dominated by the Victorian pile of Balfour Castle, which it is possible both to tour and stay in. Its accessibility (a 25-minute ferry ride from Kirkwall) makes up for a lack of striking sights.

●**Stronsay** If you want to leave fellow tourists behind, this is the place to come to: Stronsay is probably the least visited of all the islands, with neither outstanding sights nor outstanding scenery.

●**Wyre** This tiny arrow-shaped island has the remains of Scotland's oldest stone castle on it. There is also a partly restored twelfth-century chapel.

SHETLAND

Sumburgh

The long, thin ridge of land that forms the tail of Shetland ends in the cliffs of **Sumburgh Head**. If you have just arrived by air, spend some time exploring the area before setting off on the journey north. From Sumburgh Head itself you look out over the tide-race of Sumburgh Roost to the angular profile of Fair Isle on the horizon. There is a colony of seabirds, and a cluster of sandy beaches. Within the shadow of the airport lies the most important archaeological site in Shetland.

Jarlshof

(HS, standard times; closed in winter)
Walter Scott coined the name in his novel *The Pirate*, long before the existence of a Norse settlement here was confirmed. Jarlshof was inhabited from prehistoric times right down to the seventeenth century, so there is a profusion of buildings dating from the late Neolithic period onwards. From the Bronze Age there is a metal-worker's workshop; from the Iron Age, earth houses and the substantial remains of a broch. The best-preserved houses, however, are wheel houses from the third to the eighth centuries. These are comfortable-looking designs, with a series of individual rooms radiating round a central hearth, giving everyone privacy and warmth in equal measure. The Norse settlement would seem to have spanned the next 500 years, and the foundations of a number of long houses remain. Then there is a medieval farmstead and finally the shell of a seventeenth-century house. A platform on one corner of this gives an aerial view of the jumble of buildings. In the background, helicopters from the oil rigs shuttle in and out of the Sumburgh airport.

Dunrossness

Oil wealth is responsible for the fine road which runs up the eastern side of Dunrossness (Da Ness) towards Lerwick. It is easy enough to speed along it, but exploring the side roads to either side leads you immediately into more typical Shetland scenery: clusters of small modern croft houses, small fields, and boats drawn up at the edge of shallow bays.

The **Shetland Croft House Museum** (open June to Sept, daily 10 to 1, 2 to 5) near Boddam on the east coast shows how things have changed since the last century. Almost all the furniture in the house is made from driftwood, for Shetland has no trees to speak of and even the cabbages have to be salt-resistant. The old farmstead has its separate water mill and corn-drying kiln, well restored.

On the west side of the peninsula the **Loch of Spiggie** is a shallow patch of water famous for its gathering of whooper swans, and also well known for duck. A little further north on the back roads you come to **St Ninian's Isle**. This is a place of remarkable beauty where a small near-island is linked to the mainland only by a double oxbow of white shell sand, like two parentheses back to back. This unusual formation is known as a tombolo, and this is the only sandy one in Britain. The island is the site of a ruined twelfth-century church where a treasure of silver objects from the eighth or ninth centuries was found in a larch box buried beneath a slab. There are replicas in the Lerwick museum.

Mousa Broch

This is the best-preserved broch (see page 437) in Scotland. It stands on the edge of the island of Mousa, opposite Sandwick on the east coast. The broch is just visible from the main road, but to see it properly you must take the boat from Sandwick, run by Tom Jamieson (ring 095 05 367 in advance) during the summer months. The walls stand 45 feet high, probably to within a few feet of the original top, and, from inside, the impression is of standing in the base of an enormous chimney. Galleries run up the middle of the massively thick walls, and you can get to the top of the tower via one of them. Mousa (or Moseyjarborg, as the Norsemen called it) leapt into written history in the *Orkneyinga Saga* as the scene of an elopement: the absconding couple took refuge in the broch from their pursuer, Earl Harald, and forced him to negotiate.

Lerwick

Shetland's capital, sheltered by the offshore island of Bressay, exists by and for the sea. In the narrow Bressay Sound, ships of every description lie at anchor while their crews roam the shops. You will hear northern languages at every step – Russian, Polish and Norwegian in particular. Lerwick is a wonderful source of goods for eastern European fishermen; second-hand cars are winched aboard factory ships, sailors appear laden with parcels. It is also the closest shopping centre for Norwegians who want to escape their own high prices.

Consequently, Lerwick's shops are a step up on Kirkwall's, despite being much further north. A pleasant half-day's shopping is to be had here, fingering the knitwear (though the best shop for this is in Scalloway), thumbing through the books about Shetland – look especially for short stories in the local dialect – or simply window-shopping along with half the visiting mariners. All the action takes place on Commercial Street, a flagstoned alleyway which runs parallel to the seafront. Some of the houses at its southern end – gable on to the sea in the best Scottish tradition – rise straight out of the water.

The hill behind Commercial Street is topped by **Fort Charlotte** (HS, June to Sept 9 to 10pm; Oct to May 9 to 4), the only intact Cromwellian fortress in Britain. The pentangle of walls and gunports were put in place to deter the Dutch, by whom the fort was burnt in 1673. Nearby, the **Shetland Museum** (open Mon, Wed, Fri 10 to 7, Tues, Thurs, Sat 10 to 5) is old-fashioned but lovingly kept, with masses of material about fishing, finds from ancient sites, geological specimens, and curiosities enough to keep anyone happy. The **Up-Helly-Aa exhibition** (open mid-May to Sept, Tues 2 to 4, Thurs 7 to 9, Fri 7 to 9, Sat 2 to 4) is in a shed off St Sunniva Street.

Suburban Lerwick surrounds the fortified settlement of **Clickhimmin Broch** (HS, access from keykeeper; details at site), which stands in the centre of a small loch. The broch does not match that on Mousa, but its walls still stand 18 feet thick and 15 feet high. Together with the broch and the muddle of walls from various periods around it, there is a remarkable 'blockhouse', probably an intimidating Iron Age gateway.

Scalloway and west Mainland

Scalloway used to be Shetland's capital before Lerwick, but now it is a small place by comparison. Attractively situated on the edge of a curving bay looking over to the island of Trondra, it is a town of narrow streets and ancient cottages. The ruins of Earl Patrick's castle loom over the town. It was built in 1600 by labour exacted from the locals, but the castle was abandoned when the notorious Stewart earl was executed.

A drive south from Scalloway over the bridges to the islands of Trondra, West Burra and East Burra leads you through a tangle of sea lochs (called voes in Shetland) with some fine views, while a tour north-west from Scalloway to Walls takes you through scenery which grows ever wilder as you head west. Bleak moorland gives way to patches of green as you loop round the head of the voes. White cottages stand out against the dazzling sea or vanish into the grey gloom of heavy showers. Shetland sheep are everywhere, their colours ranging from deep chocolate to pure white, their knowing, pinched faces gazing at you with goat-like intensity. Their wool used to be gathered by plucking rather than shearing, and the finest Shetland shawls could be drawn through a wedding ring. Shetland ponies graze beside the road, and many rolls of film are used up on them. In the past they were bred as pit ponies, their small stature making them ideal for underground work.

There are a few distractions on this journey – the view from Wormadale Hill on a clear day, for one. Silverwork and knitting workshops are clearly signposted. Often you will find knitwear for sale in the front room of small croft houses while the knitting machines chatter in the back. At the sea's edge you will come across the characteristic Shetland yoals – small boats pointed at each end derived from ancient Norse designs.

Beyond Walls, the road heads out to the tiny village of Melby, a sudden haven of green fertility, with the island of Papa Stour a short distance offshore. A longish walk south-wards along the coast takes you to some fine cliff scenery.

North of Lerwick

Like the rest of Shetland, north Mainland is a country of sheep, birds, cottages, sea and wind. However, there is one difference: oil. Sullom Voe terminal is the biggest in Europe,

---

Up-Helly-Aa

Shetland's new year festival takes place on the last Tuesday of January (though 'the Helly' means the weekend) and reaches its climax in the burning of a Viking-style longship. The festival may have originated in pagan Yule but it is more of a nineteenth-century tradition, now tamer than it was when blazing tar barrels were rolled through the streets of Lerwick and 40 special constables had to be enrolled. Guisers dressed as Vikings sing rousing choruses – 'We are the sons of mighty sires, whose souls were staunch and strong; We sweep upon our serried foes, the hosts of Hate and Wrong'. If you cannot go to Shetland in the last week of January, the Up-Helly-Aa exhibition will give you a flavour. As well as a longship, there are samples of the shields, costumes and torches used by the celebrants, and plenty of photographs. If your enthusiasm for the Vikings mounts, you can take a trip round the harbour in season on a replica longship, the *Dim Riv*.

but also the least conspicuous. The effect on landscape and wildlife has been minimal. Only the flickering flares at night, like something from Norse mythology, or the huge tankers threading their way between islands, tell you that it is there.

Voe is worth a quick pause on the journey north to see the old post office, where spinning wheels and ancient order books have survived from earlier times. A diversion east takes you to **Lunna Ness**, where Lunna House was the headquarters of the Norwegian resistance in World War II. **Brae** is a village which has expanded with the coming of the terminal; there is a swimming-pool here. A trip across the bridge to the island of **Muckle Roe** is worthwhile for views and beach walks. A little further north, at **Mavis Grind**, the land is pinched into an isthmus between (somewhat fancifully) the North Sea and the Atlantic. After this, head west again, looking out for the spiny sea-stacks called **the Drongs**, half-hidden in spray, the oldest pub in Shetland at **Hillswick**, the natural arch off the coast beyond **Brae Wick**, and finally the cliffs at **Esha Ness**, where the road ends beside the chasm of Caldersgeo.

Outer islands

Shetland's inhabited outer islands divide into the big three (Unst, Yell and Fetlar), the smaller nearby ones (Bressay, Noss, Whalsay and Papa Stour) and the really isolated ones (Foula, Out Skerries and Fair Isle). If your ambition is to get to the northernmost point of Britain (and why not, now you are here?), a day trip to Unst is easy.

Yell and Fetlar

Yell is an island of desolate peat hag and rusting cars dumped behind crofts whose charms for visitors are hidden very deep. The Loch of Lumbister, an RSPB reserve, is the best area for wildlife. **Fetlar** is a different matter: small, largely green, and full of interesting nooks and crannies. Snowy owls nested on the island between 1967 and 1975, and although they no longer breed, one or more females can sometimes be seen at the RSPB reserve at Vord Hill. The rare red-necked phalarope, red-throated divers and whimbrel are all also found on Fetlar (the Loch of Funzie at the east of the island is the place to look). The Wick of Tresta has a lovely beach, bounded by the reddish moor-topped cliffs of Lamb Hoga where stormy petrels come ashore at night to breed.

Unst

Up here, where summer nights are never dark (the long twilight is called *simmer dim*), it is easy to persuade yourself that this is the edge of the world. Unst is not quite tundra country, but often looks or feels arctic. The most scenic part of this rather bleak island is the far north-west corner, and here too is the seabird colony of Hermaness (notable for puffins), at the edge of an extensive reserve of maritime heath. From the cliffs at Hermaness, you can gaze out on the rock islet of Muckle Flugga, the last piece of land before the Arctic Circle.

Haroldswick is a scattered cluster of houses where the northernmost post office in the United Kingdom will stamp your letters with a special postmark. **Muness Castle**, in the south-east of Unst, is also the northernmost British castle.

Fair Isle

Rising out of the sea, more or less half-way between Orkney and Shetland, Fair Isle is paradoxically more isolated than Shetland's other outliers yet more accessible. It is a place which is well used to visitors, but which has retained all its genuine hospitality. The residents put it simply – by the end of winter they are longing for some new faces, and then, just when they are getting fed up with visitors, they all go away and they are left to themselves again. It is birds – especially those rare migrants – which bring most visitors to Fair Isle, and in spring or autumn your fellow guests are likely to be 'twitchers'. The enthusiastically run **Bird Observatory**, which doubles as a comfortable guesthouse, can be intimidating if you cannot tell a blackbird from a thrush, but there is no need to join in if you do not want to.

Fair Isle is just the right size of island to wander around in a day, with enough variety in its scenery, inland as well as round its wild coast, to keep you happy for longer. The locals are not short of time for a chat, and you can poke round the little museum in the **George Waterston Memorial Centre**, join half the island in waiting for the *Good Shepherd IV* on its voyage from Mainland, or track down Fair Isle sweaters from cottage to cottage.

The other islands

- **Whalsay** is an important base for part of Shetland's fishing fleet, which explains its comparatively large population and

USEFUL DIRECTORY

Main tourist offices
Caithness Tourist Board
Whitechapel Road, Wick KW1 4EA
(0955) 2596

Orkney Tourist Board
6 Broad Street
Kirkwall, Orkney KW15 1NX
(0856) 872856

Shetland Islands Tourism
Market Cross, Lerwick
Shetland ZE1 0LU
(0595) 3434

Tourist Board publications: annual visitor's and
accommodation guides (all three tourist boards), also
Shetland Official Tourist Guide (very useful, £2.50), and
leaflets on individual Orkney islands with main sights,
services etc. Special-interest leaflets include diving,
cruising, archaeology, fishing and angling (Shetland); walks,
birds, fishing and golf (Caithness). Order by post or phone
from above addresses.

Local tourist information centres
Helmsdale (04312) 640 (Apr to Sept)
John o' Groats (095581) 373 (Apr to Sept)
Stromness (0856) 850716
Thurso (0847) 62371 (Apr to Oct)

Local transport
British Airways (services to Kirkwall, Lerwick, Wick)
(0345) 222111
Loganair (services to Kirkwall, Unst, Fair Isle, Lerwick,
Wick) 041-889 1311; also inter-island flights around the
Orkney (0856 872494) and Shetland (059 584 246)
Wick Railway Station (0955) 2131
Bus from Kirkwall–Houton for Hoy ferry (0856) 872866

Ferries

Scrabster–Stromness (0224) 572615 P&O

Stromness–Lerwick, P&O

Aberdeen–Lerwick, P&O

Aberdeen–Stromness, P&O

John o' Groats–Burwick, South Ronaldsay (passenger only, May to Sept, four sailings daily) (095 581) 353/342

Stromness–Moaness, Hoy (passenger only, up to three sailings a day; weekdays only winter) (0856) 850624

Kirkwall–Shapinsay (up to six sailings daily; not Sun in winter) (0856) 872044

Houton–Hoy–Flotta (up to five sailings daily; not Sun in winter) (0856) 81397

Tingwall–Rousay–Egilsay–Wyre (up to six sailings daily; not Sun in winter) (0856) 75360

Kirkwall–Eday–Stronsay (one or two sailings daily; not Sun in winter) (0856) 872044

Kirkwall–Sanday–Westray–Papa Westray–North Ronaldsay (one to two sailings a day Mon to Sat; North Ronaldsay Sat only) (0856) 872044

Westray–Papa Westray (school terms and summer, passenger only) (085 77) 216

Toft–Yell and Yell–Unst–Fetlar (frequent daily services) (095 782) 259/268

Laxo–Whalsay (frequent daily service) (080 66) 259

Lerwick–Out Skerries (twice a week) (080 65) 226

Vidlin–Out Skerries (three times a week) (080 65) 226

Sumburgh–Fair Isle (passenger only, up to three times a week) (035 12) 222

West Burrafirth–Foula (passenger only, once or twice a week) (03933) 3232

West Burrafirth–Papa Stour (passenger only, three or four times a week) (0595) 2024

Lerwick–Bressay (frequent daily service) (0595) 2024

Other

Fair Isle Lodge and Bird Observatory (035 12) 258

Nature Conservancy Council (information on reserves, plus ferry to Noss) (0595) 3345

Go-Orkney (round coach tour) (0856) 874260

the size of the harbour at Symbister. It has always been an important place of trade. Hanseatic merchants from the north German coast had booths here in the Middle Ages, and one has been fully restored, with an explanation of the trade between Bremen, Hamburg and Whalsay.

- **Bressay and Noss** Bressay lies offshore of Lerwick, and apart from having good views of the town is of little special interest except as a stepping stone to Noss (it is about an hour's walk across the island so it may be worth taking your car). Noss is the home of one of Shetland's biggest seabird cities, and is a National Nature Reserve. It is not open on Monday or Thursday, but at other times you can be ferried across the narrow Noss Sound from Bressay in a perilous-looking inflatable.

- **Papa Stour** is an island of caves and flowers with a population of around 40. Ferries leave from West Burra Firth, or you can fly.

- **Out Skerries** This cluster of three tiny islands, two of them linked together by a bridge, still supports a community of over 80, largely dependent on fishing. Few visitors make it out here, so you can be certain of a friendly welcome. Out Skerries are good for migratory birds; otherwise carpets of flowers in spring and the sense of being miles from anywhere are the attractions.

- **Foula** Though fractionally less far from Mainland than Fair Isle, Foula, with a population of around 45, is much less visited. It is a wild, almost mountainous, island which will be loved by the adventurous, but which may be too far away from urban comforts for most people. Do not come here by sea unless you are a very good sailor (the ferry is small and the waves large), and remember that Foula can still be cut off for days at a time.

WHERE TO STAY

BRAE

Busta House	££
Brae, Shetland ZE2 9QN	*Tel (0806 22) 506*

Half country-house retreat, half business hotel, Busta House is a successful compromise thanks to the old house, relaxed atmosphere and interesting food. There is a peat and wood fire in the 'Long Room', and a peaceful non-smoking library. Dinner in the restaurant draws on the best of the local produce, and the bar food is just as good.

Open: all year, exc 22 Dec to 3 Jan **Rooms**: 20 **Facilities**: fishing
Credit/charge cards: Access, Amex, Diners, Visa

KIRKWALL

Foveran Hotel £
St Ola, Kirkwall
Orkney KW15 1SF *Tel (0856) 872389*

This small, relaxed, modern hotel on the edge of Scapa Flow is the
best place to stay on Orkney's mainland. The lounge and restaurant
are in Scandanavian style, and the food makes use of fresh local
produce. Children are welcome.

Open: all year exc 2 to 3 weeks Jan **Rooms**: 9
Credit/charge cards: Access, Visa

LYBSTER

Portland Arms £
Lybster, Caithness KW3 6BS *Tel (059 32) 208*

A traditional welcoming coaching-inn offering good value and
above-average food in generous quantities. The bedrooms are
spacious (a couple have four-posters), and some bathrooms have
bidets. Under new ownership since inspected – reports please.

Open: all year **Rooms**: 20 **Credit/charge cards**: Access, Visa

THURSO

Forss House ££
Forss, By Thurso
Caithness KW14 7XY *Tel (0847 86) 201*

Bedrooms at this congenial old house are large and neat with solid
wardrobes and chairs and spacious bathrooms. The dining-room
with its Adam mantelpiece serves good food from a short set menu,
and there is a cosy bar.

Open: all year **Rooms**: 7 (2 in cottage) **Facilities**: fishing
Credit/charge cards: Access, Amex, Visa

WHERE TO EAT

STROMNESS

Ferry Inn ★
John Street, Stromness, Orkney KW16 3AA   *Tel (0856) 850280*

This inn resembles the inside of a schooner with appropriate harbour views. Generous bar food ranges from a daily roast to Stromness marinated herring and Orkney pâté, followed by Orkney cheese and clootie dumplings.

Open: daily 12 to 2, 5.30 to 9.30 or 10 in summer; closed Xmas Day and New Year **Credit/charge cards**: Access, Visa

WALLS

Burrastow House
Walls, Shetland ZE2 9PB   *Tel (059 571) 307*

This peaceful, remote eighteenth-century house provides local Shetland lamb, fish and smoked salmon, accompanied by home-grown vegetables. More adventurous dishes appear on the dinner menu, and a good vegetarian choice is also available.

Open: daily 12.30 to 2.30, 7 to 9 (bookings only); closed Jan to Mar **Credit/charge cards**: none accepted

INDEX

This index covers all the main sights and many of the lesser ones, as well as the main figures from Scottish history. Hotels and restaurants are not indexed. **Bold entries** refer to boxed sections on, for example, Robert the Bruce and the Edinburgh Festival.

THE WHICH? GUIDE TO GREECE AND THE GREEK ISLANDS

Greece, with more than 10,000 miles of coastline and some 1,500 islands, caters for all tastes. A perfect holiday destination for water-lovers and sun worshippers, it is at one and the same time a rural and undeveloped country of olive groves, laden donkeys, whitewashed houses and lively tavernas *and* a cultural paradise offering the classical attractions of Athens, Delphi and Olympia, medieval and Byzantine treasures, and the ancient sites of Mycenae and Knossos.

The second edition of this *Holiday Which?* guide covers four major regions of the mainland, Crete, and all six island groups. Fully updated, it includes descriptions of towns, villages and resorts, practical advice on how to get around, recommendations on when best to visit the archaeological sites and what to look out for.

'For anyone wanting just one book on Greece *The Which? Guide to Greece and the Greek Islands* would probably be the best choice.'

The Independent

Paperback   210 x 120mm   704 pages

Available from bookshops,
including the Which? shop at
359-361 Euston Road, London NW1,
and by post from
Consumers' Association, Dept CAZM,
Castlemead, Gascoyne Way, Hertford X, SG14 1LH.

Access/Visa card holders can phone FREE on
(0800) 252100 to place their order,
quoting Dept CAZM.

THE WHICH? GUIDE TO BRITTANY AND NORMANDY

Ideal for anyone taking a seaside holiday, camping, touring or walking in Brittany and Normandy, this discriminating guide covers two of the best-loved and most accessible regions of France. From rocky coastlines and unspoilt beaches to the pastoral landscape that is home to Camembert and Calvados, famous tourist attractions such as the dramatic island fortress of Mont St Michel, the Bayeux tapestry and Monet's house in Giverny, the area has a great deal to offer. This guide explores all the possibilities, including many lesser-known places. It also provides practical advice on travelling, shopping, food and the weather, and the *Holiday Which?* team picks out the best bases and recommends resorts, hotels, campsites and places to eat at, whatever your budget.

Paperback   210 x 120mm   304 pages

Available from bookshops,
including the Which? shop at
359-361 Euston Road, London NW1,
and by post from
Consumers' Association, Dept CAZM,
Castlemead, Gascoyne Way, Hertford X, SG14 1LH.

Access/Visa card holders can phone FREE on
(0800) 252100 to place their order,
quoting Dept CAZM.

THE WHICH? GUIDE TO FRANCE

Rural peace, cosmopolitan cities, tranquil country towns, fine sandy beaches and breathtaking mountain scenery . . . France has so much to offer its visitors. In this, the fifth edition of *The Which? Guide to France*, the team from *Holiday Which?* brings together all the essential information you need, both for planning a trip and to use while travelling within France.

As well as a profile of each area, including Corsica, the book has features on history and architecture and on food and drink. Throughout, background details are provided on the churches and cathedrals, museums and châteaux with which France is so liberally endowed. The guide also lists recommended restaurants in Paris and includes an invaluable practical information section.

Detailed maps and a hotels index help you pinpoint any of the 300-plus hotels which have been independently inspected and selected for this guide as being the best value for money.

'Arguably the best of the mid-range guides.'

The Daily Telegraph

Paperback   210 x 120mm   640 pages

Available from bookshops,
including the Which? shop at
359-361 Euston Road, London NW1,
and by post from
Consumers' Association, Dept CAZM,
Castlemead, Gascoyne Way, Hertford X, SG14 1LH.

Access/Visa card holders can phone FREE on
(0800) 252100 to place their order,
quoting Dept CAZM.

TWENTIETH-CENTURY UKRAINE

Twentieth-Century
UKRAINE

Clarence A. Manning

BOOKMAN ASSOCIATES
New York

Foreword

THE UKRAINIAN LANGUAGE is spoken by over forty million people living in Europe, Asia and America. It has a large and flourishing literature, and its leading authors of the nineteenth century, such as Taras Shevchenko, Ivan Franko and Lesya Ukrainka, rank with the best writers of the period.

Today the homeland of these people, the Ukrainian Soviet Socialist Republic, is a member of the United Nations and its Russian Communist representatives vote consistently with the Soviet delegation in the solid bloc that stands opposed to the principles and ideals of the democracies of the world. The Soviet Union regards its representatives as on a par with those of Poland and Czechoslovakia as eligible for election to the Security Council. These representatives do not, however, speak for the Ukrainian people, for the Soviet authorities lose no opportunity to stamp out Ukrainian nationalism, one of the worst doctrinal heresies to affect the Soviet Union. Ukrainian national independence, if it were to be achieved, would strike at the heart of Russian imperialism, be it Red of White.

The strength of this Ukrainian nationalism is not appreciated abroad. The world still looks at it through the eyes of either the Russians or the Poles, both of whom repudiate it as a menace to their own plans for self-aggrandizement. Both are willing to point out how the Ukrainians differ from themselves but both nevertheless persist in denying that the Ukrainian nationality now or in the past has ever existed.

It is the object of this book to give a picture of the Ukrainian struggle for independence during the twentieth century. It is a sad story of political failure after World War I and of oppression after World War II. With the exception of the *émigrés* and of the displaced persons, the bulk of the Ukrainians cannot speak for themselves. Yet they have a place in history which cannot be waved aside by calling their defenders propagandists or by stressing the fact that any discussion of their problem involves a criticism of their neighbors.

The Ukrainian question is today one of the most important in Europe, for it involves the largest group of people with a share of European traditions that is compelled to be silent. It enters into all plans for the future of Europe, for the securing and maintenance of peace, for the welfare of the United Nations and of humanity. If Ukraine is only a creature of propaganda, as its enemies assert, why was it admitted to the United Nations? If it is an independent nation of independent people, why should it be dominated by Moscow? This dilemma indicates the need for a deeper appreciation by the intelligent public of the situation that has developed in Kiev and Lviv and in the whole of Ukraine. It is an advanced stage of the same policy that is being applied in the satellite states, in China and Korea and explains Soviet aims and aspirations. If this book succeeds in throwing some light upon the matter, the author will be well satisfied.

Contents

Note on Transliteration

In this work an attempt has been made to transliterate both Ukrainian and Russian names directly into English. This involves certain differences in spelling. Thus in the transliteration of Ukrainian y and h are often used where the transliteration of Russian shows i and g.

In regard to proper names, those as Kiev, Dnieper, etc. are given in their common English form. Lesser known names are given in direct transliteration.

A special note should be made for Lviv. This city of many names is called Lvov in Russian, Lwów in Polish, Lemberg in German and Léopol in French. The Ukrainian form is used consistently.

TWENTIETH-CENTURY UKRAINE

I

The Ukrainian Revival before 1914

THE PUBLICATION OF Ivan Kotlyarevsky's *Eneida* in 1798 is usually regarded as the beginning of the modern Ukrainian national movement. This travesty of the old Latin epic of Virgil attributed to Aeneas and his followers escaping from the sack of Troy the characteristic thoughts and actions of a band of Zaporozhian Kozaks escaping from the destruction of the Sich by Catherine the Great of Russia in 1775, the year of the opening of the American Revolution. It drew heavily upon the author's knowledge of Ukrainian life, customs and traditions and it revived a vein of patriotism and of pride in national heritage that had lain dormant for nearly a century.

It appeared twenty-three years after the final destruction of the Sich, the traditional center of Ukrainian political life, and thirty years after the Russian Empress had abolished the mechanism of the hetman state, the last formal Ukrainian organization. There was thus a definite political gap between the old and the new; and the Russian attitude was such that the new movement was forced to confine itself for some decades to struggle for a national culture.

The *Eneida* not only appealed to the traditions and instincts of the people, but introduced the vernacular Ukrainian into literature. Kotlyarevsky for the first time broke with that artificial combination of Church Slavic, Polish and Russian that was the conventional written language among noble and intellectual Ukrainians. The discarding of this antiquated and rigid mode of expression brought the new literature near to the speech of the people, to their folk poetry, their *dumy*— the tales of adventure and heroism of the Kozaks of the Sich— and made them responsive to all the literary currents that were flowing from the West of Europe. It thus paved the way for the Ukrainians to develop a modern literature and take their place in the general stream of Western and European civilization and culture.

The *Eneida* was parallel to those works in the other languages of Eastern and Central Europe which marked the passing of the old order and initiated the modern national movements. All of these were at first literary rather than political. This was fortunate, for the movements were able to take root and gain strength under the very eyes of the authorities, whereas the slightest hint of political activity would have caused them to be tracked down and exterminated before they could have been fairly launched. As it was, Kotlyarevsky was able to call attention to much of the Ukrainian past and do it in what seemed to the watchful Russians a harmless way.

This is not the place to recount the ancient history of the Ukrainians.[1] In the eleventh and twelfth centuries, Kiev, Christianized from Constantinople, was one of the great cities of Europe. Its grand princes, such as Yaroslav the Wise and Volodymyr Monomakh, ranked among the leading sovereigns of the day. The state soon fell upon evil times. In 1169 its capital was pillaged by Prince Andrey Bogolyubsky of Suzdal, the original capital of the Moscow princes, and later it was mercilessly ravaged by the Tatar and Mongol invasions. Finally all vestige of independence was lost and Ukraine came to form part of that heterogeneous state which passed into history as Poland. Then came the Kozaks, bold and fearless warriors, who in the sixteenth and seventeenth centuries dared to raid the outskirts of the Turkish capital of Constantinople and became a menace to the King of Poland.

In 1654 the Hetman Bohdan Khmelnytsky made an alliance at Pereyaslav with Tsar Alexis of Moscow. The consequences were disastrous, for the tsars divided the country with Poland along the line of the Dnieper River and unilaterally abrogated one condition of the alliance after another. Finally in the latter part of the eighteenth century Catherine the Great not only wiped out the hetman regime and the Sich but she introduced the complete Russian system of administration and reduced the population to serfdom in the Russian manner. The richer landowners, many of whom had been Kozak officers, found it to their advantage to be completely Russianized, to accept the Russian language and the manners of the St. Petersburg court and to forget their Ukrainian past.

With all Ukrainian political institutions wiped out, the Russian government set to work to annihilate all distinctive elements in Ukrainian life. The name of Ukraine was abolished and there was only a grudging toleration of a somewhat confused region which passed under the name of Little Russia. The language of the Ukrainian people was blandly called a mere peasant idiom unworthy of serious consideration or development. The surviving Ukrainian customs were ridiculed as non-Russian and backward, while at the same time the government vehemently insisted that there was no recognizable difference between Ukrainians and Great Russians. When the incompatibility of these two views was pointed out, the government simply branded all interest in Ukrainian affairs an Austro-German intrigue which was to be repressed by severe measures.

This attitude of the Russian imperial government was shared to the full by the radical Russian intelligentsia. Belinsky, universally acclaimed for his liberal ideas, could not heap sufficient scorn upon the poems of Taras Shevchenko and used his pen to show that the peasant dialect spoken in "Little Russia" was not entitled to literary development.[2] His successors followed his example, and during the entire century the government and the revolutionists joined forces against the Ukrainian revival.[3]

In 1905 the Russian Academy of Sciences at last admitted that Great Russian and Ukrainian were two distinct Slavic languages,[4] but this advanced point of view was deprived of real meaning in the reaction that followed the unsuccessful revolution of that year.

It goes without saying that political action was altogether prohibited. Throughout the nineteenth century the whole empire was ruled by the bureaucracy. There were no popular elections, and the only rudimentary step toward elective government was taken with the organization of the zemstvos to handle certain local affairs. It is safe to say that up to the Revolution of 1905 there was no legal organ for the development of Ukrainian experience in public affairs and few or no means whereby the Ukrainians could secure such experience, unless they were content to serve as Russians in the Russian political machine. There were no schools where instruction was given publicly in the Ukrainian language; there were no newspapers printed in Ukrainian; and almost the only books available were those printed in Lviv and other cities of Western Ukraine and smuggled across the border in a steady stream.[5]

Of the younger and more radical Ukrainian intelligentsia, the vast majority joined the Russian revolutionary movements. On the one hand they thus gained a knowledge of Russian political techniques; on the other they were all too frequently drawn into the Russian orbit and suffered denationalization as surely as did the more conservative who bowed to the bureaucratic system.

The natural wealth of Ukraine was a significant factor in Russian plans; the coal and iron mines of the Donets basin played an important role in the industrialization of the empire. The commercial and industrial centers which were built during the nineteenth century on Ukrainian territory were settled chiefly by Great Russians who were encouraged to emigrate there, while Ukrainians who obtained posts in government service were shifted to remote sections of the land where they would be isolated amid a non-Ukrainian population. This deliberate transfer of the population created in the country definite Russian and later Soviet centers which played an important role in the modern period.

There was a slight change after the Revolution of 1905, inasmuch as the first Duma contained a number of representatives of the Ukrainians and of minorities who sympathized with them.[6] Permission was granted to publish newspapers in Ukrainian and for a while it seemed as if the Ukrainians might obtain the same rights as some of the other nationalities of the empire. But the first Duma was soon dissolved and in later elections the laws were so changed that the Ukrainians lost almost all representation.

Despite the attitude of the Academy of Sciences, the Ukrainians felt with especial rigor the force of the reaction that followed the collapse of the revolutionary wave. They were refused permission to open schools where Ukrainian would be the language of instruction and censorship was tightened over Ukrainian books and newspapers. However, for the first time in Russian history, there was a definite Ukrainian press. The *Literary and Historical Messenger* was moved from Lviv to Kiev. In a word, following this revolution, there did develop a distinct Ukrainian movement on a broader scale than had been possible earlier, even though it was hampered at every turn.

During the nineteenth century the revival spread to the Ukrainians living under Hapsburg rule in Western Ukraine.[7] This area fell into three categories, depending on the provincial boundaries of the Hapsburg Empire: Galicia, Bukovina and the area of the Carpathian Mountains. Of these Galicia contained the largest part of the Western Ukrainian population, which had passed under Hapsburg rule after the dismemberment of Poland in the eighteenth century.

Conditions here were very different and there was a definite social pressure exerted to induce the Ukrainians (or Ruthenians, as they were called after the Latin name of the area) to declare themselves Poles. Serfdom was abolished in 1848 but the dominating class was Polish and in accordance with Hapsburg policy, the Poles were favored by the central government in Vienna.

Religiously and culturally there was another difference. Most of the Western Ukrainians were Catholics of the Eastern Rite and from the time when the Hapsburgs had taken over the province, they had provided much-needed opportunities for the education of the clergy. This gave the movement a far more clerical tinge than in Eastern Ukraine and it tended to perpetuate the artificial Church Slavic language. In fact, it was not until well along in the century that the clerical and conservative supporters of Church Slavic were defeated and the way was opened for the development of the vernacular tongue.

This came about when the nationalists were called upon to struggle with the Muscophiles who advocated the introduction of Great Russian and looked to Russia for protection. Very few of this group either knew any Great Russian or were aware of the linguistic complications involved in the ideas which they were so passionately advocating. It was in the time of Michael Drahomaniv and Ivan Franko, in the seventies and eighties, that the nationalist and vernacular cause definitely triumphed; but even later there were outbreaks of Muscophilism.

In Galicia the Ukrainians had far better opportunities to acquaint themselves with the problems of government and public service than in Russia. Though rarely considered for the higher administrative posts, they could look forward to minor positions in the Hapsburg service. They could enter the learned professions as Ruthenians. They could form their own

political parties and although the elections were often controlled, they succeeded in placing a goodly number of
candidates even against Polish efforts.

In Galicia, then, there was no question of the existence of a
Ruthenian group. It was treated by the Poles as inferior but
its identity was undisputed. The people had at least a modi-
cum of protection and of opportunity.[8] In Russia, on the other
hand, the autocratic government sternly denied the Ukrainians
their identity and employed every means to deprive them of
self-expression.

In Bukovina the Ukrainians were in much the same situation
as in Galicia.

In the third section, the region of the Carpathians, conditions were less favorable, for this formed part of the kingdom
of Hungary. Under the Hungarian system of administration
the territory was divided into several counties, each of which
was dependent directly upon Budapest. The Hungarian system made it much more difficult for minority groups to work
together across county lines. Education was at a low level
and what there was, was directed to turn the young men into
patriotic Hungarians. The Russian invasion in 1848 had greatly
strengthened those factions which were Muscophile in tendency and the nationalist movement was perhaps weaker here
than in the other provinces. Yet the trend was definitely toward better living conditions and by the beginning of World
War I the Ukrainian population of this mountain area was
already becoming more self-confident and self-assured.

There was one outstanding hurdle that all Ukrainian leaders,
whether in Russia or in Austria-Hungary, had to face, and it
was something that confronted all the oppressed peoples of
Eastern Europe. Any change in their political status was dependent upon forces outside of themselves. It was evident to
all that the two empires in which they were enclosed could
not be overthrown by popular revolt. They could improve
their educational, social and economic conditions but the time

for armed uprisings was definitely past. Europe was on the surface more peaceful than it had been for centuries and although the coffee houses buzzed with gossip about the imminence of a great war, the fact remained that the rulers of Europe had been able to solve almost every crisis that had arisen since the time of the French Revolution without plunging the continent into a major struggle. It was only in such a major struggle that one could hope for the downfall of either of the two empires.

II

Ukraine and World War I

THE MURDER OF Archduke Francis Ferdinand, heir to the throne of Austria-Hungary, and his wife at Sarajevo on June 28, 1914, gave to the world its first open intimation that the long-expected test of strength in Central and Eastern Europe and in the Balkans was at hand. More specifically, it was a sign that on a world scale, a clash between the Triple Entente, composed of the British Empire, France and the Russian Empire, and the Triple Alliance of Germany, Austria-Hungary and Italy was to break out momentarily. This would be a struggle of giants.

Each of these great powers looked at the conflict in her own way. To Great Britain, the main enemy was Germany, with her aspirations for maritime supremacy and her efforts to push to the southeast and seize control of the wealth of Asia Minor and perhaps India. France thought in terms of the lost provinces of Alsace-Lorraine. Italy was torn between her desires to profit at the expense of France and her hopes of recovering Trieste and adjacent territory from her rival and ally, Austria-Hungary, and securing the east shore of the Adriatic. Germany concentrated on her rivalry with Great Britain and her long-standing feud with France. Austria-Hungary wished to put a stop to the spreading of Slav nationalism among the Southern Slavs from independent Serbia and she hoped to get rid of Russian agents working among her Slavic citizens. Russia saw an opportunity to advance toward the Straits and to win new subjects among the Slavs of the Austro-Hungarian Empire.

With these differences in the political line-up, it was only natural that the Western democracies thought of the war largely in terms of the Western front. The German invasion of Belgium and the overrunning of northern France seemed to both the British Empire and France the most *important* events. They knew relatively little of the complicated situation in Eastern Europe and they cared less. At the moment the might of the Russian Empire was to them the great factor in the East and though there might be criticism of Russian methods, there surged up a friendship for Russia and a belief in Russia that made them skeptical of any Eastern movement which was not sponsored by the tsars. This idea was fostered as always even by the Russian revolutionists abroad who were as ardently opposed to minority rights as were the bureaucrats themselves.

When the Western Powers thought at all of the future of Austria-Hungary, they were willing to divide it up. It was relatively easy to convince them of the right of the Czechs to independence, since they were familiar with the medieval kingdom of Bohemia. The problem of the Balkans was also relatively simple: the Balkan Wars of 1912-13 had publicized the desire of the Serbs to unite with them their long-separated brothers in the Southern Slav provinces of the Dual Monarchy. The case of Poland was more complex, for to the Poles the war was indeed a civil war. Relatives of all social ranks from peasants to aristocrats were called into the services of Germany, Austria-Hungary and Russia and were compelled to fight against their own cousins and even brothers. Russia promised freedom to the Poles of the Central Powers and demanded the direct annexation of the "Russians" in West

Ukraine. She confidently envisaged the establishment of a series of independent Slav countries and except in the case of the Serbs, who had already a native dynasty, she believed that she would be able to place on the thrones of the new governments Russian princes who would weld their states to the traditional Russian policy.

The Central Powers naturally saw things differently. They regarded the independence movement among the Czechs as the work of Russian propaganda and they aimed to bring all the Southern Slavs into Austria-Hungary. They were willing to liberate Russian Poland and place it under the control of a German or Austrian prince who would co-ordinate it with their own policy and who would perhaps have some influence in Austrian Poland but none in German Poland. This sharply divided the Poles at home and abroad—with a Polish National Committee operating in Paris, London and New York, and a Polish Council of the Regency working in Berlin and Vienna— and it was not until America entered the war and the Central Powers weakened that there was any agreement between the two factions.[1] The feud continued throughout the entire history of independent Poland in the hostility of the friends of Marshal Joseph Pilsudski and Ignace Jan Paderewski. The Central Powers were willing also to give at least idealistic support to all groups in the Russian Empire which might have separatist ambitions.

In all this the Ukrainians were under a special handicap. They had formed one of the latest waves of emigration to the West, and they had done so under the varied names of Galicians, Ruthenians, Russians, Little Russians and even Austrians or Hungarians. They had not yet developed a strong leadership abroad. They had no representatives with the broad popular appeal of the Czech Thomas G. Masaryk, a distinguished philosopher with an American wife, or of the musical genius Paderewski. The Russian authorities abroad redoubled their efforts to prove that there was no such people as the

Ukrainians and that the entire Ukrainian movement was of German origin. The Poles demanded the inclusion of a great part of Ukraine in a revived Polish state. The Central Powers would not promise to change their system whereby Polish influences were supreme in the Ukrainian parts of the Hapsburg Empire. Thus the Ukrainians could not look forward without misgiving to a victory of the Triple Entente nor could they be sure that a victory of the Central Powers would bring them any relief.

Despite the cheerless outlook, the Ukrainian leaders in Austria-Hungary established as early as August 5, 1914, a Holovna Ukrainska Rada to mobilize all Western Ukrainian forces against the Russian Empire. The next day a Ukrainian Military Organization was started to create a volunteer force of Sichovi Striltsi (Riflemen of the Sich).[2] This paralleled the Polish Legions of Pilsudski but it was distrusted by the authorities. The number of the Striltsi was severely limited and they were poorly supplied at the beginning. In 1918, a fully equipped regiment of them marched to the defence of Lviv.

The Ukrainians who had left Russia organized in Vienna a Society for the Liberation of Ukraine. This broadcast appeals for assistance to all enemies of Russia and hoped to find some sympathy among the Western democratic powers. At the moment it met with slight success.[3]

The wave of patriotic enthusiasm which swept over Russia demanded the suppression of all Ukrainian organizations as agents of the Central Powers.[4] Ukrainian newspapers in Kiev and elsewhere which had survived the censorship of the last years were now suppressed. New regulations were added so that authors who desired to print books of any kind in Ukrainian were compelled to file three copies of the manuscript with the censor and then the government found excuses to hold up decisions and avoid publication. Prominent Ukrainians were moved into the interior of Russia. Separate Ukrainian relief organizations were forbidden as unnecessary on the familiar pretext that the Ukrainians were not a separate people. Yet with open work barred, the Ukrainians were able to form un-official groups within the Russian organizations and thus give some aid and encouragement to, and receive information about, the Western Ukrainians who were taken prisoners. Vainly the Eastern Ukrainians, especially those of socialist tendencies, argued that they were loyal and wished to see all Ukraine united within the Russian Empire. They were not believed and the government made it clear to them that the time had come to liquidate the Ukrainian problem for good and all.

In Western Ukraine the Hapsburg government arrested the Muscophile leaders as Russian agents. It was none too soon, for three days after the declaration of war between Russia and Austria-Hungary, the Russian Army crossed the boundaries of Eastern Galicia and on September 3, 1914, entered Lviv, the capital of the province. Then it pushed on and finally it reached the summit of the Carpathian Mountains in the district of Carpatho-Ukraine, following much the same route as the Russians had taken in 1849, when they entered to aid the Hapsburgs against the Hungarians.

The Russians lost no time in putting into power the Musco-philes among the Western Ukrainians. They proceeded on the usual assumption that there was no such people as the Ukrain-ians; they appointed a Russian governor general of the "liber-ated" province and they deported prominent nationalist leaders to the interior. Thus they arrested Professor Hru-shevsky at his summer home in the Carpathians and sent him to Nizhni Novgorod; but thanks to the intercession of the Russian Academy of Sciences, he was allowed to go to Moscow and work in the libraries there. Archbishop Count Andrew Sheptitsky, metropolitan of Lviv and head of the Catholics of the Eastern rite, was taken into Russia and kept there dur-ing the entire period of the war.[5]

The lesser clergy of the Uniat church who fell into Russian hands were either deported or compelled to join the Orthodox church, on the adroit theory that the Uniat church had been forced upon the Russian Orthodox people in the sixteenth century by the papacy and the Poles[6] and that the Russian armies had therefore liberated the people from a foreign yoke and brought them back to their original faith. Again it made no difference if the people preferred their own usages and customs. They were Russians and were to make the best of it. In the words of Shevchenko, be silent and happy.

All Ukrainian cultural and economic institutions were abolished. Reading rooms were closed, co-operative societies were shut down, and the printing of Ukrainian was subjected to the same rules as in Russia itself. Everything possible was done to give an air of permanence to the new regime.

In the spring of 1915 Tsar Nicholas II visited Lviv, where he congratulated the "Russian" population on their return to the homeland and assured them that the province would never again return to alien rule. All of the imperial and other official utterances stressed the fact that special rights would be given to the Poles but that the Russians of the province would receive the same treatment as did Russians everywhere.

This was a convenient principle for the Russians. In a region already devastated by war, it gave them the right to treat all conscious Ukrainians as traitors to the cause of Russia, their native land, to confiscate their property, and deport them to regions in the Russian Empire where they would be no longer subject to German influences—and this at a time when the activities of the Baltic Germans who held high rank at the Russian court, were beginning to awake suspicion of treason within the empire.

Naturally, this principle, when applied by renegade Ukrainians who had fled into Russia before the war and by certain favored Poles who were hostile to the growth of Ukrainian influence in Eastern Galicia, could excuse the most arbitrary actions. There resulted a reign of terror and destruction which did as much harm to the population as the actual fighting

around the various cities, even including the fortress of Peremyshl, which held out against the invaders for several months.
At the end of April, 1915, the tide turned again. General
von Mackensen smashed the Russian lines along the Dunajec
River in the western part of the province and the Russians
were compelled to retreat. Since "Russian" patriots must, of
course, be kept from falling under German control, the army
command ordered them to be evacuated. The Russians hoped
to be able to move out of Western Ukraine all "Russian-speak-
ing" persons, i.e., Ukrainians. Of course they did not succeed, yet they did gather up thousands of men, women and
children who were compelled to retire eastward with the
army and were then deposited as refugees throughout the
eastern and northern provinces of European Russia and Siberia.
The forced evacuation of the Ukrainian population was attended with severe hardships, especially since the military
could ill spare any food, clothing or other supplies for the
"liberated" and "rescued" civilians.

Once the refugees had reached their new homes, they were
naturally forbidden to form any special Ukrainian associations.
What was the use of a war of liberation if any evidence could
be shown that the form of liberation was not too palatable to
those liberated? The various other national groups that had
been removed from the Western borders of Russia were allowed to form their own relief organizations, but the Ukrainians, since they were in theory Russian, were not given this
privilege. Thus they were caught again on the two horns of
the Russian dilemma. Their very existence was denied and
they were refused the aid which they could expect as Russians
while at the same time they were treated as an alien body
which could expect no sympathy or support from the Russian
population. Imperial fiat even tried to prevent help from the
"non-existent" Ukrainians of the empire.

With the Russian retreat from Galicia, the Austrian authorities returned and they allowed Ukrainian life to resume in the

evacuated areas. Once more the old institutions, now devastated, were reopened. As the German armies advanced eastward and northward, Kholm, Pidlyashshya, Volyn and Podolia each became in turn the scene of the same kind of military activities, with the Russians evacuating Ukrainian inhabitants and forgetting about them afterwards. Later a Russian offensive under General Brusilov succeeded in penetrating Galicia again in the southwest and again the process was repeated.

The inability of the Ukrainians to win any active support abroad reacted against them. The activities of the Poles in all of the capitals of both groups of powers and in the United States made it advisable for the Austro-Hungarian government to proceed with caution and try to satisfy their demands. Both the Central Powers and the Triple Entente promised the Poles an independent state of some kind, the Germans and Austrians generously offering to include in their projected territory the land of the Western Ukrainians.

As a result of Polish influence, the Austrian government now became deaf when the Society for the Liberation of Ukraine pleaded for the establishment of an independent state in the Ukrainian territory taken by the German armies from Russia. The General Ukrainian Rada established in Vienna in 1915 had urged that the Ukrainian districts of Galicia and Bukovina should be included in this state. At this moment, with the Russian armies in retreat, the attitude of the Ukrainians was similar to that of the Austrian Poles: all groups within the Hapsburg lands were agreed that a reorganization of the government was necessary to satisfy the legitimate demands of the citizens and provide a proper and efficient setup. But the rigid ideas of the old Emperor Francis Joseph I prevented any action and the vigorous foreign propaganda of the Poles won them favored treatment. Undoubtedly Vienna hoped that the refusal of the Ukrainian request would leave the people a dissatisfied core in the Polish state projected by the Central Powers and so nullify its activity. The Ukrainians became convinced that they could not look for justice to Vienna and they joined the nations ardently desiring the disintegration of the entire Hapsburg structure.

Meanwhile conditions in Russia for Ukrainians of even the noninvaded areas were going from bad to worse. The few Ukrainians in the Russian Duma again asked permission to use their own language in the schools and to implement the provisions of the Constitution of 1905 and the decrees of the Academy of Sciences. A new system of educational reforms was projected by the minister of education, Count Paul Ignatyev, but even this still preserved the old idea that Ukrainians were Russians and did not give them any of the relief granted to other nationalities in the empire. A few of the Russian Progressives utilized the scandal of the occupation in Galicia to make some interpellations but these were easily set aside by the ending of the session. The Russian liberals, as hostile as the government to the Ukrainian cause, refused to see anything extraordinary in the situation in the Ukrainian areas and the authorities continued to take every measure to suppress the Ukrainian movement and smear it both at home and abroad.

Thus the year 1916 passed. On both sides of the border there was a growing realization that the days of both Austria-Hungary and Russia were running out. No one could foresee what was going to happen but there was a growing war weariness and a sullen willingness to dream of what might happen that boded ill for the two regimes. Even the death of Francis Joseph and the accession of Charles could change nothing.

III

Ukraine and Russia in Dissolution

On March 8, 1917, began the riots in Petrograd that marked the outbreak of the Russian Revolution. These became intensified and spread rapidly until on March 15, Nicholas II abdicated the throne and the Russian Empire was no more. It was a sudden and dramatic end to the Romanov dynasty that had ruled for over three hundred years, so sudden indeed that the success of the long-expected revolution could hardly be believed, even by its foremost advocates, and days and even weeks were required after its immediate impact upon the peoples of the empire before its significance could be fully appreciated.

The Ukrainians in the capital welcomed the new movement which was taking shape as they prepared to celebrate the birthday of the national poet, Shevchenko, which occurred on March 9. This had always been a special time for tsarist persecution; now, in the midst of the rioting and disorder, the exercises were held on a scale and with a freedom that had never been possible.

When the first flush of enthusiasm was over, the serious work of the revolution began—the welding of a new organization to take the place of the old, discarded system. At this point the unanimity which had held together all classes, except the hard-shelled supporters of the old regime, broke down.

There were all kinds of questions to be decided. There was the problem of the participation of the new Russia in the World War which was still going on. There were the social problems involved in the distribution of land to the peasants, the rights of property and the position of the factory workers. There were the national problems presented by the various oppressed peoples that had been brought by force or by guile within the Russian Empire. It was soon evident that there was going to be no agreement about these or as to the ultimate form of a central government, if there was to be one.

In the capital itself a disagreement at once arose between the Provisional Government, formed largely out of the moderate parties of the old Duma, and the new Soviets of Soldiers and Workmen which had been called into existence by the more radical parties, among which the Bolshevik party was as yet almost negligible. The Provisional Government, which included only one Social Revolutionist, Kerensky, wanted to continue the war and adopt a form of government based generally upon the types of parliamentary democracy known in Western Europe. The Soviets argued for an immediate peace, the breaking up of the old army, and the organization of a government based upon soviets to be established throughout the country.

Outside of the capital the wealthier classes stood for principles fairly similar to those of the Provisional Government, while the peasants demanded the immediate distribution of the land of the great estates and were willing to use force to attain their goal. In the smaller cities or wherever there was a factory population, the revolutionary movement of the Soviets took hold.

Finally among all of the oppressed nationalities, there grew up with surprising speed an agitation for the recognition of special rights in their own territories, for permission to use their own languages, and for new relationships to the central government which usually involved either outright independence or reconstruction of the Russian Empire as a federal state.

At the same time these sections developed the same class bitterness and the same social demands that were appearing in purely Russian territory.

All this was repudiated by the Great Russians of both right and left. They could not conceive of a state which would be anything but the old monolithic unity. To win the support of the Allies they were willing to make some concessions in the cases of Poland and Finland, but that was about all. When they did grudgingly concede anything more, it was with the distinct proviso that all such questions could not receive a definitive answer until the meeting of a Constituent Convention, in which the Great Russians intended to have an absolute majority.[1]

Of great importance in this connection was the relative isolation of the Russian Empire resulting from the war. Owing to the intervention of Turkey on the side of the Central Powers and the German advance into the Balkans, there was no access to the outside world through the Dardanelles. The Baltic sea routes were completely closed by the Germans. It was possible to reach Petrograd and Moscow from the West only by rail across Sweden or by the sea route to Murmansk and Archangel, the two ports on the Arctic Ocean. An alternative route was by way of Vladivostok on the Pacific and the long journey over the demoralized Trans-Siberian Railroad. The route from the Caucasus to the British positions in Mesopotamia and across Iran had indeed been traversed by a division of Russian Cossacks who had joined the British at Bagdad but it was not a practicable means of communication.

All of these routes led directly into Great Russian territory. This meant that the various non-Russian nationalities for the most part had no means of communicating with the Western Powers except across Great Russian territory. They were dependent, if war was to come, on their domestic manufacture of munitions and on captured materiel. Even if they were recognized by the Allies, these could extend them no direct help. That could come only from the Central Powers and to accept such assistance would inevitably bring forth the charge in the West that the movements were German-inspired and would work against Allied recognition in the event of German defeat, which was already becoming evident.

There were few persons in authority in Great Britain, France or the United States (which had by now entered the war) who understood or cared to understand the real nature of the Russian Empire. The Allied representatives, often with the best intentions in the world, listened to the Great Russians of either the old regime, the Provisional Government or the revolutionary Soviets. They were only too willing to believe that all important questions would be settled in the Western manner at the Constituent Convention and when they did get into contact with the minorities, they did not have the authority to promise them anything or to carry out what they did feel inclined to offer.

The Allies, while welcoming the downfall of the tsar and of the supposed pro-German clique among his associates, still felt themselves bound by their agreements with the empire. They remembered the sacrifices that the Russians (and here they did not bother to distinguish among the various nations in the empire) had made in the common cause. They believed that Russia's internal problems would be solved without delay and that a new and democratic government would emerge from the growing chaos. They therefore again hesitated to take any action which might embarrass the Provisional Government in its efforts to maintain itself in power and they jumped at the suggestion that everything be left to the Constituent Assembly.

In this setting the Ukrainians were compelled to steer their course. They occupied an important geographical position, yet they were completely cut off from any direct contact with the West. They formed the largest group next to the Great Russians, yet for two centuries their very existence as a group had been denied by Russians of all categories and they had had no chance to present their case to the world. They had only their own abilities and their confidence in the righteousness of their cause.

At the outbreak of the revolution, Professor Hrushevsky, the foremost Ukrainian historian, left Moscow, where he was under police supervision, and made his way to Kiev. Here he almost immediately became the mainspring of the Ukrainian movement. Hrushevsky was a liberal and a member of the underground Organization of Ukrainian Progressives, which had established contacts with all of the Ukrainian socialist parties.[2] The approach of the revolution allowed it to appear openly for the first time since its foundation in 1908 and take an active part in the spreading of Ukrainian agitation.

The ranks of Ukrainian patriots were swelled by the gradual return of many of the men and women who had been imprisoned or exiled during the last years of the imperial regime. They soon gave valuable support to the new movement.

In the beginning most of the leaders and the people undoubtedly thought that with the elimination of the tsar, the new regime at Petrograd would be eager to satisfy the legitimate demands of the various nationalities. The ardent separatist demands of the small Ukrainian Independence party seemed overwrought; its insistent calls for the declaration of Ukrainian independence went unheeded and its leaders took little part in the first deliberations.[3]

There is no reason to wonder at this. For about a half century, the opponents of tsarism and of imperial control of Ukraine had been in touch with Russian revolutionary leaders of the same general type and had accepted their ideology and methods. There were no political parties in the sense known to the democratic world, these having been forbidden before the Revolution of 1905. There were only secret revolutionary groups without political or administrative experience; the parties formed in 1905 had been largely broken up in the following period of reaction and driven underground.

As we have seen, the imperial regime had taken advantage of the war to suppress even the embryonic Ukrainian press.

It was therefore necessary, in the middle of the revolution, to create among a people with a high level of illiteracy a press which would voice Ukrainian desires. By the end of March there were at least three such papers, the *New Council*, the *Labor Gazette*, and the *Will of the People*,[4] but with the breakdown of transportation it was almost impossible to circulate them among the villages where the Ukrainian sentiment was strongest.

From the beginning of the Ukrainian movement, emphasis had been laid upon its cultural aspects and little attention given to the restoration of the old Kievan state. Now in the days of the revolution, cultural rights became the chief plank in the national platform. To the masses and even to many of the intellectuals, the language question seemed to be the spearhead of their cause. They wanted to have their own language introduced into the schools and officially recognized. They had connected Russian opposition to this with tsarism and bureaucracy and it never entered their heads that a Provisional Government, which loudly proclaimed its belief in democracy, would question this right.

In common with most of the citizens of the Russian Empire, the Ukrainian leaders had almost ignored foreign affairs. Preoccupied with their cultural rights and other internal matters, they had not planned any course of action in the international arena. They had devoted far more thought to the ideology of the revolution and of socialism. It was only natural that in the enthusiasm of the first days, the growing party organizations were similar to those organized elsewhere in the Russian Empire. Soon the Ukrainian Social Revolutionary party and the Ukrainian Social Democratic party under the leadership of the writer Volodymyr Vynnychenko came to the fore. Both stressed the need for autonomy but like the corresponding parties in all European countries, they thought of themselves as members of some sort of world-wide parties which would work together without too much attention to such questions as boundaries and national feelings. They had not yet learned the full lesson of the situation in Germany in 1914, when the apparently international socialist parties had voted for the war credits in the Reichstag.

In a sense the position of most of the leaders was similar to that of the American colonists in 1775, who had taken up arms to defend their rights as Englishmen and had required more than a year to realize that their goal was independence. The Ukrainian leaders wanted social reform and a recognition of their cultural rights. This meant some form of local autonomy, the need for which was emphasized by the growing disorder throughout the country which had to be countered by local initiative.

With these objects in view Professor Hrushevsky organized at Kiev the Central Rada with the aid of the Organization of Ukrainian Progressives. In its early days this conceived itself as a committee representing the various elements of Ukrainian society rather than as the nucleus of a government. At its maiden session on March 17 its first act was to send a telegram of congratulations to the prime minister of the Provisional Government, Prince Lvov, expressing the hope that that government would recognize the autonomy of Ukraine and protect the rights of the Ukrainian people.[5]

The word autonomy was used in the same sense that it had had in Austria-Hungary. It meant the power to handle certain specific problems, especially local affairs, with the permission of the central administration. Autonomy was a gift and not a right. This distinction is at wide variance with the ideas of the Anglo-Saxon world as to the significance of local institutions. In the foundation of the United States, the rights of the states as self-governing bodies were fundamental and behind even the Articles of Confederation. Under the European understanding, autonomy could be given, extended, abridged or revoked, and in all matters outside of those specified, the power of the central regime was still supreme. It thus seemed to the nationalist leaders that the Provisional Government could confer autonomy without jeopardizing its own position.

A Russia composed of autonomous districts could hardly be called a federal state, for the central authority derived its powers from itself. In a federal state the central authority would derive its powers from the component parts. The distinction was not clear at first to the Rada, and precious weeks and months were sacrificed in fruitless negotiations with the Provisional Government, which would not hear of any variation from the old monolithic system.

It was a period of meetings of all kinds. There were meetings of teachers, of co-operative societies, of peasants, of all classes, each of which demanded autonomy. When we consider that but a few weeks before, all of these groups had been organized on an imperial scale and were now talking of local needs, we can understand the effect of the upheaval and we can see why the few men who began from the definite idea of independence were scarcely heeded.

From the first moments of the revolution, the military element and those charged with maintaining public order had a deeper appreciation of what was coming. The Volynsky Guard Regiment,[6] one of those regiments of the old Russian Army mobilized on a regional basis from Ukrainian lands, was the first to join the revolution. When its imperial insignia were discarded, the regiment demanded some local insignia and called for the use of Ukrainian in its orders. Its example was followed by others and by the volunteers who were recruited for the emergency. Many of these insisted that they be allowed to take up arms to restore order at home and wanted a local commander. Thus, almost against its own will, the Rada was forced to decide about these new and Ukrainianized organizations. Should they be sent to other sections of the empire to fight? Should they be retained as local forces? Who was to be their commander?

There was only one answer. The Rada could not act merely as a mouthpiece. It had to take over the definite task of administering the affairs of state for the Ukrainian population of Kiev. Events were rapidly passing beyond the most ardent dreams.

On March 22 the Rada issued an appeal to the people to demand their rights and on the same day the Ukrainian military leaders in Kiev formed a Ukrainian Military Council to enroll troops to maintain order. This looked to the Rada as the only possible directing head.[7]

Each step in the assumption of responsibility by the Rada built up opposition among the Russians in Kiev. They felt strongly that the course of action on which the Rada had embarked was distinctly hostile to the attitude of the Provisional Government and was a threat to the unity of the state. Yet for their part they could receive no support from the Provisional Government, which was fully occupied with protecting itself against the demands of the Soviets of Soldiers' and Workmen's Delegates in Petrograd. They could only object to every action and set up their own institutions which were forced to act independently of the central government.

On April 1, when the Rada called for a public demonstration, over one hundred thousand persons appeared. These loudly demanded autonomy for Ukraine. Yet even such a mass demonstration and the previous telegrams to Petrograd brought no reply. Nor did the capital take any steps to assert its authority in Kiev.

The growing call for action in Kiev and the inaction of the Provisional Government convinced the Rada that it had to take over some of the functions of government. Ukrainian organizations were springing up throughout the country and were looking to Kiev for guidance. The influence of the metropolis was asserting itself. From the time of the old Kievan state, the city had been the capital. It was the spiritual, intellectual and economic center of Eastern Ukraine and now it was destined to become the political center. The pressure finally became overwhelming.

The Rada summoned an All-Ukrainian National Congress to meet in Kiev on April 19.[8] This was attended by over fifteen hundred delegates from all parts of the country and was the first large public gathering to represent more than the province of Kiev. It provided for a re-organization of the Rada to include delegates from all the Ukrainian provinces and a certain proportion to represent the various professional and co-operative societies. It adopted definite resolutions for Ukrainian autonomy within the Russian federation and declared itself the supreme authority in Ukraine, with a right to be consulted in the drawing up of plans for a federated Russia. There were the usual demands for Ukrainization of the schools and army forces and an insistence that Ukraine share in any Russian participation in international conferences. Again all these resolutions passed unnoticed by the Provisional Government.

The re-organization of the Rada with the appointment of a special executive committee, or Little Rada, marked a new stage in the process of the movement. It did not lead to any better relations with the Provisional Government; and even when a delegation, after a new series of congresses and petitions, went to Petrograd, the authorities refused all recognition to the Rada, still maintaining that it could make no change in the prerevolutionary setup before the meeting of the Constituent Assembly.

This blunt rejection poured oil on the fire. A Congress of Peasants' Delegates which met soon after in Kiev declared that the Rada should not have presented a request to the Provisional Government but instead a definite program for the federation of Russia. For the first time a large congress openly mentioned the possibility that if the Provisional Government refused to accept the conditions, there could only result a positive break between Ukraine and Great Russia.

The military units which had passed under Ukrainian control grew more and more restive and their feelings were not relieved when Kerensky as minister of war forbade the holding of a second military congress in June. The sole effect of Kerensky's orders was to popularize this congress, which was held on June 18-23 and again stressed the need for Ukrainian autonomy.[9]

As the Russian elements in Kiev, both radical and reactionary, were becoming more aggressive, the Rada now decided to act and on June 23 it issued its First Universal.[10] The mood of this was still conciliatory but it advanced Ukrainian thinking to a point nearer that of the nationalists. It named the Rada as the supreme government in Ukraine and the body which would speak for Ukraine in all matters concerning its relationship with the Russian Provisional Government and the Constituent Assembly.

The First Universal was of paramount importance in Ukrainian development, for while it proclaimed Ukraine as one of the federated states of the Russian republic, it laid responsibility for the development and protection of the country on the people themselves and on the Rada as their chosen vehicle of government. It did away with the old idea of autonomy as something to be granted by Petrograd and took its stand upon inherent rights.

It could not fail to widen the breach with the Provisional Government and with the Russians in Ukraine, no matter of what party they were, for all held to the unity of the country. Only the Russian Bolsheviks in Kiev welcomed its defiance of the central government but they repudiated it for assuming that Ukraine should have something more than local autonomy.

Upon the issuance of the First Universal, the Rada could now establish itself as a government. On June 28 it organized the Council of General Secretaries, with Vynnychenko as president. This was the first real executive body of the Ukrainian state. It had nine members, eight of whom belonged to the socialist groups, for the constant addition of deputies of workmen and soldiers had driven the Rada steadily to the left.

This new action finally aroused the Provisional Government. On the eve of a new offensive against the Germans, Kerensky, Tereshchenko and Tsereteli came to Kiev to consult the Rada.[11]

They proposed among other things, that the Council of General Secretaries be subject to the Provisional Government as well as to the Rada. A compromise was finally reached under which Ukraine would be governed by the Rada but would not press its demand for autonomy until the meeting of the Constituent Assembly, and the supreme command of the Ukrainized armed forces would still be in Russian hands. The results were embodied in a Second Universal, issued jointly with the Russian Commission on July 16.[12]

This clear retreat by the Rada was bitterly opposed by the military elements. The correctness of their judgment was amply confirmed by Kerensky's disastrous offensive against the Germans which commenced a few days later and which marked the final ending of the old Russian army, despite the efforts of the Ukrainian regiments. It weakened the Rada in its general position at home and benefited no one, including the Provisional Government.

Yet even this recognition of the Rada was enough to upset the Provisional Government. The Constitutional Democrats in the cabinet resigned and threw the control to the Socialists. Lenin and the Bolsheviks started another uprising in Petrograd which, though it was finally suppressed, harassed and weakened the government still further.

The Rada, continuing on its course, proceeded to draw up a constitution, or Statute of the Higher Administration of Ukraine, which it published on July 29. It was again a moderate document, avoiding any mention of the troublesome question of boundaries and carefully preserving the rights of a Russian government. Yet even this document was too strong for Petrograd, which sent down its own instructions to the Ukrainians and treated the Council of Secretaries as its own organ. Renewed protests and congresses followed and the Provisional Government was planning to arrest the members of the secretariat when it was itself overthrown by the Bolshevik revolution.

It is easy to criticize the actions of the Rada, the first Ukrain-

ian instrument of government since the Sich of a century and
a half before. Its faults were those of all of the organizations
set up by the nationalities of the old empire. They had been
so long under the tyrannical and centralized rule of St. Petersburg that they could not grasp the fact that that rule had
vanished and that the moment had come to disregard it.
The Ukrainians did not want a civil war to be started while the
German forces were occupying part of their country. They
believed the Russians were sincerely working toward a democratic government. They had started from nothing, and
from the vague desire for a cultural and economic autonomy
they had progressed to the point of trying to help build a truly
federal Russia. They had established contact with the various
other nationalities of the empire in a congress of minority peoples held in Kiev on September 21-28 to make plans for a united
front of non-Russians at the Russian Constituent Assembly.
The Rada had grown steadily and almost consistently from
the time of its inception despite the constant and unyielding
opposition of the Provisional Government, which was bound
to the old Russian tradition of unity and uniformity. Its chief
fault was the same as that of the Provisional Government, for
each was guilty of failure to devote its main energies in time of
war and revolution to building up its armed forces and its
means of self-defense.

The Rada had shown the Ukrainian people their possibilities.
It had secured the controlling position in Kiev, but although
it had brought into its membership the representatives of the
minorities, it was still opposed by Russians of all types and
schools of thought. It could not rely upon a single foreign
friend. It had insisted that Ukraine have representatives on all
Russian delegations but it was unable to take any steps to make
this effective. The downfall of the Provisional Government
turned the struggle from words to deeds. In the coming
days the military and national aspects were to be of prime
importance, aspects that were secondary so long as the con-
ception of a federalized Russia held out hopes of peace.

IV

Ukraine, the Bolsheviks and the Germans

THE COLLAPSE OF the Provisional Government put an end to the question of whether Russia was to be a unified or a federal state and raised the more urgent and ominous question of whether Ukraine was to exist in its traditional mode of life or be swung within the Bolshevik orbit.

The new regime established in Petrograd, and soon to be moved to Moscow, was led by a man of a very different calibre from the men of the Provisional Government. Lenin was determined to carry through his ideas for the creation of a proletariat state to be entirely under the control of the Bolshevik party and to be administered through the soviets. On paper he was willing to be as liberal toward the minorities as the Provisional Government had been strict. But this was only on paper, for by insisting that the Communist soviets control everything, he provided for the continued rule of the Communist party leaders who were for the most part Russians.

The advent of the new regime thoroughly befuddled the Allied representatives in Petrograd who were trying to foster the Western form of democracy in Russia and keep Russia in the war against the Central Powers. They could not believe in the permanence of a government which preached internationalism, immediate peace and the overthrow of the social order in all of its manifestations. It seemed at best some

43

form of German intrigue, for it was known that Lenin had passed through Germany in a sealed car with the approval of the German General Staff. Yet they did not wish or feel themselves in a position to declare war on the new regime. So began a period of uncertainty and confusion, with one Allied mission disagreeing with another, while the old empire fell to pieces and part after part declared its independence.

If this was the state of mind of the trained representatives of the great powers, what could be said of the Rada and the Ukrainian people who were struggling to their feet after a century and a half of absolute political subjection?

The impact of Bolshevism upon Ukraine was in the form of arms and propaganda. The land hunger of the peasantry and the unrest among the city workmen grew daily and the Rada, following the mood of the people, swung toward the left, even against the better judgment of many who had up till now supported the revolution. The outstanding fact of the Ukrainian movement thus far had been its ability to include all classes and avoid much of the disorder that had come elsewhere. Now Bolshevik agents appeared with the frank object of stirring up discontent against the Rada, not so much on the ground of national separatism as by accusing it of reactionary tendencies which thwarted the will of the proletariat. The Rada was denounced as the agent of international capitalism, where but a few days before it had seemed to many dangerously radical.[1]

The Russians in Ukraine who had fallen under Bolshevik influence no longer argued but fought. They gathered weapons and attacked each other's parties in the various cities. For a while it seemed possible that the Rada would be able to use this internecine warfare as a means of clearing its own territory and securing control, for the Bolshevik groups even with the aid of volunteers and bands from Great Russian territory were relatively weak. But their influence became threatening among some of the Ukrainian regiments, especially those which had not yet been properly trained.

The Rada strengthened its contacts with the non-Bolshevik

leftist parties and then issued the Third Universal on November 20.[2] This announced the formation of the Ukrainian National Republic (Ukrainska Narodna Respublika). The very name shows the strain and stress of the period, for it could be interpreted in all ways by all people. The word Narodna has two almost contradictory meanings. On the one hand it definitely and clearly means National. The new organization was that of the Ukrainian nation, the Ukrainian people. On the other, it means Popular, with a strong emphasis on the masses, the workmen and the peasants, and especially the proletariat. In this sense the word had become almost a slogan of the extreme left, including the Bolsheviks, who had established at Petrograd their People's Commissariats. The word called attention to both salient problems of the Rada—the national Ukrainian movement and the social agitation which was rampant.

The Third Universal separated Ukraine from the Soviet administration of Russia. It provided for the distribution of land to the peasants, the introduction of an eight-hour day in the factories, the abolition of capital punishment, a political amnesty, personal minority rights for non-Ukrainians in the country, and the taking of steps to end the war. In this way the Rada tried to satisfy both of the great movements of the day. It realized that the old disputes had become merely academic and that it was time for Ukraine to handle her own affairs. Provision was also made to elect a Ukrainian Constituent Assembly on January 9 to meet on January 22.

The Third Universal was of course badly received by the Soviets. They demanded that the Red army be admitted into the country to follow the Don Cossacks who were retiring from the front across Ukrainian territory and that the Rada turn over its authority to the Bolshevik and Communist soviets of workers and peasants. These demands obviously were intended to bring the entire state under the control of Lenin, and when they were turned down, the Bolsheviks openly declared war on the Ukrainian Republic. The Rada accepted the challenge and began to expel Bolshevik troops from Ukrainian territory.

The Kiev soviet, composed largely of Russian Bolsheviks, called a protest meeting on December 17. The Rada allowed this meeting of over two thousand deputies but saw to it that it was properly representative of the Ukrainian population. As a result there were fewer than one hundred and fifty Bolsheviks present and they withdrew when they proved unable to disrupt the proceedings. The meeting then took on a distinctively patriotic character, voted its support of the Rada, and added to its resolution the following passage: "On paper the Soviet of People's Commissars seemingly recognizes the right of a nation to self-determination and even to separation—but only in words. In fact the government of Commissars is brutally attempting to interfere in the activities of the Ukrainian government which executes the will of the legislative organ of the Ukrainian Central Rada. What sort of self-determination is this? It is certain that the Commissars will permit self-determination only to their own party; all other groups and peoples they, like the tsarist regime, desire to keep under their domination by force of arms. But the Ukrainian people did not cast off the tsarist yoke only to take upon themselves the yoke of the Commissars."[3]

This resolution aptly summarized in clear and unmistakable language the real meaning of the Soviet claims, doctrines and threats. It is as true today as it was then and is applicable to all relations between the Soviets and the rest of the world. The events of the next days showed clearly that the Bolsheviks had no intention of using persuasion or argument or any form of democracy to extend their power but that they relied entirely on force combined with disintegrating propaganda.

The frustrated Bolshevik representatives withdrew to Kharkov and here they established a Ukrainian Soviet Republic. It was headed by two Russians, Sergeyev of the Don basin and Ivanov of Kiev, and a Ukrainian Communist Horowits. To add to the general confusion, the Soviets took over the titles of the Rada, called their leaders secretaries instead of commissars and named their gathering the Rada; and they still use the term the Rada Republic to denote the Ukrainian Soviet Republic. To support this, they sent to Kharkov, to quote Professor Hrushevsky, "a band of soldiers, sailors, and various hired hooligans, stationed at Bilhorod, as if trying to force their way to the Don." These succeeded in overcoming the Ukrainian garrison in Kharkov, and the Bolsheviks made this city their capital. It was near the border of Great Russia and it was much easier to maintain contact with Petrograd and Moscow from there than from Kiev. To give color to their Ukrainian mask, they employed as one of the leaders of their armed forces George Kotsyubinsky, the son of a prominent Ukrainian writer, who had been a friend of Gorky and Lenin.[4]

The open warfare between the democratic Ukrainian government in Kiev and the Ukrainian Soviet regime in Kharkov was accompanied by effective Bolshevik propaganda in Kiev itself. This penetrated the Ukrainian army and some of the newly formed regiments either joined the Bolsheviks or went home, ostensibly for Christmas.

Up to this time the Rada had endeavored to remain in the war against the Central Powers. In this it was listening to the Western diplomatic representatives in Kiev. These promised all kinds of assistance to the hard-pressed government but found no way to deliver any supplies. And they refused to promise categorically any formal recognition of Ukrainian independence.

The situation became even more intolerable when the Germans and Bolsheviks met at Brest-Litovsk to conclude a peace.[5] The Rada was forced to send representatives to this gathering because Trotsky was presuming to speak for Ukraine as part of the old Russia. Everyone knew that it was Ukrainian grain for which the Germans and Austrians were bidding and a German-Bolshevik peace might easily force the country into a joint war against both the Bolsheviks and the Germans. The Western Allies stormed and threatened but could offer no effective help. The Rada therefore sent to Brest on January 12, 1918, three young men, Michael Levytsky, Michael Lubinsky and Alexander Sevryuk, former students of Professor Hrushevsky. Their youth and inexperience surprised General Hoffmann, the German representative, and Count Czernin,[6] the spokesman for Austria-Hungary. But they had been well instructed as to their policy and they put forward claims not only for the recognition of Ukrainian independence but for the inclusion in the new state of the Ukrainian territories under Austro-Hungarian rule. This last clause the Ukrainians soon found it necessary to waive, for it struck too deeply at the heart of the Austro-Hungarian Empire and imperiled all other negotiations.

The conference did not run smoothly. There was little friendship or confidence between the German and Austro-Hungarian representatives, for each of them was interested in advancing his own plans for Eastern Europe; and the Austrians, demoralized by the death of the Emperor Francis Joseph I,[7] were even more desperately eager for peace and grain than were the Germans. The Ukrainian delegates were especially aware of the Austrian situation, for on their way to Brest, they had passed through Lviv and had established contacts with the Ukrainian leaders in that city.

Trotsky bitterly opposed the presence of the Ukrainian representatives. He advanced all the arguments in the Russian and Bolshevik arsenal, now asserting that there was no such country or region as Ukraine, now arguing that the Rada was not a revolutionary government of the workers and peasants, now insisting that the Bolsheviks had captured Kiev and wiped out the Ukrainian government, and then on January 30 introducing two representatives of the Kharkov Communist regime, Medvedyev and Shakray, as the real representatives of Ukraine.[8]

The young Ukrainian diplomats were in a particularly uncomfortable position, for during the conference the Bolsheviks renewed their efforts to capture Kiev and for a period at the end of the month were even able to isolate the delegation for a few days by cutting all the telegraph wires out of Kiev. Yet they persevered and proved themselves far more reasonable and intelligent than the Bolsheviks, especially when Trotsky refused to sign the peace treaty in view of the Bolshevik theory that the Soviets as the spokesmen for the proletariat of the world could not sign an agreement with capitalistic and nationalistic governments like Germany and Austria-Hungary. The Germans then renewed their advance into Russian territory, whereupon Lenin compelled Trotsky to return and sign the treaty.

The treaty was finally signed on February 7, 1918. Under it the Central Powers formally recognized the independence of Ukraine, including the territory claimed by the Rada and that section which had fallen into German hands during the war. In return Ukraine promised the Central Powers a million tons of food. The Germans and Austro- Hungarians promised to return to Ukraine all of their prisoners of war and to arm and equip them for the struggle against the Bolsheviks. This was the most valuable item, for it insured a large number of trained men and of those military supplies that could not be manufactured in Ukraine under the stress of the revolution. There was also concluded a secret protocol, whereby the Austro-Hungarians would include Eastern Galicia and the Ukrainian parts of Bukovina in a new crown land in which Ukrainian would be the official language.[9]

The Treaty of Brest-Litovsk was of the greatest significance to the young republic but it brought with it not only the expected compensations but many troubles. It secured for Ukraine international recognition by the only powers that were in a position to give her any tangible support. On the debit side it made Ukraine a German satellite state and rendered possible German interference in her internal administration. It drove a wedge between the new country and the Western Allies at a time when they were increasing in strength as a result of the active arrival of American troops. Yet it was the only possible course in view of the temporizing policy of the Allies. Its unfortunate aspects were to appear only later.

Meanwhile the Rada had been making valiant efforts to maintain itself in Kiev against Bolshevik attacks and propaganda and against the opposition of Russians of every political party. A new government was formed under Volodymyr Holubovych, one of the Social Revolutionary leaders. But even in those critical days there was far too much argumentation in the Rada and too little effective action.

To strengthen the position of the delegates at Brest-Litovsk, the Rada had issued on January 22 a Fourth Universal which in direct and dignified language proclaimed the full independence of the Ukrainian National Republic—"From today the Ukrainian National Republic becomes the Independent, Free, Sovereign State of the Ukrainian People." It had taken ten months of endless talk and fighting to bring the Rada and the people to this clear-cut decision, so needful if the new government was to function smoothly and consistently.[10]

The pressure on Kiev continued and on February 7, the very day that the treaty was concluded, the government withdrew to save the city from civil war. The troops retired into the suburbs and the Rada moved to Zhytomyr. On February 9 the Bolsheviks entered the city and commenced a reign of terror which must have been as destructive as the scarcely averted storming. Over five thousand civilians fell victims in the massacre that followed of those suspected of being anti-Bolshevik.[11]

The efforts of the Rada at Zhytomyr to solve the pressing problems of the country constantly evoked hostility from some element of the population. To many of the peasants, its attempts to divide up the big estates seemed halting and hesitant. These same attempts were too strenuous for the great landowners, many of whom were either Russian or Polish in sympathy, and these classes did everything to prevent land reform and restore the old order. Thus the Rada was assailed by both the right and the left.

All this disorder and chaos made it difficult to organize and equip a regular army. The country was overrun by various armed bands under self-appointed atamans who plundered indiscriminately in the name of the revolution. Fortunately at this moment there arrived the Riflemen of the Sich and the other units which had been formed among the prisoners of war by the Society for the Liberation of Ukraine. These new units gave the republic a stability and a reliable military force that it had hitherto lacked.

By March 1 the Bolsheviks had been driven out of Kiev and the Rada was able to return. The process of clearing the country continued and by the end of April nearly all the Bolsheviks had been expelled from Ukraine by hard fighting. On March 9 the Soviets had promised the Germans to respect the territories of the Ukrainian Republic, but it goes without saying that they broke the agreement and that the Germans, busily transferring their troops to the Western front to meet the Americans, French and British, took no steps to compel them to respect it.

On the anniversary of Shevchenko's death, the Rada announced that it intended to continue the democratic policies outlined in the Third and Fourth Universals. The government of Holubovych got the support of most of the Ukrainian parties but it had continuous difficulties with the wealthy and conservative classes and in general with the non-Ukrainian population, especially the Russians and the Poles, who would have no part of it.[12]

The Germans acted as if they were the real masters of the country. In the spring, after a year of war and turmoil, with many harvests reduced or destroyed, it was hard to collect the promised grain from the peasants. The need for food was so acute in the Central Powers that they kept pressing the Rada and the government and even instituted their own methods of collection. Field Marshal von Eichhorn at Kiev became the most influential member of the German missions but he was constantly at odds with Baron Mumm, the representative of the Berlin Foreign Office. General Groner also arrived to take an active part in the grain collection.

The major concern of the Rada was to prepare for the holding of a Constituent Assembly. This had been scheduled to meet in January but the elections had not been completed because of Bolshevik aggression and because of protests that those who had been elected in various areas no longer represented the wishes of their constituents. The Rada proposed new elections and announced that the convention would open on June 12, as soon as half of the delegates had been selected.

Nevertheless the Rada was still plagued by discord and inaction. The two great movements of nationalism and of social reform were not too closely coordinated. The parties differed widely from each other and almost every measure was stubbornly debated. There was in fact a tendency to postpone decisions until after the elections and this did not fit in with German plans for securing an immediate supply of grain.

The German authorities finally lost patience with the Rada. On April 28, 1918, they sent a force of troops to surround the Rada building. A small detachment entered and its commander ordered the Rada to disperse. Despite the protest of its president, Professor Hrushevsky, the order was carried out and the Rada, thus expelled from the seat of government, ceased to function.[13]

The next day the conservative elements of the state, especially the Society of the Agriculturists, the great landowners, held a congress and elected as a new hetman Paul Skoropadsky, who was installed at once. Skoropadsky was a member of that same family which had produced Hetman Ivan Skoropadsky, who had been selected by Peter the Great to take the place of Mazepa after his deposition in 1708. He had been educated in St. Petersburg as a Russian nobleman and despite his adherence to Ukraine, his opponents saw him still as a Russian. The new regime was as conservative as the Rada had been progressive. It repealed most of the land laws, even before they had been tried out, and it received German support to put down any dissatisfaction. The new leaders were able to secure a considerable amount of grain but they met with increasing opposition and popular anger flared up against the Germans. Marshal von Eichhorn was assassinated in Kiev on July 30. He had no able successor and throughout the summer of 1918 German influence in Ukraine ebbed along with its power on the Western front.[14]

Throughout the summer there were present in Kiev Bolshevik diplomatic representatives; their leaders were Rakovsky and especially Dmytro Manuilsky, a Ukrainian by birth who had spent most of his adult life among the Russians and was a close friend of Lenin. They were in Kiev ostensibly to draw up a peace treaty between the Ukrainian Republic and the Russian Soviet Republic but it was an open secret that they were carrying on disruptive propaganda. They had a great deal of money and they spent it lavishly. The Hetman and his officials vainly begged the Germans to allow them to limit or expel the offensive members of this group.[15]

The policy of the Germans during this period was most inconsistent. They were opposed to the extension of Bolshevism but they did not want to take an openly hostile attitude and risk the reopening of an Eastern front. Even when their ambassador, Count Mirbach, was murdered in Moscow, the Bolshevik capital, the Germans kept quiet and thus unwittingly allowed the concentration of resources and people for their own downfall.[16]

The Germans pushed on to the east. They gave aid to the Don Cossacks in their fight against Bolshevism, also to the Georgians and other peoples in the Caucasus, and under their protection a long series of more or less independent peoples sprang up along the north shore of the Black Sea. Farther to the east began that movement among the old Russian officers that was later to be led by General Denikin. This rallying of anti-Bolshevik Russians with the object of re-establishing a government for the entire country received the support of the Western Allies, who still had not adopted any concrete policy. They hampered the efforts of the anti-Bolshevik Russians by banning all tsarist formulas, yet they would not support the democratic movements of those peoples who were trying to free themselves from both Russian and Bolshevik domination.

By autumn the defeat of the Central Powers was approaching and with each week the morale of their forces fell as Bolshevism made greater and greater inroads into them. At the end of October the Austro-Hungarian Empire collapsed. Turkey went out of the war on October 29. The Kaiser abdicated on November 9 and fled to Holland; and on November 11 came the armistice on the Western front. World War 1 was over.

It was a foregone conclusion that Skoropadsky could not retain his position without German support, for although he had tried to revive the traditions of the old hetmanate, he had won no popular approval except among the extreme conservatives. The final defeat of the Germans doomed him utterly. Rioting and disorders burst out anew as the people tried to rid themselves of the German "guests."

At this moment Vynnychenko tried to rally the forces of the Rada by forming a Directory of the various Ukrainian Socialist parties. He included Simon Petlyura, who had been one of the members of the original nationalist groups. Petlyura felt that action was needed even more than words. He went to Bila Tserkva, where the Riflemen of the Sich were camped, and with them he marched on Kiev.

Then came another one of those tangles that marked Allied policy toward Ukraine and the other states. Although the Germans had been defeated, the Allies in their fear of Bolshevism ordered them not to turn over their weapons or territory to the Ukrainians of any group but to maintain control pending Allied assumption of authority. It was a foolish order, for the defeated German forces were themselves heavily permeated with Bolshevism and even those who were not infected thought only of returning home with little emphasis on the order of their going. The Germans simply melted away and before long they were only too glad to make an arrangement with Petlyura to take over. This was settled on December 11 at Kasatin; and three days later, on December 14, Colonel Evhen Konovalets entered Kiev at the head of a Ukrainian detachment. The same day Skoropadsky laid down his power and slipped out of Kiev to Berlin. Petlyura arrived on December 19 and re-established the Ukrainian Republic.

It was then almost two years since the establishment of the Rada and a year since the declaration of independence. It was necessary to begin work again in a country that was even more disorganized and devastated than it had been before. The Bolsheviks had had the opportunity of strengthening their position in Moscow and Great Russia, where they were relatively unchallenged, while to the southeast the anti-Bolshevik Russians were forming the White army to fight against Bolshevism and cement the unity of the country. The Allies still vacillated. The task of Petlyura, Vynnychenko and the Ukrainians was growing more difficult all the time.

V

The Republic of Western Ukraine

THE RUSSIAN INVASION of Eastern Galicia in 1914 had devastated the most developed portion of the Ukrainian lands, but after the Russian troops had been expelled in 1915, Ukrainian understanding of the issues of the war had definitely increased. Russian excesses had ended once and for all the old Muscophile faction, and its leaders had withdrawn with the Russian armies. Wherever these armies had penetrated, they had brought home to the population the differences that existed between the Great Russians and the Ukrainians. At the same time the presence of Eastern Ukrainian units in the Russian forces had revealed to the Western Ukrainian villagers their essential unity with their brothers under tsarist rule.

By 1917 it was clear to all the nationalities of the empire that Austria-Hungary would not emerge from the war as a unit. On December 31 the Ukrainian Student Organization in Vienna was even able to state that the future of their countrymen lay in union with the Ukrainian National Republic being formed in Kiev. The other Ukrainian organizations were perhaps less outspoken. Some of the older politicians still hoped for the creation of a Ukrainian section of the Hapsburg Empire but they were rapidly falling into a minority and when on July 22, 1918, the Austrian parliament repudiated the promise given to the Ukrainian delegates at Brest-Litovsk and were sustained by the Germans, practically all hope for a peaceful solution was abandoned and action was begun on plans to set up a new regime.

President Wilson's address on January 8, 1918, setting forth his Fourteen Points, among them the self-determination of all nations, had given impetus to this development. Yet the leaders were aware of a new danger, that of falling under Polish control, for they realized that Polish propaganda at home and abroad regarded Eastern Galicia as Polish territory and that the Poles had been more successful than they in making friends among the Western Powers.

The summer of 1918 was a strange period. The Austro-Hungarian armies were still fighting on the various fronts but all of the nationalities were almost openly making their plans for an independent existence. By autumn representatives came and went, meetings were held to arrange for the formation of new governments, and the officials of the empire seemed not to notice.

By September 14, when the Allies rejected the idea of a separate peace for Austria-Hungary, even the officials of the empire lost hope. On October 16 Emperor Charles in a last attempt ordered a reconstitution of the empire on national lines but by this time no one paid attention. One and all were determined upon independence.

On October 18 a Ukrainian National Rada[2] was established at Lviv under the presidency of Dr. Evhen Petrushevych. It embraced all the Ukrainian representatives in the provincial diets and parliament and representatives of all political parties. It at once issued a call for the formation of a republic to include all the Ukrainians within the Hapsburg Empire, including those in Eastern Galicia, northwestern Bukovina and northeastern Hungary. It summoned the minorities to send their deputies to the new government and to aid in preparing a constitution providing for universal, equal, secret and direct suffrage on the basis of proportional representation, with the right of national cultural autonomy and the right of the minorities to participate in the government. It very carefully, despite some protests, omitted the question of its relationship to the Ukrainian National Republic, which was still under the regime of Hetman Skoropadsky.

There will be noticed at once a striking difference between this movement and that of the previous year in Kiev. In Lviv there was no period of hesitation. From the moment when the Rada was established, its goal was absolute independence and the Rada applied all of its energies to determining how this was to be brought about.

The process of disintegration within the old empire gained momentum. On October 16 the Hungarians broke their bonds with the Austrians. On October 28 the Czechs declared their independence of Hapsburg rule. On October 31 the Poles raised their standard in Krakow and planned to take over the whole of Galicia.

On the same day, the Rada asked the governor general of Galicia, Count Huyn, to turn over Lviv to the Ukrainians. He declined but made it plain that he would take no counteraction, and that night the Ukrainian military raised their flag over the city. By morning the new government was in control.[3]

Yet if the break with the old order was peaceful—a mere recognition of changed conditions—the new state was faced immediately with difficulties with the revived Poland, which dreamed of restoring the position she had held in the Middle Ages in Eastern Europe. Poland's great asset was the experience which her leaders had gained during the years when they had been active in the affairs of the Dual Monarchy. The Western Ukrainian Republic, in contrast, was handicapped from the start by the dearth of men who had served in the more responsible posts in either the civil service or the army. There were a large number of lesser functionaries and officers; there were few men trained and experienced in the higher echelons. The military forces consisted of that part of the Riflemen of the Sich who had not gone to East Ukraine and some disorganized reserve units, whose ranking officers had returned to their homes. The leaders of the new state soon saw that maintaining their independence was to be a greater task than winning it.[4]

They were not mistaken. On the same day that the Ukrainian flag was raised in Lviv, the Poles of the city rose in revolt. Lacking men trained in street fighting, the Ukrainians were unable to dislodge the Poles from their center of resistance and for three weeks the struggle went on. Neither side possessed any important supplies of heavy weapons. Both had only rifles, machine guns and grenades, but the contest was none the less intense.[5]

Meanwhile the Western Ukrainian Republic assumed control of one city after another throughout Eastern Galicia, as the news of the open establishment of the republic swept the country. Everywhere there was counteraction by the Poles. On November 11 a small Polish force, raised in Krakow, recovered Peremyshl and on the 19th a group of about one hundred and twenty officers with eight guns and twelve hundred men, set out by train for Lviv. They succeeded in running through the Ukrainian lines and the addition of even this small force turned the tide. They recovered the greater part of the city, and on November 22 the Western Ukrainian government left Lviv and moved to Ternopil and later to Stanyslaviv.

Throughout the winter the republic dominated most of Eastern Galicia with the exception of the railroad from Peremyshl to Lviv which the Poles succeeded in holding. The Ukrainians also maintained a more or less desultory siege of Lviv but they were confronted with steadily increasing Polish forces, as the Western Allies and especially France poured in more supplies and enabled the Polish army to grow along conventional lines. Finally in the spring, the Polish divisions which had been in France under General Joseph Haller arrived; despite the orders of the Allied missions they were thrown into the struggle and they finally forced the Western Ukrainian army to retire eastward.

The forces of the republic in Bukovina were little more fortunate. On November 3 the Ukrainians occupied Chernivtsy, the capital. It was not for long, for on Armistice Day, November 11, a detachment of the regular Romanian army entered the city and overthrew the Ukrainian Regional Committee which had been formed under Omelyan Popovych.[6]

In the third part of Western Ukraine, the region of the Carpathians, there was even more confusion. Under the old Hungarian system it had not been possible to establish a working agreement between the residents of the various counties and the disorder was abetted by the isolation of many of the mountain valleys in which the Ukrainian population lived. Meetings were held in the three centers of Preshov, Uzhorod and Hust but the great masses of the mountaineers were not as well organized as elsewhere. In addition to that, there was more Hungarian interference. Far too many of the semi-intellectuals of the region still sympathized with the Hungarians and the split between the nationalists and the Muscophiles was far deeper than in any other section. The Czechs also put in a bid for control of the territory on the basis of an understanding between President Masaryk as chairman of the Czechoslovak National Committee abroad and the American Ruska Narodna Rada, a gathering of Carpatho-Ruthenians in Scranton, Pennsylvania.[7] This was similar to the famous Pittsburgh Agreement between Masaryk and the Slovaks in the United States and it was used in the same way to advance Czech claims.

The movement was slow in starting. There was a meeting in Hust on January 21, 1919, which voted to join Western Ukraine but this was already almost academic in view of the loss of Lviv to the Poles. Agitation continued, however, and finally, on May 5, with the republic almost in ruins, the Ukrainians of Carpatho-Ukraine voted to become an autonomous part of the new Czechoslovak Republic.

It is obvious from all this that the vital part of the Western Ukrainian Republic was the region of Eastern Galicia. It was the most developed section of the new state and it had the most compact and organized Ukrainian population. Since it was only there that the state could hope to take root, the loss of Lviv was a crushing blow.

The Allied missions did their best to put a stop to the fighting but their efforts were fruitless. France stood solidly on the side of Poland; and Great Britain and the United States, convinced that the war was over, were already thinking of demobilizing their armies. Thus alone of the peoples of the old Hapsburg empire, the Ukrainians found it impossible to get a sympathetic hearing from the victorious Allies.

They went on, nevertheless, to carry out their real desire. The Republic of Western Ukraine formally voted to unite with the Ukrainian National Republic on January 3, and on January 22 the Ukrainian National Republic in imposing ceremonies accepted the union, declaring that "from today the Ukrainian people, liberated by the mighty effort of their own strength, is able to unite all the energies of her sons for the building of an undivided, independent Ukrainian State, for the good and happiness of the Ukrainian people."[8]

Once again the Ukrainian people were united as they had not been since the fall of the Kiev state in the thirteenth century. Yet this union was not consummated in a time of peace. It represented the spontaneous desire of the people but it was begotten under the shadows of two conflicts, that of the Western Ukrainians against the Poles, and that of the Eastern Ukrainians against the Bolsheviks and the White Russians, neither of whom would recognize the new state.

VI

The Decline of the Ukrainian National Republic

WITH THE RETURN of Petlyura and the directory to Kiev and the union of the two parts of Ukraine, there was again a momentary chance for the successful liberation of the country. The situation was not as favorable, however, as it had been a year earlier.

The signing of the armistice between the Western Powers and Germany had completely changed the situation and still more the temper of the times. From the very outbreak of hostilities, the Western Powers had always looked upon the Kaiser and the German general staff as the chief enemies. After the Kaiser had abdicated and the German army had been reduced to impotence, the object of the war seemed to be achieved. Austria-Hungary had disintegrated. Turkey had yielded. The old stories about an alliance between Germany and the Bolsheviks had lost all their point. The Allies were confident that Lenin and his associates could not maintain their power and they were no longer inclined to take an active part in the various conflicts raging in the east of Europe.

More than that, during the war they had worked with and recognized certain of the new governments of Eastern Europe through their national committees in Paris, London and Washington and on the whole they made little effort to ascertain whether these bodies and the governments into which they turned were representative of the wishes of the people. They made no effort to maintain order in the new countries or to provide for a peaceful arrangement of boundaries by sending even token forces to the main centers to keep up transportation and similar services. They relied entirely upon the innate democracy of the new governments and seemed to believe that the boundaries would settle themselves automatically.

In their relations with the peoples of the former Russian empire, the Allied policy was even more irresolute. On the one hand, to oppose Bolshevism, they encouraged the German occupying forces to hold their positions.[1] As in Ukraine, the result was disastrous. Elsewhere it was little better, for the German armies melted away or were transformed into predatory bands under more or less able adventurers. These became a nuisance to the Allies as well as to the native peoples.

The opening of the Dardanelles made it possible to move supplies by sea into the long-closed ports of Ukraine, the Don Cossacks, Georgia and the other entities that were in open revolt. But the Allies continued to feel as a result of the Treaty of Brest-Litovsk that these uprisings were primarily the work of German agents and they declined to cooperate actively with the struggling regimes. They continued to believe that the future of Russia should be decided at some sort of general meeting after Bolshevism had been overcome, and this led them to give some support to the various Russian White armies which had been formed during the preceding year and were now trying to cut their way to the north and Moscow from the Caucasus and Siberia. At the same time they were afraid that these forces would prove to be reactionary or tsaristic and they opposed so many of their actions that they nullified any success which these might win.[2]

There was thus created a real vacuum. On December 12, 1918, just as Petlyura was entering Kiev, the French landed a force of French and Greeks at Odessa and tried to set up an anti-Communist regime under the command of a White Russian officer whom they appointed. The French soldiers, now that peace had come, had no will to serve and they soon became infected with Bolshevism. Disorders broke out among them and by early spring they had withdrawn, after turning over all supplies in the seaport town to a Bolshevik band of less than two thousand men.[3]

Such episodes gave strength to the French desire to erect a strong Poland as a bulwark against both Bolshevism and Germany. The Ukrainian leaders now saw themselves forced to fight in the west against a Polish army which was receiving reinforcements and supplies from the Western Powers and of course the Poles were never weary of arguing that the Ukrainian movement was only a product of Hapsburg and Bolshevik machinations, exactly as the Russians swore that it was of German derivation.

During the winter of 1918-19, the pressure of the Poles on the Western Ukrainian armies never slackened. The Poles were supposed to be fighting the Bolsheviks but in reality and on various pretexts, they turned against the Western Ukrainian armies and drove them steadily eastward, preferring to risk national extinction and the ill will of the victorious Allies than make any concessions to the Ukrainians.

The delegates to the Peace Conference and the leaders of the victorious Allies, Woodrow Wilson, Lloyd George and Clemenceau, tried to check the warfare between the Poles and Ukrainians. Dmowski as the Polish representative in Paris played upon the Allied fear of a war of revenge by the Central Powers and charged that the Western Ukrainian Army was a hostile force because it had German or Austrian officers. In vain the Ukrainians offered to replace any such officers with persons nominated by the Allies. To every appeal the Poles made the answer that Galicia was an inalienable part of the Polish territory. Even at the very moment of receiving the Treaty of Saint-Germain, the Polish delegates in May and June refused to sign if any provision was made to recognize the Ukrainian population of Eastern Galicia.[4]

This put an end to the many proposals which had been drifting around as to the future of the province. Few of these had been truly realistic. Proposals had been submitted to set up an Eastern Galician state and every one recognized the folly of this. It was obvious that it would be dangerous to annex the territory to the Soviets and thus bring them to the Carpathian Mountains and make them a neighbor of Hungary which was just throwing off a Bolshevik experiment. It seemed the most practical move to make Eastern Galicia at least autonomous under Polish sovereignty; but this the Poles refused to admit.

The Allies, faced with the prospect of restraining Poland by force of arms and thereby weakening her stand against Bolshevism, finally yielded. On June 25 the Supreme Allied Council notified Poland that to check the Bolshevik bands, her army could advance to the river Zbruch, but that this did not affect the future political status of Eastern Galicia. This was a transparent fraud but it was enough for the Poles. Their new armies under General Haller rapidly pushed forward and by July, 1919, they had conquered the entire province.[5] Then some seventy-five thousand men of the West Ukrainian army retreated to join Petlyura at Kamyanets-Podolsky.

These events in West Ukraine merely added to the difficulties of the directory in Kiev. Scarcely had the act of union between the two republics been proclaimed, when new troubles arose. The old differences between Petlyura and Vynnychenko were sharply accented. Vynnychenko as a leftist theorist was attacked, even by the Allies, as a Bolshevik. Petlyura, as a man of action, was assailed as a reactionary. A new attack by the Bolsheviks ended in Vynnychenko's resignation and Petlyura's accession to power as chief ataman of the army and chief of the cabinet.[6]

On February 4 Petlyura, with his government and army, was forced to evacuate Kiev under Bolshevik pressure. He wandered toward the northwest until he reached the city of Kamyanets-Podolsky, where he was joined in July by the

remains of the Western Ukrainian army. Under the conditions, it was futile to talk of plans for detailed legislation or
even a unified military policy. All over Ukraine the way was
open for ambitious leaders to raise their own private armies
and operate in the name of the Ukrainian National Republic,
the Bolsheviks or themselves.

The exactions of these men brought the Ukrainian forces
into disrepute, for they often changed sides with amazing
frequency. Thus Hryhoryev, the Bolshevik commander who
took over Odessa from the French, had formerly been in the
Ukrainian army and only a short time afterwards had assumed
an independent position. The country was ravaged in a way
that was strongly reminiscent of the ruin in the seventeenth
century, when the various Kozak leaders were fighting for individual supremacy and seemed oblivious of the welfare of
the state as a whole.

Even so, order began again to come out of chaos. The united
Eastern and Western Ukrainian armies had so far recovered
from the catastrophes of the spring that they were able to re-
enter Kiev and re-establish their government. They decisively
defeated the Bolsheviks, who were now posing as the army of
the Ukrainian Soviet Socialist Republic with its capital at
Kharkov, the product of a new Soviet declaration of May
5, 1919. Whatever the Allies might think, the Ukrainian movement had become so widespread that even the Bolsheviks in
Moscow tried to profit by it by recognizing the independence
of their own Soviet republic and preaching an independent
Ukrainian Communism.

Once more and almost immediately fortune turned against
the new state. This time the threat came not from the Bolsheviks but from the White Russian armies under General Denikin
which with Allied blessing were pushing across Ukraine
from the southeast. Denikin was of course anti-Bolshevist but
he was dedicated to the idea of Russian unity. Everywhere he
went, he declined to compromise with any non-Russian anti-
Bolshevist force and as he advanced in Ukraine, he expended

all his energies in trying to bring back the situation as it existed before the Revolution of 1917. Ukraine was to become again Little Russia. The Ukrainian language and Ukrainian newspapers were suppressed. Ukrainian officers and soldiers were punished as severely for their disloyalty to Russia as were the Bolsheviks. The large estates were returned to the former owners. The old Russian laws were reintroduced. The only concession made was the utterly meaningless statement that when Bolshevism was overthrown, there would be a Constituent Assembly which would then consider what changes needed to be made in the old Russian regime. It was the exact policy that had led the Provisional Government of 1917 to its doom at the hands of Lenin.

The White Russians, with their better-trained officers and the supplies furnished by the Allies, were able to win victory after victory. But these victories accomplished little or nothing. Behind their lines a continuous series of local revolts burst out among outraged populations which saw all their scanty gains of the last years completely nullified. Even after Denikin had taken Kiev, he was unable to hold it and before long the forces of the Ukrainian Soviet Socialist Republic reappeared in its streets and resumed their career of murder and devastation.[7]

An epidemic of typhus broke out in the Ukrainian army which decimated its ranks and wrought havoc among the civilians. It seemed to be the last straw, yet the struggle for independence did not end.

The epidemic, the shortage of supplies and the military defeats in both east and west opened a new period of friction between the two armies. Hemmed in between the Poles, the White Russians and the Bolsheviks, the Western Ukrainians saw their worst enemy in the Poles. Unwilling to end this struggle, Dr. Petrushevych and his followers crossed into Romania and from there the *émigré* Western Ukrainian government went on to Vienna and continued its work.

The Eastern Ukrainians under Petlyura took advantage of

the new opportunities offered them and gradually retreated into Polish territory to prepare for a new onslaught against the Bolsheviks. These were offered by the policies of Marshal Pilsudski.

Pilsudski, the outstanding Polish military leader of the day, had been born near Wilno and differed in one respect from his fellow Poles. As a product of the old Polish-dominated Lithuania and a bitter enemy of Russia, Red or White, he conceived the idea not of forming a unified Polish state but of preparing around it a series of allies who as satellites would round out Polish influence and restore the country to its seventeenth-century position.

Petlyura, a man of eastern Ukraine, could not feel that deep personal antagonism to the Poles that was characteristic of the Western Ukrainians. Perhaps he sympathized with some of the broader aspects of Pilsudski's ideas. Perhaps he was merely impelled by the extreme straits to which the Ukrainian cause was reduced at the moment. At all events a *rapprochement* took place between Pilsudski and Petlyura and this involved a break with the Western Ukrainians.

On April 24, 1920, the Ukrainian National Republic, with Petlyura at its head, made a formal military alliance with the government of Poland. Under this the Ukrainians of the east omitted all references to Eastern Galicia. In return it secured Polish recognition, the first which it had received since the Treaty of Brest-Litovsk and the only formal recognition from one of the powers associated with the Allies.

Immediately after this the Polish and Ukrainian armies commenced to advance. On May 7 the first units entered Kiev and two days later they established a bridgehead on the eastern bank of the Dnieper. Many of the Ukrainian factions were angered at the appearance of the Poles and Petlyura was hotly denounced for abandoning Western Ukraine. The population in and around Kiev did not rally as expected.[8]

On May 14 the Soviets cut behind the Polish lines and severed their communications. The Polish army, still bound

to the tactics of the World War, was helpless against the unexpected attack and once again the Ukrainians saw their allies
retire and had to leave with them. This was the last time that
the troops of the Ukrainian National Republic penetrated their
capital.[9]

The campaign of 1920 was one of rapid movement. In quick
succession the Soviets pierced the Polish positions wherever
they were established and by the early part of August they
were in the neighborhood of Warsaw. Poland as well as
Ukraine seemed doomed. The Allies again and again tried
to bring about a peace. The Poles refused to listen to any
propositions as to the future of Eastern Galicia or any other
of the Ukrainian or Byelorussian lands. Yet despite this the
French sent General Weygand to defend Warsaw. At the
crucial moment Pilsudski, by a brilliant attack, placed his
forces behind the Soviet lines and completely annihilated the
Red army. It was then the turn of the Poles to advance and
they reoccupied almost the same positions that they had had
at the time of the alliance with Ukraine.

During the battle of Warsaw the southern Red armies with
whom Joseph Stalin was acting as a leader and the cavalry
forces of Budenny moved toward Lviv and tried to cut their
way to the Carpathians to reach Hungary. The Ukrainian
divisions played an important part in checking this movement
and distinguished themselves in many battles in Eastern Galicia
where they joined with the Poles in clearing the province of
the last Red soldiers, who were forced again to the east.

Peace negotiations were opened at Riga, and on November
12 a treaty of peace was signed between Poland and the Russian Soviet Republic and the Ukrainian Soviet Republic. No
mention was made of the Ukrainian National Republic.[10]
Despite the services of its troops to Poland during the war, it
was as completely forgotten as if it had never existed. The
Poles made no allusion to the alliance which they had signed
only a few months before.[9]

This doomed the republic. The Ukrainian troops under

Petlyura continued to fight on but without hope of success. Deprived of their base in Poland, they had to face without supplies the entire force of the reorganized Red army. Peace was slowly coming to Eastern Europe. The White Russian movement had ended, except for the continuing resistance of Baron Wrangel; but this was not serious and on November 16 the White army was evacuated by sea from the Crimea. The Ukrainian forces lasted a few days longer; after a defeat at Bazar on November 21, they too were forced to give up and seek refuge in Poland.

Thus ended the military phase of the Ukrainian National Republic. It was a heroic struggle against overwhelming odds, a struggle of men with ideals but without supplies, without bases, without any of the necessities of modern warfare. It marked the end of one phase of the Ukrainian struggle for liberty. Not since the days of Bohdan Khmelnytsky in the seventeenth century had the initial moment been so favorable. With the Russian empire and Austria-Hungary in dissolution and Poland not yet reborn, Ukraine had a golden opportunity to become master of her own destiny. The movement failed. The prejudices of the past were too strong. The Allies who had it in their power to recognize the new state and to carry out their ideals of a free, democratic Europe were still under the spell of the old Russian and the new Polish propaganda and they allowed Ukraine to be overwhelmed.

Yet in estimating the significance of the movement, we must not forget that the Russian Communists, in order to maintain the grasp of the old empire over the wealth of Ukraine, found it necessary to create a Ukrainian puppet state, which could sign treaties and arrange its own affairs, albeit under the dominating control of the party in Moscow.

The fate of Ukraine was shared almost immediately by the smaller states that had likewise struck for national independence. Georgia, Armenia, Azerbaijan, and many other groups in Europe and Asia had lashed out against the Russian tyranny. One and all failed. Only Finland and the three Baltic states of

Estonia, Latvia and Lithuania with their access to the sea survived the debacle.

The technique that was used against one was used against all. Ukraine was the model and the pattern by which the Russian Communists hoped to extend their control throughout the world. The system used in Ukraine was improved and standardized but it was never fundamentally changed. It called for the arousing of discontent, the encouraging of internal discord and confusion, the fomenting of disorder, the playing upon false idealism, and then the launching of an ostensibly independent Communist government which would call upon the Red army for support and assistance. There would be an immediate military response, and then would come massacres, the confiscation of property and the execution or deportation of the old leaders, while the country remained nominally free but in the chains of its masters.

For three years and more the Ukrainians had worked for their independence. For two years and a half they had fought for it, while the world had looked on with indifference. Poland, Romania and Czechoslovakia had hoped to profit and so they did for a while but the same tactics were later to be applied to them. At the time it seemed a mere episode on the Continent but in 1950, in retrospect, the fall of the Ukrainian National Republic was but the first step in the creation of the modern Frankenstein that is threatening by the same policies to cause World War III and has forced an open struggle with the United Nations in Korea.

VII

Between the Wars

THE SERIES OF treaties that were drawn up at the Peace Conference in 1919 opened a new period in European history. It was confidently assumed that they had permanently limited the power of Germany as they had certainly wiped out the empire of the Hapsburgs by dismemberment. All of the important peoples of the Dual Monarchy except the Ukrainians received an independent position in the new Europe. Yet these treaties had completely sidestepped the problems offered by the dissolution of the Russian empire. The Treaty of Riga in 1920 had indeed given Poland for the first time an eastern boundary but this had been done at the expense of the Ukrainians at a moment when for the first time in centuries Poland and Ukraine had been fighting as allies. The "peace" that was thus made in Europe was destined to a precarious existence of only some twenty years.

Under the conditions of that peace there was little hope for the Ukrainians to advance far in the direction of their long-desired independence. The new situation presented even more ominous possibilities than they had faced in 1914. Western Ukraine was divided between Poland, Czechoslovakia and Romania, largely according to the old provincial districts and regimes of Austria-Hungary. Eastern Ukraine, under the Ukrainian Soviet Socialist Republic, was an unwilling victim

72

of the new form of Russian imperialism which was substantially the old system coated with the theories of Marx, Lenin and later Stalin.

The situation was a sharp letdown from the high hopes with which the Ukrainians and the whole of Eastern Europe had arisen at the moment of the Russian revolution and the collapse of Austria-Hungary. Then independence, peace and prosperity had seemed so near. Now all of these ideals had been relegated to the distant future.

Yet the years of struggle were not a total loss. The Ukrainians had acquired a certain self-confidence during the hard experiences of those eventful three years that was to stand them in good stead. They had learned to work together in a common cause. The masses were largely freed from their political apathy, had become conscious of their national identity and were willing to proclaim themselves for what they were. The two parts of Ukraine had learned to know each other better and to feel their kinship more strongly. Personal contacts had been formed in different areas and these were by no means confined to the outstanding scholars and writers; even ordinary citizens who had served in the armies had gotten to know their fellows from other sections of the country.

Some of these contacts were of short duration, for soon the paths of Eastern and Western Ukraine began again to diverge. In the early years there was a more or less brisk interchange of certain ideas between Lviv and Kiev but this soon dried up as the Iron Curtain erected by the Soviets across Europe became ever more impassable.

A large and active *émigré* group had developed abroad. The leaders of both east and west, after the failure of the political and military movement, made their way to Western Europe and spent the next years in the capitals of the democratic powers, endeavoring, as did Orlyk and his friends after the defeat of Mazepa in 1709, to arouse interest in the fate of the Ukrainian people and enlist public sentiment in their cause. Late in the nineteenth century Professor Michael

Drahomaniv had left Kiev to undertake work of this kind in Switzerland and then in Bulgaria, but that was about all. If Ukraine was known abroad before 1914, it was only through the laborers and peasants who had gone as seasonal workers across Europe or had settled down to build a new life in the lands across the Atlantic.

The struggle for independence had its effect on emigrant Ukrainians. Many had gone to the United States and Canada as simple laborers and had prospered. The World War woke them to a full consciousness of their feelings as Ukrainians. Made the targets of Russian, Polish and German propaganda, they commenced a counteraction. They were not able at the moment to sway American and Canadian public opinion as did some of the other groups but they went to work actively for the cause of a free Ukraine. They organized relief work for their relatives abroad and seriously undertook through their various societies and especially the Ukrainian National Association the difficult task of enlightening American and Canadian public opinion on the Ukrainian problem. They sent representatives to the Peace Conference in Paris and much to the annoyance of their enemies made sure that the voice of free Ukraine would not be silenced.[1]

Even though the Ukrainian representatives failed, the Peace Conference served to introduce them to Western diplomats and statesmen. It gave them the opportunity to speak of their national cause and laid the foundation, even if only very sketchily, for future relationships.[2]

At the same time the leaders of the Ukrainian missions in Washington, Dr. Julian Bachynsky for the Ukrainian Republic and Dr. Longin Cehelsky and Dr. Luke Myshuha for the Republic of Western Ukraine worked steadily until 1923 to explain the situation. As the accredited diplomats of their state, they received broad powers and courtesies but not official recognition and their words far too often fell on deaf ears.

When all has been said, the period between the wars was disappointing for the Ukrainians but it was no less disappointing for all the other peoples of the world. The swing of public sentiment which had begun immediately after the signing of the armistice with Germany continued and resulted in an atmosphere in which all unconsciously the groundwork was laid for a new catastrophe.

The new world order was one of strange contradictions. In a physical sense the world had become united as never before. The discoveries and inventions of material science had seemingly annihilated space and time. The airplane and the radio had brought the nations nearer together. The spread of manufactures, the automobile and the motor bus had almost eliminated the self-contained life of the villages and the isolation of certain areas. The motion picture in all provincial centers and towns and in many villages had given even the most secluded individual some concept of the outside world.

Yet man had not risen to the level of these new inventions. The passport and the *carte d'identité*, regarded before 1914 as the signs of a backward government, now became almost universal. The free movement of populations was stopped. New political barriers were erected as a result of new political philosophies, while at the same time man was proclaiming as never before his belief in universality.

The treaties of 1919 had been amply provided with guarantees for the protection of minorities. They had visualized the application of the standards of civilized life to all communities. Suddenly it was discovered that these clauses either did not mean what they said or could be twisted to produce results entirely foreign to their intentions.

The statements of the Communists which had seemed alluring even to many people who did not fully sympathize with them were now revealed as little better than the brutal actions perpetrated in the height of the civil wars. The naked reality was even less palatable than the theoretical picture. The Ukrainians in the days of the conflict had realized this but they had done so unconsciously and often dimly. Now it was to be brought home to them at every moment.

The result was again a curious contradiction. During the twenty years from 1918 to 1939 not a single country on the borders of the Soviet paradise ever joined it by its own wish. It required intrigue and the intervention of the Red army. Yet abroad there were still well-meaning believers in human dignity and human rights who could somehow salve and deaden their consciences and in a kind of spiritual hypochondria place the minor mistakes of their own lands on a par with the terrors of the new system. Others were able to look upon the Soviet Union as a noble experiment and refused to condemn it. Still others believed or affected to believe that the government had been chosen democratically by its own people and insisted that the constant appeals of both the nationalities and the White Russians were mere propaganda of an undemocratic stripe. Finally some were so infatuated with the greatness and charm of Russia that they were willing to accept as perfect any government that was set up in Moscow.

War weariness became the dominant note of the new pacifism and the ideals of internationalism and the love of peace had a stronger influence on the minds and hearts of men than did justice and a secure social order. The intellectuals in their visions of a higher humanity forgot the dictates of common decency and their duty to protect their own countries, homes and firesides. In a word, it was a period when World War II was in the making and ambitious dictators could freely plot the downfall of disarmed and peaceful democratic powers.

It was a period when the old ideas of government were discarded, the old concert of European powers, the old codes under which mankind had advanced for centuries. New theories were spawned, concerned on paper with means of reforming democracy but in reality with the exaltation of the state over the individual. Idealism without a basis ran riot, and Communism, Fascism and Nazism were able to appeal to both the highest and the lowest instincts of man.

It was under such circumstances that the various Ukrainian *émigrés* abroad were compelled to live and carry on their work.

As they wandered from land to land, from capital to capital, they found different modes of thought, different ideas, different ideals, and different receptions. Now the more liberal went to one capital, the more conservative to another. They found it easy to build up groups of similar thinkers and to promote themselves to various offices in a multitude of parties and societies but there were few to follow and new divisions and new organizations sprang up like mushrooms, only to disintegrate or be dissolved in their turn.

For a while Czechoslovakia offered a safe refuge. Here the government helped to establish a free Ukrainian university, an agricultural school, a library. It was done largely because of the hostility between Czechoslovakia and Poland and had little or no connection with the development of the situation in Carpatho-Ukraine under Czechoslovak rule. Later, as Czech policy became more pro-Russian, this support for the Ukrainians tended to disappear.

Berlin and Vienna for a while after the defeat of Bolshevism in both lands welcomed the conservative *émigrés*. After his withdrawal from Kiev, Hetman Skoropadsky made his way to Berlin. The survivors of the Western Ukrainian government met regularly in Vienna. In both cases their presence in these cities was used to give color to the charges that the Ukrainian movement was a mere Austro-German phenomenon without any basis at home.

Later Paris became more hospitable and many who were disgusted with the rule of Hitler made their way to the French capital. They were only to move again when the French government turned to the left and sought the friendship of the Soviet Union.

Most of these *émigrés* remained aliens but there were others who went to the United States and Canada and the temperate countries of South America to settle down. They retained their Ukrainian feelings but many of them were swallowed up in the task of building their new homes in developing regions. They found themselves again as parts of a non-Ukrainian life but one that welcomed them as individuals and gave them abundant opportunities to live and prosper.

It was a strange time between the wars. The world seemed to have forgotten all for which it had fought so stubbornly up to 1918. Yet those ideals did not die and by 1938 they were beginning to make themselves heard again. About that time, on the eve of World War II, all the old accusations against the Ukrainians were refurbished and recirculated, whether true or false. No one paid any attention to the strange and complicated developments in Europe which heralded the next stage of Ukrainian struggle. This had a different form in each country which had seized part of Ukraine but there was a tacit agreement everywhere that at all costs the essence of Ukrainian democracy must be wiped out in one way or another, by conversion or by extermination. It is to this situation that we must now turn.

VIII

The Ukrainian Soviet Socialist Republic

I. Ukrainization

LENIN AND HIS associates had definite ideas as to the type of new world which they wished to produce. It was to be a world in which the proletariat would rule but their definition of the proletariat was peculiarly their own. It was to be a world of Communists, by Communists and for Communists. It was to be an international world in which the "proletariat" of all countries was to feel at home.

There was less agreement as to the cultural significance of this new creation. In the early days of Brest-Litovsk, when leaders like Trotsky had momentarily expected a world revolution, there had been some hesitation as to the position that the Russian variety was to hold in the Communist structure. A successful revolution, according to theory, in Germany, France or England would have been carried on by men who had come on a par with the Russian leaders.[1]

It did not happen and Lenin quickly discovered that the Third International on which he had built such high hopes was not the gathering of the heads of dominant Communist parties meeting in Moscow as a world center. It was rather a group of more or less discredited failures coming to learn from him who alone had found the path to success. In view of the accepted infallibility of Marxian dialectics, it was strange that it was in the relatively undeveloped Russian empire where the new regime saw light and gained strength and not in the industrialized areas where there was a strong proletariat. It was men trained in the Russian revolutionary technique who had been able to overthrow a government and it was only natural that from every ground these men came to accept their methods as the only correct ones.

They conveniently forgot and the world forgot with them that their victory was due to the indecision of their opponents. It was easy for them to overlook the fact that it was German policy, or lack of it, that had set Lenin up in Russia and allowed him to carry on his propaganda. It was easy to forget that it was American, British and French wavering between the independent republics which had liberated themselves from Russia and the White Russians that had facilitated the downfall of these lands. It was easy for them to gloss over and explain away the fall of the Ukrainian National Republic and to besmirch the reputations of its leaders. At first they remembered and acted with caution.

Lenin had the shrewd idea that it was going to be impossible to unify and standardize the world, or even Russia, as rapidly as he wished. More than any of the leaders of the former Russian Provisional Government or any of his Communist associates, he realized the possibilities in the cry for self-determination that was being raised on all sides. He appreciated to the full the extent to which the triumph of Bolshevism had been aided by the fighting between the White Russians and the struggling nationalities and he cleverly saw that he could use the conflicting claims of nationality and of government to further his cause in Poland and elsewhere. So he deliberately set about a policy of encouraging the growth of nationalist movements.[2]

There was another aspect to his policy. Bolshevism had not yet destroyed or exiled all of its "reactionary" enemies. The encouragement of the nationalities would develop and bring to light those men who possessed the natural gifts that might make them dangerous to him. Even a temporary catering to the nationalities would bring these men into the open and put them within his power, whenever he was ready for the next step. In 1917 the meeting at Kiev had bluntly condemned the Communist policy. The defeat of the Ukrainian National Government had disheartened many of the leaders. They did not want to live in exile but they were suspicious of the power that had profited by their downfall. It was necessary to lull their suspicions and bring them into the net. Ukrainization might help.[3]

Lenin had no intention of allowing the Ukrainian Soviet Socialist Republic to slip out of his control. The Communist party would hold the reins but in the beginning it would be done behind a façade of nationalism. For this reason the Ukrainian Soviet Socialist Republic was called upon to play an independent role in the events of the day. The Russians emphasized its independence.[4] They went through all the motions of treating it as a sovereign state. They allowed it to have its own foreign minister, its own army, its own school system, its own administration. But all these were to be under the thumb of the Kremlin. This was effected by insisting upon the unity of the Communist party and by demanding that the Communists should hold all the key positions, especially those that had to do with the maintenance of order.[5]

So it came about that the Ukrainian Soviet Socialist Republic signed a treaty of peace with Poland at Riga. It sent diplomatic representatives to all those capitals that had formerly recognized the Ukrainian National Republic. These persons were often either Russians or Ukrainians who had spent many years in Russian Communist circles but the farce continued. The democratic powers who did not believe in the existence of Ukraine and did not try to follow all the windings of Communist policy were completely deceived.

Meanwhile there was continuous activity by armed bands under men like Nestor Makhno who had played a role as more or less isolated guerilla leaders in the last days of the republic.[6] They rallied liberty-loving peasants and malcontents and

proved a thorn in the side of the new regime which was based
so largely upon the cities and their non-Ukrainian elements.
However, their efforts were futile and merely added to the
misery of the population without accomplishing any positive
good.

In 1921-22 a new misfortune came upon the country. A
long and severe drought completely destroyed the crops.
Throughout the centuries this phenomenon has been spasmodic-
ally repeated. Due to climatic conditions, the spring and the
autumn rains sometimes fail to appear. The results are serious
for a land which is so uniformly fertile. Again and again these
droughts have not only affected the material well-being of
the population but their intensity has had a pronounced effect
upon the grain markets of the entire world. In 1921 and 1922,
the effects were catastrophic. War, revolution and turmoil had
seriously curtailed production of food in earlier years. The
dispossession of the great landowners who alone had the means
to store up harvests and let them gradually pass upon the
market and the demands of the organized and unorganized
armies had reduced reserves to almost nothing. Famine broke
out and large numbers of people perished.

The loss of the grain supply threatened not only the Soviet
regime in Ukraine but even the masters in Moscow. It led to
serious discontent which the authorities dreaded to quell. They
appealed for world assistance. The American Relief Administration directed by Herbert Hoover came to the rescue and
huge quantities of food were sent to the affected area. No
attempt was made to exploit the revolt latent in the people and
the relief workers brought aid to all without discrimination.
There was no political upheaval and the Soviet government
emerged more deeply entrenched than before.

Yet it was evident that something had to be done to remedy
the persistent suffering and the lack of organized production.
In 1921, therefore, the old period of militant Communism was
ended and the New Economic Policy was proclaimed. Under
this, while the fundamental principles of Communism were

retained, there was granted a considerable freedom for small, private trade. The peasant was allowed to raise and sell his grain on a relatively free market. The small shopkeeper was allowed to do business without fear of punitive actions by the authorities. Almost immediately the prosperity of Ukraine began to revive. The peasants worked harder and saved their money. The cities began to brighten and a freer air pervaded the countryside. The outside world looked on with approval, believing that the Soviets were now coming to see the advantages of capitalism and that a real *rapprochement* might be possible.[7]

There were of course dark sides to the picture. By one device or another the contributions that Ukraine was forced to make to the central regime became heavier and heavier, so that even some of the Ukrainian Communists who had the welfare of their homeland at heart began to complain that the country was being ruined and its wealth drained off. The entire life of the country was under the control of the OGPU, the secret police, which had succeeded the Cheka, and was later to be replaced by the NKVD (the forces of the People's Commissariat for Internal Affairs). Yet all this was indirect and the average citizen was unaware of the general purpose and the methods that were being applied.

The wealthy landowners had already been dispossessed and driven into exile or liquidated. Attempts were made to form communal farms but the various cooperative organizations were allowed to flourish and the police rule was none too severe.

The first step toward limiting Ukrainian power and influence was undertaken with the establishment of the Soviet Union in 1922. This was ostensibly a higher union to include the Russian Soviet Socialist Republic, the Ukrainian, the Georgian, and in fact all of the countries that Moscow dominated. But however it appeared on paper, it meant a legal justification for control by the Moscow regime of all the governments of the other Soviet republics and it soon became evident that the higher administration was composed of exactly those persons who had sat in Moscow previously.

The whole field of foreign affairs and defense was handed over to the All-Union government, although for a while the custom continued of having a Ukrainian secretary in all the Soviet missions abroad. Yet even this was not too much of a blow, for there were a good many people in 1917 who would have been satisfied with the setting up of Ukraine as one of the federated states of a Russian republic and it seemed as if this ideal was now being realized under the rule of the Soviet Union.

Of course the real bond of union was the Communist party which itself was under the direction of Moscow. This made little appeal to the Ukrainians themselves and the bulk of its members in Ukraine were of non-Ukrainian origin. Even as late as 1927 there were at most only about one hundred and twenty-two thousand Ukrainian Communists, approximately thirty-nine for every ten thousand of the population—one of the smallest ratios of any of the Soviet republics.[8]

Yet during these years national sentiment was to a considerable degree appeased and canalized into nonpolitical paths by the emphasis that was laid upon the development of Ukrainian culture in all senses of the word. Before the outbreak of World War I, Ukrainian literature, art and music had been developing with great rapidity and broadening its scope and adapting the artistic methods of the West. National independence naturally lent zest to the movement but the stormy life of the republic made it impossible for the younger writers and artists to come to their mature status. The downfall of the republic hardly checked the flowering of the renaissance, for the Soviet regime was on the whole even more liberal than it was in the Russian Soviet Republic. Authors were compelled to pay a certain lip service to Communist ideals or at least not devote themselves to openly anti-Communist notions but within a broad range, they were free to express themselves and a little ingenuity in avoiding taboo subjects enabled them to function with little fear of censorship. This was especially true during the period up to 1925 when in Moscow the "Fellow Travelers," who included all the leading authors, were gradually winning esteem at the expense of the more distinctively proletarian writers.[9]

This period saw not only the development of literature, art and music but the foundation and growth of the Ukrainian Academy of Sciences in Kiev. This had taken shape under the presidency of Professor Volodymyr Vernadsky during the hetmanate of Skoropadsky, but the rapid change of control in Kiev had precluded serious work. The Ukrainian Soviet Republic allowed the academy to reopen and granted it relative freedom, even though the bylaws were amended to turn it into a typical Communist institution. Still, these were disregarded and the academy was allowed to correspond freely with Ukrainian scholars abroad and elect members from Western Ukraine and elsewhere.[10]

To strengthen its staff, the academy was allowed to call back many of the outstanding figures of the republic. Professor Hrushevsky, the first head of the old Rada, returned to Kiev from an *émigré* life in Vienna, and became the head of the historical division. He resumed his researches as the dean of Ukrainian scholars. There was Serhey Efremiv, the literary historian and critic, who had played a part also in the various Ukrainian national governments. Then men who had been primarily politicians and statesmen, like Holubovych, prime minister at the time of Brest-Litovsk, were induced to return.

We can well pardon and understand the point of view of optimists who saw in the Ukrainian Soviet Republic the fulfillment of many of their hopes and dreams. The Ukrainian language was introduced into the schools and the administration. It was the theoretical language of command in the Ukrainian army. Every official in the republic was supposed to be able to speak Ukrainian and use it in his office, even though exemptions were made for non-Ukrainian citizens. This was more than the Ukrainians had dared expect, even fifteen years before.[11]

The situation promised well for the future. The gradual improvement in living conditions brought about by recovery from the war, the flowering of the culture, the increasing prosperity of the peasants, the new opportunities all seemed to justify the inclusion of the country within the Soviet Union and the optimists—and these included all except the most bitter and fanatical opponents of Communism—were tolerably well satisfied with the progress that was being made.

The OGPU in the background, the attacks on religion, the other drawbacks, all seemed to be passing phases. They were little felt in the villages, although in the cities with a non-Ukrainian population they played a larger role.

The men selected to administer the state were also reassuring. The dominant figures in the Communist party were men like Rakovsky, a Romanian and an old Bolshevik, the prime minister; Gregory Petrovsky, the president; and above all Mykola Skrypnyk, the commissar of internal affairs. Rakovsky had passed through the usual routine of the professional international revolutionary but Skrypnyk was a more unusual character.

He had early enlisted in the Bolshevik party, when it was still but a struggling group largely in exile. He had become a friend of Lenin and had been prominent in the Cheka in Petrograd. He was a confirmed and ruthless Communist[12] but when he was transferred to the Ukrainian Republic, he showed at first a surprising kindliness toward the new renaissance. For some years he allowed conditions to develop as they would but always with an eye to the future triumph of the general principles of Communism as he understood them and as he had learned them from Lenin. He proved himself to be a true Ukrainian Communist and during this golden age, despite his Communist ideas, he used his influence on the whole in beneficent ways.

Thus during the twenties, the Ukrainian urge for independence in the political sphere seemed to slumber. The cultural autonomy which was given to the people, the opportunities that they had to shape Ukrainian culture along the lines of the Ukrainian tradition seemed to replace that fervor for independence which had been so marked in the earlier years.

IX

The Ukrainian Soviet Socialist Republic

II. The New Standardization

MEANWHILE CHANGES WERE taking place in Moscow. Nikolai Lenin died on January 21, 1924. A bitter struggle to be his successor broke out among the leading Bolsheviks of the Soviet Union. The power finally passed into the hands of Joseph Vissarionovich Stalin (Djugashvili). A Georgian by birth, he was a man of indomitable will and character, hence his pseudonym of Stalin (Steel). Unlike Lenin, he had scarcely been outside of Russia and he did not have that respect for foreign cultures and leaders that had been a marked characteristic of Lenin. He had risen to power as commissar of nationalities and as secretary of the Communist party and had thus created and developed its organizational framework. His accession meant the triumph of those elements that in the full sense regarded the party and the party only as the guarantee of the stability of the regime.

In the winter of 1926 at the 15th Congress of the party, Stalin made it clear that he regarded the moment as past for the encouragement and toleration of bourgeois elements and he emphasized the fact that the Soviet Union must become internally strong and developed. In due time followed the first Five-Year Plan, which aimed at the rapid industrialization of the country.

The essence of the new plan was the solidifying of the state and the standardizing of its political and cultural life on the Moscow model. The new Communist culture that had been the dream of the state's original creators was destined to be all-embracing and it was now extended to cover far larger spheres of activity than many thoroughgoing Communists in the various republics had anticipated. The institutions of the Soviet Union were all to be modeled on those of the Russian Soviet Republic and it was the distinct understanding of the Stalinists that the Great Russians were to be the elder-brothers to guide all Soviet thinking.

The early stages of this new policy were hardly noticeable. Measures were taken to provide for proper instruction in Russian in all the schools of the union. The same was true of the various military services. As the central military schools were established and developed, ambitious young men from the armies of the various republics were sent to them. When they had finished their course of studies, they were available for service anywhere in the Soviet Union. Young Ukrainians who had received a state education and distinguished themselves were liable to be assigned to Russian units or units of the Caucasian or Central Asian republics. Similarly, Russians or non-Ukrainians were assigned to staff and command posts in the Ukrainian army. This process soon introduced a considerable measure of Russification and brought the situation back to what it had been prior to the revolution.

The same thing was done in the case of such scientific and educational institutions as the Ukrainian Academy of Sciences. Under one pretext or another, this now became a branch of the All-Union Academy of Sciences and once that was done, there was no reason why Russian and other non-Ukrainian scholars should not be assigned to membership and to the administrative staff. The pressing demand for men in the natural sciences furnished a convenient excuse for the gradual suppression of those sections that dealt primarily with Ukrainian subjects. Thus slowly but surely Ukrainian institutions were transformed into branches of All-Union institutions and lost their old contact with the native regions and populations.

During the height of the movement for Ukrainization which had served to call out the latent human resources of the Ukrainian intellectual world, the promotion of Communism had been relatively disregarded. When Kaganovich in 1928 came to Ukraine to speed up matters and put pressure upon the leaders of the party and of the republic, a series of investigations was begun to find out how far the various institutions were actively engaged in pushing Communism. The results were on the whole negative and new orders were issued.

In 1929 the Academy of Sciences was discovered to have no Communists in its membership. This was a glaring defect and under pressure from Skrypnyk, new members were elected by a "socialistic" method. Candidates were proposed by various Communist groups, societies, trades unions, and for the first time something else than scientific ability was adopted as a criterion for membership. On the whole Skrypnyk kept the situation within bounds in the beginning and the academy even with a few Communist members continued to function. It was only the first step. As increased Communization was demanded, these Communists formed a group to work against their colleagues and when the president of the academy died in 1929, a full-fledged Communist was elected to succeed him.

The final step was the purging of the old membership. Attacks were made in what is now the familiar fashion on the outstanding scholars for their ignorance of Communist truth. In 1930 Professor Hrushevsky was bitterly attacked for inculcating nationalism with his historical theories. In a short time, after a series of disorderly trials before the laboring masses of the city, he was condemned for doing harm to the proletariat by his obnoxious and un-Marxist notions. He was expelled from the academy and put under arrest in a place near Moscow where he could not read or study and where he finally became blind. Then, when he was near his end, he was allowed to go to a rest house in the Caucasus to die.[1]

We have spoken at some length of Hrushevsky's case because he had played an important role in the history of the Ukrainian National Republic and was widely respected. His fate was shared by almost all of the men who had been persuaded in the period of Ukrainization to return home. In 1929 the Soviets discovered a secret Society for the Liberation of Ukraine and they arrested and sentenced to long prison terms the literary critic Efremiv and many others. The next year they found other traces of political opposition and of nationalism. This time it was the political men like Holubovych who were arrested and executed, imprisoned or exiled.[2]

It was soon the turn of the writers and artists. Those who declined to mold their thought into the accepted pattern were speedily silenced. A Ukrainian version of the Russian RAPP, whereby the writers were given specific assignments to cover the Five-Year Plan, was introduced and this provided an easy weapon for the coercion of the entire literary and artistic life of the state.

The Five-Year Plan introduced in 1929, with its emphasis on speedy industrialization, soon brought the laboring classes under the thumb of the authorities to an unprecedented degree while the outside world was regaled with stories of the triumph of Soviet construction. Furthermore these plans were so drawn as to exploit the natural resources of Ukraine and make its industry more and more dependent upon that of the Russian Soviet Republic. Certain plants for the use of the coal and iron resources were built and in most cases the half-finished materials were then transported to plants in the Russian republic for final manufacture. In this way a colonial regime was again implanted in the ostensibly independent republic. Even at this, the new factories, thanks to the laws permitting the definite assignment of labor, were filled with non-Ukrainians, and Ukrainians who heeded the government plea to go into the factories were transported away from their homes to other sectors where they could be severed from the life of the community.[3]

Yet the changes that were made in Ukrainian life by the

industrialization program were nothing compared with the results of the collectivization of agriculture which was begun in 1929. The Great Russians had always practiced a form of communal ownership of land and the change from this to working on collective farms was relatively minor. The situation in Ukraine was very different. Here, even in the old days of serfdom, the peasant had remained attached to his hut and his own plot of ground. They were his and his alone. Now he was abruptly ordered to turn over to a newly constituted authority everything that he possessed on pain of being expelled from his home. The order aroused instant opposition. The peasants—and they were not only the rich kulaks or the medium farmers—rose in opposition. More than in any other part of the union, they killed off their cattle and horses before they would turn them over. They burned the reserves of grain which the Soviet authorities had counted upon for their export trade and for the feeding of the cities. The situation speedily became serious but Stalin, pausing only to prosecute a few local authorities for excessive zeal in collectivization, pressed on.

Sterner and sterner methods were introduced to force grain from the unwilling peasants. Then in 1931 there came another drought and poor harvest. This was the opportunity for which the Kremlin had been waiting. Collecting parties ranged the countryside and compelled the peasants to hand over the specified amounts of grain and arrested, shot or exiled them if they did not do so. The result was the artificial famine of 1931-32, with the peasants being left at the approach of winter without food supplies and with no way of securing any, even though there was an abundance of grain in the hands of the government. The authorities refused to allow even the slightest amounts of food to be brought into the area from any source on the ground that the shortage had been caused by anti-governmental activity.[4]

When news of the famine began to reach the outside world, the Soviet government denied its existence and forbade the Soviet papers to publish any reports. Foreign correspondents were denied permission to visit the stricken area and far too many of them, including some of the most respected names, meekly accepted the Soviet version of events. William Henry Chamberlin was almost the only man to report on the extent of the horror.

It is possible to estimate the number of deaths that occurred. It was apparently nearly 10 per cent of the rural population or in the neighborhood of five million. This figure is reached by at least two methods. Ten per cent was the approximate proportion in those villages about which detailed information was received through devious channels. If we compare the population of Ukraine according to the census of 1927 with that of 1939, which reported a net decrease of about two hundred thousand, and check against the average normal yearly increase of population, we reach the same estimate.

The world has seen cold-blooded massacres and mass starvation before but in almost every case these have been the result of war or plague or catastrophes of nature and the governments involved have done their best to alleviate the human suffering. In the case of the Ukrainian famine, the situation was different. The government deliberately profited by the shortage of crops to starve an unwanted portion of the population. This had not been its policy in 1921, just ten years before, when it was trying to cement its position. Now it was sure of itself and felt safe in resorting to any action necessary to curb a discontented population instead of meeting its demands even in part. There is no question that the Ukrainian famine was deliberately engineered to break opposition and disintegrate the population.

Starvation was supplemented by deportation in order to clear the land for the introduction of alien elements who would be more loyal to the central regime, while the Ukrainians were uprooted from their homes and scattered in heterogeneous groups throughout the country. Perhaps no act of the Soviet government has been more revealing of its essentially callous attitude toward human life than the satisfaction which it received from this famine and its accompanying arrests and executions.

If we can possibly interpret the Soviet statements as even partially true, the net result of the increased pressure upon the Ukrainian people was merely to spread discontent and confirm the feeling that the future of Ukraine did not lie in affiliation with the Soviet Union. Year by year as an excuse for each new trial, each new act of oppression, there was discovered a new society, a new organization, a new tendency toward the strengthening of Ukrainian nationalism. The official Soviet reports during the thirties, in their apprehension of the spreading of nationalism, are comparable only to the reports of Tsar Nicholas I who was in constant fear that the "nonexistent" Little Russians who were consciously yearning for a union with their Great Russian brothers and only desirous of acquiring their superior culture were still planning an insurrection and dreaming of the days when they would be free from the Muscovite yoke.

Professor Hrushevsky's teachings as to the difference in origin and development between the Ukrainians of Kiev and the Great Russians of Moscow were found everywhere and were fiercely suppressed. Every manifestation of interest in any part of Western Europe was treated as a deliberate desire to separate from the Soviet Union and a deliberate insult to the elder brothers who had brought to all the true light of Marxist-Leninist-Stalinist knowledge.

A few years before the general trend in Ukrainian Soviet thought had been to emphasize the unity of the Ukrainians in the republic with those under Polish rule. Now this was reversed. Even the Academy of Sciences which had had at least tacit Communist approval in electing to membership some of the outstanding men in Western Ukraine dropped them quietly and without fanfare.[5] The academy refused to correspond with the scholars in the West and its members were brought to trial on the charge of corresponding with Ukrainians abroad. It was an unanswerable accusation, for the correspondence had been inspired by the governmental organs themselves during the period when the country was permitted to develop its Ukrainian consciousness.

It was the same with all subjects that had to do with the Ukrainian past or culture. After the arrest of Professor Hrushevsky the Philological-Historical center of the Academy of Sciences was wiped out in order to put an end to his teachings. The publications of the academy "for greater usefulness" were now published chiefly in Russian and then they were rarely on Ukrainian subjects, except in the field of archaeology where they could be developed on a purely materialistic basis. The plan of the academy to create a dictionary was disapproved by the central authorities in Moscow for it demanded that emphasis should be laid on all phenomena that would tend to bring the Russian and Ukrainian languages closer together. Russian words were inserted in the dictionary at the expense of Ukrainian idioms and even then the dictionary could not escape the charge of Ukrainian nationalism and the tendency to separate the Russian and Ukrainian peoples.[6]

The most ardent supporters of the claims of the Ukrainian nationalists were hardly prepared to accept the evidences of the widespread success of nationalist ideas that were seriously exposed to public view by the Soviet regime. Even at the height of the Ukrainian National Republic, it is hard to find any more evidence of the desire for separation than was printed in the reports of the Soviet prosecutors of everything that the Kremlin could imagine as Ukrainian nationalism. The thought naturally comes to the mind that the efforts of the Communist regime to suppress it had fanned the movement to a greater intensity than even the struggle for independence had been able to do.

During the thirties technical changes in the administration of the laws rendered the position of the peasants on the collective farms somewhat more tolerable. The exactions which were made by the central government were standardized and were somewhat eased, so that the peasants could know what they had to do. The old will to private property remained. The government was forced again and again to clamp down on the collective farms and even their Communist leadership because of the many efforts of the peasants to better their condition. Now the peasants were accused of giving too much care to the little individual plots which they were allowed to have for their own use, now they were accused of trying to add to these at the expense of the collective property, now they were attacked for stealing even a few handfuls of grain for their own use from the communal stores and were executed as dangerous conspirators. Village after village was uprooted and its inhabitants were scattered throughout the far north and Siberia and in the prison camps where they were destined to perish.[7].

Yet these casualties of the village population were as nothing in comparison with those of the Ukrainian Communists. After Kaganovich returned to Moscow, he was succeeded in 1933 by Postyshev as a trusted subordinate of Stalin. He called loudly upon the Ukrainian Communists to purge their ranks, recounted the discovery of the Society for the Liberation of Ukraine, then of the Ukrainian Nationalist Center, then of the Ukrainian Military Organization. His reign was one of terror as he pushed on the work of ferreting out all opposition but by 1935 he too was on the verge of arrest for nationalism and committed suicide. Skrypnyk, who had starred in the beginning of the campaign for standardization and Communization, committed suicide under suspicion of nationalism in 1933.[8] George Kotsyubinsky, who had led the Red army against the Ukrainian National Republic, was executed for nationalism in 1932. Kosyor, secretary of the Communist party for many years, was liquidated. So too were Prime Minister Chubar and President Petrovsky of the Ukrainian Soviet Socialist Republic. Another prime minister, Lubchenko, who had boasted that he had finally liquidated nationalist sentiment, was forced to end his life. Bondarenko, a successor, also disappeared. The controlling power then passed into the hands of Khrushchov, a Russian and a member of Stalin's inner circle, who retained

the confidence of the Russian authorities and has been promoted to work in Moscow.

There can be but one explanation. These people who
vanished, were liquidated or committed suicide were fanatical
Communists but they were Ukrainians who still had some regard for the essentials of Ukrainian life and tradition. That, to
the Kremlin, was an unpardonable sin like that of Marshal Tito
in Yugoslavia. They had to be prepared not only to defend the
doctrines of Communism but to prove that at every point
where the ideas and customs of Ukraine differed from those
of the Great Russians, they were nationalistic and treasonable.
They had to be prepared to accept without murmur or hesitation the latest statements that were issued by the supreme
authority.

Take an illustration. In 1935 Moscow issued the large Soviet
Encyclopedia. In it[9] Soviet scholars declared that Bohdan
Khmelnytsky, who had won the independence of the country
from the Poles in the great revolt of 1649, was a mere servant
of the Polish nobles and an enemy of the Ukrainian people.
That meant that all the songs that had been handed down in
the villages praising his heroism and exploits were anti-Communist and anti-Moscow, even though Khmelnytsky had later
brought Ukraine under Russian influence by signing the alliance of Pereyaslav. It casts a lurid light upon Stalin's dictum
that there can be but one Communist culture and that the
differentiation between the peoples of the Soviet Union can only
be in non-essentials. But there are no non-essentials for a totalitarian regime, however it cloaks itself in pseudo-democratic
dress.

Moscow and the Ukrainian Communists had done their best
at the beginning of the revolution to eliminate the wealthier
classes and the *bourgeoisie*. They had succeeded but that was
not enough. Step by step they were led unhesitatingly to
attack the fundamental forms of life, the teachings of the Socialist parties, the ideas of the poets and the writers, the historians and the retellers of the ancient legends, the advocates

of the popular poetry, the individuals who ventured to practice even the most harmless and unpolitical custom, lest in some way they conduce to a separation from the elder brothers of Moscow, the center of Russian and of Communist culture. Imperial Russia never forgave Mazepa for his attempt to join Charles XII of Sweden and the Communists share their view. By 1939 practically every Ukrainian was regarded by Stalin as a potential Mazepa, even if he only indulged in some local quirk of custom.

It brings into high relief the whole problem of the relations between international and national Communism, between the fundamentals of Communism with its class struggle, its collectivization and its regimentation and the additional demands of Moscow that the Russian version of Communism be followed in all details. Even the wildest advocates of Russification under the tsars never contemplated such an absolute and lifeless unification. The very men who had worked fanatically against the efforts of the Ukrainian to recover their independence and free themselves from the old Russian influence in broad outlines were unable to pass the new and more stringent tests and they had to choose between execution or suicide..

A mood and a temperament were developed that might prove fatal to the Soviet system if it were once aroused. Terror can succeed to a certain degree. It can silence and coerce but too much of terror will produce a revolt just as will an excess of weakness. The OGPU and the NKVD were able to prevent outbreaks. They were able to maintain the Soviet position but they were not able to win any inherent loyalty from a population that was already becoming aware that no matter what it did, it was still under suspicion. Such was the situation in 1939.

X

The Ukrainians in Eastern Asia

IN SPEAKING OF the general position of the Ukrainians within the Russian empire and later the Soviet Union, some mention must be made of that large number who for one reason or another during the nineteenth and twentieth centuries had made their way to the east. In various places they had formed entire Ukrainian-speaking settlements and in these the Ukrainian spirit developed very much as it did on its native soil.

Eastern Asia had been used as a place of deportation for the various hetmans of the seventeenth and eighteenth century who had escaped execution at the hands of the tsars. The continuous procession of these men and their sympathizers to the desolate Far East led them to wild dreams of re-establishing the ruined hetmanate in those regions. These never assumed any serious form.

About the middle of the nineteenth century, however, there began a flow of emigration from Ukraine. The movement was inspired by the imperial authorities and despite the hardships of the journey across central Asia, many made it and added to the growing number of Siberians who looked for a freer regime than was possible in the more settled European parts of the empire. Later when the imperial government actively fostered the movement, it transported the emigrants from Odessa to Vladivostok by sea; after the completion of the

Trans-Siberian Railroad the largest number went by rail to Chita and from there by boat down the river Amur.

By the outbreak of World War I almost two million Ukrainians were scattered in the Kazakh areas of Siberia, and in two additional sections the Ukrainians far outnumbered the Great Russians. These were the so-called Gray and Green Wedges. The former lay between the territory of the Kirghiz and the Kazakhs, a land in which the Kazakhs still formed the largest single element of the population. In the Green Wedge, the area along the Amur and in the old region of Primorye, the Ukrainians formed an absolute majority, except in Vladivostok and a few other communities. In some regions they formed nearly 90 per cent of the population and throughout the entire area, they rarely fell below 50-60 per cent.

Ukrainian sentiment grew rapidly and even in Vladivostok there existed prior to 1914 illegal groups of Ukrainians who were pressing for more recognition of their specific national rights. Some of these groups were even more outspoken than were the groups in Kiev, which were more closely watched by the authorities, for with them the tsarist regime relied for its control on the great distance between settlements just as it relied on the expanses of wilderness which escaping political prisoners would be compelled to traverse. This was an old tradition; Dostoyevsky in *Memoirs from a Dead House*,[1] written in 1861, alludes to the fact that the authorities allowed many convicts to escape in the spring with the knowledge that they would be forced to return before the approach of winter or perish and meanwhile the officials could pocket the money appropriated for their support.

With the Revolution of 1917 Ukrainian fervor flared up as it did in Ukraine, and it followed a similar course. Representatives from the area took part in the great Ukrainian meetings which were held in Kiev during the spring of 1917 and on June 11 there was held in Mykolsko-Ussuriysky the First Ukrainian Far-Eastern Congress. This was attended by fifty-three delegates from the various Ukrainian Hromady (Communities), representatives of Ukrainian co-operative societies, newly formed military units, etc.[2] It demanded the organization of a Ukrainian army with officers and men to be chosen from those units which were composed of Ukrainians; the organization of a permanent Ukrainian organization to be called the Secretariat of the Rada of the Green Wedge; and the drawing up of a constitution for a Far-Eastern Ukrainian Rada which was to be approved by a Second Congress.

The first actual military unit was formed in Harbin, Manchuria, by Lieutenant Theodore Tvardovsky. It was welcomed by the Chinese, who allowed it to cross the border into the Russian Empire at a time when the Chinese in Manchuria, in an effort to shake off the Russian yoke, were disarming all the old Russian military organizations.[3]

After the Ukrainian National Republic declared its independence, it sent in 1918 the same Lieutenant Tvardovsky as the first Ukrainian consul in the Green Wedge and as a result of the Treaty of Brest-Litovsk, Ukrainian consuls were established in most of the important cities to open up relations between the Ukrainians in the Far East and those in the Ukrainian National Republic. This was one of the conditions of the Treaty of Brest-Litovsk which had been signed in the early spring of 1918.

All of these measures for the organization of the Ukrainians of the Far East were opposed by the Russian Provisional Government exactly as they had been in the homeland. Russian remonstrations were, however, of no practical importance at the moment, for the various Allied armies and the Japanese moved into Vladivostok to protect the supplies of war materials which were awaiting transportation over the Trans-Siberian Railroad.

Ukrainian hopes were thus entangled with the futile efforts of the Allied Expeditionary Forces to keep open the Trans-Siberian Railroad and stop the advance of the Bolsheviks without the formal recognition of the White Russian regime of Admiral Kolchak. It was the same policy that had proved so costly to the Ukrainians and the Allies in European Russia. The Allies could not count upon the Provisional Government; they would not countenance a White military regime which sought to bring back a tsar or a conservative government; they would not cater to the Bolsheviks; and above all they would give the barest of promises to any group that was trying to help itself outside of the fixed Russian orbit.

The secretariat of the Far-Eastern Ukrainian Rada established contact with General Janin of the French army and with other leaders. At times some of the Allied officers seemed sympathetic to the movement but sooner or later a change of heart would come, the old question of the unity of Russia would again be raised and Ukrainian hopes would again be shattered.

Yet the Ukrainian population became more and more unified. More and more co-operatives and other institutions were founded; plans were made for Ukrainian schools and some of them were opened. Peter Ivanovich Horovy[4] succeeded in uniting many of the co-operatives into one union, the Chumak (Teamster), with headquarters in Vladivostok and acting under the Ukrainian banner. He and Dmytro Vorovyk were the leading figures in this movement.

There was, as in the homeland, much hesitation as to the extent of autonomy which the Ukrainians should receive. For a long while the secretariat wavered as to a demand for complete control of the Ukrainian territories in the Far East. Some hoped to be a colony of the Ukrainian National Republic. Others had less drastic ideas and remained in the general position of the Ukrainian National Rada in 1917.

As the hour neared for the withdrawal of their forces, the Allies employed a new device. This was the formation of the Far-Eastern Republic, supposedly an anti-Bolshevik democratic state able to protect itself and prevent the eastward extension of Communism. Its capital was at Chita. The Ukrainians supported it and one of their number, Peter Marchyshyn, from Lviv, became its minister of Ukrainian affairs.[5]

It was again a disillusionment and its failure led the Ukrainians to plan for a Fifth Ukrainian Far-Eastern Congress in 1923. This planned to proclaim the entire Far East, including the Primorye, the region of the Amur and the shore of the Pacific Ocean as far as Bering Strait, including Kamchatka, an independent republic, Green Ukraine. The movement was belated.

On the eve of the congress the Bolsheviks, who had recognized the independence of the Far-Eastern Republic, changed their policy and replaced it by a Communist government. Throughout the whole of the area, they arrested in December, 1922, all of the leading Ukrainian leaders, intellectuals and persons of prominence, even as they promised to open Ukrainian schools in the Ukrainian areas and did so in isolated cases.

The prisoners were held and examined for months. Then in January, 1924, a large state trial was held in Chita.[6] The prisoners were accused of trying to tear away "the Russian Far East from Russia and to hand it over to international capitalists and bourgeois." Soviet practice had not been so finely developed then and the accused refused to make any confessions. The trial went on for some days and then the accused were convicted. The leaders were sentenced to death, although this was later commuted to a long term of imprisonment. Some of the defendants succeeded in escaping and making their way to Harbin.

In that city they continued their work. At first they were able to communicate with their compatriots across the Soviet border. This steadily became more difficult and almost impossible after 1929 when the friction between the Chinese and the Soviets developed into open warfare. During these years, however, the Ukrainian group kept its independence and did not co-operate with the Russian and Siberian groups working in Tokyo, although this course was urged upon them by some of their members.[7]

With the Japanese occupation of Manchuria new difficulties arose. Japanese policy wavered between encouraging the Ukrainian activities and discouraging them as hostile to a single Russian monarchist movement which they might be able to create. The prolonged uncertainty barred active work and finally in 1940 the Japanese suppressed almost all the Ukrainian societies and stopped their newspapers.

The occupation of the city by the Soviets in 1945 put a decisive end to the movement. As in Great Ukraine proper, although the Ukrainian element of the population continued to grow because of new deportations, it was systematically suppressed. Those of the old leaders who had not succeeded in escaping from Manchuria disappeared and the Iron Curtain closed over another attempt of the Ukrainians to secure their rights. Some finally got to Shanghai and a fortunate part of these escaped from that city before its capture by the Chinese Communists. These are now in the Philippine Islands, where they share the lot of other displaced persons. The vast majority have, however, like so many of their compatriots, disappeared without a trace.

XI

Western Ukraine and Poland

As WE HAVE seen, the Western Ukrainians took advantage of the collapse of the Austro-Hungarian Empire in October, 1918, to set up the Republic of Western Ukraine. This was at once attacked by the Poles, who demanded control of the whole province of Galicia. The officers of the republic were finally forced into exile and by the late summer of 1919, the Poles were able to extend their military control over the territory at stake.

Throughout the whole of 1919 the situation greatly disturbed the representatives of the Allied Powers and their confusion was reflected in the Treaty of Saint Germain which brought about peace between Austria and the victorious Allies. The latter, while anxious about the warfare that was still going on in Eastern Galicia, were in a way helpless in the face of circumstances. They were already deeply involved in the attempts of the White Russians to overthrow the Bolsheviks and they were not fully aware of the seriousness of the problem that was offered by the independence drive among the various nationalities in the old Russian Empire. So long as they were undecided about the future of Russia, it was hopeless for them to think of a final solution of the problem of Eastern Galicia.

It was obvious that if there were a Russia with a Ukraine

peacefully and willingly incorporated in it, Eastern Galicia
should be added to it. Sober realism recognized that that condition was not going to prevail in the near future. On the
other hand there were the Poles to be reckoned with. The
wave of nationalism that had followed the independence of
the Polish state led them to demand the restoration of the
boundaries of 1772 before the first division of the country and
they were not content with a Poland that comprised merely
the Polish ethnographical territory where they formed a
majority of the population. At times Pilsudski seems to have
had a vision of a federation of the adjacent nations of Ukraine,
Lithuania and Byelorussia under the aegis of Poland but the
opposing groups headed by Dmowski and Paderewski demanded a unified state based on their interpretation of the
Union of Lublin of 1569. Above all they demanded the inclusion in Poland of the two cities of Wilno, formerly the
capital of Lithuania, and Lviv, the most important city in
Western Ukraine. Furthermore, they wanted the whole of
Eastern Galicia and were willing to fight for it.[1]

The Allies vainly advanced one compromise after another.
France, conscious of the danger from a reviving Germany, was
an ardent and consistent supporter of a strong Poland and in
all international gatherings could be relied upon to plead the
Polish cause. Great Britain was inclined to be critical of the
Polish claims, while President Wilson and the United States
were more interested in securing support for the League of
Nations. No Great Power understood or tried to understand
the Ukrainian position or seriously defended the Ukrainian
cause.

The Treaty of Saint Germain recognized the abnormal status
of Eastern Galicia by leaving open its future disposition. On
November 21, 1919, the Council of Ambassadors prepared a
Statute for Eastern Galicia under which Poland would have
control of the province for twenty-five years but the province
would be fully autonomous with its own diet, school system
and military units.[2] At the end of the period there was to be

a plebiscite in the area, for it was hoped that by that time the problem of Russia and of Bolshevism would have been solved. The Poles rejected the proposal on the ground that, having occupied the area to bar the spread of Bolshevism with the permission of the Allies, they were entitled to remain there. They rejected also the notion of the "Curzon line" as a boundary. This was a vague attempt to bound Polish territory at the time when the Allies were asking the Poles to occupy and organize territory farther east to bar Bolshevism.[3]

Under these circumstances the government of the Republic of Western Ukraine continued to flounder. In one sense its reason for existence had ended when it merged with the Ukrainian National Republic but this was so tenuous and so disturbed by the Bolsheviks that the regime of Petrushevych continued to speak for the Western Ukrainians. This was the more true when in the spring of 1920, in last efforts to secure Polish aid, Petlyura tacitly waived Ukrainian claims to Eastern Galicia at the time of his campaign against Kiev. Petrushevych and his followers moved to Vienna, where they remained as a government in exile, and later they went to Prague and finally to Berlin. Throughout they were the recognized leaders of their people and their influence on the life of the country was far greater than we might assume.

Ukrainian refusal to accept Polish rule and Allied indecision as to the future of Western Ukraine (Eastern Galicia) had the inevitable consequence that the Ukrainians (and the other minorities) boycotted the Polish elections in the spring of 1919 and were not represented in the Constituent Assembly which drew up the Polish Constitution and remained the legislative body of the country until 1922.[4] Thus at the critical period in the development of the Polish state, the advocates of a strong centralizing policy were put in absolute control.

It was very much the same in 1922, when again most Ukrainians stayed away from the polls.[5] They had been promised by the Allies autonomy for Eastern Galicia and the creation of their own diet there and so they naturally stayed outside of the Polish political arena. At the same time the Poles had no intention of granting them these privileges and the dispute over Eastern Galicia appeared constantly on the agenda of the diplomatic meetings, without any solution ever being reached.[6]

In the fall of 1922 another attempt was made to settle the long-smoldering question. The Polish Diet passed a resolution providing for the setting up of "Ruthenian" diets in the districts of Lviv, Ternopil and Stanyslaviv. The law was purposely vague as to the powers and functions of these diets but it was clear that it did not presuppose any possibility of co-operation between them on a provincial level and it did not extend any privileges to the Ukrainians living in Volyn and Pidlashshya, whom the Poles classed as a different people from the "Ruthenians." It was quite evident that there was no honest intention of granting this autonomy, such as it was. The measure was adopted to impress the Council of Ambassadors, which finally swallowed the bait and on Polish assurances that all would be well and that they would grant some sort of autonomy duly recognized Eastern Galicia as a part of Poland on March 15, 1923.[7] The Ukrainian National Rada sent delegates to Paris to register its protests, but these were never heard and the decision was allowed to stand.[8]

From 1919 on, conditions in the Ukrainian areas were unsettled, to speak mildly. The Poles arrested large numbers of the more patriotic Ukrainians and sent them to jail for long periods. The turbulence and the Polish reprisals heightened the tension between the two nationalities and renewed the ancient clashes which had been so disastrous for medieval Ukraine and medieval Poland.

The final denial of all their hopes for international action brought about a change in the thinking of Ukrainians. They were forced to accept the fact that Western Ukraine would remain under Polish sovereignty until the next European upheaval and they began to take measures accordingly. Their attitude had been expressed by a Ukrainian delegate, Samuel

Pidhirsky, in the Diet of 1922, when he declared: "The creation of an independent Ukrainian nation is the goal of the Ukrainian people, but counting on the practical condition, the Ukrainians are ready to co-operate with the Polish people and all peoples who are within the Republic, if they will be assured full and free development in all fields of life."[9] By 1928 most Ukrainians were electing members to the Polish Diet and exercising their duties as Polish citizens without giving up their hopes for independence.

Almost without exception the Ukrainian political parties formed a solid bloc of opposition to the government. They advocated measures of social reform which would benefit Ukrainians. At times they boycotted the parliament, but (what the Poles would never appreciate) they were still more bitterly opposed to the Ukrainian Soviet Republic and had no desire to join it. Some of the conservative parties seemed to acquiesce more willingly in Polish domination and were regarded as collaborationists by their fellows.[10]

There was an irreconcilable core of Ukrainians who rejected all co-operation. These were represented first by the Ukrainian Military Organization and then after 1929 by the Organization of Ukrainian Nationalists under Colonel Evhen Konovalets. He was the officer who had led the Ukrainian troops into Kiev after the fall of Hetman Skoropadsky and he now became the head of a secret militant organization which was responsible for the murder of a number of Polish leaders noted for their anti-Ukrainian tendencies. This group naturally had the sympathy of much of the population and could count on their support, especially in moments of crisis. Konovalets was finally forced out of Poland and was murdered in Amsterdam in 1938 by a Bolshevist secret agent who handed him a disguised bomb.[11]

The establishment of a *modus vivendi* between the Poles and the Ukrainians would have been delicate but the Poles completely misjudged the situation. They insisted that all the Ukrainians were eager to become Poles except a small

minority that had been bribed by the Germans. At the time
when the followers of Pilsudski were planning for German
support, they covered their actions by accusing the Ukrainians
of being a German inspired party.

The Polish hope of eliminating the Ukrainians by assimilation
was equally tactless. Count Grabski, minister of education
and a statesman, declared that within twenty-five years there
would not be a Ukrainian left in Poland and the government
attempted a policy of forced assimilation and of disintegration
of the Ukrainian communities and of pressure against outstanding Ukrainian leaders.[12]

The Polish land reform bills were applied in Ukrainian territory for the distribution of the estates of the large Polish landowners there, but the land was not given to the Ukrainian
villagers in the neighborhood but to groups of Polish veterans
who were brought into the Ukrainian districts in order to alter
the character of the population.

In the same way pressure was applied on the educational
system. The government refused to allow the formation of
a Ukrainian university in Lviv, a demand that had been put
forward in the days of Austria-Hungary. They admitted
only a negligible number of Ukrainian students to the Polish
university in Lviv and to get an education, Ukrainians were
obliged either to go abroad or to study informally in a secret
Ukrainian university that was established in Lviv without the
knowledge of the Polish authorities.[13] While there were a few
Ukrainian high schools in the area, the Polish language was
the real medium of instruction and the work in Ukrainian in
most of the so-called "Ukrainian" schools was usually confined to the most elementary grades and taught largely by
Poles who had an inadequate knowledge of the Ukrainian
language.

On a higher scale, the work of the Shevchenko Scientific
Society was hampered in every way. Its funds were either
confiscated or lost in the periods of inflation. Many of its
collections were stolen and the institution was under constant

suspicion. In an effort to counterbalance its influence and remove Ukrainian influence from Lviv, the Poles in Warsaw agreed to allow the establishment of a Ukrainian Scientific Institute. The new institution did a great deal of valuable work but it shared the sentiments of the older organization and the two maintained the same point of view.[14]

In addition to these general policies, there came moments of especial attempts at suppression. Thus in 1929 and 1930 the government attacked Ukrainian Boy Scout troops, closed Ukrainian libraries and reading rooms, seized the property of various co-operative societies, and forced the situation to a point where there was something very close to an armed revolt. This was suppressed with cruelty by units of the Polish army.

These actions were of course contrary to and in violation of the minorities treaty which Poland had signed under protest in 1919 at the conclusion of the World War. The Ukrainians and their friends presented petition after petition to the League of Nations but to little or no effect. Even after the Pacification of 1930, when a specially strong protest was made not only by the Ukrainian representatives but by many leaders of world opinion, the League contented itself with a mild reprimand for the Polish government and a statement that some of its lesser officials were undoubtedly guilty of excessive zeal in maintaining order.[15] It was merely another example of the helplessness of the League when it came to fulfill its functions against one of its members and only added to the growing weakness of the entire organization, on which the peace of Europe and of the world seemed to depend.

In 1934 the Polish government denounced the clauses of the treaties signed in Paris which guaranteed the protection of minority rights and it then opened concentration camps in which large numbers of Ukrainians were incarcerated without trial on the flimsiest pretexts.

By 1935 both sides were weary of the *impasse*. In that year the UNDO, the Ukrainian National Democratic Union, representing most of the Ukrainian parties, worked out a compromise with the government, especially Professor Koscial-kowski, the minister of internal affairs. In return for ceasing their opposition, they were offered nineteen seats in the re-organized Polish parliament and promises were held out to them of the establishment of a Ukrainian university in Lviv. Yet this "normalization" meant little, for the government continued to make mass arrests of so-called members of the Organization of Ukrainian Nationalists, intern Ukrainians and close their institutions.[16]

Next the government turned against the Ukrainian Ortho-dox. In 1938 it seized over a hundred Orthodox churches on the ground that they had been Catholic at some time in the past, and demolished several. The measure was protested not only by the Orthodox but also by the Uniat Greek Catholics, especially Archbishop Sheptytsky. On the whole the move completely backfired, and served only to solidify all Ukrain-ians under Polish rule without regard to religious affiliation.[17]

Despite this sad picture of conflict with the government, the Ukrainian position constantly improved, especially in the economic and cultural spheres. The Ukrainian co-operative societies not only remained in existence but multiplied many times in memberships and in capital. They established a flourishing Ukrainian bank for which they were able to supply the funds. One Ukrainian agricultural society alone grew to have 160,000 members.[18]

Cultural work grew in the same proportions. Literature and journalism flourished. Institutions for the youth, like the Sokols, grew in number and various athletic groups such as the Luh (Meadow) came into being and increased rapidly despite Polish opposition. With each year the Ukrainians gained in wealth and power, despite the incoherent and brutal efforts of the government to check and undermine them.

It is easy to see the difference between the position of Ukrainians in Poland and of those in the Ukrainian Soviet Republic. With all of their reactionary, unjust and brutal policies, the Poles made no attempt to wipe out the Ukrainian population as a whole or to alter the fundamental characteristics of their life. The Ukrainian villagers were able to take advantage of the rise in living conditions and to adapt themselves to the modern European civilization. They were able to accept and assimilate the new ideas that were spreading throughout civilized Europe. They were able to vote and to elect their own people to the Polish Diet as they would, even though the authorities would frequently interfere on behalf of Polish candidates, break up election meetings and arrest anti-Polish candidates on trumped-up charges and employ every other means of stealing elections. In a word the repression of the Ukrainian cause was carried on by the methods of a traditionally reactionary and often unenlightened government machine.

Poland placed herself under a tremendous handicap by this all-absorbing effect to subdue and master a large minority. It was perhaps natural, for the sense of historical continuity between the independent Poland of the past and the present revived state was strong. During the last centuries of the old Polish Republic the Ukrainians had been forced into a subordinate position and subjected to a strong Polonizing influence. In the new state the average Pole could not imagine any change. The Poles were well aware of the harm which had been done to them in the seventeenth century by the Kozak revolts but they could not see their way clear to initiating a new policy of friendship and true co-operation.

As the most powerful of the revived states of Eastern Europe, Poland could have become the natural leader of those peoples between Germany and the Soviet Union. At times Pilsudski realized the possibilities of this but he was never able to formulate a working policy to bring it about. The trend toward a unified state was so strong that it swept the entire Polish population with it and gave the idea that their national existence depended upon their success in dominating the minorities. This unfortunate mode of thinking drove the Poles from one unhappy situation to another and cost them abroad much of that wholehearted support which they had won during World War I, when the population almost with one accord was striving to recover its lost liberty.

The record of the Polish dealings with that part of Western Ukraine that was under its control contrasts sharply with its many positive achievements in other lines. It left behind it a hostility and a discontent which boded ill for the new state if it were to be involved in a major struggle with its neighbors. Yet it must be emphasized again that although almost all the Ukrainian parties were opposed to Poland, few were tempted to turn that opposition to the profit of Communism. The Ukrainian Soviet Republic had done its work so well that it proved to the Western Ukrainians that whatever was their hostility to Poland, their hatred for Russian Communists was still of necessity more intense and more fundamental.

XII

The Ukrainians and Romania

Those Western Ukrainians who had not passed under the control of Poland found themselves in either Romania or Czechoslovakia. In neither of these countries did they form as large or as concentrated a minority as in Eastern Galicia but their numbers were not unimportant.

There were nearly one million Ukrainians living in the provinces of Bukovina and Bessarabia who went to Romania. In the early days these had sought to join themselves to the Western Ukrainian Republic but in both provinces their hopes had been quickly dashed to the ground by the energetic action of the Romanian army in seizing Chernivtsy and other centers before the Ukrainians could mobilize their volunteer detachments and cement their regime. From that point on, they were denied all opportunities of organization.

As a Latin-speaking race, the Romanians were suspicious of all Eastern Slavs. In past centuries the Zaporozhian Kozaks had had close relations with the people of Moldavia and Wallachia. Vasil Lupul, the hospodar of Moldavia, had given his daughter in marriage to Timosh, the son of the hetman Bohdan Khmelnytsky. The union of the two Danubian principalities in the kingdom of Romania in the nineteenth century and the growth of Latin ties had changed this old feeling and the Romanians were perhaps the most unreasonably anti-Ukrainian of all the states which succeeded to their control.

Slowly but surely the Romanians liquidated practically the entire Ukrainian school system by introducing into it the Romanian language.[1] This was accelerated by a law in 1924 which declared the Ukrainians "Romanians who had forgotten their native language"—a highly original solution of the problem which flattered the Romanian argument that the entire population was descended from the ancient Roman settlers in Dacia.

The process was a little slower in Bessarabia, where there were conflicting political crises, arising from the fact that the United States did not fully recognize the Romanian occupation of the province, since it had formed part of the old Russian Empire.

After 1928 there came some small alleviation of the Ukrainian status. But Ukrainian political, journalistic and economic institutions were almost non-existent; in fact, during the entire period between the two world wars, it is hardly possible to speak of organized Ukrainian work in any field under Romanian rule. The Romanians, even more than the Poles, were firmly convinced that they had to repress all manifestations of Ukrainian activity, since it was motivated only by the desire to join the Soviet Union and might be regarded as indicating a lack of unity among the inhabitants of Greater Romania.

XIII

The Ukrainians and Czechoslovakia

WHILE OPEN CONFLICT marked the relations between the Ukrainians and the Poles and a creeping paralysis affected all Ukrainian work in Romania, the situation in Czechoslovakia was far more complicated. The Czechoslovak government followed a policy of not letting its right hand know what its left hand was doing. The situation in Prague and Bohemia was very different from that which prevailed in the Ukrainian section in the east of the republic, later to be known as Podkarpatska Rus, or Carpathian Ukraine, and this divergence was so sharp that it is necessary to consider separately the relations between the Ukrainians and the Czechoslovak government in the various parts of the country.

There was a scarcely hidden antipathy between Czechoslovakia and Poland which arose largely from the difference in the two national characters and partly from boundary disputes.[1] There was a theatrical and romantic side to the Polish character which made it naturally unsympathetic to the essentially sober and almost commonplace temper of the Czechs. There was a verve, a flash in the makeup of Warsaw and Krakow that was almost entirely lacking in Prague. On the other hand there was a sense of realism in the Czech capital that was not found among the Poles.

In addition the attitude of the Poles toward the Russians

differed widely from that of the Czechs. The Poles fought for supremacy for centuries with the Great Russians. They had had enough experience of Russian domination. They therefore were less responsive than other Slavs to the beauties and advantages of a mystical Pan-Slavism as devised for the benefit of the Russians. Even their experiences in the campaigns through 1920 had taught them an instinctive suspicion of all Russians whether White or Communist, and fear of the U. S. S. R. was one of the important factors in their policy.

The Czechs had no common border with the Russians but they did have a romantic faith in Pan-Slavism and a firm conviction that it was relatively simple for the Slavs to work together.[2] It was the Czechs who had developed and fostered Pan-Slavism as the Pan-Slavic brotherhood and they regarded Russia as one of the mainstays of this policy. Their chief enemies were the Germans and the Hungarians. Czech foreign policy after World War I was directed toward the neutralization of these two peoples. They had a fear and distrust of the Germans that the Poles did not share and a dislike for the Hungarians that was almost fantastic.

This was reflected in the policies of the Little Entente of Czechoslovakia, Yugoslavia and Romania, of which Dr. Benes was the chief architect.[3] This was composed of the nations which surrounded Hungary and had been largely carved out of the Hapsburg Empire and its chief functions were to watch and thwart the irredentist dreams of Hungary and the efforts of the Hapsburgs to recover their power. It carefully avoided any stand on the subject of the Soviet Union and it failed to broaden into a general alliance of the post-Versailles states. Poland and Romania collaborated on the Soviet situation. Yugoslavia and Romania worked together with regard to Bulgarian claims, a subject from which Czechoslovakia stayed aloof, just as Yugoslavia and Romania did not interfere in the Czechoslovak attitude toward Germany. Poland and Czechoslovakia rarely came into close and friendly relations even on the question of Germany.

We may perhaps doubt the authenticity of the supposed letter of Jan Masaryk to Stalin before his suicide, when he stated that his father, Thomas G. Masaryk, had made it a principle that the Czechs and the Russians should never fight.[4] Yet it was a fact that during the Soviet drive into Poland in 1920, the Czechs refused to help their neighbors; and this added to the bitter feelings between the two peoples. There were strong and well-founded suspicions that the Poles really desired friendship with the Hungarians. These two nations, and especially their upper classes, shared many of the same tastes. Poland was also accused of wanting to spread her influence among the Slovaks and intensify their disagreements with the Czechs.[5]

Whatever the exact motives and the political developments, it was President Masaryk's dream to make Prague the real Slav center after the war. From this city emanated all the calls for Pan-Slavic congresses, whether of law or philology or history or politics. In these meetings the Poles were the most critical and they often revealed their latent antagonism to Czechoslovakia.

During these years the Charles University of Prague was undoubtedly not only the oldest Slav university but the greatest. It rapidly built up an international reputation and it attracted young men and women from all parts of the Slavic world. Naturally the Ukrainians, particularly those from Poland, gathered here in large numbers. As brother Slavs, the Czechs received them kindly and were happy to help them, especially in ways that would annoy the Poles in the midst of their struggle for Eastern Galicia.[6]

Hence it came about that the Czechs and the Czech government showed themselves more than hospitable toward the Ukrainians who came within their borders. At Prague the government helped to set up a Free Ukrainian University staffed by scholars who had escaped from Poland and somewhat less often from Soviet Ukraine. With Czech approval and support, this institution embarked upon an extensive program of research and publication. Its student body was drawn to a startling degree from Western Ukraine under Polish domination, and it proved itself in a few years not only the freest and best of the various Ukrainian institutions but a worthy companion of the Slav organizations that came into being around Prague.[7]

The Czechs also helped to establish a Ukrainian agricultural school at Podebrady. In Prague they allowed a Ukrainian museum and library. There were a Ukrainian Historical and Philological Society, a Union of Ukrainian Physicians of Czechoslovakia, and many other organizations. Prague became a center of *émigré* Ukrainian cultural life and the institutions there were liberally supported also by Ukrainians of the United States and Canada.

The policy of the Czechoslovak government toward these foundations fluctuated with the years. From the first, the Czechoslovaks had been against support of the more conservative groups of Slav *émigrés*, whether they were Ukrainians, White Russians or others. In the course of time, these rightists found themselves in a more congenial milieu in either Berlin or Paris, with the latter city growing in popularity after the rise of Hitler. On the other hand, the steadily growing *rapprochement* between the Czechoslovak government and the Soviet regime which coincided with the increasing age and lessening activity of President Masaryk led to some withdrawal of support from these institutions and it was widely believed that some restriction of their activity was a condition of the Czechoslovak-Soviet alliance of 1935. Incidentally this was the first voluntary alliance between an independent Slav government and the Soviet Communists and it had serious repercussions on the European situation.

The relationship of these Ukrainian organizations and of the *émigrés* in and around Prague to the Czechs was handled apart from the relations between the Czechoslovak government and the population of Carpatho-Ukraine. This area offered the Prague regime some of its most troublesome questions.

We are poorly informed as to the early history of this part of the Ukrainian population. We know that they existed in the later Middle Ages, but it is hard to decide whether they formed part of the pre-Magyar population of the area, whether they followed the Magyar hordes as they cut their way from the east through Ukraine and into the plains of Hungary before the Christianization of Kiev towards the end of the first millennium A. D., or whether they were fugitives from the fighting in Galicia that followed the collapse of the Kiev state. Perhaps they arrived in these isolated valleys in various waves of settlement. It was the only point where a Ukrainian population had crossed the summits of the Carpathians and was living on the southern slopes.[8]

The population was poor and backward and had little opportunity for large-scale joint action. Most of the educated or semi-educated classes were more or less pro-Hungarian in sympathy and in 1918, with the collapse of the Hungarian regime, had taken refuge in Budapest. Some steps had been taken to educate the Catholic clergy of the Byzantine Rite, and the Russians had sought to influence the Orthodox. All in all the population in these isolated mountain valleys was perhaps the least integrated of all the Ukrainians and represented the attitude which had generally prevailed a century earlier in Lviv and elsewhere before Ivan Franko and his associates had begun their work.

The slowness of the revolution in this area made it impracticable after the fall of Lviv for the Carpatho-Ukrainians to join the Western Ukrainian Republic. The dismemberment of Hungary made it impossible for them to remain in that state. By the late spring of 1919 public opinion, if we may speak of it at this time, inclined toward a union with Czechoslovakia and this was duly carried out. In return the region was promised local autonomy, that same elastic word that was heard so often in 1917 and 1918, and its own diet, although the Czechs carefully refrained from deciding whether the language of the people was Ukrainian or Russian.[9]

Possession of the area was important to the Czechs with their

fear of a revived Hapsburg empire and of Hungarian irre-
dentism, for it gave them land connection with Romania and
thus with the independent states of the Balkans. This was
especially desirable in view of the clashes between the Czechs
and the Poles, and the fact that their other neighbors, Germany,
Austria and Hungary were their bitter enemies.

Relations between Prague and the province ran an uneasy
course but there was not the train of uprisings and violence
that marked Ukrainian-Polish contacts. The conflicts were
largely confined to the political, educational and administrative
spheres. The Czechoslovak government did an enormous
work in establishing schools and other modern institutions but
it staffed these largely with Czechs and Slovaks at the expense
of the educated natives of the province, whom it suspected
of being under Hungarian influence.

There can be little doubt that the Carpatho-Ukrainian leaders
thought of the proposed union with Czechoslovakia in the
same terms as those that had held prewar Hungary within the
Hapsburg Empire. They regarded it as an independent state
within the Czechoslovak Republic and predicated a Ruthenian
or Ukrainian governor appointed by the president of the republic and choosing his own administration. The final agreement included in the Minority Treaty signed by Czechoslovakia spoke of "the widest autonomy compatible with the
unity of the Republic," a separate diet, and the filling of "official positions so far as possible by natives."

In reality the Czechs placed the administrative power in the
area in the hands of Czech officials. When they appointed a
native governor, his powers were extremely limited. The local
diet that had been promised was never introduced. It seem
likely that the Czechs were waiting until they could train in
Prague a new generation of men fit for high posts, while the
return of many of the old semi-intellectuals from Budapest
after the Hungarian financial reforms introduced by Jeremiah
Smith in 1924 sharpened the demands for a rapid transfer of
the province into the hands of its population. In 1928 there

was a reorganization of the government by Prague but the administrative institutions in Podkarpatska Rus were not acceptable to the population.[10]

The founding of new schools spread knowledge of the writings of the great figures of Ukrainian literature and strengthened the sense of Ukrainian nationality in large parts of the population. This was counterbalanced by a growth of Russianism reminiscent of the old Muscophile party in Eastern Galicia. The Czechs wavered between support of the two elements.[11]

The Prague government could not decide whether the province was to be a link between the Czechoslovak Republic and the Soviet Union, whether it was to be a Ukrainian center to give an example to the Ukrainians under Polish rule, or whether its chief value was to be as a link between Czchoslovakia and Romania. At various times it adopted each of these three policies. Communism of a sort was rife. Yet the general trend was distinctly upward, despite the increased hardships brought into the area by the depression of 1929. Yet, again, the growing *rapprochement* with the Soviets as a foil to Hitlerism and the unrest among the Sudeten Germans in the western part of the republic led the government to look with some disfavor on the Ukrainian tendencies. It is very possible that the future of the region was considered in the negotiations leading up to 1935 and the Czechoslovak-Soviet alliance.

On the whole it must be concluded that the period between the wars was profitable to the population of this area. However galling Czech rule might have been, it undoubtedly brought educational and political training to a region that had been almost completely deprived of them. It developed a group of men who thought in terms of the province, men whose primary interests were with the people of the region. In this sense it prepared for the brief restoration of independence to the area which came for a few days amid the preparations for World War II.

XIV

Ukraine on the Eve of World War II:

The Republic of Carpatho-Ukraine

Early in the thirties the shadow of another world war began to fall over Europe. Just as the Italo-Turkish War and the Balkan Wars of 1912-13 had heralded the cataclysm of 1914, so the disturbances in Manchuria, in Ethiopia and in Spain forecast a new struggle. Adolph Hitler was gaining strength almost daily, while the Stalinists were purging their ranks and preparing themselves for a new step in the development of world Communism.

Under these threats the United States, Great Britain and France seemed singularly asleep. The confidence in an uninterrupted peace that had emerged with the signing of the armistice in 1918 seemed unshaken by even the clearest intimations that all was not well. The great depression had destroyed the optimism of the twenties. Totalitarianism in its several forms, Fascism, Nazism and Communism, was raising its head and daring to question all of those postulates that had been accepted for centuries by civilized Europe. Yet no one took the threat seriously.

We have seen how Ukraine was faring under its new masters. It had no accepted spokesman. On the surface of events, it was growing apart. The Ukrainians in the Ukrainian Soviet

Republic, those living under Poland and those in Carpatho-Ukraine and Romania were being subjected to different influences, to different systems of law and administration and to different economic conditions. How was it possible to speak of a Ukraine?

Abroad the Ukrainian *émigrés* were divided. The old Ukrainian National Republic still maintained a shadowy existence. Petlyura was killed by a Soviet agent in 1926 and the head of the Organization of Ukrainian Nationalists, (Colonel Konovalets), was murdered by Soviet agents in 1938. The various political factions which had remained from the old organizations, the followers of Hetman Skoropadsky and new groups which had arisen under younger leaders continued abroad their verbal jousts. Each group was sure that it had the ear of the people and a program that would save the national spirit.

Yet, as events showed, there was a deepening of Ukrainian consciousness during these years. There was a steadily increasing consensus of opinion as to the significance of Ukraine, its importance to the world, and the essential nature of its possible contribution to humanity. Much of this was due to underground activity led by the Ukrainian nationalists, much of it was barely conscious to the people who shared it. But it existed and that was the main thing.

It would have been well for the democratic world, had it attempted to evaluate all of these new currents of thought. The Western mind still kept the same logical presuppositions that it had had twenty years earlier. Despite mounting evidence of the tyrannies and outrages of the Soviet system and of world Communism, liberal opinion still believed that the Soviet leaders did not mean what they said or were in their own way trying to introduce a new and better form of democracy. Western leaders strained to draw some line of distinction between the tyrannies of Hitler and those of Stalin, so as to condemn the one and condone the other. Some put their faith in the old thesis of the unity and contentment of all peoples within the old Russian Empire. Some apologists for Kerensky and the Provisional Government turned to a glorification of the Communists as maintaining the old Russian idea. Others, anti-Communist, cherished the hope that the Provisional Government or something similar would return. Lovers of peace were afraid of annoying the Soviet government by uttering aloud what they privately believed. In fact public opinion was as averse to recognizing the facts of Soviet life as they were of suspecting Hitler of aggressive intentions and acting upon their feelings.

Yet the fear of a new war and the part Ukraine would play in it opened the way for the Communists and their allies of the popular fronts to revive all the old accusations against the Ukrainian independence movement. The mere fact that some of the leaders had taken refuge in Berlin (when all other capitals were closed to them) was enough to prove that the entire movement was Nazi-inspired, even though these leaders had appeared on the national stage long before Hitler had even begun to write his script. During the period just before the outbreak of World War II, when there were already hidden contacts between the two totalitarian systems, it became fashionable once again to damn the Ukrainians.

It was just at this moment that an enlightening episode occurred in Carpatho-Ukraine. Following the dismemberment of Czechoslovakia after the Munich meetings in 1938, that republic was reorganized on a federal basis and, on October 11, for the first time, Carpatho-Ukraine was able to organize the diet which it had been promised in 1919 and 1920. Almost immediately the regional Prime Minister Andrew Brody was arrested by the Czechs on the charge that he was trying to unite the entire area with Hungary. He was succeeded by Monsignor Voloshyn but the new regime was handicapped by the decision of Hitler and Mussolini to transfer to Hungary the area surrounding the two principal cities of the region, Uzhorod and Mukachevo. This left a truncated Carpatho-Ukraine and its government was forced to take up its abode in the little town of Hust.[1]

Disheartening as this was, the Ukrainians set to work with a will to construct even this small semi-independent state. For the first time since the fall of the Ukrainian National Republic, they might dream of something that they could call their own. Ukrainians of all groups made their way from the various countries to this new center. Trained veterans of the wars of 1918-20 came to prepare a new Ukrainian army, even though the possibilities of getting modern equipment were non-existent. Professional men of every kind gathered here and the little town during the winter was a hive of industry.[2]

Ukrainians in the United States sent aid to the new state, when they were allowed, and were prepared to establish formal contact with its leaders, but the representatives were prevented from arriving. The British refused to take any notice of the new state.

On February 12, 1939, elections were held for a diet. This held its first meeting on March 14, 1939, formally installing Monsignor Voloshyn as president.

In the early spring Slovakia was induced to declare its independence of the Czechs and was taken under the protection of the "Führer." This completely isolated Carpatho-Ukraine and rendered impossible any connection with Bohemia and Moravia. Voloshyn then declared the complete independence of the state.

His only hope of salvation was to receive at least beneficent support from the Germans, for the region was surrounded by enemies. There was little to be feared on the west, where Slovakia was already struggling with her own problems. Romania too was relatively disinterested. Poland was, as we might expect, openly hostile. She had no desire to see an independent Ukrainian state, no matter how weak and helpless, lest it prove too great an attraction for the Ukrainians living under her own rule.[3] Hungary was even more violent. That country had never been reconciled to her territorial losses of 1918 and the present moment seemed highly favorable for the restoration of her own borders in the Carpathian region. Ever since the fall of Benes, the Hungarian government had been making plans for further action. It had been fairly well armed by the Germans and could expect to defeat the Carpatho-Ukrainians, with their rifles and antiquated weapons.

On March 14, the same day that the German troops set out for Prague, the Hungarian government ordered the withdrawal of all Czech troops from Carpatho-Ukraine and invaded the province with a demand that the new government submit. When Voloshyn, trusting to the indirect assurances he had already received from the German government, appealed for help, he was coldly informed that the Germans were no longer interested.

The tragedy soon followed. The little Carpatho-Ukrainian army composed of the Riflemen of the Carpathian Sich was attacked by the Hungarian army with modern weapons. Opposition was futile but it took several days before the resistance of the mountaineers, fighting on their own terrain for their homes and liberty, was crushed. There were numerous executions of officials who fell into the hands of the Hungarian army. Voloshyn and some officials escaped to Romania and safety.

There is much mystery about this episode. It seems fairly certain that for many years Hungary had maintained contact with certain Hungarian elements in Carpatho-Ukraine and had been engaged in fomenting discontent against the Czechs. They had followed the same policy in Slovakia. After the Munich appeasement, German influence had replaced the Hungarian and the German leaders had tried to get control of the Ukrainian movement in the province.

We know that Hitler had long cast covetous eyes at Ukraine, for he realized as the Allies had never done that it was the key to the Russian problem. He realized as the Allies had never done the strained relations between the Ukrainians under Polish rule and the Polish government. An independent Carpatho-Ukraine would serve as a magnet to draw first the other Western Ukrainians and then the oppressed people in the Ukrainian Soviet Republic. Apparently he had made this clear even as late as the beginning of March, 1939, to Voloshyn and the leaders who were trying to find a way out of the *impasse* in which the Ukrainians had been placed by the collapse of Czechoslovakia. He gave Voloshyn to understand that he did not wish Poland and Hungary to have a common border, and he fostered the opposition between Carpatho-Ukraine and her neighbors.

Why, then, at the first moment of an attack by Hungary did he abandon the new state? One word would have held back the Hungarian army. He certainly did not do so in order to promote better relations with the Poles against whom he continued to intrigue. The only obvious answer is that already by March, 1939, the negotiations were under way between Hitler and Stalin which were to become public a few months later and under which Western Ukraine was to fall into the hands of the Communists. It adds a strange footnote to the negotiations between the Western Allies and Stalin, which were checked because none of the states between the two giants were willing to admit the Red army as saviors, for they well knew what the end would be.

There was another result of the collapse of Carpatho-Ukraine. Until this time it was confidently bruited about in many Polish and pro-Polish circles that the German attack on Poland would be preceded by an uprising in Western Ukraine. This was part of the Polish plan to present the Ukrainian movement as one made in Germany. The incident in Carpatho-Ukraine proved to the Ukrainians that they could not rely upon Germany. It emphasized again the same unfortunate truth that had been made so clear in 1918—i.e., that Germany was not interested in Ukrainian liberty, that the Allies refused to understand the situation, and that, fighting against overwhelming odds, the Ukrainians would have to solve their own problems or be overcome.

With the Hungarian conquest of the new state, conditions reverted to 1918. The region was reorganized as Ugro-Rus. The new institutions that had come into being between the wars were abolished. Ukrainian schools were closed. In short the region went back into Hungary as shorn of privileges as it had been during the preceding centuries.[4]

During the next months the fate of Carpatho-Ukraine was overshadowed by the better-understood events taking place in Prague, as the German armed forces wiped out the Second Republic and reshaped the area into the protectorate of Bohemia and Moravia. Even the formation of the republic of Slovakia under German protection received little notice. Diplomats came and went, newspapers were filled with accounts of the conferences leading up to World War II, and there was little space or inclination to discuss the heroic struggle of these mountaineers and the part their fate was to play in the tragedy of the world and of the continent of Europe.

XV

World War II, 1939-41

On August 23, 1939, the Nazis and the Soviet Union signed
a pact of friendship and nonaggression. It came as a bombshell
to the Allied diplomats who were at the moment negotiating
in Moscow for Soviet aid against Nazi aggression and it utterly
confused those liberal American and Western authorities on the
Soviet Union who regarded Moscow as the great bulwark
against Nazism and Fascism. Yet it was no sudden development. Hitler's speech on April 28, 1939, had given good
warning that something of the sort was in the air.[1] Besides,
the speed with which events developed after the formal signing
of the pact and the ease with which later agreements were
made suggest that there was a thorough understanding between the two totalitarian powers as to many questions which
were not openly included in the formal pact.[2]

The immediate result was the German attack on Poland on
September 1. The campaign went as expected. The better
armored and equipped Nazi forces speedily destroyed organized opposition and despite Polish valor in the defense of
Warsaw and other cities, the Polish armies were forced to the
south and east. By September 17 the Germans were besieging
Lviv. Taught by the spring events in Carpatho-Ukraine and
distrustful of the Nazi-Soviet alliance, the Ukrainian troops
fought in the Polish ranks against the invaders.[3]

They certainly could have gained nothing had they taken an opposite course, for on September 17 the Soviet Union, which had a non-aggression pact with Poland, announced that the Polish government had fallen and the Red army invaded the country from the east "to take under their protection the lives and property of the population of Western Ukraine and Western Byelorussia."[4] As if matters were already arranged, the Germans on the approach of the Soviet troops withdrew from Lviv without a battle. On September 28 Ribbentrop and Molotov signed a new agreement in Moscow and on the next day at Brest-Litovsk the German and Soviet commanders signed an agreement for the delimitation of their holdings in Poland. The Soviets had already commenced their expansion in the Baltic republics. While the line was never publicly delimited,[5] the Germans continued their retirement back of the San and Bug rivers and turned over the territory to the east to their Soviet allies.

This left in German hands four districts of Western Ukraine. The region along the San and Lemkivshchyna were added to the governor generalship of Krakow and the other two, Kholmshchyna and Pidlyashshya, were placed in the governor generalship of Lublin, for the Germans had determined to eliminate as many as possible of the old territorial divisions. All the areas became filled with refugees from the territories which had been handed over to the Soviets.[6]

In the first phase of occupation the Germans were apparently intent upon increasing the enmity between the Ukrainians and the Poles. Thus they allowed the Ukrainians to introduce Ukrainian schools in those areas where the Poles had forbidden them. They permitted quite liberally the publication of Ukrainian books. Finally they permitted the organization of a Ukrainian Central Committee in Krakow in March, 1940, to act as a general contact organ similar to those that they allowed to the Poles and the Jews. As a subsidiary of this, they approved the organization of relief organizations which would care for the needs of the local communities and of the refugees who came in ever-increasing numbers with their stories of developments in Western Ukraine under Soviet rule. To some of these the Germans contributed funds apportioned from the enormous exactions that they made upon the population. Of course, no political activity was tolerated, even though for a while they looked with some kindness upon the Organization of Ukrainian Nationalists as a body which had been prohibited by the Poles. Yet this favor was soon withdrawn as it became evident that the Ukrainians were not going to acquiesce peacefully in the new restricted life mapped out for them by the Nazis and were seeking their own style of secret organization.[7]

In the rest of Western Ukraine the Soviets were not slow in getting into action. All the lessons that they had learned in Eastern Ukraine in twenty years were at once applied. There were mass arrests of the intellectuals, the richer elements of the population, the Uniat priests, and all other persons who might be regarded with suspicion. Communist views of history and of atheism were applied in the schools. Bands of hoodlums murdered those persons whom the Soviets wished to eliminate but did not care to arrest. Deportations to the interior of the Soviet Union were common.

After a month of this procedure the Soviets judged that it was time to take the next step and proceed to the election of a People's Assembly of West Ukraine. The candidates were nominated by Communist labor groups and by peasant delegations which the Communists could control. The names of all the candidates were never published but they were largely Soviet officials and officers of the Red army. Among the names announced were the writer Korniychuk from Eastern Ukraine, Grechukha, chairman of the Supreme Soviet of the Ukrainian Soviet Republic, and many members of the NKVD. Then the Soviets took care to make it clear that anyone who voted against this new assembly or suggested other candidates was counter-revolutionary. When the elections were held on October 22, 91 per cent of the population was, to no one's surprise, announced as voting for the new regime. The only act of the People's Assembly was to appoint Stalin and other members of the Soviet Politbioro to the honorary presidium, to elect Stalin honorary president of the meeting, to congratulate the Soviet leaders, and to request admission to the U.S.S.R. and nationalization of banks and heavy industry.

The requests were kindly granted by the Soviet Union at Moscow and the hand-picked delegates were graciously received and welcomed into the Ukrainian Soviet Republic in the Kremlin on November 21. During the entire performance there was no independent word from the Ukrainian Soviet Republic which was supposed to be the state which they were joining. It was a caricature of the symbolic act of union between the Republic of Western Ukraine and the Ukrainian National Republic in 1919.[8]

The next step was the introduction of the Soviet economic system. Nationalization of the land was commenced almost immediately, also of the factories and industrial plants, whether they belonged to Poles or Ukrainians. Soviet hours of labor, at least ten hours a day, and the Stakhanov piecework system were introduced. The upsetting of all of the channels of trade and commerce and the requisitioning of grain and other foodstuffs from the peasants increased the general misery. Mass massacres at Vynnytsya[9] and elsewhere rivaled the massacre of the Polish officers at Katyn.

This first period of Soviet occupation, which extended from the entrance of the Red army until the German attack upon the Soviet Union, was a sort of preliminary period. We can compare it in many ways with the first period of the history of the Ukrainian Soviet Republic and perhaps we can find details that are reminiscent of the period of Ukrainization.

The first act of the invaders was to build up a corps of natives on whom they could rely. Communism had made little inroad into the population that was under Polish rule. There were of course individuals who had accepted the idea that their brothers across the closed border were happy but it did not take long to disillusion all who were honest enough to form an opinion. Ukrainian co-operative societies were closed or merged with those in the Ukrainian Soviet Republic. The independent educational institutions, such as the Shevchenko Scientific Society,[10] that had existed under Polish rule were now standardized and their financial resources were confiscated and placed at the disposal of the new regime, with its representatives brought in from the east.

In this phase the task of separating the Poles and the Ukrainians was given the largest place. Lviv was declared a Ukrainian city and the University of Lviv was renamed in honor of Franko, the greatest intellectual leader of the Western Ukrainians. Its staff was purged both of the old Polish professors and of Ukrainians who did not seem responsive to the new ideas. The Soviets replaced them with trustworthy Russian Communists, as they had done in Kiev and elsewhere.[11]

The masses were in a strange mood. They had heard for years of the opposition between Nazism and Communism and now the two dictatorships were working in apparently the best of relations. Supplies from the Soviet Union were going to Germany and likewise, in view of the blockade of the Atlantic coast of Germany, the Nazis were able to maintain contact with the world abroad across Siberia.

In the West the winter of 1939-40 was the period of the "phony war." The French armies were entrenched behind the Maginot Line and made few attempts to leave it and invade Germany. The Nazis were entrenching themselves in Poland and preparing to absorb the lands which they had already seized.

The dictators were not idle. Ribbentrop and Molotov had already come to an understanding as to the future of the Baltic states of Estonia, Latvia and Lithuania, which were compelled to sign treaties of mutual assistance with the Soviets and admit Soviet garrisons to their important posts. During the winter the Soviets attacked Finland. World sentiment in the democracies was on the side of Finland and despite the efforts of the Germans to secure information and turn it over to their Soviet allies the courageous Finns were able to give a good account of themselves and hold back the Red army during most of the winter.

The period also saw the formal expulsion of the Soviet Union from the League of Nations in Geneva.[12] The Soviet attack on Finland, even more unprovoked than Mussolini's invasion of Ethiopia, had shocked whatever was left of a world conscience. It was ironical that the League which had sidestepped every decisive action while there was time, should, past the eleventh hour, give a definite moral judgment and brand Moscow as an imperialistic aggressor.

Then Moscow turned her attention to the south. With the support of Hitler she requested Romania to turn over to her Bukovina and Besserabia. That part of the two provinces which had a Ukrainian population was obligingly annexed to the Ukrainian Soviet Republic. The other sections were grouped with the Autonomous Moldavian Republic to form the Moldavian Soviet Republic, a small and unimportant district created for the sole purpose of annexing Romanian territory under the guise of self-determination.[13] Again the same measures of Communization were introduced. There were the same nominations by Communist-dominated organizations, the same controlled elections, the same resolutions of gratitude to the great Stalin and the same massacres and deportations.

Then as Germany attacked in the West and her armies swept on to the Atlantic across the Netherlands, Belgium and France, Moscow repeated her tactics in the north and by the familiar devices accepted the submission of the three Baltic states, turned them into Soviet Republics and began to wipe out the people and nationalize all their possessions.

The Ukrainians could have little hope. The OUN (Organization of Ukrainian Nationalists) indulged in acts of sabotage but there was little positive action. With Germany and the Soviet Union in alliance and with the Western powers evidently losing the war, the future seemed dark indeed.

The only ray of light was the hope of a split between the two ruthless machines that held the country in their grip. The Ukrainian patriots sought eagerly for any sign of a dis-agreement, though they had few illusions as to the philanthropic motives of either party. The fate of Carpatho-Ukraine and the German surrender of Lviv and other Western Ukrainian territory to Stalin had shown them that Hitler was not in-terested in their problems. On the other hand their experiences with the Red army had shown them likewise that there was nothing to be expected in that direction. Renewed contact with the Eastern Ukrainians brought home to them in all of its horror the meaning of Communism and the sham of the Ukrainian Soviet Republic.

This gave the period a strange and unreal aspect. The Ukrainians realized perfectly that they could have no allies, even if they rose in revolt. Finland had been left to stand alone. The Byelorussians were in the same boat as themselves and the Baltic states still farther to the north were silenced. Wait-ing was the only course open. Meanwhile the patriotic leaders had to try to save their own lives, protect their followers, and prepare for whatever might come.

XVI

Ukraine between the Armies

On June 21, 1941, Nazi Germany denounced her treaty with the Soviets and her armies invaded the Soviet Union. They pushed ahead rapidly and soon the Communists were in full retreat from all the territories which they had acquired during their friendship with Hitler.

The next few days were to be decisive. As the Soviet forces withdrew, they indulged in another orgy of murder and deportation. As if doubting that they would ever return, they ruined or destroyed everything they could not carry away with them and in their haste did as much harm as possible to the local population, including the massacre of those political prisoners whom they could not remove.[1]

On June 30, as the Germans were approaching Lviv, a Ukrainian National Assembly proclaimed a Ukrainian National Government in the West with Yaroslav Stetsko as prime minister; a few days later a Ukrainian National Rada was formed with Dr. K. Levytsky, a veteran of the old Republic, as prime minister.[2] The Ukrainians in Lviv called for the restoration of an independent Ukraine. They acted quickly to forestall any possible decisions by the Germans and set to work to prepare armed forces to join in the campaign against the Bolsheviks. Similar action was taken by the Lithuanians in Kaunas, the

Latvians in Riga, and the Estonians in Tallinn.³ The way was open for the resurrection of the governments which had been overthrown during the alliance of Hitler and Stalin.

The Germans at once made it clear that they had no intention of recognizing or co-operating with any of the newly formed governments. In accordance with Hitler's theories the lands which the German army was recovering from the Communists were not intended for use and development by their own population. They were intended to furnish supplies and men for the ruling and superior Germans. Thus in the very first weeks after the advance to the east started, it was certain that the Germans were not coming as liberators but as conquerors. All leaders of the new governments who fell into their hands were imprisoned in concentration camps.

The Nazis soon played another card. Under Soviet law the land and all industrial establishments had been confiscated from the original owners and possessed by the state. The Germans (and we must remember that in Western Ukraine and the Baltic states, Soviet control had lasted under two years, so that it might have been possible to find a considerable number of the original owners) calmly announced that since the property had belonged to the Soviet Union, it was legitimate spoils. The Soviet collective farms, etc. were maintained intact. The Soviet masters were replaced by Germans, who were ordered to extract from the helpless population the greatest possible returns at any cost. Corrupt, degenerate and brutal Nazis took the place of the old corrupt, degenerate and brutal commissars. This removed the last possibility of any active co-operation between the Germans and the citizens, who would have welcomed almost any government that would free them from Communist tyranny. The Germans acquired easy title to all the property in Ukraine and elsewhere, but they paid for it with the antagonism of the entire population, Communist and anti-Communist alike.⁴

The Nazis went much further than had the imperial German officials at the time of the Treaty of Brest-Litovsk in 1918.

Those, in their search for supplies, had granted favors to the landowning class. The current crop of war lords turned against this class as resolutely as had the Communists during their occupation. They made certain that in their war against Communism, they would have the open hostility of everybody and by their defiance of any form of self-determination, they made it clear that they intended to rule by terror exactly as the Communists had done. It may have been flattering to German self-esteem but it was to prove costly during the next four years, for it entirely changed the nature of the struggle and deprived the Nazis of any peaceful source of supply. The Gestapo was to be the pillar of German domination of Ukraine, and as the armies swept eastward, they extended this system wherever they went.

There seems little doubt that in the beginning the leaders who proclaimed at Lviv the independence of Ukraine were confident that they would receive the support of the Nazis as avowed anti-Communists. In the first stages there was apparently little more secrecy made about it than in the corresponding movement in 1917. The leaders acted in Western Ukraine before the Germans reached Kiev so as to prevent a gap in the administration of the country and give an excuse for some other solution of the problem than Ukrainian independence. They set to work to create a government and incidentally an army which could be thrown into the struggle against the Communists.

For this they already had some scattered forces. Among these were such groups as the Luh (Meadow) which had offered some military training to the Ukrainians during the Polish occupation of the country. There were the Kamenyary (Stone-Crushers), who had played a similar role but were under the control of the Socialist Radical Party. There were similar groups under the Ukrainian Nationalists, and it was these specifically that were led by Borovets, better known under his pseudonym of Taras Bulba, the Kozak hero of Gogol's novel of that name. Such groups could be used either as the nucleus of an army or for police purposes, until an army could be formed.[5]

The Germans planned differently. They showed their hand on August 11, when they formally annexed Eastern Galicia to the Polish Government-General, the truncated body of the Polish state which was left after they had taken away the areas that they had decided to annex to Germany. Then they restored Bukovina and Bessarabia to Romania and they added to the Romanian share a large slice of Ukrainian territory on the left bank of the Dniester and the city of Odessa. The rest of Ukraine was formed into the Reichscommissariat of Ukraine under the supervision of Erich Koch and some of the eastern districts were placed under open military rule. This of course showed clearly that for Hitler, Ukraine did not exist in any form.[6]

Soon after, the Germans issued their first order for the transportation of physically fit Ukrainians to Germany for compulsory labor. They followed this up on September 15 with an order for the arrest of all officers of the new Ukrainian government and the internment of all known nationalists.[7] This was not done until the Germans were sure that they were going to be the masters of all Ukraine and had taken not only Lviv but Kiev, which they reached early in September.

During the summer the new Ukrainian movement spread behind the German lines to include the old Ukrainian capital. In the first rush of the German forces the Ukrainian nationalists were able with relative immunity to spread their cause on the heels of the retreating Communists, who carried off with them everything that was movable. The Reds destroyed all available food supplies and seized as many prominent individuals as they could for transportation to Central Asia. The Ukrainian Academy of Sciences was moved to the east to Ufa with part of its scientific institutes. Other sections were wantonly destroyed. Old churches and other historical monuments were blown up and everything was done to ruin the city before the Nazi arrival. Later on the responsibility for all this was placed on German shoulders despite the inconsistency with the Soviet boasts of the "scorched earth" policy.

This devastation by the retreating Communists proved fertile soil for the advancing representatives of the revived Ukrainian independence movement. They made such headway that it became obvious to the Germans that the call for an independent Ukraine was answering a popular demand. Hence the sudden swooping down upon the group and the mass arrests.

The German terror continued and soon the new masters were imprisoning or shooting well-known Ukrainian patriots. The writer Olena Teliha was executed in Kiev in 1942.

From this moment there could be no talk of any compromise with the Nazi invaders. The various groups that had been looking forward to a war on Communism saw their energies diverted to a struggle with the present enemy, the Hitler forces. It was obviously impossible to construct a regular Ukrainian army in the face of the German military control, but it was easy to organize a large number of small, independent bands of guerilla fighters.

These same tactics were adopted in all the countries that were overrun by the Nazis and the Fascists. Small bands numbering from fifty to one thousand men, largely from the same village, town or region, maintained themselves in the woods and swamps, and from these they would sally forth to harass German supply trains, cut off small columns of troops, and commit acts of sabotage on a consistent scale. Their tactics were those of the Greeks, of the Serbs under Mihaylovich, of the Norwegians, and of other peoples. There had been the rudiments of similar opposition in Western Ukraine to the Communist rule in 1940 and 1941.

These bands illustrate the difference between guerilla warfare of the present and of the not too distant past. Not many centuries ago, before the development of the modern rifle and machine gun, the bands came directly out of the village. The revolt of Khmelnytsky in 1648 and of the Haydamaki during the eighteenth century were outpourings of villagers armed with their scythes and axes to assist some little nucleus of devoted lovers of liberty who were preying on the tyrants of the day. Then the crudely armed peasants were almost a match for even the heavy cavalry and on many a field of battle they were able to give a good account of themselves.

Under modern conditions, once guerilla bands were organized under men who preferably had had some military training, their first job was to secure an adequate supply of powerful weapons, build secret ammunition dumps and gird themselves with as many of the accoutrements of modern warfare as they could secure. This was not easy and in some areas for weeks at a time the guerilla forces were hardly able to operate.

German tactics during the winter of 1941-42 facilitated guerilla work. In their desire to push on and reach the oil fields of the Caucasus, the Germans trusted to their motorized equipment to force supplies through any given area with little trouble. They did not try to keep open their main supply routes but rather despatched flying columns to outlying regions while holding their grip upon the populated or strategic areas. This gave guerilla partisans a chance to dominate almost continuously large sections of the country away from the main arteries of communication and permitted them under terrible odds to take the first steps in perfecting their organizations on a large scale.

It was no easy task to bring together the scattered bands. Now and then two or more, operating in the same neighborhood, would combine for a joint enterprise, but more often the leaders were jealous of one another. Isolated detachments meeting unexpectedly would not recognize each other and would engage in bloody conflict.

The situation was made worse when the Communists, particularly after the checking of the German advance, and in Eastern Ukraine, outfitted similar detachments which were equally ready to fight both Germans and non-Communist groups. Many of the Ukrainian leaders lost their lives in these early attempts to create some form of liaison between the different groups, especially in the autumn and winter of 1941 and the summer of 1942.

Very little information about this movement reached the outside world. It was not to the German interest to let it be known that they were meeting with opposition. They much preferred to emphasize their successes and lay the blame for any partisan activities on the Communists.

For their part the Soviets were enjoying the sympathy of the entire anti-Nazi world, which was shipping all possible supplies to the Soviet Union. To encourage this, Stalin issued grandiose statements that the Soviets alone were not bothered with a fifth column but that all citizens of the Soviet Union were united against the Nazi invaders. He had expediently relaxed the vigorous fight against nationalism and even tolerated the appearance of stories and novels that stressed the heroism and devotion of non-Communists. It would never do for him to admit that he was confronted with an uprising of peoples who wished democratic and independent governments. Later he stated that the basis of the Soviet defense was the Great Russian population and the truth leaked out only when it was officially announced that several of the smaller autonomous republics had been liquidated because of their aid to the invaders. He might have said with more truth that it was because of their unwillingness to remain Soviet citizens, when they saw even a desperate chance to recover some of their human rights. According to Soviet theory all clashes of the Red army with hostile forces were exclusively with German-supported guerillas, exactly as the Germans admitted the existence of only Soviet-supported groups.

By the end of 1942 the more serious guerilla leaders had been brought together in a loose military organization called the Ukrainian Insurgent Army (UPA). This possessed a general staff and, especially in the swamps of Polissya and the forests of Volyn, was able to develop a well-defined military base where it could gather supplies and train officers and men. The individual leaders still needed a considerable amount of independence but they paid more than nominal respect to the central authority. Those who did not and who swung too far in concentration on one or the other of the enemies, i.e., the German occupying forces or the Soviet partisan bands which were sent into the area, were often disarmed or rendered powerless to do harm to the general cause.[8]

As an aid to their operations, the Ukrainians paid particular attention to the lower German administrative organs in the areas where they were in the greatest strength. The Nazis had retained the former administrative divisions of the country. They did not have the necessary men and equipment to maintain strong guards around these lesser centers and the Ukrainians were able to wipe them out in considerable numbers and install informal administrations which would meet the minimum needs of the population and incidentally collect supplies for the fighting men.[9]

The guerilla units were able in many cases to protect themselves against strong punitive expeditions which were sent to burn entire villages and massacre the local population. When these were too strong, the bands scattered or took refuge in the woods and swamps together with the villagers and reappeared when the invaders moved on.

We must not think of this movement as merely the spasms of some hopeless and feeble men. When need be, they were able to execute difficult assignments and even do away with high Nazi officials. Thus in May, 1943, they waylaid along the line of the Kovel-Brest Railroad no less a person than Victor Lutze, a chief of the Nazi SS forces and one of Himmler's most trusted aides. The official Nazi excuse was death in an automobile accident.[10] A year later, when the Soviets were entering the same area, they surprised and mortally wounded Marshal Vatutin, perhaps one of the highest Red army officers to be killed during the war and this time the explanation was assault by bandits.[11] There was a long series of attacks on German trains deporting Ukrainians to Germany for slavery, when the guards were overpowered and the prisoners released to find places in the ranks of the UPA or return to their families and continue activities in other fields.

In the spring of 1942 Marshal Timoshenko attempted to recover Kharkov by an attack from Great Russian territory and failed. The Germans did not renew their attacks on Moscow that year when the spring thaws made army movements possible but they pushed east through Ukraine to Stalingrad on the Volga in Great Russian territory and to the southeast into the Caucasus. Their defeat at Stalingrad, with the capture of their entire army, was fatal to their hopes and from then on the Soviet armies advanced westward.

This soon brought the Soviets back into Ukrainian territory. There were new and bitterer clashes with the UPA. The Red army advance was as ruthless toward the Ukrainians as toward the Germans.[12] To cover up, the army was now reorganized into Ukrainian and Byelorussian armies to give the impression that it was the natives of those Soviet republics who were doing the fighting for the Kremlin. The move was accompanied by a pseudo-reform of the Soviet constitution, granting to each Soviet republic its own commissar for foreign affairs and serving to make plausible the Soviet demand that each of the republics should be represented in the United Nations organization which was being planned to come into being after the ending of the war.

Thus in 1945 at Yalta, Stalin won the consent of both President Roosevelt and Winston Churchill to the admission of Ukraine and Byelorussia into the United Nations. In the height of pro-Soviet enthusiasm no one bothered to ask whether the representatives of those countries would speak for Moscow or for the people. It is of interest that the Ukrainian representative hand-picked by the Russian Communists was the same Dmytro Manuilsky who had acted as the Russian Soviet agent in Kiev during the regime of Hetman Skoropadsky about twenty-five years before. He had improved his Communist techniques in the meantime by acting as co-ordinator for Communist interests in Germany. His appointment was a guarantee that the spokesmen of Ukraine in the new organization would be men absolutely and exclusively loyal to the interests of Moscow. Apparently Stalin had won this concession from Churchill and Roosevelt by vague illusions to some sort of difficulties that the Soviet regime was facing. At Yalta he was not prepared to say that these difficulties were being caused by nationalist groups that would have none of the Kremlin but his companions apparently were too polite to pin him down on this question and allowed him to secure their approval of his farce by comparisons with the British Commonwealth of Nations, etc.

The Ukrainians were not alone in their struggle. The Soviet seizure of the Baltic states of Lithuania, Latvia and Estonia and the German refusal to recognize the newly constituted democratic republics after their attack on the Soviets had made a common cause for the peoples extending between the two dictatorships. The Byelorussians, while they were less nationally conscious than the other groups, soon felt their kinship with the movement. They all developed the same type of guerilla warfare against the two invading armies and it was only natural that the various leaders established contact to carry on their operations along their ethnographical boundaries. It was then but a short step to a joint consideration of their general problems.

Furthermore, even during 1942, the UPA found that it could enroll as reliable members not only citizens of the countries that had been recently seized by the Soviet Union but many Red army deserters belonging to the other nationalities which had passed under Soviet domination at the same time as Ukraine, the period around 1920. The Stalinists were intent on destroying the essence not only of Ukrainian culture but that of the whole galaxy of nations within the Iron Curtain. The Germans tried to form units out of their prisoners of war from these same nationalities but in many cases the new recruits were susceptible to the propaganda of the UPA and passed over almost as units to the Ukrainian camp. There they found leaflets on the efforts of their own nations to obtain liberty, prepared by men who had already joined the Ukrainian army. In a short time units were formed of Georgians, Tatars, Azerbaijanians and Uzbeks.[13]

So widespread were these reactions that in November, 1943, there was held in one of the UPA strongholds between Western Ukraine and the Dnieper a conference to set up the United Liberation Struggle of the Oppressed Nations. This was attended by thirty-nine delegates from thirteen peoples that had been caught in the Soviet net, including men from Ukraine and from Azerbaijan, Bashkirs, Kabardins, Kazakhs, Byelorussians, Armenians, Ossetes, Cherkassians and Chuvash. They issued an appeal to the Oppressed Peoples of Eastern Europe and Asia to join in the creation of national democracies.[14]

It was similar in scope to the conference called in Kiev in 1917 to lay plans for the creation of a federalized Russian state. This had met just as the Bolsheviks were taking over power. It had aided in the disruptive movements within the Russian Empire and had served as an inspiration for the various national states which had developed on the imperial ruins and then been overthrown by Communist infiltration and military conquest.[15] The tendency had been kept alive by the governments-in-exile of those republics and by other patriots through the Promethean League which published in Paris a journal devoted to the cause of the free peoples that had been overwhelmed by Communism. This movement had naturally been opposed by the Soviet Union but it had also incurred throughout its entire history the enmity of the Germans, who saw in it a weapon which might bar their expansion to the vital East.[16]

Although the UPA extended its activities throughout all Ukraine, its headquarters were in the West, where it was at first able to concentrate against the Nazis. Later as the Red army began to push westward, the Germans made strenuous efforts to enlist its members in the army of General Vlasov which they were forming out of prisoners of war and Red army deserters. Few of the members yielded to the temptation and the UPA continued its fight against both aggressors.

It passed from Volyn and Polissya into the region of the Carpathians. It expanded its work in Galicia, where the Germans became more and more terroristic as they saw their hopes of victory evaporate. In these regions the advance of the Red army from the Balkans and Hungary again brought it up against the UPA, which in the meantime had had trouble with the Polish underground forces. The UPA had been able to establish contacts with these, especially during the Warsaw uprising of 1944, but many of the Polish bands were so strongly nationalistic that they declined to co-operate with other groups which might have a justifiable claim on territory that the Poles affected to own. Naturally the UPA could have no relations with the groups that were connected with the Communist-inspired center at Lublin.[17]

Finally in June, 1944, another important step was taken. This was the organization of the Supreme Ukrainian Council of Liberation, formed just before the Soviet troops entered West Ukraine. It aimed to consolidate politically all parties and it issued a Universal proclaiming its position as the supreme organ of the Ukrainian people in their fight for liberation. It adopted the following declaration of principles:

"It will fight to make you the sole master of your soil;

For a just social order without oppression and exploitation;
For the destruction of serfdom.

For free enterprise of the peasant on his own land;

For free enterprise for the worker;

For wide initiative of the working people in all branches of the economic order;

For the widest possible development of the Ukrainian national culture.[18]

These were the goals that were outlined in the comparative quiet of 1917-18 and they are still held behind the Iron Curtain by all Ukrainians worthy of the name.

The UPA endeavored to create a definite military force

and a definite political body under the most adverse circumstances. It was unfortunate that the response was not unani-
mous because of a split in the leadership of the Ukrainian Nationalists. Nevertheless, the various groups of the UPA, north,
east, south and west, have acquired a real military discipline.

Thus during the entire period of Nazi occupation and Soviet
reoccupation the population strove to bring back those democratic principles and rights which the Ukrainian National
Republic had proclaimed in 1918. It was a desperate struggle that offered little hope of final success but it showed
that the Ukrainian national spirit was not dead, even after
twenty years of Communist misrule, and it suggested the
possibilities for Ukrainian assistance to the free nations of the
world whenever they were ready to accept it.

XVII

Across the Iron Curtain

With the re-entrance of the Soviet army into Ukraine, rumors began to trickle out that not all of the partisan fighters who had helped disrupt German communications were devoted to the Communist cause. It was darkly hinted that at least part of these were organized into bands that were equally hostile to both Red and Nazi imperialism. Such rumors were not welcomed during the war—nor in the days when the West was seeking the co-operation of the Soviet Union in building the United Nations—for they seemed to indicate that all was not well and the public mood insisted upon the need for unity among the foes of Hitler.

The Communists knew how to capitalize on this mood of the moment to cement their power over Eastern and Central Europe. As the Soviet troops swept west in a wide arc, they used it to install their own governments in Bulgaria, Yugoslavia, Albania and Hungary and to dominate the regime in Czechoslovakia. Slowly but surely they made away with all of their opponents. On one excuse or another they virtually eliminated all other Allied representatives on the various control commissions and pursued their own policy of "liberation."

It was assumed by the Soviets and tacitly agreed by the other powers that the Soviets would recover that part of Western

Ukraine which they had occupied under their pact with Hitler in 1939. So they found themselves again in control of Lviv and the old Eastern Galicia and they were free to make such boundary settlements with a subservient Communist government of Poland as they might wish.[1]

They fared just as well in Carpatho-Ukraine. When the Soviets recognized Dr. Benes as head of the Czechoslovak government-in-exile soon after they entered the war, they promised to respect the old boundaries of the republic.[2] But when the Red army entered upon its territory, they met at once in their usual manner enthusiastic appeals to include Carpatho-Ukraine in the Ukrainian Soviet Republic. With their love for democracy, they could not fail to be moved; accordingly, on June 29, 1945, they annexed the area, while Dr. Benes yielded graciously in the name of Slav solidarity.[3]

In May, 1945, the Germans surrendered and the Red army formally met the Western troops in the middle of Germany to inaugurate the new era in human civilization. Up to this moment Soviet plans had proceeded without a hitch and the West had accepted the Soviet point of view on almost all disputed questions without protest or criticism.

After the first flush of jubilation over the joint victory and the first extensive contacts between soldiers of the West and those of the Soviet Union, the reservoir of good will began to empty rapidly. Soon the way was open for a new evaluation of all the reports that had been filtering across what was now commonly called the Iron Curtain.

There were three factors mainly responsible for this change. These were the unprecedented looting and plundering by the Red army, the problem of the displaced persons, and the open announcements of "banditry" by the Red command and the governments of the satellite states.

There is little need to dwell here upon the orgy of crime that was committed by the Red army. Even if a certain amount is almost inevitable in military occupation, the raping of the occupied lands reached a new high and was so reminiscent of the excesses of the Reds in Ukraine in 1918 and in 1939 that it inevitably drew attention to this characteristic of the Soviet regime. The stories about Western Ukraine were so exceeded by the developments in Germany that their truth was easily rendered not only possible but probable. Contact with the Western armies threw a revealing light not only upon the cultural level of the masses of the Red army and their discipline or lack of it but upon the Soviet determination to shield their men from an accurate knowledge of what was going on in the rest of the world.[4]

The second factor was the problem of the displaced persons. In an evil hour at the Yalta conference in the spring of 1945, Roosevelt and Churchill accepted Stalin's idea that all displaced persons should be sent back to their own homes, by force if necessary. This seemed a senseless addition. The victims of German deportation from the Western countries were only too happy to receive governmental aid in returning to their homes. They literally swarmed back to pick up the threads of their old lives where they had been broken off by the Nazi invasion.

Not so, however, the persons who had been brought to Germany from the Eastern nations. It was to be expected that the refugees from the Baltic states which had been seized by Stalin in 1940 would refuse to go home. They were joined by millions of persons from states like Poland which had been placed under new Communist-dominated regimes including enormous numbers who had deserted from the Red army and had preferred even to starve with the Nazis under the command of the Russian General Vlasov in their zeal to combat the Communists. Of this group the Ukrainians formed perhaps the largest contingent and they had come not only from Western Ukraine, which had been seized in 1939, but even from the Ukrainian Soviet Republic where they had enjoyed the paradise of Communist rule for a quarter of a century.

In the first heat of enthusiasm for their Soviet allies, the Western nations obediently handed over the vast majority of these people, who were immediately marched off to arrest and liquidation, for Soviet rules prescribed punishment not only for Red army deserters but for all persons who had fallen into enemy hands. The attempts to turn these people over led to disgraceful scenes and many preferred to commit suicide rather than return behind the Iron Curtain. Life under the most uncertain and trying conditions in the British and American zones of occupation in Germany still seemed better than life in the prison of nations that is the U.S.S.R. It was in vain that Soviet sympathizers in such organizations as the UNRRA tried to put pressure on the unwilling victims. Their minds were made up and gradually the Western Powers became convinced of this and began to try to find ways and means of balking the Soviet slave hunters. It is these implacable foes of the Soviet Union who form the overwhelming portion of the displaced persons and are able from their past experiences to supply hitherto unknown details about conditions of life in the Soviet Union and the opposition which exists against the Stalin regime.

The third factor was the announced outbreak of banditry behind the Soviet lines. This seemed strangely inconsistent with the boasted order and efficiency of the Red army. The Soviets made much of the so-called deserters and Fascists who were operating in parts of Poland and in Carpatho-Ukraine. The strength of the bands was shown by the fact that in May, 1945, they were even able to kill General Swierczewski, the Polish Communist vice minister of war.[5] A little later these were identified to newspaper reporters as the Banderivtsy, the followers of one Bandera, who seemed to be everywhere preying on small isolated detachments of the Red army.[6]

Eventually the constant flow of official announcements combined with the rumors that seeped out made it known that the "bandits" were the Ukrainian Insurgent Army, part of which had been organized out of the branch of the Union of Ukrainian Nationalists headed in Western Ukraine by Stephen Bandera. It was soon evident that these foes of both the Nazis and the Soviets at periods actually controlled relatively large sections of territory and proved a formidable enemy with which the Red army was not prepared to cope.

By the spring of 1947 the raids of these men had become so annoying that the Soviets actually made an agreement with both Poland and Czechoslovakia for joint military action against them.[7] It was evident also that they enjoyed the sympathy and support of large sections of the population, especially in Slovakia, and cases were even known where they were aided by the Czechs. The prisoners taken from these bands were publicly tried in Poland and in Czechoslovakia and were usually sentenced to death.[8]

It is now becoming possible to trace out in general lines the later history of this force. After the retreat of the Nazis from Ukraine and the re-occupation by the Soviets, large detachments made their way to the Carpathian Mountains, fighting as they went. They were apparently part of the UPA-West forces and were under strict military discipline. In the fall of 1947 one of the detachments of this group even succeeded in cutting across Czechoslovakia to the American zone in Bavaria, where its members were disarmed and interned. At first the American authorities were suspicious of them but the soldiers were later given the status of prisoners of war and were added to the large number of displaced persons, despite the demands of the Soviets and their satellite states that they should be returned as deserters or war criminals. Since then, many other detachments have made the dangerous trip successfully.[9]

These detachments have small immediate hope of winning the independence of their country from the armies which the Reds have constructed to maintain the Communist regimes in power. Their primary object seems to be to maintain themselves in existence in expectation of the outbreak of World War III while carrying on propaganda work among the Red forces, especially the non-Russian troops coming from the other Soviet republics. Though they are thus much more of a potential than a present menace to the Soviet Union, they are an outstanding example of the discontent that lurks at the core of Soviet power.

They are perhaps of even greater significance in keeping alive the ideals of liberty in the newly mastered states to the west of the Soviet Union. With the latent spirit of resistance still unextinguished in states like Czechoslovakia in which the governmental machinery has been seized by the Communists, these raiding detachments of disciplined and well-equipped men serve as a rallying point for all who prefer to die rather than live in slavery. They are of course pursued by vastly superior forces of both Soviet and satellite armies but they can be sure of support from sympathetic elements of the population.

Again and again the Communist press has issued appeals to the population not to assist them on pain of heavy reprisals but these have largely fallen upon deaf ears. The people of these countries, like the Ukrainians, are already learning that they will meet with the same reprisals and persecutions whatever action they take, and it is often safer for them to join these bands than to wait meekly for the inevitable.

The range of the UPA is gradually spreading. From the earliest days when it was chiefly occupied with the war against the Nazis, it has remained in close contact with kindred movements in the Baltic states. In fact it is rapidly becoming the center of armed resistance among all the oppressed peoples of Eastern Europe and taking the lead in building up an underground coalition of fighters against Communism and the Soviet Union.

This military activity is only one part of the story of modern Ukraine, even though it is perhaps the most spectacular. Discontent, scarcely more passive, reigns throughout the entire region.

Whatever hopes any part of the population may have had of better living conditions at the end of World War II were badly shattered almost at once. Any relaxations of Communist discipline which were tolerated during the war when the

Soviet leaders were in need of all possible support were soon revoked. The hostility of the Communists for the Western Powers which was scarcely veiled during the war flared up openly as soon as the war was over. Attacks on Anglo-American imperialism replaced the diatribes against the Poles and the Nazis of the prewar period. The new Five-Year Plan was openly described as a means of improving the military position of the Soviet Union and not of improving living conditions.

When the Soviet armies returned to Ukraine, Stalin made no bones of asserting that the Soviet victory had been won almost exclusively by the Great Russians. Several of the autonomous republics were liquidated and their populations scattered. The secret police, now renamed the MVD, continued to hound all of those people who had escaped deportation to Germany or the Soviet East. The innocent peasant who had remained on his own collective farm and who perhaps had on more than one occasion taken up arms against the Nazi invader now became a dread rebel or he would have retired with the Red army.

There came a new flood of deportations to Siberia and the Far North as the Soviet government set itself to wipe out the dangerous poison of Ukrainian nationalism and the independence movement. Again many of those Ukrainian authors were condemned and persecuted who had fancied themselves slavish followers of the new regime. They had, willingly or unwillingly, made mistakes in their ideology and in their choice of the settings of their works, which alone could be Ukrainian. Rylsky, a poet who had put himself entirely at the disposal of the Soviet government, was censured for giving way to nationalism and was thrown out of his political posts, even though in the last days of the war he had been sent from one satellite capital to another to praise Stalin's intelligence and kindness and break down anti-Communist feelings in the non-Russian Slav world.

The Communists themselves are today not immune to attack. Exactly as in the period of the purges after 1928, the slightest sign of sympathy for or understanding of the fundamentals of Ukrainian life is sufficient for the accusation of disloyalty. Khrushchov, for years prime minister of the Ukrainian Soviet Republic, has been promoted to service in Moscow, but before he left he had needed assistance and Kaganovich was sent down again as he was in 1928 to institute the reforms so much desired by the Kremlin.[10] The Soviets themselves have announced that over sixty per cent of Ukrainian Communists have been found to be infected with the nationalistic ideas of Professor Hrushevsky and have been purged.

Hardly a week passes without some attack upon the ideas of Hrushevsky, who bids fair to rival in unpopularity in Moscow the hetman Ivan Mazepa who in the eighteenth century led Ukraine in her last great futile rebellion against Muscovite domination by joining Charles XII of Sweden against Peter the Great. The name of Hrushevsky is connected with all of the individuals purged and his teachings are running wild through the country, as the intellectual expression of the conscious and unconscious aspirations of the Ukrainian people. There can be little doubt that his serious studies have received a far more sympathetic hearing among the oppressed Ukrainians of the postwar period than they ever did during his working years.

To counterbalance these manifestations of Ukrainian spirit, the Kremlin has only the answer of force and this force produces a reaction which demands more force for its suppression. Shortly after the ending of hostilities against Germany, Marshal Zhukov, one of the leading Soviet generals, was transferred to the command of the Odessa Military District, apparently to cope with the discontented Ukrainians. There have been rumors of actual outbreaks against the hard conditions of life in both Odessa and Kharkov. It is perhaps fair to say that the entire Ukrainian Soviet Republic is in a state of potential revolt.

If this is true in Eastern Ukraine, which has been under Communist domination for a quarter of a century, it is even more true in Western Ukraine and Carpatho-Ukraine, which are just undergoing the throes of collectivization. The collective farms being established to take the place of the old system of independent landholding are meeting with the same resistance that they did in the east during the years of the artificial famine created by Moscow.

Everywhere all that was Ukrainian in culture is being stifled. The great writers and leaders of the Ukrainians are being represented by the Russian Communists as the friends and supporters of their cause and their works and history are being shamelessly rewritten in order to vindicate the policies of the new masters. Russian theatrical troupes and musicians are appearing everywhere in the Ukrainian Soviet Republic to advertise the duty of the people to have unlimited respect for their elder brothers who have liberated them from the foreign yoke. The Russian language, as the language of Lenin, Stalin and Moscow, is being forced into prominence either directly or by being touted as the Communist model for a Slav language. Old traditions and local customs are being treated as products of American imperialism and Moscow makes no scruples about asserting that Ukraine must have no connections with the West politically, economically or culturally.

No happier a fate awaited those Ukrainians who found themselves at the end of the war under the various satellite governments. The boundaries of these states were drawn in Moscow and the people were given the choice of moving to the countries to which they belonged racially or remaining where they were. Naturally very few in the districts formerly in Slovakia or in Poland preferred to move to the Soviet Union. The satellite governments immediately found excuses for uprooting the population. In the case of Poland the Ukrainians who remained under the control of the puppet regime were gathered up and forced to go to the western boundaries of the country, from which the native German population had been expelled. Here they were carefully scattered among the villages in the hope that they might be completely absorbed by the Polish population.

The immediate result was a widening of the area of Ukrainian resistance for the UPA now had increased opportunities to come into contact with the fighters for freedom among the oppressed peoples of the Baltic. This gave the satellite states further excuse for attacks on the luckless population and this again swelled the ranks of the UPA and its sympathizers.

While this persecution of the Ukrainian population continued, the Soviets were devoting a certain amount of energy to the restoration of the factories, mines and hydro-electric plants which they or the Nazis had destroyed during the war. The celebrated Dnieprostroy, the great electric plant on the Dnieper, the building of which had been highly publicized in earlier years, received early attention. It became clear that the primary object of Soviet restoration was to bind the economy of Ukraine still closer to that of Moscow, and the main efforts of the authorities were expended on the areas of Moscow, the Urals and Central Asia. Machinery which had been moved to the East was not returned.[11] So far as work was done in Ukraine, it became a pretext to bring in non-Ukrainians to populate the restored cities. Ukrainians going into industry were filtered off into other republics, while their places were taken by outsiders. The unparalleled destruction in the country left the Kremlin free to work even more openly and unhesitatingly in carrying out its plans but results were not always according to its desires. Again and again it found that its methods tended to infect Soviet citizens of non-Russian origin with the nationalistic heresy rather than persuade the local population of the advantages of the Soviet regime. But its decrees and policy are inexorable.

Flattery of Stalin must go on, even in the grimmest circumstances. In the very first days, before any reconstruction was even possible, the world was astonished to read of the most liberal donations by Ukrainian villages to their benefactor Stalin for the help of the Great Russians who had been injured by the Nazi advance. Villages which faced starvation could still find the grain to give thousands of tons to their elder brothers and to the great Joseph Stalin as a small expression of their gratitude.[17]

Thus the ending of World War II has not eased the predicament of the Ukrainians. On the contrary the old processes that were applied during the preceding decade to break the spirit of the people have been intensified. The same men who came from Moscow to break Ukrainian resistance in 1928 are back at their work. The uprooting of Ukrainian ideas and ideals is being pushed more vigorously, the population is being decimated and dispersed ever more widely, and in their desperation the people are resorting to violence which is met with countermeasures. Amid all this the Ukrainian Insurgent Army is doing what it can and waiting for the hour when the world will awaken to the full significance of both the internal and external policies of the Soviet Union and come to their assistance.

XVIII

The Displaced Persons

During World War II the democracies became familiar with the work of the governments-in-exile from the nations that were overrun by the Nazis. They were composed of outstanding statesmen who had been able to escape the hurricane that swept over their countries and they not only enjoyed the general esteem of the democratic governments but were the truest guide to the ideas of the people who were compelled to remain at home. They included all parties save the Communists, for these found their spiritual and actual home in Moscow and worked at cross purposes with all of their fellows. It was a sad day for the world when the democratic powers, fired by the hope of appeasing Stalin and securing a lasting peace, withdrew their support from these groups of men and transferred it to the Communist-dominated regimes.

During the years when Hitler and Stalin were actively cooperating against democracy, these exiles and refugees had an important role not only in preserving to the world the ideals of their people but in voicing their hopes and aspirations. It is even truer today in the case of Ukraine, for it is only among the displaced persons that we can hear the voice of the true Ukraine; it cannot come from that Communist organization which has been admitted to the United Nations as the trusted mouthpiece of the Russian Communist party.

It has been a tremendous and heartbreaking task to create amid the hardships of the refugee camps in Germany and Austria the organs which can speak for the thousands of displaced persons who found themselves on the western side of the Iron Curtain. It has been even harder to prove to the Western Allies that the refugees speak not only for themselves but for their people and to secure the financial means to spread their message.

From the moment of Allied victory and the formation of the refugee camps a certain amount of relief work was undertaken by the refugees themselves. It was on a small and disconnected scale. In the autumn of 1945, however, there was held in the American zone of Germany at Aschaffenburg a meeting of representatives of the various Ukrainian camps and this formed a Central Representation of the Ukrainian Emigration, under the leadership of Vasyl Mudry, a prominent statesman among the Ukrainians previously under Poland. This committee was given the right to speak for their countrymen and their work was completed by the formation in 1947 in the British zone of a Ukrainian Central Relief Committee. In 1945 was also formed the Ukrainian Central Relief Union in Austria.[1]

These committees exercised a general supervision and guidance over all cultural work done among the displaced persons. In a strikingly short time an energetic and well-edited Ukrainian press sprang to life. The publication not only of newspapers but of school textbooks and of serious works of science and literature proceeded as rapidly as the means of financing them could be found. Ukrainian schools were set up and religious organizations flourished.

In 1945, before the approach of the Communists, the Ukrainian Free University which had existed in Prague since 1921 was transferred to Munich and despite great difficulties it began to do good work in training the younger Ukrainians and in enabling the older scholars to continue their scientific work.[2]

This was by no means an isolated institution. In 1947 a

Ukrainian Technical-Agricultural Institute was organized in Regensburg and in 1945 a Ukrainian Higher Economic School in Munich. The Ukrainian Free Academy of Science was started in Augsburg in 1945 under the leadership of Professor Dmytro Doroshenko. Then in 1947 the members of the Shevchenko Scientific Society who had survived the Soviet and Nazi occupations of Lviv came together at Munich and renewed the work of the society. In addition there was started throughout the camps a network of Ukrainian lower educational institutions.[3]

We can add a large number of other organizations—a Society of Ukrainian Co-operatives, a Society of Ukrainian Journalists, a Central Society of Ukrainian Students. There was hardly a field in which some grouping was not formed—at first largely confined to one of the Western zones of Germany or Austria but gradually spreading through the entire area, as the Western Powers came closer together in their appreciation of the real problem offered by the displaced persons and Soviet opposition to anything Western.

Similarly the MUR, the Artistic Ukrainian Movement, brought into its membership writers, artists of all kinds, actors and musicians. Exhibitions of Ukrainian art produced under its inspiration, performances of Ukrainian plays and concerts of Ukrainian music all combined to reveal to the Western Powers the range and quality of Ukrainian cultural achievements, even under difficulties.[4]

All this organizational work together with the circumstances of their life has created a stronger sense of unity among Ukrainians of all areas and all walks of life. The displaced persons represent a good cross-section of Ukrainian culture and political life, all uprooted by the devastating tactics of two totalitarian powers. They have had the opportunity to compare their experiences, from the days of the Ukrainian National Republic, and to test their ideas against a background of military occupation and political oppression. Many have escaped from both German and Soviet concentration camps and perhaps more than ever before they are coming to understand both the advantages and the defects of Western democracy and to understand also the similarity of their problems to those of persons from other occupied lands.

It was more difficult to organize political life and to co-ordinate the views of the various refugees. There had been an abundance of political parties in the area under Polish rule but none had been allowed in Eastern Ukraine. Finally in 1946, thanks to the efforts of the representatives of the Ukrainians in North America, a Co-ordinating Ukrainian Committee was organized to which most of the political parties, old and new, sent their delegates.

Once this was done, the trend toward unity was strengthened by the foundation in July, 1948, of an All-Ukrainian National Rada (Council) which is in a unique position to speak for Ukrainians of almost all political parties. At least eight of the leading Ukrainian groups took part in this meeting. They are the Ukrainian National Democratic Union, the Ukrainian National-Statehood Union, the Ukrainian Social Democratic Workingmen's Party, the Ukrainian Socialist Radical Party, the Ukrainian Democratic Revolutionary Party, the Organization of Ukrainian Nationalists, and the Organization of Ukrainian Nationalists-Revolutionaries.[5]

These parties embrace the entire gamut of Ukrainian political life with the exception of a few of the more extreme factions on the right and left and it is likely that some of these will join ultimately. The Rada includes veterans of the Ukrainian cause who have survived from World War I and those who have come into the movement at various times since then. It occupies exactly the same position as the various national committees which were organized in Great Britain, France and the United States during World War I and the various governments-in-exile from World War II.

Through this body which have drawn their membership from all classes of patriotic Ukrainian citizens, Ukraine can for the first time in years express her real feeling for democracy, her desire to take her place among the self-governing and independent nations of the world and her undying opposition to the totalitarian rule of the Soviet Union. It is these men and not the representatives of the Ukrainian Soviet Republic in the United Nations who are the real spokesmen of the Ukrainians as a definite factor in the life and organization of civilized Europe.

This concentration of Ukrainian life in Germany and Austria is obviously but a passing phase. It would be impossible to build up a normal life for the mass of displaced persons under the conditions of overcrowding and ruin in Germany and Austria. Adequate means of productive livelihood do not exist. The acute sufferings are relieved by such organizations as the United Ukrainian Relief Committee, in the American zone, and the Canadian Ukrainian Relief Fund working in the British zone, but more and more the efforts of these organizations are turning to the pressing task of moving the Ukrainians out of the devastated regions.

The dream of some of the refugees that they might be transported in a body to renew their active Ukrainian life somewhere in the New World soon proved unrealistic. There was no nation that would welcome an organized mass of several hundred thousand people carrying on their own life. The task is, then, to move the Ukrainians individually or in small groups to new homes, not only in North America but in South America, Australia, Great Britain, France and Belgium.

This new dispersal of Ukrainians throughout the world has broken up the unity of many of their organizations but it has also given them the opportunity to broaden the scope of their activity and to interest ever-widening circles of the Western world in their cause. For example, the Shevchenko Scientific Society is now represented by an American branch in New York. Many distinguished Ukrainian scholars have found posts and opportunities for work in various institutions in the United States and Canada, although unfortunately too many are still unable to utilize their distinctive skills and knowledge. The best off are undoubtedly those who have been trained in scientific pursuits, for they have been able to fit themselves into the general reservoir of scientific men and have been hampered only by their lack of English. It has been far harder for men trained in the humanities and especially in Ukrainian subjects. Yet many of these in the course of time will be able to establish themselves satisfactorily.

It means a scattering of the already attenuated Ukrainian resources but the damage would be far greater except for the period of intense concentration that followed the World War. Men from all parts of Ukraine were able for the first time to get to know one another personally, compare notes, formulate their own ideas, and build up a real spirit of unity based on solid reality and not on the purely intellectual level. Whatever may be the future, Ukrainian society abroad is far more unified than it has ever been and we can confidently expect that the gains of the last years and the real renaissance of the Ukrainian spirit will not be lost.

XIX

Ukrainian Literature

With the nation thus torn apart and under a constant strain, it is no wonder that the literature constantly reflects the interplay of the dominating forces. The contrast between those authors who were imbued with the Ukrainian spirit and those who were loudly praised by the Communist masters is indeed striking, and the list of literary victims of the Soviet regime has steadily grown to include a large proportion of the outstanding artists of the written word.

From its origin with the *Eneida,* Ukrainian literature has sounded the note of democracy and freedom. Perhaps of no other literature can it be so truly said that it is a literature of the common man, his hopes and aspirations, his fears and difficulties.[1] The Ukrainian revival in its early stages was predominantly literary in character, for it was only in prose and poetry that there could be any national expression. During much of the nineteenth century all political work was impossible, but the writers at the risk of Siberia or prison dared to voice, sometimes openly and sometimes in guarded language, those ideals which otherwise would have been expressed in the political arena.

The literary revival started in Eastern Ukraine under Russian rule. The fate of Taras Shevchenko, the great poet who dared to lash out at the Moskals and their system and then found himself in a Russian penal battalion in central Asia was a warning against too much plain speaking as to the people's suffering. As a result the ethnographical school gained in prominence. Here the difference in psychology, culture and modes of living between the Great Russians and the Ukrainians were stressed. The ideas of the authors were often cloaked in almost scientific descriptions of the life of the villages and they conveyed in the most diverse ways the real character and thoughts of the Ukrainians.

In 1863 the Russian minister of education denied and proscribed any separate Ukrainian language and an edict forbidding the publication in the language of books for popular use was interpreted by the censors to mean utter suppression of all literary work in Ukrainian. In 1876 these rules were made even more all-embracing and not until the revolution of 1905 were they at all relaxed. In the meantime most of the authors published their works at Lviv or elsewhere in the Austro-Hungarian Empire and thus undesignedly helped to knit together the two sections of the dismembered country.

The revival in Western Ukraine under the conditions of the Hapsburg system was slower but after it had taken firm root, it progressed somewhat more evenly. Its standard-bearer, Ivan Franko, a hard-working journalist of Lviv, showed himself not only a conscientious writer and critic but a man of keen insight. Through him and his associates Ukrainian literature was able to draw upon the literary development of Vienna and the West for broadening its outlook and its ideas.

By the first decade of the twentieth century Ukrainian literature was ready to break its original ethnographical bonds and stand out as a modern literature with its own aspirations and styles. It was able to express, despite unfavorable conditions, the Ukrainian version of all those tendencies which were dominant in the literatures of Western Europe as well as of Poland and Russia. The leading writers of the day, such as Lesya Ukrainka and Kotsyubinsky, shared in the literature of Western Europe. They sympathized with the developments of the modern period; their literary techniques were modern; and although they were criticized by the more conservative and static elements of the day, they justified their ambitions to place Ukrainian on a par with the other Slav and European literatures.

By the beginning of World War I most of these giants of the past were no more. Franko had died in 1916 after the retreat of the Russians from Galicia. Lesya Ukrainka had passed away in 1913 and so had Kotsyubinsky. The new phase of the Ukrainian movement which began with the war needed new talents and new modes of expression.

The enthusiasm for the establishment of an independent Ukrainian National Republic called back into literature such a man as Ivan Stefanyk, who had become silent many years before, and gave him new hope and inspiration. He was not alone. New resources of Ukrainian energy were tapped by the enthusiasm of the days of liberty but it proved to be a false dawn when the continued succession of wars and the Soviet conquest carried down the newborn state. Still, the relative freedom of the years of Ukrainization brought forth many new writers.[2]

The most promising of these, like Pavlo Tychyna, were in the group of Ukrainian Symbolists. They developed the musical resources of the language and broadened its philosophical concepts more or less on the pattern of French poetry which had inspired the international Symbolist school.[3] The common sense which had characterized Ukrainian literature kept the authors from imitating the more decadent and abnormal aspects of Symbolism. What they saw in the movement was not the desire to shock the manners and morals of the *bourgeoisie* but the opportunities to adapt to Ukrainian the ideals and techniques of Western Europe. The leading authors were men of education and culture, and following in the path of Lesya Ukrainka, they felt that the Ukrainians were heir to the poetic culture of Europe. Thus they became another link in the chain which connected Ukraine with the whole of European civilization.

Another aspect of this longing of the Ukrainian people can be seen in the Neo-Classic group headed by Mykola Zerov, a lover of Greek and Roman literature. Zerov was tremendously impressed by the fact which had been so often overlooked by writers and scholars that the Black Sea coast of Ukraine had formed an integral part of the ancient Greek world. All along it were scattered the ruins of ancient Greek colonies and the region had been visited by classical writers, such as Herodotus and the exiled Ovid, who had died there. Zerov's imagination played on these scenes of the past and he sought to win for the literature of his country some part of that clarity and sta- tuesqueness which had marked the ancient world. Among his followers were such men as Maksym Rylsky, with wide erudi- tion and appreciation of the masters of world literature.[4]

The third tendency which developed in Ukraine, as in many other countries, was Futurism, whose leading exponent was Mikhaylo Semenko. The Futurists preached destruction for the sake of destruction. They broke with all the accepted canons of art, with the ideals and traditions of the past, the respect for the peasantry and the village, the poetic systems which had been developed for the language, the normal uses of meter, rhyme and even words. While they paid lip service to the fact that they were working to build something in line with the new proletarian culture, they reveled in the negative aspects of both the old and the new, sneered at everything, and went their own way.[5]

Both the Symbolists and the Neoclassicists sought support in the long history of civilization and culture. The Futurists denied and rejected the past and were vague about the future. They were all in a way apart from the writers who accepted in one form or another the Ukrainian Soviet Republic and tried to work in harmony with the new philosophy.

The outstanding feature of these early Communistic writers was their almost pathetic endeavor to organize groups and to announce platforms as to the precise ideological program for which they stood. In the beginning there were many of these groups, each of which interpreted Communism in its own way. Thus, for example, the group of Muzahet through the pen of Yu. Ivaniv-Mezhenko concludes a long discussion of the functions of creative art with these words: "The creative individual can only create, when he considers himself as a being higher than the collective, and when, without submitting to the collective, he yet feels his national kinship with it."[6] Other groups under the name of the Red Crown, the Vineyard, etc., brought forward other ideas, while the VUOPP (All-Ukrainian Federation of Proletarian Writers) followed in the same path as the Russian school of the same name and proclaimed that the only possible literature for the new day was that produced by definitely proletarian writers—most of whom were on a relatively low educational level.

The discussion over the rights of the fellow travelers, those persons who sympathized with at least part of the Communist program, though they were not Communists, lasted for some years, but about 1922 the groups and factions became more rigid; each had its own organs for publication and each indulged in lively polemics with all of its rivals.

In the course of time the groups tended to consolidate and the feuds became more bitter. There was first the Pluh (Plough) which rested its case on the theory that the basis of Ukrainian Communism must be the village and the peasant, since these had best preserved the fundamental Ukrainian characteristics and the new Communist culture was to be built by adapting these characteristics to Marxism and the teachings of Lenin. The Hart (Hardening) of the Lovers of the Workers' Theatres took its stand on a more purely proletarian and Communist basis and declined to recognize the peasant as superior to the factory worker. It denied the territorial basis of proletarian literature within Ukraine and had a generally broader foundation. Then there was the AsPanfut (Association of Pan-Futurists), later the AsKK (Association of Communist Culture), which stressed the international character of Communism and cared little or nothing in its later developments for the purely Ukrainian, while the VUOPP (Pan-Ukrainian Society of Proletarian Writers) continued its original course.[7]

Soon out of the Pluh developed the Molodnyak (Young) which appealed for support to the more youthful classes of writers. The Hart after numerous dissensions developed into the VAPLITE (Free Academy of Proletarian Literature) and this was to be for some years the leading organization.

The discussions between these groups were wordy and sterile but the issues which gradually emerged were clear and well-defined. These concerned the independence of Ukraine even within the Communist union of the USSR. On the one side were those writers who treasured the traditions of Ukraine and wanted to develop them through Communism. On the other were the men who were completely entranced by the visions of a great Communist Soviet Union with little variation between the Soviet republics and who accepted eagerly the slightest hint from the Kremlin, as it commenced its course of enforcing the ideas of the Russian Soviet Republic upon all of its satellite states.

In this feud Mikhaylo Khvylovy came to the front as a defender of a specific Ukrainian Communism. Undoubtedly the foremost prose writer of the day, Khvylovy was a strong supporter of Communism and of the proletarian literature that was to be but at the same time he rebelled against the narrow cultural outlook of too many of the Communists. He insisted that Ukraine had the right to a life and a Communism of its own. He called for the strengthening of Ukrainian bonds with Europe, for the continuation of an interchange of cultural ideas and methods, and he warned against the utter dependence upon the Russian Soviet Republic, which was in the throes of an Asiatic renaissance. More than that, he was disgusted by the uselessness of the orgies of murders that had been carried on during the Communist conquest of Ukraine.[8]

Such ideas were rank heresy to the powers of the Kremlin and even before the final acts of repression, he was continually under attack both by fanatical Communists and the Russian sympathizers. In *The Woodsnipes* (1927) he clearly stated his ideas and indicated his lack of faith in the new paradise. He was compelled to apologize and burn the second part of the novel which was still unpublished, and it was a foregone conclusion that he was to be an outstanding victim of the purge that was to come.

In greater or lesser degree most of the capable poets and prose writers sympathized with Khvylovy. Whether Romanticism or Realism was their predominant style, whether they wrote about the present or the adventures of the past, whether they worked in poetry, prose or the drama, authors like Pidmohylny, Yanovsky, Slisarenko and Pylypenko tried to express something of the old Ukrainian spirit. They realized the difference between the ideals of Communism for which they had fought and the steadily growing power of the inhuman and cold-blooded bureaucracy and terror that they saw creeping over the country. Mykola Kulish in *The People's Malakhy* pictured an innocent and sincere Communist going up to Kiev to see the millennium which he could not find in his native village, only to be even more disillusioned. In the *Sonata Pathetique* he pictured all aspects of Ukrainian and Russian life and the entanglements of the revolution, when nationality and ideas were hopelessly confused.[9] Borys Antonenko-Davydovych in *Death* showed a Communist coming to the realization that he has been but a tool for Moscow imperialism. The list could be increased almost indefinitely, as during the years 1925-29 old illusions began to pass away under persistent signs that the era of Ukrainization was nearing its end.

The Modernists and the Neo-Classicists remained apart from these disturbing questions as long as possible. In the first years men like Tychyna, Rylsky and Bazhan were able to maintain their point of view and to consider the changes that were taking place from a disinterested standpoint. Slowly but surely they found it advisable to take their part in the various political questions of the day. Tychyna, for example, could keep up his old interest in the eighteenth-century Ukrainian philosopher Skovoroda but step by step he drifted away from the philosophical attitude that had inspired that remarkable figure. He came to introduce motifs that had a definite connection with modern life and to review his past works. It led him into the VAPLITE along with Khvylovy and made him a convert to the newer ideas.

Then came the end of Ukrainization. Special representatives of the Kremlin came down to Kiev and Kharkov to liquidate nationalist influences. The old liberties that had been accorded to the fellow travelers and nonparty writers were abridged. In Moscow this was done by placing the RAPP (Russian Association of Proletarian Writers) in practical control.[10] In Ukraine the same thing happened but here, besides the demand for proletarian control, there was a condemnation of everything connected with the name of Professor Hrushevsky.

It was quite to be expected that measures would be taken to put an end to such literary tendencies as the VAPLITE. Khvylovy was roundly denounced for speaking of the necessity of having relations with Europe and for his ideas of an Asiatic renaissance in Moscow. In return he established another organ, the *Literary Market*, which ostensibly published articles of all schools but added pungent introductions and comments which finally attracted the attention of the authorities.

During 1931 and 1932, as part of the general campaign for collectivization outlined by the Five-Year Plan, there came the artificial famine which proved that the Soviet leaders would stop at nothing to eliminate the old Ukrainian spirit, even when it was presented through a Communist prism. Henceforth there was to be no gainsaying the position of the Moscow-dominated Kremlin. The letters of Stalin and the arrests ordered by such leading agents as Postyshev and Kaganovich confirmed this truth.

In 1933 Skrypnyk, the Ukrainian Soviet commissar for education, was under fire and committed suicide. In the same year Khvylovy ended his life with a bullet. He was just in time to

escape the holocaust of writers, for some seventy-nine leading
authors were liberated from their nationalist errors by execution or deportation. The list included most of the names
that had already become famous in writing or the theatre—
Zerov, Mykola Kulish, Kosynka, Les Kurbas, Antonenko-
Davydovych and Pidmohylny. The list accommodated with
impartiality men who had been ardent Communists as well as
those who had sought to remain apart from the struggle.[11] In
many cases, as in that of Dmytro Falkivsky, their fault was
that they had dared to say that they loved their village and
its environs far better than Tibet, the Urals or the Caucasus,
which was easily taken to be a hostile criticism of that greatest
of all Russians, the Georgian Stalin.[12]

A few, like Tychyna and Rylsky, saw the light and were
able to adapt themselves to the new conditions by abjuring
all that they had formerly believed in. For example, Tychyna
was not above emphasizing Skovoroda's weakness in maintaining an aloof attitude toward the affairs of men[13] and he was
able to go so far as to write of Kiev, "Although old Sofia stands
within it, yet industry is all around" and to state that "we do
not need the golden-domed, weakly dark, simple Kiev, stifled
in its aged self but the new Kiev full of strength, with gold
and silver, young of the young."[14] He could turn from mystical themes to glorification of a tractor driver, and bring himself to flattering eulogies of Derzhinsky,[14] the first leader of
the Cheka, whose tortures and massacres had horrified the
entire world. Rylsky was little better and the same was true
of all the old writers who bought their personal safety with
their personal integrity.

More and more the prime essential of poetry was unreserved
adulation of Stalin and his associates, praise of the omniscience
of the great master and of the devotion of Kirov and other
Communists. Aspiring writers waxed lyrical over the great
writers of Russia and the Soviets and passed over in silence
their views on the development of Ukrainian literature. Some,
like Yanovsky, who were more fortunate, wrote tales of the

civil wars and the fighting against the Poles and Petlyura.[15] Abuse of the most scurrilous kind was heaped upon the men who had founded the Ukrainian National Republic and with each successive year Ukrainian history and literature became more unrecognizable.

Yet the most abject flattery of the powers in control did not satisfy the new master. Men like I. Kulyk could declare then that Tychyna and Rylsky were still only lukewarm in their devotion to the Communist fatherland. Praise was reserved for those young men like Mykytenko and others who had never been led astray and had consecrated themselves from the beginning of their literary careers to the building of socialism and the condemnation of the dregs of society, the old industrious peasants and workmen.

Yet even those men who had formed the nucleus of the VUAPP (Pan-Ukrainian Association of Proletarian Writers) were soon themselves found guilty of the charge of Ukrainian nationalism. Their turn came as soon as the old literature was entirely broken or ended. They had not gone far enough in realizing that the new man must be built purely on the models set out by the Kremlin for the content of socialist realism and that anything specifically Ukrainian was to be restricted to the mildest form of scenic background.

The later thirties passed under this depressing picture, as the writers who wished to live and work vied with one another in adapting their language to Great Russian and their themes to the adulation of Stalin and his circle and to the glorification of the Soviet Union, with especial reference to the friendship and unanimity which Stalin had created between the Ukrainians, the Great Russians and the Soviet Georgians. At the same time Ukraine and her fighting against the Poles and Petlyura came to play a bigger role in Soviet Russian literature. But there was one significant factor in it—the Russian writers made no mention of the Ukrainian Soviet Republic. We might overlook their acceptance of the Ukrainian National Republic as consisting solely of Fascists and White Guards but their failure to pay any attention to the machinery of their own Ukrainian Soviet Republic in literature illustrates beautifully their rabid insistence on the unity of the Soviet Union and their denial of all semblance of independence to their subordinate Soviet republics. Even Nikolay Ostrovsky, held up by his compatriots as possessing the highest type of Communist conscience, does not feel it necessary in his novels to mention the Ukrainian Soviet Republic as part of the Communist machinery which he describes in detail, along with the fighting on Ukrainian territory.[16]

The new literature naturally developed that hardness and inhumanity which had been introduced by the Communists into Ukrainian life. The older writers had depicted a harsh and often a forbidding life. The lot of the Ukrainians in the days of serfdom and afterwards had not been pleasant but it had not deprived the people of a sense of sympathy or at most there was an unconscious brutality which enlightenment and better living conditions could mitigate. The new regime and the new literature boasted of brutality and Kulyk could condemn a novel written by the proletarian and Communist author Holovko, because in one of the characters "we distinctly sense the symbol sadly familiar to us of 'Mother Ukraine' whose heart aches 'equally' for all of her sons; for the workingman Artem, for the peasant Ostap and for the intellectual-nationalist Yurko."[17] Here in one sentence we have the whole difference between Communist and non-Communist Ukrainian literature. The more honest and sincere Communists, like Khvylovy, could not bring themselves to this attitude and they perished under the wheels of the Moscow juggernaut. The Tychynas and the Rylskys did their best to stifle their senses and so in Rylsky's *Marina*, which was glorified as the equal of Shevchenko's *Haydamaki* and Mickiewicz's *Pan Tadeusz*, we have a grotesque vulgarization of all human qualities which reduces even the possibly sympathetic characters to monsters and turns the unsympathetic into devils in human form. The slightest touch of human understanding was enough to bring charges of

Ukrainian nationalism against the most inveterate Communist. It was one of those things that so powerfully stirred up Ukrainian sentiment against the Soviet regime.

Meanwhile the literature of Western Ukraine continued the old Ukrainian traditions. Despite the difficulties with both Poland and Romania, the authors worked with relative intellectual freedom. There was no command for them to do more than to avoid too open seditious material. Thus, under the influence of Ivan Franko, the literature of Western Ukraine continued its bonds with the West. Some authors, such as Stefanyk, who very soon relapsed into silence, Marko Cheremshyna with his descriptions of the Hutsuls in the Carpathians and Les Martovych, continued the older ethnographic school.

The newer impulses were represented by Bohdan Lepky, who approximated Symbolism and showed a keen sensitivity for all the thoughts and aspirations of the individual. For a while he had withdrawn into exile but he later returned and became a professor of Ukrainian literature in the University of Krakow. A still younger group of Western Ukrainian authors flourished in the thirties in Galicia. Its leading representatives as Bohdan Ihor Antonych and Svyatoslav Hordynsky and Bohdan Kravtsiv, all show the influence of the West and also the results of the Ukrainian renaissance of the twenties, especially the work of the neo-classicists. During the same years a group of emigres in Prague headed by Oleksander Oles and embracing such varied names as Olena Teliha and Yury Lipa did good work in reviving the idea of the state in the Middle Ages in contradistinction to the purely ethnographical and popular treatments of the people.[18]

The hopes that had been kindled after the Revolution of 1905 that Kiev might become the center of the thought of a united Ukraine were gradually shattered. The center of Ukrainian progressive thought drifted back to Lviv, where it had been in the late nineteenth century, or to the Ukrainian circles of Prague. It was a severe disappointment, especially after the liquidation of Professor Hrushevsky and the other intellectuals who had returned to Kiev during Ukrainization. Most of them disappeared or perished.

It was in Western Ukraine and especially in that part under Polish rule that progressive Ukrainian thought developed most strongly. Here the ideas and the emotions which worked around Europe in the twenties and the thirties could receive a Ukrainian coloring. Writers like Ulas Samchuk might follow ideas similar to those of Khvylovy and spread them in the *Scientific Literary Messenger*. It was in Western Ukraine and in Vienna that philosophers and sociologists like Lypynsky were able to work. Some of these naturally adapted the ideas of the twenties and thirties to Ukrainian thought in their dreams of a future Ukrainian state. They could not fail to be influenced by the ideas of the Polish intellectuals but they remained Ukrainian and there was none of that slavish adaptation of their own ideas to the will of an alien conqueror that was seen in the Ukrainian Soviet Republic.

Then in 1939 came World War II and the Communist rod was extended over Western Ukraine. Refugees fled to the West to escape the engulfing tide. For those who remained there was the choice of submission, death or deportation, the same choice which had confronted their Eastern brothers ten years before. There was the same necessity to pour out the grossest adulation of Stalin and his friends as the price of liberty. Those authors in the East who had made their peace with the Soviets heaped new compliments upon the dictator for his great generosity in "freeing" Western Ukraine and adding it to the Ukrainian Soviet Republic. Tychyna was especially perfervid in his praise of the great event.

To win popular support the Kremlin for a while carefully withdrew some of their restrictions but not those which had evoked laudation of the ruler. In fact more than ever it was made perfectly clear in the literature published under the Soviets that national defense was entirely the result of Stalin's inspiration. The war poems of Tychyna, of Rylsky, the prose and dramas of Korniychuk and of all other writers are one long paean to Stalin as the head of the Red army, to the Kremlin as the wellspring of Ukrainian courage and patriotism, to the Great Russian brother as the protector and supporter of Ukraine, to the peoples of the Soviet Union as the direct and willing executors of the will of the master. There is not a word that can appeal to a Ukrainian nationalist, no matter how mild his sentiments. Of course there is not a mention of the desperate struggle of the Ukrainians to become masters in their own home. Such would be summarily dismissed as the work of Nazi and Fascist imperialists.

A striking commentary on this passing bid for support by the people of Russian policy is the changed attitude toward Khmelnytsky. A few years before he had been declared the enemy of the Ukrainian people; now he was restored to favor because it was he who at the Treaty of Pereyaslav had taken the first step toward connecting the Zaporozhian Kozaks with Tsar Alexis. For this act all else was forgotten and the once despised and rejected hetman now became the symbol of Russian and Ukrainian oneness. There was even a decoration founded in his honor but it is to be remembered that this was done by the Kremlin and not by the Ukrainian Soviet Republic, which might as an independent entity be supposed to possess some power to confer its own honors.[19]

It cannot be denied that for certain types of war stories, the Russian and Ukrainian Soviet literatures possessed an adequate technique. Communist writers who had worked during the civil war and the fight against Ukrainian independence had built up a simple and direct type of writing in which the enemy were only black and the Communists white as the driven snow. They had an excellent supply of condemnatory epithets and knew how to use them and they never ceased to supply to their readers examples of this genre. They were able to turn out during the war a flood of forceful narratives exhibiting their hatred and disgust for the Nazis and their brutalities. Stories of the heroism of the individual soldier of the Red army and of the bravery of the civil popu-

lation in resisting the invaders and in enduring the tortures of
the Nazis were supplied wholesale as much for propaganda as
for literature. In most there was the same note that it was all
done for Stalin.[20]

With the ending of the war, Ukrainian Soviet literature
continued in the same vein. In the first days of the new puppet
governments, the old standbys were sent around to Prague,
Warsaw and Belgrade, to meetings of the Slav Congress, to
testify to Ukrainian gratitude for the beneficent works of
Stalin and to inspire in the people of the other Slav states
the same sentiments.

This era of good feeling did not last long. Almost at once
there was a reversion to strict Communist doctrines. Once
again the range of literature was narrowed and the political
and authoritative critics began to criticize and suspect even
Rylsky of going too far in lauding the services of the Ukrainians. He was at once accused of Ukrainian nationalism. The
task was resumed of wiping out any vestiges of the old Ukrainian spirit in the name of the new Communist man as dictated
by the Kremlin and the time-serving Korniychuk can deplore
even in works with a national coloring, the overemphasis on
the old mode of life.[21]

It was also the turn of many of the successful writers of
war stories. They were accused of not practicing socialist
realism, in that they had not sufficiently motivated the heroic
actions of their leaders by linking them up with a conscious
acceptance of the ideas of Stalin and the Great Russian masters
of the Kremlin. It was not enough for an author to picture
the heroic deed of a man defending his family and his village
and his Ukrainian people. He had to do it purposefully because he was following the teachings of Stalin and acting on
behalf of all the peoples of the great Soviet Union—or he
risked the accusation of being a Ukrainian nationalist.[22] Attacks
were renewed on the vestiges of religion even while the subservient Orthodox church of Moscow with its hand-picked
patriarch was thanking God for selecting Stalin to rescue

Russian religion.

It made the postwar Ukrainian Soviet literature even more schematic and sterile than it had been in the thirties and it made the Ukrainian elements even more obviously a mere background setting for the ordinary Communist tale. The process of denationalizing the literature and of eliminating the personal and the individual was carried even further, as the popular authors fell more and more under the ban.

It is small wonder then that it is only among the displaced persons and escaped authors that we can find any traces of literature imbued with a national spirit in its highest and best sense. Even under the hardships of life abroad there came a revival of Ukrainian literature which cannot be overestimated. These authors, often on the verge of starvation and in the most dire physical circumstances, are yet freer to write of their thoughts, feelings and experiences than they have been for nearly a quarter of a century. Men like Vasyl Barka are able to pick up once again the threads of contact with Western civilization and from the Ukrainian symbolism of the period of Ukrainian independence they can go on to describe their personal moods without reference to the directives of the Kremlin. There is a large number of novels and stories, like Dokia Humenna's *Children of the Chumak Path* and Ulas Samchuk's *East* which picture the forced introduction of Communism into the Ukrainian village and its devastating effects. Authors like Oleksy Zaporozhets describe, often with humor, the chaos and stupidity of the new bureaucracy which can see only rebellion and sedition in resistance to the mad whims of incompetent Communists who force their slaves to perform the most foolish and unprofitable actions in the attempt to make records for Communist efficiency. Others depict the tyranny and atrocities of the Soviet secret police. Others treat of the patriotic and personal motives that drove so many thousands to join the Ukrainian Insurgent Army. Other young writers as Michael Orest and Ivan Bahryanny have made their appearance. These men also have the sad advantage that they have become as intimately familiar with the works of the Western Ukrainian authors who have shared their fate in the camps.

Literary critics are able again to write honest and intelligent estimates of the great Ukrainian writers of the past and see them as they are and not as they must be in order to fit into the Communist ideology. They can discuss Shevchenko without feeling bound to point out that he was one in sympathy with the Russian radicals in his hatred of the tsar and was opposed to all of his high-placed friends because they were aristocrats. They can discuss Franko without shaping him to a Marxian sociology against which he was struggling for the sake of humanity. They can picture Lesya Ukrainka as a profound student of world literature without making her an adjunct of the Bolshevik party of 1905. They can bring back to Ukrainian literature and criticism the traditional meanings of liberty and freedom that have been buried in Soviet writings under the interpretations of Lenin and Stalin and have there lost all their original and normal sense.

It is still too early to know how permanent an effect this literature in exile will possess. It was the product of unusual circumstances. From 1945 for over three years the bulk of the free writers from all parts of the country were forced together. Now they are again scattering as they take up their new homes abroad.

We cannot overlook the few authors who have been writing abroad, especially in Canada, on the efforts of the Ukrainian immigrants before and after World War I to adapt themselves to the new life into which they have been plunged. In some cases these writers have been tempted to incorporate words and expressions which are not of the purest Ukrainian; they have translated English phrases; but their sins in this respect are no greater than those of Soviet authors who have edited and emended their writing into a Great Russian Ukrainian to please the Kremlin. They furnish valuable material for the student of Ukrainian character in its widest aspects and with all their defects they are often more valuable and appealing than the machine-made literature that has been duly passed by the Communist censors.

A rich and valuable store of memoirs and reminiscences by refugees, is accumulating. The world is already familiar with the stories of certain ex-Communists who have succeeded in escaping to the outside world. It does not realize how many of these same tales have been written by victims of the Nazi and Soviet prisons, who are able to describe in horrible detail their own experiences in the dread past. We can confidently expect more such books as Ukrainian writers settle down in the New World and recount their experiences in acclimating themselves.

The history of Ukrainian literature during the last quarter of a century is a sorrowful tale. With World War I a new era opened which crowned the efforts of the past to make Ukrainian a truly modern and European literature. Then the Ukrainian National Republic suffered shipwreck before the growing pressure of Communist dictatorship. The list of literary martyrs who strove to express Ukrainian ideals was a long one. The republic has survived only in the truly amazing flowering of Ukrainian literature in exile. That literature can only be sad and depressing but it reflects the unquenchable spirit of liberty and democracy which has distinguished Ukrainian literature during the nineteenth and twentieth centuries and which found earlier expression in the *dumas* and folksongs. We can only hope that that spirit may once again infuse the literature at home, that the fetters which bind it may be speedily broken and that the traditions of Shevchenko, Franko and Lesya Ukrainka may be restored in their native land.

XX

The Religious Development of Ukraine

THE LAST THIRTY years have witnessed the same upheavals in the religious life of the Ukrainians as in all other fields. Each conqueror has tried to use religion as a means of breaking Ukrainian national consciousness.

At the outbreak of World War I, when Ukraine was divided between the Russian Empire and Austria-Hungary, the people were divided between the Orthodox and the Catholics of the Byzantine Rite. This line did not exactly coincide with the boundaries of the two empires, for in Bukovina and to a lesser extent in the Carpathian region under Hungarian rule there were numbers of Orthodox. In Eastern Galicia the prevailing religion was Catholicism of the Eastern Rite and in Russia there was only Orthodoxy. As a result of this geographical division, there was the same difference in development that we have seen in other fields.

Let us look first at the situation on the ruins of the Russian Empire. The original Christian see was that of the metropolitanate of Kiev and of all Rus. It was in Kiev that Yaroslav the Wise had in the eleventh century founded the great Church of St. Sophia, one of the glories of Kiev architecture. Then at the time of the great sacking of Kiev in 1169 by Prince Andrew Bogolyubsky the person of the metropolitan was one of his greatest conquests. For all practical purposes the seat of the ecclesiastical authority was moved to Suzdal and then to Moscow and the metropolitan became a creature of the Moscow princes and tsars. The manners of the Muscovite regime were impressed upon the church and long before the fall of Constantinople, all feeling of ecclesiastical dependence upon the patriarch of Constantinople was swallowed up in the pride of Muscovy.

In Kiev the metropolitanate was finally restored, after the region had passed under the control of Lithuania. The Orthodox of Kiev were not received favorably at Moscow and it was not until the revolt of Khmelnytsky in 1649 that the northern capital attempted to renew friendly relations with them. Then, after the Treaty of Pereyaslav, the patriarch of Moscow demanded that the Orthodox of Kiev submit to his jurisdiction and by political pressure the patriarch of Constantinople was forced to acknowledge this in 1685. Immediately all the rights of the Kiev metropolitan were abolished and the sterner system of Moscow was introduced, with strict censorship over all books that appeared in Kiev.

When the Ukrainian independence movement started in 1917, demands were immediately put forward for the separation of the Russian and the Ukrainian Orthodox churches and the resumption by the metropolitan of Kiev of his position as the head of an independent Ukrainian Orthodox church, exactly as the churches of Serbia and Greece had won their independence from the patriarch of Constantinople in the nineteenth century. It goes without saying that the liberal Russian Provisional Government and all the Russian ecclesiastics, including the Patriarch Tikhon, refused the request, if they deigned to notice it at all. This was naturally the case also after the triumph of the Communists. Patriarch Tikhon was not in a position to take any action and most of the Russian bishops in the Ukrainian dioceses in 1918 and 1919 sympathized with the efforts of the White armies to restore the unity of Russia.

This left the Ukrainians in a difficult position. They appealed to the patriarch of Constantinople but at this moment the Greeks in Constantinople were anxious about the attempts of the Turks under Mustapha Kemal to re-establish Turkish sovereignty and they had no desire to take any action which might involve them in a clash with the representatives of the Western or Eastern powers. The West had, as we have seen, tried to avoid action on the form of Russian governmental organization, and as a result the Ukrainian Orthodox found their hopes thwarted. They discussed possible solutions, some indeed rather fantastic, but the fall of the Ukrainian National Republic put an end to efforts to secure their own episcopate and the Ukrainians like the Great Russians were subjected to the fury of the Communist anti-religious persecutions.

Meanwhile in 1924 the patriarch of Constantinople did answer an appeal of the Polish government to set up an Orthodox church in their country and take it under his protection. This was for the Orthodox living within the boundaries of the Polish Republic as worked out after 1920—primarily Ukrainians and Byelorussians.[1] It was never recognized by any official or unofficial body of the Russians in the Soviet Union or by the *émigrés*.

On the other hand the legal establishment of this church did not relieve pressure upon the Ukrainians living under Polish rule. The civil government and a part at least of the Roman Catholic clergy were bitterly opposed to anything that might lead to a Ukrainian organization and found all kinds of excuses to annoy them and subject them to legal disabilities. In 1938 they went so far as to close a number of Orthodox churches on the ground that they had at one time or another been the property of Catholics of the Eastern Rite.[2] This led to disturbances and in some cases even the Polish courts refused to countenance the charges drawn against the Ukrainian Orthodox.

The chief result of these attempts was an improvement in the relations of the Orthodox and the Catholics of the Eastern Rite. The leader of the latter, Archbishop Andrew Sheptytsky, openly protested on behalf of the Orthodox.

During nearly half a century the progress that was made by the Ukrainians of East Galicia was greatly aided by the work of Archbishop Sheptytsky, metropolitan of the Catholic church of the Eastern Rite. He was in every sense a great religious and cultural leader. His benefactions were limitless; he was a wise administrator of the church and he engaged in the most diverse religious and secular activities. There was hardly any aspect of Ukrainian life in which his influence was not felt. As a result he was bitterly hated by all the foes of his people. When the Russians entered Lviv in 1914, they at once deported him to Russia, from which he was not able to return until 1920, and even then the Poles did not allow him to return to his diocese. A little later, when he returned from a visit to the Ukrainians in the New World, he was interned for some months by the Polish government. This persecution by the two enemies of the Ukrainian movement only enhanced his prestige and his following and until his death in 1944 he was the very incarnation of Ukrainian hopes and aspirations.[3]

There is less to be said about the situation in Carpatho-Ukraine and Bukovina. In the case of the Orthodox under Czechoslovak rule, the patriarch of Constantinople exercised a nebulous control as in the past, despite efforts to establish an independent Czechoslovak Orthodox church. In Bukovina the Orthodox Ukrainians were brought under the control of the Romanian Orthodox church. In neither case were there any remarkable movements, although among the Ukrainian Orthodox of Carpatho-Ukraine the Russianizing tendency was very strong. In both cases the Catholics of the Eastern Rite led an uneventful existence without any strong leadership.

The equilibrium which had been attained in the religious life of Ukraine was rudely upset when Hitler and Stalin made their alliance in 1941 and the Red army invaded Poland and occupied Lviv. Almost at once there were signs that it would repeat the actions of the Russian army of 1914 and move against the Catholics of the Eastern Rite. Some of the clergy were

forced to join the Orthodox church and a number of Catholic
churches were seized. No direct action was taken against
Archbishop Sheptytsky. He was forced into practical retirement but he continued to serve his people and his church until
the German advance on Lviv in 1941.[4]

Then he threw his energy into the attempts to reorganize
a Ukrainian government. As we have seen, these were promptly blocked. In 1944 the Archbishop passed away and was
succeeded by Archbishop Joseph Slipy, who was head of the
Ukrainian Catholic church when the Soviet forces re-occupied
the city and the area. This time they had come to stay and
they acted accordingly.

On their arrival in both Carpatho-Ukraine and West
Ukraine, the Communists demanded that the Catholic church
of the Eastern Rite formally join the Russian church under
Patriarch Alexis. When they found no support among either
the clergy or the laity, they resorted to force and trickery.
All of the bishops were arrested and disappeared, including
the archbishop.[5] Then the Soviets formed a "Committee of
Initiative for the Transference of the Greek Catholic Church
to Orthodoxy." This committee consisted of three priests,
Rev. Dr. Havriil Kostelnyk, Rev. M. Melnyk and Rev. A.
Pelvetsky. These men shortly appealed to the other Greek
Catholic priests for support on the ground that the Soviet
government would recognize no other body as competent to
speak for them. A favorable response was soon forthcoming
from the representative of the Council of People's Commissars
for the affairs of the Russian Orthodox church on the Council
of People's Commissars of the Ukrainian S.S.R.

Despite protests by most of the clergy, the Committee of
Initiative arranged a synod in Lviv on March 8, 1946. It was
attended by some 216 priests and was of course thoroughly
uncanonical. The "synod" requested that it be admitted to
the Russian Orthodox church; of course the request was
granted and the three leaders were consecrated Orthodox
bishops.[6] The full resources of the Soviet machine were

applied to the task of deporting or executing any priests who refused to act in accordance with their orders.

The consequences have been appalling. Churches, including the Cathedral of St. George at Lviv, have been seized by the agents of the patriarch. There is yet no complete list of the priests and other clergy and laity who have died as martyrs to their faith. The entire property, printing houses, etc., of the church have been turned over to the Russian Orthodox. In a word the Soviets are carrying out the traditional policy of the Russian tsars and the Holy Synod which forbade the reading of the Liturgy in Russian-dominated territory in any other form than that ordered by the Russian church. Thus another dark chapter has been added to the bloody proceedings which went on as each new Ukrainian province was added to the Russian Empire and the people were forcibly converted from their centuries-old devotion to the Catholic church of the Byzantine Rite.

The Orthodox fared little better. At the first appearance of the Germans the Ukrainian Orthodox renewed their attempts to establish a Ukrainian Orthodox church. The Germans were, however, opposed to the development of any institutions to help the Ukrainians or any of the Slavs. Later some of the bishops who had served in the Polish Orthodox church consented to take part in the movement and consecrate Ukrainian bishops for the Ukrainian Autocephalous Orthodox church, and on the whole the church flourished in the regions which came under the control of the Ukrainian Revolutionary army. The Germans tried to prevent all these developments by encouraging the Autonomous Ukrainian church, which stood in some sort of relationship to the patriarch of Moscow. When successful attempts were made to unite these two groups, the German authorities interfered lest the movement be able to accomplish something for the Ukrainian national spirit. Under German pressure the Autonomous church soon withdrew from the union and then passed into insignificance because of its surrender to the enemy. After this flurry the Germans turned against the church authorities and arrested or imprisoned many of the clergy.[7]

When the Soviets returned, they speedily turned against all the Orthodox clergy who had aided in the movement and they asserted their own control over the Ukrainian Orthodox. Deportation and liquidation followed and once again the hopes for the establishment of a Ukrainian Orthodox church were doomed.

At the present time the patriarch in Moscow in his reorganization of the church has remained true to the old Russian principle. The sees in the Ukrainian Soviet Republic are held by men who are loyal to Moscow and no concessions are made to the feelings of the Ukrainians. For religious purposes the Ukrainian Soviet Republic does not exist and the Orthodox church in Ukraine is as closely[8] dependent upon the patriarch of Moscow as it had formerly been under the Holy Synod of St. Petersburg.[9]

All this is merely another sign of the fictitious quality which the Soviet Union attaches to the Ukrainian Soviet Republic. Just as in the economic, intellectual and political fields, Ukraine is felt by them as an integral part of Russia but without any of those possibly mitigating provisions which would come into effect if the republic were formally annexed. Moscow now claims precedence over all the Eastern Slavs and refuses them even those scanty privileges which are enjoyed by the citizens of the Russian Soviet Republic. At the same time it constantly harps upon the nationalistic desires of the Ukrainians and liquidates right and left.

XXI

The Economic Development of Ukraine

It is a truism for all students of Ukraine that the country is potentially one of the richest sections of Europe. It is equally obvious that the wealth of the region has never been employed for the benefit of the population. This was true under imperial rule and is just as true under the Soviets.

What are some of the resources which are available for development? They fall into the two great divisions of agriculture and mineral deposits. In both the area is unusually well endowed.

A large part of Ukrainian territory falls within the famous "black earth" region[1] which is admirably suited for the raising of grain. Even in classical times the importation into Greece and Rome of wheat from the area to the north of the Black Sea was of the greatest economic importance. After a temporary reduction of grain production in the Middle Ages because of the Tatar invasions, interest in the wheat fields of Ukraine freshened and since the annexation of the country by the Moscow tsars, Ukraine has been one of the chief sources for feeding not only Great Russia but the whole of Europe. Absence of Ukrainian grain from the world market has led to many of the difficulties in Western Europe.

Ukraine is the greatest beet sugar area of Europe. Fruits and other products of the temperate zone are also produced in large

quantities. In 1937 Ukraine produced 25 per cent of the total
grain of the Soviet Union, 78 per cent of the sugar, 75 per cent
of the canned goods, 15.2 per cent of the cattle and 30 per cent
of the pigs.[2]

The yield per acre is far lower than in less favored countries
of Europe. The methods of agriculture employed are primitive. Efforts to improve them were thwarted by the imperial
bureaucracy and the methods of administration of the large
estates. With the establishment of the Ukrainian National
Republic a drive was made toward efficiency and many agricultural stations were set up. These were for a while continued
during the period of Ukrainization but their scope was gradually restricted.[3]

There have been few attempts to diversify crops. The soy-
bean has been planted more widely but that has been the chief
development. The area devoted to tobacco has remained almost
constant. Cotton has not been successful owing to failure to
introduce a proper system of rotation and to fertilize properly.
Other crops, like rice, which might profitably be grown in
certain areas have not been developed, in view of the necessity
of fitting Ukrainian economy into the general pattern adopted
by the central organs of Moscow.[4] It is fair to say that less
than one-third of the agricultural resources of the country are
being systematically developed, and that in strict accordance
with Soviet plans.[5]

The breeding of livestock has not progressed. The number
of animals diminished sharply during World War I and the
period of the revolution. Then it began to increase but it fell
off sharply in 1929 when the peasants killed their animals rather
than hand them over to the collective farms. The period from
1933 to 1937 witnessed an increase but World War II again
ravaged the country, so that the industry is hardly yet on a
par with what it was in 1912.[6]

It is a striking fact that the percentage of many of the products of Ukraine is shrinking when compared with other sections of the Soviet Union which are regarded as less suscept-

ible to national movements. This does not mean that conditions are improving for the population of the area. It only emphasizes the greater and greater exactions that are being demanded of the unfortunate people. Thus Ukraine produces 25 per cent of the total grain supply of the union but this is 2 per cent less than it was in 1913. On the other hand, despite the population increase, the Soviet Union expanded the export of Ukrainian grain from 41 per cent in 1913 to 71 per cent in 1937. The fixed policy of the Soviet Union has been to export the largest part of the Ukrainian grain crop without regard to the needs of the population. Total grain exports from the Soviet Union have paralleled the Ukrainian crop. As a result in 1937, despite the growth of the cities of Ukraine, nearly four million tons of grain less were available for the population than in 1913, after export. This contrasts with an increase of some twenty-one million tons for the population outside of Ukraine during the same period. Since the annexation of West Ukraine after World War II, the disparity is even greater.[7]

The mineral resources of Ukraine consist primarily of coal and iron. The coal deposits of the Donets basin are among the largest in Europe and were developed on a large scale long before World War I. It is estimated that some seventy billion tons of high quality are available—an almost inexhaustible supply.[8]

Near by are the iron mines of Kriviy Rih, which contain ore that is often 55 per cent pure. These furnished the nucleus for the imperial metal industry.[9]

The ease of bringing together the coal of the Donets basin and the iron of Kriviy Rih has long been recognized and has facilitated the development of the metallurgical industry in Russia. In imperial times the government encouraged the movement into the area of large numbers of non-Ukrainians and it was from these imported workers that the Soviets obtained many of the Communists who worked against the

Ukrainian National Republic. De-Ukrainization of the mines has long been a definite policy of the Soviet Union and has perhaps succeeded better than in any other enterprise.

In the neighborhood enormous plants were established for the production of pig iron. About eight million tons are produced each year and Ukrainian production has formed about 61 per cent of the total.[10]

The steel industry produces 47 per cent of all the country's steel. With this production we already find the first step in the diversion of industry. The production of steel is only a little over half of the total, while that of pig iron is three-quarters. When it comes to finished products, the proportion produced in the steel and iron area of Ukraine sinks still lower. Only 17 per cent of the machines produced in the Soviet Union come from Ukraine.[11]

This is a continuation of the old imperial process which had concentrated around St. Petersburg and Moscow all the final manufacturing processes of the empire. Under that system Ukraine was to be only the source of raw material. The Soviets have sharpened and intensified this process with the idea of keeping the Ukrainian Soviet Republic completely dependent for all the necessities and conveniences of life.

The importance of Ukraine to the needs of the Soviet Union is being reduced by the development of Ural and Siberian centers of manufacture. Much money and energy are being expended to create these new plants and the German invasion gave the Kremlin a good pretext for moving a considerable number of the factories to the east. There are no plans for replacing these. The new Five-Year Plan adopted since the war provides for an increase of only 10 per cent in Ukrainian coal and iron production and of only 4 per cent in Ukrainian steel production. On the other hand, the energy with which this transfer of industry is being effected is shown by the fact that while in 1927 Ukraine produced 77 per cent of the coal, 75.9 per cent of the iron ore, and 72 per cent of the pig iron, in 1937 these figures had dropped to 53.8, 61.9 and 61.5 per cent. At the completion of the new plan, these figures are to drop to 34.4 per cent of the coal and 49.7 per cent of the pig iron.[12]

This change is significant. Of course, part of it can be explained by the need of the Soviet Union for exploiting the rich mineral deposits to be found in the Asiatic regions. It is hardly to be expected that Moscow would work hard at enlarging the already existing facilities of the Ukrainian Soviet Republic when other resources were available. In addition, however, the factories of Ukraine are far better known to foreigners than are the completely new developments in the east. The latter are regarded as in a safer position in time of war, since they are further removed from the frontiers. The creation of such facilities had been planned by the imperial regime but the revolution had prevented the carrying out of the process.[13] The aid given to the Soviet Union in World War II during the period of appeasement of Stalin made it possible to proceed with this work and it has been pushed even more vigorously since the German-Communist clash. Now it is to be extended still further, so that under the Moscow yoke Ukraine can look forward to a static period of its industry. No one in authority is interested any longer in treating Ukraine, with its mineral supplies, as the manufacturing base of the Soviet Union. The Kremlin hopes that it will still play an important role but its widespread discoveries of the living character of Ukrainian nationalism and its hostility to the West have persuaded it to leave Ukraine as it was and to perform on its territory only the rough fabrication of raw materials which could be dispensed with in case of an outbreak of hostilities. All this bears out Khvylovy's statement that the Soviet Union was experiencing an Asiatic renaissance in which the Russian Soviet Republic and the western Asian regions were to profit.

Agriculture, coal and iron do not exhaust the natural

wealth of Ukraine. There are enormous deposits of peat in parts of the area. The Nikopil supply of manganese is perhaps the largest in the world and there is an unlimited quantity of potassium and other minerals. These of course must be worked until the authorities can find other sources of supply in the wide expanses of Siberia and elsewhere.[14]

We can understand now the relative indifference with which Moscow regarded the reduction of the population of the Ukrainian Soviet Republic even before World War II. It has given up any possible intention of making Ukraine an important source of supply. This explains too the relative lack of attention shown in many other ways.

Here in an industrial area which can surpass any European part of the Russian Soviet Republic, there is no development of any forms of light industry. Petitions to start textile plants or other necessary factories are uniformly turned down. The budget of the Ukrainian Soviet Republic, which comprises 18 per cent of the population of the country, formed 4 per cent of the total budget of the Soviet Union in 1927 and this later dropped to 3 per cent.[15]

Practically all of the projected plants are on the east bank of the Dnieper, rather than the west. While a few new plants are to be built in Lviv, we can be sure that West Ukraine will not benefit by its absorption and that her industries which were staggering along under Polish rule will not receive any substantial aid.

There may seem to be an exception in the production of hydroelectric power. Perhaps the best-known and best-advertised work in the U.S.S.R. is the Dnieprostroy. In the old days, when there was still the pretext of Ukrainization, American engineers were hired to construct this plant, largely destroyed during the Nazi-Soviet war. It is being rebuilt but its power will be conveyed mostly to Moscow and other points in the Russian Soviet Republic where the Kremlin wants to promote manufactures on a larger scale. As it is now, the Dnieprostroy stands as one of the first great enterprises undertaken by the Soviet Union, and its outcome is regarded by the world as a measure of Soviet achievement. It has become more of a propaganda symbol than anything else, since the military preparations of the Union demand the strengthening and multiplication of plants which are less well known and less accessible.

Another important asset of Ukraine is its ports on the Black Sea. It is often forgotten that it was the securing of control over the Zaporozhian Kozaks in the seventeenth century that first seriously turned the thoughts of the Moscow tsars toward an interest in the problems of Constantinople and the Straits. Before that time what seaborne commerce was carried on by Moscow came through the White Sea and the port of Archangel, which was closed by ice for much of the year. Then came the interest in the Baltic through St. Petersburg. The eighteenth century saw Russian control extended along the shores of the Black Sea. In New Russia, as it was called, the imperial government concentrated upon the ports of Odessa and Mykolayiv.

Before the Revolution, Odessa ranked as the second port of the Russian Empire, surpassed in total commerce only by St. Petersburg, although as a center for exporting grain it was second to Mykolayiv and equalled by Rostov on the Don.[16] Since the establishment of the Soviet regime, Odessa has been more or less superseded by Mykolayiv and Kherson, largely because it is located too near the border of Bessarabia, which was under Romanian control.

The Black Sea ports have always been closely connected with the export of Ukrainian grain and Caucasian oil. Neither during the imperial nor the Soviet regime have they been used extensively for the importation of manufactures and other articles from the West. This is only natural in view of the general purposes to which Ukraine has been put by her Russian neighbors. It was the two capitals and the Great Rus-

sian areas which were intended to receive the benefits of Western civilization which was being favored by the tsars. It was
the Russian Soviet Republic which was to be the kernel and
the heart of the Soviet Union; and for that Ukraine, even
though it was declared a Soviet republic and admitted into
the United Nations, was only an appendage to be exploited
in whatever way was convenient.

It is easier to understand the imperial policy toward Ukraine than the Soviet policy, although they are one and the
same. The imperial regime recognized the wealth of the area
but obstinately refused to admit that it existed as an entity.
To the bureaucrats of the old order, the rich mineral and agricultural resources of "Little Russia" were a godsend but
it was largely the force of inertia that impelled them to work
for the well-being of the capitals and they were as reluctant
to develop ports on the White Sea as on the Black.[17] The
Baltic was their center of interest, for they viewed everything through the eyes of St. Petersburg, itself a Baltic port.
The Soviets broadcast throughout the world their interest
in all the peoples of the Soviet Union. They recognized, at
least in the period of Ukrainization, the differences that existed
between the Great Russians and the Ukrainians. But despite
their international slogans they were as obstinate in insisting
that progress should be Russian as had been the old regime.
With their fear of the growth of Ukrainian nationalism, they
naturally lost all desire to push the development of the area.

The wealth of Ukraine was for them a purely colonial
possession. Throughout their entire history, they have expended less on the Ukrainian Soviet Republic than they have
on the one region of Moscow, where they have concentrated
their institutions and their progress. Now with the preparations for war and their appreciation of the potentialities of
the Ural and Siberian areas, they are content to squeeze from
the unfortunate republic whatever they can. They do not feel
sure of their position there and they are trying to strengthen

it by famine, by deportation, by liquidation.

As early as 1927 the first Five-Year Plan announced that each one of the Soviet republics was to fit into a definite place in the whole. This was to be determined by the interests not of the people but of the Kremlin. From this point of view the position of Ukraine was clear and its function definite. It was to be an advanced storehouse in the economic sense. It was to be an accessible source of raw materials and foodstuffs and nothing else. The main base of the Soviet Union was to be in Asia, in the great expanses of the Russian Soviet Republic.

History hardly knows an example where a naturally rich area has been treated with such unconcern. From 1918 on, the interest of Moscow in the region was merely for the purposes of acquisition and exploitation. So it will continue to be and Ukraine has no more to expect from the economic development of the Soviet Union than it has from the political or the cultural.

XXII

Ukraine and the East-West Conflict

ON JUNE 24, 1950, the army of the North Korean Republic which had been established and dominated by the Soviet Union in defiance of the strict terms of the agreements made with the democratic nations during World War II, crossed into Southern Korea with the purpose of setting up a Communist government by force of arms. Of course the invasion was attended with the usual Communist outcry that North Korea had been attacked by the undemocratic and warmongering government of South Korea. It was the same story which has been repeated in varying forms for over thirty years.

Then came the surprising and unusual turn of events. The United Nations which the Soviet Union and its satellites had been boycotting declared North Korea the aggressor and the United States and the other United Nations began to give active military aid to Korea, while Stalin and his associates declared that it was undemocratic and warmongering to assist persons and nations on the bad books of the Soviet Union to defend themselves. The world is waiting now to see whether an aggressive Soviet Union directly or through its puppets feels itself ready to complete its task of communizing the world by force.

What is the fate of Ukraine in this struggle? With the exception of a few rather small areas Ukraine is united under one government for the first time since the days of Hetman Bohdan Khmelnytsky in the seventeenth century and a few months in 1919, but that government is not a government of Ukrainians, by Ukrainians and for Ukrainians. It is a government of Communist Russians, by Communist Russians and for Communist Russians; and even Communist Ukrainians cannot hope to find secure preferment in their Communist "Ukrainian" state.

Meanwhile there is a steady flow of Ukrainians to the Soviet paradise of Siberia and the frozen north, to the concentration camps, and to the grave. For those who were left under the satellite Polish government, there is exile and deportation to the new lands acquired by Poland in the West. For those who remain at home in both East and West Ukraine, there is only misery and persecution. In the words of Taras Shevchenko, "the people are happy, for they are silent," and they will remain so, in so far as the Kremlin can accomplish it.

Culture, language, traditions and institutions are being remodeled on the pattern of the Kremlin so that the Ukrainians may become worthy associates and followers of their Great Russian brothers. Their past is being rewritten for them, their present is being controlled, and their future is ultimate absorption or annihilation. The representative of the Ukrainian Soviet Republic in the United Nations, Dmytro Manuilsky, speaks in the name of Ukraine but with the voice of Moscow.

Where, then, can we find the real Ukraine? First and loudest, it speaks today through the Ukrainian Insurgent Army which is carrying on its operations not only in Ukraine itself but within the borders of Poland and Czechoslovakia and which has made itself the mouthpiece of all the oppressed peoples of Eastern Europe. Now and then small groups of it appear, well-trained and well-disciplined, in the American zones of Germany and Austria. Now and then the satellite governments release a few notes about its activities, chiefly notices of executions.

Abroad there are the displaced persons, living under the most terrible conditions but still free to live and write. There is the flowering of a new, old literature. There is the attempt to continue the old Ukrainian tradition of scholarship. There is the newly organized Ukrainian National Rada, which is composed of all parties and which is in effect the same form of organization as was adopted by the Czechs and the Poles during World War I.

What can they accomplish? They can speak and act clearly and distinctly but they cannot reach the world if the world is unconcerned.

It was the same situation in the days of the Ukrainian National Republic, when the great powers of the West declined to consider the Russian situation, supported halfheartedly the White movement, and then allowed the Communists to remain the masters of the territory. The world has seen the results of that error, and now the shadow of the Soviet Union is falling over Europe and Asia and the threat which it offers to humanity is exercising the minds and thoughts of intelligent men on every continent.

We can hope that history does not repeat itself. Already the anti-Communist Russian imperialists, the remains of the monarchists, and Kerensky and his followers, are raising their voices to demand that with the overthrow of Communism there shall be restored the one and indivisible Russia. They are using the same slogans as the tsars, the intelligensia, and Stalin, the same slogans that Taras Shevchenko and all the Ukrainians of the past cursed and opposed. They go still further and at a time when the British Commonwealth of Nations, the French Republic and the Dutch are working to extend liberty, they demand the inclusion in their Russia of all the territories that not only the tsars but Stalin has seized and dominated.

They advance the same arguments as before. Napoleon felt the weight of the power of holy Russia. Hitler tried to conquer the Communists and failed. All movements which refuse to recognize the power of Russia must fail. They overlook the fact that the White Armies in 1918, 1919 and 1920, by spurning the cooperation of the various nations which were struggling for independence and by insisting upon their indivisible Russian state and culture, doomed themselves to absolute and humiliating failure. They ignore the fact that Hitler in his insane racial theories deliberately spurned the help of Ukrainians, Lithuanians, Latvians and Estonians, and set himself to reduce them to slavery. They forget conveniently that the greatest danger to the advance of Moscow was the campaign of Charles XII of Sweden, when mere chance determined that he and the Ukrainian Kozaks under Mazepa did not become the victors at Poltava.

As opposed to this Great Russian theory, the Ukrainians and with them all of the oppressed nationalities of the Russian Empire and the Soviet Union appeal for a democratic solution of the problems of Eastern Europe. They believe that those great principles of respect for human dignity and human rights for which two world wars have been fought are more important to the world than the universalizing theories of a Belinsky or a Chernyshevsky, than the doctrines of Marx, Lenin and Stalin, or the mystic visions of a Third Rome and the universal dominance of Moscow, be it White or Red. They believe that the principle of self-determination enunciated by President Wilson, the Four Freedoms and the Atlantic Charter outlined by President Roosevelt, can be made guides to a future warless world through the United Nations and that these doctrines have the same meaning to all peoples except Stalin and the imperialists of the Kremlin.

They understand today—and it is time for the democratic world to join them in this—that the steps which have been taken to reduce the countries on their western border to the position of satellite states are nothing new. The world has seen with amazement mixed with unbelief the process whereby Poland, Czechoslovakia, Hungary, Bulgaria and Romania have been brought under the power of an organized group of men, trained in the Russian Communist schools in Moscow and sent into those lands during the period of nominal alliance with the Allies, to worm their way into key positions of government and then take over. It is only in Yugoslavia that Communists like Tito who have some interest in their own country are carrying on a successful resistance to the demands of Stalin, while in the other satellite countries, the native Communists are being marched to prison or the gallows at the orders of the Kremlin, exactly as were Skrypnyk and his companions in Ukraine. The civilized nations are still scarcely able to credit the steps that were taken in Estonia, Latvia and Lithuania to reduce them to Soviet republics and admit them into the Soviet Union.

The Ukrainians understand all this, for they have seen how the process was worked among them in 1918, 1919 and 1920. They have seen how the way was prepared by appeals for assistance against the imperialists, how it was carried on slowly but methodically during the period of Ukrainization, and how it was accomplished during the period of collectivization. They have seen it and felt it for over a quarter of a century, and they have seen how it was applied when the Red armies invaded West Ukraine in 1939 and again in 1944 and 1945. They have seen the same process as it was developing in the other peoples of the Russian Empire, Georgia, Armenia, Azerbaijan and Central Asia.

It is all the same process and Ukraine has been the great testing ground for the new methods of Soviet imperialism, not only under Stalin but under Lenin. The Russian Communists have made temporary truces with the capitalists, the Fascists, the peasants and the nationalistic workmen of each country which they wished to conquer and have continued them only so long as it served their nefarious purposes. Western thought will do very wrong, unless it too learns that the process of 1950 is but a refined version of that which was worked out in 1918 and 1919 and improved in 1944 and 1945.

It was a bitter blow when democratic statesmen were forced to realize that their compromises with the Soviets and their abandonment of the governments in exile advanced Soviet power into the heart of Europe and put it in a position to threaten France and Italy. It was a sad blot upon their principles when they accepted the Soviet interpretation of the Yalta agreements and returned to deportation or death millions of wretched men and women who had succeeded in escaping outside the Iron Curtain.

Today the democratic powers have gone further. They are intent upon stopping the extension of Communism. They are trying desperately to keep it from conquering Greece and Turkey. They are hoping that it can be held in check in Italy and they are actively working to maintain some touch of freedom in Germany and Berlin. They are offering refuge to democratic leaders from the satellite states but as yet they have not ventured to form a plan to liberate their populations, while the Soviet colossus swallows China and advances throughout Asia.

Again and again in the patient discussions of the foreign ministers, the angry exchanges in the Security Council and the United Nations, the Western Powers have stressed the fact that they do not want to take from the Soviet Union what is rightfully her own. It is a noble sentiment. There is only one question more that should be asked: What is rightfully her own?

In view of the situation in St. Petersburg and Moscow in 1917, it might be held that the Great Russians have chosen Soviet rule. This cannot be said of any other people within the old Russian Empire and it can even less be said of any of the recent acquisitions. The world knows today the meaning of Soviet elections, where almost the entire population votes in open ballot for the program dictated by their masters—or else. The world knows today how the Red army and the secret police, be it called Cheka, OGPU, NKVD or MVD, work to carry out that "or else." The world knows today, as it never knew before, how the Red army and armed forces of various kinds can be called into action to support the Soviet Union. It knows the significance of the Soviet fifth columns in all the countries of the world.

All this is nothing new for Ukraine. The people there have seen the flowering of this system. They have seen it from the very beginning and it is their certainty that there is no hope of change that has led to the development of the Ukrainian insurgent army and the desperate struggle of the Ukrainian people. They prefer death as free men to death as slaves.

One leader after another who has awakened from the mirage of the past years is calling upon the democratic nations to take the lead in a positive message to the world, in formulating a program which can rally all men to their cause and arouse an echo even within the Iron Curtain. That program is simple. It is to offer true democratic liberty to the oppressed peoples of the Soviet Union, to the people of the satellite states as distinct from their puppet governments, even if they temporarily look askance at the Cominform. It is to offer just as certainly the same democratic liberty to the peoples of the oppressed republics of the Soviet Union, to demand that they be represented in the United Nations by people chosen by themselves in a democratic way and not picked by the Kremlin.

It is idle to put forward the plea that in the new democratic world Russia must exist in the boundaries of 1914 and of 1950. The very statistics put out by the Soviet Union emphasize that the Asiatic renaissance, the development of the eastern spaces of the Russian Soviet Republic, can supply satisfactorily all the needs of the Great Russians. They show conclusively that the satellite republics are doomed to a lower standard of living to furnish the Russian war potential in good measure. If Ukrainian grain is to be used solely for export by Moscow, why should not that grain bring in returns for the Ukrainian people? Why should the Ukrainian peasant be expelled from his fields and subjected to famine, in order that the masters of the Kremlin should secure the means of spreading their propaganda?

Ukraine has always maintained close connections with the West. She has never voluntarily merged her fate with the East as has Moscow. Every attempt at the liberation of the country has approached the West and the West has not listened. Today the West is threatened as never before. It is but the part of prudence for it to open its ears and eyes and recognize the efforts of the Ukrainian people to shake off the yoke that has lain upon them for centuries, to assist them in their struggle, and to admit them to the new Europe and the union of free and democratic nations.

Bibliography

ALLEN, W. E. D., *The Ukraine*. Cambridge, 1940.

AMENDE, DR. EVALD, *Die Nationalitëten in den Staaten Europas*. Vienna, 1931.

ANDRUSIAK, M., *Nazva "Ukraina"* (The Name of "Ukraine"). Prague, 1941.

BORODAYEVSKY, S. V., *Istoriya kooperatsii* (History of Cooperation). Praha, 1925.

BORSCHAK, ELIE, *L'Ukraine à la Conference de la Paix, 1919-1923*. Paris, 1938.

    Traité de Paix à Brest Litovsk, Le Monde Slave, 1937.

BRÉGY, PIERRE and PRINCE SERGE OBOLENSKY, *L'Ukraine—Terre Russe*. Paris, 1939. Eng. trans., London, 1940.

BUELL, R. L., *Poland—Key to Europe*. New York, 1939.

The Cambridge History of Poland, 1697-1935. Cambridge, 1941.

CHAMBERLIN, WILLIAM HENRY, *The Russian Revolution, 1917-1921*. New York, 1935.

    The Ukraine: A Submerged Nation. New York, 1944.

CHMELAR, JOS., *Podkarpatská Rus*. Praha, 1923.

CHOULGINE, ALEXANDRE, *L'Ukraine contre Moscou*. Paris, 1935.

COLEMAN, A. P., *Brief Survey of Ukrainian Literature*. New York, 1936.

CZUBATYJ (CHUBATY), NICHOLAS, *Literatur der ukrainischen Rechtsgeschichte, 1919-1929*, Revue d'histoire du droit, v. II-III Lvow, 1930.

Die deutsche Okkupation der Ukraine, Geheime Dokumente, Strasbourg, 1934.

DOLENGA, SV., *Skoropadshchyna* (The Regime of Skoropadsky). Warsaw, 1934.

DOROSHENKO, DMYTRO, *History of the Ukraine.* Edmonton, 1939.
> *Istoria Ukrainy, 1917-1923* (The History of Ukraine, 1917-1923). Uzhorod, 1930-1932.
> *The Uniate Church in Galicia, 1914-1917,* The Slavonic Review, v. XII, London, 1934.

DUSHNYCK, WALTER, *Martyrdom in Ukraine.* New York, 1946.

EVAIN, EMMANUEL, *Le Probleme de l'independence de Ukraine à Paris.* Paris, 1931.

FELINSKI, M., *The Ukrainians in Poland.* London, 1931.

FRANKO, IVAN, *Poems,* (trans. by Percival Cundy). New York, 1948.

FREDERIKSEN, OLIVER J., *The Ukraine,* in *Handbook of Slavic Studies.* Cambridge, Mass., 1949.

GAUTIER, G., *Histoire ukrainienne. Publications en langue ukrainienne parues dans l'U.R.S.S. de 1917 a 1928,* Revue historique v. 162, Paris, Sept.-Oct., 1929.

Gelb und Blau. Moderne ukrainische Dichtung in Auswahl, Zusammengestellt von Wolodimir Derzawin, Augsburg, 1948.

HALECKI, O., *The History of Poland.* London, 1942.

HRDLICKA, ALES, *The Peoples of the Soviet Union.* Washington, 1942.

HRUSHEVSKY, *A History of Ukraine* (trans. by O. J. Frederiksen). New Haven, 1941.
> *Osvobozhdenie Rossii i Ukrainsky Vopros* (The Liberation of Russia and the Ukrainian Question), St. Petersburg, 1906.
> *Die Ukrainische Frage in Ihrer Historischen Entwickelung,* Vienna, 1915.

Istoriya Naukovoho Tovaristva im. Shevchenka (History of the Shevchenko Scientific Society. New York and Munich, 1949.

IVANYTSKY, B., *Lis i lisove hospodarstvo Ukrainy* (Forestry in Ukraine). Warsaw, 1939.

IVASYUK, V., *Suchasni Problemy ekonomiky Ukrainy* (Present day Problems in Ukrainian Economy). Warsaw, 1931-1936.

KARPOVICH, MICHAEL, *The Russian Revolution of 1917*, Journal of Modern History, Vol. II. Chicago, 1930.

KHRUSHCHOV, N. S., *Shvidshi Vidrod silske hospodarstva radyanskoi Ukrainy* (Rapid Recovery of village agriculture in Soviet Ukraine). Kiev, 1946.

KRYPYAKEVYCH,I., *Istoriya Ukrainskoi Kultury* (History of Ukrainian Culture). Lviv, 1938.

KRUPNYTSKY, BORYS, *Geschichte der Ukraine*. Leipzig, 1939.

KUBIYOVYCH, V., *Geografiya ukrainskykh i sumeshnykh zemel* (Geography of Ukrainian and surrounding lands). Lviv, 1938.

KUBIJOWYTCH,W., *Die Verteilung der Bevolkerung in der Ukraine*. Berlin, 1934.

KUTSCHABSKY, W., *Die Westukraine im Kampfe mit Polen und der Bolschevismus in den Jahren 1918-1923*. Berlin, 1934.

LAWTON, LAUNCELOT, *Ukraine: Europe's Greatest Problem*, East Europe and Contemporary Russia, v. III, 1939.

LEBED, MYKOLA, *UPA—Ukrainska Povstanska Armiya* (UPA—The Ukrainian Insurgent Army). Western Europe, 1946.

LEVICKI, E., *La Guerre Polono-Ukrainienne 1918-1919*. Bern, 1919.

LEVITSKY, K., *Istoriya Vyzvolnykh Zmahan Halytskykh Ukraintsiv z chasu Svitovoy Viyny* (History of the Revolutionary Uprisings of the Galician Ukrainians during the World War). Lviv, 1929-1930.

LOBAY, DANYLO, *Neperemozhna Ukpaina* (Unconquered Ukraine). Winnipeg, 1950.

LOS, STANISLAW, *The Ukrainian Problem in Poland*, The Slavonic Review, v. X. London, 1931.

LOTOTSKY, AL., *Simon Petlyura*. Warsaw, 1936.

LUTOSLAWSKI, W. and ROMER, E., *The Ruthenian Question in Galicia*. Paris, 1919.

MALEVSKY-MALEVITCH, P. ed., *Russia-U.S.S.R. A Complete Handbook*. New York, 1933.

MANNING, C. A., *Outline of Ukrainian History*. Winnipeg, 1949.

The Story of the Ukraine. New York, 1947.

Ukrainian Literature, Studies of the Leading Authors. Jersey City, 1944.

MARGOLIN, A., *From a Political Diary, Russia, the Ukraine, and America*. New York, 1946.

MARTEL, RENÉ, *La Ruthenie subcarpathique*. Paris, 1935.

MIRSCHUK, J., *The Ukrainian Uniat Church*, The Slavonic Review, v. X. London, 1931-1932.

OKHOTNIKOV, J. and N. BATCHINSKY, *La Bessarabie et la Paix Europeenne*. Paris and Prague, 1927.

OBERMAIER, FRANZ, *Ukraine, Land der schwarzen Erde*. Wien, 1942.

PANEYKO, V., *Galicia and the Polish-Ukrainian Problem*, The Slavonic Review, v. IX. London, 1931.

PELENSKY, EVHEN YU, *Ucrainica v zahidno-evropeyskykh movakh, Vybrana Bibliographia* (Ucrainica in Western European Languages, A selected Bibliography). Munich, 1948.

PILSUDSKI, J., *L'Année 1920*. Paris, 1929.

Poland, ed. Robert J. Kerner. Berkeley & Los Angeles, 1945.

Polish Encyclopedia. Fribourg, 1917.

POPOVYCH, O., *Vidrodzhennya Bukovyny* (The Renaissance of Bukovina). Lviv, 1933.

POSTYSHEV, PAVEL and S. V. KOSSIOR, *Soviet Ukraine To-day; The Results of the Agricultural Year 1933 and the Immediate Tasks of the Communist of the Ukraine by P. P. Postyshev and Results and Immediate Tasks of the National Policy in the Ukraine by S. V. Kossior*. Moscow and Leningrad, 1934.

PRZYBYLSKI, A., *La Pologne en lutte pour ses frontières, 1918-1920*. Paris, 1925.

RAKHMANNY, ROMAN, *Ukraina z chasu Vtoroy Svitovoy Viyny* (Ukraine during World War II). Ukrainian Press Service, 1946.

REVYUK, E. comp., *Polish Atrocities in Ukraine*. New York, 1931.

REVYUK, EMIL, *Ukraine and the Ukrainians, a Handbook of Concise Information Regarding the Country, People, History and Industry of Ukraine.* Washington, 1920.

ROMANOVSKY, YU, *Ukrainsky separatism i Nyemtsy* (Ukrainian Separatism and the German). Tokio, 1920.

SCHMIDT, AXEL, *Ukraine, Land der Zukunft.* Berlin, 1939.

SCHUMANN, HANS, *Der Hetmanstaat,* Jahrbücher für Geschichte Osteuropas v. IV, 1936.

SHULGIN, ALEXANDER, *Ukraine and its Political Aspirations,* The Slavonic Review, v. XIII. London, 1934-1935.

SIMPSON, GEORGE WILFRED, *Ukraine: A Series of Maps and Explanations Indicating the Historic and Contemporary Geographical Position of the Ukrainian People.* London and New York, 1941.

SKRZYPEK, ST., *The Problem of Eastern Galicia.* London, 1948.

SLAVUTYCH, YAR, *Moderna Ukrainska Poeziya.* Philadelphia, 1950.

SMOLKA, ST., *Les Ruthènes et les problèmes religieuses du monde russe.* Berne, 1917.

STEBER, CHARLES, *L'Ukraine: son histoire et ses richesses. Les dessous des menées hitleriennes.* Paris, 1939.

SVIT, IVAN, *Zelena Ukraina* (Green Ukraine). New York and Shanghai, 1949.

Syohochasne i Mynule (The Present and Past). Munich and New York, 1948.

TILTMAN, H., *Peasant Europe.* London, 1934.

TISSERAND, R., *La Vie d'un People: L'Ukraine.* Paris, 1933.

Ukraine and its People, edited by I. Mirchuk. Munich, 1949.

Ukraine, a short sketch of economic, cultural and social constructive work of the Ukrainian Soviet Socialist Republic. Charkiv, 1929.

The Ukrainian Bulletin. New York, 1948.

The Ukrainian Quarterly. New York, 1944.

Ukrainian Weekly. Jersey City, 1933.

Ukrainian Resistance, The Story of the Ukrainian National Liberation Movement in Modern Times, New York, 1949.

Velyka Istoriya Ukrainy (Great History of Ukraine). Winnipeg, 1948.

VOLOSHYN, A., *Carpathian Ruthenia*, The Slavonic Review, v. VIII. London, 1935.

VOWLES, HUGH PEMBROKE, *Ukraine and its People*. London and Edinburgh, 1939.

WASILEWSKI, L., *Ukraina i Sprawa Ukrainska* (Ukraine and the Ukrainian Question). Warsaw, 1934.

WHEELER-BENNETT, JOHN, *The Forgotten Peace, Brest-Litovsk, March, 1918*. New York, 1938.

WIEDEMAYER, GERHARD, *Ukraine, brot für Europa*. Berlin, 1942.

WINTER, ED, *Byzanz und Rom im kampf um die Ukraine, 955-1939*. Leipzig, 1942.

YEFREMOV, S., *Istoriya ukrainskoho pysmenstva* (History of Ukrainian Literature). Kiev, 1924.

ZELENY, PETRO, *Petro Ivanovych Horovy*. New York and Shanghai, 1949.

Notes

CHAPTER ONE

1. For a brief history of Ukraine, see C. A. Manning, *The Story of the Ukraine* (New York, 1947), and M. Hrushevsky, *A History of Ukraine* (New Haven, 1941).
2. See V. G. Belinsky, "The Gaydamaki," *Polnoe Sobraniye Sochineniy* (St. Petersburg, 1904), VII, 214 ff.
3. See Hrushevsky, *op. cit.*, p. 496.
4. See Hrushevsky, *op. cit.*, p. 512.
5. See C. A. Manning, *Ukrainian Literature, Studies of the Leading Authors* (Jersey City, 1944), p. 69.
6. Seven Ukrainians were elected from the one guberniya of Volyn.
7. See Hrushevsky, *op. cit.*, chap. XXI.
8. *Poland*, ed., Bernadotte E. Schmidt (Berkeley and Los Angeles, 1945), pp. 68 ff.

CHAPTER TWO

1. R. L. Buell, *Poland, Key to Europe* (New York, 1939), pp. 65 ff.
2. *Velyka Istoriya Ukrainy*, ed. Ivan Tyktor (Lviv, Winnipeg, 1948), pp. 748 ff.
3. *Velyka Istoriya Ukrainy*, pp. 756 ff.
4. Hrushevsky, *op. cit.*, pp. 518 ff.
5. *Velyka Istoriya Ukrainy*, pp. 758 ff.
6. For earlier cases, seé A. H. Hore, *Student's History of the Greek Church* (London, 1902), pp. 447 ff. Cf. Hrushevsky, *op. cit.*, pp. 516 ff.

CHAPTER THREE

1. Historians of all schools of thought agree as to the nature of the problems confronting the Revolution and vary only as to the emphasis which they place upon the different factors. However, most Russian historians and others trained under their influence pass over almost in silence the problem of the nationalities. Thus Bernard Pares, *Russia* (New York, 1943), hardly refers to it. Geroid Tanquaray Robinson, *Rural Russia under the Old Regime* (New York, 1932), pp. 148-49, mentions the rise of nationalism in the border states prior to 1905 but pays no attention to its development between the Revolutions as affecting the rural population. On the other hand, C. Tcheidze in *Russia —U.S.S.R.* (New York, 1933), pp. 103 ff. notes the increasing tension between the Russians and the other nationalities and in the same volume, p. 65, Peter Malevsky-Malevitch mentions the important role of the separatist movements in the events of 1918. He emphasizes that by 1918 the opponents of the Communists were of "two very different groups: One comprising the property-owning classes (who had been deprived of their all by the Bolsheviks), the officers, the civil servants and all those devoted to the ideals of the Russian State as constituted before the October Revolution; the other, the national separatist groups, which desired complete separation from Russia. It is easy to see that, no matter how antagonistic these groups might be to Communism, their aims were absolutely dissociated. The unity of the Russian State could only be re-established in one of two ways: either by a restoration of the Monarchy or by federation. Neither alternative appealed to the anti-Bolshevik groups."

2. Nicholas D. Czubatyj, "National Revolution in Ukraine," *The Ukrainian Quarterly*, I, 23.

3. Czubatyj, *op. cit.*, p. 23.

4. Hrushevsky, *op. cit.*, p. 522.

5. See *Velyka Istoriya Ukrainy*, p. 763.

6. Pares, *op. cit.*, p. 86, does not mention that the bulk of the soldiers in this regiment were Ukrainian.

7. Hrushevsky, *op. cit.*, p. 524.
8. *Velyka Istoriya Ukrainy*, p. 763.
9. Czubatyj, *op. cit.*, p. 25.
10. See *Velyka Istoriya Ukrainy*, pp. 766 ff.; Czubatyj, *op. cit.*, p. 27; Hrushevsky, *op. cit.*, pp. 526 ff.
11. Chubatyj, *op. cit.*, p. 29.
12. Hrushevsky, *op. cit.*, p. 527. This precipitated the downfall of the cabinet in Petrograd and was contemporary with the July uprising in that city.

CHAPTER FOUR

1. Hrushevsky, *op. cit.*, p. 532.
2. Hrushevsky, *op. cit.*, p. 532.
3. Czubatyj, *op. cit.*, p. 32.
4. *Velyka Istoriya Ukrainy*, p. 768. Chubatyj, *op. cit.*, p. 33. This was in connection with the Russian Council of Soviets of the Donets and Kriviy Rih. D. Doroshenko, *Istoriya Ukrainy*, Uzhorod, 1930-2, Vol. I, pp. 222 ff.
5. The interpretation of the Conference of Brest-Litovsk is highly controversial. Russian and anti-German writers use it consistently to discredit the Ukrainian movement. Cf. Pares, *op. cit.*, p. 97; John Wheeler-Bennett, *The Forgotten Peace, Brest Litovsk, March, 1918* (New York, 1938), etc. *Russia—U.S.S.R.*, pp. 65-6. On the other hand Ukrainian historians as Hrushevsky, *op. cit.*, pp. 536 ff. and D. Doroshenko, *Istoriya Ukrainy* (Uzhorod, 1930-32), p. 202 emphasize that the Rada had no other course open to it.
6. O. Czernin, *In the World War* (New York, 1920), p. 258.
7. Francis Joseph had died November 21, 1916, and the young emperor Charles was still floundering in his policies.
8. James Mavor, *The Russian Revolution* (London, 1928), pp. 202 ff.
9. *Velyka Istoriya Ukrainy*, pp. 779 f.
10. Hrushevsky, *op. cit.*, pp. 539 ff.
11. Hrushevsky, *op. cit.*, p. 543.
12. Hrushevsky, *op. cit.*, p. 546.
13. *Velyka Istoriya Ukrainy*, p. 786.

14. Doroshenko, *op. cit.*, p. 154.
15. Doroshenko, *op. cit.*, pp. 162 ff.
16. Doroshenko, *op. cit.*, p. 181.

CHAPTER FIVE

1. *Velyka Istoriya Ukrainy*, p. 790.
2. *op. cit.*, p. 791.
3. For the Polish explanation of this occupation as aided by the old government, see A. Przybylski, *Wojna Polska, 1918-1921* (Warszawa, 1930), p. 24.
4. *Velyka Istoriya Ukrainy*, p. 792 f.
5. Przybylski, *op. cit.*, pp. 45 ff. *Velyka Istoriya Ukrainym*, p. 798 ff.
6. *Velyka Istoriya Ukrainy*, p. 832.
7. R. W. Seton-Watson, *A History of the Czechs and Slovaks* (London, New York, 1943), p. 324. *Velyka Istoriya Ukrainy*, p. 833 f.
8. Czubatyj, *op. cit.*, pp. 37 ff.

CHAPTER SIX

1. For similar cases in the Baltic area, see E. W. Polson Newman, *Britain and the Baltic* (London, 1930), pp. 80 ff., in the cases of Von der Goltz and the still more complicated case of Bermondt-Avalov.
2. All histories of the White Armies point this out.
3. Hrushevsky, *op. cit.*, p. 555; W. H. Chamberlin, *The Ukraine, A Submerged Nation* (New York, 1944), p. 48.
4. Buell, *op. cit.*, pp. 268 ff.
5. Buell, *op. cit.*, p. 270.
6. *Velyka Istoriya Ukrainy*, p. 812.
7. Chamberlin, *op. cit.*, p. 49.
8. *Velyka Istoriya Ukrainy*, pp. 825 ff.; Przybylski, *op. cit.*, pp. 130 ff.
9. *Velyka Istoriya Ukrainy*, p. 827.
10. See extracts from the treaty printed in Stanislaw Skrzypek, *The Problem of Eastern Galicia* (London, 1948), pp. 72 ff.

CHAPTER SEVEN

1. Ukrainian-American Political Action in the Years 1914-1920, *Golden Jubilee Almanac of the Ukrainian National Association 1894-1944.* Jersey City, N. J. 1944, pp. 112ff.
2. Margolin, *From a Political Diary, Russia, the Ukraine and America.* New York, 1946.

CHAPTER EIGHT

1. This is shown by the outline of the Communist International (the Comintern) published in *Russia—U.S.S.R.* (pp. 332 ff.) and resting on the declaration of 1924. The Comintern took definite shape in Moscow in 1919 before the ending of hostilities. Ruth Fischer in *Stalin and German Communism* (Cambridge, 1948, p. 547) says: "Comintern life and Comintern policy should have been divorced from the Russian party." Still she notes that as early as 1920 Russian methods were already being applied in Germany. The failure of the Communists outside of Moscow had the inevitable result of emphasizing the success of Lenin and his followers but it is difficult to decide at exactly what date Russian domination became a matter of right and not of policy.
2. See the citations in *Russia—U.S.S.R.*, p. 171.
3. See Yuriy Sherekh, "Trends in Ukrainian Literature under the Soviets," *The Ukrainian Quarterly*, IV, 154.
4. The Constitution of the Uk.S.S.R. of March 14, 1919, definitely declares it to be a state completely independent of the R.S.F.S.R. (the Russian Socialist Federal Soviet Republic) *Russia—U.S.S.R.*, p. 174.
5. Thanks to the statutes of the Communist International and its theories of class and not of geographical membership, there is no inconsistency on this point.
6. Makhno did not leave Ukraine until 1921. Chamberlin, *op. cit.*, p. 50. The guerilla movement died away of itself as the guerillas sank to mere bandits. Soviet literature of these years loves to reproduce this type. Compare the sequence in Boris Savinkov's *Black Horse* (London, 1924).

7. Chamberlin, *op. cit.*, pp. 56 f.
8. *Russia—U.S.S.R.*, p. 115.
9. See Gleb Struve, *Soviet Russian Literature* (London, 1935), pp. 224 ff.
10. Nicholas D. Czubatyj, "Silver Jubilee of the Ukrainian Academy of Sciences, 1918-1943," *The Ukrainian Quarterly*, I, 236 ff.
11. See W. E. D. Allen, *Ukraine* (Cambridge, 1940), p. 280.
12. For an estimate of Skrypnyk in Moscow, see Reuben Darbinian, "A Mission to Moscow," in *The Armenian Review*, Vol. I, No. 3, pp. 28 ff.

CHAPTER NINE

1. Nicholas D. Czubatyj, "The Silver Jubilee of the Ukrainian Academy of Sciences, 1918-1943," *The Ukrainian Quarterly*, I, 244 ff.
2. Chamberlin, *op. cit.*, p. 57 f.
3. Allen, *op. cit.*, p. 366.
4. Chamberlin, *op. cit.*, pp. 59 ff.
5. Chubatyj, *op. cit.*, p. 248.
6. Chubatyj, *op. cit.*, p. 248.
7. Chamberlin, *op. cit.*, p. 62.
8. The following paragraph can perhaps be cited here: "The Ukrainian Soviet literature arose, grew and developed in the throes of bitter class struggle. Its young and as yet frail forces had to blaze their path through the barriers that were raised by the Ukrainian nationalist bourgeoisie, by kulakdom and its ideologists in the domains of literary theory and literary policy, headed by the school of the 'academician' S. Yefremov. Preaching the 'united national front,' they withheld recognition from all forces which, opposing this front, sought to strengthen the proletarian dictatorship and to cement the brotherly alliance with the republics of the Soviet Union. These chauvinists further enjoyed active support of those elements which represented the nationalist deviation in the ranks of the Ukrainian Communist Party. Not without reason did

Skrypnik (the head of the nationalist deviation in the Communist Party of the Ukraine who worked hand in hand with the imperial interventionists) even in 1929 write of the "diminished" role of literary work. His object was to make out a case for prerevolutionary Ukrainian literature (which, according to Skrypnik and Yefremov, supposedly represented the "united front of the creative forces of our people"), as though it had been stronger, more influential and effective than the contemporary Soviet literature of the Ukraine. The reactionary roots of these arguments are quite apparent. The ideology of bourgeois nationalism reflected, after all is said and done, the aim of the Ukrainian kulak to fence off his farmyard from the proletarian revolution. It was a reflection of the hopes of the Ukrainian bourgeoisie for unhindered and "independent" exploitation of the workers and peasants of the Ukraine.

"Quite in accord with this kulak program was another slogan that was launched later by the Ukrainian nationalists (Khyylevy), that of "orientation psychology of Europe." This slogan, if carried out, would have meant the transformation of Soviet Ukraine into a colony of foreign imperialism." I. Kulik, in *Literature of the Peoples of the U.S.S.R.* VOKS Illustrated Almanac, Nos. 7-8, Moscow, 1934, p. 53 f. It is to be noted that the author of these lines was himself later liquidated on the same charges, Cf. Yury Sherekh, in *The Ukrainian Quarterly*, IV, 166.

9. Bolshaya Sovyetskaya Entsiklopediya, 1935, Vol. LIX, p. 816.

CHAPTER TEN

1. F. M. Dostoyevsky, *Zapiski iz Mertvago Doma*, Part II, Chap. V.
2. Ivan Svit, *Zelena Ukraina* (New York-Shanghai, 1949), pp. 11 f.
3. Svit, *op. cit.*, p. 12.
4. Petro Zeleny, *Petro Ivanovych Horovy* (New York-Shanghai, 1949), 11 pp.

5. Svit, *op. cit.*, p. 13.
6. Zeleny, *op. cit.*, pp. 9 f.
7. Svit, *op. cit.*, pp. 20 ff.

CHAPTER ELEVEN

1. See Malbone W. Graham, "Polish Politics, 1918-1939," in *Poland* (Berkeley and Los Angeles), pp. 81 ff.
2. See the summary of this statute in the article of Basil Paneyko, "Poles and Ukrainians in Galicia," *Slavonic and East European Review*, IX, 580 f.
3. See Buell, *op. cit.*, pp. 269 ff.; *Poland,* pp. 81 ff.; *Velyka Istoriya Ukrainy*, pp. 820 ff. For the extreme Polish point of view, see A. Bruce Boswell, *Poland and the Poles* (New York, 1919), pp. 163-66.
4. See Buell, *op. cit.*, p. 85.
5. See Buell, *op. cit.*, p. 272. Hrushevsky, *op. cit.*, p. 562.
6. Hrushevsky, *op. cit.*, p. 563. See also Paneyko, *op. cit.*, p. 581-82. It is to be noted that the Poles here drew a distinction between the Uniats (Catholics of the Byzantine Rite) and the Orthodox Ukrainians who were formerly in the Russian Empire. This can be seen in the article of Stanislas Srokowski, "The Ukrainian Problem in Poland," *Slavonic and East European Review*, IX, 588 ff., especially 593 f. This distinction is not made in the Treaty of Riga (see summary in Skrzpek, *The Problem of Eastern Galicia* [London, 1948], pp. 72 ff.). It is not made either in the *Polish Encyclopedia*, Vol. II, Nos. 3 and 5, Geneva, 1921, which uses the old terminology, regards Ukraine as the gubernia of Kiev and uses the term Ruthenia for the entire area, exactly the reverse of modern usage.
7. The Council of Ambassadors recognized the Polish boundaries as set by the Treaty of Riga. See Skrzypek, *op. cit.*, pp. 74 f. This decision, recognizing the legality of Polish control over regions to the east, made the question of Eastern Galicia as mentioned in the text academic and meaningless.
8. See Hrushevsky, *op. cit.*, p. 563.

9. *Velyka Istoriya Ukrainy*, p. 853.
10. *Poland*, pp. 118 ff.
11. Chamberlin, *op. cit.*, p. 67.
12. See Paneyko, *op. cit.*, p. 585.
13. See Czubatyj, "Silver Jubilee," p. 242.
14. See Hrushevsky, *op. cit.*, pp. 504, 509, 562; C. A. Manning, "The Jubilem of the Shevchenko Scientific Society (1873-1948)," in *The Ukrainian Quarterly*, V, 29-36.
15. See Hrushevsky, *op. cit.*, p. 568; Buell, *op. cit.*, pp. 276 ff.
16. See Buell, *op. cit.*, pp. 277 f.
17. *Velyka Istoriya Ukrainy*, pp. 856 f.
18. Roman Olesnicki, "The Ukrainian Cooperative Movement," *The Ukrainian Quarterly*, II, 36-42.

CHAPTER TWELVE

1. *Velyka Istoriya Ukrainy*, p. 859 f.

CHAPTER THIRTEEN

1. See *Poland*, pp. 381 ff.
2. The idealistic Pan-Slavism had been founded by the Lutheran Slovak, Jan Kollar, publishing in 1824 his collection of sonnets, *Slavy Dcera* (The Daughter of Slava). This inspired many of the Czech developments and indirectly had a great influence upon Taras Shevchenko and the Ukrainian movement as a whole. At the time of the foundation of the Czechoslovak Republic, there was a sharp cleavage between the openly pro-Russian and anti-Bolshevik policies of Dr. Karel Kramar and the attitude of President Masaryk and Dr. Eduard Benes, who hoped for continued co-operation with Russia despite the Bolshevik government. See R. W. Seton-Watson, *History of the Czechs and Slovaks* (London, New York, 1943), p. 314.
3. See Seton-Watson, *op. cit.*, p. 339.
4. The authenticity of this was denied by Dr. Jan Papanek, *New York Times*, August 30, 1948.
5. See Buell, *op. cit.*, p. 344.

6. *Velyka Istoriya Ukrainy*, p. 867.
7. *Velyka Istoriya Ukrainy*, pp. 867 f.
8. See *Hrushevsky, op. cit.*, pp. 427 ff.
9. The Treaty of Saint Germain (Articles 10-13) provided for the autonomy of the area (Podkarpatska Rus) and also stated, "Yet these deputies (to Prague) will not enjoy the right of voting in the Czechoslovak Diet in all legislative matters of the same type as those assigned to the Ruthenian Diet." (Article 13). Dr. Jiri Hoetzel in an article "The Definitive Constitution of the Czechoslovak Republic" prefixed to a text of the Constitution, Prague, 1920, p. 12, stresses that by inserting the provisions of the Treaty as paragraph 3 of the Constitution, "the Republic clearly shows that she desires fully to guarantee the autonomic existence of the territory of Russinia." This paragraph promises Carpathian Russinia "the widest measure of self-government compatible with the unity of the Czechoslovak Republic." Other provisions specify that the laws passed by the Diet shall be approved by the President of the Republic and listed separately and that the Governor shall be appointed by the President and responsible also to the Diet and that "public officials shall be selected, in so far as possible, from the population of Russinia" (*op. cit.*, p. 22). The question of language was handled in paragraph 6 of a law dated February 29, 1920, declaring the Czechoslovak language the official language of the State. "The Diet which shall be set up for Russinia shall have the right reserved to it of settling the language question for this territory in a manner consonant with the unity of the Czechoslovak State. Until this settlement has been made, this law shall apply, due regard, however, being paid to the special circumstances of that territory in respect to language" (*op. cit.*, p. 49).
10. *Velyka Istoriya Ukrainy*, pp. 860 f.
11. Dr. Josef Gruber, *Czechoslovakia, A Study of Economic and Social Conditions* (New York, 1924), p. 9, shows this ambiguity by citing the census of 1921 which gives "Russians (Great Russians and Ukrainians) 461, 849."

CHAPTER FOURTEEN

1. Seton-Watson, *op. cit.*, pp. 374 f.
2. *Velyka Istoriya Ukrainy*, pp. 862 ff.
3. See Hrushevsky, *op. cit.*, p. 571.
4. Seton-Watson, *op. cit.*, p. 379.

CHAPTER FIFTEEN

1. *New York Times*, April 29, 1939.
2. Dallin, *Soviet Union's Foreign Policy, 1939-1942* (New Haven, 1943).
3. Skrzypek, *op cit.*, p. 11.
4. See *Velyka Istoriya Ukrainy*, p. 873; Skrzypek, *op. cit.*, p. 75.
5. Skrzypek, *op. cit.*, pp. 75-76. Note that the agreement in Moscow was apparently a fairly rough line, as shown by Article I.
6. *Velyka Istoriya Ukrainy*, p. 873.
7. *Velyka Istoriya Ukrainy*, pp. 874 ff.
8. *Velyka Istoriya Ukrainy*, p. 877; Skrzypek, *op. cit.*, pp. 13 ff., 82 f.; *Pravda*, October 29, 1939.
9. See M. Seleshko, "Vinnytsya—the Katyn of Ukraine," *The Ukrainian Quarterly*, V, 238-48.
10. *Istoriya Naukovoho Tovaristwa im. Shevchenka* (New York-München, 1949), p. 45; Ya. Pasternak, "Naukove Tovaristvo im. Shevchenka v chas druhoi svitovoi viyny," *Syohochasne i Mynule*, Vol. I, München-New York, 1948, pp. 37 ff.
11. *Velyka Istoriya Ukrainy*, p. 878.
12. *New York Times*, December 15, 1939.
13. *Velyka Istoriya Ukrainy*, p. 879.

CHAPTER SIXTEEN

1. *Ukrainian Resistance* (New York, 1949), pp. 43 f.
2. Mykola Lebed, *UPA, Ukrainska Povstanska Armiya* (Western Europe, 1946), p. 15.

3. For the situation in the Baltic, see Thomas G. Chase, *The Story of Lithuania* (New York, 1946), pp. 303 f.; Dr. Alfred Bilmanis, *Latvia and her Baltic Neighbors* (Washington, 1942), p. 114.

4. See Lebed, *op. cit.*, pp. 16 f. Compare Chase, *op. cit.*, pp. 304 f. *Deutsche Zeitung im Osland*, October 19, 1941 (quoted in Bilmanis, *op. cit.*, p. 115 f.

5. Lebed, *op. cit.*, Nicholas D. Czubatyj, "The Ukrainian Underground," *The Ukrainian Quarterly*, Vol. II, p. 161 f.

6. *Velyka Istoriya Ukrainy*, p. 880.

7. Nicholas D. Chubatyj, "The Ukrainian Underground," *The Ukrainian Quarterly*, Vol. II, p. 157.

8. See *Ukrainian Resistance*, pp. 67 ff.; Lebed, *op. cit.*, pp. 25 ff.

9. *Ukrainian Resistance*, pp. 76ff.

10. *Ukrainian Resistance*, p. 79.

11. *Ukrainian Resistance*, pp. 88f.

12. *Ukrainian Resistance*, p. 109.

13. Lebed, *op. cit.*, pp. 32 ff.

14. *Ukrainian Resistance*, p. 84.

15. Roman Smal Stocky, "The Promethean Movement," *The Ukrainian Quarterly*, III, 330.

16. *Ibid.*, pp. 324 ff.

17. Lebed, *op. cit.*, 77ff.

18. Chubatyj, *op. cit.*, *The Ukrainian Quarterly*, II, 162 f.

CHAPTER SEVENTEEN

1. Arthur Bliss Lane, *I Saw Poland Betrayed*.

2. See Seton-Watson, *op. cit.*, p. 387. Jan Papanek, *Czechoslovakia*, New York, 1945, p. 103 f. "Now Carpatho-Russia and the other liberated parts of Czechoslovakia, outside the immediate military zone, are under the civil administration of the Czechoslovak Government, whose delegate from London took it over on October 28, 1944, from the Soviet military authorities, according to the Soviet-Czechoslovak administrative agreement of May 8, 1944."

3. *New York Times*, June 30, 1945. See P. Tychyna "Bud' zdorova, Zakarpatska Ukraina," *Vybrani Tvory*, Kiev, 1947, p. 281 f.
4. W. H. Chamberlin, "Stirrings of Ukrainian Unrest," *The Ukrainian Quarterly*, III, 113.
5. Nicholas D. Chubatyj, "The UPA Fights the Kremlin," *The Ukrainian Quarterly*, III, 359.
6. *New York Times*, May 4, 1946.
7. Chubatyj, *op. cit.*, p. 359.
8. *New York Times*, May 6, 1946, etc.
9. *New York Times*, September 19, 1947.
10. See Chamberlin, "Stirrings of Ukrainian Unrest," *The Ukrainian Quarterly*, III, 109.
11. Stephen Protsiuk, "The Evacuation of Industry in 1941 and the Postwar Economy of Ukraine," *The Ukrainian Quarterly*, V, 215 ff.

CHAPTER EIGHTEEN

1. *Velyka Istoriya Ukrainy*, p. 888.
2. *U.F.U. Newsletter, Ukrainian Free University in Munich*, I year, April, 1948, No. I.
3. *Velyka Istoriya Ukrainy*, p. 890 ff.
4. *Velyka Istoriya Ukrainy*, p. 892 f.
5. *Velyka Istoriya Ukrainy*, p. 895 f.

CHAPTER NINETEEN

1. C. H. Andrusyshen, "Ukrainian Literature—A Mirror of the Common Man," *The Ukrainian Quarterly*, IV, 44 ff.; Clarence A. Manning, "The Democratic Trend of Ukrainian Literature," *The Ukrainian Quarterly*, I, 40 ff.
2. Serhey Efremov, *Istoriya Ukrainskoho Pismenstva*, II, 337.
3. This does not prevent I. Kulyk (*Literature of the Peoples of the U.S.S.R.*, Moscow, 1934, p. 58) from declaring, "His early works (1910) were saturated with symbolism, mysticism and abstract 'cosmic' ideals, which, in the long

run, expressed the ideology of the Ukrainian bourgeoisie."
Again, "Stronger organizational ties with the realities,
emancipation from artificial, at times purely bookish culture, such are the conditions on which depends further
progress by Tychina along the new road chosen by this
great Ukrainian poet." Yuriy Sherekh, "Trends in Ukrainian Literature under the Soviets," *The Ukrainian Quarterly*,
Vol. IV, p. 151.

4. See Sviatoslav Hordynsky, "The Fivefold Cluster of Un-
vanquished Bards," *The Ukrainian Quarterly*, V, 249 ff.
Also the introduction of Volodymyr Derzhavyn to Mykola
Zerov, *Sonnetarium* (Berchtesgarten, 1948).

5. See Efremov, *op. cit.*, II, 387. Sherekh, *op. cit.*, p. 153.

6. Yuriy Sherekh, "Trends in Ukrainian Literature under
the Soviets," *The Ukrainian Quarterly*, Vol. IV, p. 163.

7. Sherekh, *op. cit.*, p. 164.

8. See note II, Chapter Nine. S. Mykolyshyn, *Natsionalism
u literaturi na Skhidnykh Ukrainskykh Zemlyakh* (Paris,
1938), pp. 18 ff. Honore Evach, "Mykola Khvylovy—
Communist and Patriot," *The Ukrainian Quarterly*, I, 272
ff.; Sherekh, *op. cit.*, p. 156.

9. Sviatoslav Hordynsky, "Ideas on the Scaffold, Mykola
Kulish and his Sonata Pathetique," *The Ukrainian Quarterly*, V, 331 ff.

10. Ernest J. Simmons, *An Outline of Modern Russian Literature (1880-1940)* (Ithaca, 1943), p. 49.

11. See Sherekh, *op. cit.*, 165. Yar Slavutych, *Moderna Ukrainska Poeziya* (Philadelphia, 1950), pp. 62 f.

12. See *"Dmytro Falkivsky" Samostiyna Dumka*, Chernivtsy,
1936, parts 3-5, p. 166 ff.

13. Pavlo Tychyna, *"Davyd Guramishivili chytae Hryhoriyu
Skovorodi 'Vytyazya v Tigroviy Shkuri',"* *Vybrani Tvori*,
Kiev, 1946, Vol. I, p. 248, ff.

14. Tychyna, "Feliks Dzerzhinski," *op. cit.*, Vol. I, p. 242 f.

15. Yanovsky, *Vsadniki.*

16. Nikolay Ostrovsky, *Kak Zakalyalos Stal* (Moscow, 1936).

17. Kulyk, *op. cit.*, p. 57.

18. Yar Slavutych, *op. cit.*, pp. 37 ff.

19. Clarence A. Manning, "The Soviets and Khmelnitsky," *The Ukrainian Quarterly*, III, 12 ff.
20. Clarence A. Manning, "Socialist Realism and the American Success Novel," *South Atlantic Quarterly*, XLVIII, 213-19.
21. Yuriy Kobiletsky, "Shlyakhi Narisu," *Dnipro*, Year 3, No. 2, pp. 101 ff.

CHAPTER TWENTY

1. The number of Russian refugees in Poland was small. The Orthodox were chiefly centered in the so-called eastern provinces inhabited by the minorities and of this population again, few were Russian.
2. See Buell, *op. cit.*, p. 279.
3. Clarence A. Manning, Archbishop Andrey Sheptytsky, *Review of Religion*, IX, pp. 282 ff.
4. Walter Dushnyck, *Martyrdom in Ukraine* (New York, 1946), p. 15.
5. Dushnyck, *op. cit.*, p. 21.
6. Dushnyck, *op. cit.*, pp. 25 ff. It was reported in the *Ukrainska Pravda*, September 26, 1948, that Bishop Kostelnik had been murdered, Patriarch Alexis claimed that it was the work of Ukrainian agents but there is also a suspicion that he was liquidated for some reason by the MVD. *The Ukrainian Quarterly*, IV, 375.
7. *Velyka Istoriya Ukrainy*, pp. 881 ff.

CHAPTER TWENTY-ONE

1. According to *Ukraine and Its People*, edited by I. Mirchuk, Munich, 1949, p. 131, three-quarters of Ukrainian territory consists of black earth.
2. Prof. T. S., "Ukraine in the Economy of the U.S.S.R.," *The Ukrainian Quarterly*, III, 224 f.
3. Prof. Hryhory Makhiv, "Agricultural Science in Ukraine," *The Ukrainian Quarterly*, V, 53 ff.
4. Hryhory Makhiv, "New Cultivated Crops in Ukraine," *The Ukrainian Quarterly*, V, 319 ff.

5. Prof. Hryhory Makhiv, "Agricultural Science in Ukraine," *The Ukrainian Quarterly*, V, 58.

6. Wasyl Marchenko, "The Basic Features of the Development of Farming in Ukraine under the Soviets," *The Ukrainian Quarterly*, IV, 353 ff.

7. Prof. T. S., *op. cit.*, p. 225.

8. *Ukraine and Its People*, p. 150.

9. *Ukraine and Its People*, p. 155.

10. Prof. T. S., *op. cit.*, p. 225.

11. Prof. T. S., *op. cit.*, p. 228.

12. V. Marchenko, "The Role of Ukraine in the Present Five-Year Plan," *The Ukrainian Quarterly*, V, 124 ff.

13. *Russia—U.S.S.R.*, p. 395.

14. *Ukraine and Its People*, pp. 153, 158 ff.

15. T. S., "Ukraine and the Budget of the U.S.S.R.," *The Ukrainian Quarterly*, IV, 26 ff.

16. *Russia—U.S.S.R.*, p. 454.

17. It was only during World War I that steps were taken to utilize the ice-free port of Murmansk in the north.

INDEX